THE COLLECTED WORKS OF
ABRAHAM LINCOLN

THE COLLECTED WORKS OF
ABRAHAM LINCOLN

THE ABRAHAM LINCOLN ASSOCIATION
SPRINGFIELD, ILLINOIS

VI

ROY P. BASLER, *EDITOR*

MARION DOLORES PRATT AND LLOYD A. DUNLAP

ASSISTANT EDITORS

RUTGERS UNIVERSITY PRESS
NEW BRUNSWICK, NEW JERSEY

SOURCES
AND LOCATION SYMBOLS

DESCRIPTION OF SOURCES

THE following symbols provide a description of sources as cited at the beginning of the first footnote to each item. In addition to the customary symbols for describing manuscripts, the editors have employed symbols or single words to identify other sources which have been cited repeatedly in the first footnote.

AD	Autograph Document
ADS	Autograph Document Signed
ADf	Autograph Draft
ADfS	Autograph Draft Signed
AE	Autograph Endorsement
AES	Autograph Endorsement Signed
AL	Autograph Letter
ALS	Autograph Letter Signed
ALS copy	Autograph Letter Signed, copied by Lincoln and preserved in his papers
Copy	Copy not by Lincoln
D	Document
DS	Document Signed
Df	Draft
DfS	Draft Signed
ES	Endorsement Signed
F	Facsimile—following any of the preceding symbols
LS	Letter Signed
P	Photostat—following any of the preceding symbols

Angle	*New Letters and Papers of Lincoln.* Compiled by Paul M. Angle. Boston and New York: Houghton Mifflin Company, 1930.
Herndon	*Herndon's Lincoln: The True Story of a Great Life.* By William H. Herndon and Jesse W. Weik. 3 volumes. Chicago, New York, and San Francisco: Belford, Clarke & Company, [1889].
Hertz	*Abraham Lincoln: A New Portrait.* By Emanuel Hertz. 2 volumes. New York: Horace Liveright, Inc., 1931.
Lapsley	*The Writings of Abraham Lincoln.* Edited by Arthur Brooks Lapsley. 8 volumes. New York: P. F. Collier and Son, 1905.

SOURCES

NH	*Complete Works of Abraham Lincoln.* Edited by John G. Nicolay and John Hay. 12 volumes. New York: Francis D. Tandy Company, 1905.
OR	*The War of the Rebellion: A Compilation of the Official Records of the Union and Confederate Armies.* 4 series; 70 "volumes"; 128 books. Washington: Government Printing Office, 1880-1901. Roman numerals are used for Series, Volume, and Part (if any); pages are in arabic.
Tarbell	*The Life of Abraham Lincoln. . . .* By Ida M. Tarbell. 2 volumes. New York: The Doubleday & McClure Company, 1900.
Tracy	*Uncollected Letters of Abraham Lincoln.* Edited by Gilbert A. Tracy. Boston and New York: Houghton Mifflin Company, 1917.
Wilson	*Uncollected Works of Abraham Lincoln.* Edited by Rufus Rockwell Wilson. 2 volumes. Elmira, New York: Primavera Press, 1947-1948.

LOCATION SYMBOLS

CCamStJ	St. John's Seminary Library, Camarillo, Calif.
CLCM	Los Angeles County Museum Library, Los Angeles, Calif.
CSmH	Henry E. Huntington Library, San Marino, Calif.
CoHi	State Historical Society of Colorado, Denver, Colo.
CoU	University of Colorado Library, Boulder, Colo.
Ct	Connecticut State Library, Hartford, Conn.
CtHi	Connecticut Historical Society, Hartford, Conn.
CtLHi	Litchfield Historical Society, Litchfield, Conn.
CtSoP	Pequot Library, Southport, Conn.
CtWat	Watertown Library Association, Watertown, Conn.
CtY	Yale University Library, New Haven, Conn.
DLC	Library of Congress, Washington, D. C.
DLC-HW	Herndon-Weik Collection, Library of Congress
DLC-RTL	The Robert Todd Lincoln Collection of the Papers of Abraham Lincoln, Library of Congress
DLM	Lincoln Museum, Ford's Theatre, National Park Service, Washington, D. C.
DNA	National Archives, Washington, D. C. All additional abbreviations and numbers given with this symbol are those employed by the National Archives at the time the manuscript was located.
DNM	National Museum Library, Washington, D. C.

DeHi	Historical Society of Delaware Library, Wilmington, Del.
DeWI	Wilmington Institute Free Library, Wilmington, Del.
I-Ar	Archives Division, Illinois State Library, Springfield. Ill.
IBloHi	McLean County Historical Society, Bloomington, Ill.
ICHi	Chicago Historical Society, Chicago, Ill.
ICU	University of Chicago Library, Chicago, Ill.
IDecJ	James Millikin University Library, Decatur, Ill.
IFre	Freeport Public Library, Freeport, Ill.
IHi	Illinois State Historical Library, Springfield, Ill.
IJI	Illinois College Library, Jacksonville, Ill.
ISLA	The Abraham Lincoln Association, Springfield, Ill.
IU	University of Illinois Library, Urbana, Ill.
IaCrM	Iowa Masonic Library, Cedar Rapids, Iowa
IaDaM	Davenport Public Museum, Davenport, Iowa
IaHA	Iowa State Department of History and Archives, Des Moines, Iowa
In	Indiana State Library, Indianapolis, Ind.
InFtwL	Lincoln National Life Foundation, Fort Wayne, Ind.
InHi	Indiana Historical Society, Indianapolis, Ind.
InLTHi	Tippecanoe County Historical Association, Lafayette, Ind.
InU	Indiana University Library, Bloomington, Ind.
KyBC	Berea College Library, Berea, Ky.
KyU	University of Kentucky Library, Lexington, Ky.
LU	Louisiana State University Library, Baton Rouge, La.
MB	Boston Public Library, Boston, Mass.
MCon	Free Public Library, Concord, Mass.
MFai	Millicent Library, Fairhaven, Mass.
MH	Harvard University Library, Cambridge, Mass.
MHi	Massachusetts Historical Society, Boston, Mass.
MS	Springfield Library Association, Springfield, Mass.
MSHi	Connecticut Valley Historical Society, Springfield, Mass.
MdAA	Hall of Records, State of Maryland, Annapolis, Md.
MdHi	Maryland Historical Society, Baltimore, Md.
MeHi	Maine Historical Society, Portland, Me.
MiD	Detroit Public Library, Detroit, Mich.
MiK-M	Kalamazoo Public Library Museum, Kalamazoo, Mich.
MiU-C	William L. Clements Library, University of Michigan, Ann Arbor, Mich.

MiU-Hi	Michigan Historical Collection, University of Michigan, Ann Arbor, Mich.
MnHi	Minnesota Historical Society, St. Paul, Minn.
MnSM	Macalester College Library, St. Paul, Minn.
MoHi	State Historical Society of Missouri, Columbia, Mo.
MoSHi	Missouri Historical Society, St. Louis, Mo.
N	New York State Library, Albany, N. Y.
NAuE	Fred L. Emerson Foundation, Auburn, N. Y.
NBLiHi	Long Island Historical Society, Brooklyn, N. Y.
NBuG	Grosvenor Library, Buffalo, New York
NBuHi	Buffalo Historical Society, Buffalo, N. Y.
NDry	Southworth Library, Dryden, N. Y.
NHi	New-York Historical Society, New York City
NIC	Cornell University Library, Ithaca, N. Y.
NN	New York Public Library, New York City
NNC	Columbia University Library, New York City
NNP	Pierpont Morgan Library, New York City
NRU	University of Rochester Library, Rochester, N. Y.
NSh	John Jermain Memorial Library, Sag Harbor, N. Y.
NSk	Skaneateles Library Association, Skaneateles, N. Y.
NWM	U. S. Military Academy Library, West Point, N. Y.
NbO	Omaha Public Library, Omaha, Nebr.
NcGu	Guilford College Library, Guilford, N. C.
NhExP	Phillips Exeter Academy, Exeter, N. H.
NjP	Princeton University Library, Princeton, N. J.
OCHP	Historical and Philosophical Society of Ohio, Cincinnati, Ohio
OClCS	Case Institute of Technology, Cleveland, Ohio
OClWHi	Western Reserve Historical Society, Cleveland, Ohio
OFH	Hayes Memorial Library, Fremont, Ohio
OMC	Marietta College Library, Marietta, Ohio
ORB	Oliver R. Barrett Collection, Chicago, Ill.*
OSHi	Clark County Historical Society, Springfield, Ohio
OrHi	Oregon Historical Society, Portland, Ore.
PHC	Haverford College Library, Haverford, Pa.
PHi	Historical Society of Pennsylvania, Philadelphia, Pa.

* After the *Collected Works* was in press, the collection of the late Oliver R. Barrett was sold at auction by Parke-Bernet Galleries (Catalog 1315) on February 19-20, 1952. It has been impossible to trace all new owners of the more than two hundred items, and impracticable to change the source citations for those which are known, but many of the more important items went to such well-known collections as those in the Library of Congress (Debates Scrapbook, purchased for the Alfred Whital Stern Collection) and Illinois State Historical Library (letters to Joshua F. Speed, etc.).

PMA	Allegheny College Library, Meadville, Pa.
PP	Free Library of Philadelphia, Philadelphia, Pa.
PPDrop	Dropsie College Library, Philadelphia, Pa.
PSt	Pennsylvania State College Library, State College, Pa.
PU	University of Pennsylvania Library, Philadelphia, Pa.
RPAB	Annmary Brown Memorial Library, Providence, R. I.
RPB	Brown University Library, Providence, R. I.
THaroL	Lincoln Memorial University, Harrogate, Tenn.
THi	Tennessee Historical Society, Nashville, Tenn.
ViU	University of Virginia Library, Charlottesville, Va.
VtU	University of Vermont Library, Burlington, Vt.
WBeloHi	Beloit Historical Society, Beloit, Wis.
WHi	State Historical Society of Wisconsin, Madison, Wis.
WvU	West Virginia University Library, Morgantown, W. Va.

Courtesy of Frederick Hill Meserve

AUGUST 9, 1863
By Alexander Gardner

THE COLLECTED WORKS OF
ABRAHAM LINCOLN

━━━━◀◆▶━━━━

To the Senate[1]

To the Senate of the United States: December 13, 1862

In the list of nominations transmitted to the Senate under date of the 1st instant, Captain Wm. M. Glendy, U.S. Navy, was included therein for promotion to the grade of commodore.

Since submitting this nomination it appears that this officer was ineligible for the advancement to which he had been nominated, in consequence of his age, being sixty-two on the 23d of May, 1862, and under the law of 21 December, 1861, should, had this fact been known to the Navy Department, have been transferred to the retired list on the day when he completed sixty-two years.

The nomination of Captain Glendy is accordingly withdrawn.

It is due to this officer to state that at the period of the passage of the law of December, 1861, he was, and still is, absent on duty on a foreign station, and the certificate of his age, required by the Navy Department, was only received a few days since.

Washington, D.C., 13 December, 1862.   ABRAHAM LINCOLN.

[1] *Senate Executive Journal*, XIII, 11. Captain William M. Glendy of Maryland was placed on the retired list and is listed in the *U.S. Official Register*, 1863, as "Prize Commissioner" at Washington, D.C.

To Edwin M. Stanton[1]

December 13, 1862.

Will the Secretary of War please direct that Mr. Thoroughman may be disposed of at the discretion of Abram Jonas and Henry Asbury of Quincy, Ill., both of whom I know to be loyal and sensible men?   A. LINCOLN.

December 13, 1862.

[1] Leslie J. Perry, "Appeals to Lincoln's Clemency," *The Century Magazine*, LI (December, 1895), 252. Perry describes Lincoln's endorsement as "on the face of a large official envelop which probably originally contained all the papers relating to the case. . . . Inside in a single-paper the report of Henry Asbury and Abra[ha]m Jonas—from which it appears that Mr. Thoroughman

was duly paroled and permitted to go to his home." Thomas Thoroughman of St. Joseph, Missouri, was arrested for disloyalty in May, 1862, and afterwards sent to Quincy, Illinois.

To Simon Cameron[1]

Hon. Simon Cameron   Executive Mansion,
Harrisburg, Pa.   Washington, Dec. 14, 1862.
   Please come to Washington so soon as you conveniently can.

                                   A. LINCOLN

[1] ALS, RPB. No reply has been found, but see Lincoln to Cameron, February 13, 1863, *infra*.

To Samuel R. Curtis[1]

                   Executive Mansion, Washington,
Major-General Curtis, Saint Louis, Mo.:   December 14, 1862.
   If my friend Dr. William Fithian, of Danville, Ill., should call on you, please give him such facilities as you consistently can about recovering the remains of a step-son and matters connected therewith.   A. LINCOLN.

[1] Tarbell (Appendix), p. 355. William Fithian's stepsons, Lieutenant Colonel John C. Black of the Thirty-seventh Illinois, and his brother William P. Black, had been badly wounded in the Battle of Prairie Grove in northwest Arkansas on December 7, 1862. Ward H. Lamon relates, "I shall never forget the scene, when I took to Mr. Lincoln a letter written by Dr. Fithian to me, describing the condition of the 'Black boys,' and expressing his fears that they could not live. Mr. Lincoln read it, and broke into tears. . . ." (*Recollections of Abraham Lincoln*, pp. 104-105). John C. Black survived to a distinguished career in politics.

To John G. Nicolay[1]

                             War Department.
John G. Nicolay, Headquarters: [December 14, 1862]
     What news have you?   A. LINCOLN.

[1] Tarbell (Appendix), p. 355. No answer has been found, but see note, Lincoln to Burnside, December 12, *supra*.

To Edward Bates[1]

This letter being written by the U.S. District Attorney I have concluded to grant the pardon requested.   A. LINCOLN
   Dec. 15. 1862

[1] AES, DNA RG 204, U.S. Pardon Attorney, A 453. Lincoln's endorsement is written on the back of a letter from William P. Price, U.S. District Attorney at Baltimore, December 11, 1862, recommending pardon of First Mate Rasmus Benson, convicted of cruel and unusual punishment of a seaman.

[2]

To Isaac R. Diller[1]

Captain Dahlgren, of the U.S. Navy, having tested, to some extent, the new powder mentioned within, and having expressed the opinion that a fuller test should be made, which he thinks cannot be satisfactorily done with less than one thousand pounds, I agree to the within terms, as modified by what is written below. The quantity of powder produced for the test may be more, but not less than one thousand pounds, and the sum to be paid for preparing this quantity, shall not be more than the actual cost, nor more than two dollars per pound, nor in the aggregate more than five thousand dollars. When the officers, or other skilled person or persons, I shall select to make the test, shall advise me that in their opinion, the powder possesses all the advantages represented within, and that it has no important fault, I will advise the payment of the one hundred and fifty thousand dollars, for the transfer to the United States, the secret of composing and making said powder, and the exclusive right, within the United States, of making, using, and vending it to others, to be used. I only promise to advise the payment, because I have not the money at my control which I could, by law, absolutely promise to pay.

December 15. 1862.   A. LINCOLN

[1] Copies, DLC-RTL; copy, DNA WR RG 74, Navy Branch, Bureau of Ordnance, Letters Received 1862-1863. See Lincoln to Welles, August 2, *supra*, and endorsement of January 15, 1863, *infra*. On September 10, 1862, Isaac R. Diller wrote Lincoln as follows:

"After consultation with Captain Dahlgreen, I have come to the conclusion not to attempt to make the large quantity of the new powder which he will require for full tests, in this City. In my opinion it would not be safe to do so, on account of the secrecy necessary to be observed in its manufacture.

"In my opinion the expense, incurred in the manufacture of the required amount will not exceed five hundred dollars,—provided I have permission to draw from the public stores such articles as are on hand.

"The sum specified will be used only for the purpose of purchasing certain necessary means for making it, which will always be found useful in the public laboratory connected with the Agricultural Department of the Government.

"Before commencing these experiments it will be positively necessary for me to return to the West for a few days and I respectfully ask that transportation be furnished me for that purpose.

"I propose to do this work in Philadelphia, and in this determination Capt. Dahlgreen concurs.

"When I am prepared to commence operations, I have the honor to ask that Dr. Charles M. Wetherill, Chief Chemist of the Agricultural Department, be again assigned to me to conduct the manufacture, and experiments, as he is the only person, except myself, familiar with the process of manufacture, in this country.

"The expenses already incurred, not counting my time or that of the Chemist, amounts to two hundred & fifty-five dollars." (DLC-RTL).

On October 17, 1862, Charles M. Wetherill wrote Lincoln as follows:

"Having understood that Captain Diller is ready to have me detailed back to the Department of Agriculture, I desire to make the following statement. I have brought my chemical apparatus (which I value at $3000) to Washington by Captain Dillers directions. I have used it in the experiments without charge to the Government.

"I have placed this apparatus together with my scientific library (which I value at $2000) at the disposal of the Department of Agriculture to be used by me in the prosecution of researches in agricultural chemistry, until Congress shall provide for the Chemistry of the Department. As I place $5000 of my Capital at the disposal of the Government, without interest I think I should be made secure in its ownership. As soon as I am detailed back to the Dept. of Agriculture I lose possession of my apparatus unless said room is in the possession of the Commissioner. I have therefore respectfully to request that this laboratory tranfer be made or that I be otherwise made secure in my ownership before I am detailed back to my Department." (DLC-RTL).

Shortly afterwards, Wetherill was appointed chemist in the Department of Agriculture (New York *Tribune*, October 27, 1862), and the experiment was undertaken. On December 10, Diller submitted the following document to the president and received Lincoln's endorsement (dated December 15, as given above):

"The undersigned, Isaac R. Diller, a citizen of the United States, and resident of the State of Illinois, would respectfully represent; that I am the owner and possessor of a process of making an article of gunpowder entirely unknown and unused in the United States.

"I propose to place the art of manufacturing the said powder and every thing pertaining to the complete understanding of its composition, in the possession of the Government of the United States, on the condition, that as soon as the amount hereafter specified has been made, and the article being tested by said Government, and being found to possess the qualities and advantages claimed for it, then and in that case in consideration therefor, the said Government is to pay, or cause to be paid, to the undersigned, the sum of one hundred and fifty thousand dollars ($150,000).

"The said tests to be carried on and conducted by officers of the said Government, to be selected by the President, in the presence of the undersigned, and at as an early a day as possible, after a notification from the undersigned that the material is prepared.

"When the said tests are completed, if successful and satisfactory to the said Government, I will then place them in possession of the said art and mode of compounding the said article of gunpowder, whereupon the above sum is then to be paid, as above stipulated.

"I further propose to proceed immediately, upon the approval of these propositions, by the President of the United States, to prepare a sufficient quantity of the said article for the tests aforesaid, not exceeding one thousand pounds, the said Government agreeing to pay all charges and expenses incurred in the preparation of the said quantity, and the machinery necessary therefor.

"I propose to file full specifications of the advantages claimed for the new powder, in the office of Captain J. A. Dahlgren, chief of the Bureau of Ordnance in the Navy Department, within ten days from the date and approval of the above propositions by the President.

"I have the honor to be Very Respectfully Your Obedient Servant

ISAAC R. DILLER."

"Specification of the advantages claimed for the 'R.R.R. Gunpowder' made a part of this paper by direction of the President.

"1. It contains neither saltpetre nor sulphur. It bears no relation to gun-cotton. The ingredients can always be obtained in the United States.

"2. The manufacture of the powder is simple, requiring no complicated apparatus, and is attended with less danger than the manufacture of ordinary gunpowder.

"3. Atmospheric changes, whether of moisture, or heat, do not injure the powder. Like ordinary gunpowder, it requires a great pressure or friction for its explosion. It does not ignite under 300° Celsius. It may be ignited by a spark, or percussion cap, like common gunpowder.

"4. In smooth-bored guns, *seven* parts by weight of this powder, are, as effective as *nine* parts by weight of ordinary gunpowder, while in rifled guns, this advantage is in the proportion of *one* to *two*.

"5. Neither this powder, nor its ingredients in store, are liable to deteriorate.

"6. The heating effect of this powder is less than that of ordinary powder, in the proportion of one to two. It gives a weaker report, less smoke, and fouls the gun much less than ordinary gunpowder. It does not damage the gun.

"7. In comparing equal weights of this with ordinary gunpowder, the estimated cost is about equal—but the smaller amount required of this powder, renders it greatly advantageous on the score of economy.

ISAAC R. DILLER."

See further Lincoln to Stanton and Welles, July 21, 1863, and Lincoln's memorandum of instructions for testing Diller's powder, November 2, 1863, *infra;* also references indexed under Isaac R. Diller and Charles M. Wetherill.

To Edwin M. Stanton[1]

Hon. Sec. of War   Washington,
Sir: Dec. 15, 1862.

Hon. Mr. Covode wishes Col. Crossman to be made a Brigadier General, and I wish to oblige him if it can be consistently done. Yours truly   A. LINCOLN

[1] ALS, owned by Frederick M. Dearborn, New York City. On March 7, 1863, Lieutenant Colonel George H. Crosman, deputy quartermaster general in charge of the depot of clothing and equipment at Philadelphia, was recommended for promotion by brevet to the rank of colonel from January 1, 1862, and to the rank of brigadier general by brevet from October 1, 1862. The promotions were confirmed by the Senate on March 10, 1863.

To Ambrose E. Burnside[1]

Washington City, D.C.

Majr. Gen. Burnside   Dec. 16 1862

Your despatch about Gen. Stahl, is received. Please ascertain from Gen. Sigel, & his old corps, whether Stahl or Schurz is preferable, & telegraph the result, and I will act immediately. After all I shall be governed by your preference.

A. LINCOLN

[1] ALS, IHi. The address "Falmouth" is added following Burnside's name by Stanton. Burnside's reply, received at 6 P.M., reads as follows: "My application for the appointment of Gen Stahl is based upon the recommendation of Gen Sigel who has been a very useful and efficient officer during the time that I have had command of this army. He is decidedly of the opinion that Gen Stahl is the best man." (NHi). On the back of the telegram Lincoln endorsed "Let Gen.

Stahl be appointed. Dec. 16. 1862. A. LINCOLN." Colonel Julius Stahel of the Eighth New York Infantry was appointed brigadier general on November 12, 1861, and assigned to temporary command of the Eleventh Corps on December 18, 1862, during the absence of General Sigel (OR, I, LI, I, 960), and on January 10, 1863, he was named to the command when Sigel assumed command of the Division comprising the Eleventh and Twelfth Corps (OR, I, XXI, 962). Stahel became major general on March 14, 1863.

To Samuel R. Curtis[1]

Majr. Gen. Curtis   Executive Mansion,
St. Louis, Mo.   Washington, Dec. 16. 1862.

N. W. Watkins, of Jackson, Mo. (who is half brother to Henry Clay) writes me that a Col. of ours has driven him from his home at Jackson. Will you please look into the case, and restore the old man to his home, if the public interest will admit?

A. LINCOLN

[1] ALS, RPB. No reply from Curtis has been found. Nathaniel W. Watkins, a prominent old Whig, had led a force of Missouri State Guards (Confederate) in the early months of the war. On November 30, 1862, he wrote Lincoln as follows:

"In December of last year Mr. [John W.] Noell the member of Congress . . . wrote to my son saying . . . that he had an interview with you in relation to me, that you had expressed kind feelings for me and that if I would come Home, and give my word that . . . I would be loyal, and take no part in the Rebellion you would restore me to my rights, and protection as a citizen. . . . Afterwards you were kind enough in the month of February last to cause the indictment pending against me to be dismissed, and restored me to all my rights as a citizen.

"So soon as I learned this . . . I returned to Missouri, and reached my home at this place in July where I have resided with my Family . . . doing nothing in any way prejudicial to the Government. . . .

"On the day before yesterday . . . Coln. Albert Jackson . . . without cause or provocation forceably drove me and my family from our House giving but three hours notice. . . ." (DLC-RTL).

To Henry H. Sibley[1]

Brigadier General H. H. Sibley   Executive Mansion,
St. Paul, Minnesota.   Washington, Dec. 16. 1862

As you suggest, let the executions fixed for Friday, the nineteenth (19th.) instant, be postponed to, and be done on, Friday the twentysixth (26th.) instant.   A. LINCOLN

Private

Operator please send this very carefully and accurately.

A. L.

[1] ALS, RPB. On December 15 General Sibley replied to Lincoln's letter of December 6 *supra* as follows: "Your order of 6th Inst. for the Execution of 39 Indians just recd by Special messenger They are imprisoned at Mankato 90

miles distant & the time fixed 19th is too short for preparation & for concentrating the troops necessary to protect the other Indians & preserve the peace The excitement prevails all sections of the state & secret combinations Exist Embracing thousands of citizens pledged to execute all the Indians matters must be managed with great discretion & as much secrecy as possible to prevent a fearful collision between the U.S. forces & the citizens. I respectfully ask for authority to postpone the Execution one week from the 19th Inst if I deem necessary Please reply at once. Your directions of 9th relative to Chakaydon rec'd today by mail & will be obeyed." (DLC-RTL). The communication referred to in the last sentence of Sibley's despatch has not been located. On December 27, Sibley telegraphed as follows: "I have the honor to inform you that the 38 Indians and half-breeds ordered by you for execution were hung yesterday at Mankato, at 10 a.m. Everything went off quietly, and the other prisoners are well secured." (OR, I, XXII, I, 880). One of the thirty-nine listed in Lincoln's communication to Sibley, December 6, *supra*, "Chaska-don" or "Chaskay-etay," alias Robert Hopkins, was not executed. On August 18, 1864, Lincoln endorsed a petition for Hopkins "Pardons [*sic*]. A. LINCOLN" (DNA WR RG 153, Judge Advocate General, NN 2323).

To Ambrose E. Burnside[1]

Executive Mansion,
Major General Burnside   Washington, December 17, 1862.

George Patten says he was a class-mate of yours and was in the same regiment of artillery. Have you a place you would like to put him in? and if so what is it?   A. LINCOLN.

[1] Tarbell (Appendix), p. 356. Burnside replied at 3:30 P.M., "Telegraph Lines have been down all day. Will answer you in reference to George Patten in a day or two. . . ." (DLC-RTL). No further communication in regard to Patten has been found. George Patten of South Carolina, graduated at West Point in 1847, and resigned from the Army July 21, 1851. He was professor in the Military Institute at Chester, Pennsylvania, from 1861 to March 11, 1863, when he was appointed captain and assistant adjutant general of Volunteers, from which appointment he resigned on July 2, 1863. On February 10, 1864, he was appointed first lieutenant in the Third New Jersey Cavalry and served until May 15, 1865.

To Abraham C. Corder[1]

Abraham C. Corsey, of 7th. Ills. Vols.
Grand Junction, Miss.   Dec. 17. 1862
Your despatch of yesterday received. Not now.

A. LINCOLN

[1] ALS, RPB. The roster of the Seventh Illinois lists no Abraham C. Corsey, and no correspondence from him or further reference to him can be found. Lincoln probably erred in writing the name. Abraham C. Corder of Brooklyn and New Haven, Illinois, was a wagon master in the Seventh Illinois Cavalry. On March 16, 1863, he telegraphed Lincoln from Memphis, "Your dispatch of Decr 18th recd. states 'not yet.' Am now ready to go to work." (DLC-RTL). No satisfactory explanation has been found for this cryptic exchange of telegrams.

[7]

To John J. Crittenden, John W. Crisfield, and William A. Hall[1]

Hon. J. J. Crittenden   Executive Mansion,
"   J. W. Crisfield   Washington,
"   W. A. Hall.   Dec. 17. 1862.

Gentlemen: Your note of to-day asking me to designate a time when I can receive you as a committee, is at hand. Let 10. A.M. to-morrow be the time. Your Obt. Servt.   A LINCOLN

[1] ALS, DLC-Nicolay Papers. The note from Representatives Crittenden and Crisfield, and Representative-elect William A. Hall of Missouri, soliciting an interview to present the views of people in the border states is also in the Nicolay Papers.

To Samuel R. Curtis[1]

                       Executive Mansion,
Major-General Curtis: Washington, December 17, 1862.

Could the civil authority be reintroduced into Missouri in lieu of the military to any extent, with advantage and safety?
                         A. LINCOLN.

[1] Tarbell (Appendix), p. 356. General Curtis replied at 9:15 P.M., "Dispatch received. The peace of this State rests on military power. To relinquish this power would be dangerous. It would allow rebels to rule some sections and ruin the Union men who have joined the military power to put down the rebellion. The civil authority is gradually coming into use, but sneaking rebels are in office, anxious to encourage new raids, and secure revenge for past military surveillance. It requires a considerable military force to keep things quiet in Missouri." OR, I, XXII, I, 839.

On December 19, Lieutenant Colonel Franklin A. Dick, provost marshal general of the Department of the Missouri, wrote Lincoln in support of General Curtis' reply, "Officially I have most complete and reliable information as to the condition of this State. I have been in Missouri nearly all the time during the rebellion, and I say positively that at no previous time have the efforts and evil purposes of the Rebels in this State and city been more active and hopeful than now. . . . I therefore most respectfully ask of the President, that he will not require that we relax in our efforts to fight this enemy in the most effective manner. . . ." (DLC-RTL).

Memorandum Concerning William H. Johnson[1]

                       December 17, 1862

I decline to sign the within, because it does not state the thing quite to my liking. The colored man William Johnson came with me from Illinois, and I would be glad for him to be obliged, if he can be consistently with the public service; but I can not make an

order about it, nor a request which might, in some sort, be construed as an order.   A. LINCOLN.
    Dec. 17, 1862

    [1] Hertz, II, 889. John E. Washington speculates that this memorandum refers to a request for leave of absence for Johnson in order to earn extra money (*They Knew Lincoln*, p. 131).

To Jacob Collamer[1]

Hon. Jacob Collamer.   Executive Mansion,
My dear Sir: Washington, Dec. 18. 1862.
    I will see the Committee named, at 7 P.M. to-day.
                                                      A. LINCOLN

    [1] ALS, RPB. Senator Collamer's note of December 18 notified the president that "A committee of the Republican Senators desire an interview with the President at as early an hour after six oclock this evening as may suit his convenience." (DLC-RTL). The purpose of the interview was to discuss the resignation of Secretary Seward which had been submitted to the president on December 16. See Lincoln's letter to Seward and Chase, December 20, *infra*.

To Hamilton R. Gamble[1]

Gov. Gamble   Executive Mansion,
St. Louis, Mo   Washington, Dec. 18, 1862.
    It is represented to me that the enrolled militia alone would now maintain law and order in all the counties of your State North of the Missouri river. If so, all other forces there, might be removed South of the river, or out of the State. Please post yourself, and give me your opinion upon this subject.   A. LINCOLN

    [1] ALS, RPB. Governor Gamble replied to Lincoln's telegram on the same day, "I can maintain law & order north of the Missouri River with the Enrolled Militia alone if they can be certainly provided for with subsistence clothing & pay for time they may be in actual service   Many of them are very poor   taking other troops would help rather than hinder me   I would keep the small number in service that could protect the country (DLC-RTL)." See further Lincoln to Curtis, December 19, *infra*.

To the Senate and House of Representatives[1]

December 18, 1862

To the Senate and House of Representatives:
    I transmit a copy of a despatch to the Secretary of State from Mr. Adams, United States Minister at London, and of the correspondence to which it refers, between that gentleman and Mr. Panizzi, the Principal Librarian of the British Museum, relative to

certain valuable publications presented to the Library of Congress.
Washington, 18 December 1862.   ABRAHAM LINCOLN

[1] DS, DNA RG 46, Senate 37A F2; DS, DNA RG 233, House Executive Document No. 15. Minister Charles F. Adams' letter to Seward, November 21, 1862, transmitted correspondence with Sir Anthony Panizzi relative to the presentation to the Library of Congress of the early volumes of *Description of Ancient Marbles; Select Papyri in the Hieratic Character;* and the entire series of zoological catalogs published by the Museum. Lincoln's communication was referred in both Senate and House to the joint committee on the Library.

To Edwin M. Stanton[1]

I wish this appointment to be made if it can be done consistently.
Executive Mansion   A. LINCOLN
Dec. 18, 1862.

[1] AES, IHi. This copy of an autograph endorsement by Lincoln appears on a copy of a letter from Joshua F. Speed, written on Executive Mansion stationery, December 9, 1862, recommending Captain Charles L. Thomasson of the Fifth Kentucky Infantry for an appointment "in the pay department." No record has been found of Thomasson's appointment.

To Ambrose E. Burnside[1]

Washington, December 19, 1862.
Major-General Burnside: Come of course, if in your own judgment it is safe to do so.   A. LINCOLN.

[1] NH, VIII, 147. Lincoln replied to Burnside's telegram received at 11:50 P.M., "I want very much to see you   If all is quiet can I come up tomorrow afternoon" (DLC-RTL). At 3 P.M. on December 20, Burnside telegraphed, "I will be with you tonight." (*Ibid.*). See further Lincoln's message to the Army of the Potomac, December 22, *infra.*

To Samuel R. Curtis[1]

Majr. Gen. Curtis   Executive Mansion,
St. Louis, Mo.   Washington, Dec. 19, 1862
Hon.   Hall,[2] M.C. here, tells me, & Gov. Gamble Telegraphs me, that quiet can be maintained in all the counties *North* of the Missouri river, by the enrolled militia. Confer with Gov. Gamble, and telegraph me.   A. LINCOLN

[1] ALS, RPB. Curtis' reply received at 6 P.M. is as follows: "Only 2 skeleton Regts united States troops north of River   the Governor is absent. Some Enrolled Militia not so reliable   Will write you" (DLC-RTL). On December 20, he wrote:
"In regard to your telegraphic inquiry as to the propriety of relying entirely on the Enrolled Militia . . . I proceed to enlarge on my telegraphic reply.
"We have just driven the rebels out of Missouri, and hold them south by a force almost continuous along the southern border. . . . Their anxiety exists to return . . . where the wealthy secessionists in many neighborhoods are ready

to receive and replenish them. In such neighborhoods the pro-slavery influence seeks to exclude the Union troops, hoping to hold their negroes better under the Enrolled Militia, many of whom are commanded by pro-slavery officers. I try to study the surrounding elements, and move troops away just as fast as I think the safety of community will permit, and will probably soon withdraw all or nearly all the volunteers from Northern Missouri. Another trouble intervenes. The Enrolled Militia when in actual service are fed by the United States, and levy contributions from the secessionists to indemnify themselves for losses. . . . So far I have got along without much difficulty with mixed forces, but I have required of my officers and acted myself with great caution and courtesy toward State troops, for fear of trouble. . . . I, and all good Union men, dread the least conflict of sovereignties. . . . The object of all this is to present . . . the delicacy of my position . . . . wherever a community can maintain the peace with civil laws and the Enrolled Militia, I shall gladly relinquish military authority. . . ." (DLC-RTL).   2 William A. Hall.

To Salmon P. Chase[1]

Secretary of the Treasury, please do not go out of town.

December 20, 1862.   A. LINCOLN.

1 Warden, *Life of Chase*, p. 508. Chase's lengthy reply of the same date is as follows:

"I intended going to Philadelphia this afternoon, but shall, of course, observe your 'direction' not to leave town

"Will you allow me to say that something you *said* or looked, when I handed you my resignation this morning, made on my mind the impression that, having received the resignations both of Gov. Seward and myself, you felt you could relieve yourself from trouble by declining to accept either and that the feeling was one of gratification.

"Let me assure you few things could give me so much satisfaction as to promote in any way your comfort, especially if I might promote at the same time the success of your administration, and the good of the country which is so near your heart.

"But I am very far from desiring you to decline accepting my resignation—very far from thinking, indeed, that its non-acceptance and my continuance in the Treasury Department will be most for your comfort or further benefit of the country.

"On the contrary I could not if I would conceal from myself that recent events have too rudely jostled the unity of your cabinet and disclosed an opinion too deeply seated and too generally received in Congress & the Country to be safely disregarded that the concord in judgment and action essential to successful administration does not prevail among its members.

"By some the embarrassment of administration is attributed to me; by others to Mr. Seward; by others, still to other Heads of Departments. Now neither Mr Seward nor myself is essential to you or to the Country; we both earnestly wish to be relieved from the oppressive charge of our respective Departments; and we both have placed our resignations in your hands.

"A resignation is a grave act; never performed by a right minded man without forethought or with reserve. I tendered mine from a sense of duty to the country, to you, and to myself—and I tendered it to be accepted. So did, as you have been fully assured, Mr. Seward tender his.

"I trust therefore that you will regard yourself as completely relieved from all personal considerations. It is my honest judgment that we can both better serve you and the country at this time, as private citizens, than in your cabinet. . . ." (DLC-RTL).

To Thomas J. Henderson[1]

Executive Mansion, Washington,
Hon. T. J. Henderson. December 20, 1862.

My dear Sir:— Your letter of the 8th to Hon. William Kellogg has just been shown me. You can scarcely overestimate the pleasure it would give me to oblige you, but nothing is operating so ruinously upon us everywhere as "absenteeism." It positively will not do for me to grant leaves of absence in cases not sufficient to procure them under the regular rules.

It would astonish you to know the extent of the evil of "absenteeism." We scarcely have more than half the men we are paying on the spot for service anywhere. Yours very truly,

A. LINCOLN.

[1] Lapsley, VI, 222. Colonel Thomas J. Henderson of the One Hundred Twelfth Illinois Volunteers was at Camp Ella Bishop, Lexington, Kentucky. No letter from him at this time has been found.

Memorandum:
Appointment of Henry W. Streeter[1]

I want to oblige Mr. Speaker Grow in this case if it can consistently be done. A. LINCOLN
Dec. 20. 1862.

[1] AES, DNA WR RG 94, U.S. Military Academy, 1863, Box 82, No. 148. Lincoln's endorsement is written on a letter from Galusha A. Grow, December 19, 1862, asking appointment to West Point of "*Henry W. Streeter* of Montrose Pa. . . . the son of my *very* best friend." Streeter's appointment is not of record.

To William H. Seward and Salmon P. Chase[1]

(COPY)
Hon. William H. Seward, & Executive Mansion,
Hon. Salmon P. Chase. Washington, December 20. 1862.

Gentlemen: You have respectively tendered me your resignations, as Secretary of State, and Secretary of the Treasury of the United States. I am apprised of the circumstances which may render this course personally desireable to each of you; but, after most anxious consideration, my deliberate judgment is, that the public interest does not admit of it. I therefore have to request that you will resume the duties of your Departments respectively. Your Obt. Servt. A. LINCOLN.

P.S. Same as above sent to Gov. Chase   A L.

P.S. Same as above sent to Gov. Seward.   A L.

Note—Postscripts, like the above are to respective letters.

1 ALS copy, DLC-RTL; ALS, NAuE. Since this episode has been told a number of times, the editors do not undertake to elaborate upon it. Brief letters of resignation were submitted on December 16 by Seward and on December 20 by Chase. On December 21, Seward wrote, "I have cheerfully resumed the functions of this Department in obedience to your command." (DLC-RTL). Chase, however, replied on December 22, as follows:

"On Saturday afternoon I received your note addressed to Mr. Seward and myself desiring us to resume the charge of our respective Departments.

"I had just written you a letter expressing quite another judgment; and that you may fully understand my sentiments I now send it to you. [See note, Lincoln to Chase, *supra.*]

"Your note, of course, required me to reconsider my views; and the next [*sic*] a further reason for reconsideration was furnished by the receipt from Mr. Seward of a copy of his reply to a note from you, identical with that sent to me, announcing his resumption of the duties of the State Department.

"I cannot say that reflection has much if at all changed my original impressions; but it has led me to the conclusion that I ought, in this matter, to conform my action to your judgment and wishes.

"I shall resume, therefore, my post as Secretary of the Treasury; ready, however, at any moment, to resign it, if, in your judgment, the success of your administration may be, in the slightest degree, promoted." (*Ibid.*).

Congratulations to the Army of the Potomac[1]

Executive Mansion, Washington, December 22, 1862.

To the Army of the Potomac: I have just read your Commanding General's preliminary report of the battle of Fredericksburg. Although you were not successful, the attempt was not an error, nor the failure other than an accident. The courage with which you, in an open field, maintained the contest against an entrenched foe, and the consummate skill and success with which you crossed and re-crossed the river, in face of the enemy, show that you possess all the qualities of a great army, which will yet give victory to the cause of the country and of popular government. Condoling with the mourners for the dead, and sympathizing with the severely wounded, I congratulate you that the number of both is comparatively so small.

I tender to you, officers and soldiers, the thanks of the nation.

ABRAHAM LINCOLN.

1 Printed leaflet distributed to the Army of the Potomac, ORB; New York *Tribune,* December 24, 1862. In the Lincoln Papers there is what appears to be a draft in an unidentified handwriting of a proclamation, or order of thanks, prepared for Lincoln to issue to the Army of the Potomac on this occasion. It bears little resemblance to Lincoln's communication as issued. The editors venture no guess as to its author, but reproduce it herewith:

"The President, commander in chief, returns his thanks to the generals, the officers, and the soldiers of the Army of the Potomac for the skill, discipline, valor, and devotion displayed in the Battle of Fredericksburg.

"An army of citizen soldiers largely composed of volunteers fresh from the peaceful occupations which have been heretofore the privilege and the duty of American citizens, you have bridged and crossed a deep and wide river in the face of a powerful foe, have arrayed yourselves with the regularity and order of veterans, have attacked with heroic valor an army in positions fortified with time and skill, and unsuccessful in the assault through the unexpected strength of the position and the number and desperate courage of the foe—misguided children of the same soil and the same race as yourselves, you continued the bloody conflict until night put an end to the unequal struggle.

"Resting on your arms upon the ensanguined field, the dawning day saw you still in firm and regular order offer battle to the enemy.

"Through a whole day the gage was declined.

"The foe had learned the strength of an army of citizen soldiers striking for their country, for the cause of orderly government and human rights. He declined to quit his vantage ground and accept the contest on an equal field.

"During a dark and stormy night you recrossed on narrow bridges the river in your rear, without haste, in close and regular order, without the loss of a color, a gun, and, save in battle, of a man.

"An army which has done this, has answered all the objections heretofore made against the discipline, the steadiness, or the skill of volunteers.

"It has shown that it confides in its leaders; that it can obey orders, and that for every evolution of war, this army of the people is competent as the trained troops of mercenaries on which rulers of other lands rely for defense and for aggression.

"The land mourns the loss of many gallant dead. They are heroes, dead for Liberty.

"Their names will live in the memory of the people from whom they came and whose cause they died to defend. And while it will be a sad page which records the story of the Battle of Fredericksburg, still, it will be blazoned with the names of patriots and gilded with the fires of heroism and of self devotion.

"We fight the battle of Liberty, not in this land only, but throughout the world.

"All lands have looked to America as the home of freedom, as the refuge of the oppressed.

"Upon the courage of her sons now depend the hopes of the world, and wherever the story of Fredericksburg is read, will the lovers of Liberty take courage.

"Soldiers of freedom, again your country thanks you.

"This order will be read at the head of every regiment of the Army of the United States.

"Given at the Executive Mansion, in the City of Washington, this 21st day of December, in the year of our Lord 1862, and of the Independence of the United States the 87th."

To John A. Dix[1]

Executive Mansion,
Major Gen: Dix   Washington, December 22, 1862.

Owing to extreme pressure of business, I have neglected for a week to write this note. General Busteed is with you. I bespeak for him your kindest consideration. His case is peculiar. Without much military experience he has entered the service from purely patriotic motives. Please assign him the position best adapted to his case, which may be within your power. Yours very truly

A. LINCOLN.

1 LS (copy?), DLC-RTL. This letter is in John Hay's handwriting, but signed by Lincoln. Concerning General Busteed, see Lincoln to Stanton, August 7, *supra*. General Dix replied on December 29, "I have just received your note in regard to Genl. Busteed, and am happy to inform you that I had anticipated your wishes by assigning him to a command at Yorktown under Maj. Genl. Keyes, an experienced officer, who will put him in the way of acquiring a knowledge of his duties. He is already in charge of a Brigade. . . ." (DLC-RTL).

To William B. Franklin and William F. Smith[1]

Major General Franklin &   Executive Mansion,
Major General Smith   Washington, Dec. 22. 1862.

Yours of the 20th. suggesting a plan of operations for the Army of the Potomac, is received. I have hastily read the plan, and shall yet try to give it more deliberate consideration, with the aid of military men. Meanwhile let me say it seems to me to present the old questions of preference between the line of the Peninsula, and the line you are now upon. The difficulties you point out as per- taining to the Fredericksburg line are obvious and palpable. But now, as heretofore, if you go to James River, a large part of the army must remain on or near the Fredericksburg line, to protect Washington. It is the old difficulty.

When I saw Gen. Franklin at Harrison's Landing on James River last July, I can not be mistaken in saying that he distinctly advised the bringing of the Army away from there[2]

Yours very truly   A LINCOLN.

1 ADfS, DLC-RTL. The lengthy letter of December 20 from Major Generals Franklin and Smith advocated the return to a plan of attack via the James River and expressed the generals' opinion that "the plan of campaign already com- menced will not be successful" (OR, I, XXI, 868-70). On January 23, 1863, Burnside issued an order relieving Smith and Franklin from their commands: "It being evident [they] can be of no further service to this army. . . ." (*Ibid.*, 999); but the order was not approved by Lincoln, and Burnside himself was removed a few days later.

2 General Franklin's reply of December 26 is not in the Lincoln Papers or in the *Official Records*, but a copy in the Butler Papers (DLC) reads:

"In arguing the propriety of a campaign on the James River, we supposed Washington to be garrisoned sufficiently and the Potomac impassable except by bridges. The fortifications of Harpers Ferry is another important requisite. These matters were considered as of course and did not enter into our discussion of the two plans of campaign.

"I presume that you are right in supposing that I advised the withdrawal of the army from James River in July last. I think that under the same circumstances I would give the same advice. The Army was debilitated by what it had already gone through, was in an unhealthy position, its sick list was enormous, and there was a prospect that we would have to remain in that position during the two worst months August and September.

"The effect of this would have been to ruin the army in health. Circumstances are very different now. The army is in good health and the best months of the year are before us."

To the Senate[1]

To the Senate of the United States.   December 22, 1862

In compliance with the Resolution of the Senate of the 15th. instant, requesting a copy of the Report of the Honorable Reverdy Johnson, I transmit a communication from the Secretary of State and the documents by which it was accompanied.

Washington,   ABRAHAM LINCOLN.
22nd. December, 1862.

[1] DS, DNA RG 46, Senate 37A F3. The report of Reverdy Johnson's activities as U.S. commissioner at New Orleans from July 7 to July 29, 1862, investigating General Benjamin F. Butler's seizure of property of foreign consuls, may be found in Thirty-seventh Congress, Third Session, *Senate Executive Document No. 16.*

To Salmon P. Chase[1]

Executive Mansion,
Washington, December 23, 1862.

Dear Sir: Unless you know some strong objection, please send me a nomination for Cuthbert Bullitt as collector of the customs at New Orleans. I wish to do this at once. Yours truly,

A. LINCOLN.

[1] NH, VIII, 152. Chase replied on the same day that because "the Act of Congress of last session provides that the duties of Collectors &c in States in insurrection shall be performed by Special Agents. . . . Mr. Bullitt cannot therefore be appointed Collector. But I propose to appoint him Special Agent to perform the duties. . . ." (DLC-RTL). Cuthbert Bullitt is listed in the *U.S. Official Register,* 1863, as "Acting Collector."

To Fanny McCullough[1]

Executive Mansion,
Dear Fanny   Washington, December 23, 1862.

It is with deep grief that I learn of the death of your kind and brave Father; and, especially, that it is affecting your young heart beyond what is common in such cases. In this sad world of ours, sorrow comes to all; and, to the young, it comes with bitterest agony, because it takes them unawares. The older have learned to ever expect it. I am anxious to afford some alleviation of your present distress. Perfect relief is not possible, except with time. You can not now realize that you will ever feel better. Is not this so? And yet it is a mistake. You are sure to be happy again. To know this, which is certainly true, will make you some less miserable now. I have had experience enough to know what I say; and you need only to believe it, to feel better at once. The memory of your dear Father, instead of an agony, will yet be a sad sweet feeling in your heart, of a purer, and holier sort than you have known before.

Please present my kind regards to your afflicted mother.

Your sincere friend   A. Lincoln.

Miss. Fanny McCullough.

1 ALS, owned by Miss Alice Orme Smith, Fairfield, Connecticut. Fanny's father, Lieutenant Colonel William McCullough of the Fourth Illinois Cavalry was killed in a night battle near Coffeeville, Mississippi, on December 5. As clerk of the McLean County Circuit Court at Bloomington, McCullough had been well known to Lincoln.

To Members of the Cabinet[1]

Executive Mansion,
Washington, December 23, 1862.

Gentleman of the Cabinet   A bill for an act entitled "An Act for the admission of the State of 'West-Virginia' into the Union, and for other purposes," has passed the House of Representatives, and the Senate, and has been duly presented to me for my action.

I respectfully ask of each [of] you, an opinion in writing, on the following questions, towit:

1st. Is the said Act constitutional?

2d. Is the said Act expedient?

Your Obt. Servt.   ABRAHAM LINCOLN

1 ALS (copy?), DLC-RTL. The opinions submitted by members of the cabinet are too long for adequate quotation here. The originals are in the Lincoln Papers, and an adequate presentation may be found in Nicolay and Hay, *Abraham Lincoln: A History* (VI, 300 ff.). Seward, Chase, and Stanton replied affirmatively on both questions; Welles, Blair, and Bates negatively. Governor Peirpoint telegraphed Lincoln on December 18 that veto of the bill "will be death to our cause," and again on December 20 that "great feeling exists . . . in reference to your delay in signing the bill for the new state." (DLC-RTL). Lincoln wrote his own opinion on December 31, *infra*, and signed the bill on the same day.

To John G. Nicolay[1]

Mr. Nicolay, please run over this & tell me what is in it.

Dec. 23, 1862.   A.L.

[1] AES, DLC-RTL. Lincoln's endorsement, and one by David Davis, are written on an envelope containing a fifteen-page letter from the Reverend Henry P. Tappan, president of the University of Michigan, November 22, 1862, reporting from a trip to Europe on the prevailing opinion abroad as unfavorable to the Union because of military reverses and indecisive administration.

To Edwin M. Stanton[1]

I think Senator Henderson should be obliged in this case.

Dec. 23, 1862 A. LINCOLN

[1] AES, DNA WR RG 107, Secretary of War, Letters Received, P 246. Lincoln's endorsement is written on a letter from John D. L. Dryden of St. Louis, Missouri, to Senator John B. Henderson, December 13, 1862, forwarding a petition for discharge of Reverend E. Kirby Miller from prison.

To Edwin M. Stanton[1]

December 23, 1862.

I really wish the writer of this letter—Uri Manly—appointed a Quarter-Master, or Commissary. Sec. of War please do not overlook this. A. LINCOLN

Dec. 23. 1862.

[1] AES, DLC-RTL. Lincoln's endorsement is written on the envelope of a letter from a loyal Democrat, Uri Manly of Marshall, Illinois, December 12, 1862, asking appointment. With the letter is an unsigned memo "Respectfully returned to the President, with the information that Uri Manly was appointed Quarter Master prior to Decr. 1st. His Commission has been made out and signed, and is now in the office of the Adjutant General." Manly's appointment as captain and quartermaster was dated November 26, 1862.

To Francis Joseph I[1]

December 24, 1862

Abraham Lincoln,
President of the United States of America.

To His Imperial Royal Majesty Francis Joseph I,
    Emperor of Austria,
        &c., &c., &c.

Great and Good Friend: I have received the letter which Your Majesty was pleased to address to me on the 28th. of October, last, announcing the marriage of His Imperial Highness the Archduke Charles Louis, Your Majesty's brother, to Her Royal Highness, the Princess Mary Annunziata, sister of His Majesty the King of the Two Sicilies.

I participate in the satisfaction afforded by this happy event and pray Your Majesty to accept my sincere congratulations upon the occasion.

May God have Your Majesty always in His safe and holy keeping! Your Good Friend, ABRAHAM LINCOLN.
Washington, December 24, 1862.
By the President:
WILLIAM H. SEWARD, Secretary of State.

[1] Copy, DNA FS RG 59, Communications to Foreign Sovereigns and States, III, 194.

To the Senate and House of Representatives[1]

December 24, 1862

To the Senate and House of Representatives.

I transmit, for the consideration of Congress, a Report from the Secretary of State on the subject of Consular Pupils.

Washington ABRAHAM LINCOLN
December 24. 1862

[1] DS, DNA RG 46, Senate 37A F3. Seward's report of December 24, 1862, reads in part as follows:
"By the act of Congress of August 18, 1856 . . . the President was authorized to appoint a class of officers called consular pupils . . . . as consuls were forbidden to employ clerks at the public expense . . . if one or more pupils were attached to the consulate they could, while learning the general duties of the consular service, perform those of clerk. . . . The sudden repeal . . . February 7, 1857, of the section of the act . . . referred to, authorizing the appointment of consular pupils, was consequently regretted . . . and the expediency of asking Congress again to confer the authority for the appointment of such officers . . . is now submitted to your consideration. . . ." (Thirty-seventh Congress, Third Session, *Senate Executive Document No. 14*).
No legislation concerning Seward's suggestion was passed.

To Edwin M. Stanton[1]

Executive Mansion, Washington, December 24, 1862.

To-day Hon. Mr. Cox calls, and asks that Col. Samuel A. Gilbert, of Ohio be a Brigadier Genl. He is now near Lexington, Ky. Has been in service from the beginning. Papers on file in his favor from Gen. Wright & others.

He also says a word for Col. Wood, as also does Senator Sherman. Papers on file in this case also.

[1] AD, IHi. Colonel Samuel A. Gilbert of the Forty-fourth Ohio Volunteers was brevetted brigadier general March 13, 1865. No record has been found of the promotion of Colonel Oliver Wood of the Twenty-second Ohio.

To Edwin M. Stanton[1]

Hon. Sec. of War: Executive Mansion,
Sir: Washington, December 26, 1862

Two Ohio regiments and one Illinois regiment were captured at Hartsville, have been parolled, and are now at Columbus Ohio. This brings the Ohio regiments substantially to their homes. I am strongly impressed with the belief that the Illinois regiment better be sent to Illinois, where it will be recruited and put in good condition, by the time they are exchanged, so as to re-enter the service. They did not misbehave, as I am satisfied; so that they should receive no treatment, nor have anything withheld from them, by way of punishment. Yours truly   A. LINCOLN

[1] ALS-F, ISLA. See Lincoln to Halleck, December 8, *supra*. The One Hundred Fourth Illinois were ordered to Camp Douglas, Illinois.

To Samuel R. Curtis[1]

Maj. Gen. Curtis   Executive Mansion,
St. Louis, Mo.   Washington, Dec. 27. 1862.

Let the order in regard to Dr. McPheters and family be suspended until you hear from me again.   A. LINCOLN

[1] ALS, RPB. On December 19, Provost Marshal F. A. Dick of the Department of the Missouri issued *Special Order No. 152*, that Reverend Samuel B. McPheeters, Pastor of the Pine Street Presbyterian Church of St. Louis, and his wife, leave the state within ten days because of "unmistakeable evidence of sympathy with the rebellion." Reverend McPheeters' congregation were split, some advocating his expulsion and others opposing it. The Unionist portion of the congregation themselves eventually succeeded in expelling McPheeters from his pastorate, but he was not made to leave the state. See further Lincoln to Curtis, January 2, 1863, and Lincoln's endorsement concerning McPheeters, December 22, 1863, *infra*.

Endorsement Concerning John J. Key[1]

December 27, 1862

The within, as appears, was written some time ago. On full re-consideration, I can not find sufficient ground to change the conclusion therein arrived at   A. LINCOLN
Dec. 27. 1862.

[1] AES, DLC-RTL. Lincoln's endorsement is written on the envelope containing a signed copy of the letter to Major Key of November 24, 1862, *supra*.

[20]

To Hamilton R. Gamble[1]

His Excy. Gov. Gamble   December 27, 1862

I do not wish to leave the country North of the Missouri to the care of the enrolled militia, except upon the concurrent judgment of yourself and Gen. Curtis. His I have not yet obtained. Confer with him, & I shall be glad to act when you and he agree.

                                                        A. LINCOLN

[1] ALS, RPB. Lincoln's telegram replied to one from Governor Gamble of 10:30 A.M., December 27, asking Lincoln to direct that the country "north of the Missouri" be placed under "care of enrolled militia." See Lincoln to Curtis, December 19, *supra*.

To Caleb B. Smith[1]

Hon. Sec. of Interior &   Executive Mansion
Comr. of Indian Affairs   Washington December 27. 1862

Mr DePuy was appointed Indian Agent. Charges were made against him, and another was appointed to the same office. The charges fail in the proof & Mr DePuy's reappointment is sought. But Mr. Daily,[2] the territorial delegate, asks that the other appointee be not removed. Please call Mr. Daily & Mr DePuy before you & give them a fair hearing, decide what is proper to be done & I will do it. Yours truly   A. LINCOLN

[1] ALS, owned by Gordon A. Block, Philadelphia, Pennsylvania. Henry W. DePuy's successor at the Pawnee Agency, Genoa, Nebraska Territory, was Benjamin F. Lushbaugh who is listed in the *U.S. Official Register* as of September, 1863.   [2] Samuel G. Daily of Peru, Nebraska Territory.

To Hiram Walbridge[1]

General Hiram Walbridge   Executive Mansion
My Dear Sir   Washington December 28th. 1862.

I have twice declined to see you on the ground that I understood the object of your desired interview, and that it was a matter of embarrassment to me. My real respect and esteem for you makes me unwilling to leave the matter in quite so abrupt a form. My embarrassment is that the place you seek not selfishly I think, is greedily sought by many others; and there is sure to be opposition both fierce and plausible to the appointment of any one who up to this time has not been in the military service. What answer to it will I make? Shall I say I did it for political influence? That will be the more loudly objected to. I need not point out to you where this objection will come from. It will come from your competitors; it will come from party spirit; it will come from indignant members of Congress who will perceive in it an attempt of mine to set a guardian over them.

The longer I can get along without a formal appointment the better. Yours Very truly   A. LINCOLN

1 Copy, ISLA. Lincoln's original letter has not been found, but the contemporary copy from which our text is reproduced seems to be authentic. There is no reply from Walbridge in the Lincoln Papers, but there are numerous letters in November and December, 1862, pressing Lincoln to appoint "General" Walbridge military governor of the District of Columbia. Walbridge's only claim to military distinction seems to have consisted in his appointment as brigadier general of Ohio Militia in 1843.

To Benjamin F. Butler[1]

Major General B. F. Butler   Executive Mansion,
My dear Sir: Washington, December 29, 1862.

I believe you have a family, and I dislike to deprive you of an early visit to them. But I really wish to see you at the earliest moment. I am contemplating a peculiar and important service for you, which I think, and hope you will think, is as honorable, as it is important. I wish to confer with you upon it. Please come immediately upon your arrival at New-York. Yours very truly

A. LINCOLN.

1 ALS, DLC-Butler Papers. Major General Nathaniel P. Banks assumed command at New Orleans on December 16, and on December 18, Butler wrote Lincoln for permission to visit his family (DLC-RTL). See further Lincoln to Stanton, January 23, and to whom it may concern, February 11, 1863, *infra.*

To Ambrose E. Burnside[1]

Washington City, D.C.
Major General Burnside   December 30, 1862 [3:30 P.M.]

I have good reason for saying you must not make a general movement of the army without letting me know.

A. LINCOLN

1 ALS, owned by Dale Carnegie, New York City. Brigadier Generals John Newton and John Cochrane had gone to the president to tell of the great dejection and demoralization of the Army of the Potomac and had expressed the opinion that to fight under such conditions would bring destruction. Burnside's *General Orders No. 8,* January 23, 1863, ordered Newton and Cochrane dismissed from the service for their action, but the order was not approved by Lincoln and was not issued (OR, I, XXI, 998). Burnside replied to Lincoln's telegram at

7:45 P.M., "Your dispatch is received. I have rescinded some orders that had already been given. I am summoned to give evidence in Court Martial tomorrow at Washington and will see you." (DLC-RTL).

To Hamilton R. Gamble[1]

Order No. 416.[2]

His Excncy. Gov. Gamble   Executive Mansion,
My dear Sir   Washington, December 30, 1862.

Inclosed is an order, substantially, and I believe exactly, such as I directed to be made nearly a month ago. After a good deal of reflection, I concluded that it was better to make a rule for the practical matter in hand, (the removal of officers and acceptance of resignations) than to decide a general question, towit, whether the force are *State troops*, which, while it might embrace the practical question mentioned, might also be the nest in which forty other troublesome questions would be hatched. I would rather meet them *as* they come, than *before* they come, trusting that some of them may not come at all. Yours very truly   A. LINCOLN

[1] ADfS, DLC-RTL; ALS, owned by James D. Randles, Los Angeles, California. See Lincoln to Stanton, December 2, *supra*.

[2] "Order No. 416" appears on the draft but not on the letter sent, and refers to the enclosure, a copy of AGO *Special Orders No. 417* [*sic*], December 28, 1862, as printed in the *Official Records* (III, II, 955).

Preliminary Draft of
Final Emancipation Proclamation[1]

[December 30, 1862]

Whereas, on the twenty second day of September, in the year of our Lord one thousand, eight hundred and sixty-two, a proclamation was issued by the President of the United States, containing among other things the following, to wit:

[Blank space for insertion]

Now therefore I, Abraham Lincoln, President of the United States, by virtue of the power in me vested, as Commander-in-Chief, of the Army, and Navy of the United States in time of actual armed rebellion against the authority and government of the United States, and as a proper and necessary war measure for suppressing said rebellion, do, on this first day of January in the year of our Lord one thousand eight hundred and sixty three, and in accordance with my intention so to do, publicly proclaimed for one hundred days as aforesaid, order and designate as the States and parts of States in which the people thereof respectively are this day in rebellion against the United States, the following to wit:

Arkansas, Texas, Louisiana, except the Parishes of

[Blank space for insertion]

Mississippi, Alabama, Florida, Georgia, South Carolina, North Carolina, and Virginia, except the forty-eight counties designated as West Virginia, and also the counties of

[Blank space for insertion]

And by virtue of the power, and for the purpose aforesaid, I do order,[2] and declare, that all persons held as slaves within said designated States, and parts of States, are, and henceforward forever shall be free; and that the Executive government of the United States, including the military and naval authorities thereof, will recognize and maintain the freedom of said persons and[3] will do no act, or acts to repress said persons, or any of them, in any suitable efforts they may make for their actual freedom. And I hereby appeal to[4] the people so declared to be free, to abstain from all disorder, tumult, and violence, unless in necessary self defence; and[5] in all cases, when allowed, to labor faithfully, for[6] wages.

And I further declare, and make known, that such persons of suitable condition, will be received into the armed service of the United States to garrison and defend forts, positions, stations, and other places, and to man vessels of all sorts in said service.

[1] Copies, DLC-RTL. Lincoln's autograph draft has not been found, but copies were prepared and distributed to members of the cabinet at the meeting on December 30. Each member was requested to offer suggestions. The copies received by Stanton and Welles have not been located, but those of Bates, Blair, Chase, and Seward are in the Lincoln Papers together with each member's suggestions for revision. In addition to submitting an entirely new redrafting of his own, which Lincoln did not use, Chase on December 31 made the following suggestions:

". . . It seems to me wisest to make no exception of parts of States from the operation of the Proclamation, save the Forty-eight Counties designated as West-Virginia. . . .

"I think it would be expedient to omit from the proposed Proclamation the declaration that the Executive Government of the United States will do no act to repress the enfranchised in any efforts they may make for their actual freedom.

"This clause in the September Proclamation has been widely quoted as an incitement to servile insurrection. In lieu of it, and for the purpose of shaming these misrepresentations, I think it would be well to insert some such clause as this: 'not encouraging or countenancing, however, any disorderly or licentious conduct.' If this alteration is made, the appeal to the enslaved may properly enough be omitted. It does not appear to be necessary, and may furnish a topic to the evil-disposed for censure and ridicule. . . .

"I think it absolutely certain that the rebellion can in no way be so certainly, speedily and economically suppressed as by the organized military force of the loyal population of the insurgent regions, of whatever complection. In no way can irregular violence and servile insurrection be so surely prevented as by the regular organization and regular military employment of those who might otherwise probably resort to such courses.

"Such organization is now in successful progress. . . .

"Considering these facts, it seems to me that it would be best to omit from the Proclamation all reference to the military employment of the enfranchised population, leaving it to the natural course of things already well begun; or to state distinctly that in order to secure the suppression of the rebellion without servile insurrection or licentious marauding, such numbers of the population declared free as may be found convenient will be employed in the military and naval service of the United States. . . .

"Finally, I respectfully suggest that on an occasion of such interest, there can be no just imputation of affectation against a solemn recognition of responsibility before men and before God; and that some such close as follows will be proper:—

" 'And upon this act, sincerely believed to be an act of justice warranted by the Constitution, and of duty demanded by the circumstances of the country, I invoke the considerate judgment of Mankind and the gracious favor of Almighty God.' "

Bates' suggestions (undated but either December 31 or January 1) are as follows:

"I respectfully suggest that

"1. The President issues the proclamation 'by virtue of the power in *him* vested, as *commander in chief of the army & navy* of the United States, in time of *actual, armed rebellion*' &c— 'and as a proper & necessary *war measure*, for suppressing said rebellion—' Date January 1863.

"2. It is done *in accordance with* the first proclamation—of Sept 22d 1862.

"3. It distinguishes between *States & parts of States*, and designates those States & parts of States, 'in which the people thereof, respectively, ARE THIS DAY, (Jan 1, 1863) *in rebellion* against the United States.'

"These three propositions being true, I think they ought to be followed out, without excess or diminution, by action, not by the declaration of a principle nor the establishment of a law, for the future guidance of others. It is a *war measure* by the President—a matter of fact—not a law by the legislature.

"And as to what is proposed to be done in the future, the least said the better. Better leave yourself free to act in the emergencies, as they arise, with as few embarrassing committals as possible.

"Whether a particular State or part of a State, is or is not in *actual rebellion*, on the 1st. Jany 1863, is a simple matter of fact, which the President, in the first proclamation, has promised to declare in the second. Of course, it must be *truly* declared: It is no longer open, to be determined, as a matter of policy or prudence, independently of the *fact*.

"And this applies, with particular force, to Virginia. The Eastern shore of Virginia & the region round about Norfolk, are now (Dec. 31, 1862) more free from *actual* rebellion than are several of the 48 Counties spoken of as West Virginia.

"If the latter be exempt from the proclamation, so also ought the former. And so, in all the States that are considered *in parts*.

"The last paragraph of the draft, I consider wholly useless, and probably injurious—being a needless pledge of future action—which may be quite as well done without as with the pledge."

Blair's suggestions (undated but either December 31 or January 1) and Seward's (December 30) are given in the succeeding footnotes appended to the particular passages affected.

2 Blair's suggested revision of the remainder of the draft is as follows (portions in parentheses are on a separate sheet marked for insertion as given here):

"I do order & declare that all persons held as slaves within said designated states & parts of states shall be free; and that the Executive Government of the United States, including the Military & Naval authorities will recognize & maintain the freedom of said persons. And in order that they may render all the aid they are willing to give to this object & to the support of the Government, authority will be given to receive them in to the service whenever they can be usefully employed & they may be armed to garrison forts, to defend positions & stations and to man vessels. And (whilst) I appeal to them to show themselves worthy of freedom by fidelity & diligence in the employments which may be given to them by the observance of order & by abstaining from all violence not required by duty or for self defence. (It is due to them to say that the conduct of large numbers of these people since the war began justifies confidence in their fidelity & humanity generally)."

³ Seward suggested: "Omit the words . . . between 'and' and 'freedom'."
⁴ Seward suggested: "for 'appeal to' substitute 'command and require'."
⁵ Seward suggested: "after 'and,' insert 'I do recommend to them'."
⁶ Seward suggested: "after 'for,' insert 'just and reasonable'."

To John A. Dix[1]

Major Gen. Dix   Executive Mansion,
Fort-Monroe, Va.   Washington, Dec. 31, 1862.

I hear not a word about the Congressional election of which you and I corresponded. Time nearly up.   A. LINCOLN

[1] ALS, RPB. Dix telegraphed on the same day, "I did not receive until Yesterday, the returns of the conductors of Election of Norfolk & Princess Anne Counties & of the Cities of Norfolk & Portsmouth. Mr [John B.] McCloud the successful Candidate, leaves for Washington to-day. I will write by mail" (DLC-RTL). His letter of the same date added further information as follows:

"The Union men of the Second Congressional District of Virginia in the counties in our possession being desirous of an opportunity of manifesting their fidelity to the Government and of securing their exemption from the penalties of disloyalty, by electing a member of Congress so as to be represented by the 1st Jany. 1863, I issued the Proclamation of which a copy is enclosed marked A. calling an election on the 22nd inst. . . . I felt assured that my act would meet your approval.

"Previously to the election . . . Governor Pierpont . . . issued writs of elections for the day, and the election was held with all the legal sanctions of which the case was susceptible. . . . The aggregate vote cast was 1402. . . ." (*Ibid.*).

John B. McCloud's election was contested by his opponent W. W. Wing. The House committee on elections recommended on February 4, 1863, that neither be seated, and on February 14 this recommendation was adopted by the House.

Opinion on the Admission of West Virginia into the Union[1]

[December 31, 1862]

The consent of the Legislature of Virginia is constitutionally necessary to the bill for the admission of West-Virginia becoming a law. A body claiming to be such Legislature has given it's consent. We can not well deny that it is such, unless we do so upon the outside knowledge that the body was chosen at elections, in which a majority of the qualified voters of Virginia did not participate.

[1] ADf, DLC-RTL. Although the draft is undated, Nicolay and Hay (VIII, 157) give December 31, 1862, the date upon which Lincoln signed the act admitting West Virginia, as the date of Lincoln's opinion. See Lincoln's letter to members of the cabinet, December 23, *supra*.

But it is a universal practice in the popular elections in all these states, to give no legal consideration whatever to those who do not choose to vote, as against the effect of the votes of those, who do choose to vote. Hence it is not the qualified voters, but the qualified voters, *who choose to vote,* that constitute the political power of the state. Much less than to non-voters, should any consideration be given to those who did not vote, *in this case:* because it is also matter of outside knowledge, that they were not merely neglectful of their rights under, and duty to, this government, but were also engaged in open rebellion against it. Doubtless[2] among these non-voters were some Union men whose voices were smothered by the more numerous secessionists; but we know too little of their number to assign them any appreciable value. Can this government stand, if it indulges constitutional constructions by which men in open rebellion against it, are to be accounted, man for man, the equals of those who maintain their loyalty to it? Are they to be accounted even better citizens, and more worthy of consideration, than those who merely neglect to vote? If so, their treason against the constitution, enhances their constitutional value! Without braving these absurd conclusions, we can not deny that the body which consents to the admission of West-Virginia, is the Legislature of Virginia. I[3] do not think the plural form of the words "Legislatures" and "States" in the phrase of the constitution "without the consent of the Legislatures of the States concerned &c" has any reference to the *new* State concerned. That plural form sprang from the contemplation of two or more old States contributing to form a new one. The idea that the new state was in danger of being admitted without its own consent, was not provided against, because it was not thought of, as I conceive. It is said, the devil takes care of his own. Much more should a good spirit—the spirit of the Constitution and the Union—take care of it's own. I think it can not do less, and live.

But is the admission into the Union, of West-Virginia, expedient. This, in my general view, is more a question for Congress, than for the Executive. Still I do not evade it. More than on anything else, it depends on whether the admission or rejection of the new state would under all the circumstances tend the more strongly to the restoration of the national authority throughout the Union. That which helps most in this direction is the most expedient at this

[2] This sentence is written on the right-hand margin of the first page, and the place for its insertion marked by an asterisk.

[3] This sentence and the next two following are written on the right-hand margin and bottom of the second page, and the place for their insertion marked by an asterisk.

time. Doutless those in remaining Virginia would return to the Union, so to speak, less reluctantly without the division of the old state than with it; but I think we could not save as much in this quarter by rejecting the new state, as we should lose by it in West-Virginia. We can scarcely dispense with the aid of West-Virginia in this struggle; much less can we afford to have her against us, in congress and in the field. Her brave and good men regard her admission into the Union as a matter of life and death. They have been true to the Union under very severe trials. We have so acted as to justify their hopes; and we can not fully retain their confidence, and co-operation, if we seem to break faith with them. In fact, they could not do so much for us, if they would.

Again, the admission of the new state, turns that much slave soil to free; and thus, is a certain, and irrevocable encroachment upon the cause of the rebellion.

The division of a State is dreaded as a precedent. But a measure made expedient by a war, is no precedent for times of peace. It is said that the admission of West-Virginia, is secession, and tolerated only because it is our secession. Well, if we call it by that name, there is still difference enough between secession against the constitution, and secession in favor of the constitution.

I believe the admission of West-Virginia into the Union is expedient.

To Solomon Foote[1]

Hon. S. Foote   Executive Mansion
My dear Sir: Washington, 1863

Mrs. L. requests me to invite you to accompany us to the opera this evening. If you accept, be here at half past 7 P.M. Please answer by bearer. Yours truly,   A. LINCOLN

1 Copy, ISLA. No reply has been discovered and efforts to supply a specific date have not succeeded.

Emancipation Proclamation[1]

January 1, 1863

By the President of the United States of America:

A Proclamation.

Whereas, on the twentysecond day of September, in the year of our Lord one thousand eight hundred and sixty two, a proclamation was issued by the President of the United States, containing, among other things, the following, towit:

"That on the first day of January, in the year of our Lord one thousand eight hundred and sixty-three, all persons held as slaves within any State or designated part of a State, the people whereof shall then be in rebellion against the United States, shall be then, thenceforward, and forever free; and the Executive Government of the United States, including the military and naval authority thereof, will recognize and maintain the freedom of such persons, and will do no act or acts to repress such persons, or any of them, in any efforts they may make for their actual freedom.

"That the Executive will, on the first day of January aforesaid, by proclamation, designate the States and parts of States, if any, in which the people thereof, respectively, shall then be in rebellion against the United States; and the fact that any State, or the people thereof, shall on that day be, in good faith, represented in the Congress of the United States by members chosen thereto at elections wherein a majority of the qualified voters of such State shall have participated, shall, in the absence of strong countervailing testimony, be deemed conclusive evidence that such State, and the people thereof, are not then in rebellion against the United States."

Now, therefore I, Abraham Lincoln, President of the United States, by virtue of the power in me vested as Commander-in-Chief, of the Army and Navy of the United States in time of actual armed rebellion against authority and government of the United States, and as a fit and necessary war measure for suppressing said rebellion, do, on this first day of January, in the year of our Lord one thousand eight hundred and sixty three, and in accordance with my purpose so to do publicly proclaimed for the full period of one hundred days, from the day first above mentioned, order and designate as the States and parts of States wherein the people thereof respectively, are this day in rebellion against the United States, the following, towit:

Arkansas, Texas, Louisiana, (except the Parishes of St. Bernard, Plaquemines, Jefferson, St. Johns, St. Charles, St. James[,] Ascension, Assumption, Terrebonne, Lafourche, St. Mary, St. Martin, and Orleans, including the City of New-Orleans) Mississippi, Alabama, Florida, Georgia, South-Carolina, North-Carolina, and Virginia, (except the fortyeight counties designated as West Virginia, and also the counties of Berkley, Accomac, Northampton, Elizabeth-City, York, Princess Ann, and Norfolk, including the cities of Norfolk & Portsmouth [)]; and which excepted parts are, for the present, left precisely as if this proclamation were not issued.

And by virtue of the power, and for the purpose aforesaid, I do order and declare that all persons held as slaves within said designated States, and parts of States, are, and henceforward shall be free; and that the Executive government of the United States, including the military and naval authorities thereof, will recognize and maintain the freedom of said persons.

And I hereby enjoin upon the people so declared to be free to abstain from all violence, unless in necessary self-defence; and I recommend to them that, in all cases when allowed, they labor faithfully for reasonable wages.

And I further declare and make known, that such persons of suitable condition, will be received into the armed service of the United States to garrison forts, positions, stations, and other places, and to man vessels of all sorts in said service.

And upon this act, sincerely believed to be an act of justice, warranted by the Constitution, upon military necessity, I invoke the considerate judgment of mankind, and the gracious favor of Almighty God.

In witness whereof, I have hereunto set my hand and caused the seal of the United States to be affixed.

[L.S.]   Done at the City of Washington, this first day of January, in the year of our Lord one thousand eight hundred and sixty three, and of the Independence of the United States of America the eighty-seventh.

By the President: ABRAHAM LINCOLN

WILLIAM H. SEWARD, Secretary of State.

¹ ADS-P, DLC-RTL; DS, DNA FS RG 11, Proclamations. Lincoln's original autograph of the proclamation was sold in 1863 (see Lincoln's letter to Ladies in charge of North Western Fair, October 26, *infra*), at the Chicago Northwestern Sanitary Fair, to Thomas B. Bryan, who presented it to the Soldiers' Home in Chicago. It was lithographed "and thousands [of dollars] were realized by the Chicago Soldiers Home from the sale of copies. . . ." (Charles Bryan, son, to Nicolay, November 24, 1886, DLC-Nicolay Papers. See also Lincoln to Bryan, January 18, 1864, *infra*.) In 1871 the original was burned in the Chicago Fire. Prior to the Chicago Fair in 1863 the historian Benson J. Lossing also had prevailed upon Lincoln to allow him to have a facsimile made for use in his *Pictorial History of the Civil War*. On October 29, 1863, John Hay forwarded to Lossing a photograph made at Lincoln's direction, with apologies for "blots on the edges" which were "incidental to the copying, and are not in the original" (ALS, RPB). Three photographic copies of the original preserved in the Lincoln Papers, presumably made at the same time as the copy sent to Lossing, have provided the present text. The official engrossed document in The National Archives follows Lincoln's original. (For a detailed study of the various printings of the proclamation, see Charles Eberstadt, "Lincoln's Emancipation Proclamation," *The New Colophon*, 1950, pp. 312-56.)

Lincoln's final proclamation was not completed until January 1 after consultation with the cabinet and study of the suggestions for revision submitted by the several members on December 31. Nicolay telegraphed Horace Greeley and Henry J. Raymond on the afternoon of December 31 that "The Proclamation cannot be telegraphed to you until during the day tomorrow (telegrams, RPB). Telegrams from John A. Dix and Michael Hahn on December 31 defined the parts of Virginia and Louisiana not then in rebellion which were to be exempted by the proclamation (DLC-RTL).

The photographic copies of the original autograph show the superscription "By the President of the United States of America: A Proclamation." to be in the hand of a clerk. The excerpt from the preliminary proclamation of September 22, which appears as paragraphs two and three in the final proclamation, is in the form of a clipping from the State Department circular printing of the preliminary proclamation, with quotation marks added by Lincoln. The formal close, "In witness whereof," etc., is also added in the handwriting of a clerk. Otherwise the body of the proclamation is in Lincoln's handwriting.

Endorsement Concerning John McNeil[1]

[c. January 1, 1863?]

531 citizens justifying Gen McNeil for hanging the ten men, & asking that he shall not be surrendered to Jeff Davis 146, more names.

[1] AE, DLC-RTL. Lincoln's endorsement is written on the envelope containing a printed petition January 1, 1863, justifying General McNeil's conduct and asking that he not be surrendered to Jefferson Davis, signed by "loyal citizens of Northern Missouri." Brigadier General John McNeil of the Missouri State Militia had on October 18, 1862, executed ten rebel guerrillas at Palmyra, Missouri. On November 17, Jefferson Davis ordered Theophilus H. Holmes, commanding the Confederate Trans-Mississippi Department, to demand surrender of McNeil, and if it was refused, to execute the first ten Union officers to fall into his hands. McNeil remained active in the Union cause, and no further action seems to have been taken in the matter by Lincoln.

To Henry W. Halleck[1]

Major Gen. Halleck   Executive Mansion,
My dear Sir: Washington, January 1. 1863.

Gen. Burnside wishes to cross the Rappahannock with his army, but his Grand Division commanders all oppose the movement. If in such a difficulty as this you do not help, you fail me precisely in the point for which I sought your assistance. You know what Gen. Burnside's plan is; and it is my wish that you go with him to the ground, examine it as far as practicable, confer with the officers, getting their judgment, and ascertaining their temper, in a word, gather all the elements for forming a judgment of your own; and then tell Gen. Burnside that you *do* approve, or that you do *not* approve his plan. Your military skill is useless to me, if you will not do this. Yours very truly   A LINCOLN

[*Endorsement*]

Withdrawn, because considered harsh by Gen. Halleck.   A.L.
Jan. 1. 1862 [1863]

[1] ALS, DLC-RTL. Lincoln's endorsement, incorrectly dated "Jan. 1. 1862" is written on the back of the letter. On January 1, Major General Burnside wrote Lincoln as follows:

"Since leaving you this morning, I have determined that it is my duty to place on paper the remarks which I made to you, in order that you may use them or not, as you see proper.

"I am in command . . . of nearly 200,000 men, 120,000 of whom are in the immediate presence of the enemy, and I cannot conscientiously retain the command without making an unreserved statement of my views.

"The Secretary of War has not the confidence of the officers and soldiers, and I feel sure that he has not the confidence of the country. In regard to the latter statement, you are probably better informed than I am. The same opinion applies with equal force in regard to General Halleck. It seems to be the universal opinion that the movements of the army have not been planned with a view to co-operation and mutual assistance.

"I have attempted a movement upon the enemy, in which I have been repulsed, and I am convinced, after mature deliberation, that the army ought to make another movement in the same direction, not necessarily at the same points on the river; but I am not sustained in this by a single grand division commander in my command. My reasons for having issued the order for making this second movement I have already given you in full, and I can see no reasons for changing my views. Doubtless this difference of opinion between my general officers and myself results from a lack of confidence in me. In this case it is highly necessary that this army should be commanded by some other officer, to whom I will most cheerfully give way.

"Will you allow me, Mr. President, to say that it is of the utmost importance that you be surrounded and supported by men who have the confidence of the people and of the army, and who will at all times give you definite and honest opinions in relation to their separate departments, and at the same time give you positive and unswerving support in your public policy, taking at all times their full share of the responsibility for that policy? In no positions held by gentlemen near you are these conditions more requisite than those of the Secretary of War and General-in-Chief and the commanders of your armies. In the struggle now going on, in which the very existence of our Government is at stake, the interests of no one man are worth the value of a grain of sand, and no one should be allowed to stand in the way of accomplishing the greatest amount of public good.

"It is my belief that I ought to retire to private life. I hope you will not understand this to savor of anything like dictation. My only desire is to promote the public good. No man is an accurate judge of the confidence in which he is held by the public and the people around him, and the confidence in my management may be entirely destroyed, in which case it would be a great wrong for me to retain this command for a single day; and, as I before said, I will most cheerfully give place to any other officer." (OR, I, XXI, 941-42. This letter does not appear in the Lincoln Papers, and a footnote to the text in the source specifies "This letter is printed from General Burnside's copy.")

On the same day General Halleck wrote Stanton the following letter of resignation:

"Sir: From my recent interview with the President and yourself, and from the President's letter of this morning, which you delivered to me at your reception, I am led to believe that there is a very important difference of opinion in regard to my relations toward generals commanding armies in the field, and that I cannot perform the duties of my present office satisfactorily at the same time to the President and to myself. I therefore respectfully request that I may be relieved from further duties as General-in-Chief." (OR, I, XXI, 940-41. A footnote in the source reads as follows: "As duplicates are found among General Halleck's papers, and no copy is found in the War Department files, it is presumed that the application was withdrawn upon withdrawal of the President's letter.")

To Edwin M. Stanton[1]

Hon. Sec. of War: Executive Mansion,
Dear Sir: Washington, Jany. 1, 1863.

Yesterday a piteous appeal was made to me by an old lady of genteel appearance, saying she had, with what she thought sufficient assurance that she would not be disturbed by the government, fitted up the two South Divisions of the old "Duff Green" building in order to take boarders, and has boarders already in it, & others, including M.C.s. engaged, and that now she is ordered to be out of it by Saturday the 3rd. Inst.; and that, independently of the ruin it brings on her, by her lost out-lay, she neither has, nor can find another shelter for her own head. I know nothing about it myself, but promised to bring it to your notice. Yours truly   A. LINCOLN

[1]ALS-P, ISLA. The lady has not been identified and no further reference has been discovered. The "Duff Green Building" presumably referred to the former residence of Duff Green on the north side of E Street, a short distance east of Tenth Street.

To Samuel R. Curtis[1]

           Executive Mansion,
Major General Curtis   Washington, January 2, 1863.

My dear Sir: Yours of Dec. 29th. by the hand of Mr. Strong is just received. The day I telegraphed you suspending the order in relation to Dr. McPheters, he, with Mr. Bates, the Attorney General, appeared before me, and left with me a copy of the order mentioned. The Dr. also showed me the copy of an oath which he said he had taken, which is, indeed, very strong, and specific. He also verbally assured me that he had constantly prayed in church for the President and Government, as he had always done before the present war. In looking over the recitals in your order, I do not see that this matter of the prayer, as he states it, is negatived; nor that any violation of his oath is charged; nor, in fact, that any thing specific is alledged against him. The charges are all general —that he has a rebel wife & rebel relations, that he sympathizes with rebels, and that he exercises rebel influence. Now, after talking with him, I tell you frankly, I believe he does sympathize with the rebels; but the question remains whether such a man, of unquestioned good moral character, who has taken such an oath as he has, and can not even be charged of violating it, and who can be charged with no other specific act or omision, can, with safety to the government be exiled, upon the suspicion of his secret sympathies. But I agree that this must be left to you who are on the spot; and if, after all, you think the public good requires his removal, my suspension of the order is withdrawn, only with this qualification that the time during the suspension, is not to be counted against him. I have promised him this.

But I must add that the U.S. government must not, as by this order, undertake to run the churches. When an individual, in a church or out of it, becomes dangerous to the public interest, he must be checked; but let the churches, as such take care of themselves. It will not do for the U.S. to appoint Trustees, Supervisors, or other agents for the churches. Yours very truly

A. LINCOLN

P.S. The committee composed of Messrs. Yeatman & Filley (Mr. Brodhead not attending) has presented your letter and the memorial of sundry citizens. On the whole subject embraced, exercise your best judgment, with a sole view to the public interest, and I will not interfere without hearing you.[2]   A. LINCOLN

Jan. 3, 1863.

[1] ADfS, DLC-RTL. Curtis' letter of December 29, 1862, introduced "the bearer Geo. P. Strong . . . a leading and worthy member of the Union Element of Dr. McPheter's church. Your Telegraphic order suspending the Provost Marshalls was a surprise. . . ." (DLC-RTL).

[2] Giles F. Filley, crockery merchant and stove manufacturer, and James E. Yeatman, banker, left St. Louis on December 30 to interview the president concerning the McPheeters affair and other problems of the state. (OR, I, XXII, I, 884). James O. Broadhead, a lawyer at St. Louis, was the third member who did not attend.

To the Senate and House of Representatives[1]

January 2, 1863

To the Senate and House of Representatives:

I submit to Congress the expediency of extending to other Departments of the Government, the authority conferred on the President by the 8th. Section of the Act of the 8th. of May, 1792, to appoint a person to temporarily discharge the duties of Secretary of State, Secretary of the Treasury and Secretary of War, in case of the death, absence from the seat of Government or sickness of either of those officers.   ABRAHAM LINCOLN

Washington 2nd. January 1862 [1863]

[34]

¹ DS, DNA RG 46, Senate 37A F2; DS, DNA RG 233, House Executive Document No. 24. Secretary Caleb B. Smith sent in his resignation on December 31, 1862. Seward wrote Lincoln on January 2, 1863, that since the act authorizing the president to appoint "an acting head of a department" applied only to the departments of State, Treasury, and War, "You will have to leave Mr Smith's resignation *unaccepted*," in which case the assistant could "without special appointment . . . act in the *absence* of the Secretary." (DLC-RTL). An act approved February 20, 1863, gave the president power to appoint acting heads in other executive departments. On January 5, Lincoln nominated John P. Usher to succeed Smith, and Usher was confirmed by the Senate on January 8.

Endorsement¹

Let this woman have her boy out of Old Capitol Prison.
January 3, 1863.   A. LINCOLN.

¹ Leslie J. Perry, "Appeals to Lincoln's Clemency," *The Century Magazine,* LI (December, 1895), 253. No further reference has been found.

To Joseph Holt¹

Judge-Advocate-General: Executive Mansion,
My Dear Sir: Washington, January 3, 1863.
The bearer of this [Benjamin N. Martin]² makes an appeal in behalf of General Benham. I have told him that if you can carefully examine the case, and therefore do advise the restoration of General Benham [*sic*].³ I do not order you to do this, but leave it to yourself. I send the papers in my possession. Yours, very truly,   A. LINCOLN.

¹ OR, I, XIV, 979.
² Brackets are in the source. Benjamin N. Martin was a professor at the "University of the city of New York" and a friend of General Henry W. Benham's.
³ Brackets are in the source. Benham's appointment as brigadier general of Volunteers was revoked on August 7, 1862, on recommendation of Halleck and approval of Stanton, for Benham's part in the Union repulse at Secessionville, James Island, South Carolina, June 16, 1862. Holt recommended on January 26, 1863, that Benham be restored to service, and the revocation of Benham's appointment was cancelled on February 6 (OR, I, XIV, 979-83).

To the Senate¹

To the Senate of the United States.   January 3, 1863
I transmit to the Senate for consideration with a view to ratification, a Convention for the mutual adjustment of claims between the United States and Ecuador, signed by the respective plenipo-

tentiaries of the two Governments, in Guayaquil, on the 25th. November, ultimo.   ABRAHAM LINCOLN
  Washington, 3 January, 1863.

¹ DNA RG 46, Senate 37B B4. The convention was ratified by the Senate on January 28, 1863.

To Gideon Welles¹

                                                    Executive Mansion,
Dear Sir: Washington, Jan'y 4, 1863.
  As many persons, who come well recommended for loyalty and service to the Union cause, and who are refugees from rebel oppression in the State of Virginia, make application to me for authority and permission to remove their families and property to protection within the Union lines, by means of our armed gunboats on the Potomac River and Chesapeake Bay, you are hereby requested to hear and consider all such applications, and to grant such assistance to this class of persons as in your judgment their merits may render proper, and as may, in each case, be consistent with the perfect and complete efficiency of the naval service and with military expediency.   ABRAHAM LINCOLN
  Hon. Gideon Welles
  Secretary of the Navy.

¹ LS, DNA WR NB RG 45, Executive Letters, January-February, 1864, No. 8. No reply from Welles has been located. Although definitely dated 1863, this letter is filed among 1864 documents, and may have been misdated by Lincoln.

To Samuel R. Curtis¹

                                                    Executive Mansion,
Major General Curtis   Washington, January 5, 1863.
  My dear Sir: I am having a good deal of trouble with Missouri matters, and I now sit down to write you particularly about it. One class of friends believe in greater severity, and another in greater leniency, in regard to arrests, banishments, and assessments. As usual in such cases, each questions the other's motives. On the one hand it is insisted that Gov. Gamble's Unionism, at most, is not better than a secondary spring of action—that hunkerism, and a wish for political influence, stand before Unionism, with him. On the other hand, it is urged that arrests, banishments, and assessments are made more for private malice, revenge, and pecuniary interest, than for the public good. This morning I was told by a gentleman who, I have no doubt believes what he says,

that in one case of assessments for *ten* thousand dollars, the different persons who paid, compared receipts, and found they had paid thirty thousand dollars. If this be true, the inference is that the collecting agents pocketed the odd twenty thousand. And true or not, in the instance, nothing but the sternest necessity can justify the making and maintaining of a system so liable to such abuses. Doubtless the necessity[2] for the making of the system in Missouri *did* exist, and whether it continues for the maintainance of it, is now a practical, and very important question. Some days ago Governor Gamble telegraphed me asking that the assessments, outside of St. Louis county, might be suspended, as they already have been within it; and this morning all the members of congress here from Missouri, but one, lay a paper before me asking the same thing. Now, my belief is that Gov. Gamble is an honest and true man, not less so than yourself; that you and he could confer together on this, and other Missouri questions with great advantage to the public; that each knows something which the other does not, and that, acting together, you could about double your stock of pertinent information. May I not hope that you and he will attempt this? I could at once safely do, (or you could safely do without me) whatever[3] you and he agree upon. There is absolutely no reason why you should not agree. Yours as ever

A. LINCOLN

P.S. I forgot to say that Hon. James S. Rollins, M.C. from one of the Missouri Districts wishes that, upon his personal responsibility, Rev. John M. Robinson, of Columbia, Mo. James L. Matthews of Boone county, Mo, and James L. Stephens, also of Boone county, Mo. may be allowed to return to their respective homes. Major Rollins leaves with me very strong papers from the neighbors of these men, whom he says he knows to be true men. He also says he has many constituents who he thinks are rightfully exiled; but that he thinks these three should be allowed to return. Please look into the case, and oblige Major Rollins if you consistently can.[4] Yours truly   A. LINCOLN

[1] ALS copy, DLC-RTL. This letter is misdated July 5, 1863, in Hertz, II, 899. As printed in the *Official Records* (I, XXII, II, 17-18) it carries the subscription "(Copy sent to Governor Gamble)," and we may infer from General Curtis' reply (*infra*) that as of January 15, he had not received the original. On December 31, 1862, Governor Gamble telegraphed Lincoln as follows: "I have stopped all assessments of Enrolled Militia. Please order by telegraph the suspension of all assessments by United States officers. Great distress is produced." (OR, I, XXII, I, 888). On January 3, 1863, Lincoln's interview with James E. Yeatman, Giles F. Filley, and George P. Strong took place (see postscript to Lincoln's letter to Curtis, January 2, *supra*). On January 4 six members of

Congress from Missouri petitioned Lincoln to order a discontinuance of the military assessments "as now all penalties for violations of the law, can be enforced in the civil tribunals in that State."

On January 15, Curtis replied as follows:

"I had the honor to see a letter addressed to me, but sent to Governor Gamble, of the 5th instant . . . relating to . . . affairs in this State, which you say are giving you much trouble. . . .

"In my interview with Governor Gamble, and in reference to persons charging him with selfish and ambitious motives, and doubts as to his fidelity, the Governor expressed his regrets, and evinced generous sentiments of loyalty. . . . I think with you that Governor Gamble is loyal, and I do not see any occasion for us to differ, except it may be as to some measures. . . . He goes for you and our country and some of your measures. I go for all. . . . There may be frauds, such as you name, but I doubt it. No assessment committee could commit such a fraud as you name with impunity. . . . On matters concerning the degree and direction of force against rebels, I am appealed to as the supposed head of military power in this vicinity. On complaints of too much severity, the Governor and Your Excellency are appealed to, and we do not, therefore, . . . always see both sides. As to banishments, the Governor goes further than I. . . . As to the cases named by Mr. Rollins, I will examine, and write to him. They must stand on their own merits, not on his; but I shall have due deference to his opinion as to the safety of the release. As I intimated in a former letter, I only fear some conflict with the Governor in regard to Enrolled Militia and regular volunteers. I command the volunteers, but the Enrolled Militia, it is claimed, can only be commanded by the Governor. . . ." (OR, I, XXII, II, 42-43).   2 "Necessity for the" inserted by Hay.

3 "Ever you" inserted by Hay.

4 No further reference to the disposal of these cases has been found.

Memorandum[1]

January 5, 1863

Major Rollins' three cases of exile.

I have, to-day, Jan. 5. 1863, written Gen. Curtis about this.

AL.

1 AES-DLC-RTL. See Lincoln to Curtis, *supra*.

Memorandum[1]

As to suspending Assessments. Wrote Gen. Curtis to-day Jan. 5. 1863.

A.L

1 AES, DLC-RTL. Lincoln's endorsement is written on an envelope containing a letter from Missouri members of congress asking that military assessments in Missouri be discontinued. See Lincoln to Curtis, *supra*.

To the House of Representatives[1]

To the House of Representatives.   January 5, 1863

In compliance with the Resolution of the House of Representatives of the 22nd. ultimo, in relation to the alleged interference of our Minister to Mexico in favor of the French, I transmit a report from the Secretary of State and the papers with which it is accompanied.   ABRAHAM LINCOLN

Washington, January 5, 1863.

1 DS, DNA RG 233, House Executive Document No. 23. Seward's report of December 29, 1862, transmitted by Lincoln, including all the papers involved, may be found in Thirty-seventh Congress, Third Session, *House Executive Document No. 23.* Minister Thomas Corwin and other members of the diplomatic corps in Mexico City had protested on October 2, 1862, an order expelling foreigners without "evident proofs" of their actions against the Mexican government.

To William S. Rosecrans[1]

Major General W. S. Rosecrans[2]   Executive Mansion,
Murfreesboro, Tenn.   Washington, Jan. 5. 186[3]

Your despatch announcing retreat of enemy has just reached here. God bless you, and all with you! Please tender to all, and accept for yourself, the Nation's gratitude for yours, and their, skill, endurance, and dantless courage.   A LINCOLN

1 ALS, RPB. Lincoln's erroneous date "1862" has been corrected on the manuscript in a different handwriting. Rosecrans' dispatch to Halleck on January 5, 1863, reported the Union victory in the Battle of Murfreesboro, Tennessee, as follows: "We have fought one of the greatest battles of the war, and are victorious. Our entire success on the 31st was prevented by a surprise of the right flank; but have, nevertheless, beaten the enemy, after a three-days' battle. They fled with great precipitancy on Saturday night. The last of their columns of cavalry left this morning. Their loss has been very heavy. Generals [James E.] Rains and [Roger W.] Hanson killed. [James R.] Chalmers, [Daniel W.] Adams, and [John C.] Breckinridge are wounded." (OR, I, XX, I, 186).   2 "W. S. Rosecrans" is not in Lincoln's handwriting.

To Caleb Russell and Sallie A. Fenton[1]

                                          Executive Mansion,
My Good Friends   Washington, January 5, 1863

The Honorable Senator Harlan has just placed in my hands your letter of the 27th of December which I have read with pleasure and gratitude.

It is most cheering and encouraging for me to know that in the efforts which I have made and am making for the restoration of a righteous peace to our country, I am upheld and sustained by the good wishes and prayers of God's people. No one is more deeply than myself aware that without His favor our highest wisdom is but as foolishness and that our most strenuous efforts would avail nothing in the shadow of His displeasure. I am conscious of no desire for my country's welfare, that is not in consonance with His will, and of no plan upon which we may not ask His blessing.[2] It seems to me that if there be one subject upon which all good men may unitedly agree, it is imploring the gracious favor of the God of Nations upon the struggles our people are making for the preservation of their precious birthright of civil and religious liberty. Very truly Your friend   A. LINCOLN.

To   Caleb Russell   ⎱Secretaries
       Sallie A. Fenton   ⎰

[1] LS-F, Davenport, Iowa, *Democrat and Leader*, February 14, 1928. The letter is in John Hay's handwriting signed by Lincoln. A draft in Hay's autograph indicates his composition of the letter (DLC-RTL). The following communication was sent to Senator James Harlan by Caleb Russell on December 27, 1862 (*ibid.*):

"To Abraham Lincoln President of the United States

"Esteemed Friend   On behalf of the Religious Society of Friends in the State of Iowa, whom we represent, we desire briefly to express to thee the very deep solicitude we feel that that [*sic*] in the present perilous condition of the Nations life, thou mayest be favored to ask counsel of Him who holdeth the destinies of Nations in His hand. We desire to express our united approval of thy late Proclamation of Prospective Emancipation. We believe it is intrinsically right and in the direction to bring about a permanent peace in our beloved country and we hope it may be carried out uncompromisingly. At this very late period we can do but *very* little more, than bear our testimony in favor of justice and liberty and like Aaron and Him of old would gladly hold up *thy* hands as they did the hands of Moses.

"In Christian love we subscribe ourselves thy friends.

"Signed by direction and on behalf of the monthly meeting of the Religious Society of Friends of Prairie Grove in the State of Iowa this 27th of the 12th mo A.D. 1862.   "CALEB RUSSELL

                                    "SALLIE A. FENTON"

[2] This sentence is marked for deletion in the draft, but appears in the letter.

To Mrs. Abraham H. Hoge[1]

Mrs. A. H. Hoge   Executive Mansion,
Chicago, Illinois.   Washington, January 6. 1863.

I am sorry I failed in my former note to make myself understood by you. You send me a commission, which is good as far as it goes; but it fills only *one* of the *three* conditions which I stated to you as being indispensable. The remaining conditions are that a Major-General must be found who has not already the full complement of Staff-officers, which the law allows to a Major-General, and who is willing to take your son as one of them. Without these I should violate both law, and an indispensable courtesy, to thrust your son, or any one else, upon any Major General's staff. As to Brigadier-Generals, they are not allowed any staff officers with as high rank as Major. If I were to undertake it, I probably could not, in less than a month, nor without a laborious correspondence, find the General entitled by law to have an additional staff officer with the rank of Major, and who is willing [to] take your son as the man. This your son must do this [*sic*] for himself. I hope I now make myself understood   Yours very truly   A. LINCOLN

1 ALS, ICHi. See Lincoln's letter to Mrs. Hoge, November 25, 1862, *supra*. Mrs. Hoge's letter is not in the Lincoln Papers.

Memorandum Concerning Alban B. Botsford[1]

Executive Mansion, Washington, Jan. 6. 1863.
Col. Ulmann, calls with Capt. Alban B. Botsford, now of 78th. N.Y. Inftry.—both at National Hotel. Has property in Mississippi and is well acquainted in La. When time comes would like to aid in organizing blacks there.

1 AD, DLC-RTL. On March 2, 1863, Botsford was appointed colonel of the Seventy-eighth U.S. Colored Troops and served until September 22, 1863, when he resigned. Daniel Ullmann, colonel of the Seventy-eighth New York Infantry, was recruiting a cadre of officers to organize a brigade of Negro troops in Louisiana. See Lincoln to Banks, March 29, *infra*.

Memorandum Concerning Meredith Clymer[1]

Executive Mansion, Washington, Jan. 6. 1863.
To-day, Col. Ulmann calls & urges that Dr. Meredith Clymer be appointed one of the new Medical Inspectors. Thinks he is of superior fitness for the place.

1 AD, IHi. Dr. Meredith Clymer was appointed surgeon of Volunteers on December 25, 1861, and had received praise from Dorothea Dix (see Lincoln to Stanton May 5, 1862, *supra*), but no record of his appointment as inspector has been found.

To William H. Seward[1]

Executive Mansion, Washington, 6th. January, 1863.
The Secretary of State is directed not to countersign the within contract, or to affix the seal of the United States thereto, but to retain the instrument under advisement.   ABRAHAM LINCOLN.

1 DS, DNA FS RG 59, Miscellaneous Letters. The accompanying contract between Bernard Kock "formerly of New Orleans" and the U.S. government, December 31, 1862, called for transporting and colonizing five thousand Negroes on Vache Island, a dependency of Haiti. Seward wrote Lincoln on Jan-

uary 3, "I think it necessary to have a few precautions taken before I certify the contract of Bernard Kock, and I will speak with you on the subject when we meet." (DLC-RTL). Kock, who signed himself "Governor of A'Vache Island," had secured a twenty-year concession from the government of Haiti. His letter of January 17 implies that he had asked the government for $50,000 in advance (DLC-RTL). On March 20, 1863, Kock transferred his contract to Leonard W. Jerome, Charles K. Tuckerman and Paul S. Forbes. On April 16, Lincoln issued his proclamation (*infra*), cancelling the contract.

To Green Adams[1]

Executive Mansion,
Hon. Green Adams   Washington, January 7, 1863.

My dear Sir: In answer to your inquiries of this morning I have to say I am very anxious to have the special force in Kentucky raised and armed. But the changed conduct towards me of some of her members of congress, and the ominous out-givings as to what the Governor and Legislature of Kentucky intend doing, admonish me to consider whether any additional arms I may send there, are not to be turned against the government.[2] I hope this may clear up on the right side. So far as I can see, Kentucky's sons in the field, are acting loyally and bravely, God bless them! I can not help thinking the mass of her people feel the same way. Yours truly

A. LINCOLN

[1] ADfS, DLC-RTL; LS, owned by Mrs. Henry C. Adams, Pittsburgh, Pennsylvania. No letter from Green Adams has been found to which this can be a reply. The probability is that Adams presented his request in person. An act approved on February 7, 1863, authorized the Governor of Kentucky to raise a force of 20,000 twelve-months volunteers to serve in Kentucky, with discretion of the president to use them outside the state.

[2] This reference may be explained by Horatio G. Wright's communication to Halleck of December 30, 1862, "I have information, on which I am inclined to rely, that in case the President issues his proclamation . . . on the 1st proximo, the Legislature of Kentucky, which meets on Monday next, will legislate the State out of the Union, and that the Governor's message will favor such action; also that the court of appeals has a disloyal majority, and will reverse all judgments of loyal inferior courts against rebels. . . ." (OR, I, XX, II, 282).

To B. Gratz Brown[1]

Hon. B. Gratz Brown   Washington, D.C.,
Jefferson City, Mo.   Jan. 7. 1863 [5:30 P.M.]

Yours of to-day just received. The Administration takes no part between it's friends in Mo, of whom, I at least, consider you one; and I have never before had an intimation that appointees there, were interfering, or were inclined to interfere.   A. LINCOLN

[1] ALS, RPB. The time sent does not show on the original, the clerk's notation at the top left of the page having been trimmed off. The telegram from Brown, received at 5:15 P.M., reads as follows: "Does the administration desire my defeat if not why are its appointees here working for that end" (DLC-RTL).

To John A. Dix[1]

Major Gen. Dix   Washington, D.C.,
Fort-Monroe, Va   Jan. 7, 1863

Do Richmond papers of 6th. say nothing about Vicksburg? or, if anything, what?   A. LINCOLN.

[1] ALS, RPB. Dix replied at 5:55 P.M., "The only 2 Richmond papers of the Sixth I have seen say nothing of Vicksburg but they admit & mourn over the Rebel defeat at Murfreesboro" (DLC-RTL). A later telegram from Dix received at 8:40 P.M., quotes a despatch of January 2 in the Richmond *Examiner* of January 6, "It expresses a confidence of holding Vicksburgh against any force the Federals can bring against it It adds 'this morning our forces advanced against the Enemy who were erecting works on the Lake causing them to evacuate their position, leaving fifty stand of arms nine prisoners & all their implements for erecting fortifications. Our forces now occupy the whole country bordering on the Lake.

"'The Enemy having returned with their transports & gone down the Yazoo. The Enemy have left Chickasaw Bayou & are reported going on their transports to Snyder's Bluff on the Yazoo where it is supposed they will make an attempt to storm our works.

"'Our forces are well advised of their movements'" (DLC-RTL).

To Henry W. Halleck[1]

Executive Mansion.
Maj Genl Halleck.   Washington, January 7th. 1863.

My dear Sir: What think you of forming a reserve Cavalry Corps of, say 6000 for the Army of the Potomac? Might not such a corps be constituted from the Cavalry of Sigels and Slocums corps, with scraps we could pick up here and there? Yours truly,
                                                    A LINCOLN.

[1] Copy, DNA WR RG 108, HQA, December file 1863, 137L. No reply from Halleck has been found and none is given in the *Official Records* where Lincoln's communication is printed (I, XXI, 954). On January 14, however, General Carl Schurz wrote Lincoln, "To-day I went with Gen. Sigel to see Gen. Burnside, who fully agreed to it that I should command the Eleventh Corps and Gen. Stahel the Cavalry Reserve. Gen. Stahel also is very well satisfied with it. All concerned now agreeing upon that point the only thing that is wanted is that you should be kind enough to issue an order placing me in command of the Corps and Gen. Stahel in command of the Cavalry-Reserve, consisting of the Cavalry now with the Grand Reserve Division and such regiments as will be attached to it. . . ." (DLC-RTL). See further Lincoln to Stanton, January 12, *infra*.

[43]

To William A. Hammond[1]

January 7, 1863

Will the Surgeon General please see Rev. Mr. Alvord, and give his opinion to me in writing whether he should be appointed a Chaplain as he desires?   A. LINCOLN

Jan. 7. 1863.

[1] AES, OFH. Lincoln's endorsement is written on an envelope on which the following endorsements also appear:

"Will the President please give me a commendation to any Regt. in the Army of the Potomac in need of a chaplain. Dr. Hammond promises to transfer me to the first permanent Hospital which shall be opened on the front. In the mean time I will do what I can in connection with a Regiment. Very respectfully   J. W. ALVORD"

"Respectfully returned to the President. There is no Law which will permit of a chaplain being appointed to a hospital and assigned to duty in the field. Mr Alvord thinks he can obtain the appointment of Regimental Chaplain which will be sati[sfactory] to him and cover the case.

"W. A. HAMMOND   Surg. Gen."

No record of the Reverend Alvord's appointment has been found.

To Edwin M. Stanton[1]

Allow Col. Peyton the additional time required, unless there be reason to the contrary unknown to me.   A. LINCOLN

Jan. 7. 1863.

[1] AES, CSmH. Lincoln's endorsement is written on a letter from Jesse E. Peyton to Adjutant General Lorenzo Thomas, Philadelphia, January 3, 1863, asking an extension of time for recruiting his regiment, since the draft and restrictions imposed upon his recruiting had seriously handicapped recruitment. Stanton's endorsement below Lincoln's is as follows: "There is good & valid reason for not extending the time & the Secretary of War declines to do it." See further Lincoln to Stanton, January 8, *infra*.

To Edwin M. Stanton[1]

If it is lawfully competent for me to make the appointments within requested, let it be done at once.   A. LINCOLN

Jan. 7. 1863.

[1] AES-P, ISLA. Lincoln's endorsement is written on a letter from Major General John A. McClernand, Memphis, Tennessee, December 29, 1862, asking appointment of "Major Adolph Schwartz, 2nd. Illinois Light Artillery, to be Asst. Inspector General of my corps, with the rank of Lt. Colonel; also Major Walter B. Scates A. A. General, for promotion to the same rank; also Capt. James Dunlap for promotion to the same rank in the Qr. Mast. Dept." Major Scates apparently brought this letter from McClernand along with another of the same date (see Lincoln to McClernand, January 8, *infra*). No record has been found of Major Schwartz's promotion. Dunlap and Scates were appointed lieutenant colonels as of January 1, 1863.

To José M. Acha[1]

January 8, 1863

Abraham Lincoln,
President of the United States of America.

To His Excellency Señor Don Jose M. Acha
Constitutional President of the Republic of Bolivia.

Great and Good Friend: I have received the letter of your Excellency of the 16 August last informing me of your election by the popular suffrage to the Constitutional Presidency of the Republic at the expiration of the Provisional term of service which the national assembly had entrusted to you.

I felicitate Your Excellency on this renewed mark of the confidence of the people in your Excellency's administration, and I sincerely hope that under your continued direction of affairs the national prosperity may be greatly enlarged and the happiness of the people secured.

The sentiments of friendship expressed by your Excellency are cordially reciprocated. It is equally my desire and study to strengthen the friendly relations which have, happily, always subsisted between our respective countries. The Treaty just exchanged by our respective plenipotentiaries which I will immediately proclaim as the law of the land, will, I am confident, aid us both in giving effect to our good intentions.

I beg your Excellency to accept the expressions of my high regard and sincere friendship, and I pray God to have &c. Your Good Friend   ABRAHAM LINCOLN.

By the President:
WILLIAM H. SEWARD, Secretary of State.
Washington, 8 January, 1863.

[1] Copy, DNA FS RG 59, Communications to Foreign Sovereigns and States, III, 196-97.

Order to Edward Bates[1]

Executive Mansion
Ordered by the President: January 8. 1863.

Whereas on the 13th day of November, 1862, it was ordered "that the Attorney General be charged with the superintendence and direction of all proceedings to be had under the Act of Congress of the 17 of July 1862 entitled "an Act to suppress insurrection, to punish treason and rebellion, and to seize and confiscate the property of rebels, and for other purposes" in so far as may concern

[45]

the seizure, prosecution and condemnation of the estate, property and effects of rebels and traitors as mentioned and provided for in the fifth, sixth, and seventh sections of the said Act of Congress."

And whereas, since that time it has been ascertained that divers prosecutions have been instituted in the Courts of the United States, for the condemnation of property of rebels and traitors under the Act of Congress of August the 6th 1861, entitled "an Act to confiscate property used for insurrectionary purposes" which equally require the superintending care of the Government: Therefore—

It is now, further ordered by the President: That the Attorney General be charged with the superintendence and direction of all proceedings to be had under the said last-mentioned Act (the Act of 1861) as fully in all respects, as under the first-mentioned Act (the Act of 1862).   ABRAHAM LINCOLN.

[1] Copy, DLC-Nicolay Papers. In the *Official Records* (III, IV, 408-409) this order is printed as an enclosure in a letter from Bates to General Lewis Wallace, May 25, 1864. See also Lincoln's order to Bates, November 13, 1862.

To Ambrose E. Burnside[1]

Jan. 8. 1863.

I understand Gen. Halleck has sent you a letter of which this is a copy. I approve the letter. I deplore the want of concurrence with you, in opinion by your general officers, but I do not see the remedy. Be cautious, and do not understand that the government, or country, is driving you. I do not yet see how I could profit by changing the command of the A.P. & if I did, I should not wish to do it by accepting the resignation of your commission.

Gen. Burnside.   A. LINCOLN

[1] AES-P, ISLA; AES copy, DLC-RTL. Lincoln's endorsement is written on an official copy of Halleck's letter to Burnside of January 7, 1863. The autograph copy of the endorsement is written on the back of Burnside's letter to Lincoln of January 5, 1863, and is headed "Answered by indorsement on copy of Gen. Halleck's letter as follows."

On January 5, Burnside tendered his resignation "as Major General of Volunteers" and wrote Lincoln as follows:

"Since my return to the Army I have become more than ever convinced that the General Officers of this command are almost unanimously opposed to another crossing of the river; but I am still of the opinion that the crossing should be attempted, & I have accordingly issued orders to the Engineers and Artilery to prepare for it. There is much hazzard in it as there always is in the majority of Military Movements, and I cannot begin the movement without giving you notice of it, particularly as I know so little of the effect that it may have upon other movements of distant armies. The influence of your telegraph the other day is still upon me, and has impressed me with the idea that there are many parts of the problem which influence you that are not known to me. In order to relieve you from all embarassment in my case, I enclose with this my resignation of my commission of Major General of Volunteers which you can have accepted, if my movement is not in accordance with the views of yourself, and your military advisers. I have taken the liberty to write to you personally upon this subject because it was necessary as I learn from Genl Halleck for you to approve of my general plan written at Warrenton, before I could commence the movement, and I think it quite as necessary that you should know of the important movement I am about to make—particularly as it will have to be made in opposition to the views of nearly all my General Officers, & after the receipt of a dispatch from you informing me of the opinion of some of them who had visited you.

"I beg leave to say that my resignation is not sent in, in any spirit of insubordination, but as I before said simply to relieve you of any embarrassment in changing commanders where lack of confidence may have rendered it necessary.

"The bearer of this will bring me any answer, or I should be glad to hear from you by telegraph in cipher." (DLC-RTL).

As printed in the *Official Records* (I, XXI, 944-45) Burnside's letter has an additional paragraph, third from the last, which is reproduced from "Burnside's copy of this letter, but is not in that received by the President," as follows:

"In conversation with you on New Year's morning, I was led to express some opinions which I afterward felt it my duty to place on paper, and to express them verbally to the gentlemen of whom we were speaking, which I did in your presence after handing you the letter. You were not disposed then, as I saw, to retain this letter, and I took it back, but I now return it to you for record, if you wish it."

The copy of Halleck's letter to Burnside of January 7, which bears Lincoln's original endorsement, reads as follows:

"In all my communications and interviews with you since you took command of the Army of the Potomac, I have advised a forward movement across the Rappahannock. At our interview at Warrenton, I urged that you should cross by the fords above Fredericksburg rather than to fall down to that place, and, when I left you at Warrenton, it was understood that at least a considerable part of your army would cross by the fords, and I so represented to the President. It was this modification of the plan proposed by you, that I telegraphed you had received his approval. When the attempt at Fredericksburg was abandoned, I advised you to renew the attempt at some other point, either in whole or in part to turn the enemy's works, or to threaten their wings or communications; in other words, to keep the enemy occupied till a favorable opportunity offered to strike a decisive blow. I particularly advised you to use your cavalry and light artillery upon his communications, and attempt to cut off his supplies and engage him at an advantage.

"In all our interviews I have urged that our first object was, not Richmond, but the defeat or scattering of Lee's army, which threatened Washington and the line of the Upper Potomac. I now recur to these things simply to remind you of the general views which I have expressed, and which I still hold.

"The circumstances of the case, however, have somewhat changed since the early part of November. The chances of an extended line of operations are now, on account of the advanced season, much less than then. But the chances are still in our favor to meet and defeat the enemy on the Rappahannock, if we can effect a crossing in a position where we can meet the enemy on favorable or even equal terms. I therefore still advise a movement against him. The character of that movement, however, must depend upon circumstances which may change any day and almost any hour. If the enemy should concentrate his forces at the place you have selected for a crossing, make it a feint and try another place. Again, the circumstances at the time may be such as to render an attempt to cross the entire army not advisable. In that case theory suggests that, while the enemy concentrates at that point, advantages can be gained by crossing smaller forces at other points, to cut off his lines, destroy his communication, and capture his rear guards, outposts, &c. The great object is to occupy the enemy, to prevent his making large detachments or distant raids, and to injure him all you can with the least injury to yourself. If this can be best accomplished by feints of a general crossing and detached real crossings, take that course; if by an actual general crossing, with feints on other points, adopt that course. There seems to me to be many reasons why a crossing at some point should be attempted. It will not do to keep your large army inactive. As you yourself admit, it devolves on you to decide upon the time, place, and character of the crossing which you may attempt. I can only advise that an attempt be made, and as early as possible." (OR, I, XXI, 953-54).

To Andrew Johnson[1]

Gov. Johnson.   Executive Mansion,
Nashville, Tenn.   Washington, January 8. 1863.

A despatch of yesterday, from Nashville, says "the body of Capt. Todd of 6th. Ky, brought in to-day.["] Please tell me what was his Christian name, and whether he was in our service, or that of the enemy. I shall also be glad to have your impression as to the effect the late operations about Murfreesboro, will have on the prospects of Tennessee.   A. LINCOLN

[1] ALS, RPB. The operator's notation of time sent for this telegram appears in the upper left hand corner "2.15 P.M." Johnson telegraphed his reply at 9 P.M., "Body of Capt Charles S Todd of Shelbyville Ky belonging to federal 6th Ky is here in metallic case awaiting transportation Your order in regard thereto will be promptly attended to" (DLC-RTL). Captain Charles S. Todd, a relative of Mrs. Lincoln, had been killed in the Battle of Murfreesboro. See Lincoln to Johnson, January 10, *infra*.

To John A. McClernand[1]

                         Executive Mansion,
Major General McClernand   Washington, January 8. 1863.

My dear Sir Your interesting communication by the hand of Major Scates is received. I never did ask more, nor ever was willing to accept less, than for all the States, and the people thereof, to take and hold their places, and their rights, in the Union, under the Constitution of the United States. For this alone have I felt authorized to struggle; and I seek neither more nor less now. Still, to use a coarse, but an expressive figure, broken eggs can not be mended. I have issued the emancipation proclamation, and I can not retract it.

After the commencement of hostilities I struggled nearly a year and a half to get along without touching the "institution"; and when finally I conditionally determined to touch it, I gave a hundred days fair notice of my purpose, to all the States and people, within which time they could have turned it wholly aside, by simply again becoming good citizens of the United States. They chose to disregard it, and I made the peremptory proclamation on what appeared to me to be a military necessity. And being made, it must stand. As to the States not included in it, of course they can have their rights in the Union as of old. Even the people of the states included, if they choose, need not to be hurt by it. Let them adopt systems of apprenticeship for the colored people, conforming substantially to the most approved plans of gradual emancipation; and, with the aid they can have from the general government, they may be nearly as well off, in this respect, as if the present trouble had not occurred, and much better off than they can possibly be if the contest continues persistently.

As to any dread of my having a "purpose to enslave, or exterminate, the whites of the South," I can scarcely believe that such dread exists. It is too absurd. I believe you can be my personal witness that no man is less to be dreaded for undue severity, in any case.

If the friends you mention really wish to have peace upon the old terms, they should act at once. Every day makes the case more difficult. They can so act, with entire safety, so far as I am concerned.

I think you would better not make this letter public; but you may rely confidently on my standing by whatever I have said in it. Please write me if any thing more comes to light. Yours very truly

A. LINCOLN.

[1] ALS-P, ISLA; LS copy, DLC-RTL. The autograph letter is incorrectly dated "1862," but the signed copy is correctly dated. Two letters from McClernand dated December 29, 1862, were carried to Lincoln by Major Walter B. Scates (see Lincoln's endorsement to Stanton, January 7, *supra*). The lengthy letter to which Lincoln here replied reported that, "A gentleman of the first respectability just arrived from the rebel army . . . brings suggestions of . . . import from officers of high rank in the rebel service, who were formerly my warm personal and political friends.

"These officials desire the restoration of peace and are represented to be willing to wheel their columns into the line of that policy. They admit that the South West and the North West are geographically and commercially identified. . . ." (DLC-RTL).

To Caleb B. Smith[1]

Executive Mansion,

Hon. Caleb B. Smith   Washington, January 8. 1863.

My dear Sir: I wish you would tell me in writing, exactly what you did promise Watt about going to Europe last Spring. If it was

in writing send me a copy; if merely verbal, write it as accurately as you can from memory, and please send it to me at once. Yours as ever
A. LINCOLN

[1] ALS, CSmH. No reply from Smith has been found, but his endorsement of approval appears on a copy of a letter from David P. Holloway to John Watt, March 14, 1862, which reads as follows:

"Understanding that you are about to go to Europe, I wish to engage your services for the Agricultural Division of the Patent Office, in the selection and purchase of seeds, commencing on the first of July next. You will receive full instructions about that time, informing you of the services required in detail. Your compensation will be at the rate of fifteen hundred dollars per annum and your actual travelling expenses" (DLC-RTL).

But see also Lincoln to Lorenzo Thomas, November 16, 1861, *supra*, and note.

To Edwin M. Stanton[1]

Hon. Sec. of War: Executive Mansion,
My dear Sir,   Washington, January 8, 1863.

We shall need all the men we can get. Is there a special reason why Col. Peyton should not finish up his Regiment? If there is such special reason please tell me what it is. Yours truly
A. LINCOLN.

[1] ALS, The Hill School, Pottstown, Pennsylvania. See Lincoln's endorsement to Stanton, January 7, *supra*. Senators Samuel C. Pomeroy, James A. Mc-Dougall, and Edgar Cowan wrote Lincoln on January 8 as follows:

"Will you listen for a moment to Col. *Jesse E. Peyton* of Philadelphia Pa.

"I hope no injustice will be done and that he may be encouraged to fill up his Regiment. He comes to me very highly recommended.

"And in that spirit is most cordially commended to you. . . ." (DLC-RTL). No record of Peyton's appointment has been found.

Memorandum Concerning William S. Pryor, J. O'Hara, and Thomas L. Jones[1]

Executive Mansion, Washington, January 9, 1863.
To-day Mr. Senator Powell calls and demands the unconditional release William S. Pryor, of New-castle, Henry Co. Ky   J. O'Hara, of Covington, Ky, who have been imprisoned at Camp Chase, & are now on parol at Cincinnati, not allowed to go to Kentucky. Col. Thomas L. Jones has a similar case except he has the previleges of New-port.

[1] AD, DLC-RTL. No further reference has been found to the cases of Pryor and O'Hara. The case of Thomas L. Jones of Newport, Kentucky, is amply recorded in the *Official Records* (II, V, 247, 250, 296). Jones had been paroled by Governor Tod of Ohio and upon expiration of his parole was recommended to be released upon taking an oath of allegiance in February, 1863.

Memorandum Concerning Sandwich Islands[1]

I have a new reason for holding on to this a little while.

Jan. 9. 1863.   A. LINCOLN

[1] AES, DNA FS RG 59, Appointments, Box 373. Lincoln's endorsement is written on a letter to Seward from James S. Rollins, January 6, 1862[3], concerning activities of French Roman Catholics and the possibility of French intervention in the Sandwich Islands. The memorandum probably refers to the imminent replacement of Thomas J. Dryer by James McBride as commissioner to the Sandwich Islands on January 26, 1863. See Lincoln to Seward March 7 and 15, 1862, *supra*. Although Dryer seems to have been incompetent, his difficulties as commissioner were aggravated by the presence of former commissioner David L. Gregg, Lincoln's old friend whom President Pierce had appointed commissioner in 1853 and who remained in the Islands as adviser to King Kamehameha IV (Sumner to Lincoln, October 11, 1862, DLC-RTL).

To the Senate and House of Representatives[1]

January 9, 1863

To the Senate and House of Representatives.

I transmit for the consideration of Congress, and with a view to the adoption of such measures in relation to the subject of it as may be deemed expedient, a copy of a note of the 8th instant, addressed to the Secretary of State by the Minister Resident of the Hanseatic Republics accredited to this Government, concerning an International Agricultural Exhibition to be held next summer in the City of Hamburg.   ABRAHAM LINCOLN.

Washington, 9th January, 1863.

[1] DS, DNA RG 46, Senate 37A F2; DS, ICU. Lincoln transmitted a copy of R. Schleidu's letter to Seward, January 8, 1863, presenting a prospectus of the international agricultural exhibition to be held at Hamburg. Resolutions to facilitate a proper representation of the U.S. at the Hamburg Fair were introduced in the House on February 11 and the Senate on February 26, but neither seems to have been adopted.

To William H. Seward[1]

January 9, 1863

Dr. Smith, mentioned within, is an intimate personal friend of mine; and I have unconsciously superseded him, if at all. Sec. of State please inform me how it is   A. LINCOLN

Jan. 9. 1863.

[1] AES, DNA FS RG 59, Appointments, Box 383. Lincoln's endorsement is written on a letter from John Forsythe, Chicago, January 6, 1863, to Orville H. Browning, in regard to the removal of Forsythe's father-in-law, Dr. James Smith, as acting consul at Dundee, Scotland. Smith's son Hugh was appointed consul at Dundee in 1861 but because of poor health had to turn over the man-

agement of the office to his father. Lincoln's nomination of James Smith for the consulship was confirmed by the Senate on February 18, 1863. See further Lincoln to Seward, January 14, *infra*.

To Gideon Welles[1]

My dear Sir   Executive Mansion   Jan. 9, 1863

Capt Boggs of the Navy, thinks he ought to be recommended to Congress for a vote of thanks, and I am anxious to give the due reward of merit in all cases. Please give special attention to his case, & let me know the result Yours truly   A. LINCOLN

[1] Stan. V. Henkels Catalog 1342, January 4, 1924, No. 26. Charles S. Boggs of New Jersey, who had been nominated for promotion to captain on December 1, 1862, was probably the officer concerned, but no reply from Welles or record of a recommendation for a congressional vote of thanks has been found.

To David Wilmot[1]

Executive Mansion,   Washington, Jan. 9, 1863.
Hon. D. Wilmot,   I will do that.   A. LINCOLN

[1] ALS, DLC-RTL. An undated note from Wilmot to which Lincoln replied, reads as follows: "I leave for Harrisburg at 5 o'c to day. Not having heard from you I have called for an answer. Will you please give an answer on this sheet." (DLC-RTL).

Another undated letter from Wilmot, probably written on or near this date, is as follows:

"Yesterday Mr Grow informed me you had determined to make my appointment. I tender you my gratitude and thanks.

"Will you allow me a word, I dislike exceedingly to sever my identity with my State. I am known to its people, and hope that I have the love and respect of many of them. A position on the Court of Claims is *national*, the Bench of the District is *local*. I feel that Mr President very much—more perhaps than I ought. Again, while *able to labor*, in quiet and without excitement, I am satisfied that I have not many years in which to make provision for the family I must leave behind. The salary on the court of claims is $1000 greater than on the District Court.

"I trust that my name would not impair public confidence in the Courts and that your friends throughout the country would feel that you had not unworthily bestowed the appointment." (DLC-RTL).

On March 6, 1863, Lincoln appointed Wilmot judge of the Court of Claims.

To Samuel R. Curtis[1]

Maj. Gen. Curtis   Executive Mansion,
St. Louis, Mo.   Washington, Jany. 10. 1863.

I understand there is considerable trouble with the slaves in Missouri. Please do your best to keep peace on the question for two or three weeks, by which time we hope to do something here towards settling the question, in Missouri.   A. LINCOLN

[1] ALS, owned by Alfred W. Stern, Chicago, Illinois. Curtis replied on January 11, "Dispatch received. Hear of no negro troubles. Rebel raid on Springfield some trouble. My forces are coming on them from two directions." (OR, I, XXII, II, 32). A bill introduced in the House on December 22, 1862, by Representative Albert S. White for giving aid to Missouri toward abolishment of slavery passed the House on January 6 and as amended passed the Senate on February 12, 1863. No record of Lincoln's approval has been found, however, and a similar bill introduced in the Senate on December 19, 1862, by Senator John B. Henderson was reported unfavorably on January 14 by Senator Lyman Trumbull from the committee on the judiciary.

To William A. Hammond[1]

Respectfully submitted to Surgeon General, for his opinion whether Mr. Bushnell should be appointed, as recommended.

Jany. 10. 1863.   A. Lincoln

[1] AES, CCamStJ. Lincoln's endorsement is written on an envelope of the U.S. Sanitary Commission, Washington, D.C. Below it Hammond endorsed on January 13: "Respectfully returned to His Excellency the President with the recommendation that Mr. Bushnell be appointed as there is a place for him at Louisville." Bushnell has not been identified and no record of his appointment has been found.

To Andrew Johnson[1]

Gov. Johnson.   Executive Mansion,
Nashville, Tenn.   Washington, January 10, 1863.

Yours received. I presume the remains of Capt. Todd are in the hands of his family friends, & I wish to give no order on the subject.

But I do wish your opinion of the effects of the late battles about Murfreesboro, upon the prospects of Tennessee.   A. Lincoln

[1] ALS, RPB. See Lincoln to Johnson, January 8, *supra*. Johnson's telegram in reply was received at 11:10 P.M., January 11, "The battle of Murfreesborough has inspired much confidence with Union men of the ultimate success of the Government, and has greatly discouraged rebels, but increased their bitterness. If the rebel army could be expelled from the State, and Union sentiment developed without fear or restraint, I still think Tennessee will be brought back into the Union by decided majority of popular vote. Eastern portion of the State must be redeemed before confidence can be inspired with the mass of the people that the Government has the power to assert and maintain its authority in Tennessee. . . ." (OR, I, XX, II, 317).

To Jacob Collamer[1]

If not going to church please call & see me at once; & if to church, please call as soon after, as convenient   A. Lincoln

Jan. 11. 1863.

[1] ALS, owned by Charles W. Olsen, Chicago, Illinois. Lincoln's note is written on a small card. No specific data has been located concerning this conference, but the possibility is that Lincoln discussed the serious public reaction against the Emancipation Proclamation, the possibility of getting action on pending legislation to aid Missouri to free the slaves in that state (see Lincoln to Curtis, January 10, *supra*) and the general state of Union morale.

To William A. Buckingham[1]

Executive Mansion,
Governor: Washington, January 12, 1863.

It is with feelings of sincere pleasure and gratitude that I acknowledge the receipt of your kind favor of the 2nd. of January, conveying the Resolutions of the Legislature of Connecticut, approved December 24th, 1862.

Be assured, my dear sir, that I am deeply gratified by this new proof of the loyal and patriotic devotion of the people of your state, and that I most gratefully appreciate their expressions towards myself, which are at once so generous and so kind.

I have the honor to be Very truly Your Obt. Servt.

His Excellency   A. LINCOLN
The Governor of Connecticut

[1] LS copy, DLC-RTL. The copy or draft is in John Hay's handwriting. The resolution transmitted by Governor Buckingham reads in part as follows: "Resolved by this Assembly: That our confidence in the patriotism and integrity of the president . . . remains unshaken; and that, as the representatives of the people of this state, we pledge ourselves to support and sustain him . . . ; and . . . we tender him our sympathy in the trying and difficult circumstances in which he is placed. . . . We deprecate every attempt to impute to him such evils or disasters as may have resulted from the errors of judgement, insufficiency, or culpability of subordinate officials. . . ." (DLC-RTL).

To Joseph Holt[1]

War Department, Washington City, January 12, 1863.

The Judge-Advocate-General is instructed to revise the proceedings of the court-martial in the case of Maj.-Gen. Fitz John Porter, and to report fully upon any legal questions that may have arisen in them, and upon the bearing of the testimony in reference to the charges and specifications exhibited against the accused and upon which he was tried.   ABRAHAM LINCOLN.

[1] OR, I, XII, II (Supplement), 1134. Judge Advocate General Holt's long review appears in Thirty-seventh Congress, Third Session, *House Executive Document No. 71* and in the *Official Records*, I, XII, II (Supplement), 1112-33.

To Edwin M. Stanton[1]

Hon. Sec. of War   Executive Mansion
Dear Sir.   Washington, January 12, 1863.

I intended proposing to you this morning, and forgot it, that Schurz and Stahl should both be Maj. Genls. Schurz to take Sigel's old corps, and Stahl to command Cavalry. They, together with Sigel, are our sincere friends; and while so much may seem rather large, any thing less is too small. I think it better be done. Yours truly   A. LINCOLN

[1] ALS-F, ISLA. See Lincoln to Halleck, January 7, *supra*, and endorsement to Franz Sigel, January 26, *infra*. Carl Schurz and Julius Stahel were appointed major generals of Volunteers on March 14, 1863. AGO *Special Orders No. 29*, January 19, 1863, assigned Schurz to Sigel's old corps and Stahel to command cavalry in the newly formed Grand Reserve Division under Sigel.

To Edwin M. Stanton[1]

Hon. Sec. of War   Executive Mansion,
Dear Sir: Washington, January 12, 1863.

Dr. Thomas Sim, has been dismissed from the service for being in this City contrary to a general order. His afflicted wife assures me he had a pass from Gen. Sickles, commander of his Division, for 48 hours, and that within the 48 hours he was refused the 15 days absence he asked, and reported to Gen. Sickles, who extended his time so as to take the Dr. with him, and that he reached the army in less than twelve additional hours, to the original 48, allowed him. Please see the lady. Yours truly   A. LINCOLN

[1] ALS-P, ISLA. Dr. Thomas Sim of Illinois, surgeon-in-chief of General Daniel E. Sickles' brigade, had been dismissed January 5 on erroneous information. Although the official date of his restoration to service has not been found, the New York *Tribune* reported his restoration on January 17, 1863.

To Edward Bates[1]

Attorney General, please make out and send me a pardon in this case.   A. LINCOLN

Jan. 13. 1863.

[1] AES, DNA RG 204, U.S. Pardon Attorney, A 456. Lincoln's endorsement, preceded by one from Benjamin F. Butler recommending the pardon, is written on a recommendation signed by Ira Harris and others, January 5, 1863, in the case of Robert B. Nay, formerly of New York and Quincy, Illinois, who had served as chief of detectives in the provost marshal's department under Butler at New Orleans. Nay had been convicted of defrauding the government. See Lincoln to Bates, February 13, *infra*.

To John A. Dix[1]

Major General Dix   Executive Mansion,
My dear Sir: Washington, January 14, 1863.

The proclamation has been issued. We were not succeeding—at best, were progressing too slowly—without it. Now, that we have it, and bear all the disadvantage of it, (as we do bear some in certain quarters) we must also take some benefit from it, if practicable. I therefore will thank you for your well considered opinion whether Fortress-Monroe, and York-Town, one or both, could not, in whole or in part, be garrisoned by colored troops, leaving the white forces now necessary at those places, to be employed elsewhere. Yours very truly   A. LINCOLN

[1] ALS, IHi; ADfS, DLC-RTL. Dix replied on January 15:
"I have just received your 'private and confidential' letter, and hasten to reply to it by the special messenger who brought it.
"You do not ask my opinion in regard to the policy of employing colored troops; and I infer that this is a question, which has been decided. I therefore, answer only the special inquiry proposed to me. . . .
"I regard this Fortress . . . as second to no other in the Union. It is the key to the Chesapeake Bay. . . . In a political point of view . . . the tranquillity . . . of Maryland may depend on the possession of this Fortress. . . .
"Under these circumstances I think this post should be held by the best and most reliable troops the country can furnish. . . .
"The question of employing colored troops at Yorktown may be determined by a totally different class of considerations. The position is of little practical importance. . . .
"If it be decided to employ colored troops any where, I know no place where they could be used with less objection. The proper garrison is 4000 men. One half of that number at least should be white troops. . . ." (DLC-RTL).

To the House of Representatives[1]

To the House of Representatives: January 14, 1863

The Secretary of State has submitted to me a resolution of the House of Representatives of the 5th. instant, which has been delivered to him, and which is in the following words:

"Resolved, That the Secretary of State be requested to communicate to this House if not in his judgment incompatible with the public interest, why our Minister in New Granada has not presented his credentials to the actual government of that country. Also, the reasons for which Señor Murillo is not recognized by the United States as the diplomatic representative of the Mosquera government of that country. Also what negotiations have been had, if any, with General Herran as the Representative of Ospina's Government in New Granada since it went out of existence."

On the 12th. day of December 1846, a treaty of amity, peace and concord was concluded between the United States of America and the Republic of New Granada, which is still in force. On the 7th. day of December 1847, General Pedro Alcántara Herran, who had been duly accredited, was received here as the Envoy Extraordinary and Minister Plenipotentiary of that Republic. On the 30th. day of August, 1849, Señor Don Rafael Rivas was received by this Government as Chargé d'Affaires of the same Republic. On the 5th. day of December, 1851, a Consular Convention was concluded between that Republic and the United States, which Treaty was signed on behalf of the Republic of Granada by the same Señor Rivas. This treaty is still in force. On the 27th. of April, 1852, Señor Don Victoriano de Diego Paredes was received as Chargé d'Affaires of the Republic of New Granada. On the 20th. of June, 1855, General Pedro Alcantara Herran was again received as Envoy Extraordinary and Minister Plenipotentiary, duly accredited by the Republic of New Granada, and he has ever since remained, under the same credentials, as the representative of that Republic near the Government of the United States. On the 10th. of September, 1857, a Claims Convention was concluded between the United States and the Republic of Granada. This Convention is still in force, and has in part been executed. In May, 1858, the Constitution of the Republic was remodelled and the nation assumed the political title of "The Granadian Confederacy." This fact was formally announced to this Government, but without any change in their representative here. Previous to the fourth day of March, 1861, a revolutionary war against the Republic of New Granada, which had thus been recognized and treated with by the United States, broke out in New Granada, assuming to set up a new Government under the name of the United States of Columbia. This war has had various vicissitudes, sometimes favorable, sometimes adverse to the revolutionary movement. The revolutionary organization has hitherto been simply a military provisionary power, and no definitive constitution of Government has yet been established in New Granada in place of that organized by the Constitution of 1858. The Minister of the United States to the Granadian Confederacy, who was appointed on the 29th. day of May, 1861, was directed, in view of the occupation of the capital by the revolutionary party and of the uncertainty of the civil war, not to present his credentials to either the Government of the Granadian Confederacy or to the provisional Military Government, but to conduct his affairs informally as is customary in such cases, and to report the progress of events and await the instructions of this Government. The advices which have been received from him, have not hitherto been sufficiently conclusive to determine me to recognize the revolutionary Government. General Herran being here with full authority from the Government of New Granada, which had been so long recognized by the United States, I have not received any representative from the Revolutionary government, which has not yet been recognized, because such a proceeding would in itself be an act of recognition. Official communications have been had on various incidental and occasional questions with General Herran as the Minister Plenipotentiary and Envoy Extraordinary of the Granadian Confederacy—but in no other character; no definitive measure or proceeding has resulted from these communications, and a communication of them at present would not, in my judgment, be compatible with the public interest.

Washington, January 14, 1863.   ABRAHAM LINCOLN

[1] DS, DNA RG 233, House Executive Document No. 33.

To John G. Nicolay[1]

Will Mr. Nicolay, please make out the papers in this case.

Jan. 14. 1863.   A. LINCOLN

[1] AES, CSmH. Lincoln's endorsement is written on a letter from Attorney General Bates, January 14, 1863, asking appointment of "the Revd Wm. K. Talbot (of Columbus)" to fill the vacant hospital chaplaincy at Columbus, Kentucky.

To William H. Seward[1]

January 14, 1863

As I understand the Consulate at Dundee has not been accepted by Mr. Hall, and as I was unconscious, in appointing Mr. Hall, (if I did it) that I was interfering with my old friend, Dr. Smith, I will be obliged if the Sec. of State will send me a nomination for Rev. James Smith, of Ills. for that Consulate.   A. LINCOLN

Jan. 14. 1863.

[1] AES, DNA FS RG 59, Appointments, Box 382. Lincoln's endorsement is written on a memorandum from Seward of January 10, 1863, summarizing the facts concerning the consulship at Dundee, Scotland, and noting that since L. W. Hall, appointed as successor to Hugh Smith, had declined appointment, the place was officially vacant. See Lincoln to Seward January 9, *supra*, concerning appointment of Reverend James Smith.

To Edwin M. Stanton[1]

January 14, 1863

Will the Sec. of War please consider whether a test of this invention is not worth making; and if decided in the affirmative, have the test made.   A. LINCOLN

Jan. 14. 1863.

[1] AES, DNA WR RG 92, Quartermaster General, Consolidated File. Lincoln's endorsement, accompanied by an endorsement of Stanton's referring the matter to Montgomery C. Meigs, is written on an envelope which contained recommendations of John Schenck's "concentrated food for horses," now filed separately (RG 92, P 130, S 381).

Endorsement
Concerning Isaac R. Diller's Gunpowder[1]

January 15, 1863

The President the War and Navy Departments to take such measures as may be necessary to test the powder submitted or to be submitted by Mr. Diller, and referred to in the inclosed papers.

Jan. 15. 1863.   A. LINCOLN.

[1] Copy, DNA WR RG 74, Navy Branch, Bureau of Ordnance Letters Received. The copy of Lincoln's endorsement is with the copies of Lincoln's agreement with Diller of December 15, 1862, *supra*, and associated papers.

To Edwin M. Stanton[1]

January 15, 1863.

Secretary of War: Please see Mr. Stafford, who wants to assist in raising colored troops in Missouri.   A LINCOLN.

[1] NH, VIII, 191. Lieutenant Colonel Spencer H. Stafford of the Eleventh New York Infantry resigned March 5, 1862, and worked under Benjamin F. Butler at New Orleans. He served later as colonel of the Tenth and Seventy-third U.S. Colored Infantry.

To Editors of the Washington *Chronicle*[1]

Editors of Chronicle   Executive Mansion,
Gentlemen: Washington, Jan. 16. 1863.

If you should publish the attached letter, please make the corrections indicated. Yours &c   A LINCOLN

[1] ALS, owned by Paul Huttinger, Philadelphia, Pennsylvania. The letter which Lincoln enclosed to John W. Forney's *Chronicle* was undoubtedly a copy of his letter to McClellan of April 9, 1862, *supra*, which had been released by General Ethan A. Hitchcock at the McDowell court of inquiry then in session.

The letter was published in the *Chronicle* on January 17, 1863, with the comment that "The *Star* last evening contains the letter, but as it was full of errors, we obtained the following corrected and official copy. . . ."

Memorandum:
Appointment of Charles S. Heintzelman[1]

When the time comes I should like to make this appointment, if not pressed too hardly in other directions.   A.L.

Jan. 16. 1863.

[1] AES, DNA WR RG 94, U.S. Military Academy, 1861, No. 373, Box 78. Lincoln's endorsement is written on an envelope containing recommendations in favor of Charles S. Heintzelman, son of Samuel P. Heintzelman whom Lincoln nominated on the same date to be major general of Volunteers to rank from May 5, 1862, the date of the Battle of Williamsburg, Virginia. Charles S. Heintzelman entered West Point July 1, 1863, and graduated in June, 1867.

To Edwin M. Stanton[1]

January 16, 1863

Injustice has probably been done in this case. Sec. of War please examine it.

[1] Copy, DNA WR RG 107, Register of Secretary of War, Letters Received, P 9. The original document is missing but the Register preserves the copy of Lincoln's endorsement written on papers in the case of Lieutenant Gurdon McKay, Twenty-second Massachusetts Volunteers, dismissed from service as absent without leave. No later record of McKay's service has been found.

To the Senate and House of Representatives[1]

January 17, 1863

To the Senate and House of Representatives:

I have signed the Joint Resolution to provide for the immediate payment of the army and navy of the United States, passed by the House of Representatives on the 14th, and by the Senate on the 15th instant.

The Joint Resolution is a simple authority, amounting however, under existing circumstances, to a direction to the Secretary of the Treasury to make an additional issue of one hundred millions of dollars in United States notes if so much money is needed for the payment of the army and navy.

My approval is given in order that every possible facility may be afforded for the prompt discharge of all arrears of pay due to our soldiers and our sailors.

While giving this approval, however, I think it my duty to express my sincere regret that it has been found necessary to authorize so large an additional issue of United States notes, when this circulation, and that of the suspended banks together have become already so redundant as to increase prices beyond real values, thereby augmenting the cost of living to the injury of labor, and the cost of supplies to the injury of the whole country.

It seems very plain that continued issues of United States notes, without any check to the issues of suspended banks, and without adequate provision for the raising of money by loans, and for funding the issues so as to keep them within due limits, must soon produce disastrous consequences. And this matter appears to me so important that I feel bound to avail myself of this occasion to ask the special attention of Congress to it.

That Congress has power to regulate the currency of the country, can hardly admit of doubt; and that a judicious measure to prevent the deterioration of this currency, by a reasonable taxation of bank circulation or otherwise is needed, seems equally clear. Independently of this general consideration, it would be unjust to the people at large, to exempt banks, enjoying the special privilege of circulation, from their just proportion of the public burdens.

In order to raise money by way of loans most easily and cheaply, it is clearly necessary to give every possible support to the public credit. To that end, a uniform currency, in which taxes, subscriptions to loans, and all other ordinary public dues, as well as all private dues may be paid, is almost, if not quite indispensable. Such a currency can be furnished by banking associations, organized under a general act of Congress, as suggested in my message at the beginning of the present session. The securing of this circulation, by the pledge of United States bonds, as therein suggested, would still further facilitate loans, by increasing the present and causing a future demand for such bonds.

In view of the actual financial embarrassments of the government, and of the greater embarrassments sure to come, if the necessary means of relief be not afforded, I feel that I should not perform my duty by a simple announcement of my approval of the Joint Resolution which proposes relief only by increasing circulation, without expressing my earnest desire that measures, such in substance as those I have just referred to, may receive the early sanction of Congress.

By such measures, in my opinion, will payment be most certainly secured, not only to the army and navy, but to all honest creditors of the government, and satisfactory provision made for future demands on the treasury.   ABRAHAM LINCOLN

January 17. 1863.

[1] DS, DNA RG 46, Senate 37A F2; DS, DNA RG 233, House Executive Document No. 37. A bill (H.R. 659) to provide ways and means for the support of the government, introduced on January 8, was much amended and finally approved on March 3, 1863. It provided for issuance of $150,000,000 of U.S. notes for the payment of Army, Navy, and other creditors, for issuance of not more than $900,000,000 in bonds and $400,000,000 in Treasury notes, and that holders of U.S. notes issued under the Act of February 25, 1862, should turn them in for bonds by July 1, 1863. The act also put a tax on all banks, etc., issuing notes or bills for circulation as currency.

To John W. Forney[1]

Hon. J. W. Forney   Executive Mansion
My dear Sir: Jan. 18. 1863.

I see that "Occasional" in the "Press" appeals to Congress to make the appropriation for paying for the emancipated slaves in this District. That appropriation is already made in the emancipation act, as you will see in Sec. 7. page 378. Yours truly

A. LINCOLN

[1] ALS, IHi. On the bottom of the first page Forney endorsed in ink: "Dear Doctor—Did you know this? I did not. J.W.F." What appears to be an answer is written in pencil above and between the lines of Forney's endorsement as follows: "The Prest is right. There was $1000,000 appd. for purposes connected with the Emancipation in the District. JMB over" The verso has a further illegible note in pencil but also signed with the initials "J.M.B." "Occasional" seems to have been Forney's own column in the Philadelphia *Press*, but was probably written in part by John R. Young who was editor of the *Press*. On January 18, Forney telegraphed Young, "Let Occasional correct himself in a short letter for tomorrow by stating that he was misinformed as to the appropriation for paying emancipated slaves in the dist of columbia that the appropriation is made in the emancipation act & add that his great object was to secure prompt payment of claimants out of appropriations already made. Do your best." (DLC-Young Papers). The correction appeared in the *Press* on January 19, 1863. The identity of "J.M.B." can only be hazarded. Dr. John M. Bernhisel, a graduate of the University of Pennsylvania medical department and friend of Forney's, was delegate in congress from Utah Territory.

To Montgomery Blair[1]

                            January 19, 1863
The relations of Downey are among the best men of my acquaintance, and as Judge Treat, before whom he was convicted, recommends his pardon, I incline to pardon him, if the Post-Master General does not object. Will he please say whether he has any objection & return to me?   A. LINCOLN
Jan. 19. 1863.

[1] AES, DNA RG 204, U.S. Pardon Attorney, A 457. Below Lincoln's endorsement Postmaster General Blair endorsed on January 20, "I concur in the propriety of pardoning Downey." The endorsements are written on a letter from

Lawrence Weldon with concurring endorsements by Judge Samuel H. Treat, Stephen A. Corneau and David L. Phillips, January 13, 1863, asking a pardon for James M. Downey, convicted of robbing the mails. See Lincoln to Bates, January 20, *infra*. Downey has not been further identified.

To Edwin M. Stanton[1]

Hon. Sec. of War: Executive Mansion
Dear Sir: January 19, 1863
   Please have the Pay-Master-General examine & report upon all the evidence in his control, bearing upon the question of removal of Joseph A. Nunes, as an Additional Pay-Master. Yours truly   A. LINCOLN

1 ALS, IHi. No reply from Stanton has been found, but Joseph A. Nunes remained in service, was brevetted lieutenant colonel as of November 1, 1865, and was mustered out on November 15, 1865.

To Edwin M. Stanton[1]

If it be lawful to make the appointment within requested by Gen. Franklin, let it be done   A. LINCOLN
   Jan. 19. 1863.

1 AES-F, ISLA. Lincoln's endorsement is written on a letter from Major General William B. Franklin to Major Emeric Meszaros of the Fourth Missouri Cavalry, December 23, 1862, as follows:
   "I have received your letter of the 15 inst.
   "I shall be very glad to have you on my Staff, and if you can obtain the necessary commission, hope that you will come."
   No record has been found of Meszaros' appointment.

To the Workingmen of Manchester, England[1]

                                          Executive Mansion, Washington,
To the workingmen of Manchester: January 19, 1863.
   I have the honor to acknowledge the receipt of the address and resolutions which you sent to me on the eve of the new year.
   When I came, on the fourth day of March, 1861, through a free and constitutional election, to preside in the government of the United States, the country was found at the verge of civil war. Whatever might have been the cause, or whosoever the fault, one duty paramount to all others was before me, namely, to maintain and preserve at once the Constitution and the integrity of the federal republic. A conscientious purpose to perform this duty is a key to all the measures of administration which have been, and

to all which will hereafter be pursued. Under our form of government, and my official oath, I could not depart from this purpose if I would. It is not always in the power of governments to enlarge or restrict the scope of moral results which follow the policies that they may deem it necessary for the public safety, from time to time, to adopt.

I have understood well that the duty of self-preservation rests solely with the American people. But I have at the same time been aware that favor or disfavor of foreign nations might have a material influence in enlarging and prolonging the struggle with disloyal men in which the country is engaged. A fair examination of history has seemed to authorize a belief that the past action and influences of the United States were generally regarded as having been beneficent towards mankind. I have therefore reckoned upon the forbearance of nations. Circumstances, to some of which you kindly allude, induced me especially to expect that if justice and good faith should be practiced by the United States, they would encounter no hostile influence on the part of Great Britain. It is now a pleasant duty to acknowledge the demonstration you have given of your desire that a spirit of peace and amity towards this country may prevail in the councils of your Queen, who is respected and esteemed in your own country only more than she is by the kindred nation which has its home on this side of the Atlantic.

I know and deeply deplore the sufferings which the workingmen at Manchester and in all Europe are called to endure in this crisis. It has been often and studiously represented that the attempt to overthrow this government, which was built upon the foundation of human rights, and to substitute for it one which should rest exclusively on the basis of human slavery, was likely to obtain the favor of Europe. Through the actions of our disloyal citizens the workingmen of Europe have been subjected to a severe trial, for the purpose of forcing their sanction to that attempt. Under these circumstances, I cannot but regard your decisive utterance upon the question as an instance of sublime Christian heroism which has not been surpassed in any age or in any country. It is, indeed, an energetic and reinspiring assurance of the inherent power of truth and of the ultimate and universal triumph of justice, humanity, and freedom. I do not doubt that the sentiments you have expressed will be sustained by your great nation, and, on the other hand, I have no hesitation in assuring you that they will excite admiration, esteem, and the most reciprocal feelings of friendship among the American people. I hail this interchange of sentiment, therefore, as an augury that, whatever else may happen, whatever misfortune may befall your country or my own, the peace and friendship which now exist between the two nations will be, as it shall be my desire to make them, perpetual.

ABRAHAM LINCOLN.

[1] Thirty-seventh Congress, Third Session, *Senate Executive Document No. 49*. Although Lincoln's letter as printed in *Executive Document No. 49* is dated January 19, Seward's letter to Charles F. Adams transmitting it is dated January 16, in the same source. On January 2, Minister Charles F. Adams transmitted to Seward a letter from Mayor Abel Haywood of Manchester, January 1, forwarding "an address to the President . . . agreed upon at a public meeting of the working men and others of this city . . . last night" which reads in part as follows:

"As citizens of Manchester . . . we beg to express our fraternal sentiments. . . .

"We rejoice in your greatness. . . . We honor your free States, as a singular, happy abode for the working millions. . . . One thing alone has, in the past, lessened our sympathy with your country and our confidence in it; we mean the ascendency of politicians who not merely maintained negro slavery, but desired to extend and root it more firmly. Since we have discerned, however, that the victory of the free north, in the war which has so sorely distressed us as well as afflicted you, will strike off the fetters of the slave, you have attracted our warm and earnest sympathy.

"We joyfully honor you, as the President, and the Congress with you, for the many decisive steps towards practically exemplifying your belief in the words of your great founders, 'All men are created free and equal.' . . . .

"Accept our high admiration of your firmness in upholding the proclamation of freedom." (*Ibid.*).

To Edward Bates[1]

Hon. Attorney-General please make out and send me a pardon in this case. A. LINCOLN

Jan. 20. 1863.

[1] AES, DNA RG 204, U.S. Pardon Attorney, A 457. See Lincoln to Blair, January 19, *supra*, case of James M. Downey.

To Samuel R. Curtis[1]

I know not what to do with these letters but to submit them to Gen. Curtis. A LINCOLN

Jan. 20. 1863.

[1] AES, DLC-RTL. Lincoln's endorsement is written on the back of a letter from John J. Crittenden, January 19, 1863, enclosing a letter from Governor Yates of Illinois protesting the supposed military assessments against Derrick A. January, prominent merchant of St. Louis, Missouri, for being disloyal. Succeeding endorsements by Curtis (February 2) and Provost Marshal General

Franklin A. Dick (February 3) indicate that although January was disloyal in the early months of the war he had later established his loyalty and was not actually under assessment for disloyalty.

To Samuel T. Glover[1]

Hon. S. T. Glover   Executive Mansion
My dear Sir   Washington, D.C. Jan. 20, 1863.

Yours of January 12th. stating the distressed condition of the people in South-West Missouri, and urging the completion of the Railroad to Springfield, is just received. Of course I deplore the distress of the people in that section & elsewhere. Nor is the thought of extending the railroad, new to me. But the military necessity for it, is not so patent, but that Congress would try to restrain me in some way, were I to attempt it. I am very glad to believe that the late military operations in Missouri and Arkans[as] are at least, promising of repose to South West Missouri. Yours very truly   A. LINCOLN

[1] ADfS, DLC-RTL. Glover's letter of January 12 reads in part: "When recently in Jefferson City I found the most intense interest prevailing among members of the legislature . . . in relation to the condition of S W Mo. That country has been repeatedly ravaged by contending armies. It is now in great want . . . very great suffering already exists. . . . I promised when at Jefferson to write you and call your attention to the project of finishing our Railroad to Springfield as a military necessity. It would complete the conquest of Mo and lay all Arkansas in our power. . . ." (DLC-RTL). Concerning the extension of the Pacific Railroad see Lincoln's order of July 11, 1862, Lincoln to Curtis, October 12, 1862, *supra*, and to Rosecrans, March 4 and 10, 1864, *infra*.

To the Senate[1]

To the Senate of the United States: January 20, 1863

I transmit, herewith, a report from the Secretary of State in answer to the Resolution of the Senate relative to the correspondence between this Government and the Mexican Minister, in relation to the exportation of articles contraband of war for the use of the French Army in Mexico.   ABRAHAM LINCOLN.
Washington, January 20, 1863.

[1] DS, DNA RG 46, Senate 37A F3. Seward's report of January 19 (in reply to Senate resolution of January 13) transmitting correspondence with Mexican Minister Matias Romero may be found in Thirty-seventh Congress, Third Session, *Senate Executive Document No. 24*. The Mexican complaint was that although the French were permitted to purchase at New Orleans and New York mules and wagons for use in Mexico against the Mexican forces, a shipment of

arms to the Mexican government had been stopped at New Orleans by Stanton's order of November 20, 1862. While the order prohibited "arms," it did not prohibit mules and wagons.

To Edwin M. Stanton[1]

I have a strong inclination to give Col. McHenry another chance. What says the Sec. of War?   A. LINCOLN

Jan. 20. 1863.

[1] AES, NHi. Lincoln's endorsement is written on the margin of a broadside reprinting an account of the dismissal of Colonel John H. McHenry, Jr., of the Seventeenth Kentucky Volunteers on account of an order issued by McHenry on October 27, 1862, in regard to returning slaves to their owners. McHenry and the Seventeenth Kentucky had established a notable battle record at Donelson and Shiloh. No record of further action in the case of Colonel McHenry has been found.

To Thomas Ewing[1]

January 21, 1863

I believe your son knows, and you may now know, that I hold him in very high estimation; still, there is a reason, in no wise personal to him, why I shall have to confer the appointment mentioned to another.   A. LINCOLN

Jan. 21. 1863.

[1] AES, DLC-Ewing Papers. Lincoln's endorsement is written on a letter from Thomas Ewing recommending his son Thomas, Jr., who had "borne himself creditably . . . in three hard fought battles, but his habits & education do in my opinion fit him for civil rather than military life," for appointment as assistant secretary of the Interior. On March 13, Colonel Thomas Ewing, Jr., of the Eleventh Kansas Cavalry, was nominated brigadier general of Volunteers, and was confirmed by the Senate on the same day.

Order Approving Sentence of Fitz-John Porter[1]

January 21, 1863

The foregoing proceedings, findings, and sentence in the foregoing case of Major-General Fitz-John Porter, are approved and confirmed; and it is ordered that the said Fitz-John Porter be, and he hereby is, cashiered and dismissed from the service of the United States as a Major General of Volunteers, and as Colonel and Brevet Brigadier General in the Regular Service of the United States, and forever disqualified from holding any office of trust or profit under the Government of the United States.

January 21, 1863.   ABRAHAM LINCOLN.

[1] AGO *General Orders No. 18*, January 22, 1863.

Order Establishing Gauge of Union Pacific Railroad[1]

January 21, 1863

Whereas, by the 12th. Section of an act of Congress, entitled "An Act to aid in the construction of a Rail Road and Telegraph line, from the Missouri River to the Pacific Ocean and to secure to the Government the use of the same, for postal, military, and other purposes," Approved July 1st. 1862, it is made the duty of the President of the United States, to determine the uniform width of the track of the entire line of the said Rail Road and the branches of the same; and whereas, application has been made to me, by the Leavenworth, Pawnee and Western Rail Road Company, (a company authorized by the Act of Congress above mentioned to construct a branch of said Rail Road) to fix the gauge thereof.

Now, therefore, I, Abraham Lincoln, President of the United States of America, do determine that the uniform width of the track of said Rail Road·and all its branches which are provided for in the aforesaid Act of Congress, shall be Five (5) feet, and that this order be filed in the Office of the Secretary of the Interior, for the information and guidance of all concerned.

Done at the City of Washington, this 21st. day of January, in the Year of Our Lord One thousand eight hundred and sixty three.

ABRAHAM LINCOLN

[1] DS, DNA NR RG 48, General Records, Department of Interior, Union Pacific Railroad. On January 20, Lincoln asked the cabinet for their opinions on the relative merits of the five-foot gauge and the standard gauge of four feet eight and one-half inches. Welles' *Diary* on this date records that he as well as other members favored the standard gauge which was generally approved by Eastern interests, while California interests desired the five-foot width. Lincoln's order was superseded, however, by an act of congress approved on March 3, 1863, which established the standard gauge already widely adopted in the East as the width of the first transcontinental railroad.

To the Senate and House of Representatives[1]

Executive Mansion   Washington January 21. 1863

Gentlemen of the Senate and House of Representatives.

I submit herewith for your[2] consideration, the Joint Resolutions of the Corporate authorities of the City of Washington, adopted September 27th. 1862, and a Memorial of the same under date of October 28th. 1862, both relating to, and urging the construction of certain rail roads concentrating upon the City of Washington.

In presenting this Memorial, and the Joint Resolutions to you, I[3] am not prepared to say more than that the subject is one of great practical importance; and that I hope it will receive the attentive consideration of Congress.   ABRAHAM LINCOLN

January 21. 1863.

[1] DfS, DLC-RTL; DS, DNA RG 46, Senate 37A F2. The resolution transmitted asked the president to direct the construction of railroads from Washington to the deep waters of Chesapeake Bay and to Hagerstown, Maryland. On January 23, the message was read in the Senate and ordered to lie on the table and be printed. On January 26, the message was read in the House and referred to the committee on roads and canals. There is no record of further action.

[2] Lincoln deleted "favorable" at this point in the draft.

[3] The draft is revised in Lincoln's autograph to the present text from this point on. The original reading was: "I deemed it proper to note that it must be apparent to all, that the Nation in time of peace, will derive great advantages from these Roads, and they will be invaluable to the government in time of war. Their want has been, and is severely felt in suppressing the present rebellion."

To William H. Seward[1]

It won't do. Must have a tip-top man there next time.

Jan. 21. 1863.   A. L.

[1] Copy, DLC-RTL. The copy of Lincoln's endorsement is with a copy of Seward's note to which it replies: "What do you say as to sending Bradford R. Wood to the Sandwich Islands." Bradford R. Wood was minister to Denmark. See Lincoln's memorandum of January 9, *supra*, and note to Seward concerning James McBride, January 24, *infra*.

To John P. Usher[1]

Sec. of Interior, please send me a nomination for William T. Otto, as Assistant Sec. of Interior.   A. LINCOLN

Jan. 21. 1863.

[1] AES, DNA NR RG 48, Applications, Box 1293. Lincoln's endorsement is written on a letter of January 12, 1862[3], signed by twenty-one members of congress recommending the appointment of William T. Otto of Indiana.

To Samuel Y. At Lee[1]

If entirely convenient, will Mr. Atelee, allow William, leave of absence for to-day?   A. LINCOLN

Jan. 22. 1863

[1] ALS, N. William H. Johnson worked as messenger for At Lee at the Treasury Department in the afternoons and tended to Lincoln's wardrobe, shaved him, and did other personal services in the mornings.

To James R. Doolittle[1]

Hon. J. R. Doolittle

Executive Mansion,
Washington, Jan 22. 1863.

My dear Sir I find I can not postpone the appointment of Asst. Sec of Interior to the end of the session. I therefore shall have to try to recognize Mr. Potter in some other way. Yours very truly   A. LINCOLN.

[1] ALS-F, ISLA. Representative John F. Potter had been defeated for re-election in 1862. Lincoln later in the year appointed him consul general to Canada.

To Stephen A. Hurlbut[1]

Major Gen. S. A. Hurlbut   Executive Mansion,
My dear Sir.   Washington, January 22, 1863.

Yours of the 17th. to Mr. Washburne has been shown me. As your friend, which you know I am, I would advise you not to come to Washington, if you could safely come without leave. You now stand well with the Sec. of War, and with Gen. Halleck, and it would lessen you with both for you to make your appearance here. I advise you by all means to dismiss the thought of coming here. Yours very truly   A. LINCOLN.

[1] ALS-P, ISLA. Brigadier General Hurlbut's letter to Representative Elihu B. Washburne of January 17 specifies that he wishes "to come to Washington & see the President on matters of public as well as private importance. You will greatly oblige me by obtaining from him *orders* for me to come. . . ." (DLC-RTL). See Lincoln to McClernand, *infra*.

To John A. McClernand[1]

Major Gen. McClernand   Executive Mansion,
My dear Sir: Washington, January 22. 1863.

Yours of the 7th. was received yesterday. I need not recite, because you remember the contents. The charges, in their nature, are such that I must know as much about the facts involved, as you can. I have too many *family* controversies, (so to speak) already on my hands, to voluntarily, or so long as I can avoid it, take up another. You are now doing well—well for the country, and well for yourself—much better than you could possibly be, if engaged in open war with Gen. Halleck. Allow me to beg, that for your sake, for my sake, & for the country's sake, you give your whole attention to the better work.

Your success upon the Arkansas, was both brilliant and valuable, and is fully appreciated by the country and government. Yours truly   A. LINCOLN

1 ALS, IHi. On January 7, McClernand had written Lincoln as follows:

"I have determined, at whatever personal cost to myself, to address . . . you, upon a subject of the deepest interest. . . .

"I charge Maj. Genl. Henry W. Halleck with wilful contempt of superior authority, and with utter incompetency for the extraordinary and vital functions with which he is charged as Genl-in-Chief. . . .

"I charge him with contempt of authority in this: That in violation of the order made by the Secretary of War, under your personal direction, bearing date of October 21, 1862, assigning me to the command of the proposed 'Miss. River Expedition,' he set me aside for . . . Maj. Genl. U.S. Grant—whom he privately authorized to detach troops to Memphis, to form part of the Expedition, prior to the issue of the public order, assigning me to its command. Also in this: That, although the order, issued by the Secretary of War, was made in the presence of the Genl.-in-Chief . . . he has contumaciously refused to recognize me in the relations contemplated. . . .

"I charge him with incompetency on many grounds: 1st, For want of eminence in any profession, or calling, previous to his appointment as Maj. Genl. . . .

"Without ever having fought a battle, he curtailed the success of our arms at Fort Henry. . . . Before Corinth, . . . he permitted the enemy to escape. . . . Since he assumed the functions of General-in-Chief, scarcely anything but disaster has marked the experiences of our arms. . . .

"How can the country be saved in its dire extremity, with such a Chief at the head of our armies! . . .

"Without genius, justice, generosity, or policy, his continuance in command will not only involve continual new levies to fill up the wasting ranks . . . but must be attended by accumulating disaster. . . .

"Having full confidence in the correctness of my views, and having no concealments in regard to this letter, it is left to you to make such use of it as you may think proper. . . ." (DLC-RTL).

On January 21, Halleck further extended General Grant's authority and explained the revocation of Grant's order expelling Jews from his department:

"General: The President has directed that so much of Arkansas as you may desire to control be temporarily attached to your department. This will give you control of both banks of the river.

"In your operations down the Mississippi you must not rely too confidently upon any direct co-operation of General Banks and the lower flotilla, as it is possible that they may not be able to pass or reduce Port Hudson. They, however, will do everything in their power to form a junction with you at Vicksburg. If they should not be able to effect this, they will at least occupy a portion of the enemy's forces and prevent them from re-enforcing Vicksburg. I hope, however, that they will do still better and be able to join you.

"It may be proper to give you some explanation of the revocation of your order expelling all Jews from your department. The President has no objection to your expelling traitors and Jew peddlers, which, I suppose, was the object of your order; but, as it in terms proscribed an entire religious class, some of whom are fighting in our ranks, the President deemed it necessary to revoke it." (OR, I, XXIV, I, 9).

Memorandum
Appointment of Thomas J. C. Amory[1]

Executive Mansion, Washington, Jan. 22. 1863.
To-day, Jonathan Amory, U.S. despatch agent at Boston, call to ask that his son, Col. Thomas. J. C. Amory, may be made a Brig.

Gen. He is a graduate, is a Capt. in the Reg. Army, and a Col. of 17th. Mass vols—is at Newbern N.C. and is recommended by Gen. Foster, & also by Mass. delegation—so says the father.

[1] AD, IHi. Colonel Thomas J. C. Amory was brevetted brigadier general October 1, 1864.

Memorandum Concerning Herman Koppel[1]

Executive Mansion, Washington, January 22. 1863.
To-day, Mr. Prentiss, calls as Atty. of Herman Koppel, saying the latter is a loyal citizen, that he resided at Charleston S.C. at the beginning of the rebellion; that he converted what he had into a few bales of cotten and other articles, apparantly to break the blockade, as a mode of getting out, but really intending to surrender to the blockade, which he did of purpose & with no effort to avoid it—that his property has been condemned by a prize court, and he appeals to me to remit to him the proceeds of the property, or at least the government's moiety of it.

Admitting this all to be true, is it both lawful and proper for me to do this?

[1] AD, DLC-RTL. No further reference has been found, and the persons named have not been identified.

To Frederick Steele[1]

Executive Mansion, Washington,
Brigadier General Frederick Steele   January 22, 1863.
Sir: So far as respects your military record and reputation, it seems highly fit and proper that you should be promoted to a Major Generalship; and I should nominate you for it, at once, were it not for a document[2] presented to me, of which the inclosed is a copy. With a satisfactory explanation, I will gladly make the nomination; and in such way, that the time from now till then, shall not be lost to you. Without such explanation, I could scarcely bring myself to make the nomination; and I think it is certain the Senate would not confirm it, if made. Your Obt. Servt.

A. LINCOLN

[1] ADfS, DLC-RTL; LS, owned by William W. Steele, Pescadero, California. General Steele replied on February 15, 1863:
"In reply to your communication of the 22d ultimo. touching certain allegations made against me by J. G. Forman, I have the honor to submit the following brief explanation. . . .
"When I assumed command of the Army of the South West . . . our camps and . . . Helena were overrun with fugitive Slaves of both sexes. . . . Vice,

immorality and distress . . . followed. . . . Under the Articles of War I considered it my imperative duty to use every proper means . . . to abate these evils.

"While such a state of affairs existed . . . Mrs. [Charles] Craig, a lady of the highest respectability and wife of the planter alluded to in the allegations, came to my office, and weeping told me that a negro girl who had been raised under her own eyes, and whom she regarded as almost one of her own family was in a house of prostitution, with, I think five other negro girls. I inquired whether she could point out the house, and on being answered that she could, I gave her the order to the Provost Marshal which appears in the allegations. There was no understanding that any of these girls should be delivered up to their masters. If they had been white I should have given the same order. . . .

"Forman asserts that Craig was a rebel. . . . I assert that he was a Union man, and as loyal to the United States . . . as most people would have been under the circumstances. . . ." (DLC-RTL).

Steele also enclosed a letter of the same date from General U. S. Grant to Elihu B. Washburne, as follows:

"I have just been shown a letter from the President to Brig. Steele stating that his name had been withheld from the Senate for promotion in consequence of charges that had been made against him for returning fugitive slaves to their Masters.

"Gen. Steele is one of our very best soldiers. . . . He is in every sense a soldier. . . . No matter how far any policy of the Government might vary from his individual views he would conform to it. . . . Besides I have never heard him express an opinion against any policy of the administration and know he would do nothing to weaken the power of the President. . . .

"I hope the President & the Senate will be disabused of any opinion they may have formed prejudicial to Gen. Steele. . . ." (*Ibid.*).

Steele was appointed major general dating from November 29, 1862.

2 The document has not been located but Steele's letter of February 15 indicates the author as Jacob G. Forman, a former army chaplain who was acting as postmaster at Helena, Arkansas.

To Nathaniel P. Banks[1]

Major Gener Banks   Executive Mansion,
My dear Sir: Washington, [January 23?] 1863.

In superseding you, by returning Gen. Butler to command the Department of the Gulf, I have trusted that you will not understand me as being even indifferent to your feelings and your honor. I would be as careful of yours as of my own.

I have issued the proclamation, which, like most measures has two sides to its effects. What is evil in effect we are already enduring, and we must have the counterpart of it. For this last, as I think, there is no such place as Louisiana, and no such man as Gen. Butler. But to make the most of both, he must go with heart and will; and having been relieved from that Department it is a great point with him to be restored to it. In beginning the peculiar work alluded to there should not be another hour's delay. Hence I send him at once. I sincerely hope the Mississippi may be opened by the time Gen. Butler reaches New-Orleans; but whether it shall be or not, he must go forward without more delay. That you shall make your independent expedition into Texas is still intended; but it can not be made so long as your force is needed on the Mississippi; and while needed there, it is my purpose that you retain the immediate command of it in it's opperation, although you are to report to Gen. Butler after his arrival. When your force, or a substantial and sufficient part of it can be spared from the Mississippi, you are to go to Texas with a department independent of Gen. Butler. His orders and instructions are drawn up with a view to, and in conformity with all this.

[1] ADf, NHi. The draft was apparently never completed, nor any letter sent. See Lincoln to Stanton, *infra*.

To Edward Bates[1]

January 23, 1863

Please give me your opinion in writing whether, after a vessel and cargo is regularly condemned in a prize court, for breach of United States blockade, I, as President, have any lawful power of remission in the case? And if any, to what extent?

[1] Copy, DLC-RTL. The copy of this note appears in Bates' reply of February 9, 1863, which reads: "I . . . believe that after a regular condemnation of a vessel and cargo in a prize court, for breach of Blockade, the President has no lawful power to remit the forfeiture, and restore the property or its proceeds, to the claimant. . . ." (DLC-RTL).

To Ambrose E. Burnside[1]

Executive Mansion,
General Burnside: Washington, January 23, 1863.
Will see you any moment when you come.   A. LINCOLN.

[1] Tarbell (Appendix), p. 359. Burnside had telegraphed at 8:30 P.M. on January 23, "I have prepared some very important orders and I want to see you before issuing them Can I see you alone if I am at the White House after midnight?" (DLC-RTL). Burnside's *General Orders No. 8*, January 23, 1863, reads as follows:
"I. General Joseph Hooker, major-general of volunteers and brigadier-general U.S. Army, having been guilty of unjust and unnecessary criticisms of the actions of his superior officers, and of the authorities, and having, by the general tone of his conversation, endeavored to create distrust in the minds of officers who have associated with him, and having, by omissions and otherwise, made reports and statements which were calculated to create incorrect impressions, and for habitually speaking in disparaging terms of other officers, is hereby dismissed the service of the United States as a man unfit to hold an important commission during a crisis like the present, when so much patience, charity, confidence, consideration, and patriotism are due from every soldier

in the field. This order is issued subject to the approval of the President of the United States.

"II. Brig. Gen. W. T. H. Brooks, commanding First Division, Sixth Army Corps, for complaining of the policy of the Government, and for using language tending to demoralize his command, is, subject to the approval of the President, dismissed from the military service of the United States.

"III. Brig. Gen. John Newton, commanding Third Division, Sixth Army Corps, and Brig. Gen. John Cochrane, commanding First Brigade, Third Division, Sixth Army Corps, for going to the President of the United States with criticisms upon the plans of their commanding officer, are, subject to the approval of the President, dismissed from the military service of the United States.

"IV. It being evident that the following-named officers can be of no further service to this army, they are hereby relieved from duty, and will report, in person, without delay, to the Adjutant-General, U.S. Army: Maj. Gen. W. B. Franklin, commanding left grand division; Maj. Gen. W. F. Smith, commanding Sixth Corps; Brig. Gen. Samuel D. Sturgis, commanding Second Division, Ninth Corps; Brig. Gen. Edward Ferrero, commanding Second Brigade, Second Division, Ninth Army Corps; Brig. Gen. John Cochrane, commanding First Brigade, Third Division, Sixth Corps; Lieut. Col. J. H. Taylor, assistant adjutant-general, right grand division." (OR, I, XXI, 998-99).

Lincoln did not approve the order and hence it was never issued. See Lincoln's letter to Halleck January 25, *infra*, and note.

To Henry W. Halleck[1]

Major General Halleck   Executive Mansion
My dear Sir.   Jan. 23. 1863.

I understand you have before you the record of a Court-martial, in the case of Col. Samuel Graham. If so, and you have not already decided it, please do not, until speaking with me concerning it. Yours truly   A. LINCOLN

[1] ALS-F, ISLA. Colonel Samuel Graham of the Fifth New York Volunteer Artillery was found guilty and sentenced to be dismissed on November 17, 1862, on charges of appointing George H. Sealey as sutler for the regiment in return for $1,000 from Sealey. The court-martial recommended pardon because of Graham's inexperience, and Lincoln remitted the sentence.

Memorandum
Appointment of John J. D. Kingsbury[1]

Executive Mansion, Washington, January 23, 1863.

To-day, Mrs. Col. Kingsbury, whose husband fell at Antietam, calls and asks that John J. D. Kingsbury, cousin, and adopted son, of the Col. be appointed to West Point, for which the Col. intended him. He now resides in New-York, but is native of Conn. Will be 18. years of age next June.

[1] AD, DNA WR RG 94, U.S. Military Academy, 1863, No. 101, Box 81. With the memorandum is a letter from Governor William A. Buckingham recommending the appointment. The only Colonel Kingsbury listed as killed at

Antietam was Henry W. Kingsbury of the Eleventh Connecticut Infantry. John J. D. Kingsbury is listed at West Point in the fourth class as of 1863, but no further record has been found.

Memorandum: Promotion of John Green[1]

Executive Mansion Jan. 23. 1863

To-day, Mrs. Green, calls and urges that her husband, Capt. John Green of the 2nd. Cavalry, have brevet promotions. I am to have his case inquired into.

And now, has his name been sent for the brevet? Or, if not, ought it to be?   A. LINCOLN

[1] ADS, DLC-RTL. Below Lincoln's memorandum appears the following endorsement:

"Capt Jno Greene 2d Cavry is recommended by Genl McClellan for the brevet of Major for 'distinguished services from Camp Lincoln to James river to date July 1. 62.' Respy.   J. C. KELTON A.A.G."
"Jany 24. 63.

Captain Green was not brevetted major until later, for gallantry at Gettysburg, July 3, 1863.

To the Senate and House of Representatives[1]

January 23, 1863

To the Senate and House of Representatives:

I transmit for the consideration of Congress a report from the Secretary of State, transmitting the Regulations, Decrees and Orders for the government of the United States Consular Courts in Turkey.   ABRAHAM LINCOLN

Washington.

January 23. 1863.

[1] DS, DNA RG 46, Senate 37A F3. Seward's report transmitted by Lincoln is printed in Thirty-seventh Congress, Third Session, *Senate Executive Document No. 25.*

To Edwin M. Stanton[1]

Executive Mansion,

Hon. Secretary of War   Washington, January 23. 1863.

Sir: I think Gen. Butler should go to New-Orleans again. He is unwilling to go, unless he is restored to the command of the Department. He should start by the first of February, and should take some force with him. The whole must be so managed as to not wrong, or wound the feelings of Gen. Banks. His original wish was to go to Texas; and it must be arranged for him to do this now with a substantial force; and yet he must not go, to the endangering the opening of the Mississippi. I hope this may be done by the time Gen. Butler shall arrive there; but whether or not, I think we can not longer dispense with Gen. Butler's service. Yours truly   A. LINCOLN

[1] ALS-P, ISLA. See also Lincoln to Banks, *supra*. General Butler never got back to New Orleans but was assigned to command of the Eighteenth Army Corps and Departments of Virginia and North Carolina on October 28, 1863. See Lincoln to Butler January 28, *infra*, and Lincoln to whom it may concern regarding Butler, February 11, *infra*.

To Henry W. Halleck[1]

January 24, 1863

Will General Halleck please call over, bringing with him the letter from Genl Hooker, this morning?   A. LINCOLN
Jany 24th. 1863.

P.S. Please bring Genl Heintzelman's last return   A. L.

[1] Copy, DNA WR RG 108, HQA, No. 67, Box 60. No trace has been found of a letter from General Joseph Hooker to which Lincoln might be referring, but one is tempted to suspect that it may have been a private, rather than an official letter, containing personal views pertinent to the question of whether he was fit to command the Army of the Potomac.

To William H. Seward[1]

Sec. of State, please send me a nomination for Dr. James McBride, of Oregon, to be Commissioner at the Sandwich Islands.
Jan. 24. 1863.   A. LINCOLN

[1] AES, DNA FS RG 59, Appointments, Box 335. Lincoln's endorsement is written on a letter from Thomas Nelson of New York, January [9?] 1863, enclosing recommendations for Dr. James McBride of Oregon.

To Henry W. Halleck[1]

Maj. Gen. Halleck   Executive Mansion,
My dear Sir   Washington, Jan. 25. 1863.
    Please meet Gen. Burnside here at 10 o'clock this morning.
Yours truly   A. LINCOLN

[1] ALS, owned by C. Norton Owen, Glencoe, Illinois. AGO *General Orders No. 20*, January 25, 1863, relieved Major Generals Burnside, Edwin V. Sumner and William B. Franklin of their commands, and assigned Major General Joseph Hooker to command the Army of the Potomac. Later Halleck described his interview with Lincoln as follows:

". . . General Burnside had had an interview with the President in the night or very early in the morning. I was sent for while at breakfast. When I arrived at the President's room, he informed the Secretary and myself that General Burnside had proposed the dismissal and relieving of several high officers, and, if his order was not approved, he wished to resign. The President announced his decision to relieve General Burnside and put General Hooker in command. He asked no opinion or advice either from the Secretary or myself, and none whatever was offered by either of us. General Burnside afterward came in, and the matter of accepting his resignation was discussed. I strongly urged him to withdraw it, which he finally consented to do." (Halleck to Franklin, May 29, 1863, OR, I, XXI, 1008-1009.)

To George E. Fawcett[1]

Executive Mansion, Washington, January 26 1863
My Dear Sir   Allow me to thank you cordially for your thoughtful courtesy in sending me a copy of your "Emancipation March"
Your Obt Servt   A. LINCOLN
George E. Fawcett Esq
Muscatine Iowa

[1] LS-F, ISLA. The letter is in John Hay's handwriting. George E. Fawcett was a teacher of instrumental music at Greenwood Academy, Muscatine, Iowa.

To Joseph Hooker[1]

Major General Hooker: Executive Mansion,
General.   Washington, January 26, 1863.
I have placed you at the head of the Army of the Potomac. Of course I have done this upon what appear to me to be sufficient reasons. And yet I think it best for you to know that there are some things in regard to which, I am not quite satisfied with you. I believe you to be a brave and a skilful soldier, which, of course, I like. I also believe you do not mix politics with your profession, in which you are right. You have confidence in yourself, which is a valuable, if not an indispensable quality. You are ambitious, which, within reasonable bounds, does good rather than harm. But I think that during Gen. Burnside's command of the Army, you have taken counsel of your ambition, and thwarted him as much as you could, in which you did a great wrong to the country, and to a most meritorious and honorable brother officer. I have heard, in such way as to believe it, of your recently saying that both the Army and the Government needed a Dictator. Of course it was not *for* this, but in spite of it, that I have given you the command. Only those generals who gain successes, can set up dictators. What I now ask of you is military success, and I will risk

the dictatorship. The government will support you to the utmost of it's ability, which is neither more nor less than it has done and will do for all commanders. I much fear that the spirit which you have aided to infuse into the Army, of criticising their Commander, and withholding confidence from him, will now turn upon you. I shall assist you as far as I can, to put it down. Neither you, nor Napoleon, if he were alive again, could get any good out of an army, while such a spirit prevails in it.

And now, beware of rashness. Beware of rashness, but with energy, and sleepless vigilance, go forward, and give us victories. Yours very truly   A. LINCOLN

[1] ALS, owned by Alfred W. Stern, Chicago, Illinois. Hooker was called to the White House for an interview, and this letter presumably was handed to him at that time. It remained unknown until after Hooker's death in 1879, and the circumstances of the interview, as well as Hooker's reception of the president's views, have not been adequately recorded. All accounts known to the editors reveal an abundance of conjecture and rationalized recollection after the fact.

To the Senate[1]

To the Senate of the United States: January 26, 1863

In compliance with the Resolution of the Senate of the 13th. instant requesting a copy of certain correspondence respecting the capture of British vessels sailing from one British port to another, having on board contraband of war intended for the use of the insurgents, I have the honor to transmit a report from the Secretary of State and the documents by which it was accompanied.

Washington,   ABRAHAM LINCOLN
January 26th. 1863.

[1] DS, DNA RG 46, Senate 37A F3. Seward's report concerning the seizure of the British ships *Lilla* and *Adela* by the U.S.S. *Quaker City* on July 3 and 7, 1862, is printed in Thirty-third Congress, Third Session, *Senate Executive Document No. 27*. The *Lilla* was carrying saltpeter and the *Adela* was charged with running the blockade under guise of carrying the mails.

To Franz Sigel[1]

                                              January 26, 1863

I believe an increased Cavalry force would be valuable, but I have not promised that, to suit the convenience of any officer, I would, however inconvenient to the government, raise one immediately. I have tried, in regard to Gen. Schurz & Gen. Stahl, to oblige all around; but it seems to get worse & worse. If Gen. Sigel would say distinctly, and unconditionally, what he desires done, about the

[79]

command of the forces he has, I should try to do it; but when he has plans, conditioned upon my raising new forces, which is inconvenient for me to do, it is drawing upon me too severely.

Jan. 26. 1863.   A. LINCOLN

¹ AES, NN. Lincoln's endorsement is written on a letter from Major General Sigel, January 23, as follows:

"The order from the War Department, assigning Gen. Schurz to the command of the Eleventh Corps has been received and promulgated by me. It was my understanding and that of the officers of the Eleventh Corps that Gen. Schurz was only to take the command of the Corps in the event of his becoming a Major General; and also that Gen. Stahel was, at the same time, to be promoted and assigned to the command of a Reserve Corps of Cavalry attached to the Grand Reserve Division.

"Under existing circumstances there is much dissatisfaction among the officers, which might be damaging to our interests in case of a battle, and Gen. Stahel feels humiliated by this arrangement, since it gives him a command inferior to that he has all along had—the command of a Division together with the Cavalry of the Corps. According to the order of the War Dept. he is now assigned to the command of the Cavalry alone, which is not so strong as it was when he had the command of his Division together with the Cavalry of the Corps.

"In order to harmonize these misunderstandings, and as an act of justice to Genl. Stahel, I would respectfully recommend that an order be immediately issued for the organization of a Reserve Cavalry Corps, to be attached to the Grand Reserve Division, and that its organization and command be assigned to Gen. Stahel.

"This would at once harmonize the differences, and be at the same time to the highest interests of the army of the Potomac."

On January 29, Sigel replied to Lincoln's endorsement:

"I respectfully acknowledge the receipt of your endorsement on my letter of the 23d inst. I beg leave to submit to you the following statement:

"I believe that, in regard to Genl. Stahel and Genl. Schurz, the former is entitled by seniority to succeed me in the command of the 11th Corps, and so I represented my convictions to Genl. Burnside, and intended to be so understood by Your Excellency.

"In order to accommodate both of these officers, and because I believed a Cavalry Corps would be of great advantage . . . I recommended that, if such a Corps could be organized, Genl. Stahel could superintend its organization and take command of it, while Genl. Schurz could . . . command . . . the 11th Corps. . . . As, however, according to your endorsement . . . it seems not convenient to organize such a Cavalry force at present, I think it my duty . . . to renew my recommendation that Genl. Stahel succeed me in the command of the 11th Corps. . . ." (DLC-RTL).

See also Lincoln to Halleck, January 7 and Lincoln to Stanton, January 12, *supra,* and Lincoln to Sigel, February 5, *infra.*

To Edwin M. Stanton¹

Hon. Sec. of War   Executive Mansion,
Dear Sir.   Washington, January 26, 1863.

The bearer of this, Mr. Edward Yates, is an Englishman, who, more than a year ago, sent two small treatises on the Art of War, of which treatises he is the author. He is now passing some time in the United States, and wishes permission to visit our Army. I know not whether you consistently can oblige him, but if you can, I shall be obliged, as I feel sure he is our true friend. Yours truly   A. LINCOLN

¹ ALS, PMA. Edward Yates was the author of *Elementary Treatise on Strategy*, London, 1852, as well as an abolitionist and reformer. No further reference to his visiting the army has been found, but a friendly letter which he wrote to Lincoln from London, May 4, 1864, is in the Lincoln Papers.

To Ambrose E. Burnside¹

Major Gen. Burnside   Executive Mansion, Washington,
My dear Sir   January 28. 1862 [1863].

Gen. Humphreys is now with me saying that you told him that you had strongly urged upon me, his, Gen. H's promotion, and that I in response had used such strong language, that you were sure his name would be sent to the Senate. I remember nothing of your speaking to me; or I to you, about Gen. H. still this is far from conclusive that nothing was said. I will now thank you to drop me a note, saying what you think is right and just about Gen. Humphreys. Yours as ever   A. LINCOLN

¹ ALS, IHi. Lincoln misdated this letter as to year. On February 14, 1863, Burnside answered as follows:
"General [Andrew A.] Humphreys is the general that behaved so gallantly at Fredericksburg, and when I spoke to you of him you said he ought to be rewarded by promotion to rank of major-general, and I hope it will be done. . . ." (OR, I, XXI, 1006).
On March 28, 1863, Humphreys wrote Secretary Stanton asking for a court of inquiry in regard to a note of censure which he received from Major General Halleck, September 13, 1862, "I make this request because after having been strongly recommended for promotion for services in the field by Major-General Burnside, my promotion has not taken place. . . ." (OR, I, XIX, I, 368). Halleck endorsed this complaint with the notation that "As General Halleck did not oppose General Humphreys' promotion, but on the contrary supported General Burnside's recommendation for such promotion, the whole motive of General Humphreys' complaints falls to the ground." (OR, I, LI, I, 1000). Humphreys' promotion to major general was sent to the Senate in a list under date of December 31, 1863, but was not confirmed by the Senate until May 12, 1864.

To Benjamin F. Butler¹

Major General Butler   Executive Mansion,
Lowell, Mass.   Washington, January 28. 1863.

Please come here immediately. Telegraph me about what time you will arrive.   A. LINCOLN

¹ ALS, RPB. Butler's reply was received at 1 P.M., "Telegram received, will leave thursday morning. Be in Washington friday morning" (DLC-RTL). See Lincoln to Stanton January 23, *supra*, and his letter to whom it may concern, February 11, *infra*.

Order Approving Sentence of Justus McKinstry¹

January 28, 1863

The sentence in the foregoing case will be carried into execution by the dismissal of Major *Justus McKinstry*, Quartermaster, United States Army, from the service of the United States.

Washington, January 28, 1863.   ABRAHAM LINCOLN.

¹ AGO *General Orders No. 43*, February 13, 1863. Major McKinstry had been found guilty of neglect and violation of duty and had been sentenced to be dismissed from the service.

To the Senate and House of Representatives¹

January 28, 1863

To the Senate and House of Representatives:

In conformity to the Law of 16 July 1862, I most cordially recommend that Commander David D. Porter, U.S. Navy, Acting Rear Admiral, commanding the Mississippi Squadron, receive a vote of thanks of Congress, for the bravery and skill displayed in the attack on the Post of Arkansas, which surrendered to the combined Military and Naval Forces on the 10th. Inst.

Washington City,   ABRAHAM LINCOLN
28 January 1863.

¹ DS, DNA RG 46, Senate 37A F2. The joint resolution tendering thanks to Commander Porter was approved February 7, 1863.

To Edwin M. Stanton¹

Sec. of War, please see the bearer, and have any injustice which may have been done Gen. Keyes corrected.   A. LINCOLN

Jan. 28. 1863.

¹ AES, NHi. Lincoln's endorsement is written on the envelope of a letter from Major General Erasmus D. Keyes, January 25, 1863:

"I take the liberty to introduce to you my adjutant General, Col. C[harles]. C. Suydam. As the nominations of Sumner, Heintzleman, Hooker & Casey to be major generals to date from Williamsburg & Fair Oaks, while my name is omitted, does me injustice, I have requested Col. Suydam to state to you the facts of my conduct in those two battles with which he was personally cognizant."

Keyes' nomination as major general, dated March 5, 1863, was confirmed by the Senate on March 11.

To John A. Dix[1]

Majr. Genl. Dix   Washington City, D.C.
Fort-Monroe Va.   January 29, 1863
Do Richmond papers have *any thing* about Vicksburg?

A LINCOLN

[1] ALS, RPB. General Dix replied on the same day, "The Richmond papers up to & including the 27th, the latest date we have, were carefully examined & nothing about Vicksburgh was noticed. . . ." (DLC-RTL).

To Edwin M. Stanton[1]

Hon. Sec. of War   Executive Mansion
Dear Sir   Jan. 29, 1863.
Mr. Speed tells me you wish to appoint him to some agency about the Goose-Creek Salt works; and he wishes to decline it, & that William P. Thomason may be appointed. I personally know Mr. Thomason to be an honest & very competent man, & fully in sympathy with the administration. I think he should be appointed.
Yours truly   A. LINCOLN

[1] ALS, IHi. The Goose Creek Salt Works near Manchester, Kentucky, had been destroyed by Union forces in October, 1862. Joshua F. Speed was in Washington at this time (James F. Speed to Joshua F. Speed, January 19, 1863, DLC-RTL), but no further reference to the salt works has been found. William P. Thomasson, a lawyer in Chicago who had formerly been U.S. representative from Kentucky (1843-1847) was probably the man recommended.

To Thurlow Weed[1]

Hon. Thurlow Weed   Executive Mansion,
My dear Sir   Washington, January 29. 1863.
Your valedictory to the patrons of the Albany Evening Journal brings me a good deal of uneasiness. What does it mean? Yours truly   A. LINCOLN.

[1] ADfS, DLC-RTL. Weed's reply of February 1, 1863, reads as follows:
"I retired from an apprehension that I was doing more harm than good. I could not remain without remonstrance against a Spirit by which you are persecuted, and which I *know* will end our Union and Government. It is impossible, just now, to resist Fanaticism—a Fanaticism which divides the North and deprives you of the support essential, vital in-deed, to the Life of the Republic. Its constant cry is: 'Give! Give!' and the more you give the more it demands.
"They accuse me of 'opposing the Administration.' I answered that falsehood yesterday, and sent Mr. Nicolay a Paper. I have labored to shield the Administration from their persecution.
"There is *crazy* 'method' in Greeley's Abolitionism. He has the Presidency on his Brain. He ran 'Maine Law' into the ground expecting to make himself

Governor. His Ambition is mere lunacy, but, unfortunately, I fear he possesses the power to ruin our Country. If I could be heard by the same, and the same number, of readers, I should hope to open their eyes.

"This State was ours, in November, by 25,000 majority, with Morgan, and 50,000 with Dix, but he, and his like, would have an Abolition issue for Govnr, that they might have a Legislature in favor of Greeley or Field, for U.S. Senator.

"I may not be able to do much good, but all I am belongs to my Country, and to yourself, as its President." (DLC-RTL).

To John A. Dix[1]

Major General Dix   Washington City, D.C.
Fort Monroe, Va.   January 30 1863
    What Iron-clads, if any, have gone out of Hampton Roads within the last two day[s]?   A LINCOLN

[1] ALS, RPB. General Dix replied on the same day, "No iron-clads have left for two days. The Weehawken is at Norfolk; the Patapsco is here, waiting for favorable weather, and the Nahant is at Newport News. I have just telegraphed to General Halleck our success in a fight with [Roger A.] Pryor." (OR, I, XVIII, 530).

To John A. Dix[1]

Major Gen. Dix   Washington City, D.C.
Fort-Monroe, Va.   January 31 1863
    How has Corcoran's and Pryor's battle terminated? Have you any news through Richmond papers, or otherwise?

                                                            A. LINCOLN

[1] ALS, RPB. General Dix's reply was received at 5:30 P.M. "I am waiting for an answer from Genl Peck to a despatch I sent him three hours ago asking . . . the result of the fight at the deserted house yesterday. . . ." (DLC-RTL).

A second telegram was received at 6 P.M. "I have just recd . . . Peck's answer. . . . He has not yet received reports or lists but he has ascertained that we had twenty four killed & eighty wounded No missing reported The Enemys supposed loss in killed & wounded to be about equal to ours. We have taken 12 prisoners. . . ." (Ibid.).

To William W. Gallaer[1]

                                                        January 31, 1863
    I would like to oblige Mr. Gallaer, & other good men; but I cannot now do the thing he desires.

[1] American Art Association Anderson Galleries Catalog 4180, May 8-9, 1935, No. 204. According to the catalog description this is an autograph note signed. On February 9, 1863, William W. Gallaer of Memphis, Tennessee, wrote Lin-

coln from Willard's Hotel in Washington. Although his letter does not state specifically the subject which he laid before Lincoln, it is reproduced in part as follows:

"Although it is probable I may be considered troublesome, if not impertinent, yet I cannot resist the impression that I have failed in properly presenting the subject I had the honor personally to lay before you. Permit me to . . . briefly state some facts bearing upon that matter.

"It cannot be denied that since the occupation of Memphis . . . there has been apparent on the part of the prominent men of that vicinity, who formerly sympathized with the rebellion movement, a secret desire to withdraw their support from that unholy cause, and a desire for peace on any terms.

"The prevalence of such feelings alarmed the rebel leaders, and induced them to resort to every argument and threat to prevent the spread of union sentiment.

"The argument having most weight and used most effectually is, that the government is determined to sweep away all their property, and under no circumstances ever to restore, or permit them to enjoy it again. . . .

"The result is, that hundreds of influential men are rendered lukewarm, who would otherwise have the strongest incentives to use their influence in putting down the rebellion, for the protection of their interests if from no other motive. . . ." (DLC-RTL).

To Montgomery C. Meigs[1]

Quarter-Master-General   Executive Mansion,
Dear Sir: Washington, January 31. 1863.

The bearer of this, Mr. James C. Conkling, is successor to Mr. Thomas H. Campbell, now deceased, as agent to adjust accounts with this government for the State of Illinois. He has ample business qualifications, is entirely trustworthy; and with all is my personal friend of long standing. Please see & hear him. Yours truly   A. LINCOLN

[1] ALS, CSmH.

Memorandum Concerning
Fines Collected from Kentuckians[1]

January 31, 1863

Senator Powell calls and leaves this paper and asks that an order be made on the persons stated to have made the collections to refund the money to the persons respectively from whom collected, and all monies collected in like manner in the counties of Henderson,[2] Union, Hopkins & Webster   A. LINCOLN
Jan. 31, 1863.

[1] AES, DLC-RTL. The signature has been crossed out, but is as given. Lincoln's endorsement is written on a list of more than one hundred citizens with amount of fines collected by Colonel John W. Foster and Lieutenant Colonel Thomas Johnson of the Sixty-fifth Indiana Volunteers and Lieutenant Colonel

John Mehringer of the Ninety-first Indiana Volunteers. See Lincoln to Jeremiah T. Boyle, February 1, *infra*.

2 "Henry" has been deleted and "Henderson" written above.

To Robert C. Schenck[1]

Major Gen. Schenck   Washington City, D.C.
Baltimore, Md.   January 31 1863

I do not take jurisdiction of the pass question. Exercise your own discretion as to whether Judge Pettis shall have a pass.

A LINCOLN

[1] ALS, RPB. A purported telegram from Schenck received at 4:40 P.M. on January 31, reads: "Judge Pettis desires leave tonight to visit a sick soldier at Gloucester Point. Shall he have it?" (DLC-RTL). A second telegram from Schenck received at 11:20 P.M., replied, "I beg to say that the Telegram sent you in my name about a pass was without my authority." (*Ibid.*). "Judge Pettis" was probably S. Newton Pettis, appointed associate justice in Colorado Territory in 1861, who had returned to Pennsylvania in 1862.

To Edwin M. Stanton[1]

January 31, 1863

If the within showing of Col. Ballier's case is correct, I think he should be restored. It shows that he was sick in hospital when discharged from service, and that without knowledge of his discharge he made premature efforts to return to his duty.

[1] Copy, DNA WR RG 107, Register of Secretary of War, Letters Received, P 42. The original endorsement or note is missing but the register preserves a copy. Colonel John F. Ballier of the Ninety-eighth Pennsylvania was discharged on November 26, 1862, and re-mustered on March 12, 1863.

To Joseph P. Taylor[1]

Commissary General.   Executive Mansion,
Sir.   Washington, January 31, 1863.

Please see the bearer, Edward D. Baker, who is a son of my old friend Col. Baker, who fell at Ball's Bluff. He is now a first Lieut. in the 4th. U.S. Cavalry, and has been serving as Adjutant of the Regiment. He was in the battles of Perryville, and Murfreesboro. He now wishes to be a Commissary with the rank of Captain, and if you can inform me that he can be made such consistently with the rules of the service, I will oblige him. Yours truly

A. LINCOLN

[1] ALS, IHi. Lieutenant Baker was appointed captain and assistant quartermaster, March 13, 1863. See Lincoln's endorsement to Taylor concerning Baker, February 5, *infra*.

To Jeremiah T. Boyle[1]

Gen. J. T. Boyle   Executive Mansion,
Dear Sir: Washington, February 1. 1863.

Yesterday Senator Powell left a paper with me, with a request which I endorsed upon it at the time, and the contents of which paper, and request appear by the inclosed copies. You perceive at once what the object is. This course of procedure, though just and politic in some cases, is so liable to gross abuse, as to do great injustice in some others and give the government immense trouble. I will thank you, therefore, if you will, without reasonable delay, ascertain the facts of these cases and report them to me, together with such other information as may best enable me to understand the whole case. Yours truly   A. LINCOLN

[1] ADfS, DLC-RTL. See Lincoln's memorandum of January 31, *supra.* General Boyle replied on February 11, 1863, "Your letter of the 1st inst., requesting information in regard to contributions assessed . . . by Col. J. W. Foster, of 65th Regt. Ind. Vols . . . was received on 7th inst. and forwarded to Col. Foster for report.

". . . the assessment . . . was made by Col. Foster without orders from me; but I approved it after it was done, and still approve it as right, just, and politic. . . . The contributions were required of avowed secessionists . . . and it was applied honestly to reimburse loyal Union citizens in part for their losses by rebel guerrillas. . . . As far as I am advised, Mr. President, I believe the matter should be left as it is, without any interference with it. . . ." (DLC-RTL).

On February 20 Boyle enclosed a copy of Colonel John W. Foster's report of January 6, 1863, and a letter from Foster dated February 16, which reads in part:

"I am in receipt of the letter of . . . President Lincoln, with your endorsement . . . instructing me to report on the names contained in the paper submitted by Senator Powell.

"You will remember that I made full report of all my action in these matters at the time, giving in detail the condition of the country, the causes which led to my action, the amount levied, the manner in which it was distributed, and the effect which it had upon the community. This report has been read by yourself and Maj. Gen. Wright . . . and . . . fully approved.

"I desire that this report be sent to the President. It was made upon my honor as an officer, and by it I desire that I may be judged. The money levied has been . . . paid out . . . to the citizens of Hopkins County, who were the sufferers by the action of these very men and their friends, who ask the President for redress. . . ." (DLC-RTL).

To Oliver P. Morton[1]

"Cypher"

Gov. O. P. Morton   Washington, D.C.,
Indianapolis, Ia: Feb. 1. 1863

I think it would not do for me to meet you at Harrisburg. It would be known, and would be misconstrued a thousand ways. Of

[87]

course if the whole truth could be told and accepted as the truth, it would do no harm, but that is impossible.   A. LINCOLN

[1] ALS, RPB. On January 31, Governor Morton telegraphed, "It is important that I should see you a few hours, but I cannot leave long enough to go to Washington. Can you meet me at Harrisburg?" (OR, III, III, 23). Peace Democrats were advocating a Northwest Confederacy. The Indiana legislature had gone Democratic in the 1862 elections, and Morton was having a great deal of trouble. On February 9, he sent Lincoln by Robert Dale Owen a letter outlining the plans of the Democrats to end the war by whatever means, to recognize the Confederacy, and to propose a reunion leaving out the New England States. The letter also dealt with the secret societies which were being organized with the avowed purpose of sabotaging the Union.

Memorandum:
Appointment of Eliphalet N. Chester[1]

Executive Mansion, Washington, Feb. 2. 1863.
To-day Senator Doolittle, Mrs. Spaulding, and Col. Root, call and ask that Eliphalet Nott Chester, of Buffalo N.Y. 17 the 18th. of next July, be sent to West-Point. Two of his brothers have served in this war, (one of them still in the service) and he, as a private, has been through the battles of South-Mountain, Antietam, and Fredericksburg. Col. Root is his Col., and gives the strongest testimony, both as to his general worthiness, and his particular talent for Military matters.

[1] AD, DNA WR RG 94, U.S. Military Academy, 1862, No. 55, Box 80. Private Eliphalet N. Chester of the Ninety-fourth New York Infantry, commanded by Colonel Adrian R. Root, entered West Point September 9, 1863, and graduated June 17, 1867. "Mrs. Spaulding" was probably the wife of U.S. Representative Elbridge G. Spaulding of Buffalo, New York.

To the Workingmen of London[1]

Executive Mansion, Washington,
To the workingmen of London: February 2, 1863.
I have received the new year's address which you have sent me with a sincere appreciation of the exalted and humane sentiments by which it was inspired.

As those sentiments are manifestly the enduring support of the free institutions of England, so I am sure also that they constitute the only reliable basis for free institutions throughout the world.

The resources, advantages, and powers of the American people are very great, and they have, consequently, succeeded to equally great responsibilities. It seems to have devolved upon them to test whether a government, established on the principles of human freedom, can be maintained against an effort to build one upon the exclusive foundation of human bondage.

They will rejoice with me in the new evidences which your proceedings furnish, that the magnanimity they are exhibiting is justly estimated by the true friends of freedom and humanity in foreign countries.

Accept my best wishes for your individual welfare, and for the welfare and happiness of the whole British people.

ABRAHAM LINCOLN.

[1] Thirty-seventh Congress, Third Session, *Senate Executive Document No. 49.* On February 2, Lincoln's letter was forwarded to Minister Charles F. Adams by Secretary Seward with instructions to "submit it informally to the notice of Earl Russell and if he offers no objection, then to deliver it to the parties to whom it is addressed." The address of the Workingmen adopted at a meeting on December 31, 1862, printed in the London *Daily News* of January 1, 1863, was forwarded by Adams to Seward on January 8, and reads in part:
"We who offer to you this address are Englishmen and workingmen. We prize as our dearest inheritance . . . the liberty we enjoy—the liberty of free labor upon a free soil. We have . . . been acustomed to regard with veneration and gratitude the founders of the great republic in which the liberties of the Anglo-Saxon race have been widened beyond all the precedents of the old world, and in which there was nothing to condemn or to lament but the slavery and degradation of men guilty only of a colored skin or an African parentage. . . . We have watched with the warmest interest the steady advance of your policy along the path of emancipation; and on the eve of the day on which your proclamation of freedom takes effect, we pray God to strengthen your hands, to confirm your noble purpose, and to hasten the restoration of that lawful authority which engages, in peace or war, by compensation or by force of arms, to realize the glorious principle on which your Constitution is founded—the brotherhood, freedom, and equality of all men." (*Ibid.*).

To Edward Bates[1]

Let a pardon be made out in this case.   A. LINCOLN
Feb. 3, 1863

[1] AES, DNA RG 204, U.S. Pardon Attorney, A 459. Lincoln's endorsement appears on a petition signed by Samuel Brereton and others, asking a pardon for Albert C. War, convicted of assault with intent to kill.

Memorandum:
Appointment of William H. Hodges[1]

Executive Mansion, Washington, February 3. 1863.
To-day Senator Foote calls and asks that William H. Hodges, of Mass. 17 next June, and nephew of Mrs. Foote, may be sent to

West-Point. He says the boy is a fine scholar, and of uncommonly fine physical developement

[1] AD, DNA WR RG 94, U.S. Military Academy, 1863, No. 91, Box 81. William H. Hodges is listed at West Point as of September 1863, but is not in the *Official Register* in 1865.

To Edwin M. Stanton[1]

February 3, 1863

Sec. of War, please see Mr. Conkling, a good man, who comes as successor of Mr. Campbell, now deceased, as agent to settle accounts for Illinois.   A. LINCOLN

Feb. 3. 1863.

[1] ALS, IHi. See Lincoln to Meigs, January 31, *supra*.

To the House of Representatives[1]

To, the House of Representatives: February 4, 1863

In compliance with the resolution of the House of Representatives on the 5th. December last, requesting information upon the present condition of Mexico, I transmit a report from the Secretary of State, and the papers by which it was accompanied.

Washington, February, 4th. 1863.   ABRAHAM LINCOLN

[1] DS, DNA RG 233, House Executive Document No. 54. Seward's eight hundred-page report transmitted by Lincoln may be found in Thirty-seventh Congress, Third Session, *House Executive Document No. 54*.

To Robert C. Schenck[1]

Cypher

Major Gen. Schenck   Washington, D.C.,
Baltimore, Md.   Feb. 4 1863

I hear of some difficulty in the streets of Baltimore yesterday. What is the amount of it?   A. LINCOLN

[1] ALS, RPB. No reply from General Schenck has been located. A Washington despatch of February 5 appearing in the New York *Herald*, February 6, suggests the occasion of Lincoln's telegram: "The practical feeling of white soldiers towards negroes is seen in the fact that yesterday morning a lot of one hundred and fifty convalescents from Philadelphia, in charge of a guard of ten men, armed at the Soldiers' Rest, and at once showed their antipathy to the colored people by assaulting the contrabands employed about the quarters. . . . The Baltimore papers state that in coming through that city they attacked every colored person coming in their way, and assaulted the police who endeavored to protect them."

To the Senate[1]

To the Senate of the United States: February 4, 1863

In pursuance of the joint resolution of Congress approved 3 February, 1863, tendering its thanks to Commander John L. Worden, U.S. Navy, I nominate that officer to be a captain in the Navy, on the active list, from the 3d February, 1863.

It may be proper to state that the number of captains authorized by the 2d section of the act of 16 July, 1862, is now full, but presuming that the meaning of the 9th section of the same act is that the officer receiving the vote of thanks shall immediately be advanced one grade, I have made the nomination.

Washington, D.C., February 4, 1863. ABRAHAM LINCOLN.

[1] *Executive Journal*, XIII, 113-14. John L. Worden's appointment was confirmed by the Senate on February 21.

To Francisco S. Lopez[1]

February 5, 1863

Abraham Lincoln,
President of the United States of America,

To His Excellency Señor Don Francisco Solano Lopez,
President of the Republic of Paraguay.

Great and Good Friend: I have received the letter which under date of 30 October, last, you addressed to me, announcing the death of the late most excellent President, Señor Don Carlos Antonio Lopez and of your subsequent elevation to the Presidency of the Republic by the unanimous vote of the Representatives of the nation.

I offer your Excellency my sincere sympathy in the sad bereavement which you have experienced in the death of your distinguished Father, under whose government the Republic of Paraguay enjoyed many years of peace and prosperity. The election of your Excellency to succeed him is the best proof of the satisfaction of the Republic with his administration.

I congratulate you upon this mark of the confidence of the nation, and sincerely reciprocate the desire Your Excellency has expressed for the continuance of the good relations so happily subsisting between the United States and Paraguay, to which desirable end my own best efforts shall not be wanting.

Wishing peace, progress, and prosperity for the Republic, and health and happiness to your Excellency I pray God to have you always in His most holy keeping.

Written at the city of Washington this 5th. day of February 1863 and of the Independence of the United States of America the eighty-seventh. Your Good Friend, ABRAHAM LINCOLN.
By the President:
WILLIAM H. SEWARD, Secretary of State.

[1] Copy, DNA FS RG 59, Communications to Foreign Sovereigns and States, III, 198-99.

To the Senate[1]

To the Senate of the United States.　　　　February 5, 1863

I submit to the Senate for consideration with a view to ratification a "Convention between the United States of America and the Republic of Peru, providing for the reference to the King of Belgium of the claims arising out of the capture and confiscation of the ships Lizzie Thompson and Georgiana"—signed at Lima on the 20th, December, 1862.　　　　ABRAHAM LINCOLN
Washington, 5 February, 1863.

[1] DS, DNA RG 46, Senate 37B B17. The convention was ratified by the Senate on February 18, 1863.

To the Senate[1]

To the Senate of the United States:　　　　February 5, 1863

I submit to the Senate, for consideration with a view to ratification, a "convention between the United States of America and the Republic of Peru, for the settlement of the pending claims of the citizens of either country against the other," signed at Lima on the 12th January, ultimo, with the following amendment:

Article 1.　Strike out the words, "The claims of the American citizens Dr. Charles Easton, Edmund Sartori, and the owners of the whale ship William Lee, against the Government of Peru, and the Peruvian citizen Stephen Montano against the Government of the United States," and insert *all claims of citizens of the United States against the Government of Peru, and of citizens of Peru against the Government of the United States, which have not been embraced in conventional or diplomatic agreement between the two Governments or their plenipotentiaries, and statements of which soliciting the interposition of either Government may, previously to the exchange of the ratifications of this convention have been filed in the Department of State at Washington, or the Department for Foreign Affairs at Lima, &c.*

This amendment is considered desirable, as there are believed to be other claims proper for the consideration of the commission which are not among those specified in the original article, and because it is at least questionable whether either Government would be justified in incurring the expense of a commission for the sole purpose of disposing of the claims mentioned in that article.

Washington, February 5, 1863.   ABRAHAM LINCOLN.

[1] *Executive Journal*, XIII, 122. Lincoln's suggested amendment of Article 1 was adopted and appears in the convention as printed in *U.S. Statutes at Large*, XIII, 639.

To William H. Seward[1]

Sec. of State please see these gentlemen, representative of the shipping interests.   A. LINCOLN
Feb. 5, 1863

[1] Copy, ISLA. A note from Senator Sumner, February 4, 1863, requests Lincoln to receive three men named Frazer, [Samuel?] Hall, and Eldredge, "a committee from Boston of gentlemen interested in the Navy & familiar with ships & the sea. They have important suggestions to offer. . . ." (DLC-RTL). The men have not been identified, but it seems possible that they were the gentlemen whom Lincoln sent to Secretary Seward.

To Franz Sigel[1]

Executive Mansion,
Major General Sigel   Washington, February 5. 1863.

My dear Sir   Gen. Schurz thinks I was a little cross in my late note to you. If I was, I ask pardon. If I do get up a little temper I have no sufficient time to keep it up.

I believe I will not now issue any new order in relation to the matter in question; but I will be obliged, if Gen. Hooker consistently can, and will give an increased Cavalry command to Gen. Stahl. You may show Gen. Hooker this lettter if you choose. Yours truly
A. LINCOLN

[1] ALS, NN. See Lincoln's endorsement to Sigel, January 26, *supra*. On February 5, General Hooker broke up the Grand Division organization of the Army of the Potomac and assigned Sigel to command of the Eleventh Corps. On February 12, Sigel wrote Joseph Dickinson, assistant adjutant general, Army of the Potomac, "I beg leave respectfully to represent that the reduction of my command in the Army of the Potomac makes it exceedingly unpleasant . . . to remain longer in my present command, and therefore request that I be immediately relieved from my command. . . ." On February 19, Lincoln directed Stanton to telegraph Hooker that the president "has given General Sigel as good a command as he can, and desires him to do the best he can with it." (OR, I, XXV, II, 71). Sigel insisted, however, "Either, that I be relieved from my command, or that my resignation be accepted, as my present position and relations . . . are so unsatisfactory and dispiriting to me, that it would be in the highest degree unpleasant for me to continue in command of my Corps." (Sigel to Stanton, March 11, 1863, DLC-RTL). Later Sigel took a subordinate command in the Department of the Susquehanna.

To Edwin M. Stanton[1]

Let Thomas J. C. Amory be appointed a Brigadier General.

Feb. 5, 1863   A. LINCOLN

[1] Copy, ISLA. Colonel Thomas J. C. Amory of the Seventeenth Massachusetts Volunteers was nominated brigadier general on February 6, 1863. On February 12, his nomination was returned to the president along with others, on recommendation of the Senate Committee on Military Affairs that there was "no law authorizing said appointments" (*Executive Journal*, XIII, 128). Appointed brevet brigadier general as of March 13, 1865, Amory was confirmed by the Senate on March 12, 1866.

To Joseph P. Taylor[1]

[c. February 5, 1863]

I would like to give the son of my old friend, Col. Baker one of the places or vacancies created by this act, Will the Com. Genl. please arrange it for me?   A. LINCOLN

[1] AES, MHi. Lincoln's endorsement is written on the bottom of the printed bill H.R. 658 "An Act to promote the efficiency of the commissary department." The date of the bill ("In the Senate . . . February 5, 1863. Read the first and second times.") suggests the date of Lincoln's endorsement. See further, Lincoln's endorsement to Meigs, February 27, *infra*.

Endorsement: Appointment of Joseph Hertford[1]

I should be glad for my friend Swett to be obliged; and besides, Mr. Hertford is a very worthy and competent gentleman.

Feb. 6. 1863.   A. LINCOLN

[1] Copy, DLC-RTL. The copy of this endorsement is contained in a letter from Joseph Hertford, March, 1863, reminding Lincoln of a letter from Leonard Swett in favor of Hertford's appointment as special agent of the Treasury. Joseph Hertford is listed in the *U.S. Official Register*, 1863, as a clerk in the Bureau of Internal Revenue.

To Bartolomé Mitre[1]

February 6, 1863

Abraham Lincoln,
President of the United States of America.

To His Excellency Señor Don Bartolomé Mitre,
President of the Argentine Republic.

Great and Good Friend: I have received the letter which Your Excellency has addressed to me under date of the 23d. October, last, announcing your election to the Presidency of the Republic by the free suffrages of your fellow-citizens.

[94]

I assure Your Excellency that this event has inspired me with the liveliest gratification. After so many years of discord and strife the Provinces of the Argentine Confederation have buried their jealousies and again present themselves to the world as a united nation having a common interest and a common destiny.

No one knows better than Your Excellency that it has been the uniform desire and effort of this Government so far as it could properly do so by the friendly offices of its Ministers in the Plata, to promote conciliation and to effect the consolidation which has happily been accomplished.

I congratulate the nation and Your Excellency upon this result, and upon the elevation of Your Excellency to the Chief Magistracy of the reunited Republic. And I do not doubt that the earnest patriotism and enlightened statesmanship of Your Excellency will speedily obliterate all painful remembrances of the past and inspire the people of the nation to give you a hearty and unanimous support in the developement of their best interests.

Sincerely reciprocating Your Excellency's sentiments of friendship for this Government and people and praying God to have your Excellency always in His most holy keeping, I am your Good Friend, ABRAHAM LINCOLN.

By the President:
    WILLIAM H. SEWARD, Secretary of State.
Washington 6 February, 1863.

1 Copy, DNA FS RG 59, Communications to Foreign Sovereigns and States, III, 200-202.

To the Senate[1]

To the Senate of the United States: February 6, 1863

I transmit herewith a report from the Secretary of State with accompanying documents in answer to the resolution of the Senate on the 30th ultimo.   ABRAHAM LINCOLN

Washington, February 6th, 1863.

1 DS, DNA RG 46, Senate 37A F3. Seward's report of February 5 and accompanying documents are printed in Thirty-seventh Congress, Third Session, *Senate Executive Document No. 33.* The resolution of January 30, 1863, asked the president to communicate ". . . whether or not any commissioner, representative, or agent of the United States has received from the Japanese government, or from any agent thereof, any sum of money to be used and expended in the construction of a ship or ships of war; and if so, who was that commissioner, representative, or agent of this government; how much money he received; into whose hands did he deposit it; in whose hands or under whose control is it now; and what disposition is proposed to be made of it." Robert H. Pruyn, minister to Japan, had arranged for the building of three warships

and guns, a field battery of six guns, and a rifling machine, for the government of Japan. Thurlow Weed and Charles B. Lansing of Albany, New York, were selected as agents by Pruyn.

To the Senate[1]

To the Senate of the United States: February 6, 1863

In compliance with the resolution of the Senate of the United States of yesterday, requesting information in regard to the death of General Ward, a citizen of the United States, in the military service of the Chinese Government, I transmit a copy of a despatch of the 27th. of October, last, and of its accompaniment, from the Minister of the United States in China.   ABRAHAM LINCOLN

Washington, 6th. February, 1863.

[1] DS, DNA RG 46, Senate 37A F2. Seward's report enclosed a copy of a despatch from Anson Burlingame, October 27, 1862, informing him of the death of Frederick T. Ward of Salem, Massachusetts, killed by rebels at Tse-Kzi near Ning Po during the Tai-Ping rebellion.

To Edwin M. Stanton[1]

[c. February 8, 1863]

If another Quarter Master is needed in Gen. McClernand's Corps, I would like for the appointment within requested to be made. Sec. of War, please refer to Q.M. Genl.   A. LINCOLN

[1] AES, IHi. Lincoln's endorsement is written on a letter from Mrs. Abraham H. Hoge, February 8, 1863, asking a quartermastership for her son. Holmes Hoge was appointed captain and assistant quartermaster on March 13, 1863. See Lincoln's letters to Mrs. Hoge, November 25, 1862, and January 6, 1863, *supra.*

To James M. Edmunds[1]

February 9, 1863

I shall be obliged if the Commissioner of the General Land-Office will give Mr. Morris a full hearing on the business indicated within, and do what may be directed by the law in the case. Please give Mr. Morris an early hearing.   A. LINCOLN

Feb. 9. 1863.

[1] AES-P, ISLA. Lincoln's endorsement is written on a letter from Governor Richard Yates, January 13, 1863, asking that Isaac N. Morris be given a hearing in regard to "the claim of Illinois to the two per cent fund, due the State from the General Government." The claim had to do with net proceeds of the sale of public lands in Illinois from January 1, 1819, to be used for roads. Morris'

report (*Illinois Reports*, 1865) indicates that as of December 24, 1864, the claim had not been allowed. See Lincoln's memorandum and letter to Morris, August 24, 1863, *infra*.

To William A. Hammond[1]

February 9, 1863

Will the Surgeon General please have an examination of the physical condition of Henry Williams, named within, made by a competent Surgeon, and report to me.   A. LINCOLN

Feb. 9. 1863.

1 AES, DLC-RTL. Lincoln's endorsement is written on a letter of February 3 from Ambrose W. Clark to Hiram Berdan concerning a physical examination of Private Henry Williams of Company D, First U.S. Sharpshooters, under sentence of imprisonment for desertion. On February 14, Hammond returned the letter with additional endorsements and a report "from which it appears that no apprehension need be entertained as to the health of Henry Williams."

To Edwin M. Stanton[1]

February 9, 1863

I know nothing as to whether the transfer sought, is admissable. I have a very strong impression, however that Gen. Frye is a worthy gentleman and meritorious officer.   A. LINCOLN

Feb. 9. 1863.

1 AES, NHi. Lincoln's endorsement is written on a letter signed by Representatives John J. Crittenden, Aaron Harding, and Senator Garrett Davis, January 6, 1863, asking that Brigadier General Speed S. Fry be transferred from the Army of the Cumberland to the Army of the Ohio. On May 26, 1863, General Fry was placed in command of the Eastern District of Kentucky under the Department of the Ohio.

To Edwin M. Stanton[1]

Will Mr. Stanton please see Col. Kirkham and read the letter of Mr. Butler, one of our wisest and most reliable men at Springfield

Monday. Feby. 9. 1863.   A. LINCOLN.

1 LS, NHi. William Butler's letter has not been located, but Governor Richard Yates wrote Lincoln on January 30, 1863, that Colonel Robert Kirkham of Shawneetown, Illinois, who had resigned command of the Fifty-sixth Illinois Infantry on June 26, 1862, was going to Washington. "He knows what is going on here. The Government must let us nave at least 4 Regiments of well armed men in Illinois. Hope you will give friend Kirkham a careful hearing." (DLC-RTL). On February 9, Stanton ordered four regiments to be raised as Illinois home guards, but the order was countermanded on March 31 when matters had somewhat quieted down (OR, III, III, 109).

To Edwin M. Stanton[1]

I personally know John W. True; and think him both competent and worthy to be an Additional Paymaster.   A. LINCOLN
Feb. 9. 1863.

[1] AES, IHi. Lincoln's endorsement is written on a letter from F. G. True, a banker at Mattoon, Illinois, February 1, 1863, to Lyman Trumbull, asking that Major John W. True of the Fifty-fourth Illinois Infantry be made a paymaster. John W. True resigned from service on July 17, 1863. See Lincoln to Stanton, December 4, 1862, *supra.*

To Edward Bates[1]

Let a pardon be made out in this case.
Feb. 10, 1863

[1] AE, DNA RG 204, U.S. Pardon Attorney, A 460. Lincoln's endorsement appears on a petition signed by Bernhardt Weiss and H. P. King, February 5, asking pardon for Henry Williams of Baltimore convicted of manslaughter.

To David Hunter and Others[1]

Executive Mansion
Washington. February 10th. 1863
To David Hunter, Major General U.S.A., Rufus Saxton,
   Brig: Genl. U.S.A., A. C. Smith, W. E. Wording and W. H. Brisbane Esquires:
                   You are hereby authorized and directed agreeably to an Act of Congress, approved on the 6th. day of February inst. to select for Government use, for war, military, naval revenue, charitable, Educational or police purposes, such tracts, parcels or lots of land, within the State of South Carolina, from the lands which may have been or which may hereafter be offered for sale by the Direct Tax Commissioners in said State, appointed under an Act of Congress, approved June 7th. 1862. as may seem to you necessary and proper for the purposes aforesaid. And I do direct and order that either of the two persons first named, together with two of the three persons last named, shall constitute a quorum for the purpose of making such selections; and in case of the absence of the two persons first named, the last named three persons, or the major part of them, are authorized to make the selections, as hereinbefore directed. And you are hereby authorized and empowered to execute and perform the duties herein specified, according to Law. You will report your proceedings to the Secretary of the Treasury.   ABRAHAM LINCOLN

[1] LS-P, ISLA. The act of June 7, 1862 (amended February 6, 1863), provided that the President appoint a board of three tax commissioners for each state in which insurrection existed.

Memorandum: Appointment of Philip Reade[1]

Executive Mansion   Feb. 10. 1863.

To-day Gen. B. F. Butler calls and asks that Philip Read of Mass (Dracut) may be sent to West-Point. Is now just past 17.

[1] AD, DLC-RTL. Philip Reade entered West Point in 1865, but did not graduate.

To the Senate[1]

To the Senate of the United States: February 10, 1863

In answer to the resolution of the Senate of yesterday, requesting information touching the visit of Mr. Mercier to Richmond, in April last, I transmit a report from the Secretary of State, to whom the resolution was referred.   ABRAHAM LINCOLN

Washington, 10th. Feby., 1863.

[1] DS, DNA RG 46, Senate 37A F2. Seward's report of February 9 concerning the visit of Henri Mercier, the French minister, reads in part:

"That no suggestions were made to M. Mercier by the Secretary of State that induced, or were designed or calculated to induce, him to undertake a mission to Richmond in April last, or at any other time. He was not then, nor has he or any other person ever been, authorized by this government or by the Secretary of State to make any representations of any·kind or on any subject to the . . . so-called authorities at Richmond, or to hold any communication with them on behalf of this government. . . .

"Since the fourth of March, 1861, no communication, direct or indirect, formal or informal, has been held by this government, or by the Secretary of State, with the insurgents, their orders, or abettors. No passport has been granted to any foreign minister to pass the military lines except by the President's direction, and each of such ministers who has received such passport has, on his return, waited upon the President as well as the Secretary of State, and given them such account, unasked, as he thought proper of the incidents of his journey.

"Of course, these statements are to be qualified so far as the facts relating to communications concerning the exchange of prisoners and other military matters. . . ."

To Edwin M. Stanton[1]

I suppose these papers are superseded, by what the Secretary did yesterday.   A. LINCOLN

Feb. 10. 1863.

1 AES, DLC-Stanton Papers. Lincoln's endorsement is written on a letter from Governor Richard Yates, Ozias M. Hatch and Jesse K. Dubois, February 2, 1863, relating the danger of insurrection in Illinois. The Democrats had won the election in 1862, and as in Indiana were attempting to rule as well as legislate. See Lincoln's note to Stanton introducing Colonel Robert Kirkham, February 9, *supra*.

To Edwin M. Stanton[1]

Hon. Sec. of War   Executive Mansion
My dear Sir   February 11, 1863.

Mr. Senator Henderson and Mr. Representative Rollins, are so anxious to have something done for Edward H. Castle [Casth?], of Mo, that I ask you to see them, and oblige them if you can consistently with law and propriety.   [A. LINCOLN]

1 ALS, IHi. The signature has been cut off this letter. No further reference has been found, and Edward H. Castle (Casth?) has not been further identified.

To Whom It May Concern[1]

                                                   Executive Mansion
Whom it may concern.   Washington, February 11, 1863.

Major General Butler, bearer of this, visits the Mississippi River, and localities thereon, at my request, for observation. The Military and Naval Commanders, whom he may meet, will please facilitate his passage from point to point, and make him as comfortable as possible during his stay with them respectively. I will thank them also to impart to him such information as they may possess, and he may seek, not inconsistent with the military service.

                                                   A. LINCOLN

1 ADS, DLC-Butler Papers. See Lincoln to Stanton January 23 and to Butler January 28, *supra*. A draft of an order is preserved in the Lincoln Papers with emendations in Stanton's autograph and dated February 17, 1863, which ordered (1) Butler's return to command of the Department of the Gulf and the creation of a separate department in Texas under command of General Nathaniel P. Banks; (2) the creation of a new department "as soon as the navigation of the Mississippi is opened . . . to consist of the Department of the Gulf, —and so much of the Mississippi valley as is contained south of Cairo, in the States of Missouri and Arkansas on the west Bank and of Kentucky west of the Cumberland River, Western Tennessee and Mississippi on the Eastern Bank of the River, . . . to be called the Department of the Gulf and the Mississippi. . . . command assign[ed] to Maj. Gen Butler," and (3) authorized Butler "to enlist and organize such forces as he may deem expedient within these Departments. . . ." (DLC-RTL). The order was never issued, however, and Butler did not return to New Orleans.

To Henry W. Halleck[1]

Major Gen. Halleck

Executive Mansion
Feb. 12. 1863.

Gen. Meagher, now with me, says the Irish Brigade has had no promotion; and that Col. Robert Nugent &; Col. Patrick Kelly, both of that Brigade have fairly earned promotion. They both hold commissions as Captains in the regular army. Please examine their records with reference to the question of promoting one or both of them. Yours truly   A. LINCOLN

[1] ALS, owned by Charles W. Olsen, Chicago, Illinois. Colonel Patrick Kelly was killed in action June 16, 1864, and Colonel Robert Nugent was not brevetted brigadier general until March 13, 1865.

To William S. Rosecrans[1]

Majr. General Rosecrans.
Murfreesboro, Tenn.

Executive Mansion
Washington, Feb. 12, 1863.

Your despatch about "River Patrolling" received. I have called the Sec. of Navy, Sec. of War, and General-in-Chief, together and submitted it to them, who promise to do their very best in the case. I can not take it into my own hands without producing inextracable confusion.   A. LINCOLN

[1] ALS, RPB. General Rosecrans telegraphed on February 11: "The enemy will direct all its operations to intercept our connection. To prevent this it is absolutely necessary to patrol the rivers. Information in possession of the commanding General and post Commanders must be promptly acted upon. It is, therefore, absolutely necessary to have the gunboats which co-operate in that work directed to report to, and receive instructions from, the general commanding, or, in his absence, the commanders along the river districts. The officers commanding gunboats express a willingness to co-operate with the department, but in order to make their aid effective and prompt, such arrangements should be made." (OR, I, XXIII, II, 57).

To the Senate[1]

To the Senate of the United States: February 12, 1863

In answer to the resolution of the Senate of the 10th. instant, requesting information on the subjects of mediation, arbitration, or other measures looking to the termination of the existing civil war, I transmit a report from the Secretary of State and the documents by which it was accompanied.   ABRAHAM LINCOLN

Washington, 12th. Feby., 1863.

¹ DS, DNA RG 46, Senate 37A F3. Seward's report of February 12, enclosing copies of letters and extracts of letters which passed between the Department of State and various representatives of foreign powers relative to mediation, arbitration, and other proposals for ending the war, may be found in Thirty-seventh Congress, Third Session, *Senate Executive Document No. 38.*

To the Senate¹

To the Senate of the United States: February 12, 1863

On the 4th of September, 1862, Commander George Henry Preble, U.S. Navy, then senior officer in command of the Naval force off the harbor of Mobile, was guilty of inexcusable neglect in permitting the armed steamer Oreto, in open daylight, to run the blockade. For his omission to perform his whole duty on that occasion and the injury thereby inflicted on the service and the country, his name was stricken from the list of Naval officers and he was dismissed the service.

Since his dismissal earnest application has been made for his restoration to his former position by Senators and Naval officers, on the ground that his fault was an error of judgment, and that the example in his case has already had its effect in preventing a repetition of similar neglect.

I therefore, on this application and representation, and in consideration of his previous fair record, do hereby nominate George Henry Preble to be a commander in the Navy, from the 16th July, 1862, to take rank on the active list next after Commander Edward Donaldson, and to fill a vacancy occasioned by the death of Commander J. M. Wainwright.²   ABRAHAM LINCOLN.

Washington, D.C., 12 February, 1863.

¹ *Executive Journal*, XIII, 129. Commander George H. Preble of Maine was supported for reinstatement principally by William P. Fessenden. His restoration was confirmed by the Senate on February 21, 1863.

² Jonathan M. Wainwright was killed in action at Galveston, Texas, on January 1, 1863.

To the Senate¹

To the Senate of the United States: February 12, 1863

On the 24th August, 1861, Commander Roger Perry, U.S. Navy. was dismissed from the service under a misapprehension in regard to his loyalty to the Government, from the circumstance that several oaths were transmitted to him and the Navy Department failed to receive any recognition of them. After his dismissal, and upon his assurance that the oath failed to reach him and his readiness to execute it, he was recommissioned to his original position on the 4th September following. On the same day, 4th September, he was ordered to command the sloop-of-war Vandalia; on the 22d this order was revoked and he was ordered to duty in the Mississippi squadron, and on the 23d January, 1862, was detached sick, and has since remained unemployed. The Advisory Board, under the act of 16th July, 1862, did not recommend him for further promotion.

This last commission having been issued during the recess of the Senate expired at the end of the succeeding session, 17 July, 1862, from which date, not having been nominated to the Senate, he ceased to be a commander in the Navy.

To correct the omission to nominate this officer to the Senate at its last session, I now nominate Commander Roger Perry to be a commander in the Navy, from the 14th September, 1855, to take his relative position on the list of commanders not recommended for further promotion.   ABRAHAM LINCOLN.

Washington, D.C., 12th February, 1863.

1 *Executive Journal*, XIII, 129-30. Commander Roger Perry of Maryland was confirmed by the Senate on February 21, 1863.

To Edward Bates[1]

Attorney General will please have a pardon made out for Robert B. Nay, mentioned within.   A. LINCOLN

Feb. 13. 1863.

1 AES, DNA RG 204, U.S. Pardon Attorney, A 456. Lincoln's endorsement is written on a letter from Major General Nathaniel P. Banks, January 24, 1863, transmitting the record in the case of Robert B. Nay, former chief of police in New Orleans. See Lincoln to Bates, January 13, *supra*.

To Simon Cameron[1]

Hon. Simon Cameron   Executive Mansion,
Harrisburg, Penn.   Washington, Feb. 13, 1863.

Gen. Clay is here, & I suppose the matter we spoke of will have to be definitely settled now. Please answer.   A LINCOLN

1 ALS, RPB. Cameron replied to Lincoln's telegram on February 15, as follows:

"I was in Phila Friday & yesterday, and only got your Telegram this morning.

"I will come to Washington, as soon as I can leave Harrisburg—but it may not be until Saturday next. I hope this short delay will put Mr Clay to no inconvenience." (DLC-RTL).

On February 23 Cameron tendered his resignation as minister to Russia, and on the next day Lincoln nominated Cassius M. Clay to replace him.

Endorsement Concerning Mr. Wright[1]

Would see Mr. Wright any time.   A. LINCOLN
Feb. 13. 1863.

[1] AES, RPB. The endorsement has been clipped from an envelope.

To Galusha A. Grow[1]

Washington, February 13, 1863.

Sir: I herewith communicate to the House of Representatives, in answer to their resolution of the 18th of December last, a report from the Secretary of the Interior, containing all the information in the possession of the department respecting the causes of the recent outbreaks of the Indian tribes in the north-west, which has not heretofore been transmitted to Congress.

Hon. Galusha A. Grow,   ABRAHAM LINCOLN.
Speaker of the House of Representatives.

[1] Thirty-seventh Congress, Third Session, *House of Representatives Executive Document, No. 68*. Secretary Usher's report, concluding that the "real cause of outbreak is difficult, if not impossible, to determine," may be found in the same source.

Memorandum
Concerning Transfer of Richard W. Johnson[1]

Executive Mansion, Washington, Feb. 13. 1863.

To-day, Hon. Mr. Yeaman, of Ky, calls and asks that Gen. R. W. Johnson, may be transferred from Gen. Rosecrans command to that of Gen. Wright. Mr. Yeaman says he does this at the request of Gen. Johnson   A. LINCOLN

[1] ADS, CSmH. Brigadier General Richard W. Johnson had commanded the Second Division of the right wing of the Fourteenth Corps, Army of the Cumberland, in the Stone's River campaign, December 26, 1862–January 5, 1863. The returns for January, 1863, list Colonel William H. Gibson in command of the Second Division, but those for February and later list Johnson back in the same command. George H. Yeaman was congressman from Owensboro, Kentucky.

To the Senate[1]

To the Senate of the United States.   February 13, 1863

I transmit to the Senate, in answer to their Resolution of the 12th instant, the accompanying report from the Secretary of State.

Washington, February 13th, 1863.   ABRAHAM LINCOLN

[1] DS, DNA RG 46, Senate 37A F3. The resolution of February 12, 1863, introduced by Lot M. Morrill, called upon the president for information concerning the employment by the French Emperor of African Negro troops in Mexico. Secretary Seward's report of February 13 enclosed along with other corroborating evidence a copy of a letter from William S. Thayer, consul at Alexandria, Egypt, January 9, 1863, reporting that the viceroy of Egypt had placed 450 Negro soldiers on the French transport *La Seine* to be used in the expedition to Mexico.

To Edwin M. Stanton[1]

Sec. of War, please examine & give me his opinion of this case.

Feb. 13. 1863.   A. LINCOLN

[1] AES, DLC-RTL. Lincoln's endorsement is written on a letter from Major General William W. Burns, February 12, 1863, asking an investigation of the stoppage of royalties on a tent which he and Colonel Ebenezer S. Sibley had jointly patented and which the army had adopted in 1861. Stanton replied on February 14 that payment was stopped by order of Secretary Cameron "probably on the ground that an officer in the service cannot charge the government for the use of his invention," and added that upon his own request for an opinion, the judge advocate general had likewise decided against the payments. "The ruling is not satisfactory to my mind. . . . But the claim being decided against by my predecessor and by the law officer of the Department whose opinion . . . is entitled to great consideration I have not felt myself authorised to allow a claim. . . ." (*Ibid.*).

To Henry W. Halleck[1]

February 14, 1863

Submitted to Gen. Halleck, with the remark that the object— matching the Cavalry raids of the enemy—is a most desireable one. The particular project, the Gen. in-Chief must judge of.

Feb. 14. 1863.   A. LINCOLN

[1] AES, DNA WR RG 108, HQA, A 1755, Box 56. Lincoln's endorsement is written on what seems to be a copy, with no signature or date, of a request from an officer in the Army of the Cumberland that he be permitted to organize an independent command of cavalry and mounted infantry to counter the effect of Confederate cavalry raiders. No clue has been found as to its authorship, but see Lincoln's letter to Rosecrans, February 17, *infra*.

To Edwin M. Stanton[1]

Hon. Sec. of War.   Executive Mansion,
My dear Sir: Washington, February 14, 1863.
Will you please let me see the papers mentioned to us some time last summer, by Gen. Halleck as convicting Fitz Henry Warren of fraud in connection with the payment of a regiment. Yours truly
                                                    A. LINCOLN

[1] ALS, NHi. Brigadier General Fitz-Henry Warren, formerly editor of the Burlington, Iowa, *Hawk-Eye* (1844-1849) and assistant editor of the New York *Tribune* (1861), wrote Lincoln from Rolla, Missouri, February 8, 1863:
"I appeal to your sense of justice, and your impartial intelligence for permission to defend myself against a false charge of 'fraud'"
"For that purpose, I most respectfully ask permission to visit Washington" (DLC-RTL).
The Register of letters received by the Adjutant General's Office lists a presidential request of March 21, 1863, for leave for General Fitz-Henry Warren to visit Washington to explain his case, but the original letter is missing (DNA WR RG 94, P 178). General Warren remained in service and was brevetted major general on August 24, 1865, after being mustered out of service on August 5.

To Edward Bates[1]

Hon. Attorney General   Executive Mansion,
Dear Sir: Washington, Feb. 16. 1863.
Nathan Darling, Captain of the Capitol Police, was fined forty dollars and charged with costs, for arresting two persons in the Lobby of the Gallery of the H.R. on the occasion of Reading Washington's Farewell Address Feb. 22. 1863.[2] He supposing he was performing his official duty. The fine was imposed in the Criminal Court upon indictment. I have concluded to remit the fine, if considered lawful for me to do so. Please make out the proper paper, if you deem it within my power. Yours truly,   A. LINCOLN

[1] ALS, DNA RG 204, U.S. Pardon Attorney, A 460. On February 22, 1862, Washington's birthday was elaborately observed in Washington. Part of the scheduled ceremony was the presentation to congress of captured Confederate flags, to be followed by the reading of Washington's Farewell Address. Representative John J. Crittenden, however, introduced a resolution opposing acceptance of the flags on the ground that they were flags of pirates and rebels and represented no recognized government. After heated debate his resolution was adopted 70 to 61, to the vast disappointment of the crowd in the gallery, and the pursuant ceremony was disrupted by a commotion in the audience. (Washington *Daily Globe*, February 22, 1862). Captain Nathan Darling was indicted by a grand jury in March, on the complaint of Milton L. Brosius that he "with force of arms did make assault did then and there beat and ill treat. . . ." The case was continued to the June term of the Criminal Court, when Darling entered a plea of guilty, and on July 25 was sentenced to pay a fine of twenty

dollars and costs. The envelope containing Lincoln's letter to Bates bears the following endorsement by Benjamin B. French, commissioner of public buildings: "The President wrote the within & handed it to me this morning. Will you have the kindness to attend to it as soon as you conveniently can and oblige." On February 18, 1863, Lincoln signed Darling's pardon.

2 Lincoln's date is obviously an error for "1862."

To Edwin M. Stanton[1]

Submitted to the War-Department. If consistent with the public interest I would like for *Gen. Logan* to be obliged in this case.

Feb. 16. 1863.   A. LINCOLN

1 AES, IHi. Lincoln's endorsement appears on a letter from General John A. Logan, January 3, 1863, recommending Lieutenant C. C. Williams, his acting assistant quartermaster, for appointment as quartermaster. No further reference has been found.

To Edwin M. Stanton and Gideon Welles[1]

Hon. Secretary of War &   Executive Mansion,
Hon. Secretary of the Navy.   Washington, February 16, 1863

Gentlemen   Please appoint an officer from each of your Departments, for the purpose of testing the incendiary shell, & incendiary fluid, of A. Berney, and reporting to me whether it would be proper to introduce the shell, or the fluid, in some other form, one or both, into the Military or Naval service of the United States.
Yours truly   A. LINCOLN.

1 ALS, ICHi. This letter has been separated from the documents which once accompanied it in the War Records, but a copy of Stanton's endorsement dated February 17 is preserved in the Naval Records, indicating appointment of Captain Stephen V. Benét of the ordnance department, who was stationed at West Point. A copy of a later (undated) endorsement of the Navy Department indicates appointment of three officers, Captain Timothy A. Hunt, Captain John S. Chauncey, and Commodore John S. Missroon, to act for the Navy in making the tests (DNA WR NB RG 45, Executive Letters, No. 114a). An unsigned report dated February 20, 1863, summarized several tests by the Navy of Alfred Berney's fluid and incendiary shells, dating from March and April, 1862, all of which indicated unsatisfactory results (DLC-RTL). On April 28, 1863, Assistant Secretary of War Peter H. Watson enclosed a report from Captain Benét dated April 10, which stated that "the trial was satisfactory, & for incendiary purposes I do not hesitate to recommend it to the Department." (*Ibid.*). Alfred Berney was a chemist at Jersey City, New Jersey.

Memorandum: Appointment of Edgar Harriott[1]

[c. February 17, 1863]

A direct descendant of one who never was a father.

¹ AE, DLC-RTL. Lincoln's endorsement is written on a florid letter from Edgar Harriott, New York, February 17, 1863, to Mrs. Lincoln, asking her influence in obtaining his appointment as acting assistant paymaster in the Navy and claiming to be "a direct decendent of John Randolph of Roanoke." Harriott was indeed poorly informed as to his ancestry, in view of what the *Dictionary of American Biography* refers to as the "universal contemporary opinion that he [John Randolph] was impotent . . . verified after his death."

Memorandum Concerning Interview with W. H. Tyler and Committee¹

The President will be pleased to see the Committee at 7. P.M. today.

Feb. 17. 1863.

¹ AE, DLC-RTL. Lincoln's endorsement is written on the envelope containing a letter from W. H. Tyler, chairman of a committee of citizens of New York, February 17, 1863, asking an interview in which to present resolutions concerning colonization of Florida with "armed free labor colonies." The resolutions prepared by William C. Bryant and adopted by a meeting at Cooper Institute on February 7 had been sent to Lincoln on February 8, and as early as November 6 and 28, 1861, the scheme had been the subject of letters written to the president by Eli Thayer (DLC-RTL).

To William S. Rosecrans¹

Executive Mansion, Washington,

Major General Rosecrans.   February 17, 1863.

My dear Sir: In no other way does the enemy give us so much trouble, at so little expence to himself, as by the *raids* of rapidly moving small bodies of troops (largely, if not wholly, mounted) harrassing, and discouraging loyal residents, supplying themselves with provisions, clothing, horses, and the like, surprising and capturing small detachments of our forces, and breaking our communications. And this will increase just in proportion as his larger armies shall weaken, and wane.² Nor can these raids be successfully met by even larger forces of our own, of the same kind, acting merely on the *defensive*. I think we should organize proper forces, and make *counter-raids*. We should not capture so much of supplies from them, as they have done from us; but it would trouble them more to repair railroads and bridges than it does us. What think you of trying to get up such a corps in your army? Could you do it without any, or many additional troops (which we have not to give you) provided we furnish horses, suitable arms, and other appointments? Please consider this, not as an order, but as a suggestion. Yours truly   A LINCOLN

[*Endorsement*]

While I wish the required arms to be furnished to Gen. Rosecrans, I have made no promise on the subject, except what you can find in the within copy of letter   A. LINCOLN
    March 27, 1863.

1 ADfS, DLC-RTL; copy and AES, DLC-Stanton Papers. Lincoln sent a copy of this letter to Stanton with the endorsement as reproduced. See Lincoln's endorsement to Halleck, February 14, *supra*. No reply from General Rosecrans has been located.
2 Lincoln deleted semicolon and "if they ever shall" after "wane."

To the Senate[1]

To the Senate   Executive Office,
    of the United States,   February 17. 1863,
    I transmit, herewith, for the constitutional action of the Senate thereon, a Treaty made and concluded, on the 3d. day of February 1863, between W. W. Ross, Commissioner, on the part of the United States, and the Chiefs and Head-men of the Pottowatomie Nation of Indians, of Kansas, which, it appears from the accompanying letter, from the Secretary of the Interior, of the 17th. instant, is intended to be amendatory of the treaty concluded with said Indians, on the 15th. November 1862.   ABRAHAM LINCOLN

1 DS, DNA RG 46, Senate 37B C11. On February 18, the treaty was referred to the committee on Indian Affairs and ordered to be printed. On December 18, 1868, it was recommitted, and on February 16, 1869, finally rejected.

To Timothy P. Andrews[1]

PayMaster-General,   Executive Mansion
Dear Sir   Washington, Feb. 18. 1863.
    You will oblige me if you will send me in writing the items, and amount of each, in which *Major Wilson received* or *charged,* more than was lawful for him to take. Yours truly   A LINCOLN

1 ALS, DLC-RTL. Paymaster General Andrews wrote his answer on the back of Lincoln's letter the same day:
"The charges referred to were made of the money received by Major N. G. Wilcox, late an addl. Pay Master, for the transportation of two servants, never transported on various journeys from Illinois to Louisville—Louisville to St. Louis—St. Louis to Leavenworth—Leavenworth to St. Louis—in 1861 & 1862.
"I was in St. Louis & several PM's informed me of the abuse & of his boasting of having done so: and, in giving him an order to return to Louisville Kentucky

gave him an order to refund all the monies so drawn from the Qr. Masters Dept., which he alledges he did do. I cannot give the dates or names records being at St. Louis except that the order to him to refund was in the Spring or Summer of last year 1862."

On February 23, Lincoln directed that Major Wilcox's dismissal be rescinded and that his resignation be accepted to take effect February 21, 1863 (AGO *General Orders No. 47*, February 23, 1863).

Memorandum:
Appointment of Henry R. Tucker[1]

Executive Mansion   Feb. 18. 1863

To-day, Hon. I. N. Arnold calls with Col. Tucker, of Chicago, and asks that his son, Henry Russell Tucker, 16 next July, be sent to West-Point. Col. T. has just lost his only other son in battle, & has himself been in charge of Camp Douglas.

[1] AD, DNA WR RG 94, U.S. Military Academy, 1863, No. 168, Box 82. Joseph H. Tucker, a Chicago commission merchant, was colonel of the Sixty-ninth Illinois Infantry, a three-months regiment. His son Henry R. is not listed at West Point. His other son, Captain Lansing B. Tucker, also of the Sixty-ninth Illinois, died in August, 1862.

To the Senate[1]

To the Senate of the United States: February 18, 1863

I transmit to the Senate for consideration, with a view to its rati-fication, an Additional Article to the treaty between the United States and Great Britain, of the 7th. of April, 1862, for the sup-pression of the African slave trade, which was concluded and signed at Washington on the 17th. instant by the Secretary of State and Her Britannic Majesty's Minister accredited to this Gov-ernment.   ABRAHAM LINCOLN

Washington, 18th. Feby. 1863.

[1] DS, DNA RG 46, Senate 37B B7. On February 27 the Senate unanimously agreed to the additional article, and ratifications were exchanged by Great Britain and the United States on April 1, 1863. The article added the coasts of Madagascar, Puerto Rico, and San Domingo to those of Africa and Cuba stipu-lated in the treaty as the areas to be patrolled.

To William H. Seward[1]

Hon. Sec. of State   Executive Mansion
My dear Sir   Feb. 18. 1863

I have two not *very* important matters, upon which I wish to consult the Cabinet. Please convene them, say at 10. A.M. to-morrow. Yours truly   A. LINCOLN

¹ ALS, owned by Richard F. Lufkin, Boston, Massachusetts. Welles' *Diary* records the meeting on February 19 as discussing the expediency of an extra session of the Senate, which Chase favored and Seward opposed and the others expressed "no very decided opinion." The proclamation convening the Senate on March 4 was issued on February 28, *infra*. Welles also mentions discussion of whether the president should accept an invitation to preside at a religious meeting on Sunday evening, February 22. "Chase favored it. All the others opposed it but Usher, who had a lingering, hesitating, half-favorable inclination to favor it. . . ." Concerning this meeting see Lincoln's letter to Alexander Reed, February 22, *infra*. Bates' *Diary* mentions an additional discussion of "brevetting the meritorious *regular* officers, among whom promotion is so slow. . . ."

To John P. Usher¹

Sec. of Interior, please see my old friend, Dr. Henry, now from Oregon   A. LINCOLN.

Feb. 18. 1863.

¹ ALS, ORB. On February 3, Anson G. Henry, surveyor general of Washington Territory, had written Lincoln a ten-page letter concerning affairs in Oregon and Washington Territory in general and Indian affairs in particular (DLC-RTL).

To William H. Herndon¹

William H. Herndon   Washington, D.C.,
Springfield, Ills.   February 19. 1863

Would you accept a job of about a month's duration at St. Louis, five dollars a day & mileage? Answer.   A LINCOLN

¹ ALS, RPB. Herndon's reply to Lincoln's telegram is not in the Lincoln Papers and has not been located, but a letter from Herndon to Nicolay, March 3, 1863, requested that, ". . . If you preserved the letter which I wrote to you declining the office which the Presdt offered me please send it to me. I didn't save a copy. Don't forget to write to me & send the letter." (DLC-RTL).

To the Senate¹

To the Senate of the United States: February 19, 1863

Congress on my recommendation passed a resolution, approved 7th February, 1863, tendering its thanks to Commodore Charles Henry Davis for "distinguished service in conflict with the enemy at Fort Pillow, at Memphis, and for successful operations at other points in the waters of the Mississippi River."

I therefore, in conformity with the 7th section of the act approved 16th July, 1862, nominate Commodore Charles Henry Davis to be a rear-admiral in the Navy, on the active list, from the 7th February, 1863.

Captain John A. Dahlgren, having in said resolution of the 7th

February, in like manner, received the thanks of Congress "for distinguished service in the line of his profession, improvements in ordnance, and zealous and efficient labors in the ordnance branch of the service, I therefore, in conformity with the 7th section of the act of 16th July, 1862, nominate Captain John A. Dahlgren to be a rear-admiral in the Navy, on the active list, from the 7th February, 1863.

The 9th section of the act of July, 1862, authorizes "any line officer of the Navy or Marine Corps to be advanced one grade, if, upon recommendation of the President by name, he receives the thanks of Congress for highly distinguished conduct in conflict with the enemy, or for extraordinary heroism in the line of his profession;" and Captain Stephen C. Rowan and Commander David D. Porter having each, on my recommendation, received the thanks of Congress for distinguished service, by resolution of the 7th February, 1863, I do therefore nominate Captain Stephen C. Rowan to be a commodore in the Navy, on the active list, from the 7th February, 1863.

Commander David D. Porter to be a captain in the Navy, on the active list, from the 7 February, 1863.

If this nomination should be confirmed there will be vacancies in the several grades to which these officers are nominated for promotion.   ABRAHAM LINCOLN.

Washington, D.C., 19th February, 1863.

[1] *Executive Journal*, XIII, 151. The promotions of Davis and Dahlgren were confirmed by the Senate on February 27, 1863, and those of Rowan and Porter on February 2, 1864.

To Thurlow Weed[1]

Mr. T. Weed: Executive Mansion,
Dear Sir   Washington, Feb. 19, 1863.

The matters I spoke to you about are important; & I hope you will not neglect them. Yours truly   A. LINCOLN

[1] ALS, NRU. On the bottom of the page and continuing on the back are the signatures of New York merchants who pledged $1,000 each as follows: Charles Knapp; Marshall O. Roberts; Alexander T. Stewart; Isaac Bell; William H. Aspinwall; Cornelius Vanderbilt; James Mitchell; H. B. Cromwell; Novelty Iron Works, Horace Allen, Pres.; James T. Sanford; Spofford & Tileston; J. F. Winslow; Secor & Co.; and P. S. Forbes. Russell Sturges and Henry W. Hubbell pledged $1,000 together. In the *Life of Thurlow Weed, Including His Autobiography and a Memoir* . . . , edited by Harriet A. Weed, Boston, 1883-1884 (II, 434-35) an account of the circumstances which occasioned Lincoln's note and Weed's raising of the money is quite specific about everything except the purpose for which the money was needed, but quotes Lincoln as follows: "Mr. Weed, we

are in a tight place. Money for legitimate purposes is needed immediately; but there is no appropriation from which it can be lawfully taken. I didn't know how to raise it, and so I sent for you." It is more likely that the money was raised to finance party machinery than that it was needed for purposes of government. Welles' *Diary* on February 10 noted Weed's presence in Washington: "He has been sent for, but my informant knows not for what purpose. It is, I learn, to consult in regard to a scheme of Seward to influence the New Hampshire and Connecticut elections. . . ." On March 8, Weed wrote Lincoln that "The Secession 'Petard,' in Connecticut, has probably 'hoisted' its own Engineers. Thank God for so much." (DLC-RTL). Governor Buckingham was re-elected over Democrat Thomas H. Seymour by a 2,000 majority.

To Edwin M. Stanton[1]

If consistent with the service, I would like for my friend, Major Fell, to be obliged, as within requested.   A. LINCOLN

Feb. 20. 1863.

[1] AES, IHi. Lincoln's endorsement is written on a letter from Jesse W. Fell to David Davis, February 20, 1863, asking that he present to Lincoln, Fell's case for a leave of absence of two or three months for reasons of health and business. Fell resigned his commission on December 26, 1863.

To Edward Bates[1]

Attorney General please send me a nomination according to the within.   A LINCOLN

Feb. 21, 1863

[1] Copy, ISLA. Lincoln's endorsement is written on a letter from California members of congress, February 20, 1863, requesting appointment of Stephen J. Field as circuit judge in California. Field's appointment was confirmed by the Senate on March 10, 1863.

Memoranda: Appointment of John Wilson[1]

Executive Mansion, Washington, Feb. 21, 1863.

To-day Hon. John S. Watts, and many others from Arizona, ask that John Wilson, of Chicago be Surveyor General for that territory.

John Wilson—Chicago.
Surveyor General
     Arizona.

I now understand Mr. Wilson does not desire this appointment.

[February 23, 1863?]

[1] AD, DLC-RTL. The second of the two notations is written on the envelope containing the first and is dated on the basis of a report that John Wilson of Chicago had declined the appointment during an interview with the president on February 23 (New York *Times*, February 25, 1863).

To Edwin M. Stanton[1]

Hon. Sec. of War   Executive Mansion
My dear Sir.   Washington, Feb. 21. 1863.

George W. Phipps, of Philda., is brother-in-law to Senator Foster; and I am led to think, he has more than common qualifications for, say, a Pay-Mastership. I shall really be glad if an Additional Pay Mastership can be given him. Yours truly

A. LINCOLN

[1] ALS, NHï. No record has been found of an appointment for Lafayette S. Foster's brother-in-law George W. Phipps, but see Lincoln's letters to Mrs. L. H. Phipps and to Stanton, March 9, *infra.*

To Edwin M. Stanton[1]

February 21, 1863

What says the Pay Master General to the case?

[1] Copy, DNA WR RG 107, Secretary of War, Register of Letters Received, P 30. The original endorsement and papers are missing, but the register indicates that Lincoln's endorsement referred papers in the case of Major Ezra Wolf, dismissed from service as paymaster. No further record of Ezra Wolf has been located.

To Alexander Reed[1]

Rev. Alexander Reed   Executive Mansion
My dear Sir   Washington, February 22, 1863

Your note by which you, as General Superintendent of the U.S. Christian Commission, invite me to preside at a meeting to be held this day at the Hall of the House of Representatives in this city, is received.

While, for reasons which I deem sufficient, I must decline to preside, I can not withhold my approval of the meeting, and it's worthy objects. Whatever shall be sincerely, and in God's name, devised for the good of the soldier and seaman, in their hard spheres of duty, can scarcely fail to be blest. And, whatever shall tend to turn our thoughts from the unreasoning, and uncharitable passions, prejudices, and jealousies incident to a great national trouble, such as ours, and to fix them upon the vast and long-enduring consequences, for weal, or for woe, which are to result from the struggle; and especially, to strengthen our reliance on the Supreme Being, for the final triumph of the right, can not but be well for us all.

The birth-day of Washington, and the Christian Sabbath, co-

[114]

inciding this year, and suggesting together, the highest interests of this life, and of that to come, is most propitious for the meeting proposed. Your Obt. Servt.   A. LINCOLN

¹ ADfS, DLC-RTL; LS-F, ISLA. See note to Lincoln's letter to Seward, February 18, *supra*. The letter of invitation from the U.S. Christian Commission of February 12, 1863, signed by George H. Stuart and others, reads in part:

"Under the auspices of the U.S. Christian Commission public meetings have been recently held in Phila. and New York, to be followed up by another next Sunday night in Boston, and it is proposed to complete the series by a final one in Washington.

"These meetings are doing great good for our countrys cause as well as for the noble men of our Army and Navy.

"If we may believe the united testimony of press and people their influence to check distrust and disloyalty and to restore confidence and support to the Government has been very great. . . .

"To give the meeting in Washington the greatest possible weight for the Sacred interests involved the House of Representatives as the place, the 22nd of February the anniversary of Washingtons birth day, as the time, and the President of the United States as the Chairman, have been suggested. . . .

"Rev Alex Reed General Superintendent for the Christian Commission is commended to your kindness, and is authorized to act in regard to the meeting. . . ." (DLC-RTL).

To Senator Wilson¹

Will Senator Wilson please call and see me.   A. LINCOLN
     Feb. 23. 1863.

¹ ALS, RPB. Whether this note was to Senator Henry Wilson of Massachusetts or to Senator Robert Wilson of Missouri is not certain.

To Henry W. Halleck¹

Major Gen. Halleck   Executive Mansion,
Dear Sir: Washington, February 24. 1863.

This morning the West-Virginia delegation call and say that the enemy contemplate invading & over-running them, in the early Spring; and that, for this object, among other things they are building a plank-road from Staunton to Beverly. To meet this our friends are anxious, first, that the 7 Virginia Infantry, and the 1st. Virginia Cavalry both now under Gen. Hooker, may be sent back to West-Virginia. These regiments are greatly reduced, ours having not more than one hundred and sixteen men. Secondly, they desire that, if, possible, a larger portion of their force in West-Virginia, should be mounted, in order to meet the increasing guerallaism with which they are annoyed & threatened.

Can these things, or some of them, be done? Yours truly
                    A. LINCOLN

[115]

[1] ALS-P, ISLA. No reply from Halleck has been located. References in the *Official Records* indicate that the Seventh Virginia Infantry and First Virginia Cavalry were not transferred as requested.

To Hannibal Hamlin[1]

The President of the   War Department, Washington City,
United States Senate.   February 25th. 1863.

Sir. In answer to the Senate Resolution of the 21st inst. I have the honor to enclose herewith a letter of the 24th Inst. from the Secretary of War, by which it appears that there are 438 Assistant Quartermasters, 387 Commissaries of Subsistence, and 343 Additional Paymasters, now in the Volunteer Service, including those before the Senate for confirmation.

I am, Sir, Very Respectfully Your Ob't Servant

ABRAHAM LINCOLN

[1] DS, DNA RG 46, Senate 37B A6, Box 9. A resolution submitted by Senator Lyman Trumbull on February 21 asked that the secretary of War be "directed to inform the Senate how many paymasters, and how many assistant quartermasters, and how many assistant commissaries, including those nominated to the Senate, there now are in the Volunteer force." (*Executive Journal*, XIII, 158).

To the Senate[1]

To the Senate of the United States: February 25, 1863

I nominate Passed Midshipman Samuel Pearce and Nathaniel T. West, now on the retired list, to be ensigns in the Navy on the retired list.

These nominations are made in conformity with the 4th section of the act to amend an act entitled "An act to promote the efficiency of the Navy," approved 16 January, 1857, and are induced by the following considerations:

The pay of a passed midshipman on the retired list as fixed by the "Act for the better organization of the military establishment," approved 3d August, 1861, amounted, including rations, to $788 per annum. By the "Act to establish and equalize the grade of line officers of the U.S. Navy," approved 16 July, 1862, the grade or rank of passed midshipman, which was the next below that of master, was discontinued and that of ensign was established, being now the next grade below that of master and the only grade in the line list between those of master and midshipman. The same act fixes the pay of officers on the retired list, omitting the grade of

passed midshipman, and prohibits the allowance of rations to retired officers. The effect of this was to reduce the pay of a passed
midshipman on the retired-list from $788 to $350 per annum, or
less than half of previous rate.

This was no doubt an unintended result of the law, operating
exclusively on the two passed midshipmen then on the retired-list,
and their promotion or transfer to the equivalent grade of ensign
would not completely indemnify them, the pay of an ensign on the
retired-list being only $500 per annum. It is the only relief how-
ever which is deemed within the intention of the existing laws,
and it is the more willingly recommended in this case as there
is nothing in the character of the officers to be relieved which
would make it objectionable. These are the only cases of the kind.

Washington, D.C., February 25, 1863.   ABRAHAM LINCOLN.

[1] *Executive Journal*, XIII, 194-95. The nominations of Samuel Pearce and
Nathaniel T. West were confirmed by the Senate on March 10, 1863.

To Edward Bates[1]

Attorney General please send me a nomination according to the
within.   A. LINCOLN
    Feb. 26. 1863.

[1] AES, CSmH. Lincoln's endorsement is written on a letter from the senators
and three of the four representatives from Michigan, February 2, 1863, asking
appointment of Solomon L. Withey of Grand Rapids as U.S. judge for the
Western District of Michigan. See Lincoln to Russell and Dickey, February 27,
infra. Withey's appointment to the new district was confirmed by the Senate on
March 11, 1863.

To Jesse K. Dubois[1]

Hon. J. K. Dubois   Washington, D.C.,
Springfield, Ills.   February 26, 1863
    Gen. Rosecrans repeatedly urges the appointment of William P.
Carlin as a Brigadier General. What say you now?

                                            A LINCOLN

[1] ALS, RPB. General Rosecrans telegraphed Lincoln on January 28, 1863,
that Colonel William P. Carlin of the Thirty-eighth Illinois "ought to have been
made Brigadier long ago. His conduct in the recent battle of Stone river doubly
deserves it. . . . I hope you will promote him." (DLC-RTL). Carlin's promotion was confirmed by the Senate on March 9, 1863. The reason for Lincoln's
telegram to Dubois may be suggested by Dubois' letter of December 3, 1862,
complaining that the army was controlled by Democrats and that Democrats
received all the promotions (DLC-RTL). No reply from Dubois has been found.

Memorandum:
Appointment of William W. Danenhower[1]

Feb. 26. 1863.

To-day William W. Danenhower says that the Fourth Auditor of the Treasury will probably resign in April next; and that if so, and when, he wishes to be appointed to the place.

[1] AD, DLC-RTL. Stephen J. W. Tabor of Iowa received the appointment, but Danenhower is listed as chief clerk under Tabor in the *U.S. Official Register,* 1863.

To Edward Bates[1]

If the judgment of the Attorney General concurs, let a pardon be made out, conditioned on taking oath and giving bond, as within.

Feb. 27. 1863.   A. LINCOLN

[1] AES, DNA RG 204, U.S. Pardon Attorney, A 465. Lincoln's endorsement is written on a letter from Bland Ballard, February 21, 1863, accompanying a petition from William Welch of Jefferson County, Kentucky, for pardon of his son William G. Welch, who had joined the Confederate army and who had an indictment for treason pending against him, but wished to take the oath of allegiance and return home.

To Joseph Hooker[1]

Executive Mansion,
Major Gen. Hooker   Washington, Feb. 27. 1863.

If it will be no detriment to the service I will be obliged for Capt. Henry A. Marchant, of Company I, 23rd. Pennsylvania Vols, to come here, and remain four or five days.   A. LINCOLN

[1] ALS, IHi. Hooker's chief-of-staff, General Daniel Butterfield, replied on the same day, "The necessary order, as requested, has been issued in the case of Captain Merchant. . . . General Hooker just left for Washington." (*Report of the Joint Committee on the Conduct of the War,* 1865, I, 198). Henry A. Marchant of Philadelphia was an artist who had been associated with his brother Edward D. Marchant in the painting of portraits and miniatures. During February, 1863, Edward D. Marchant was engaged in painting the portrait of Lincoln which is now owned by the Union League Club of Philadelphia. The genesis of this portrait is explained by John W. Forney's letter to Lincoln, December 30, 1862, introducing Edward D. Marchant, who "has been empowered by a large body of your personal and political friends to paint your picture for the Hall of American Independence. . . ." (DLC-RTL). Presumably Edward D. Marchant may have suggested to Lincoln the desirability of a consultation with his relative and associate, Captain Henry A. Marchant. See further, Lincoln to Hooker, March 5, *infra.*

To Montgomery C. Meigs[1]

What I said within for Lieutenant Baker to be a Commissary I now say for him to be a Quarter Master.   A. LINCOLN.

Feb 27– 1863,

1 AES, owned by Anson M. Henry, Olympia, Washington. Lincoln's endorsement is written on an envelope which at one time contained Lincoln's letter to Taylor, January 31, *supra.* See also Lincoln's endorsement to Taylor, February 5, *supra.* Edward D. Baker was appointed captain and assistant quartermaster on March 13, 1863.

Memorandum: Appointment of John C. Mallery[1]

Executive Mansion, Washington, Feb. 27. 1863.

To-day Hon. Mr. Babbitt, of Penn. strongly urges the appointment of *John C. Mallery,* son of Judge Garrick Mallery, for West-Point. Mr. Babbitt is very earnest & anxious on this subject.

1 AD, DNA WR RG 94, U.S. Military Academy, 1862, No. 187, Box 80. John C. Mallery, son of Garrick Mallery, a Philadelphia lawyer who had served in the Pennsylvania legislature (1827-1831) and as judge of the Third District of Pennsylvania (1831-1836), entered West Point in 1863 and graduated in 1867.

Memorandum
Concerning Report on California Trade[1]

Several Senators and Representatives call this day and urge that this Resolution be attended to by the next meeting of Congress.

Feb. 27. 1863.

1 AE, DLC-RTL. Lincoln's endorsement is written on a duplicate copy of a resolution adopted in the Senate on July 12, 1862: "Resolved, That the President be requested to have prepared a full Report of the Foreign and Domestic Trade and commerce of the States of California and Oregon and Washington Territory, to be submitted at the next Session of Congress for the use of the Senate." No record has been found of any communication from Lincoln to the Senate in answer to this request.

To Alfred Russell and Charles Dickey[1]

Alfred Russell & Charles Dickey   Executive Mansion,
Detroit, Mich.   Washington, Feb. 27, 1863.

The bill you mention in your despatch of yesterday was approved and signed on the 24th. of this month.   A LINCOLN

1 ALS, RPB. The despatch from Russell and Dickey has not been located, but it probably referred to the act approved on February 24 "to divide the State of Michigan into two Judicial Districts and to provide for holding the District and

Circuit Courts therein." Alfred Russell and Charles Dickey were U.S. Attorney and U.S. Marshal, respectively, for the Eastern District of Michigan, as listed in the *U.S. Official Register* for 1863.

To Barney Williams[1]

Mr. Barney Williams   Executive Mansion
My dear Sir—   Washington, Feb. 27, 1863.

Your note of today is received. I do not think I can put your nephew among the first ten appointments now soon to be made. I really wish to oblige you; but the best I can do is to keep the papers, and try to find a place before long. Yours truly,

A. LINCOLN

[1] Copy, CSmH. The letter from Williams has not been located. Barney Williams (Bernard O'Flagerty) was a popular blackface minstrel and Irish comedian who amassed a considerable fortune. His nephew has not been identified, but it is probable that he was asking a West Point appointment.

Memorandum
Concerning the New York *Herald*[1]

[February 28, 1863?]

It is important to humor the Herald. Is there any objection to Hanscoms telegraphing the proclamation?

[1] AD, DLC-RTL. The date assigned to this memorandum in the Lincoln Papers has been followed because of insufficient evidence to the contrary. Simon P. Hanscom was reporter for the New York *Herald* and in 1863 became editor of the Washington, D.C., *National Republican*. Lincoln's memorandum (probably to Seward) concerning Hanscom's request may have referred to the proclamation of February 28 *infra*, convening the special session of the Senate, but in view of the interest of New York papers in receiving advance copies of the Emancipation Proclamation, it seems possible that the undated note may have been written *circa* December 31, 1862.

Proclamation Convening the Senate[1]

February 28, 1863
By the President of the United States of America:

A Proclamation.

Whereas objects of interest to the United States require that the Senate should be convened at twelve o'clock on the fourth of March next, to receive and act upon such communications as may be made to it on the part of the Executive:

Now, therefore, I, Abraham Lincoln, President of the United States, have considered it to be my duty to issue this my Proclamation, declaring that an extraordinary occasion requires the Senate of the United States to convene for the transaction of business at the Capitol, in the City of Washington, on the fourth day of March next, at twelve o'clock at noon on that day, of which all who shall at that time be entitled to act as members of that body are hereby required to take notice.

Given under my hand and the seal of the United States at Washington, the twenty-eighth day of February, in the [L.S.] year of our Lord one thousand eight hundred and sixty-three, and of the Independence of the United States of America, the eighty-seventh.   ABRAHAM LINCOLN

By the President:
WILLIAM H. SEWARD, Secretary of State.

[1] DS, DNA FS RG 11, Proclamations. See note from Lincoln to Seward, February 18, *supra.* The necessity for the special session was a backlog of appointments and promotions which required Senate confirmation.

To the Senate[1]

To the Senate of the United States: February 28, 1863
In compliance with the resolution of the Senate of the 26th. instant, requesting a copy of any correspondence which may have taken place between me and working men in England, I transmit the papers mentioned in the subjoined list.

Washington, 28th. Feby. 1863.   ABRAHAM LINCOLN

[1] DS, DNA RG 46, Senate 37A F2. See Lincoln's letters to the Workingmen of Manchester, January 19, and to the Workingmen of London, February 2, *supra.* The correspondence transmitted is printed in Thirty-seventh Congress, Third Session, *Senate Executive Document No. 49.*

To the Senate and House of Representatives[1]

February 28, 1863
To the Senate and House of Representatives:
I transmit for the consideration of Congress, a despatch to the Secretary of State from the United States Consul at Liverpool, and the address, to which it refers, of the distressed operatives of Blackburn, in England, to the New York Relief Committee, and to the inhabitants of the United States generally.

Washington, 28th. Feby. 1863.   ABRAHAM LINCOLN

[1] DS, DNA RG 46, Senate 37A F2. The despatch from Thomas H. Dudley, U.S. Consulate, Liverpool, England, February 3, 1863, enclosed a memorial from "the distressed operatives of Blackburn," expressing thanks for kindness and sympathy and the hope that the war might come "to a speedy termination in favor of freedom, regardless of race or color." The memorial suggested further that "the benevolent object you have in view would be more effectually accomplished by affording to distressed operatives free or assisted passages to some port in the United States, where employment could be afforded them. This plan, your memorialists feel convinced, would be infinitely preferable to that of sending provisions for distribution by the relief committee of England. . . ."

To Edwin M. Stanton[1]

Executive Mansion, Washington,
Hon. Sec. of War.   Feb. 28, 1863.

My dear Sir   Mr. Eastman says you said he would have to come to me about the guns, or something to that effect. Do you know any law giving me control of the case? If so, please say so in writing. Yours truly   A. Lincoln

[1] ALS, IHi. Arthur M. Eastman of Massachusetts was a manufacturer of arms. Stanton's reply has not been located.

To Salmon P. Chase[1]

Executive Mansion, Washington,
Hon. Secretary of the Treasury: March 2, 1863.

My Dear Sir: After much reflection, and with a good deal of pain that it is adverse to your wish, I have concluded that it is not best to renominate Mr. Howard, for collector of internal revenue, at Hartford, Connecticut. Senator Dixon, residing at Hartford, and Mr. Loomis, representative of the district, join in recommending Edward Goodman for the place, and, so far, no one has presented a different name. I will thank you, therefore, to send me a nomination, at once, for Mr. Goodman. Yours truly,   A. Lincoln.

[1] Robert B. Warden, *Account of the Private Life and Public Services of Salmon Portland Chase* (1874), p. 524. Mark Howard's appointment as collector of internal revenue for the First District in Connecticut had been opposed by Senator James Dixon, with the result that the Senate rejected the appointment on February 26. Chase replied on March 2:

"This morning I received your note directing me to send the nomination proposed by Mr. Dixon & Mr. [Dwight] Loomis & was about replying to it, when the Senator called & we talked the matter over. The result of our conversation was an agreement to call on you as soon as practicable and submit the matter to you for further consideration. I do not insist on the renomination of Mr. Howard and Mr. Dixon & Mr. Loomis, as I understand, do not claim the nomination of his successor.

"I shall be glad if this shall prove acceptable to you. My only object—and I think you so understand it—is to secure fit men for responsible places, without

[122]

admitting the right of Senators or Representatives to control appointments for which the President & the Secretary as his presumed adviser must be responsible. Unless this principle can be practically established I feel that I cannot be useful to you or the country in my present position." (DLC-RTL).

On March 9, Welles' *Diary* records, "Had a call from Senator Dixon. Is depressed and unhappy. Regrets that he opposed the confirmation of Howard. Says if the subject was to be gone over again his course would be different. . . . He proposed several names for the place. I had no other candidate than my old friend James G. Bolles, and he, though naming two or three others, fell in with it." The appointment of James G. Bolles was confirmed by the Senate on March 12.

To Salmon P. Chase[1]

Executive Mansion, Washington, March 2, 1863.

My dear Sir: Your note in relation to the collectorship at Hartford is just received. It is a little difficult for me to read; but as I make it out, the matter is now temporarily suspended by agreement of yourself and Senator Dixon; and with which, of course, I am satisfied. Yours, truly,   A. LINCOLN

[1] NH, VIII, 222.

To Salmon P. Chase[1]

Executive Mansion, Washington, March 2, 1863.

My dear Sir: I see an act under which an assistant collector of the port of New York is to be appointed. Nobody has applied to me for it. Have you any applications or any particular wishes upon the subject? Yours truly,   A. LINCOLN.

[1] NH, VIII, 221. No reply from Chase has been located. The *U.S. Official Register*, 1863, lists Charles P. Clinch as assistant collector for the Port of New York. An act approved March 3, 1863, provided for the appointment.

To the Senate and House of Representatives[1]

March 2, 1863

To the Senate and House of Representatives

I transmit to Congress a copy of a Preamble and Joint Resolutions of the Legislative Assembly of the Territory of New Mexico, accepting the benefits of the Act of Congress approved the 2d of July, last, entitled "An Act donating public Lands to the several States and Territories, which may provide colleges for the benefit of Agriculture and the Mechanic Arts."   ABRAHAM LINCOLN

Washington, 2d March, 1863.

[123]

[1] DS, DNA RG 46, Senate 37A F2. The resolutions of the territorial legislature accepted the grant and instructed the governor that all monies accruing should be placed in the hands of curators of the industrial college to be located at Santa Fe.

To David P. Holloway[1]

March 4, 1863

The writer of this letter is an acquaintance and friend of mine, & I believe, an honest and true man, & I introduce him as such.

A. LINCOLN.

[1] Parke Bernet Catalog 272, April 2, 1941, No. 438. According to the catalog description, Lincoln's endorsement is written on a letter from Jonathan Haines asking an introduction to the commissioner of patents in order to press his claim for an extension of his patent on a harvesting machine.

To Miguel de San Roman[1]

March 4, 1863

Abraham Lincoln,
President of the United States of America.

To His Excellency The Marshal Don Miguel San Roman,
Constitutional President of the Republic of Peru.

Great and Good Friend: I have received the letter which you addressed to me on the 29th. October last, informing me of Your Excellency's elevation to the Presidency of the Republic by the free suffrages of your fellow-citizens and offering to me assurances of your desire to cultivate the relations established between our respective Governments.

I congratulate your Excellency upon this token of the confidence of the people of Peru, and I am satisfied that your Excellency's experience and statesmanship will be constantly exerted for the best interests of the Republic. It shall be my constant desire so to conduct the relations of this Government that Your Excellency may always look to the United States as a faithful and true friend.

I pray Your Excellency to accept the assurances of my earnest wishes for your personal happiness and for the prosperity of Peru.

And so, commending you to the care of the Almighty, I remain Your Excellency's Good Friend.   ABRAHAM LINCOLN.

By the President:

WILLIAM H. SEWARD, Secretary of State.

Washington, 4 March, 1863.

[1] Copy, DNA FS RG 59, Communications to Foreign Sovereigns and States, III, 202-203.

To Joseph Hooker[1]

Executive Mansion, Washington D.C., March 5, 1863.
Major General Hooker, Commanding Army of the Potomac:
For business purposes, I have extended the leave of absence of
Capt. Henry A. Merchant, [Marchant] 23d Pennsylvania volun-
teers, five days, hoping that it will not interfere with the public
service. Please notify the regiment to-day.   A. LINCOLN.

[1] Thirty-eighth Congress, Second Session, *Report of the Joint Committee on
the Conduct of the War* (1865), I, 200. See Lincoln's letter to Hooker February
27, *supra*. No reply from Hooker has been found.

Receipt from Francis E. Spinner[1]

March 5, 1863
Received, March 5. 1863. of A. Lincoln, President of the United
States the sum mentioned within, in "Green-backs"

F. E. SPINNER
Treasurer of the United States

[1] AD, DLC-RTL. With the exception of Spinner's signature, the receipt is in
Lincoln's autograph accompanying a letter dated at Brooklyn, March 2, 1863,
and signed "Candide secure," as follows:
"Enclosed you will find Eight hundred and sixty eight dollars which came
by in a dishonest manner and which I return to the United States through you
"Being tempted, in an unguarded moment, I consented to take it being very
much in want of money but thanks be to my Saviour I was led by the influences
of the Holy Spirit to see my great sin and to return it to you as the representative of the United States
"Hoping you will pardon, me in the name of the government you represent
as I trust I will be pardoned by my Father who is in heaven (through the
merits and mediation of Jesus Christ his son)."
The envelope which contained the letter and money is addressed to Lincoln
"Care of 'Adams & Co Express.' " In the upper left-hand corner the envelope is
endorsed in an unidentified hand "$900 from Wm Johnson," and on the verso
Lincoln endorsed first in pencil and later in ink, "Stolen money returned." It
is uncertain whether the "from Wm Johnson" is meant to designate the person
who stole and returned the money, or merely the messenger who carried the
money from Lincoln to the Treasurer's office. William H. Johnson, Lincoln's
part-time valet and messenger of the Treasury Department, was probably the
person designated.

Memorandum Concerning Henry Baxter[1]

[Executive Mansio]n
[Washington, Mar]ch 6. 1863.
Senator Chandler says Col. Baxter crossed the Rappahannock
with boats when Pontoniers shrunk back.

[125]

¹ AD, IHi. The bracketed portion has been restored by the editors. Severely wounded at Fredericksburg, Lieutenant Colonel Henry Baxter, commanding the Seventh Michigan Volunteers, had secured a bridgehead across the Rappahannock while a pontoon bridge was completed by Union forces. He was appointed brigadier general of Volunteers on March 12, 1863.

To Edwin M. Stanton¹

If this appointment can be consistently made, I shall be glad.
March 6. 1863.   A. LINCOLN

¹ AES, owned by Gordon A. Block, Philadelphia, Pennsylvania. Lincoln's endorsement, as well as concurring endorsements by General William T. Sherman and Colonel Giles A. Smith of the Eighth Missouri Volunteers, is written on a letter from Colonel George B. Hoge of the One Hundred Thirteenth Illinois Volunteers, February 2, 1863, recommending Lieutenant William A. McLean, quartermaster of Hoge's regiment, for appointment as assistant quartermaster in the Regular Army. McLean was not appointed to the Regular Army, but was appointed captain and commissary of subsistence of Volunteers on May 18, 1864.

To William H. Seward¹

Hon. Sec. of State   Executive Mansion,
My dear Sir   Washington, March 7, 1863.
Please call over, and bring the "Marque & Reprisal" bill with you. Yours truly   A LINCOLN.

¹ ALS, RPB. The act approved March 3, 1863, authorized the president to issue to private armed vessels letters of marque and general reprisal and to make all needful rules and regulations for the government and conduct thereof. The act was passed as a possible counterstroke to rebel vessels being built in English shipyards. Employment of such letters was discussed in cabinet meetings on March 10, 13, and 17. Seward and Chase favored, and Bates and Welles opposed the action, on the ground that it might lead to war with Great Britain. See Bates' and Welles' *Diaries* under these dates.

To Edwin M. Stanton¹

                                                    March 7, 1863
I incline to think there is some mistake in this case. Will the Sec. of War please inquire what Gen. Hooker personally knows about it?   A. LINCOLN
    March 7. 1863.

¹ AES, DLC-RTL. Lincoln's endorsement is written on a letter from Colonel Moses N. Wisewell of the Twenty-eighth New Jersey Volunteers, March 3, 1863, asking investigation of the dismissal of Lieutenant William Berdine on charges of disloyalty. Succeeding endorsements are concluded by General Joseph Hooker's endorsement of March 24, "The investigation which has been had . . . seems to establish the propriety of the order dismissing Lieutenant Berdine." See Lincoln's endorsement, April 8, *infra*.

To Edwin M. Stanton[1]

March 7, 1863

According to appointment I had a talk with Gen. Fremont last evening. I promised to try to have him told something definite by this evening. Please see Gen. Halleck to-day; and if you can get him half agreed, I agree.

[1] Stan. V. Henkels Catalog 1243, October 22, 1919, No. 311. According to the catalog description, this communication is an autograph letter signed. No reply from Stanton has been located. The proposed new command for Frémont did not materialize, reportedly because of Halleck's opposition, and on March 17, Frémont left Washington for New York highly disgruntled (New York *Tribune*, March 18, 1863).

To Edwin M. Stanton[1]

I understand the Secretary of War, knows of this case, and I incline to think something should be done in it.   A. LINCOLN

March 7, 1863.

[1] AES, IHi. Lincoln's endorsement is written on a letter from James W. Fenton, Kankakee, Illinois, March 2, 1863:

"Having been for many years past a hearty supporter and laborer in your cause . . . I take the liberty of imploring you to discharge the poor Boys in the U.S. service that were recruited from this state for the Marine Artillery, and at least to discharge my son Alonzo Fenton and prospective son in law George M Wood

"My son, a weak & feeble boy, having had for some years past the consumption, and desirous of serving his country, but unable to endure the hardship of the Land service, . . . was induced to enlist in the Marine Artillery. Both he & Wood are lying in prison at Newbern N.C. . . where they have been imprisoned by the Provost Marshall . . . for no reason but refusing to join a different branch of the service from that in which they enlisted. . . . The *United voice* of the State cries against retaining those men in the service. The Legislature have had to demand their discharge as they should never have been called upon to do, & I believe never would have been necessary, if you had known all the facts. . . ."

The letter is also endorsed by Peter H. Watson, assistant secretary of War, referring the matter to the adjutant general "for investigation and report," but no further reference has been found.

A somewhat different picture is presented by Headquarters Department of North Carolina, *General Orders No. 64*, December 4, 1862: "A portion of the Marine Artillery having forfeited their right to any benefits from the investigating court now sitting on their case by their disgraceful and mutinous conduct in refusing work, threatening to seize an armed United States boat, threatening to abandon a post of the United States left under their care, and other conduct most subversive to good order and military discipline, it is ordered that these men be distributed as follows: To . . . First United States Artillery . . . 50 men; to Third New York Volunteer Artillery . . . 100 men, the balance . . . to the volunteer regiments in this department. . . ."

To Benjamin F. Wade[1]

Will the Committee please call and see me at, say 8. o'clock this evening? A. LINCOLN

March 7. 1863.

[1] AES, DLC-RTL. Lincoln's endorsement is written on a letter from Senator Wade, chairman of the committee on the conduct of the war, March 7, 1863, asking that "copies of all papers & documents connected with the movements of the Army of the Potomac," requested by a Senate resolution of December 5, 1862, but never received, be furnished "with as little delay as possible, as they are very necessary to enable us to complete our labors." Wade's endorsement appearing below Lincoln's is as follows: "I will see you this evening at 8 o'clock as you suggest." No record has been found of the conference nor of Lincoln's transmittal of the requested papers. A joint resolution of March 2, 1863, extended the life of the committee for thirty days.

To Montgomery Blair[1]

I very cheerfully indorse the above indorsers, knowing nothing of Mr. Christy. A. LINCOLN

March 9. 1863.

[1] AES, IaHA. Lincoln's endorsement is written below a note signed by Senators James Harlan and James W. Grimes and others: "If the Post Master General finds it possible to make the promotion solicited within the undersigned would be personally gratified." These endorsements are no longer with the papers designated as "within," and "Mr. Christy" has not been identified.

Endorsement[1]

Can any thing be done for this Lady-friend of Marshal Lamon? I do not see how. A. LINCOLN

March 9. 1863

[1] AES-P, ISLA. Lincoln's endorsement has been clipped from an envelope. The only clue to the lady mentioned is in an extract from a letter received from Miss Maria A. Donnelly of Martinsburg, Virginia, by Ward H. Lamon, dated March 11, 1863, giving information as to conditions in Richmond from the sister of Miss Donnelly, recently released from imprisonment there. (DLC-RTL).

To Anson G. Henry[1]

March 9, 1863

I know not except the Secretary of the Treasury tells me the report shows that Mr. Stevens has already had a full hearing of the charges and evidence. The report is to be shown to me.

March 9, 1863. A. LINCOLN

¹ Copy, ISLA. Lincoln's endorsement is written on the back of a letter from Anson G. Henry, March 9, 1863, which states: "I have just heard from Stevens of the Mint. He asks for a copy of the Charges Against him, and promises to disprove them so far as they affect his integrity & management of the Mint, if a little time is allowed him." Robert J. Stevens, superintendent of the Mint at San Francisco, was reported to have "appointed or retained in office dishonest or vicious men" (New York *Tribune*, March 11, 1863). He was removed from office and replaced by Robert B. Swain.

To Joseph Holt¹

Hon. Joseph Holt   Executive Mansion,
Judge Advocate General.   Washington,
My dear Sir   March 9. 1863.

I understand there is one vacancy of a Judge Advocate, under the 6th. section of the same act under which you hold your appointment. If so, please indorse on this sheet, your opinion as to whether, with reference to the service, the vacancy should now be filled; and also what army the appointee shall be assigned to. Yours truly   A LINCOLN

¹ ALS, IHi. Holt did not endorse the letter and no reply from him has been found.

Memorandum Concerning Joseph W. Fisher¹

Executive Mansion, Washington, March. 9, 1863.

Hon. Mr. Stevens asks that J. W. Fisher, now Colonel of a Penn. Regt. & commanding a Brigade, may take the place of the Gen. caught at Fairfax last night.

¹ AD, IHi. Colonel Joseph W. Fisher of the Fifth Pennsylvania was not appointed a brigadier. Brigadier General Edwin H. Stoughton of Vermont was captured in bed at 2 A.M. on March 9 during a raid by Confederate General John S. Mosby. It was of this episode that Lincoln was reported to have said "that he did not mind the loss of the Brigadier as much as he did the loss of the horses. 'For,' said he, 'I can make a much better Brigadier in five minutes, but the horses cost a hundred and twenty-five dollars apiece.'" (New York *Times*, March 11, 1863).

Memorandum Concerning William F. Smith¹

Executive Mansion, Washington, March 9, 1863.

To-day, Gen. Wm. F. Smith calls and asks that his nomination heretofore as a Major General, and his acceptance of it, by being assigned to, and taking command as a Major General, may be taken and held to be a vacation of his office as a Brigadier General of Volunteers, so that he can again take his place in the regular army.

He would also like to have a leave of absence of as long as the service will admit.

[1] AD, DLC-Stanton Papers. General William F. Smith was in command of the Ninth Corps, Army of the Potomac, from February 4 to March 17, 1863, and his next assignment was to command of a division in the Department of the Susquehanna, which he held from June 17 to August 3, 1863.

Memorandum Concerning Joseph Snider[1]

Executive Mansion, Washington, March 9, 1863.
To-day, Senator Bowden, with Mr. Boyd, & Mr. Hawxhurst,[2] one an editor & one a member of the Legislature, call and ask that Col. Joseph Snider, of the 7th. Va. now in the A.P. be a Brigadier General. He has been three times hit,—twice at Antietam with but slight injury, and once very serverly at Fredericksburg. Also has had two horses shot under him. They say Gov. Pierpoint & many of the Legislature [are] for him. He resides in Monongalia Co. West Virginia.

[1] AD, IHi. No record has been found of Colonel Joseph Snider's appointment as brigadier general.
[2] Boyd has not been further identified, but John Hawxhurst was a member of Governor Peirpoint's government at Alexandria after the admission of West Virginia to the Union.

To Mrs. L. H. Phipps[1]

Executive Mansion,
Mrs. L. H. Phipps   Washington, March 9, 1863.
Yours of the 8th. is received. It is difficult for you to understand, what is, nevertheless true, that the bare reading of a letter of that length requires more than any one person's share of my time. And when read, what is it but an evidence that you intend to importune me for one thing, and another, and another, until, in self-defence, I must drop all and devote myself to find a place, even though I remove somebody else to do it, and thereby turn him & his friends upon me for indefinite future importunity, and hindrance from the legitimate duties for which I am supposed to be placed here.? Yours &c.   A. LINCOLN

[1] ADfS, DLC-RTL. Lincoln probably did not send this letter. See his letter to Stanton, *infra.* The letter from Mrs. L. (S.?) H. Phipps of March 8, 1863, reads in part: "Mr Stanton declined making another appointment to a *Pennsylvanian* . . . but I have been told that had I applied for Mr Phipps as from Memphis . . . Mr Stanton w'd probably have nominated him—& that it is not

now too late. . . . Mr. Phipps was in business in Tennessee some years—& was driven from Memphis in the outbreak of the Rebellion—as an Abolitionist . . . &. . . . cast . . . upon the world penniless. . . . deprived of the power to support his family. . . . Can President Lincoln wonder at my coming to his aid in this way? . . ." (DLC-RTL). See also Lincoln's letter to Stanton concerning George W. Phipps, February 21, *supra.*

To Edwin M. Stanton[1]

Hon. Sec. of War: Executive Mansion,
Dear Sir   Washington, March 9. 1863.

A few days since I gave the lady, bearer of this, Mrs. Phipps, some sort of writing, favoring the appointment of her husband to be an Additional PayMaster. She thinks she failed because the application was made as from Pennsylvania, and says that it could & can be justly made from Tennessee. Please let her have it, if you consistently can either from Tennessee or any where else. Yours truly   A LINCOLN.

[1] ADfS, DLC-RTL. See Lincoln's letter to Stanton, February 21, and to Mrs. L. H. Phipps, *supra.* In addition to some uncertainty as to whether Mrs. Phipps signed her letter of March 8 as "Mrs. L. H." or as Mrs. "S. H.," and also as to whether the George W. Phipps, about whom Lincoln wrote on February 21 was the husband referred to, there is no further record available which would indicate that Lincoln ever sent either of his letters of March 9.

To Edwin M. Stanton[1]

Hon. Sec. of War.   Executive Mansion,
My dear Sir   Washington, March 9. 1863.

Please make up the order to-day, sending Gen. Sumner to Missouri—it being understood that he finishes up the Court-Martial, which will be done in two or three days. Yours truly

A. LINCOLN

[1] ALS, MeHi. AGO *Special Orders No. 114,* March 10, 1863, ordered General Edwin V. Sumner to proceed to St. Louis to relieve General Samuel R. Curtis in command of the Department of the Missouri. Sumner died on March 23, however, and Curtis remained in command until May 24, when he was succeeded by General John M. Schofield. See also Lincoln to Stanton, May 11, *infra.*

To David Tod[1]

Gov. David Tod   Executive Mansion,
Columbus, O.   Washington, March 9. 1863.

I think your advice, with that of others, would be valuable, in the selection of Provost-Marshals for Ohio.   A. LINCOLN

[1] ALS, RPB. No reply from Governor Tod has been found.

Memorandum:
Appointment of Leopold O. Parker[1]

Executive Mansion, Washington, March 10, 1863.
To-day, Leopold C. P. Cooper, of Norfolk, Va. asks that his adopted son, Leopold O. Parker, may go to West-Point. Is now in his 20th. year. Mr. Cooper says there are papers on file, from Senators Bowden & Willey. Also Messrs. Brown, Blair & Segar.[2]

[1] AD, DNA WR RG 94, U.S. Military Academy, 1863, No. 127, Box 82. Leopold O. Parker was not appointed to West Point, but he became a second lieutenant of Volunteers on January 14, 1865. Senator Lemuel J. Bowden's letter of introduction, March 7, 1863, gives the father's name as Leopold C. P. Cowper.
[2] Representatives William G. Brown, Jacob B. Blair, and Joseph E. Segar.

Proclamation Granting Amnesty to Soldiers Absent without Leave[1]

Executive Mansion, March 10, 1863.
In pursuance of the twenty-sixth section of the act of Congress, entitled "An act for enrolling and calling out the National Forces, and for other purposes," approved on the third day of March, in the year one thousand eight hundred and sixty-three, I, ABRAHAM LINCOLN, President and Commander-in-Chief of the Army and Navy of the United States, do hereby order and command, that all soldiers enlisted or drafted into the service of the United States, now absent from their regiments without leave, shall forthwith return to their respective regiments.

And I do hereby declare and proclaim, that all soldiers now absent from their respective regiments without leave, who shall, on or before the first day of April, 1863, report themselves at any rendezvous designated by the General Orders of the War Department number fifty-eight, hereto annexed, may be restored to their respective regiments without punishment, except the forfeiture of pay and allowances during their absence; and all who do not return within the time above specified shall be arrested as deserters, and punished as the law provides.

And whereas evil disposed and disloyal persons at sundry places have enticed and procured soldiers to desert and absent themselves from their regiments, thereby weakening the strength of the armies and prolonging the war, giving aid and comfort to the enemy, and cruelly exposing the gallant and faithful soldiers remaining in the ranks to increased hardships and danger, I do therefore call upon all patriotic and faithful citizens to oppose and resist the aforementioned dangerous and treasonable crimes, and to aid in restoring to their regiments all soldiers absent without leave, and to assist in the execution of the act of Congress "for enrolling and calling out the national forces, and for other purposes," and to support the proper authorities in the prosecution and punishment of offenders against said act, and in suppressing the insurrection and rebellion.

In testimony whereof, I have hereunto set my hand.

Done at the city of Washington, this tenth day of March, in the year of our Lord one thousand eight hundred and sixty-three, and of the Independence of the United States the eighty-seventh.   ABRAHAM LINCOLN.

[L.S.]

By the President:

EDWIN M. STANTON, Secretary of War.

[1] AGO *General Orders* (not numbered but between No. 57 and No. 58), 1863. In *U.S. Statutes at Large* (XIII, 775-76) this order is termed "Executive Order No. 1."

To Edward Bates[1]

Attorney General, please make out & send me a pardon for Wilbur Buckheart. The papers are with you.   A. LINCOLN

March 11. 1863.

[1] ALS, DNA RG 204, U.S. Pardon Attorney, A 439. Wilbur Buckheart (Buckhart?), who was convicted of mail robbery, has not been identified further.

Memorandum:
Appointment of Edward E. Cross[1]

Executive Mansion, Washington, March 11. 1863

This morning Senator Hale calls with Col. Edward E. Cross of 5. N.H. volunteers, asking that he may be a Brig. Gen. The Col. says he is the senior Colonel of the A.P. He has been in several battles, has been nine times hit, and appeals to his military record.

[1] AD, owned by Milton H. Shutes, Oakland, California. Colonel Cross died on July 3 of wounds received at Gettysburg on July 2, 1863.

Memorandum: Appointment of Odon Guitar[1]

Executive Mansion, Washington, March 11. 1863.

Major Rollins calls and again urges that, if possible, Col. Odon Guitar, be a Brigadier General. I believe the case is a meritorious [one].

[1] AD, IHi. Representative James S. Rollins had been a major in the Black Hawk War. His recommendations of Colonel Guitar of the Ninth Missouri State Militia Cavalry came to naught. Lincoln had nominated Guitar as brigadier general of Volunteers on January 19, but the nomination was not confirmed by the Senate. As of June 27, 1863, Guitar became brigadier general in the Missouri Militia.

To Edwin M. Stanton[1]

March 11, 1863

Submitted to the Sec. of War, with the remark, that the experiment of filling up the authorized four regiments better be made, without wasting time to get up the framework of two more.

March 11. 1863.   A. LINCOLN

[1] AES, NHi. Lincoln's endorsement is written on a telegram from Brigadier General Daniel Ullmann, New York, March 11, 1863, "I can in less than ten days organize from the names I have corps of officers for at least Two more Regiments. Please authorize me." See Lincoln to Banks, March 29, *infra*.

To Charles Sumner[1]

Hon. Charles Sumner   Executive Mansion,
My dear Sir   Washington, March 11. 1863

I still have no name for Solicitor to go to Peru. Have you? Yours truly   A. LINCOLN.

[1] ALS-F, ISLA. An act approved March 3, 1863, to carry into effect the Convention with Peru signed at Lima on January 12, 1863, authorized the appointment of a solicitor "learned in the Spanish language." No reply from Sumner has been found. The *U.S. Official Register*, 1863, lists Henry R. La Reintrie of Maryland as solicitor to Peru.

To John P. Usher[1]

March 11, 1863

If there be a vacancy at the place named, let the appointment within requested, be made. If there be two vacancies, let this appointment be to the lower one   A. LINCOLN

March 11. 1863.

[1] AES-P, ISLA. Lincoln's endorsement is written on a letter from Senator James Harlan, March 9, 1863, recommending appointment of Mahlon Wilkinson of Dakota Territory "as Indian Agent on the Missouri river above Ft. Randal." Wilkinson's appointment was made during the recess of the Senate and confirmed on March 2, 1864.

To the Senate[1]

To the Senate of the United States: March 12, 1863

I herewith transmit to the Senate, for its consideration and ratification, a treaty with the chiefs and headmen of the Chippewas of the Mississippi and the Pillagers and Lake Winibigoshish bands of Chippewa Indians.   ABRAHAM LINCOLN.

Executive Mansion, March 12, 1863.

[1] *Executive Journal*, XIII, 293. The treaty was ratified by the Senate on March 13.

To Joseph Hooker[1]

Executive Mansion,
Major General Hooker: Washington, March 13, 1863.

General Stahl wishes to be assigned to General Heintzelman, and General Heintzelman also desires it. I would like to oblige both if it will not injure the service in your army or incommode you. What say you?   A. LINCOLN.

[1] Thirty-eighth Congress, Second Session, *Report of the Joint Committee on the Conduct of the War* (1865), I, 203. Hooker replied on March 14, "No serious loss will result to the service by the transfer of General Stahl to General Heintzelman's command, provided Colonel [Percy] Wyndham, now on duty with General H., be ordered to join his regiment [First New Jersey Cavalry]." (*Ibid.*). On February 2, Samuel P. Heintzelman had been placed in command of the Twenty-second Corps and Department of Washington, and on March 17, Brigadier General Julius Stahel was assigned to command the cavalry under Heintzelman.

To William W. Morris[1]

Executive Mansion,
To the Commandant at Fort McHenry: March 13, 1863.

General:—You will deliver to the bearer, Mrs. Winston, her son, now held a prisoner of war in Fort McHenry, and permit her to take him where she will, upon his taking the proper parole never again to take up arms against the United States.

ABRAHAM LINCOLN.

[1] Allen T. Rice, ed., *Reminiscences of Abraham Lincoln*, p. 507. As described by E. W. Andrews in his reminiscence, Lincoln's order was written on an envelope containing a letter from Andrews to Lincoln stating the case of Mrs. Winston's wounded son. Andrews does not give Mrs. Winston's full name, nor that of the son, but states that she resided near Nashville, Tennessee. For details see the source.

To Isabel II[1]

March 14, 1863

Abraham Lincoln.
President of the United States of America.

To Her Majesty Dona Isabel II.
By the Grace of God and the
Constitution of the Spanish
Monarchy, Queen of Spain

Great and Good Friend I have received the letter which your Majesty was pleased to address to me on the 28th. of December announcing that the Duchess of Montpensier Your Majestys beloved sister had on the 12th of the same month happly given birth to a Prince who has received at the holy baptismal font the names of Petro de Alcantana Maria de Gudalupe Isabel Francisco de Asis Gabriel Sebastian Christina

I participate in the satisfaction afforded by this happy event and offer my sincere congratulations upon the occasion May God have, Your Majesty always in His holy keeping Your Good Friend   ABRAHAM LINCOLN

Washington 14. March 1863
By the President
WILLIAM H. SEWARD Secretary of State.

[1] Copy, DNA FS RG 59, Communications to Foreign Sovereigns and States, III, 224.

Memorandum: Promotion of George Sangster[1]

Executive Mansion,
Washington, March 14, 1863.

To-day, Gov. Hicks, with Col. Walton, Member of Md. Leg. & Mr. Ireland, Post-Master at Anapolis, and ask that Col. George Sangster, of N.Y. be promoted. These Md. people make his acquaintance [from] his commanding paroled camp at Anapolis. Senator Harris, is also for him.

[1] AD, IHi. No record has been found of a promotion for Lieutenant Colonel George Sangster of the Forty-seventh New York Militia. Thomas Ireland was the Annapolis postmaster, and "Col. Walton" was doubtless John Walton, who served one term in the House of Delegates 1861-1863.

Memorandum Concerning Isaac H. Duval[1]

March 16. 1863

H. W. Crothers, aid to Gov. Pierpoint, on behalf of the Governor & himself, asks that Col. Isaac H. Duval, of W. Virginia, & now

[136]

at Winchester with Milroy, be a Brigadier General. They want him in West-Virginia, Lightburn[2] being in Tennessee with Rosecrans. Senator Bowden joins in the request.

Both say they wish Milroy to command in West-Virginia

[1] AD, IHi. Hugh W. Crother's recommended promotion of Colonel Isaac H. Duval, Ninth West Virginia Infantry, was not fulfilled until September 24, 1864.
[2] Colonel Joseph A. J. Lightburn of the Fourth West Virginia Infantry.

Memorandum: Appointment of Henry Stevens[1]

March 16. 1863.

To-day Mr. Whaley of W. V. calls and says he has nothing to fall back upon now, except to have Rev. Mr. Stevens, appointed a chaplain for the hospital at Charleston, Kanhawa Co. Va

[1] AD, DLC-RTL. Following Representative Kellian Van Rensalear Whaley's recommendation, Reverend Henry Stevens of West Virginia was appointed hospital chaplain of Volunteers on April 13, 1863.

To Jesse O. Norton[1]

Hon. J. O. Norton   Executive Mansion,
Joliet, Ills.   Washington, March 16. 1863.

William Chumasero, is proposed for Provost-Marshal of your District. What think you of it? I understand he is a good man

A. LINCOLN

[1] ALS, RPB. No reply from former congressman Norton has been located. William Chumasero, a lawyer at Peru, Illinois, was not appointed, the appointment going to Abel Longworth.

To Edwin M. Stanton[1]

Sec. of War, please see & hear Capt. Deaw [Dean?].
March 16, 1863   A. LINCOLN

[1] Charles Retz Catalog 51, 1947. Captain Deaw has not been identified. It seems possible that the source may be in error as to the name.

Memorandum: Removal of John Lockwood[1]

[c. March 17, 1863]

I agree to this when P.M.G. sends me the papers.

[1] AE, DLC-RTL. Lincoln's endorsement is written on the envelope of a letter from Senator James R. Doolittle, March 17, 1863, recommending removal

of John Lockwood and appointment of C. Latham Sholes, as postmaster at Milwaukee. Lockwood "resigned," and Charles Wells was appointed, April 22, 1864, to take over the post effective May 1, 1864.

To William S. Rosecrans[1]

Major Genl. Rosecrans   Executive Mansion,
Murfreesboro, Tenn.   Washington, March 17, 1863.

Your telegram of yesterday just received. I write you more fully than I could communicate by the wires.   A. LINCOLN

[1] ALS, RPB. This telegram was followed by the letter, *infra*.

To William S. Rosecrans[1]

Executive Mansion,
Major General Rosecrans   Washington, March 17, 1863.

My dear Sir. I have just received your telegram saying that "The Secy. of War telegraphed after the battle of Stone River" 'Anything you & your command want, you can have,' " and then specifying several things you have requested, and have not received.

The promise of the Secretary, as you state it, is certainly pretty broad; nevertheless it accords with the feeling of the whole government here towards you. I know not a single enemy of yours here. Still the promise must have a reasonable construction. We know you will not purposely make an unreasonable request; nor persist in one after it shall appear to be such.

Now, as to the matter of a Pay-Master. You desired one to be permanently attached to your Army, and, as I understand, desired that Major Larned should be the man. This was denied you; and you seem to think it was denied, partly to disoblige you, and partly to disoblige Major Larned—the latter, as you suspect, at the instance of Paymaster-General Andrews. On the contrary, the Secretary of War assures me the request was refused on no personal ground, whatever, but because to grant it, would derange, and substantially break up the whole pay-system as now organized, and so organized on very full consideration, and sound reason as believed. There is powerful temptation in money; and it was and is believed that nothing can prevent the Pay-Masters speculating upon the soldiers, but a system by which each is to pay certain regiments so soon after he has notice that he is to pay those particular regiments that he has no time or opportunity to lay plans for speculating upon them. This precaution is all lost, if Pay-masters respectively are to serve permanently with the same regiments, and pay them over and over during the war. No special application of this has been intended to be made to Major Larned, or to your Army.

And as to Gen. Andrews, I have, in another connection, felt a little agrieved, at what seemed to me, his implicit following the advice and suggestions of Major Larned—so ready are we all to cry out, and ascribe motives, when our own toes are pinched.

Now, as to your request that your Commission should date from December 1861. Of course you expected to *gain* something by this; but you should remember that precisely so much as you should gain by it others would lose by it. If the thing you sought had been exclusively ours, we would have given it cheerfully; but being the right of other men, we having a merely arbitrary power over it, the taking it from them and giving it to you, became a more delicate matter, and more deserving of consideration. Truth to speak, I do not appreciate this matter of rank on paper, as you officers do. The world will not forget that you fought the battle of "Stone River" and it will never care a fig whether you rank Gen. Grant on paper, or he so, ranks you.

As to the appointment of an aid contrary to your wishes, I knew nothing of it until I received your despatch; and the Secretary of War tells me he has known nothing of it, but will trace it out. The examination of course will extend to the case of R. S. Thoms, whom you say you wish appointed.

And now be assured, you wrong both yourself and us, when you even suspect there is not the best disposition on the part of us all here to oblige you. Yours very truly   A. LINCOLN

1 ADfS, DLC-RTL. Rosecrans' telegram of March 16 is as follows:
"The Secretary of War telegraphed after the battle of Stone's River: 'Anything you and your command want you can have.' I asked that paymasters like other staff officers, should serve with the troops in the field. It was not granted. I then asked as a personal favor that my commission should date from December, 1861. It was not granted. I then asked that Major [Charles T.] Larned, chief paymaster of this department, might be left here, and not removed, as I have reason to believe he has been, to gratify the spleen of Colonel [Timothy P.] Andrews, who hates him on account of his dislike of the old Colonel [Benjamin F.] Larned. That was refused. When I asked that the major might stay to expedite the payment of the troops, Major [Charles M.] Terrell being then sick, that was not granted. Now I find an aide has been appointed, whom, having once recommended, I requested not to be appointed, because he went off on a spree the very night after I told him I had recommended him, hoping that he would at least quit drinking.

"After telegraphing the withdrawal, and explaining to his brother-in-law, Col. Donn Piatt, the reason, I nominated R[obert] S. Thoms, esq., a young lawyer of Cincinnati, who, paying his own way, served at the battle of Stone's

River with as much gallantry and effect as any one of the staff. This request was disregarded, and an aide appointed in spite of my request. . . ." (OR, I, XXIII, II, 146-47).

Rosecrans' appointment as major general took effect as of March 21, 1862, Grant's, as of February 16, 1862. Robert S. Thoms' nomination as captain and aide-de-camp had gone to the Senate under date of February 26, 1863, but the nomination incorrectly gave his name as "Thomas." He was appointed as of April 25, 1863. The appointment of Donn Piatt's brother-in-law, Byron Kirby, as captain and aide-de-camp to Rosecrans was confirmed by the Senate on March 11.

To Joshua F. Speed[1]

Confidential.

Executive Mansion,

My dear Speed   Washington, March 17. 1863.

I understand a Danville, Illinoisian, by the name of Lyman Guinnip, is under an indictment at Louisville, something about slaves. I knew him slightly. He was not of bad character at home, and I scarcely think he is guilty of any real crime. Please try if you can not slip him through. Yours as ever   A. LINCOLN

[1] ALS-P, ISLA. No reply from Speed has been found. Lyman Guinnip, a dealer in agricultural implements at Danville, Illinois, had served as colonel of the Seventy-ninth Illinois Volunteers from August 28 to October 17, 1862. He was indicted October 24, 1862, together with one C. G. Bradshaw for aiding a slave to escape; John Smith Speed, brother of Joshua, was foreman of the grand jury. The Circuit Court Order Book No. 9 records the disposal of the case in the May term of court, 1863: "The defendants having in the three foregoing cases deposited in court thirty-six hundred dollars in lieu of bail for their appearance and having failed to appear and suffered a default on motion of Commonwealth by attorney It is ordered that the Trustee of the jury fund pay over to him one thousand and eighty dollars being the thirty percent damages on said forfeiture which was accordingly done."

To Henry W. Davis[1]

Hon. H. W. Davis   Executive Mansion,

My dear Sir   Washington, March 18. 1863.

There will be, in the new House of Representatives, as there were in the old, some members openly opposing the war, some supporting it *unconditionally,* and some supporting it with "buts" and "ifs" and "ands." They will divide on the organization of the House—on the election of Speaker.

As you ask my opinion, I give it that the supporters of the war should send no man to congress who will not[2] go into caucus with the unconditional supporters of the war, and abide the action

of such caucus, and support in the House,[3] the person therein
nominated for Speaker. Let the friends of the government first
save the government, and then administer it to their own liking.
Yours truly   A. LINCOLN.

P.S. This is not for publication, but to prevent any[4] misunderstanding of what I verbally said to you yesterday.   A. L.

[1] ALS, MdHi; ADfS, DLC-RTL. Representative Davis replied on March 20,
1863, "Your favor of the 18th is all that could be desired & will greatly aid us
in bringing our friend to a conclusion such as the interests of the country require." (DLC-RTL). The congressman referred to has not been identified.
[2] "Pledge himself to" appears at this point in the autograph draft in the
Lincoln Papers.
[3] "Support in the House," is substituted for "vote for" in the autograph draft.
[4] "Any" does not appear in the autograph draft.

To Edwin M. Stanton[1]

Hon. Sec. of War.   Executive Mansion,
Sir.   Washington, March 19, 1863.
    Hon. John A. Gurley, Gov. of Arizona, wishes one of the Colo-
rado regiments, to be placed where it can give protection to that
Territory; and he also wishes authority to raise one regiment in
the territory. I wish you and the General-in-Chief, would consider
whether these things, one or both, can not be safely & profitably
done? Yours truly   A. LINCOLN

[1] ALS, NHi. Defeated for re-election to the House of Representatives in 1862,
John A. Gurley was appointed governor of Arizona Territory, but died in Ohio,
August 19, 1863, before his departure to take over his duties. No reply from
Stanton has been found.

To Edwin M. Stanton[1]

Will the Secretary of War please give Mr. Theobald as early an
appointment as possible, for a hearing of his business?
March 19. 1863.   A. LINCOLN

[1] ALS, KyU. Lincoln's endorsement is written on an envelope containing a
letter from Governor James F. Robinson of Kentucky, March 9, 1863, introducing Edward S. Theobald as financial agent of the state, who sought federal
funds in repayment of state funds expended in raising militia to repel Confederate raids. Robinson set forth information that Confederate forces were preparing to invade Eastern Kentucky again and plead the inability of the state
to raise troops for defense unless her treasury were reimbursed for the prior
expenditures. Stanton also endorsed the envelope, referring the matter to Brigadier General William S. Ketchum. See further, Lincoln to Stanton, March 24,
infra.

To John P. Usher[1]

Hon. Sec. of Interior   Executive Mansion,
Sir.   Washington, March 19, 1863.

Levi J. Keithly was nominated for Indian Agent for New-Mexico, and the nomination fell by the non-action of the Senate. Please send me a recess appointment for him. Yours truly

A. LINCOLN

[1] ALS, MnHi. Levi J. Keithly is listed as agent for New Mexico in the *U.S. Official Register*, 1863.

To Stephen A. Hurlbut[1]

"Cypher"

Major Gen. Hurlbut   Executive Mansion,
Memphis, Tenn.   Washington, March 20 [25?], 1863

What news have you? What from Vickburg? What from Yazoo-Pass? What from Lake Providence? What generally?

A. LINCOLN.

[1] ALS, RPB. This telegram is dated March 25 in the *Official Records,* also by Nicolay and Hay (VIII, 232), and in view of the fact that Hurlbut replied from Memphis at 4 P.M. on March 25, it seems barely possible that Lincoln dated his message erroneously. However, Hurlbut's reply was not received at Washington until 9:50 P.M. on March 27, and the condition of the telegraph may have been such as to delay receipt of Lincoln's despatch for a period of five days. Hurlbut's reply is in part as follows: "Two divisions of General Sherman's command are in Steele's Bayou, above Haynes' Bluff, and two divisions in Yazoo Pass, near Greenwood. Water runs freely into Lake Providence, but Bayou Macon is encumbered with trees. About 900 square miles of Upper Louisiana under water. Canal at Vicksburg deep enough but not wide enough. . . . All indications point to a steady abandonment of Vicksburg and concentration on Rosecrans. . . ." (OR, XXIV, III, 147).

To Whom It May Concern[1]

Executive Mansion,
Washington, March 20. 1863.

Whom it may concern   Whereas it appears to my satisfaction that Thomas W. Knox, a correspondent of the New-York Herald, has been, by the sentence of a Court-Martial, excluded from the Military Department under command of Major General Grant, and also that Gen. Thayer,[2] president of the court Martial which rendered the sentence, and Major General McClernand in command of a corps of that Department, and many other respectable persons, are of opinion that Mr. Knox's offence was technical,

[142]

rather than wilfully wrong, and that the sentence should be revoked, now therefore said sentence is hereby so far revoked as to allow Mr. Knox to return to Gen. Grant's Head-Quarters, and to remain, if Gen. Grant shall give his express assent; and to again leave the Department, if Gen. Grant shall refuse such assent.

A. LINCOLN

[1] ALS-F, ISLA. This item is misdated May 20, 1863, in Hertz (II, 895). In an article appearing in the *Herald* on January 18, 1863, Thomas W. Knox had been highly critical of General William T. Sherman's competence. Having violated Sherman's order prohibiting civilians from accompanying the expedition to Vicksburg, Knox was arrested on Sherman's orders, and tried before a general court-martial at Young's Point, Louisiana, on February 5, for "giving intelligence to the enemy directly or indirectly" (found not guilty) and for "disobedience of orders." Found guilty on the latter charge he was sentenced to be banished from the lines, not to return under penalty of imprisonment.

On April 6, Knox presented Lincoln's "To whom it may concern" to Sherman, and expressed "regret at the want of harmony between portions of the army and the press, and the hope that there may be a better feeling in the future. . . ." (OR, I, XVII, II, 893).

General Grant replied to Knox on April 6, as follows:

"The letter of the President . . . authorizing you to return to these headquarters, and to remain with my consent, or leave if such consent is withheld, has been shown me.

"You came here first in positive violation of an order from General Sherman. Because you were not pleased with his treatment of army followers, who had violated his order, you attempted to break down his influence with his command, and to blast his reputation with the public. You made insinuations against his sanity, and said many things which were untrue, and, so far as your letter had influence, calculated to affect the public service unfavorably.

"General Sherman is one of the ablest soldiers and purest men in the country. You have attacked him and been sentenced to expulsion from this department for the offense. Whilst I would conform to the slightest wish of the President, where it is formed upon a fair representation of both sides of any question, my respect for General Sherman is such that in this case I must decline, unless General Sherman first gives his consent to your remaining." (*Ibid.*, p. 894).

General Sherman replied to Knox on April 7:

"Yours of April 6, inclosing a copy of President Lincoln's informal decision in your case, is received.

"I certainly do regret that Generals McClernand and Thayer regard the disobedience of orders emanating from the highest military source and the publication of willful and malicious slanders against their brother officers as mere technical offenses, and notwithstanding the President's indorsement of that conclusion, I cannot so regard it. After having enunciated to me the fact that newspaper correspondents were a fraternity bound together by a common interest that must write down all who stood in their way, and that you had to supply the public demand for news, true if possible, but false if your interest demanded it, I cannot be privy to a tacit acknowledgment of the principle.

"Come with a sword or musket in your hand, prepared to share with us our fate in sunshine and storm . . . and I will welcome you . . . but come as you now do, expecting me to ally the reputation and honor of my country and my fellow-soldiers with you, as the representative of the press, which you yourself say makes so slight a difference between truth and falsehood, and my answer is, Never." (*Ibid.*, pp. 894-95). [2] Brigadier General John M. Thayer.

To Salmon P. Chase[1]

March 21, 1863

Will the Secretary of the Treasury do me the favor to hear my old friend Dr. Henry briefly, about Victor Smith.

A. LINCOLN.

[1] Charles F. Heartman Catalog 199, December 8, 1928, No. 111. According to the catalog description this is an autograph note signed. On April 13, Henry wrote Chase a reminder of his application for the removal of Victor Smith, collector at Port Angelos, Puget Sound, "on account of the unfortunate influence which his continuance in office will exert and does exert upon the public estimation of the Administration in Washington Tery. . . ." (Copy, DLC-RTL). See further, Lincoln's letter to Chase, May 8, *infra*.

Memorandum
Appointment of Erasmus Dennison[1]

[c. March 21, 1863]

West-Point—for next year—now 1863, then 1864.

[1] AE, DNA WR RG 94, U.S. Military Academy, 1863, No. 46, Box 81. Lincoln's endorsement is written on the envelope of a letter from Governor William Dennison to Montgomery Blair, March 21, 1863, concerning appointment of his son to West Point. There is no record of Erasmus Dennison's appointment.

To Edwin M. Stanton[1]

If the Sec. of War approves, let the man Martin, be released

March 21. 1863   A. LINCOLN

[1] AES, IHi. Lincoln's endorsement appears on an undated letter from Green Adams: "I left with you some time since a letter from Mr. Walters, with a request written on it and signed by Mr. Pomeroy and my self asking that a man by the name of Martin, now in Prison in Kansas, be released. I hope it will be done I am satisfied it ought to be done & that the effect would be beneficial."

The letter from Walters endorsed by Samuel C. Pomeroy has not been found, and Martin and Walters have not been identified.

To Salmon P. Chase[1]

March 23, 1863

Submitted to the Sec. of Treasury. Mr. Williamson, writer of the within was our "Willie's" teacher; and I would be really glad for him to be obliged.   A. LINCOLN

March 23. 1863.

1 Copy, DNA FI RG 56, Treasury Department, General Records. Lincoln's endorsement is written on a letter from Alexander Williamson, March 21, 1863, which states: "There are several appointments to be made by Secretary Chase on Monday first in the 2nd., 3rd., and 5th. Auditors and also in the Quarter Masters Department. I therefore respectfully request your recommendation for a position in either of these offices." On March 28, Williamson was appointed to a temporary clerkship in the Second Auditor's Office at a salary of $1200 per year.

Memorandum[1]

[c. March 23, 1863]

The President would like to see the gentlemen who sent in a letter from the Philadelphia Board of Trade, dated the 23rd. Inst.

1 AD, DLC-RTL. Accompanying this undated note is a letter from the Office of the Board of Trade, Philadelphia, March 23, 1863, signed by Lorin Blodget, William B. Thomas, and George L. Buzby, recommending that the president order the testing of a new weapon called "Solidified Greek Fire," to be used in filling shells. On March 31, William B. Thomas acknowledged receipt of a non-extant letter from Lincoln, as follows:

"I have the honor to acknowledge the receipt of your letter of yesterdays date.

"Mr Levi Short of the state of New York is the inventor of the article known as 'Solidified Greek Fire.' I have written to him informing him of your desire to witness his experiments.

"He will doubtless await upon you in a very few days." (DLC-RTL).

The New York *Herald* reported that on March 31 "Mr. G. Rush Duer, one of the patentees of the 'liquified and solidified Greek fire,' gave a private exhibition last night in the presence of the President . . . General Martindale and Assistant Secretary of the Navy Fox, and others. . . ." (New York *Herald*, April 1, 1863).

To Horatio Seymour[1]

Private & Confidential

His Excellency   Executive Mansion,
Gov. Seymour   Washington, March 23, 1863.

Dear Sir:[2] You and I are substantially strangers; and I write this chiefly that we may become better acquainted. I, for the time being, am at the head of a nation which is in great peril; and you are at the head of the greatest State of that nation. As to maintaining the nation's life, and integrity,[3] I assume, and believe, there can not be a difference of *purpose* between you and me. If we should differ as to the *means,* it is important that such difference should be as small as possible—that it should not be enhanced by unjust suspicions on one side or the other. In the performance of my duty, the co-operation of your State, as that of others, is needed—in fact, is indispensable. This alone is a sufficient reason why I should wish to be at[4] a good understanding with you.

Please write me at least as long a letter as this—of course, saying in it, just what you think fit. Yours very truly   A. Lincoln

¹ ALS-F, ISLA; ADfS, DLC-RTL. On April 14, Governor Seymour replied in part as follows: "I have delayed answering your letter for some days with a view of preparing a paper in which I wished to state clearly the aspect of public affairs from the stand point I occupy. . . . I have been prevented from giving my views in the manner I intended by a pressure of official duties. . . . In the mean while I assure you that no political resentments, or no personal objects will turn me aside from the pathway I have marked out for myself—I intend to show to those charged with the administration of public affairs a due deference and respect and to yield them a just and generous support in all measures they may adopt within the scope of their constitutional powers. For the preservation of this Union I am ready to make every sacrifice. . . ."

² "Dear Sir:" appears only in the autograph draft in the Lincoln Papers.

³ The autograph draft has a phrase deleted at this point as follows: "and relieving it from it's peril."

⁴ In the autograph draft Lincoln substituted "at a good understanding" for "on good terms."

To Salmon P. Chase¹

March 24, 1863

Hon. Secretary of the Treasury: Please see and hear Miss Upton (Upton's Hill) who now has employment in your department and fears she may lose it.   A. Lincoln.

March 24. 1863.

¹ Copy, IHi-Nicolay and Hay Papers. No record of Miss Upton's employment has been found.

Memorandum Concerning Charles Wiegand¹

March 24, 1863

I think this man, Charles Wiegand, called on me once, or oftener; but I really know nothing as to his capacity or merit. If a Brigade was promised him by the War Department I know nothing of it; and not knowing whether he is fit for any place I could not with propriety, recommend him for any.   A. Lincoln

March 24. 1863.

¹ AES, DLC-RTL. Lincoln's endorsement is written on a letter signed "Charles Wiegand Col. I Arkansas Inft.," and dated at Washington, March 24, 1863, asking "after a long illness and suffering from wounds," to be restored "to my command, or rather the command of the brigade as promised by the War Department." Apparently a letter in reply to Wiegand gave substantially the consent of this endorsement, for on March 26 Wiegand wrote again, "Your answer to my application of March 24th is in my hands and regret that through pressure of business a former favorable decision on Your part has been obliterated and therefor would most respectfully request Your Excellency,

to have the official records as to my conduct of Generals Sigel & [Alexander] Asboth of the battle of Pea Ridge Mar 6, 7 & 8– '62; the official report from July 11-22 '62 and of the battles of Kam Hill & Boston Mountain; and the official reports of General Rosecrans in Septemb. 1862—battle of Corinth—re-examined, which I trust will refresh Your memory and no doubt will reverse Your decision above mentioned." (*Ibid.*).

Although Wiegand submitted with his letter an autograph testimonial from General Sigel, there is no further record of Lincoln's action, or of Wiegand's service.

To Edwin M. Stanton[1]

March 24, 1863

Let James H. Ledlie . . . be made a Brigadier General, if it is legally possible. I doubt if it is admissable, but if it is, let his appointment date from the Goldsboro battle.

[1] *The Collector*, July 1948, No. M 1345. According to the catalog description Lincoln's note is on a letter from John G. Foster to Henry W. Halleck, asking that Ledlie's nomination be submitted to the Senate. Colonel James H. Ledlie of the Third New York Artillery was appointed brigadier general of Volunteers as of December 24, 1862, but the appointment expired on March 4, 1863. His re-appointment was dated October 27, 1863.

To Edwin M. Stanton[1]

Can not this sum of 250,000 be paid at once? Sec. of War, please tell me.   A. LINCOLN

March 24. 1863.

[1] AES, DLC-RTL. Lincoln's endorsement is written on a letter from Joshua F. Speed and James Guthrie, March 22, 1863, which states:

"Mr. Theobald the attorney and agent for the state of Ky. who came here with an earnest letter from Governor Robinson to you, to have the accounts of the state audited and settled— finds that the 3d auditor makes requirements before he will go into an adjustment of the balance, which will cause some six or eight weeks delay.

"If this is done we fear that the very object for which the Governor asks, so small a sum as $250.000. will pass by reason of the delay. It is to aid in raising new troops that the Governor asks this money."

Stanton answered on March 25 that "An examination of the disbursements must first be made to ascertain how much is available." (*Ibid.*) On March 29, Stanton reported further:

"Upon investigation of the state of the appropriation for the supply of arms to loyal citizens of States in rebellion—July 31st 1861, p. 283, it appears that there will not remain sufficient [funds] for the purpose specified in the letter of Messrs. Speed and Guthrie herewith returned.

"Accounts are pending in the Treasury Department, which when passed, will afford to . . . Kentucky a very large sum that may be applied . . . to the purpose mentioned." (*Ibid.*).

See also Lincoln to Stanton, March 19, *supra*.

Commutation of Sentence
of James S. Pleasants[1]

March 25, 1863.

The sentence of death in this case is hereby commuted to imprisonment for during the war, in one of the military prisons to be designated by the Secretary of War.   A. LINCOLN

[1] AGO *General Orders No. 76*, March 31, 1863. Lincoln's endorsement is on the court-martial record of James Snowdon Pleasants, a citizen of Montgomery County, Maryland, convicted March 8, 1863, of feeding the enemy and knowingly harboring and protecting them.

To Benjamin Gratz[1]

Mr. Benjamin Gratz.   Executive Mansion,
Lexington, Ky.   Washington, March 25, 1863.

Show this to whom it may concern as your authority for allowing Mrs. Shelby to remain at your house, so long as you choose to be responsible for what she may do.   A. LINCOLN

[1] ALS, RPB. No communication from Benjamin Gratz which accounts for Lincoln's telegram has been located, but a letter from Gratz to Montgomery Blair, April 18, 1863, asks that "Mrs. Susan Shelby the daughter of the late Alfred Shelby and Grand-daughter of Gov. Shelby" be given a pass to visit her wounded husband, who was Colonel J. Warren Grigsby of the Confederate Sixth Kentucky Cavalry. Although Gratz's reference to her as both "Mrs. Shelby" and "Mrs. G." are confusing, other sources confirm that Mrs. Susan Shelby Grigsby was probably the woman meant.

To William S. Rosecrans[1]

Major Gen. Rosecrans   Executive Mansion,
Murfreesboro Tenn.   Washington, March 25, 1863.

Your despatches about Gen. Davis and Gen. Mitchell are received. Gen. Davis' case is not peculiar, being simply one of a great many recommended, and not nominated, because they would transcend the number allowed by the law. Gen. Mitchell was nominated and rejected by the Senate; and I do not think it proper for me to re-nominate him without a change of circumstances, such as the performance of additional service, or an expressed change of purpose on the part of at least some Senators who opposed him.

A. LINCOLN

[1] ALS, RPB. General Rosecrans telegraphed on March 24, midnight, asking appointment of Brigadier General Jefferson C. Davis, formerly colonel of the Twenty-second Indiana Infantry, as a major general. On March 25 Rosecrans telegraphed a similar request for appointment of Brigadier General Robert B.

Mitchell, formerly colonel of the Second Kansas Infantry. Neither was appointed, but Davis was brevetted major general of Volunteers as of August 8, 1864.

To Edwin M. Stanton[1]

March 25, 1863

The writer of the within,—Charles King—is President of Columbia College, N.Y.—son of *the* Rufus King of revolutionary memory, and, I believe, father of our Gen. Rufus King. If his request within, can be consistently granted, I shall be glad.

March 25. 1863.   A. LINCOLN

[1] AES, IHi. Lincoln's endorsement is written on a letter from Charles King, March 21, 1863, introducing Louis Peugnet whose son Ernest Peugnet had been appointed assistant quartermaster of Volunteers on March 16, and who wished the appointment changed to that of aide-de-camp. No further reference to the matter has been found.

To Edwin M. Stanton[1]

I remember nothing about this case; but if there is an order of mine, such as stated within, let the appointed at once [*sic*]?

March 25. 1863.   A. LINCOLN

[1] AES, DLC-RTL. Lincoln's endorsement is written on a letter from William Lilley, March 20, 1863, reviewing his inability to get action on Lincoln's "order" to Stanton of August 9, 1862, *supra*. Lilley's letter complains that "For a period of seven months therefore he [Stanton] has kept me idle, on hotel expenses, awaiting his action on *your written order*, giving me from time to time, such answers as would seem to preclude my right to leave the city." See further Lincoln to Lilley, April 2, and to Stanton, April 20 and May 9, *infra*.

To Andrew Johnson[1]

Private

Hon. Andrew Johnson   Executive Mansion,
My dear Sir: Washington, March 26. 1863.

I am told you have at least *thought* of raising a negro military force. In my opinion the country now needs no specific thing so much as some man of your ability, and position, to go to this work. When I speak of your position, I mean that of an eminent citizen of a slave-state, and himself a slave-holder. The colored population is the great *available* and yet *unavailed* of, force for restoring the Union. The bare sight of fifty thousand armed, and drilled black soldiers on the banks of the Mississippi, would end the rebel-

[149]

lion at once. And who doubts that we can present that sight, if we but take hold in earnest? If you *have* been thinking of it please do not dismiss the thought. Yours truly   A. LINCOLN

[1] ALS, NNP; ADfS, DLC-RTL. No reply from Governor Johnson has been found.

To Montgomery C. Meigs[1]

Quarter-Master-General please see the bearer a moment.
March 26. 1863.   A. LINCOLN

[1] ALS, owned by Carl E. Wahlstrom, Worcester, Massachusetts. Beneath Lincoln's note is written: "Given to me by the President. Eli Parker." Eli (Ely) S. Parker of New York was appointed assistant adjutant general with rank of captain as of May 25, 1863, but it is not certain that he was the bearer of this note.

To Edward Bates[1]

I do not remember how the record stands. Have appointments been made, as indicated within?   A. LINCOLN
March 27. 1863.

[1] AES, DNA RG 60, Papers of Attorney General, Appointments. Lincoln's endorsement is written on a letter from Lyman D. Stickney, chairman, U.S. Direct Tax Commission, and Rufus Saxton, military governor of Florida, Beaufort, South Carolina, March 16, 1863, asking that Judge Philip Fraser of the U.S. District Court for the Northern District of Florida, "with a marshall & district attorney be assigned to active duty in Florida. A vigorous effort is now being made to restore that State. . . ." Below Lincoln's endorsement is written "No Marshal & no District Attorney. In regard to Marshal recommendations of a strong character for Mr Remington—of Jacksonville. March 28. 1863." Joseph Remington's appointment as marshal was confirmed by the Senate on January 20, 1864.

To Salmon P. Chase[1]

Executive Mansion,
Washington, March 27, 1863.
Dear Sir: Governor Dickinson's business was rather with you than with me. His friend with him, Edward J. Westcott, has been trading at Newbern, and is hindered from renewing his business there. Please oblige the governor and Mr. Westcott so far as you consistently can. Yours truly,   A. LINCOLN.

[1] NH, VIII, 233-34. Daniel S. Dickinson's friend, Edward J. Westcott, has not been further identified.

To Robert B. Nay[1]

[c. March 27, 1863]

I will not say thee "Nay."

[1] AE, DLC-RTL. Lincoln's endorsement is written on a letter from Robert B. Nay, March 27, 1863, requesting an interview. See Lincoln to Bates, January 13 and February 13, *supra*.

Speech to Indians[1]

March 27, 1863

"You have all spoken of the strange sights you see here, among your pale-faced brethren; the very great number of people that you see; the big wigwams; the difference between our people and your own. But you have seen but a very small part of the pale-faced people. You may wonder when I tell you that there are people here in this wigwam, now looking at you, who have come from other countries a great deal farther off than you have come.

"We pale-faced people think that this world is a great, round ball, and we have people here of the pale-faced family who have come almost from the other side of it to represent their nations here and conduct their friendly intercourse with us, as you now come from your part of the round ball."

Here a globe was introduced, and the President, laying his hand upon it, said:

"One of our learned men will now explain to you our notions about this great ball, and show you where you live."

Professor Henry then gave the delegation a detailed and interesting explanation of the formation of the earth, showing how much of it was water and how much was land; and pointing out the countries with which we had intercourse. He also showed them the position of Washington and that of their own country, from which they had come.

The President then said:

"We have people now present from all parts of the globe—here, and here, and here. There is a great difference between this pale-faced people and their red brethren, both as to numbers and the way in which they live. We know not whether your own situation is best for your race, but this is what has made the difference in our way of living.

"The pale-faced people are numerous and prosperous because

they cultivate the earth, produce bread, and depend upon the products of the earth rather than wild game for a subsistence.

"This is the chief reason of the difference; but there is another. Although we are now engaged in a great war between one another, we are not, as a race, so much disposed to fight and kill one another as our red brethren.

"You have asked for my advice. I really am not capable of advising you whether, in the providence of the Great Spirit, who is the great Father of us all, it is best for you to maintain the habits and customs of your race, or adopt a new mode of life.

"I can only say that I can see no way in which your race is to become as numerous and prosperous as the white race except by living as they do, by the cultivation of the earth.

"It is the object of this Government to be on terms of peace with you, and with all our red brethren. We constantly endeavor to be so. We make treaties with you, and will try to observe them; and if our children should sometimes behave badly, and violate these treaties, it is against our wish.

"You know it is not always possible for any father to have his children do precisely as he wishes them to do.

"In regard to being sent back to your own country, we have an officer, the Commissioner of Indian Affairs, who will take charge of that matter, and make the necessary arrangements."

The President's remarks were received with frequent marks of applause and approbation. "Ugh," "Aha" sounded along the line as the interpreter proceeded, and their countenances gave evident tokens of satisfaction.

¹ Washington *Daily Morning Chronicle*, March 28, 1863. The *Chronicle* account of the ceremonies which preceded Lincoln's speech reads in part:

"The Executive Mansion was yesterday morning the scene of a very interesting ceremony. The Indian chiefs now in the city met the President of the United States and had a formal interview with him. The meeting took place in the East room. Quite a number of persons were present, among whom we noticed Secretaries Seward, Chase, and Welles, Daniel S. Dickinson, of New York, Professor Henry, and other celebrated personages. The Indians were all seated on the floor in a line, and around them the spectators formed a ring which, notwithstanding the assiduous yet polite efforts of Mr. Nicolay, was still too contracted to permit all to see the principal actors. The silence, which would seem to be the part of common propriety on such an occasion, was by no means observed by the restless and eager crowd of visitors. Everybody seemed to find some one's bonnet or shoulder in the way, and to think himself or herself entitled to the best and most conspicuous place. The ladies, too, could not refrain from audible comments on the speeches.

"Still everything went off very well. These Indians are fine-looking men. They have all the hard and cruel lines in their faces which we might expect in savages; but they are evidently men of intelligence and force of character. They were both dignified and cordial in their manner, and listened to everything with great interest. At half-past eleven the President entered the circle, and each one of the chiefs came forward and shook him by the hand, some of them adding a sort of salaam or salutation by spreading out the hands, and some contenting themselves with a simple shake of the hand and the inevitable 'how' of the Indians of the Plains. The following is a list of the chiefs:

"*Cheyennes.*—Lean Bear, War Bonnet, and Standing Water.

"*Kiowais.*—Yellow Buffalo, Lone Wolf, Yellow Wolf, White Bull, and Little Heart.

"*Arapahoes.*—Spotted Wolf and Nevah.

"Comanches.—Pricked Forehead and Ten Bears.

"*Apache.*—Poor Bear.

"*Caddo.*—Jacob.

"Mr. Commissioner Dole introduced them. . . .

"The President said: 'Say to them I am very glad to see them, and if they have anything to say, it will afford me great pleasure to hear them.' "

Speeches were made by Lean Bear and Spotted Wolf, through an interpreter, and by Lincoln as reported above.

To Edwin M. Stanton[1]

Executive Mansion,
Washington, March 27. 1863.

To-day Mr. Blake, of Indianapolis, asks

1. Capt. Aiken be promoted
2. Col. William H. Blake of the 9th. be promoted.
3. Col. John W. Blake of the 40th. be promoted.
4. That himself—James Blake—have something.

[Endorsement]

Submitted to the Secretary of War.   A. LINCOLN

March. 30. 1863.

[1] AD and AES, DLC. A letter from Caleb B. Smith, Indianapolis, March 23, 1863, introduced "James Blake Esq one of the oldest and most worthy citizens of this City," who "has sacrificed a very large estate to meet liabilities incurred in an effort to promote an important public enterprize." (DLC-RTL). No record has been found of his appointment or of the other promotions mentioned.

To Edwin M. Stanton[1]

Sec. of War, please have me informed as to what ground Capt. O'Hara was dismissed upon.   A. LINCOLN

March 27, 1863.

[1] AES, DLC-RTL. Lincoln's endorsement is written on a letter from Assistant Adjutant General James B. Fry to Captain Daniel O'Hara, January 22, 1863, notifying him that his appointment as assistant quartermaster of Volunteers "is hereby revoked." Stanton endorsed in reply to Lincoln's query, that O'Hara's name had been stricken from the list of nominations "upon satisfactory evidence that the appointment was one not fit to be made."

To Edwin M. Stanton[1]

March 27, 1863

Sec. of War, please see this man, who is well recommended by Mayor Opdyke.   A. LINCOLN

[1] AES, DNA WR RG 107, Secretary of War, Personnel Appointments, Box 24. Lincoln's endorsement is written on an envelope containing recommendations of Jacob Wilson by George Opdyke and others.

To Gideon Welles[1]

If there be any vacancy of a Lieutenant of Marines, I really wish the appointment within requested to be made.   A. LINCOLN
March 27. 1863.

[1] AES, ORB. Lincoln's endorsement is written on a letter of John J. Hughes, Roman Catholic archbishop of New York, February 4, 1863, asking appointment of the son (unnamed) of "Mrs. Emily Duke of Washington" as a lieutenant of Marines. No such appointment has been found.

To Nathaniel P. Banks[1]

Private

Major General Banks   Executive Mansion,
My dear Sir: Washington, March 29, 1863.

Hon. Daniel Ullmann, with a commission of Brigadier General, and two or three hundred other gentlemen as officers, goes to your department and reports to you, for the purpose of raising a colored brigade. To now avail ourselves of this element of force, is very important, if not indispensable. I therefore will thank you to help Gen. Ullmann forward with his undertaking, as much, and as rapidly, as you can; and also to carry the general object beyond his particular organization if you find it practicable. The necessity of this is palpable if, as I understand, you are now unable to effect anything with your present force; and which force is soon to be greatly diminished by the expiration of terms of service, as well as by ordinary causes. I shall be very glad if you will take hold of the matter in earnest.

You will receive from the Department a regular order upon this subject. Yours truly   A. LINCOLN.

[1] ALS, CSmH; ADfS, DLC-RTL. On January 13, Colonel Daniel Ullmann was authorized to raise a brigade of Negro Volunteers in Louisiana (OR, III, III, 14). A later order of March 24 authorized him to raise six companies of Louisiana Volunteer Infantry (*ibid.*, pp. 99-100). On March 25, Stanton issued instructions to Banks and Ullmann covering the assignment (*ibid.*, pp. 101-102). Banks acknowledged receipt of Lincoln's letter on April 17, "It gives me pleasure to assure you that I shall give him [Ullmann] every assistance . . . in carrying out your instructions. . . ." (DLC-RTL). On September 3, 1863,

Special Orders No. 50 revoked Ullmann's special powers and ordered him to report to Banks (*ibid.*, p. 766).

To Edwin M. Stanton[1]

Hon. E. M. Stanton   March 29. 1863

Sir   I fear—in fact, believe—the despatch you mentioned is utter humbuggery. I have tracked it up & found that it came from Cairo last-night to the New-York-Mercury, was printed in that paper of this morning, which came by mail to Philadelphia & is thence telegraphed to Capt. Fox.[2] Now, is it not past belief that such news would be at Cairo that length of time, and not be sent directly to us—especially as Pennock[3] is under strict orders to send every thing promptly. Besides there are no six-iron-clads, nor 15000 men at Vicksburg to pass through the canal, even if the Mississippi river had risen fifteen feet in as many minutes. Yours truly   A. LINCOLN

[1] ALS-P, ISLA. On Sunday, March 29, the New York *Mercury* printed a dispatch dated Cairo, March 28, 8 P.M., announcing the successful use of one of the canals which Grant's army was engaged in digging to by-pass the Vicksburg fortifications. A telegram from M. J. Roberts, manager of the New York telegraph office to Thomas T. Eckert, March 30, 12:10 P.M., verified that the purported dispatch was a hoax, "No dispatch for the 'Mercury' appears on the . . . Line Books Saturday." (DLC-RTL).   [2] Gustavus V. Fox.

[3] Captain Alexander M. Pennock, commanding the Naval Station at Cairo, Illinois.

Proclamation
Appointing a National Fast Day[1]

March 30, 1863

By the President of the United States of America.

A Proclamation.

Whereas, the Senate of the United States, devoutly recognizing the Supreme Authority and just Government of Almighty God, in all the affairs of men and of nations, has, by a resolution, requested the President to designate and set apart a day for National prayer and humiliation:

And whereas it is the duty of nations as well as of men, to own their dependence upon the overruling power of God, to confess their sins and transgressions, in humble sorrow, yet with assured hope that genuine repentance will lead to mercy and pardon; and to recognize the sublime truth, announced in the Holy Scriptures and proven by all history, that those nations only are blessed whose God is the Lord:

And, insomuch as we know that, by His divine law, nations like individuals are subjected to punishments and chastisements in this world, may we not justly fear that the awful calamity of civil war, which now desolates the land, may be but a punishment, inflicted upon us, for our presumptuous sins, to the needful end of our national reformation as a whole People? We have been the recipients of the choicest bounties of Heaven. We have been preserved, these many years, in peace and prosperity. We have grown in numbers, wealth and power, as no other nation has ever grown. But we have forgotten God. We have forgotten the gracious hand which preserved us in peace, and multiplied and enriched and strengthened us; and we have vainly imagined, in the deceitfulness of our hearts, that all these blessings were produced by some superior wisdom and virtue of our own. Intoxicated with unbroken success, we have become too self-sufficient to feel the necessity of redeeming and preserving grace, too proud to pray to the God that made us!

It behooves us then, to humble ourselves before the offended Power, to confess our national sins, and to pray for clemency and forgiveness.

Now, therefore, in compliance with the request, and fully concurring in the views of the Senate, I do, by this my proclamation, designate and set apart Thursday, the 30th. day of April, 1863, as a day of national humiliation, fasting and prayer. And I do hereby request all the People to abstain, on that day, from their ordinary secular pursuits, and to unite, at their several places of public worship and their respective homes, in keeping the day holy to the Lord, and devoted to the humble discharge of the religious duties proper to that solemn occasion.

All this being done, in sincerity and truth, let us then rest humbly in the hope authorized by the Divine teachings, that the united cry of the Nation will be heard on high, and answered with blessings, no less than the pardon of our national sins, and the restoration of our now divided and suffering Country, to its former happy condition of unity and peace.

In witness whereof, I have hereunto set my hand and caused the seal of the United States to be affixed.

Done at the City of Washington, this thirtieth day of March, in the year of our Lord one thousand eight hundred [L.S.] and sixty-three, and of the Independence of the United States the eighty seventh.

By the President: ABRAHAM LINCOLN
    WILLIAM H. SEWARD, Secretary of State.

¹ DS, DNA FS RG 11, Proclamations. The Senate Resolution requesting the president to proclaim a day for "national prayer and humiliation" was introduced by Senator James Harlan on March 2, and adopted on March 3, 1863.

To William A. Hammond¹

Let Rev. James Gubby be appointed Hospital Chaplain, to serve at the Hospital at Hilton-Head South-Carolina.

March 31. 1863.   A. LINCOLN

¹ AES, IHi. Lincoln's endorsement is written on a letter from Judge H. D. Smith, chairman of the tax commission at Hilton Head, South Carolina, to Senator Charles Sumner, February 26, 1863, introducing Reverend James Gubby "late chaplin of 3d R.I. Regt. and for some time detailed to the Genl. Hospital at Hilton Head. He is now desirous of being appointed as chaplain to the Genl. Hospital at Hilton Head. . . ." Reverend Gubby was appointed on April 1, 1863.

License of Commercial Intercourse¹

Washington, Executive Mansion,
March 31, 1863.

Whereas, by the act of Congress approved July 13, 1861, entitled "An act to provide for the collection of duties on imports, and for other purposes," all commercial intercourse between the inhabitants of such States as should by proclamation be declared in insurrection against the United States and the citizens of the rest of the United States, was prohibited so long as such conditions of hostility should continue, except as the same shall be licensed and permitted by the President to be conducted and carried on only in pursuance of rules and regulations prescribed by the Secretary of the Treasury; and whereas it appears that a partial restoration of such intercourse between the inhabitants of sundry places and sections heretofore declared in insurrection in pursuance of said act, and the citizens of the rest of the United States, will favorably affect the public interests:

Now, therefore, I, Abraham Lincoln, President of the United States, exercising the authority and discretion confided to me by the said act of Congress, do hereby license and permit such commercial intercourse between the citizens of loyal States and the inhabitants of such insurrectionary States in the cases and under the restrictions described and expressed in the regulations prescribed by the Secretary of the Treasury, bearing even date with these presents, or in such other regulations as he may hereafter, with my approval, prescribe.   ABRAHAM LINCOLN.

¹ NH, VIII, 238-39.

To David Hunter[1]

Private

Executive Mansion
Major General Hunter   Washington D.C. April 1. 1863.

My dear Sir: I am glad to see the accounts of your colored force at Jacksonville, Florida. I see the enemy are driving at them fiercely, as is to be expected. It is important to the enemy that such a force shall *not* take shape, and grow, and thrive, in the South; and in precisely the same proportion, it is important to us that it *shall.* Hence the utmost caution and vigilance is necessary on our part. The enemy will make extra efforts to destroy them; and we should do the same to preserve and increase them. Yours truly   A. LINCOLN

[1] ALS, CSmH. On March 10, 1863, the First South Carolina Volunteers commanded by Colonel Thomas W. Higginson and a portion of the Second South Carolina Volunteers commanded by Colonel James Montgomery reoccupied Jacksonville, Florida. Both were Negro regiments.

Order for Pardon and Release of John O. Brown[1]

War Department   Washington City,
Ordered   April 1 1863

That John O Brown under sentence of death by judgment of a Court Martial at Indianapolis be and he is hereby pardoned and absolved from the sentence aforesaid; and that he be released from imprisonment and discharged from the service of the United States. By order of the President.   A. LINCOLN

EDWIN M STANTON
Secretary of War

[1] DS, owned by Emanuel A. Gardiner, New York City. The order is in Stanton's handwriting, signed by Lincoln. On March 19, 1863, Colonel Henry B. Carrington submitted a report to Stanton and Lincoln on the activities of the Knights of the Golden Circle, "organized to break up the army. I have abundant affidavits and . . . proof. . . . Their success was considerable until the arrest and conviction of John O. Brown, now under sentence of death suspended at my request, that he may be used as a witness before the U.S. district court in May next." (OR, II, V, 363-67). See further Lincoln to Morton, July 18, *infra.*

To William Lilley[1]

Capt. William Lilly   Executive Mansion,
Sir: Washington, April 2, 1863.

Possibly there has been some misunderstanding in your case. You were nominated to, and rejected by the Senate. I have thought

[158]

it a good rule, and have tried to act upon it, not to renominate any one whom the Senate has already rejected, unless I have evidence that the Senate would do differently on a second trial. In your case I now distinctly say that if any Senator, continuing in the Senate, will say in writing, that he voted against you, and that he has since investigated the case, and would now vote for you, and that he believes you would now be confirmed, I will renominate you. Without this, or something as strong, I can not do it.
Yours truly   A. LINCOLN

1 ALS, DLC-RTL. See Lincoln's communication to Stanton concerning Lilley, March 25, *supra*, and April 20 and May 9, *infra*.

Proclamation about Commercial Intercourse[1]

April 2, 1863

By the President of the United States of America.

A Proclamation.

Whereas, in pursuance of the Act of Congress, approved July 13, 1861, I did, by Proclamation dated August 16, 1861, declare that the inhabitants of the States of Georgia, South Carolina, Virginia, North Carolina, Tennessee, Alabama, Louisiana, Texas, Arkansas, Mississippi and Florida (except the inhabitants of that part of Virginia lying West of the Alleghany mountains and of such other parts of that State and the other States hereinbefore named as might maintain a legal adhesion to the Union and the Constitution or might be, from time to time, occupied and controlled by forces of the United States engaged in the dispersion of said insurgents) were in a state of insurrection against the United States and that all commercial intercourse between the same and the inhabitants thereof, with the exceptions aforesaid, and the citizens of other States and other parts of the United States was unlawful and would remain unlawful until such insurrection should cease or be suppressed, and that all goods and chattels, wares and merchandise, coming from any of said States, with the exceptions aforesaid, into other parts of the United States, without the license and permission of the President, through the Secretary of the Treasury, or proceeding to any of said States, with the exceptions aforesaid, by land or water, together with the vessel or vehicle conveying the same to or from said States, with the exceptions aforesaid, would be forfeited to the United States:

And whereas, experience has shown that the exceptions made

in and by said Proclamation embarrass the due enforcement of said Act of July 13, 1861, and the proper regulation of the commercial intercourse authorized by said Act with the loyal citizens of said States:

Now, therefore, I, Abraham Lincoln, President of the United States, do hereby revoke the said exceptions, and declare that the inhabitants of the States of Georgia, South Carolina, North Carolina, Tennessee, Alabama, Louisiana, Texas, Arkansas, Mississippi, Florida and Virginia (except the forty-eight counties of Virginia designated as West Virginia, and except, also, the ports of New Orleans, Key West, Port Royal and Beaufort in North Carolina) are in a state of insurrection against the United States, and that all commercial intercourse not licensed and conducted as provided in said Act between the said States and the inhabitants thereof, with the exceptions aforesaid, and the citizens of other States and other parts of the United States, is unlawful and will remain unlawful until such insurrection shall cease or has been suppressed, and notice thereof has been duly given by Proclamation; and all cotton, tobacco and other products, and all other goods and chattels, wares and merchandise, coming from any of said States, with the exceptions aforesaid, into other parts of the United States, or proceeding to any of said States, with the exceptions aforesaid, without the license and permission of the President, through the Secretary of the Treasury, will, together with the vessel or vehicle conveying the same, be forfeited to the United States.

In witness whereof, I have hereunto set my hand and caused the seal of the United States to be affixed.

Done at the City of Washington, this 2d. day of April, A.D. 1863, and of the Independence of the United States [L.S.] of America, the eighty seventh.

By the President: ABRAHAM LINCOLN
WILLIAM H. SEWARD, Secretary of State.

1 DS, DNA FS RG 11, Proclamations.

To Charles F. Adams[1]

Hon. Charles F. Adams.   Executive Mansion,
My dear Sir.   Washington, April 3. 1863
    This will introduce to you, Rev. John M. Sturtevant, President of Illinois College. He visits Europe in no official character. He is a worthy and capable gentleman; and also is one of my most highly valued personal friends. I shall be much obliged for any

kind attentions you may find it convenient to show him. Your
Obt. Servt.   A. LINCOLN

¹ ALS copy, DLC-RTL. Reverend Julian M. Sturtevant wrote Lincoln on
March 27, 1863, that on the "advice and request of many friends" he would
visit England in order to present "the cause of our dear country and of universal liberty." (DLC-RTL).

To Joseph Hooker[1]

Executive Mansion,
Major General Hooker   Washington, April 3, 1863.
Our plan is to pass Saturday-night on the boat; go over from
Acquia-creek to your camp Sunday morning; remain with you
till Tuesday morning, and then return. Our party will probably
not exceed six persons of all sorts.   A LINCOLN

[1] ALS, IHi. General Hooker replied to Lincoln's telegram at 5 P.M., "Your
telegram of today has just been received by me I am rejoiced to learn that
you have appointed a time to visit this Army and only regret that your party
is not as large as our hospitality. . . ." (DLC-RTL). Bates' *Diary* records that
the party consisted of the president, Bates, Mrs. Lincoln, "Tad" Lincoln, Dr.
Anson G. Henry, Noah Brooks, and Captain Medorem Crawford of Oregon.

To Edwin M. Stanton[1]

The writer of this is a true man to my personal knowledge; and if
there can be a way found to oblige him I shall be glad.
April 3, 1863.   A. LINCOLN

[1] AES, IHi. Lincoln's endorsement appears on a letter of Brigadier General
James C. Veatch to John P. Usher, March 26, 1863, asking assistance in procuring a commission for his son Harry Veatch, who "has been with me over
a year, sharing the toils and dangers of a soldiers, without rank or pay." No
record of Harry Veatch's appointment has been found.

To John P. Usher[1]

What, if anything, does the Sec. of Interior know about this?
Apl. 3. 1863.   A LINCOLN

[1] AES, DLC-RTL. Lincoln's endorsement is written on a telegram signed "B.
Pickett," Rock Island, Illinois, April 3, 1863, "Am removed from agency Island
Rock Island without chance to be heard in defense desire investigation; will
send evidence by mail" (DLC-RTL). A clerk endorsed in reply on April 5,
"This Dept. has no information . . . & no officer there." The telegram was in
error as to the name. Lincoln's old friend Thomas J. Pickett wrote Montgom-
ery C. Meigs on April 18, that he had been removed "from the agency of the
Q.M. Department (on the Island of Rock Island) on newspaper charges, ema-

nating . . . from J. B. Danforth, editor of the Rock Island Argus. Capt. [Henry B.] Hendershott, to whom the matter was referred, gave me no opportunity to defend myself from the very serious accusation of selling (for my private benefit) government timber and stone. *I utterly and positively deny the truth of these charges.*" (DLC-RTL). On April 23, Meigs referred Pickett's letter to Stanton and Lincoln. See further Lincoln's letter to Calvin Truesdale, April 20, *infra.*

To Isabel II[1]

April 4, 1863

Abraham Lincoln.

President of the United States of America

To Her Majesty Doña Isabel II.

By the Grace of God and the Constitution of the Spanish Monarchy, Queen of Spain, &c. &c

Great and Good Friend: I have received the letter which Your Majesty was pleased to address to me on the 30th. of January last announcing that Her Royal Highness the Infanta Doña Maria Cristina, had, on the 17th. of that month happily given birth to a son, who has received at the holy baptismal font the names of Luis Jesus, Maria Isabel, José, Francisco de Asis Sebastian

I participate in the satisfaction afforded by this happy event, and offer my sincere congratulations upon the occasion.

May God have Your Majesty always in His safe and holy keeping
ABRAHAM LINCOLN

Washington, April 4th 1863

By the President

WILLIAM H. SEWARD   Secretary of State.

[1] Copy, DNA FS RG 59, Communications to Foreign Sovereigns and States, III, 226.

Memorandum:
Appointment of John M. K. Davis[1]

Executive Mansion,
Washington, April 4, 1863.

Miss Davis calls & asks for the appointment of her brother—John M. K. Davis—as a cadet—Nineteen last January—resides here where also he was born. If any of the present batch slip up I am to consider young Mr. Davis.

[1] AD, DNA WR RG 94, U.S. Military Academy, 1861, No. 215, Box 77. John M. K. Davis entered West Point in 1863 and graduated in 1867.

Memorandum Concerning Harbor Defenses[1]

April 4, 1863

On this general subject, I respectfully refer Mr. Browne to the Secretaries of War and Navy for conferrence and consultation.

I have a single idea of my own about harbor defences It is a Steam-ram, built so as to sacrifice nearly all capacity for carrying, to those of speed and strength, so as to be able to split any vessel having hollow enough in her to carry supplies for a voyage of any distance. Such ram, of course could not her self carry supplies for a voyage of considerable distance; and her business would be to guard a particular harbour, as a Bull-dog guards his master's door.

April 4, 1863. A. LINCOLN

[1] ADS, CtLHi. Mr. Browne has not been identified, but may have been the well-known boatbuilder Joseph Brown. See Lincoln to Joseph Smith and others, March 28, 1862, *supra*.

To Isaac Newton[1]

Executive Mansion
Dear Sir: Washington, April 4th. 1863.

You will please detail Dr. C. M. Wetherill Chief Chemist and F. G. Murray, Esq both of your Department for special service, to report to Capn. I. R. Diller at Philadelphia Pa for one month from date, also giving Dr. Wetherill permission to close his laboratory in the Agricultural Department during that period, and to take its key with him for the security of its contents during his absence.

Yours Truly ABRAHAM LINCOLN

The Commissioner of Agriculture

[1] Copy, DLC-RTL. On the same day, Secretary Newton wrote Wetherill as follows: "Agreeably to the request of the President . . . I detail you for special service for the period of one month from date, to report to Capt. I. R. Diller, at Philadelphia Pa. You will close your laboratory for that period, taking the key with you." (DLC-RTL). See further Lincoln to Newton, August 5, *infra*.

To Edwin M. Stanton[1]

April 4, 1863

Sec. of War please see Hon. Mr. Marvin, who recommends J. P. Butler, for Provost-Marshal for his Dist. I think attention to this case is necessary. A. LINCOLN

April 4, 1863.

[1] AES, owned by Charles W. Olsen, Chicago, Illinois. Lincoln's endorsement is written on a letter from Edwin D. Morgan, April 3, 1863, introducing Representative-elect James M. Marvin, of the Eighteenth Congressional District of

New York, who "wishes to confer with you in relation to the appointments from his district under the conscription act." James P. Butler was appointed captain and provost marshal as recommended.

Appointment of Charles E. Mix[1]

Executive Office   April 6th. 1863.

I hereby appoint Charles E. Mix to be Acting Commissioner of Indian Affairs, during the temporary absence of the Hon. William P. Dole, from the Seat of Government.   ABRAHAM LINCOLN

[1] DS, DNA NR RG 75, Office of Indian Affairs, Letters Received, Miscellaneous, p. 27. Mix was chief clerk in the Office of Indian Affairs.

Memorandum of Army Strength[1]

[c. April 6, 1863]

Technically Present for duty	136,724 —	
On other duty	33,188 —	169,912
Sick, absent & in arrest	44,855	

214,767

[1] AE, DLC-RTL. Lincoln's memorandum, jotted down on his visit to Hooker's headquarters, accompanies a confidential report submitted by Brigadier General Henry J. Hunt, chief of artillery of the Army of the Potomac, April 6, 1863.

Memorandum on Joseph Hooker's Plan of Campaign Against Richmond[1]

[c. April 6–10, 1863]

My opinion is, that just now, with the enemy directly ahead of us, there is *no* eligible route for us into Richmond; and consequently a question of preference between the Rappahannock route, and the James River route is a contest about nothing. Hence our prime object is the enemies' army in front of us, and is not with, or about, Richmond—at all, unless it be incidental to the main object.

What then? The two armies are face to face with a narrow river between them. Our communications are shorter and safer than are those of the enemy. For this reason, we can, with equal powers fret him more than he can us. I do not think that by raids towards Washington he can derange the Army of the Potomac at all. He has no distant opperations which can call any of the Army of the Potomac away; we have such operations which may call him away, at least in part. While he remains in tact, I do not think we should take the disadvantage of attacking him in his entrenchments; but we should continually harrass and menace him, so that he shall have no leisure, nor safety in sending away detachments. If he weakens himself, then pitch into him.

¹ ADf, DLC-RTL. This undated memorandum written on lined note paper is given the date April 11 by Nicolay and Hay, but since Lincoln returned to Washington on April 11, it is highly probable that the memorandum was written during his visit at Hooker's headquarters some time between April 6 and 10. Hooker's letter of April 11 (see note to Lincoln's letter to Hooker, April 12, *infra*) suggests that the plan of attack was developed in accordance with Lincoln's views as expressed in the memorandum.

Authorization for Peter H. Watson¹

April 7. 1863.

Peter H. Watson, Esq, Assistant Secretary of War is authorized to perform the duties of Secretary of War during the temporary absence of Secretary Stanton from Washington

ABRAHAM LINCOLN

¹ ADS-P, ISLA. Stanton left Washington on April 7 to attend the funeral of his brother-in-law C. P. Walcott. Peter H. Watson sent a despatch to Lincoln, who had not yet returned to the city (see Lincoln to Hooker, April 3, *supra*), notifying him of Stanton's departure and requesting that the authorization be sent by special messenger (DLC-RTL).

Endorsement Concerning William Berdine¹

[April 8, 1863?]

Lieut. William Berdine—a curious case, to be shown to Gov. Newell.

¹ AE, DLC-RTL. Lincoln's endorsement is on an envelope from the War Department which contained the record in Berdine's case (see Lincoln to Stanton, March 7, *supra*). The date April 8, 1863, is written on the envelope but not by Lincoln. It is possible that Lincoln carried the papers with him to Hooker's headquarters in order to discuss the case.

To Gideon Welles¹

Hon. Sec. of Navy   Falmouth April 8. 1863

I have Richmond papers of the 7th. They contain nothing of interest to us except a despatch as follows—

"Charleston, April 5–

Important movements are taking place here; but for military reasons no particulars can yet be telegraphed."

And an editorial in these words.

"On yesterday morning eight Monitors and iron-clads were off the bar at Charleston. This brief, but significant telegram, which we received early in the day tells of work. The storm so long prepared for Charleston has burst at last. We await the issue with buoyant hopes but not without the solicitude due so important a struggle. May Heaven shield Charleston from all the rage of her enemies and ours."

A. LINCOLN

[1] ALS, NHi. Rear Admiral Samuel F. Du Pont reported to Welles on April 8 that his attack on Fort Sumter on April 7 had been unsuccessful:

"This vessel [*New Ironsides*] could not be brought into such close action as I endeavored to get her. Owing to the narrow channel and rapid current she became partly unmanageable, and was twice forced to anchor to prevent her going ashore, once owing to her having come into collision with two of the monitors. She could not get nearer than 1,000 yards. . . . Toward evening, finding no impression made upon the fort, I made the signal to withdraw the ships, intending to renew the attack this morning. But the commanders of the monitors came on board and reported verbally the injuries to their vessels, when . . . I determined not to renew the attack, for, in my judgment, it would have converted a failure into a disaster, and I will only add that Charleston can not be taken by a purely naval attack, and the army could give me no cooperation. . . ." (*Naval Records*, I, XIV, 3).

To Gideon Welles[1]

Office of U.S. Military Telegraph,
War Department. Hd Qrs Army Potomac

Hon Secy of Navy—

Apl 9 1863.

Richmond Whig of the 8th has no telegraphic despatches from Charleston but has the following as editorial.

"All thoughts are now centred upon Charleston. Official intelligence was made public early yesterday morning that the enemies iron clad fleet had attempted to cross the bar & failed but later in the day it was announced that the gun boats & transports had succeeded in crossing and were at anchor—our iron clads lay between the forts quietly awaiting the attacks. Further intelligence is looked for with eager anxiety. The Yankees have made no secret of their vast preparation for an attack on Charleston & we may well anticipate a desperate conflict. At last the hour of trial has come for Charleston. The hour of deliverance or destruction for no one believes the other alternative, surrender, possible. The heart of the whole country yearns towards the beleagured city with intense solications [solicitude?] yet with hopes amounting to confidence. Charleston knows what is expected of her and what is due to her fame and to the relation she sustains to the cause.

The devoted, the heroic, the great hearted Beauregard is there & he too knows what is expected of him & will not disappoint that expectation. We perdict a Sarragossa defense and that if Charleston is taken it will be only a heap of ruin."

The rebel pickets are reported as calling over to our pickets to-day that we had taken some rebel fort. This is not very intelligible and I think is entirely unreliable. A LINCOLN

[1] Copy (telegram received), DNA WR NB RG 45, Executive Letters, No. 33. See Lincoln to Welles, April 8, *supra*.

Endorsement Concerning William Kellogg[1]

[c. April 11, 1863]

I understand my friend Kellogg is ill-natured—therefore I do not read his letter. A L

[1] AES, DLC-RTL. Lincoln's endorsement is written on the envelope containing ex-congressman Kellogg's letter of April 8, 1863, which reads in part:

"I am in receipt of a note from your private secretary informing me that as a 'mark' of your 'confidence and esteem' you had appointed me Consul at Valaparaiso, Chile.

"Certainly the *Honor*, attached to the office ought to satisfy the ambition of the most aspiring, and the salary (which would but little if any more than defray the expenses of myself and family to & from the place of duty,) is as much as a reasonable man should desire. Yet I feel myself compelled to decline the appointment.

"At one time, I was indiscreet enough to indicate to your Excellency a desire for an appointment to an office, for which, I was vain enough to believe I was qualified but from the position now offered, I am forced to conclude, that your Excellency held a decidedly different opinion from my own on that subject, or that my political status was such that the administration would suffer by my appointment to an office of the grade of those held by Peck, Wilmot, Olin, Fisher, Swett, Gurley and Carter and many other recent appointees.

"If I have lost the confidence and regard of those for whom I have had a most ardent esteem and whom I have most *faithfully served*, I must not loose my own self respect. I am therefore compelled to decline the position tendered."

Ebenezer Peck and David Wilmot had been appointed to the U.S. Court of Claims; Abraham B. Olin, George P. Fisher, and David K. Cartter to the U.S. Court, District of Columbia; John A. Gurley as governor of Arizona; and Leonard Swett as commissioner on Peruvian claims.

To Robert B. Mitchell[1]

Officer in Command Executive Mansion,
at Nashville, Tenn. Washington, April 11. 1863.

Is there a soldier by the name of "John R. Minnick" of Wynkoop's Cavalry, under sentence of death, by a Court-Martial, or

Military Commission, in Nashville? and, if so, what was his offence? and when is he to be executed?   A. LINCOLN

If necessary let the execution be staid till I can be heared from
again.   A. LINCOLN

[1] ALS, RPB. Brigadier General Robert B. Mitchell was in command at Nashville. John R. Minick was a private in Company K, Seventh Pennsylvania
Cavalry, commanded by Colonel George C. Wynkoop. Minick served until discharged January 6, 1865, at expiration of his term of enlistment. No reply to
Lincoln's telegram has been found.

To Carl Schurz[1]

Major General Schurz   Executive Mansion,
My dear Sir,   Washington, April 11. 1863.

I can not comply with your request to take your Division[2] from
the Army of the Potomac. Gen. Hooker does not wish it done. I do
not myself see a good reason why it should be done. The Division
will do itself, and it's officers, more honor; and the country more
service, where it is. Besides these general reasons, as I understand,
the Army of the Potomac will move, before these proposed changes
could be conveniently made. I always wish to oblige you, but I can
not in this case. Yours truly   A. LINCOLN

[1] ALS, DLC-Schurz Papers; ALS copy, DLC-RTL. Schurz's letter to Lincoln
of April 6, reads in part:
"You remember that I received the command of the 11th Corps by your order
under the Grand Division arrangement. When the latter was abolished, Gen.
Sigel resumed command of the Corps. Soon afterwards he left it on leave of
absence and . . . I assumed the command. But Gen. Hooker assigned Maj. Gen.
Howard to the command of the Corps, which reduced me to my old Division.
. . . I do not want to interfere with the arrangements already made but should
be happy to be assigned to another Department, but I cannot go without my old
troops. . . . I should be glad to be ordered off to Gen. Burnside or Gen. Rosecrans, and I am sure every man in my command would hail the order with
enthusiasm. We have always been outsiders in this Army . . . and I have no
doubt this Army will see us leave without regret, provided our place be filled
by an equal number of American troops. . . . Gen. Howard agrees with me. . .
and Gen. Hooker . . . will have no objection, if the gap left by my Division,
which is one of the smallest anyhow, can be filled with other troops. . . . If
you send me West with my boys, which I sincerely hope you will, I will take
my chance without asking for anything more, except a good opportunity to
fight." (DLC-RTL).
That Schurz did not speak for all his men is indicated by a letter from
Brigadier General Adolph von Steinwehr to Major General Oliver O. Howard,
April 5, "I am informed, that General Schurz endeavors to obtain the command of the German troops of this corps & to be ordered with them to Kentucky
or elsewhere. . . . I . . . earnestly beg you, that you will retain us in this
Corps & under your command. I hope the time is not far of[f], when these
political moves may cease. . . ." (DLC-RTL).
[2] The copy in the Lincoln Papers has the word "away" at this point.

To Edwin M. Stanton[1]

I decline to interfere in behalf of Lieut. Williams
April 11. 1863.   A LINCOLN

[1] AES, IHi. Lincoln's endorsement is written on a letter from Joseph Holt to Stanton, March 30, 1863, summarizing the facts in the case of West Point graduate, First Lieutenant John Benson Williams of the Third Infantry, dismissed from service on February 11, 1863, for deserting his company in the presence of the enemy. An unsigned endorsement preceding Lincoln's indicates that Holt's letter is "Respectfully submitted to . . . the President as requested by his note of the 18th. Ulto." Lincoln's note of March 18 has not been located.

To Joseph Hooker[1]

Washington, D.C., April 12, 1863.

Major-General Hooker: Your letter, by the hand of General Butterfield, is received, and will be conformed to. The thing you dispense with would have been ready by midday to-morrow.

A. LINCOLN.

[1] OR, I, XXV, II, 200. Hooker's letter of April 11, 1863, brought by Major General Daniel Butterfield, reads as follows:

"After giving the subject my best reflection, I have concluded that I will have more chance of inflicting a serious blow upon the Enemy by turning his position to my right, and if practicable to sever his communication with Richmond with my Dragoon force, and such Batteries as it may be deemed advisable to send with them. I am apprehensive that he will retire from before me the moment I should succeed in crossing the river, and over the shortest line to Richmond, and thus escape being seriously crippled.

"I hope that when the Cavalry have established themselves on the line between him and Richmond, they will be able to hold him and check his retreat until I can fall on his rear—or if not that, I will compel him to fall back by the way of Culpepper, and Gordonsville over a longer line than my own with his supplies cut off.

"The Cavalry will probably cross the river above the Rappahannock bridge, thence to Culpepper and Gordonsville, and across to the Aquia Railroad somewhere in the vicinity of Hanover Court House. They will probably have a fight in the vicinity of Culpepper, but not one that should cause them much delay or embarrassment.

"I have given directions for the Cavalry to be in readiness to commence the movement on Monday morning next. While the Cavalry are moving, I shall threaten the passage of the river at various points, and after they have passed well to the Enemies rear, shall endeavor to effect the crossing.

"I hope Mr. President, that this plan will receive your approval. It will obviate the necessity of detaching a force from Washington in the direction of Warrenton, while I think it will enhance my chances for inflicting a heavy blow upon the enemies forces.

"We have no news from over the river today, the enemy refusing to let us have the newspaper.

"I sincerely trust that you reached home safely, and in good time yesterday.

"We all look back to your visit with great satisfaction." (DLC-RTL).

To Andrew G. Curtin[1]

Hon. Andrew G. Curtin   Executive Mansion,
My dear Sir: Washington, April 13. 1863.

If, after the expiration of your present term as Governor of Pennsylvania, I shall continue in office here, and you shall desire to go abroad, you can do so with one of the first class missions. Yours truly   A. LINCOLN

[1] ADfS, DLC-RTL; ALS-F, ISLA. Governor Curtin's letter of April 14 seems to be in reply to this letter although referring to a letter of "the 12th instant," as follows: "I have the honor to acknowledge the receipt from your own hands of your letter of the 12th instant. . . . I am urged by many of our personal and political friends in Penna. to become a candidate for relection, but the condition of my health and considerations of public policy admonish me to accept your generous offer and devote my whole energies to the discharge of my duties and the support of the Government until the close of my official term when I will be prepared to enter upon the new official position to which you have been pleased to assign me. . . ." (DLC-RTL).

To Samuel F. Du Pont[1]

         Executive Mansion,
Admiral Dupont   Washington, April 13. 1863.

Hold your position inside the bar near Charleston; or if you shall have left it, return to it, and hold it till further orders. Do not allow the enemy to erect new batteries or defences, on Morris-Island. If he has begun it, drive him out. I do not, herein, order you to renew the general attack. That is to depend on your own discretion, or a further order.   A LINCOLN

[1] ALS, RPB. For Du Pont's report on the Charleston operation, see note to Lincoln's despatch to Welles, April 8, *supra.* On April 13, Halleck notified General David Hunter as follows: "Dispatches have been sent to Admiral Du Pont to continue operations against Charleston. You will co-operate with your forces with Admiral Du Pont as you and he may deem best. It is the President's desire that these operations be continued." (OR, I, XIV, 440). See further Lincoln to Hunter and Du Pont, April 14, *infra.*

To Frederic, Grand Duke of Baden[1]

         April 13, 1863
         Abraham Lincoln.
President of the United States of America

To His Royal Highness Frederic,
Grand Duch of Baden

Great and Good Friend: I have received the letter which Your Royal Highness was pleased to address to me on the 28th of February last announcing the marriage of His Grand Ducal Highness the Prince William of Baden with Her Imperial Highness the Princess Mary of Leuchtenberg.

I participate in the satisfaction afforded by this happy event and pray Your Royal Highness to accept my sincere congratulations upon the occasion together with the assurances of my highest consideration. Your Good Friend   ABRAHAM LINCOLN.

Washington April 13. 1863

By the President

WILLIAM H. SEWARD Secretary of State.

1 Copy, DNA FS RG 59, Communications to Foreign Sovereigns and States, III, 228.

To Montgomery C. Meigs[1]

April 13, 1863

I will be personally obliged, if the Quarter-Master-General can conveniently arrange to have the change made, as within requested.   A. LINCOLN

April 13. 1863.

1 AES, IHi. Lincoln's endorsement is written on a letter from Governor Richard Yates, April 2, 1863, recommending Second Lieutenant James R. Hosmer of the Eighth Maryland Volunteers for appointment as assistant quartermaster. Hosmer was appointed with rank of captain on May 12, 1863.

To Edwin M. Stanton[1]

Hon. Sec. of War   Executive Mansion,

Dear Sir   Washington, April 13, 1863

You remember my calling on you some time ago with the bearer, Mr. Asbury Waddell of Arkansas. I feel warranted to believe him a reliable man. Francis Springer who signs a letter he will show you, is one of my best friends, & than whom there is no more reliable man. Mr. Waddell says he can easily raise a regiment in his state—we need the regiment; and I therefore think you better fix him out with some authority to raise the regiment. Yours truly

A. LINCOLN

1 ALS, owned by Edward C. Stone, Boston, Massachusetts. The letter from Reverend Francis Springer has not been located, but a letter from Major General Francis J. Herron, St. Louis, March 17, 1863, introduced Waddell as "just through from the Rebel lines and has important information concerning matters in the South West, and also in regard to the Indians. . . ." (DLC-RTL). No record has been found of Waddell's appointment to raise troops.

To John P. Usher[1]

Hon. Sec. of Interior   Executive Mansion,
My dear Sir   Washington, April 13. 1863.

Please see Mr. Dickey a friend, and son of a friend, of mine. He is a gentleman of very high standing; and I will be glad if you will hear him patiently, and oblige him if possible. Yours truly

A. LINCOLN

[1] ALS, owned by Oliver J. Keller, Springfield, Illinois. Oliver J. Dickey was the law partner of Representative Thaddeus Stevens at Lancaster, Pennsylvania, and son of John Dickey, who had been a member of congress with Lincoln in 1847-1849 and lived at the same boarding house. No reference has been found concerning Oliver J. Dickey's business with the Department of Interior.

To John E. Bouligny[1]

Executive Mansion,
Hon. J. E. Bouligny   Washington, April 14. 1863.

My dear Sir: I did not certainly know the object of your call yesterday, but I had a strong impression in regard to it. When our national troubles began you and I were not personally acquainted; but all I heard of you placed you, in my estimation, foremost among Louisianians, as a friend of the Union. I intended to find you a position, and I did not conceal my inclination to do so. When, last autumn, you bore a letter from me to some parties at New-Orleans, you seemed to expect, and consequently I did expect, you would return here as a member of one or the other branch of Congress. But you were not so returned; and this negative evidence, with other of like character, brings me to think that the Union people there, for some reason, prefer others for the places there [here?]. Add to this that the Head of the Department here, in which finding a place for you was contemplated, is not satisfied for the appointment to be made, and it presents, as you see an embarrassing case for me. My personal feelings for Mr. Bouligny are not less kind than heretofore. Yours very truly

A LINCOLN

[1] ADfS, DLC-RTL. On April 23, Bouligny wrote Lincoln in part as follows:
"Domestic affliction has prevented me from complying with the request indicated by your memorandum on my note of the 16th inst. in which I requested a personal interview in answer to the contents of your favor of the 14th.
"Whilst I avail myself of your kind suggestion to reply by letter, still I would have much preferred to meet you and give a full explanation. . . . All the sacrifices I have made . . . were not made for the hope . . . of *reward*, but for the *sake of the union*. . . . Yet I complain . . . that some insidious enemy should be permitted to poison the mind of those who have all *power*; that *simple*

justice should be denied me. I most solemnly assert . . . that *I received a majority of the loyal votes cast at that election.* I did not contest the same, because I did not desire to embarass my government. . . . When I went to New Orleans in the autumn (alluded to by you) it was at the earnest request of my friend Gen Jno A. McClernand—but I had no hopes of being elected upon my personal popularity, and so expressed myself to you. It was for that reason, I requested *your letter*, expecting to get assistance from the parties to whom you wrote. I was at the time of the canvass very sick. . . . My tickets were [gath] ered up at the polls and destroyed, yet I repeat that I received a *majority of the loyal votes,* of my district. . . . You had promised to appoint me to the position of Surveyor of the Port of N. Orleans, & I did not suppose my being a Candidate for a short term of Congress . . . would prejudice my claims. . . . Through the frankness of Hon W. H. Seward . . . I believe I know the cause of Mr. Chase's opposition . . . Mr Seward has informed me that it has been represented to you & Mr Chase, that I was a dissipated man. I do not deny that sometimes in times past, I have acted imprudently, but that I was *ever* . . . addicted to drink . . . is a most base . . . falsehood. . . ." (DLC-RTL).

To Joseph Hooker[1]

Washington, D.C.,
April 14, 1863– 5.30 p.m.

Major-General Hooker: Would like to have a letter from you as soon as convenient.　　　　　　　　　　　　　A. LINCOLN.

[1] OR, I, XXV, II, 209. Hooker replied to Lincoln's telegram at 11 P.M., "I had supposed the enemy were attacking [John J.] Peck to prevent his reenforcing [John G.] Foster; but if with the numbers alleged, it must be for a more important purpose. As soon as [George] Stoneman's designs are discovered to the enemy, Peck will be relieved. The enemy have not to exceed 30,000 men between Richmond and Suffolk, including both of those towns." (*Ibid.*). On April 12, Hooker had ordered Stoneman to take his cavalry force to turn the enemy's position on his left and cut communications with Richmond. See further Lincoln to Hooker, April 15, *infra.*

To David Hunter and Samuel F. Du Pont[1]

Private　　　　　　　　　　　Executive Mansion, Washington,
Gen. Hunter & Admiral Dupont　　　　　　　　April 14, 1863.

This is intended to clear up an apparent inconsistency between the recent order to continue operations before Charleston, and the former one to move to another point in a certain contingency. No censure upon you, or either of you, is intended. We still hope that by cordial and judicious co-operation, you can take the batteries on Morris Island and Sullivan's Island, and Fort-Sumpter. But whether you can or not we wish the demonstration kept up for a time, for a colatteral and very important object. We wish the attempt to be a real one, (though not a desperate one) if it affords any considerable chance of success. But if prossecuted as a *demonstration* only, this must not become public, or the whole effect will be lost. Once again before Charleston, do not leave till further orders from here. Of course this is not intended to force you to leave unduly exposed, Hilton Head, or other near points in your charge. Yours truly   A. LINCOLN

P.S. Whoever receives this first, please send a copy to the other immediately.   A. L.

[1] ALS, CSmH. See Lincoln's communication to Du Pont, April 13, *supra*. The "apparent inconsistency" to which Lincoln refers is indicated by Welles' communication to Du Pont on April 2, "The exigencies of the public service are so pressing in the Gulf that the Department directs you to send all the iron-clads that are in a fit condition to move, after your present attack upon Charleston, directly to New Orleans, reserving to yourself only two." (OR, I, XIV, 436).

John Hay delivered Welles' order of April 2, and on April 16 he wrote Nicolay from Hilton Head, South Carolina, of the reception of Lincoln's order of April 13, as follows:

"The General and the Admiral this morning received the orders from Washington, directing the continuance of operations against Charleston. The contrast was very great in the manner in which they received them. The General was absolutely delighted. . . . He said, however, that the Admiral seemed in very low spirits about it. . . . Whether the intention of the Government be to reduce Charleston now . . . or by powerful demonstration to retain a large force of the enemy here, he is equally anxious to go to work again. . . ." (Tyler Dennett, ed., *Lincoln and the Civil War in the Diaries and Letters of John Hay*, pp. 60-61).

Du Pont wrote Welles on April 16 as follows:

"I am . . . painfully struck by the tenor and tone of the President's order, which seems to imply a censure, and I have to request that the Department will not hesitate to relieve me by an officer who . . . is more able to execute that service in which I have had the misfortune to fail—the capture of Charleston. . . ." (Daniel Ammen, *The Navy in the Civil War*, II, 108).

To William H. Seward[1]

April 14, 1863

This petition asks me to appoint the petitioner to the "regular mechanical department" I know of no such Department, with which I, by law, as President, have anything to do.

April 14. 1863.   A. LINCOLN

[1] AES, NAuE. Lincoln's endorsement appears on the back of a petition of William R. Nevins of New York, an inventor of machinery and baking ovens who had brought a regiment of bakers and engineers to Washington in 1861, but failing to get it mustered had been compelled to disband his regiment. He asked for a commission or "appointment into the Regular mechanical Department." No record has been found of Nevins' appointment.

To Salmon P. Chase[1]

Hon. Sec. of Treasury, please give Louis, whom you know, an audience of a few minutes.   A. LINCOLN
April 15, 1863

[1] Thomas F. Madigan, *A Catalogue of Lincolniana* (1929), p. 24. "Louis" was Louis Bargdorf, doorkeeper at the White House.

Endorsement[1]

I have no sufficient time to hear appeals in cases of this sort.
Apl. 15. 1863.   A. LINCOLN

[1] AES, RPB. Lincoln's endorsement is written on a portion of an envelope, without clue to its original contents.

To Joseph Hooker[1]

                                   Executive Mansion,
Major General Hooker   Washington, April 15. 1863

It is now 10-15. P.M. An hour ago I received your letter of this morning, and a few minutes later your despatch of this evening. The latter gives me considerable uneasiness. The rain and mud, of course, were to be calculated upon. Gen. S. is not moving rapidly enough to make the expedition come to any thing. He has now been out three days, two of which were unusually fine weather, and all three without hindrance from the enemy, and yet he is not twentyfive miles from where he started. To reach his point, he still has sixty to go; another river, the Rapidan, to cross, and will be hindered by the enemy. By arithmetic, how many days will it take him to do it? I do not know that any better can be done, but I greatly fear it is another failure already. Write me often. I am very anxious. Yours truly   A. LINCOLN

[1] ALS-F, ISLA. Hooker's letter of April 15 is as follows:
"A letter from Maj Genl. Stoneman dated 1 o'clock P.M. yesterday, informs me that his command will be across the river before daylight this morning the 15th. It was his intention to cross at three points, all above the Rappahannock Station. I sent him six days rations, for men and animals, by wagons to be distributed just before his passage of the river. The wagons are now on their return. From the Rappahannock, if he should meet with no unusual delay, he will strike the Aquia and Richmond Rail Road on the night of the second day. Meanwhile I shall do what I can to keep the Enemy up to their works in my front and if they should fall back shall pursue with all the vigor practicable.
"Up to late last night the Enemy appeared to have no suspicion of our designs. This morning I can see nothing, from the storm.

[175]

"I am rejoiced that Stoneman had two good days to go up the river and was enabled to cross it before it had become too much swollen.

"If he can reach his position the storm and mud will not damage our prospects.

"He has been furnished with a copy of Maj. Genl Peck's despatch regarding the Enemy in his immediate front. If it should be true Richmond can have no soldiers in the city at this time." (DLC-RTL).

Hooker's telegram of 8 P.M. the same day is as follows:

"Just heard from Genl. S[toneman]. His Artillery has been brought to a halt by the mud   One Division only having crossed the river. If practicable, he will proceed without it. All the streams are swimming." (*Ibid.*).

On April 17 Hooker replied to Lincoln's letter of the 15th:

"I have the honor to acknowledge your communication of the night of the 15th inst. and in compliance with your request, transmit herewith a letter from Genl. Stoneman dated the 16th inst, as it will fully inform you of the circumstances attending his march up the river. . . . The letter was this moment received.

"His failure, to accomplish speedily the objects of his expedition, is a source of deep regret . . . but I can find nothing in his conduct . . . requiring . . . censure. We cannot control the elements.

"From your letter I conclude that you had misapprehended the position of his advance the night of the second day out . . . which was on the South Side of the Rappahannock and fifty miles from this camp. . . .

"I have given directions for him to remain in his present position, holding himself in readiness to march as soon, after, the roads and rivers will permit. . . . I still hope to turn his movement to some good account. . . .

"No one, Mr President can be more anxious, than myself to relieve your cares and anxieties and you may be assured that I shall spare no labor, and suffer no opportunity to pass unimproved, for so doing.

"We have no reason to suppose that the enemy have any knowledge of the design of Genl. Stoneman's movement." (*Ibid.*).

Resolution on Slavery[1]

[April 15, 1863]

Whereas, while *heretofore*, States, and Nations, have tolerated slavery, *recently*, for the first in the world, an attempt has been made to construct a new Nation, upon the basis of, and with the primary, and fundamental object to maintain, enlarge, and perpetuate human slavery, therefore,

Resolved, That no such embryo State should ever be recognized by, or admitted into, the family of christian and civilized nations; and that all ch[r]istian and civilized men everywhere should, by all lawful means, resist to the utmost, such recognition or admission.

[1] AD-F, ISLA. The resolutions are written on the back of a page of Executive Mansion stationery. On the front page appears the following notation by John Bright:

"Extract from a letter from the Honble. Chas. Sumner, dated Washington April 17th. 1863.

" 'Two days ago the President sent for me to come to him at once. When I arrived, he said that he had been thinking of a matter on which we had often spoken, the way in which English opinion should be directed, & that he had drawn up a resolution embodying the ideas which he should hope to see adopted by public meetings in England. I inclose the resolution, in his autograph, as he gave it to me. He thought it might serve to suggest the point which he regarded as important.' "

No record has been found of the adoption of these resolutions in England. On November 30, 1863, Sumner wrote Lincoln concerning articles in the London *Post* which threatened " 'recognition' of the rebel slave-mongers, in the event of any reverse to the national arms." Sumner suggested that "in yr message you should refer to the resolutions of Congress [reported by Sumner on February 28, 1863, expressing regret that foreign powers had not informed the confederate States that they could not expect recognition], and mention that they have been sent to Foreign Courts;—and then add to this statement the enunciation of the principle you so well expressed in the memdm. you gave to me last spring—to the effect, that, while in times past there have been nations where slavery was an incident, now, for the first time in human history a new Power presents itself & asks 'recognition' in the Christian Family, whose only declared reason of separate existence is the support of slavery — & that no such power can expect any such 'recognition,' but that Christian states are bound to set their faces against it." (Copy, DLC-Nicolay Papers). Lincoln did not follow Sumner's suggestion by incorporating the reference in his Annual Message to Congress of December 8, 1863.

To Edwin M. Stanton[1]

I do not remember about this case. How is it?

Apl. 15. 1863.   A. LINCOLN

[1] AES, DLC-RTL. Lincoln's endorsement is written on a letter from Ezra Webb, Washington, April 11, 1863, "On 14th. ult. my friend Senator Wade who attended to my restoration, as Paymaster, informed me *you* had (through him restored me some 10 days previously). I then said I would return to Cincinnati and return here and file my accounts and vouchers with as little delay as possible. . . . I was paying troops on big Sandy in Jany & could not file accts as early as those who quit in Nov & Decr." Stanton endorsed "I know nothing about the case." Ezra Webb's appointment as additional paymaster of Volunteers was confirmed by the Senate on June 30, 1862. No further reference to his removal or restoration has been found.

Memorandum
Concerning William H. W. Horner[1]

William H. W. Horner—   [c. April 16, 1863]
      For West-Point.
A very excellent recommendation. Born March 23. 1845.

[1] AE, DNA WR RG 94, U.S. Military Academy, 1861, No. 392, Box 78. Lincoln's endorsement is written on a letter from Governor Oliver P. Morton, April 16, 1863, recommending appointment of William H. W. Horner of Wisconsin, at the request of General John Love of Indiana. No appointment is of record.

Memorandum Concerning Patronage in St. Louis, Missouri[1]

April 16, 1863

In answer to the within question "Shall we be sustained by you?" I have to answer that at the beginning of the administration I appointed one whom I understood to be an editor of the "Democrat" to be Post-Master at St. Louis[2]—the best office in my gift within Missouri. Soon after this, our friends at St. Louis, must needs break into factions, the Democrat being, in my opinion, justly chargeable with a full share of the blame for it. I have stoutly tried to keep out of the quarrel, and so mean to do. As to contracts, and jobs, I understand that, by the law, they are awarded to the best bidders; and if the government agents at St. Louis do differently, it would be good ground to prossecute them upon.   A. LINCOLN

April 16. 1863.

[1] AES, DLC-RTL. Lincoln's endorsement is written on a letter of April 9, 1863, from Truman Woodruff, newly elected auditor of St. Louis. Woodruff enclosed a newspaper clipping showing results in the city election of April 6 and complained that the government was neglecting loyal Republicans in favor of secessionists, with particular reference to printing contracts which had not been given to the *Missouri Democrat*.
[2] Peter L. Foy.

Proclamation Cancelling Contract with Bernard Koch[1]

April 16, 1863

Abraham Lincoln,
President of the United States of America.

To all to whom these presents shall come: Greeting.

Know ye that, Whereas a paper bearing date the thirty first day of December, last, purporting to be an agreement between the United States and one Bernard Kock, for immigration of persons of African extraction to a dependency of the Republic of Hayti; was signed by me on behalf of the party of the first part; but whereas the said instrument was and has since remained incomplete, in consequence of the seal of the United States not having been thereunto affixed; And whereas I have been moved by considerations, by me deemed sufficient, to withhold my authority for affixing the said seal;

Now, therefore, be it known, that I, Abraham Lincoln, President

[178]

of the United States, do hereby authorize the Secretary of State to cancel my signature to the instrument aforesaid.

Done at Washington, this sixteenth day of April, in the [L.S.] year of our Lord, 1863.

By the President: ABRAHAM LINCOLN
WILLIAM H. SEWARD, Secretary of State.

[1] DS, DNA FS RG 11, Proclamations. See Lincoln to Seward, January 6, *supra.*

To Edwin M. Stanton[1]

Hon. Sec. of War.   Executive Mansion,
Sir.   Washington, April 16, 1863.

I understand that Major Easton, Q.M. in regular Army, and now serving at Leavenworth, Kansas, is sought to be dismissed on a charge of disloyalty. The present Governor of Kansas,[2] Senator Pomeroy, and U.S. Judge Williams,[3] (the latter of whom I have known nearly thirty years) all say he is not disloyal, but is a worthy and efficient officer. I therefore think we better not act without positive evidence. Perhaps better wait to hear from the Governor after he shall have reached home. Yours truly

A. LINCOLN

[1] ALS, NHi. No reply from Stanton has been found. Major Langdon C. Easton served as quartermaster at Fort Leavenworth until December 3, 1863, when he became chief quartermaster of the Army of the Cumberland.
[2] Thomas Carney.   [3] Lincoln's old friend Archibald Williams.

Memorandum Concerning D. M. Leatherman[1]

I shall not be ready for Mr. Leatherman till 9. o'clock to-morrow morning   A LINCOLN
April 17. 1863.

[1] ADS, owned by George P. Leatherman, Hot Springs, Arkansas. General Stephen A. Hurlbut wrote Lincoln on March 28, 1863, introducing "Mr D. M. Leatherman of Memphis who represents many persons largely interested in lands in this neighborhood. . . ." (DLC-RTL). No indication is given of Leatherman's business with the president, but see Lincoln to Stanton, July 11, *infra.*

Appointment of George Harrington[1]

Washington April 18th. 1863
George Harrington, is hereby appointed to discharge the duties of Secretary of the Treasury, during the absence of Salmon P. Chase, the Secretary.   ABRAHAM LINCOLN

[179]

[1] DS, CSmH. An endorsement indicates that "The Secretary resumed his duties on the 9th of May 1863." Chase was in New York and Philadelphia "to ascertain if a loan, say of fifty millions, to pay off all arrears cannot now be obtained. . . ." (Chase to Lincoln, April 22, 1863, DLC-RTL).

To Edwin M. Stanton[1]

Executive Mansion,
Washington, April 18. 1863.

This man, Rosenberg, who, it seems was with Fremont & Sigel, in several battles, can get no pay in any way. Gen. Hooker testifies to have seen him doing efficient service at the 2nd. Bull-Run.

A. LINCOLN

[Endorsement]

Submitted to the Sec. of War.   A LINCOLN
April 20. 1863.

[1] ADS and AES, NHi. Rosenberg has not been identified, but was probably one of several officers appointed by Frémont and Sigel who never received commissions.

To Edward Bates[1]

Hon. Attorney General.   Executive Mansion,
My dear Sir   Washington, April 20. 1863.

I have promised this lady to ask your attention to the application of her husband, James E. Dunawin, for a pardon—the application said to now be before you. Yours truly

April 20. 1863.   A. LINCOLN

[1] ALS, DNA RG 204, U.S. Pardon Attorney, A 411. James E. Dunawin has not been identified.

To Heads of Departments and Bureaus[1]

April 20, 1863

This young man, or boy, rather, asks a Messengership; and I think, by the letters of Gov. Cannon & Hon John W. Houston, he is shown to have peculiar claim to so small a place. I will thank any Head of a Department or Bureau, who can & will find it for him.   A. LINCOLN

April 20. 1863.

[1] ADS, DeWI. The young man recommended by Governor William Cannon and former congressman from Delaware, John W. Houston, has not been identified.

Proclamation Admitting West Virginia into the Union[1]

April 20, 1863

By the President of the United States of America.

A Proclamation.

Whereas, by the Act of Congress approved the 31st. day of December, last, the State of West Virginia was declared to be one of the United States of America, and was admitted into the Union on an equal footing with the original States in all respects whatever, upon the condition that certain changes should be duly made in the proposed Constitution for that State;

And, whereas, proof of a compliance with that condition as required by the Second Section of the Act aforesaid, has been submitted to me;

Now, therefore, be it known, that I Abraham Lincoln, President of the United States, do, hereby, in pursuance of the Act of Congress aforesaid, declare and proclaim that the said act shall take effect and be in force, from and after sixty days from the date hereof.

In witness whereof, I have hereunto set my hand and caused the Seal of the United States to be affixed.

Done at the city of Washington, this twentieth day of April, in the year of our Lord one thousand eight hundred and sixty-three, and of the Independence of the United States the eighty-seventh.

[L.S.]

By the President: ABRAHAM LINCOLN

WILLIAM H. SEWARD, Secretary of State.

1 DS, DNA FS RG 11, Proclamations. The Act of December 31, 1862, provided that West Virginia be admitted when the people had ratified a change in the seventh section of the eleventh article of the proposed constitution. The change ratified was the substitution of the following in place of the original section seven: "The children of slaves born within the limits of this State after the fourth day of July, eighteen hundred and sixty-three, shall be free; and that all slaves within the said State who shall, at the time aforesaid, be under the age of ten years, shall be free when they arrive at the age of twenty-one years; and all slaves over ten and under twenty-one years shall be free when they arrive at the age of twenty-five years; and no slave shall be permitted to come into the State for permanent residence therein."

To Edwin M. Stanton[1]

April 20, 1863

The conditions of this note being complied with by the attached letters of Senators Wilson & Nesmith, it is hereby directed that

William Lilley be re-appointed a Quarter Master; and, if not inconsistent, let the appointment date with the original appointment
April 20. 1863   A LINCOLN

[1] AES, DLC-RTL. Lincoln's endorsement is written on his letter to William
Lilley, April 2, *supra*. Accompanying letters from James W. Nesmith, April 12,
and Henry Wilson, April 20, state that Lilley's rejection had been based on
misinformation and that if he were renominated they would vote to confirm
him. See further Lincoln's letter to Stanton, May 9, *infra*.

To Calvin Truesdale[1]

Calvin Truesdale, Esq   Executive Mansion,
Post-Master   Washington,
Rock-Island, Ills.   April 20, 1863.

Thomas J. Pickett, late agent of the Quarter-Master's Department for the Island of Rock-Island, has been removed, or suspended from that position, on a charge of having sold timber and
stone from the Island for his private benefit. Mr. Pickett is an old
acquaintance and friend of mine; and I will thank you if you will
set a day or days, and place, on & at which, to take testimony on
the point; notify Mr. Pickett, and one J. B. Danforth Jr. (who, as
I understand, makes the charge) to be present with their witnesses;
take the testimony in writing, offered by both sides,[2] and report
it in full to me. Please do this for me. Yours truly
                                                            A. LINCOLN

[1] ALS, owned by John H. Hauberg, Rock Island, Illinois; ADfS, DLC-RTL.
This letter is misdated in the *Complete Works* (X, 80) April 20, 1864. See
Lincoln to Usher, April 3, *supra*, and to Meigs, May 4, *infra*.
[2] The autograph draft in the Lincoln Papers has "parties" instead of "sides."

To Frederic VII[1]

                                                          April 21, 1863
                            Abraham Lincoln,
           President of the United States of America
To His Majesty Frederic VIII [VII]
           King of Denmark
Great and Good Friend: I have received the letter which Your
Majesty was pleased to address to me on the 12th. ultimo, an-
nouncing the marriage of Her Royal Highness the Princess Alex-
andra Caroline Mary Charlotte Louisa Julia, of Denmark, with
His Royal Highness Albert Edward Prince of Wales.

I participate in the satisfaction which this happy event has afforded to Your Majesty, and to Your Majesty's Royal House and offer to you my sincere congratulations upon the occasion.

May God have Your Majesty always in His safe and holy keeping Your Good Friend   ABRAHAM LINCOLN

Washington, 21st April, 1863

By the President

WILLIAM H. SEWARD Secretary of State

¹ Copy, DNA FS RG 59, Communications to Foreign Sovereigns and States, III, 229.

To William H. Seward and Gideon Welles¹

Hon. Secretaries of   Executive Mansion,
State & of the Navy.   Washington, April 21. 1863.

Gentlemen: It is now a practical question for this government, whether a government mail of a neutral, power, found on board a vessel captured by a beligerent power, on charge of breach of blockade, shall be forwarded to it's designated destination, without opening; or shall be placed in custody of the prize court, to be in the discretion of the court, opened and searched for evidence to be used on the trial of the prize case. I will thank each of you to furnish me

First, a list of all cases wherein such question has been passed upon, either by a diplomatic, or a judicial decision.

Secondly, all cases wherein mails, under such circumstances, have been without special decision, either forwarded unopened; or detained, and opened, in search of evidence.

I wish these lists to embrace as well the reported cases in the books generally, as the cases pertaining to the present war in the United States.

Thirdly, a statement, and brief argument, of what would be the dangers and evils, of forwarding such mails unopened.

Fourthly, a statement and brief argument, of what would be the dangers and evils of detaining and opening such mails, and using the contents, if pertinent, as evidence.

And lastly, any general remarks that may occur to you, or either of you. Your Obt. Seryt.   A. LINCOLN.

¹ ADfS, DLC-RTL; LS, DNA WR NB RG 45, Executive Letters, No. 79. Welles' *Diary* on April 27 states that he delivered his thirty-one page reply, as did Seward on that day. Neither of the replies has been located. The questions concerning the *Peterhoff* were a major issue between Welles and Seward —Welles insisting that opening the mails was the only way to get concrete evidence of the intentions of the vessel, and Seward dissenting from that view. The problem was settled before the secretaries rendered their arguments, however, when on April 23, U.S. District Attorney E. Delafield Smith asked the

court to release the mails to the British government. Editorials from the Chicago *Tribune* and Boston *Transcript* of April 24, attacking Smith's action, are filed in the Lincoln Papers along with the autograph draft of Lincoln's letter of April 21.

Memorandum Concerning John G. Foster[1]

Executive Mansion, Washington, April 22. 1863.

To-day, Gov. Stanley, calls and asks that Gen. Foster, may have his commission dated back. Gen. F.'s conduct at Washington N.C. I think, entitles him to additional consideration.   A. LINCOLN

[1] ADS, NHi. On April 19 Brigadier General John G. Foster in command of the Department of North Carolina drove Confederate forces under Major General Daniel H. Hill from Washington, North Carolina, which the Confederates had taken on March 30, 1863. Foster's appointment as major general, dated from July 18, 1862, was confirmed by the Senate on March 10, 1863. Governor Edward Stanly's request therefore seems to have been unnecessary.

To Edwin M. Stanton[1]

April 22, 1863

The vouchers within, of Col. Bendix, by Gens. French, Couch, Butterfield, Hooker, Wool, & Butler, are ample. Whether what Col. Bendix desires, can be done, consistently with the service, I must refer to the Secretary of War. In considering the case, Gen. Hooker's late order, and also the Gov. of New-York, must be rem[em]bered, as well as general principles and regulations.

April 22. 1863.   A. LINCOLN

[1] AES, owned by Solomon Foster, East Orange, New Jersey. Colonel John E. Bendix of the Tenth New York Infantry was mustered out of service May 7, 1863, the term of his regiment's enlistment being expired. The vouchers referred to are no longer with Lincoln's endorsement, but they probably were concerned with Colonel Bendix's desire to retain his commission after his regiment was mustered out. *General Orders No. 44*, Army of the Potomac, April 20, 1863, provided that all officers were to be mustered out with their regiments, but if the regiment re-enlisted officers were to be retained.

To Edwin M. Stanton[1]

April 22, 1863

Let nothing be done to the detriment of. Joseph Kitchen, until the case is better understood, nor without letting me know.

A. LINCOLN

[1] Copy, DNA WR RG 107, Register of Secretary of War, Letters Received, P 80. The copy is preserved in the Register, indicating referral of a medical certificate of disability for Joseph Kitchen endorsed by Ward H. Lamon. The original document and attendant papers have not been located in the file, and Joseph Kitchen has not been identified.

To Charles Sumner[1]

Hon. Charles Sumner   Executive Mansion,
My dear Sir   Washington, April 22, 1863.

Mrs. L. is embarrassed a little. She would be pleased to have your company again this evening, at the Opera, but she fears she may be taxing you. I have undertaken to clear up the little difficulty. If, for any reason, it will tax you, decline, without any hesitation; but if it will not, consider yourself already invited, and drop me a note. Yours very truly   A. LINCOLN.

[1] ALS-P, ISLA. No reply from Sumner has been found.

To Simon Cameron[1]

Hon. Simon Cameron   Washington City,
Harrisburg, Penn.   April 23. 1863

Telegraph me the name of your candidate for West-Point.
                                       A. LINCOLN.

[1] ALS, RPB. Cameron replied to Lincoln's telegram on the same day, "His name is John Cameron." (DLC-RTL). A letter from Cameron dated January 27, 1862, mentions John Cameron as "a remote connexion of mine." (*Ibid.*). See Lincoln's list, *infra*.

To Salmon P. Chase[1]

Hon. S. P. Chase   Washington City,
Philadelphia, Penn.   April 23. 1863

Telegraph me the name of your candidate for West-Point.
                                       A. LINCOLN

[1] ALS, RPB. Chase replied to Lincoln's telegram on the same day, "His name is Washington Hunt Walbridge of Toledo Ohio." (DLC-RTL). See Lincoln's list, *infra*.

List of Recommendations for West Point[1]

[c. April 23, 1863]

Bishop Hughes	—	William A. Cunningham
Gen. Cameron	—	John Cameron
Speaker Grow	—	Henry W. Streeter.
Gen. Heintzelman	—	Charles S. Heintzelman
Gen. Sumner.	—	George Sumner Jenkins.
Gen. Taylor	—	John J. D. Kingsbury.
Gov. Chase	—	William H. Walbridge,
Mrs. Blair	—	Charles Harrod Campbell,
Senator Foote.	—	William H. Hodges,
Mr. Stanton.	—	Christopher Wolcot, O.

[1] AD, DLC-RTL. This document is misdated [1861] in the Lincoln Papers. A similar autograph list of the names of the persons making the recommendations, but without names of candidates, is written on a letter from Galusha Grow, February 10, 1863, asking appointment of Henry W. Streeter. Lincoln's telegrams to Chase and Cameron on April 23 indicate that the present list was made up about April 23. Of the ten boys listed six entered West Point in 1863: Charles H. Campbell, Charles S. Heintzelman, William H. Hodges, John J. D. Kingsbury, and Christopher C. Walcott and Washington H. Walbridge, about whose last and first names respectively, Lincoln was in error.

To William S. Rosecrans[1]

Major General Rosecrans.　　Executive Mansion, Washington,
Murfreesboro, Tenn.　　　April 22 [23rd] 1863. [10:10 A.M.]

Your despatch of the 21st. received. I really *can not* say that I have heard any complaints of you. I have heard complaint of a Police corps at Nashville; but your name was not mentioned in connection with it so far as I remember. It may be that by inference, you are connected with it; but my attention has never been drawn to it in that light.　　　　　　　　　　A. LINCOLN

[1] ALS, RPB. Lincoln's dating of this telegram has been corrected by the clerk. Rosecrans telegraphed Lincoln on April 21 as follows: "Thrice has notice directly come to me that some complaint has been lodged in the minds of persons high in authority or in records in the War office against the working of my army policy or that there was a conflict of authority between the civil & military　each time I have stated that I know of none & asked for the specification that I might remedy the evil　No reply has been given　No information of what this all means. Can There be anything wrong　I want to know it & appeal to you to please order the complaints to be communicated to me fully. If the Fox is unearthed I will promise to skin him or pay for his hide." (DLC-RTL).

To Joseph Segar[1]

　　　　　　　　　　　　　　Executive Mansion,
Hon. Joseph Segar　　　　　Washington, April 23, 1863.

My dear Sir: My recollection is that Accomac and Northampton counties (Eastern Shore of Va.) were not exempted from a Proclamation issued some short while after the adjournment of Congress; that some time *after* the issuing of the preliminary Emancipation Proclamation, in September, and *before* the issuing of the final one on January 1st. 1863, you called on me and requested that "Eastern Shore of Va" might be exempted from both the Summer Proclamation, & the final emancipation Proclamation. I told you that the non-exemption of it from the former, was a mere omission, which would be corrected; and that it should also be exempted from the final emancipation Proclamation. The preliminary Emancipation Proclamation does not define what is included, or excluded; but only gives notice that this will be done in the final one. Both yourself and Gen. Dix, at different times, (Gen. Dix in writing) called my attention to the fact that I had omitted to exempt the "Eastern Shore of Virginia" from the first proclamation; and this was all that was needed to have me correct it. Without being reminded by either him or yourself, I do not think I should have omitted to exempt it from the final Emancipation Proclamation; but at all events, you did not allow me to forget it. Supposing it was your duty to your constituents to attend to these matters, I think you acted with entire good faith and fidelity to them. Yours truly A. LINCOLN.

[1] ADfS, DLC-RTL. No correspondence has been found from Joseph Segar which has bearing on this letter, but see Lincoln to Dix, November 20, 1862, *supra.*

To Edwin M. Stanton[1]

April 25, 1863

Gov. Johnson thinks it would be well to have the within added to his letter of instruction. If the Secretary of War sees no objection, I see none. A. LINCOLN

April 25. 1863

[1] AES, IHi. Lincoln's endorsement is written on a page of instructions corrected by Stanton. Deleted words are in italics and Stanton's changes are bracketed:

"*In fine he is hereby* [As a general instruction to guide your administration you are] authorized to exercise *any and all* [such] powers [as may be] necessary and proper to carry into full and fair effect the 4th. Section of the 4th. Article of the Constitution of the United States which declares 'The United States shall guarantee to every state in this Union a republican form of Government, and shall protect each of them against invasion and domestic violence'; and *further all* [whatever] power *necessary* [may be necessary] in restoring to the people of Tennessee their civil and political rights under the Constitution of the United States and the Constitution of the State of Tennessee and the laws made in pursuance thereof."

The orders issued by Peter H. Watson, April 2, and Edwin M. Stanton, April 18, defining Andrew Johnson's authority as military governor of Tennessee may be found in the *Official Records*, III, III, 115, 122-23. See further Lincoln's letters to Johnson on September 19, *infra.*

To Benjamin B. French[1]

Comr. of Public Buildings please see the bearer

April 27. 1863. A. LINCOLN

[1] ADS, owned by C. Norton Owen, Glencoe, Illinois. The bearer has not been identified.

To Joseph Hooker[1]

Washington, D.C.,
April 27, 1863– 3.30 p.m.

Major-General Hooker: How does it look now?

A. LINCOLN.

[1] OR, I, XXV, II, 263. Hooker replied at 5 P.M., "I am not sufficiently advanced to give an opinion. We are busy. Will tell you all as soon as I can, and have it satisfactory." (*Ibid.*).

To James H. Lane[1]

Hon. James H. Lane   Executive Mansion,
Leavenworth, Kansas—   Washington, April 27. 1863.

The Governor of Kansas is here, asking that Lieut. Col. J. M. Williams, of a colored regiment there, shall be removed; and also complaining of the military interference of Gen. Blunt in the late election at Leavenworth. I do not know how, if at all, you are connected with these things; but I wish your assistance to so shape things that the Governor of Kansas may be treated with the consideration that is extended to Governors of other States. We are not forcing a Regimental officer upon any other governor, against his protest. Can not this matter be somehow adjusted?   A. LINCOLN.

[1] ALS, DLC-RTL. The envelope addressed by Lincoln "To go by Telegraph" bears Lincoln's further endorsement "Not sent because Gov. Carney thought it best not be." Major General James G. Blunt declared martial law in Leavenworth as the result of disturbances attendant upon the city elections on April 6, and on April 18, abolished martial law upon request of the newly elected Mayor, Daniel R. Anthony (OR, I, XXII, II, 218,226). James M. Williams was colonel of the Seventy-ninth U.S. Colored Infantry.

To Joseph G. Totten[1]

Gen. Totten, please see Judge Mott, now Territorial Delegate for Nevada.   A. LINCOLN

April 27, 1863.

[1] Tracy, p. 223. No further reference has been found to Gordon N. Mott's business with General Totten.

To Peter H. Watson[1]

Hon. P. H. Watson   Executive Mansion,
Asst. Sec. of War   Washington, April 27, 1863.

My dear Sir: I have attentively considered the matter of the "Republican" in regard to which you called on me the other day; and the result is that I prefer to make no change, unless it shall again give just cause of offence, in which case I will at once withdraw the patronage it is enjoying at my hand. I believe it will not

[188]

offend again; and if not, it is better to let the past go by quietly.
Yours truly   A. LINCOLN

¹ ADfS, DLC-RTL. See further Lincoln to Stanton, July 2, *infra*.

Commutation of Sentence of John A. Chase¹

April 28, 1863.

The sentence of death in this case is commuted to imprisonment
at hard labor, with ball and chain attached to his leg, during the
remainder of the present war; all to be in Fort Delaware.

A. LINCOLN.

¹ AGO *General Orders No. 107*, April 28, 1863. Lincoln's endorsement is in the
court-martial record of Sergeant John A. Chase, Company A, Twenty-fourth
New York Volunteers, convicted on April 21, 1863, of striking and using threatening language toward his superior officer.

To Andrew G. Curtin¹

Hon. A. G. Curtin   Washington City,
Harrisburg, Penn.   April 28. 1863

I do not think the people of Pennsylvania should be uneasy about
an invasion. Doubtless a small force of the enemy is flourishing
about in the Northern part of Virginia on the "*Scew-horn*" principle, on purpose to divert us in another quarter. I believe it is
nothing more. We think we have adequate forces close after them.

A. LINCOLN

¹ ALS, RPB. Governor Curtin telegraphed Stanton on April 28 as follows:
"The following dispatch just received:
" 'Governor Curtin: Pittsburgh, 28th.
" 'An express messenger from Morgantown, by express train from Union-
town, arrived here at 2 o'clock this morning, with intelligence that 4,000 rebel
cavalry were within 2 miles of Morgantown at 2 o'clock yesterday, coming
into Pennsylvania. The Baltimore and Ohio Railroad, between Grafton and
Cumberland, is torn up.
" 'All the foregoing is confirmed by intelligence from Wheeling. We are
without arms, artillery, or ammunition here. What can you do for us?
" 'THOMAS M. HOWE,
" '*Assistant Adjutant-General, Pennsylvania.*'
"Have you any information? If it is reliable, what force, if any, can you oppose to the rebels? We have no force in the State of any kind, as you are
aware. Be pleased to telegraph me as soon as possible, as there is much alarm
in this part of Pennsylvania threatened." (OR, I, XXV, II, 278).

To Joseph Hooker¹

Executive Mansion,
Major General Hooker   Washington, April 28, 1863.

The maps, newspapers, and letter of yesterday are just received,
for all which I thank you. While I am anxious, please do not sup-

pose I am impatient, or waste a moment's thought on me, to your own hindrance, or discomfort. Yours as ever   A. LINCOLN

1 ALS, CSmH. Hooker's letter of April 27 is as follows:

"I fully appreciate the anxiety weighing upon your mind, and hasten to relieve you from so much of it as lies in my power. You know that nothing would give me more pleasure than to keep you fully advised of every movement and every intended movement made and to be made by this Army, as is my duty to do. But the country is so full of traitors, and there are so many whose desire it is to see this Army meet with no success, that it almost makes me tremble to disclose a thing concerning it to anyone except yourself. Not that there are not many as true to the cause as yourself; but all have friends and their fidelity I am not so sure of. The following is what I have done and what I propose to do. The 11th 12th & 5th Corps marched this morning, with instructions to take posts at Kelley's Ford at 4 P.M. tomorrow. The Ford being still deep for Artillery, a Ponton train will be in readiness to be thrown across the river, in season I hope, for one or two Corps to cross before morning and take the route to cross the Rapidan at Germania hills and the other Corps to cross at Ely's Ford about the same time and both to march on Chancellorsville and meet there the second night from Kelly's Ford. The Corps march light, with their pack trains of small ammunition, leaving their wagon trains to be crossed on a more direct line when they become opened.

"Simultaneous with this the 6th, 1st & 3rd Corps will cross in the vicinity of Franklin's crossing and make honest demonstrations on the Telegraph and Bowling Green roads, where the main Rebel bodies behind their defences are posted. Keeping them in their places, and if they should detach heavy forces to attack the troops coming down the river, to storm and carry those works and take possession of the enemy's short line of retreat. At the same time, Stoneman will cross with his cavalry to carry out the instructions, a copy of which has already been furnished you. This is an outline, you will be able to fill up the plan. The object in crossing high up the river is to come down in rear of the enemy holding strong positions at the U.S. and Banks Fords, and so strongly fortified that they can only be carried with great loss of life if at all, from a front attack. They are held, as you will see by the accompanying map, by a small force, but the crossings are rendered formidable by the character of the defences.

"The only element which gives me apprehension with regard to the success of this plan is the weather. How much will depend upon it. The details will readily suggest themselves to you.

"After crossing the Rapidan I can hear from the column descending the rivers, by the troops now at Bank's Ford, where I shall throw over two bridges as soon as the development of the battle will permit.

"I write in great haste as I leave for Kelley's Ford tomorrow morning and am busy in making the necessary preparations.

"I send you the Richmond papers last received. The remarkable feature in them is that they write from Fredericksburg that in their opinion we are quitting this line." (DLC-RTL).

Memorandum Concerning
Francis L. Capen's Weather Forecasts[1]

April 28, 1863

It seems to me Mr. Capen knows nothing about the weather, in advance. He told me three days ago that it would not rain again till the 30th. of April or 1st. of May. It is raining now & has been for ten hours. I can not spare any more time to Mr. Capen.

April. 28. 1863.   A LINCOLN

[1] AES, DLC-RTL. Lincoln's endorsement is written on a letter from Francis L. Capen, April 25, 1863. In the center of Capen's one-page letter appears his card, inscribed as follows: "Thousands of lives & millions of dollars may be saved by the application of Science to War. Francis L. Capen. Certified Practical Meteorologist & Expert in Computing the Changes of the Weather." The letter requests a favorable reference to the War Department and concludes, "I will guarantee to furnish Meteorological information that will *save* many a serious sacrifice." Other letters from Capen in the Lincoln Papers demonstrate that he was more of a crank than a scientist.

To William A. Newell[1]

Hon. W. A. Newell.   Executive Mansion,
Allentown, New-Jersey.   Washington, April 29. 1863.

I have some trouble about Provost-Marshal in your first district. Please procure Hon. Mr. Starr to come with you and see me; or, come to an agreement with him, and telegraph me the result.

                             A. LINCOLN

[1] ALS, RPB. No reply from Governor Newell, nor reference to a conference with Representative John F. Starr, has been found. Robert C. Johnson was appointed provost marshal for the First District of New Jersey on May 2, 1863. A letter from James M. Scovel, May 3, 1863, reads in part:

"On Saturday I had a long & friendly talk with Mr Starr about the Provost Marshalls appointment. He will I think adhere to his slate. You, I hope will not. Mr. Starr is thoroughly loyal and will sustain the Government in all measures. . . . Like other congressmen he is not without his own aspirations. . . . A combination of Trenton politicians with a few in our own district, always opposed to a young man who wants to rise,—have induced Mr Starr to name Col. Johnson for the Marshalship. He is a respectable gentleman without family and of considerable fortune.

"Mr Starr tells me he thinks I want to advance too fast. . . . No man in or out of New Jersey has suffered more from the Copperheads than I have. . . .

"Of course, after I know that I *have done my whole duty*, it is unpleasant to be asked to take a subordinate position on the Military board. . . ." (DLC-RTL).

On May 9 Scovel wrote again to express his appreciation of "the appointment of Commissioner &c notice of which I have just received from the Secretary of War." (*Ibid.*).

To David Hunter[1]

PRIVATE   Executive Mansion,
Major General Hunter   Washington, April 30, 1863.

My dear Sir   This morning I was presented an order of yours dismissing from the service, subject to my approval, a Captain

Schaadt, of one of the Pennsylvania regiments. Disloyalty, without any statement of the evidence supposed to have proved it, is assigned as the cause of the dismissal; and he represents at home, as I am told, that the sole evidence was his refusal to sanction a resolution (indorsing the emancipation proclamation I believe); and our friends assure me that this statement is doing the Union cause great harm in his neighborhood and county, especially as he is a man of character, did good service in raising troops for us last fall, and still declares for the Union & his wish to fight for it. On this state of case I wrote a special indorsement on the order, which I suppose he will present to you; and I write this merely to assure you that no censure is intended upon you; but that it is hoped that you will inquire into the case more minutely, and that if there be no evidence, but his refusal to sanction the resolution, you will restore him. Yours as ever   A. Lincoln

¹ ADfS, DLC-RTL; LS, IHi. David Schaadt was captain of Company D, One Hundred Seventy-sixth Pennsylvania, a regiment of nine-months drafted militia, mustered in on November 8, 1862, and mustered out on August 18, 1863. See Lincoln's endorsement, *infra*.

Regarding the Case of David Schaadt¹

Executive Mansion, Washington, April 30, 1863.
Such facts are brought to my notice as induce me to withhold,² my approval of the dismissal of Capt. Schaadt, named within. He is satisfactorily proved to me to be of good character for candor and manliness, and generally; and that he was most active and efficient, in Pennsylvania last autumn, in raising troops for the Union. All this should not retain him in the service, if, since then, he has given himself, in any way, to the injury of the service. How this is I must understand better than I now do, before I can approve his dismissal. What has he done? What has he said? If, as is claimed for him, he is guilty of nothing, but the withho[l]ding his vote or sanction, from a certain resolution or resolutions, I think his dismissal is wrong, even though I might think the resolution itself right, and very proper to be adopted by such as choose. Capt. Schaadt will report himself to Gen. Hunter, and deliver him this paper, for his further action.   A. Lincoln

¹ ADfS, DLC-RTL. Lincoln's draft of this endorsement is on Executive Mansion stationery, on the back of which is a copy of Hunter's *General Orders No. 28*, March 30, 1863, dismissing Captain Schaadt for disloyalty "unanimously certified to the Major Genl. Commanding by the Colonel, Lt. Col, Major &

Surgeon of the 176th. Regt. of Pa M." No further references to the case have been found.   2 "For the present," deleted at this point by Lincoln.

To Timothy P. Andrews[1]

May 1, 1863

Pay Master General, please see Rev. Dr. Van Santvoord who has a question about his pay. He only asks that it commence with the date of his commission, whereas he has served ever since & long before.   A. LINCOLN.

May 1, 1863.

[1] Herbert W. Fay, *Week-by-Week in Springfield*, May 16, 1936. Reverend Cornelius Van Santvoord was chaplain of the Eightieth New York Infantry, October 10, 1861 to November 18, 1862, and hospital chaplain of Volunteers February 2, 1863 to July 15, 1865. See also Lincoln to William A. Hammond, *infra*.

To Andrew G. Curtin[1]

Gov. Curtin   Executive Mansion, Washington,
Harrisburg, Pa.   May 1. 1863. [10:55 P.M.]

The whole disposable force at Baltimore & elsewhere in reach have already been sent after the enemy which alarms you. The worst thing the enemy could do for himself would be to weaken himself before Hooker, & therefore it is safe to believe he is not doing it; and the best thing he could do for himself, would be to get us so scared as to bring part of Hooker's force away, and that is just what he is trying to do. I will telegraph you in the morning about calling out the militia   A. LINCOLN

[1] ALS, RPB. Two telegrams from Governor Curtin, received at 4:25 P.M. and 10 P.M., reported despatches from Pittsburgh and Western Pennsylvania importuning protection against a reported invasion (OR, I, XXV, II, 346).

To Henry W. Halleck[1]

Major Gen. Halleck,   Executive Mansion
My dear Sir   Washington May 1, 1863.

Please see & confer with Gen. Totten. He thinks the public service might be advanced by Gen. Cullum going to Boston; and if you can spare him for a few days, I wish him to go. Yours truly
A. LINCOLN.

[1] Copy, ISLA. Lieutenant Colonel George W. Cullum of the Corps of Engineers, a brigadier general of Volunteers, served May 2-22 on a special board to examine the defenses of Boston harbor.

To William A. Hammond[1]

May 1, 1863

The Surgeon General will oblige me, if he can consistently assign Chaplain Van Santvoord, to the Covalesent Camp for a few months.

A. LINCOLN

May 1. 1863.

[1] ALS, RPB. See Lincoln to Andrews, *supra*.

To S. Johnson Salisbury[1]

S. Johnson Salesbury
Elgin, Illinois.

Washington, D.C.,
May 1 1863

Yours of the 28th. ult. about Post-Master at Elgin was received; and being upon a subject to which my attention had not been called, I refered the Despatch to the Post-Master General, since which I have not heared from it

A. LINCOLN

[1] ALS, RPB. S. Johnson Salesbury (Salisbury?) has not been identified, and his telegram of April 28 has not been located. George B. Raymond was post-master at Elgin, Illinois.

To Edwin M. Stanton[1]

Let this appointment be made at once.   A. LINCOLN
May 1. 1863.

[1] AES, IHi. Lincoln's endorsement appears on a letter from John Crowell, Cleveland, Ohio, April 28, 1863, asking appointment of "John Crowell Jr. to the office of Asst. Adjutant General under Brigadier Genl. William B. Hazen, 2d Brigade, 2d Division Army of the Cumberland." On December 31, 1863, John Crowell, Jr., was nominated assistant adjutant general with rank of captain dating from May 1, 1863, and was confirmed by the Senate on March 8, 1864.

To Edward Bates[1]

May 2, 1863

Will the Attorney General please make out the proper document remitting the remainder of the imprisonment in this case, letting the pecuniary punishment stand.

A. LINCOLN

May 2. 1863

[1] AES, DNA RG 204, U.S. Pardon Attorney, A 471. Lincoln's endorsement is written on a letter from Montgomery Blair and Gideon Welles May 1, 1863,

asking that William Wormley and William Ringgold, sentenced in the District
of Columbia Criminal Court on May 1, 1863, to fifty dollar fines and ten days
in jail, be released from the remainder of the jail sentence.

To Salmon P. Chase[1]

Sec. of Treasury, please see this lady, a moment.

May 2. 1863.   A. Lincoln

[1] ALS, CtLHi. The lady has not been identified.

To Andrew G. Curtin[1]

Gov. Curtin   Executive Mansion,
Harrisburg, Pa.   Washington, May 2. 1863.

Gen. Halleck tells me he has a despatch from Gen. Schenck this
morning, informing him that our forces have joined, and that the
enemy menacing Penn. will have to fight or run to-day. I hope I
am not less anxious to do my duty to Pennsylvania, than yourself; but I really do not yet see the justification for incurring the
trouble and expense of calling out the militia. I shall keep watch
and try to do my duty.   A. Lincoln

P.S. Our forces are exactly between the enemy and Pennsylvania.

A. Lincoln

[1] ALS, RPB. General Robert C. Schenck telegraphed from Baltimore, "Railroad clear and working to Grafton. . . . [John R.] Kenly has advanced to-
night to Clarksburg and joined [Benjamin S.] Roberts. They will fight to-day,
or the rebels must run." (OR, I, XXV, II, 372):

Governor Curtin's reply to Lincoln's telegram was received at 1:45 P.M.: "I
have no doubt my dispatch to Pittsburg . . . sent since yours recd will quiet
the excitement in western Penna. All the movements of the Government are
perfectly satisfactory & your conclusion as to calling militia force in harmony
with my views. I have not been seriously alarmed & in my despatches only
reflected a part of the excitement & all from west." (DLC-RTL).

To William H. Seward[1]

Hon. Sec of State.   Executive Mansion,
My dear Sir,   Washington. May 2. 1863.

Have we any committal as to the vacant consulate at Havanna?
If we have not, I am for giving it to Hon. Caleb Lyon, and of
doing it at once. Yours truly.   A. Lincoln.

[1] Copy, DLC-RTL. Seward replied the same day that he had communicated
with two other candidates and had as yet no answer (DLC-RTL). Former
congressman (1853-1855) from New York, Caleb Lyon was not appointed to
the Havana consulate, but in 1864 became the first governor of Idaho Territory.

To Daniel Butterfield[1]

Washington City,

Major General Butterfield.   May 3. 1863.

Where is Gen. Hooker? Where is Sedgwick? where is Stoneman?

A. LINCOLN

[1] ALS-F, ISLA. Major General Butterfield, Hooker's chief of staff, telegraphed Lincoln at 8:50 A.M. on May 3 that "a battle is in progress" (OR, I, XXV, II, 377). Stanton replied "The President thanks you for your telegrams, and hopes you will keep him advised as rapidly as any information reaches you." (*Ibid.*, p. 378). Butterfield replied to Lincoln's query at 4:40 P.M., "General Hooker is at Chancellorsville. General Sedgwick, with 15,000 to 20,000 men, at a point 3 or 4 miles out from Fredericksburg, on the road to Chancellorsville. Lee is between. Stoneman has not been heard from. This is the situation at this hour from latest reports, 4.30 p.m." (*Ibid.*).

To Ambrose E. Burnside[1]

Major General Burnside   Executive Mansion,

Cincinnati, Ohio   Washington, May 4, 1863.

Our friend, Gen. Sigel claims that you owe him a letter. If you so remember, please write him at once. He is here.

A. LINCOLN

[1] ALS, RPB. No answer from Burnside, nor clue as to the implications of this letter, has been found.

To Joseph Hooker[1]

Washington, D.C.,

Major-General Hooker: May 4, 1863—3.10 p.m.

We have news here that the enemy has reoccupied heights above Fredericksburg. Is that so?   A. LINCOLN.

[1] OR, I, XXV, II, 401. As printed in *Report of the Joint Committee on the Conduct of the War* (1865) I, 226, this telegram is addressed to General Daniel Butterfield. Hooker replied, "I am informed that it is so, but attach no importance to it." (*Ibid.*).

To Montgomery C. Meigs[1]

It appearing to me that Mr. Picketts fault is more apparant than real, it is my wish that he be restored to his place.

May 4, 1863.   A. LINCOLN

[1] AES, DNA WR RG 92, Quartermaster General, P 211. Lincoln's endorsement is written on an envelope containing papers in defense of Thomas J. Pickett. Meigs endorsed, "Let it be done by order of the President." See Lincoln to Usher, April 3, and to Truesdale, April 20, *supra*.

Memorandum Concerning Rufus Ingalls[1]

May 4, 1863

1. It appears Ingalls is not with Hooker, and therefore may not be acting under his special direction.

2. He may consider it a proper precaution, in view of what he knows is going on at Fredericksburg.

3. He may not know that we know about Fredericksburg, and, to keep it from us, may say 'My reasons are good'

May 4, 1863.   A. LINCOLN

[1] AES, NHi. Lincoln's endorsement is written on a note from Stanton, misdated May 5, 1862, as follows:
"Ingalls despatch was sent from U S Ford the extreme point to which the telegraph wire extends. It is as follows

" '5.10. PM   US. Ford   May 4
" 'Col D H Rucker
" 'Ship no more horses or other stores until further notice. Please advise Capt [William] Stoddard & [Colin B.] Ferguson (Quarter Masters at Alexandria)   My reasons are good.   RUFUS INGALLS.
Chf Q M'

"There is nothing else new. Yours truly EMS"

To James B. Fry[1]

Dear Sir: Washington May 5, 1863.

Please appoint the following Provost Marshals and members of Enrolling Boards for the State of Illinois:

1st District:	
Provost Marshal,	William James
2d Dist.	
Provost Marshal,	Amos B. Coon
Enrolling Board	Col. Wm Shaffer
3d Dist.	
Provost Marshal	John V. Eustace.
4th Dist.	
Provost Marshal	James Woodruff
5th Dist.	
Provost Marshal	James M. Allen
6th Dist.	
Provost Marshal,	Capt. Abel Longworth
7th Dist.	
Provost Marshal	Wm Fithian
Enrolling Board	Capt. J. S. Wolf[2]
8th Dist	
Provost Marshal	Isaac Keys.
Enrolling Board	Clinton Jones[3]
9th Dist	
Provost Marshal	Benj. F. Westlake.

[197]

10th Dist
    Provost Marshal,   Wm M. Fry
    Enrolling Board   Hon. S. W. Moulton
11th Dist.
    Provost Marshal   Hon. Mortimer O'Kean
    Enrolling Board   Hon. Wm B. Archer
12th Dist.
    Provost Marshal   Geo. Abbott
                                   John E. Deitrich comr.

13th Dist
    Provost Marshal   Capt Wm C. Carroll.[4]
    Enrolling Board   A. J. Kuykendall

Yours Truly

Col. J. B. Fry   ABRAHAM LINCOLN
Provost Marshal General.

[1] LS, IHi. Colonel James B. Fry had been appointed provost marshal general on March 17, 1863. The appointments for Illinois were made as listed except for Colonel William Shaffer who was replaced by William D. Barry.

[2] John S. Wolf's appointment was revoked on June 15, 1863, and his place filled by Samuel Frazier. [3] Replaced on May 27 by Burrel T. Jones.

[4] Replaced on May 7 by Isaac N. Phillips.

To Joseph Hooker[1]

War Department Washington City,
Major General Hooker   [May 6] 1863.
Are you suffering with *dust* this morning?

[1] ADf, DLC-Nicolay Papers. This telegram was not sent, because the telegraph lines were down until later in the morning. On the bottom of the page is a note in shorthand, probably by Nicolay, and a longhand transcription as follows: "Written by the President, but not sent out in the morning of May 6th., after a pouring rain all night and during the morning. Subsequently turned out that on the 6th Hooker had recrossed the river."

To Joseph Hooker[1]

War Department Washington City, D.C.
My dear General   May 6. 9/40. A.M. 1863
The great storm of yesterday and last night, has interrupted the telegraph; so that we think fit to send you Gen. Dix despatch of the contents of Richmond papers. I need not repeat the contents. We also try to get it to you by Telegraph. We have nothing from your immediate whereabouts since your short despatch to me, of the 4th. 4/20. P.M. We hear many rumors, but do not exactly know what has become of Sedgwick. We have heard no word of Stoneman, except what is in Dix's despatch about Col. Davis which looks well. It is no discourgement that you have already

fought the bulk of Longstreet's force, nor that Jackson is severely wounded. And now, God bless you, and all with you. I know you will do your best. Waste no time unnecessarily, to gratify our curiosity with despatches. Yours as ever   A. LINCOLN

Maj. Genl. Hooker.

1 ALS, owned by Mrs. Arthur L. Bates, Meadville, Pennsylvania. This despatch and General Dix's despatch of May 5, 11:50 P.M., were carried by Gustavus V. Fox. The telegraph lines were reopened later, and Lincoln sent the message of 11:40 A.M., *infra.*

To Joseph Hooker[1]

Washington City, D.C.

Major General Hooker.   May 6. 11/40 1863

We have, through Gen. Dix, the contents of Richmond papers of the fifth (5th) Gen. Dix's despatch in full, is going to you by Capt. Fox of the Navy. The substance is Gen. Lee's despatch of the third (3rd) Sunday claiming that he had beaten you, and that you were then retreating across the Rappahannock; distinctly stating that two of Longstreet's Divisions fought you on Saturday; and that Gen. Paxton[2] was killed, Stonewall Jackson severely wounded, and Generals Heth[3] and A. P. Hill slightly wounded. The Richmond papers also state, upon what authority, not mentioned, that our Cavalry have been at Ashland, Hanover Court-House and other points, destroying several locomotives, and a good deal of other property, and all the Railroad Bridges to within five (5.) miles of Richmond.   A. LINCOLN

1 ALS, IHi. For Hooker's reply, see note to Lincoln's telegram of 12:30 P.M., *infra.*   2 Elisha F. Paxton was killed on May 3.
3 Henry Heth.

To Joseph Hooker[1]

Washington, D.C. May 6, 1863– 12.30 p.m.

General Hooker: Just as I had telegraphed you contents of Richmond papers, showing that our cavalry has not failed, I received General Butterfield's of 11 a.m. yesterday.[2] This, with the great rain of yesterday and last night, securing your right flank, I think puts a new face upon your case; but you must be the judge.

A. LINCOLN.

1 OR, I, XXV, II, 434. Hooker replied at 4:30 P.M., as follows:
"Have this moment returned to camp. On my way received your telegrams of 11 a.m. and 12.30. The army had previously recrossed the river, and was on its return to camp. As it had none of its trains of supplies with it, I deemed this advisable. Above, I saw no way of giving the enemy a general battle with

the prospect of success which I desire. Not to exceed three corps, all told, of my troops have been engaged. For the whole to go, there is a better place nearer at hand. Will write you at length to-night. Am glad to hear that a portion of the cavalry have at length turned up. One portion did nothing." (*Ibid.*, p. 435).

Stanton replied, "The President and General-in-Chief left here this afternoon at 4 o'clock to see you. They are probably at Aquia by this time." (*Ibid.*).

[2] General Daniel Butterfield's despatch to Lincoln is as follows:

"General Hooker is not at this moment able, from pressing duties, to write of the condition of affairs. He deems it his duty that you should be fully and correctly advised. He has intrusted it to me. These are my words, not his.

"Of his plans you were fully aware. The cavalry, as yet learned, have failed in executing their orders. [William W.] Averell's division returned; nothing done; loss of 2 or 3 men. [John] Buford's Regulars not heard from. General [John] Sedgwick failed in the execution of his orders, and was compelled to retire, and crossed the river at Banks' Ford last night; his losses not known.

"The First, Third, Fifth, Eleventh, Twelfth, and two divisions of Second Corps are now on south bank of Rappahannock, intrenched between Hunting Run and Scott's Dam. Trains and Artillery Reserve on north bank of Rappahannock. Position is strong, but circumstances, which in time will be fully explained, make it expedient, in the general's judgment, that he should retire from this position to the north bank of the Rappahannock for his defensible position. Among these is danger to his communication by possibility of enemy crossing river on our right flank and imperiling this army, with present departure of two-years' and three months' [nine-months'] troops constantly weakening him. The nature of the country in which we are prevents moving in such a way as to find or judge position or movements of enemy. He may cross to night, but hopes to be attacked in this position." (*Ibid.*, pp. 421-22).

To Rufus Ingalls[1]

Washington City,
Col. Ingalls   May 6. 1863 [1.45 P.M.].

News has gone to Gen. Hooker which may change his plans. Act in view of such contingency.   A LINCOLN

[1] ALS, RPB. See Lincoln to Hooker, 11:40 A.M., *supra.*

To Edwin M. Stanton[1]

May 6 and 8, 1863
About attaching a part of Ky, now, under Grant, to Burnside.
May 6. 1863.   A.L.

Submitted to Sec. of War, & asking special attention.
May 8. 1863.   A. LINCOLN

[1] AES, THaroL. Lincoln's endorsements have been removed from the petition on which they were originally written. On June 11, 1863, James F. Robinson telegraphed Lincoln as follows: "The Public Interests will be greatly promoted & the Peace & Quiet of the State will be secured by adding to the Dept of the Ohio under the Command of Genl. Burnside all that part of Kentucky lying South & West of the Tennessee which is now in Gen Grants Dept   I most earnestly desire that this change shall be made" (DLC-RTL).

To Joseph Hooker[1]

Major General Hooker.   Head-Quarters, Army of the Potomac,
My dear Sir   May. 7 1863.

The recent movement of your army is ended without effecting it's object, except perhaps some important breakings of the enemies communications. What next? If possible I would be very glad of another movement early enough to give us some benefit from the fact of the enemies communications being broken, but neither for this reason or any other, do I wish anything done in desperation or rashness. An early movement would also help to supersede the bad moral effect of the recent one, which is sure to be considerably injurious. Have you already in your mind a plan wholly, or partially formed? If you have, prossecute it without interference from me. If you have not, please inform me, so that I, incompetent as I may be, can try [to] assist in the formation of some plan for the Army. Yours as ever   A LINCOLN

[1] ALS-F, ISLA. Copies of this letter and of Hooker's reply are preserved in the Lincoln Papers in an envelope endorsed by Lincoln "Gen. Hooker. Visit to camp, May 7 1863." Hooker's reply is as follows:

"I have the honor to acknowledge your communication of this date, and in answer have to state that I do not deem it expedient to suspend operations on this line from the reverse we have experienced in endeavoring to extricate the army from its present position. If in the first effort we failed it was not from want of strength or conduct of the small number of the troops actually engaged, but from a cause which could not be foreseen, and could not be provided against. After its occurrence the chances of success were so much lessened that I felt another plan might be adopted in place of that we were engaged in, which would be more certain in its results. At all events, a failure would not involve disaster, while in the other case it was certain to follow the absence of success. I may add that this consideration almost wholly determined me in ordering the army to return to its old camp.

"As to the best time for renewing our advance upon the enemy, I can only decide after an opportunity has been afforded to learn the feeling of the troops. They should not be discouraged or depressed, for it is no fault of theirs—if I may except one Corps—that our last efforts were not crowned with glorious victory. I suppose details are not wanted of me at this time.

"I have decided in my own mind the plan to be adopted in our next effort, —if it should be your wish to have one made. It has this to recommend it—It will be one in which the operations of all the Corps, unless it be a part of the Cavalry, will be within my personal supervision." (DLC-RTL).

To Edwin M. Stanton[1]

Hon Secretary of War.   Head Quarters A.P. May 7, 1863.

Have you any news? and if any what is it? I expect to be up to-night.   A. LINCOLN

[1] Tracy, p. 223. Stanton's reply, if any, has not been located.

To Edward Bates[1]

May 8, 1863

This resignation is accepted; and the Attorney General will please send me immediately an appointment of Joshua Tevis, to fill the vacancy.   A. LINCOLN

May 8. 1863.

[1] AES, DNA GE RG 60, Papers of Attorney General, Segregated Lincoln Material. Lincoln's endorsement is written on a letter of resignation from U.S. District Attorney Thomas E. Bramlette of Kentucky, May 4, 1863. Bramlette had accepted the nomination of the Union Central Committee as candidate for governor of Kentucky. Joshua Tevis of Louisville was appointed.

To Salmon P. Chase[1]

Executive Mansion,

Hon. S. P. Chase   Washington, May 8. 1863.

My dear Sir. I address this to you personally, rather than officially, because of the nature of the case. My mind is made up to remove Victor Smith as Collector of the Customs at the Puget Sound District. Yet, in doing this, I do not decide that the charges against him are true. I only decide that the degree of dissatisfaction with him there is too great for him to be retained. But I believe he is your personal acquaintance & friend; and if you shall desire it, I will try to find some other place for him. Yours as ever,

A LINCOLN

[1] ADfS, DLC-RTL. See Lincoln to Chase, March 21, *supra.* Anson G. Henry telegraphed Lincoln on April 27, "Has Victor Smith been removed. Am very anxious to know." (DLC-RTL). See further Lincoln to Chase, May 11, *infra.*

To Salmon P. Chase[1]

Hon. Secretary of Treasury: May 8, 1863

My dear Sir: Please send me, at once, an appointment of Henry Clay Wilson, of Washington Territory, to be collector of customs for the Puget Sound district, in place of Victor Smith. Yours truly,

A. LINCOLN.

[1] Robert B. Warden, *Account of the Private Life and Public Services of Salmon Portland Chase* (1874), p. 527.

To Joseph Hooker[1]

Executive Mansion,

Major General Hooker.   Washington, May 8. 1863.

The news is here, of the capture, by our forces of Grand Gulf— a large & very important thing. Gen. Willich,[2] an exchanged prisoner, just from Richmond, has talked with me this morning. He was there when our cavalry cut the roads in that vicinity. He says there was not a sound pair legs in Richmond, and that our men, had they known it, could have safely gone in and burnt every thing & brought us Jeff. Davis. We captured and parold three or four hundred men. He says, as he came to City point, there was an army three miles long (Longstreet's he thought) moving towards Richmond. Milroy has captured a despatch of Gen. Lee, in which he says his loss was fearful, in his late battle with you.[3]   A. LINCOLN

[1] ALS, IHi.
[2] Brigadier General August Willich had been captured December 31, 1862, at Stone River near Murfreesboro, Tennessee.
[3] General Milroy's telegram to General Schenck of 8 P.M., May 6, reads in part: "A telegraphic dispatch was received at Edenburg an hour before my forces took this place, addressed to Major Myers [Samuel B. Myers] rebel commander . . . signed by General Lee, stating that they (the rebels) had gained a glorious victory, but with fearful loss on both sides. . . ." (OR, I, XXV, II, 437).

Proclamation Concerning Aliens[1]

May 8, 1863

By the President of the United States of America:

A Proclamation.

Whereas the Congress of the United States, at its last Session, enacted a law, entitled "An Act for enrolling and calling out the National Forces and for other purposes," which was approved on the 3d. day of March, last: and whereas it is recited in the said act that there now exist in the United States an insurrection and rebellion against the authority thereof, and it is, under the constitution of the United States, the duty of the Government to suppress insurrection and rebellion, to guaranty to each state a republican form of Government, and to preserve the public tranquillity; and whereas, for these high purposes, a military force is indispensable, to raise and support which all persons ought willingly to contribute; and whereas no service can be more praiseworthy and honorable than that which is rendered for the maintenance of the Constitution and Union, and the consequent preservation of free government: and whereas, for the reasons thus recited, it was enacted by the said statute that all able bodied male citizens of the United States, and persons of foreign birth who shall have declared on oath their intention to become citizens under and in pursuance of the laws thereof, between the ages of twenty and forty-five years, (with certain exceptions not necessary to be here mentioned,) are declared to constitute the national forces, and shall be liable to perform military duty in the service of the United States when called out by the President for that purpose:

And whereas it is claimed by and in behalf of persons of foreign birth, within the ages specified in said act, who have heretofore declared on oath their intentions to become citizens under, and in pursuance of, the laws of the United States, and who have not exercised the right of suffrage or any other political franchise under the laws of the United States, or of any of the States thereof, that they are not absolutely concluded by their aforesaid declaration of intention from renouncing their purpose to become citizens, and that, on the contrary, such persons, under treaties or the law of nations, retain a right to renounce that purpose, and to forego the privileges of citizenship and residence within the United States, under the obligations imposed by the aforesaid Act of Congress:—

Now, therefore, to avoid all misapprehensions concerning the liability of persons concerned to perform the service required by such enactment, and to give it full effect, I do hereby order and proclaim that no plea of alienage will be received or allowed to exempt from the obligations imposed by the aforesaid Act of Congress, any person of foreign birth who shall have declared on oath his intention to become a citizen of the United States under the laws thereof, and who shall be found within the United States at any time during the continuance of the present insurrection and rebellion, at or after the expiration of the period of sixty-five days from the date of this proclamation; nor shall any such plea of alienage be allowed in favor of any such person who has so, as aforesaid, declared his intention to become a citizen of the United States, and shall have exercised, at any time, the right of suffrage, or any other political franchise, within the United States under the laws thereof, or under the laws of any of the several States.

In witness whereof I have hereunto set my hand, and caused the seal of the United States to be affixed.

Done at the city of Washington, this eighth day of May, in the year of our Lord one thousand eight hundred and [L.S.] sixty-three, and of the Independence of the United States the eighty-seventh.   ABRAHAM LINCOLN

By the President:

WILLIAM H. SEWARD, Secretary of State.

1 DS, DNA FS RG 11, Proclamations.

[204]

To Charles W. Rand[1]

May 8, 1863

To C. W. Rand, Esq., Marshal of the United States for the Northern District of California:

Whereas, it has come to my knowledge that one Andres Castillero, and divers persons acting or claiming to act under him as his agents or assigns, have, under and by virtue of a pretended grant or grants from the lawfully constituted authorities of the Republic of Mexico, occupied and taken possession of, and made settlement on a portion of the public lands of the United States situate in the County of Santa Clara and State of California, commonly called and known as the New Almaden Quicksilver mining property, and embracing about three thousand varas of land in all directions from the mouth of the mine commonly called and known as the New Almaden Quicksilver Mine, and have, for a long time past, by extracting valuable minerals therefrom and converting the same to their own use; by erecting buildings and other improvements thereon, and by other unauthorized acts, used and enjoyed the said portion of the public lands as if they were the lawful owners thereof, all of which acts have been without the consent, and against the rights of the United States: And whereas, by the decision of the Supreme Court of the United States in the case of Andres Castillero against the United States, at the December Term of the said Court last past, it has been adjudged that the grant or grants from the lawfully constituted authorities of the Republic of Mexico, under which the said Andres Castillero and the persons claiming under him as agents or assigns, have claimed and pretended to hold the said described portion of the public lands, is or are fraudulent and void, and conferred no right whatever to the said described portion of the public lands or to the minerals therein, whereby it appears that the said Andres Castillero and the persons claiming under him as agents or assigns, now in possession of the said described premises, are intruders thereon without right: And whereas, the said described portion of the public lands has never been surveyed and opened to settlement and sale under the laws of the United States:

Now, therefore, I, Abraham Lincoln, President of the United States, by virtue of the power and authority in me vested by the Act approved the 3d day of March, A.D. 1807, Chap. 46, entitled "An Act to prevent settlements being made on lands ceded to the United States until authorized by law," do hereby order and direct you to enter upon that portion of the public lands situate in Santa

Clara County, in the State of California, commonly called and known as the New Almaden mining property, embracing about three thousand varas of land in all directions from the mouth of the mine commonly called and known as the New Almaden Quicksilver Mine, and to remove therefrom any and every person or persons who shall be found on the same, and deliver the said premises, with all the appurtenances of whatsoever kind to the possession of Leonard Swett, an agent who has been duly authorized by me to take possession of and hold the same for the United States, and also that you take such measures and call to your assistance such military force of the United States in California as may be necessary to execute this order.

In witness whereof, I have hereunto affixed my hand, this eighth day of May, A.D. 1863. ABRAHAM LINCOLN.

[1] Gregory Yale, *Legal Titles to Mining Claims and Water Rights, in California* . . . (1867), pp. 401-402; copy, DLC-RTL. The copy in the Lincoln Papers is undated, but Yale dates this order as above. The original is apparently lost since the San Francisco fire. For a discussion of the surrounding circumstances of this order, see Samuel C. Wiel, *Lincoln's Crisis in the Far West* (1949). See also Lincoln to Leonard Swett and Frederick F. Low, July 9, *infra*.

To Peter H. Watson[1]

May 8, 1863

Will Mr. Watson please act upon this case as soon as possible.

[1] Copy, DNA WR RG 107, Register of Secretary of War, Letters Received, P 96. The original documents are missing, but the register indicates that Lincoln's note referred "Mr. Peckham's proposal to sell patent rifles and his method of making cartridges." No further reference has been found.

To Hiram Barney[1]

Hon. Hiram Barney   Executive Mansion,
My dear Sir.   Washington, May 9. 1863.

This introduces Gov. Wright, of Indiana, whose name, if not his person, you certainly know. He is trying to raise a little money, not for himself, but to carry some articles to the World's Fair at Hamburg. I shall be glad if, by your acquaintance with the rich men, you can render him some assistance. Yours truly

A. LINCOLN

[1] ALS, owned by Arthur Wendell, Rahway, New Jersey. Joseph A. Wright, Governor of Indiana 1849-1857, was commissioner to the exposition at Hamburg.

To Edward Bates[1]

May 9, 1863

In speaking of the discretion which the District Attorney might use, I alluded to such discretion as is conferred by the law; and I certainly did not mean to say, I would undertake to confer an enlarged discretion upon him.   A. LINCOLN

May 9. 1863.

[1] AES, DNA GE RG 60, Papers of Attorney General, Segregated Lincoln Material. Lincoln's endorsement is written on a letter from Charles W. Prentiss, New York attorney, May 7, 1863, endorsed by Solomon Foot in concurrence, asking that the president put in writing a verbal statement made to Prentiss to the effect that U.S. District Attorney E. Delafield Smith was "at liberty to use his discretion" in settling the case of the *John Gilpin*, a vessel seized as a prize for running the blockade loaded with cotton. Welles' *Diary* on May 12 records the cabinet discussion on the case, "There has been a good deal of outside engineering in this case. Chase thought if the parties were loyal it was a hard case. I said all such losses were hard, and asked whether it was hardest for the wealthy, loyal owners, who understood to run the blockade with their cotton, or the brave and loyal sailors who made the capture and were by law entitled to the avails, to be deprived. I requested him to say which of these parties should be the losers. He did not answer. I added this was another of those cases that belonged to the courts exclusively, with which the Executive ought not to interfere. All finally acquiesced in this view."

To John A. Dix[1]

Washington City, May 9. 1863

Major General Dix   It is very important for Hooker to know exactly what damage is done to the Railroads, at all points between Fredericksburg and Richmond. As yet we have no word as to whether the crossings of the North and South Ana, or any of them, have been touched. There are four of these crossings, that is, one on each road on each stream. You readily perceive why this information is desired. I suppose Kilpatrick or Davis[2] can tell. Please ascertain fully what was done, & what is the present condition, as near as you can, and advise me at once.   A. LINCOLN

[1] ALS, RPB. Colonel Judson Kilpatrick of the First Brigade, Third Cavalry Division, reported to Dix at 6:50 P.M., "General [David M.] Gregg was ordered to destroy the bridges referred to. I only burned those over the Chickahominy. I do not know that he succeeded, but was told by prisoners that he did." (OR, I, XXV, II, 456).

Dix replied to Lincoln's query on May 11, "Mr. Ould [Robert Ould, Confederate agent for exchange of prisoners] says neither of the two bridges over the South Anna nor the bridge over the North Anna was destroyed. The railroad communication is uninterrupted. . . ." (*Ibid.*, p. 465).

[2] Colonel Hasbrouck Davis of the Twelfth Illinois Cavalry.

To Edwin M. Stanton[1]

Hon. Sec. of War   Executive Mansion,
My dear Sir—   Washington, May 9. 1863.

I wish you would make out the appointment of Lilley at once. He has my word in writing, and I can not afford to break it. I appreciate your opposition to him; but you can better afford to let him be appointed, than I can afford to break my word with him. Yours as ever   A. LINCOLN

[1] ALS (copy?), DLC-RTL. See Lincoln to Stanton, April 20, *supra.* On May 11, Montgomery C. Meigs transmitted the papers in the case of William Lilley to Stanton, and cited the following statement from General Rufus Saxton:

"With regard to the treatment of the poor, defenceless blacks . . . I can only say that W. Lilly's course was such as to outrage all the common feelings of humanity, characterised by the most cowardly and brutal treatment, and apparently in one or two instances by criminal indecency. Habitually in a state of partial intoxication, he grossly insulted the wife of the only loyal white man in South Carolina who claimed our protection, while her husband and herself were in his house.

"Unanimously rejected by the Senate as an Assistant Quartermaster, a Court Martial held on the spot where he performed his 'efficient service,' after a long and impartial trial, justly sentenced him to be cashiered." (DLC-RTL).

On May 15, Senator Henry Wilson wrote Lincoln, "I am constrained by a sense of duty, after reading papers in the War office, to withdraw my letter in favor of Mr Lilley for Quarter Master. I had not examined the matter, and relied . . . upon the opinion of Mr. King, but I find I have made a mistake, and desire to right it." (*Ibid.*).

Presumably Lincoln dropped the matter, although Lilley wrote a further plea on June 8.

To Edwin M. Stanton[1]

Hon. Sec. of War   Executive Mansion,
My dear Sir   Washington, May 9. 1863.

Please inform me on what ground Dr. Worster of this City has been arrested. Yours truly   A. LINCOLN

[1] ALS, DLC-RTL. Lincoln's letter was returned with an endorsement by Captain Henry B. Todd, headquarters provost marshal, May 11, 1863, stating that Dr. R. J. Worster "was arrested for obtaining money from Soldiers and assisting them in obtaining fraudulent & illegal Discharges. . . ."

To John P. Usher[1]

Executive Mansion, May 9, 1863.

The Secretary of the Interior will send me a temporary commission for the within named Alfred R. Elder, as Indian Agent at Olympia, Washington Territory.   A. LINCOLN

1 ES, DNA NR RG 48, Appointments, Indian Agencies, Box 1274. The endorsement is written on a letter from Usher transmitting recommendations for Alfred R. Elder of Washington Territory. Elder was appointed agent of Medicine Creek Agency.

To Peter H. Watson[1]

Mr. Watson, Assistant Secretary of War, please see the bearer, who is the man of whom I spoke in reference to a diving invention.
May 9, 1863. A. LINCOLN.

1 Hertz, II, 866. The bearer has not been identified.

To Daniel Butterfield[1]

War Department, Washington City,
Major General Butterfield: May 11, 1863.
About what distance is it from the Observatory, we stopped at last Thursday to the line of enemys works you ranged the glass upon for me? A. LINCOLN.

1 Thirty-eighth Congress, Second Session, *Report of the Joint Committee on the Conduct of the War* (1865), I, 237. General Butterfield replied at 6:15 P.M., "About two miles in a direct line." (DLC-RTL).

To Salmon P. Chase[1]

Hon. Secretary of Treasury: May 11, 1863
My dear Sir: I have just learned that Henry C. Wilson, whom I had appointed as the successor of Victor Smith, at Puget Sound, is dead. Please send me a commission for Frederick A. Wilson. Yours truly, A. LINCOLN.

1 Robert B. Warden, *Account of the Private Life and Public Services of Salmon Portland Chase* (1874), p. 527. See Lincoln's letters to Chase, May 8, *supra*. On May 11, Chase wrote Lincoln as follows:

"Some weeks ago you verbally directed me to investigate the papers connected with the case of the Collector for the Puget Sound District. . . .

"Almost immediately afterwards important business . . . called me to the Eastern Cities. On leaving I directed the Assistant Secretary to examine all the papers . . . so that, on my return, I could at once make the investigation you required.

"I came back on Friday night (8th) & was informed . . . that you had already directed him to make out . . . a Commission for a new Collector.

"This information surprised and greatly pained me; for I had not thought it possible that you would remove an officer of My Department, without awaiting the result, although somewhat delayed, of an investigation directed by yourself; and appoint a successor . . . without even consulting me. . . .

"Today I have received your note stating that the person for whom, in my absence, a commission was prepared, is deceased; and directing one to be made out for another person of whom I know absolutely nothing. . . .

"I can ask, of course, nothing more than conference. The right of appointment belongs to you; and if . . . your judgment . . . differs from mine, it is my duty to acquiesce, cheerfully; unless, indeed, the case be one of such a character, as to justify my withdrawal from my post. I have, however, a right to be consulted. . . .

"The blank commission which you direct me to send . . . is enclosed. . . . It is enclosed, however, with my most respectful protest against the precedent; and with the assurance that if you find anything in my views to which your own sense of duty will not permit you to assent, I will, unhesitatingly, relieve you from all embarrassment so far as I am concerned by tendering you my resignation." (DLC-RTL).

Lincoln endorsed on the envelope, "First offer of resignation." Lewis C. Gunn of California was appointed to replace Victor Smith, but in 1865 Frederick A. Wilson received the post following Gunn's resignation. See Lincoln to Chase, May 13, *infra*.

To John A. Dix[1]

Washington City,
Major General Dix.   May 11. 1863
    Do the Richmond papers have anything about Grand Gulf or Vicksburg?   A. LINCOLN

[1] ALS, RPB. Dix replied (received at 4:35 P.M.), "I had but a moment to examine the papers. I have enclosed them to the Secretary of War   I saw nothing of Grand Gulf or Vicksburg" (DLC-RTL).

To Edwin M. Stanton[1]

Hon. Sec. of War.   Executive Mansion.
Dear Sir: Washington. May 11th. 1863.
    I have again concluded to relieve Genl Curtis. I see no other way to avoid the worst consequences there. I think of Gen. Schofield for his successor; but I do not wish to take the matter of a successor out of the hands of yourself and Genl Halleck. Yours truly.   A. LINCOLN.

[1] Copy, DNA WR RG 108, HQA, Letters Received, 428, Box 62. A communication signed by Samuel T. Glover and others, May 1, 1863, reads as follows:

"The disorders in this Military department are frightful. Crime in almost every form is committed with impunity. These disorders are not accidental but result from party principles and organization encouraged and assisted by the Military power which instead of being exerted for our protection is being used to promote the evils of which we complain.

"The 'Revolutionists' as they boastfully style themselves . . . whose avowed purpose is the immediate abolition of Slavery, regardless of the constitutional rights of our citizens are assisted in their operations by the Chief of this department. . . ." (DLC-RTL).

On May 2 Governor Gamble pressed for the removal of General Curtis (*ibid.*). Bates' *Diary* records on May 11 that Austin A. King and John B. Henderson "are here, urging upon the Prest the necessity to make a change of commander in Mo., and at once." See also Lincoln to Stanton, March 9, *supra.*

To Edward Bates[1]

Hon. Attorney General   Executive Mansion,
My dear Sir: Washington, May 12. 1863.

Please get me up a pardon similar to the one we gave to the son of Gen. Sterling Price, for John Orcutt Carpenter, of Kentucky. Yours truly   A LINCOLN

[1] ALS, DNA RG 204, U.S. Pardon Attorney, A 472. See Lincoln to Bates, November 19, 1862, *supra*, concerning pardon of Edwin R. Price. No further reference has been found concerning John Orcutt Carpenter.

To Joseph Holt[1]

Sentence commuted to suspension of two months rank and pay proper, to commence March 30th. 1863   A. LINCOLN
May 12, 1863.

[1] AES, DNA WR RG 153, Judge Advocate General, MM 187. Lincoln's endorsement is written on the court-martial record of Lieutenant Adelbert S. Eddy, Fourth New York Heavy Artillery, dismissed from service for absence without leave and neglect of duty. Generals Abercrombie and Heintzelman recommended the commutation as given by Lincoln. See further Lincoln to Stanton, September 11, *infra.*

To Horatio Seymour[1]

Gov. Seymour   Executive Mansion,
Albany, N. Y.   Washington, May 12. [1863]

Dr. Swinburne and Mr. Gillett are here having been refused, as they say, by the War Department, permission to go to the Army of the Potomac. They now appeal to me, saying you wish them to go. I suppose they have been excluded by a rule which experience has induced the Department to deem proper; still they shall have leave to go, if you say you desire it. Please answer.

           A. LINCOLN

[1] ALS, RPB. Letters from former Governor Edwin D. Morgan, May 5, and Governor Seymour, May 4, introduced Dr. John Swinburne and his assistant Mr. J. T. Gillett, who volunteered their services to the Army following the Battle of Chancellorsville (DLC-RTL). Seymour replied to Lincoln's telegram on May 13, "I have great confidence in Dr. Swinbourn's skill but I cannot ask the Gov't. to violate its rules. You know best the interest of the Army & I shall be contented with your decision. I am obliged to you for your courtesy." (*Ibid.*).

To Edwin M. Stanton[1]

May 12, 1863

Sec. of War, please see Mr. Dole & others about the first colored regiment. Please do the best for them you can. . . .

[1] Parke-Bernet Catalog 939, March 1-2, 1948, No. 267. This partial text is all that is available. William P. Dole and others represented the Union League of Washington, D.C., in recommending Reverend J. D. Turner and W. G. Raymond who had applied for "permission to raise a colored Regiment in this District" (W. G. Raymond to Lincoln, April 25, 1863, DLC-RTL).

To Edwin M. Stanton[1]

May 12, 1863

The within is presented with a very praiseworthy object, and is submitted to the War Department, asking the best attention that can be consistently given to it.   A. LINCOLN

May 12. 1863.

[1] AES, IHi. Lincoln's endorsement is written on a memorial from the Union League of Philadelphia recommending employment of disabled veterans in "the lighter military and civil duties connected with the Provost Guard, the Arsenals of construction . . . ordnance department. . . ." etc.

To Gideon Welles[1]

Hon. Sec. of Navy, please see & hear Hon. Mr. Casey.

May 12. 1863.   A. LINCOLN

[1] ALS, Ct. On the back of the card bearing Lincoln's note is Welles' pencilled endorsement, "Mr C. wanted special favor to trade for cotton &c &c.   not granted." Mr. Casey has not been identified, but may have been Samuel L. Casey of Kentucky.

To Pedro Diez Canseco[1]

May 13, 1863

Abraham Lincoln,
President of the United States of America,
To His Excellency
    Señor Don Pedro Diez Canseco,
    Second Vice President of the Republic
    of Peru, charged with Executive Power.
    Sir: I have been deeply touched by the announcement, contained in the letter which you addressed to me under date of the

eleventh ultimo, of the decease of the Most Excellent President of the Republic of Peru, the Grand Marshal, Don Miguel San Roman.

Regarding the interests of the Spanish American Republics with no common concern, I have not failed to observe the incidents of the brief administration of the Grand Marshal, Señor San Roman, with admiration and respect, and to anticipate for the Republic a most prosperous and brilliant future in the developemement [*sic*] of his wise and sagacious policy.

I offer to your Excellency and to the Peruvian Nation my sincere sympathy and condolence in this painful event.

As your Excellency has entered upon the duties of the Presidency, ad interim, under Constitutional sanction, prescribing to yourself such a course as must invite the approval and coöperation of other Powers, I cannot but believe that the Supreme Ruler of the Universe will guide the counsels of Your Excellency to a happy issue.

And so commending you to His safe and Holy Keeping. I remain, Your Excellency's Good Friend,   ABRAHAM LINCOLN.

By the President:

WILLIAM H. SEWARD, Secretary of State.

Washington, May 13, 1863.

[1] Copy, DNA FS RG 59, Communications to Foreign Sovereigns and States, III, 207-208.

To Salmon P. Chase[1]

                                        Executive Mansion, Washington,
Hon. Secretary of the Treasury: May 13, 1863.

My dear Sir: I return the letters of General Garfield and Mr. Flanders. I am sorry to know the general's pet expedition under Colonel Streight, has already been captured. Whether it had paid for itself, as he hoped, I do not know. If you think it proper to fill the agency mentioned by Mr. Flanders, by all means let Mr. F. be the man.[2]

Please send me over the commission for Lewis C. Gunn, as you recommend, for collector of customs at Puget Sound.[3] Yours truly,

                                        A. LINCOLN.

[1] Robert B. Warden, *Account of the Private Life and Public Services of Salmon Portland Chase* (1874), p. 528. The letters of General James A. Garfield and Benjamin F. Flanders have not been located. Colonel Abel D. Streight commanding a raiding party sent from Tuscumbia, Alabama, to cut railroads,

was captured with 1,600 men by General Nathan Bedford Forrest near Rome, Georgia, on May 3, 1863.
² Flanders was appointed supervising special agent of the Treasury Department at New Orleans.   ³ See Lincoln to Chase, May 11, *supra.*

To Salmon P. Chase[1]

May 13, 1863

I understand there are, or have been, some charges against Lieutenant Merryman, of which I know nothing. I only wish to say, he was raised from childhood in the town where I lived, and I remember nothing against him as boy or man.

His father, now dead, was a very intimate acquaintance and friend of mine.   A. LINCOLN.

[1] NH, VIII, 273. Lieutenant James H. Merryman of the revenue service was the son of Dr. Elias H. Merryman. Concerning Merryman's difficulties with Victor Smith, collector of customs at Port Townsend, Washington Territory, see OR, I, L, I, 1099, and I, L, II, 70-72. Merryman remained in the service for over twenty years. See Lincoln to Welles, April 8, 1864, *infra.*

To Salmon P. Chase[1]

Hon. Sec. of Treasury: Please see Capt. Martin, well vouched as a good man who seeks a position in the Marine Revenue service
May. 13. 1863.   A. LINCOLN

[1] Copy, IHi-Nicolay and Hay Papers. Mr. Martin has not been identified and is not listed in the *U.S. Official Register,* 1863.

To John W. Forney[1]

Col. Forney   Executive Mansion,
My dear Sir   Washington, May 13. 1863.
I wish to lose no time in thanking you for the excellent and manly article in the Chronicle on "Stonewall Jackson" Yours truly
A. LINCOLN

[1] ALS, ORB. Forney had on May 12 written Lincoln a letter of apology for "a most ungenerous criticism upon Generals Halleck and Hooker" which had appeared in the Philadelphia *Press.* The editorial on the death of Stonewall Jackson in the Washington *Chronicle* of May 13 was as generous to the enemy as the *Press* had been ungenerous to the Union leaders. Forney acknowledged Lincoln's note as follows, "Thanks for your kind letter, by the young gentleman who bears your name. I have been deeply chagrined by the *error* in my Phila. paper a few days ago, in my absence, and am therefore glad to find that you can see also what is right and just. . . ." (DLC-RTL).

To Anson G. Henry[1]

Dr. A. G. Henry   Executive Mansion, Washington,
Metropolitan Hotel   New-York.   May 13. 1863.

Governor Chase's feelings were hurt by my action in his absence. Smith is removed, but Gov. Chase wishes to name his successor, and asks a day or two to make the designation.

                                  A. LINCOLN

[1] ALS, RPB. See Lincoln to Chase, May 11, *supra*.

To Joseph Hooker[1]

Washington, D.C., May 13, 1863– 1 p.m.

Major-General Hooker: If it will not interfere with the service, nor personally incommode you, please come up and see me this evening.   A. LINCOLN.

[1] OR, I, XXV, II, 474. Hooker replied at 2:30 P.M., "Will see you at Eight this Evening." (DLC-RTL).

To Edwin M. Stanton[1]

                     Executive Mansion, Washington,
Hon. Secretary of War   May 13, 1863.

My dear Sir   Since parting with you I have seen the Secretaries of State and the Treasury, and they both think we better not issue the special suspension of the Writ of Habeas Corpus spoken of. Gov. Chase thinks the case is not before Judge Swaine,[2] that it is before Judge Levett, that the writ will probably not issue, whichever the application may be before; and that, in no event, will Swaine commit an imprudence. His chief reason for thinking the writ will not issue, is that he has seen in a newspaper that Judge Levett[3] stated that Judge Swaine & he refused a similar application last year. Yours truly   A. LINCOLN

[1] ALS, DLC-Stanton Papers. On May 4, Clement L. Vallandigham had been arrested, on orders of General Burnside. On May 8, Burnside telegraphed in reply to a non-extant telegram from Lincoln, "Your dispatch just rec'd. I thank you for your kind assurance of support & beg to say that every possible effort will be made on my part to sustain the Govt of the United States in its fullest authority." (DLC-RTL). The furor in Ohio and throughout the North over the arrest and ensuing trial was such that Secretary Stanton feared the impact on Union morale if the U.S. district judge should ignore the general proclamation suspending the writ of habeas corpus. On May 13, he therefore prepared an order especially suspending the writ in Vallandigham's case and drafted an accompanying despatch to Burnside. Both documents, unsigned, are

preserved in the Lincoln Papers. On May 19, Stanton ordered Burnside, at the direction of the president, to "send C. L. Vallandigham under secure guard to the headquarters of General Rosecrans to be put by him beyond our military lines and in case of his return within our lines he be arrested and kept in close custody for the term specified in his sentence." (OR, II, V, 657).

2 Noah H. Swayne, associate justice of the U.S. Supreme Court from Ohio, who with the U.S. district judges constituted the U.S. Circuit Court for Ohio.

3 Humphrey H. Leavitt, judge of the U.S. District Court for Southern Ohio, who later denied the motion for habeas corpus in a decision generally upholding not only Lincoln's power to suspend the writ but also General Burnside's order for the arrest of Vallandigham.

To Edwin M. Stanton[1]

Hon. Sec. of War please see Mr. Diggs. A. LINCOLN
May 13. 1863.

1 ALS, RPB. Mr. Diggs has not been identified.

To Joseph G. Totten[1]

Gen. Totten   Executive Mansion,
My dear Sir   Washington, May 13, 1863.

I wish to appoint William Whipple, son of the General who fell in the recent battle on the Rappahannock, to West-Point, next Spring, and I wish to file this with you as a remembrance upon the subject. Yours truly   A. LINCOLN

1 ALS, DNA WR RG 94, U.S. Military Academy, 1863, No. 466, Box 83. General Amiel W. Whipple was killed at Chancellorsville; Charles W. Whipple is listed in the *Official Register* (1865) as in the third class at West Point.

To William C. Bryant[1]

Executive Mansion,
Mr. W. C. Bryant.   Washington, May 14, 1863.

My dear Sir Yours requesting that Gen. Sigel may be again assigned to command, is received. Allow me to briefly explain. I kept Gen. Sigel in command for several months, he requesting to resign, or to be relieved. At length, at his urgent & repeated solicitation, he was relieved. Now it is inconvenient to assign him a command without relieving or dismissing some other officer, who is not asking, and perhaps would object, to being so disposed of. This is one of a class of cases; and you perceive how embarrassing they are. Yours very truly   A. LINCOLN

¹ ALS, in custody of Conrad G. Goddard, Roslyn, Long Island, New York. Bryant wrote on May 11, 1863, "You will . . . pardon the liberty which I take in representing to you the universal desire of our German fellow citizens that General Sigel should be again placed in command of that part of the army of the Rappahannock which is composed of German soldiery and which has suffered some loss of credit in the recent battles. The enthusiasm in his favor among our German population is unanimous. . . . It is impossible, Sir, for you, where you are, to concieve of the strength and fervor of this wish of our German population. . . . The other day when it was said that General Sigel had been called to join the army under General Hooker it was the common exclamation that that single step 'was equal to the addition of ten thousand men to the army.' " (DLC-RTL).

On July 6, 1863, Sigel was assigned to command of militia and volunteer forces at Reading, Pennsylvania (OR, I, XXVII, III, 563).

To Joseph Hooker¹

Executive Mansion, Washington,
Major General Hooker   May 14. 1863.

My dear Sir: When I wrote you on the 7th. I had an impression that possibly, by an early movement, you could get some advantage from the supposed facts that the enemies communications were disturbed and that he was somewhat deranged in position. That idea has now passed away, the enemy having re-established his communications, regained his positions and actually received re-inforcements. It does not now appear probable to me that you can gain any thing by an early renewal of the attempt to cross the Rappahannock. I therefore shall not complain, if you do no more, for a time, than to keep the enemy at bay, and out of other mischief, by menaces and occasional cavalry raids, if practicable; and to put your own army in good condition again. Still, if in your own clear judgment, you can renew the attack successfully, I do not mean to restrain you. Bearing upon this last point, I must tell you I have some painful intimations that some of your corps and Division Commanders are not giving you their entire confidence. This would be ruinous, if true; and you should therefore, first of all, ascertain the real facts beyond all possibility of doubt. Yours truly   A. LINCOLN

¹ ADfS, DLC-RTL. Hooker wrote Lincoln on May 13:

"My movements have been a little delayed by the withdrawal of many of the two-years' and nine-months' regiments, and those whose time is not already up it will be expedient to leave on this side of the river. This reduction imposes upon me the necessity of partial reorganization. My marching force of infantry is cut down to about 80,000, while I have artillery for an army of more than double that number. It has always been out of proportion, considering the character of the country we have to campaign in, and I shall be more efficient by leaving at least one-half of it in depot. In addition, Stoneman's cavalry returned to camp day before yesterday, and will require a day or two more to be in readiness to resume operations.

"I know that you are impatient, and I know that I am, but my impatience must not be indulged at the expense of dearest interests.

"I am informed that the bulk of Longstreet's force is in Richmond. With the facilities at hand, he can readily transfer it to Lee's army, and no doubt will do so if Lee should fight and fall back, as he will try to do.

"The enemy's camps are reported to me as being more numerous than before our last movement, but of this I have no positive information. They probably have about the same number of troops as before the last battle, but with these and Longstreet's they are much my superior, besides having the advantage of acting on the defensive, which, in this country, can scarcely be estimated.

"I hear nothing of Peck's movements and of the force at West Point, which is too small to be of much importance in the general movement. If it is expected that Peck will be able to keep Longstreet's force in and about Richmond, I should be informed of it, and if not, a reserve infantry force of 25,000 should be placed at my disposal in this vicinity. I merely state this for your information, not that I know even that you have such a force, or, if you have, that you would be disposed to make use of it in this way. I only desire that you should be informed of my views. In my opinion, the major part of the troops on the Upper Potomac, in and around Washington and Baltimore, are out of position, and if great results are expected from the approaching movement, every man and vessel at the disposal of the Government should be assigned their posts. I hope to be able to commence my movement to-morrow, but this must not be spoken of to any one. . . ." (OR, I, XXV, II, 473).

To Henry T. Blow, Charles D. Drake and Others[1]

Hon. H. T. Blow   Executive Mansion,
C. D. Drake & others   Washington,
St. Louis, Mo   May 15, 1863. [9 P.M.]

Your despatch of to-day is just received. It is very painful to me that you in Missouri can not, or will not, settle your factional quarrel among yourselves. I have been tormented with it beyond endurance for months, by both sides. Neither side pays the least respect to my appeals to your reason. I am now compelled to take hold of the case.   A. LINCOLN

[1] ALS, RPB. The telegram to which Lincoln replied reads as follows: "The Telegraph reports the probable appointment of Gen Schofield to command this Dept. We a committee last Monday by the largest meeting of Union people ever held in St Louis pray to suspend that appointment until you hear from us" (DLC-RTL).

In reply to a despatch from Major General Francis J. Herron, commanding at Rolla, Missouri, threatening to resign rather than serve under Schofield, Stanton replied on May 17 that the president "directs me to say that he is unaware of any valid objection to General Schofield, he having recently commanded the Department of the Missouri, giving almost universal satisfaction so far as the President ever heard. He directs me to add that he has appreciated the services of General Herron and rewarded them by rapid promotions, but that, even in him, insubordination will be met as insubordination, and that your resignation will be acted upon as circumstances may require whenever it is tendered." (OR, I, XXII, II, 285).

To James Guthrie[1]

Hon. James Guthrie   Washington City,
Louisville, Ky.   May 16 1863 [8:35 P.M.]

Your despatch of to-day is received. I personally know nothing of Col. Churchill; but months ago;[2] and more than once, he has been represented to me as exerting a mischievous influence at St. Louis, for which reason I am unwilling to force his continuance there against the judgment of our friends on the ground. But if it will oblige you, he may come to, and remain at Louisville, upon taking the oath of allegiance, and your pledge for his good behavior.   A. LINCOLN.

[1] ALS, RPB. See Lincoln to Stanton, *infra*. Guthrie telegraphed Lincoln on May 16 as follows: "Col. Samuel B. Churchill, of Saint Louis, formerly of this city, has been banished South with his wife and seven children, five of them very small. Colonel Churchill is a man of intelligence and high character, of moderate fortune. It will utterly ruin him to have to go South. I respectfully request that his sentence be commuted. He will take the oath and give bond if allowed. I ask this because I know him and rely on his honor, and he is a cousin of my children." (OR, II, V, 627).

[2] See Lincoln to Lazarus W. Powell, February 4, 1862, *supra*.

To Edwin M. Stanton[1]

Hon. Sec. of War.   War Department
My dear Sir.   Washington City, May 16. 1863

The commander of the Department at St. Louis, has ordered several persons South of our military lines, which order is not disapproved by me. Yet, at the special request of Hon. James Guthrie, I have consented to one of the number, Ṣamuel Churchill, remaining at Louiṡville, Ky, upon condition of his taking the oath of allegiance, and Mr. Guthrie's word of honor for his good behavior.
Yours truly   A. LINCOLN

[1] ALS, IHi. See Lincoln to Guthrie, *supra*, and to Stanton, May 19, *infra*.

To Edwin M. Stanton[1]

Executive Mansion May 16th. 1863

The Secretary of War will please instruct Major General Burnside to parole Major Clarence Prentice now a rebel prisoner in Camp Chase, Ohio, to remain outside the limits of both the loyal and disloyal States, or so-called "Confederate States," of the United States of America, during the present rebellion, and to abstain from in any wise aiding or abetting said rebellion.   A LINCOLN

[1] ES-F, ISLA. Lincoln's endorsement is written on a letter from George D. Prentice, May 6, 1863, requesting that the president reply to an earlier letter of April 28 which reads:

"Mr. Lincoln, I have a great favor to ask of you. Hear me! My only child, Clarence J. Prentice, God help him, is a major in the Confederate service. A few weeks ago he came into Kentucky and being cut off from his command he came by night to his home to see me and his mother and his baby. He was seen coming and in a few hours arrested. He is now at Camp Chase and his mother in Columbus. He desires I know to serve no longer in the war. He would be a great loss to the Confederates, for he has been one of their most effective officers.

"I do not suppose . . . that you can parole my boy upon his taking the non-combatant's oath to remain in the United States though I should be most happy if you could; but I fervently appeal to you to let him go upon his taking that simple oath anywhere outside of the United States and of the rebel Confederacy. I know his plans. His mother will go with him and he will never bear arms against us again. I will be surety for this with fortune and life. I have written to General Burnside to let my son remain at Camp Chase till I hear from you. Please let it be soon for I am most unhappy." (OR, II, V, 527-28).

As printed in the *Official Records*, Prentice's letter of April 28 bears three endorsements. The first, Joseph Holt to Stanton, May 16, 1863, is as follows: "Clarence J. Prentice himself has made no communication to the Government expressive of his feelings in regard to the war or of his future plans and purposes. When prisoners of war are willing to take the oath of allegiance it is the practice to permit them to do so. When they are not thus willing they have been invariably exchanged under the cartel. The intermediate course now proposed has not been pursued because the Government would thereby lose the advantage of the exchange and because no satisfactory . . . guaranty would exist that the prisoner thus tenderly dealt with would not at the first opportunity reenter the rebel military service. . . . He left his home in a State then and still loyal and voluntarily and wantonly banded with traitors. . . . It is for the Secretary to determine whether the established policy . . . shall be modified in his favor."

The second endorsement, Brigadier General Edward R. S. Canby to Colonel William Hoffman, commissary general of prisoners, is dated May 22: "Colonel: I submitted this paper to the Secretary of War yesterday and he said that he was under the impression that the President had given an order permitting Prentice to go abroad. Has it been done?"

The third endorsement, Hoffman to Canby, undated, is as follows: "There is no record in this office of any special orders in the case of Major Prentice. On the 13th instant he was sent from Camp Chase to City Point for exchange."

One infers that Prentice's letter of May 6, bearing Lincoln's order of May 16 endorsed on the verso, was "lost" in the War Department. Major Clarence Prentice was exchanged and fought on until the end of the war as major and later colonel in the Confederate Army.

To Joseph Holt[1]

Judge Advocate General please examine, and report upon, this case.

May 17. 1863.   A. LINCOLN

[1] AES, DNA RG 153, Judge Advocate General, General Court Martial, MM 187. See Lincoln to Holt, May 12, *supra*. On June 22 Nicolay returned the papers in the case of Lieutenant Adelbert S. Eddy to Holt with the notation that the case had already been decided by the president (*ibid.*). See also Lincoln to Stanton, September 11, *infra*.

Memorandum:
Appointment of Ernest L. Kinney[1]

Executive Mansion, Washington, May 17, 1863.

Ernest L. Kinney seeks the appointment of a 2nd. Lieutenant in the Regular Army. He has been five years at Churchill's Military School—not West-Point. He is a Lieutenant in the 54th. N.Y. Vols, and was assigned to Gen. Tyler's Staff last December, in which service he has continued till now, & still is. His regiment is about being disbanded by consolidation, & he fears being thrown out of service thereby. For this reason he seeks the appointment. He is a family relation of Senator Dixon of Connecticut.

1 AD, DLC-RTL. Second Lieutenant Ernest L. Kinney remained in the Volunteers until he resigned on November 14, 1864, to enlist as private in the First Cavalry on November 17, where he was commissioned second lieutenant on January 2, 1865.

Memorandum:
Appointment of Thomas J. Bishop[1]

Executive Mansion, Washington, May 18. 1863.

Hon. John S. Phelps recommends Thomas J. Bishop, to be P. Marshal, in the now, 4th. Springfield District Mo. He fought at Springfield last winter & is a good man.

1 AD, DLC-RTL. No record of Bishop's appointment has been found.

To Edwin M. Stanton[1]

PRIVATE

Hon. Secretary of War   Executive Mansion,
My dear Sir   Washington, May 18. 1863.

You will greatly oblige me, because it will be a matter of personal relief to me, if you will allow Hanscom's (the Republican's) accounts to be settled and paid. Yours truly   A. LINCOLN.

1 ALS, NHi. See Lincoln to Peter H. Watson, April 27, *supra.* The *National Republican* was designated by Lincoln as the official organ to print official government notices (see April 11, 1861, *supra*). Following a change of ownership Lincoln confirmed the designation on February 16, 1863, but for some reason the War Department failed to settle its accounts with the paper.

To Edwin M. Stanton[1]

[c. May 18, 1863]

Secretary of War please see Mr. Gibbs, with this letter from Gov. Andrew.   A. LINCOLN.

¹ Stan. V. Henkels Catalog 1494, November 20, 1935, No. 51. According to the catalog description Lincoln's endorsement is written on a letter from Governor John A. Andrew, May 18, 1863. No further reference has been found and Mr. Gibbs has not been identified.

To Queen Victoria¹

May 18, 1863

Abraham Lincoln
President of the United States of America

To Her Majesty Victoria
Queen of the United Kingdom
of Great Britain and Ireland.
&c &c. &c. Sendeth Greeting:

Great and Good Friend: I have received the letter which Your Majesty addressed to me on the 31st. day of March last, announcing the pleasing intelligence of the Marriage on the 10th. of that month of Your Majesty's dearly beloved son His Royal Highness Albert Edward Prince of Wales, Duke of Saxony, Prince of Saxe-Coburg and Gotha &c. &c. with Her Royal Highness the Princess Alexandra Caroline Maria Charlotte Louisa Julia, eldest Daughter of His Royal Highness the Prince Christian of Denmark. Feeling a lively interest in whatever concerns the Welfare and happiness of Your Majesty's illustrious House, I pray Your Majesty to receive my cordial congratulations on this auspicious event, and my fervent Wishes that it may signally promote your own happiness and that of the Prince your son and his young spouse: And so I recommend Your Majesty and Your Majesty's Royal Family to the protection of the Almighty.

Written at Washington, the 18th day of May, in the year of our Lord one thousand eight hundred and sixty-three. Your Good Friend, ABRAHAM LINCOLN

By the President
WILLIAM H. SEWARD Secretary of State.

¹ Copy, DNA FS RG 59, Communications to Foreign Sovereigns and States, III, 216-17.

To Joseph Holt¹

May 19, 1863

Judge Advocate General, please examine and report upon this case. The young man is nephew of Ex. President Fillmore, who writes the within letter A. LINCOLN
May 19, 1863.

[1] AES, owned by Charles W. Olsen, Chicago, Illinois. Lincoln's endorsement is written on a letter from Millard Fillmore, May 16, 1863, asking a court of inquiry for his nephew, First Lieutenant George M. Fillmore of the Third Artillery, dismissed on April 17, 1863, for intemperance. The register of letters received by the judge advocate general lists a missing letter or endorsement dated May 25 from John G. Nicolay (No. 410), that the president will take no action on the enclosed papers of Lieutenant Fillmore (DNA WR RG 153).

To Edwin M. Stanton[1]

May 19, 1863

Sec. of War, please make up an order & send to Mr. Guthrie according to the despatches *pro* & con, in the case of Samuel B. Churchill.   A. LINCOLN

May 19, 1863.

[1] AES, NHi. See Lincoln to Guthrie, and to Stanton, May 16, *supra.* Lincoln's endorsement is written on a telegram from Joshua F. and James Speed, May 19, 9:10 A.M., "Did you get our dispatch of Sunday about Churchill of St Louis   The time is so short & we so anxious must be our apology for this message." The telegram of Sunday, May 17, is as follows: "Samuel B. Churchill, of Saint Louis, was arrested in this city by order of General Curtis and taken to Saint Louis. We understand that he with his family . . . are ordered to leave for the South on Wednesday. We know Churchill well, being an old schoolmate and intimate friend to both of us. His father . . . . died a few months ago leaving a large estate and the prisoner one of his executors, with important and indispensable duties to discharge in which many of our and your friends are deeply interested, none of which can be discharged without his discretion. In view of all the circumstances we ask a revocation of this order, and we will hold ourselves bound for the faithful performance of any obligation which may be imposed on him. . . . The duties alluded to in connection with his father's estate are here. If his presence is hurtful in Saint Louis can he be allowed to remain here? If this is granted we will hold ourselves in honor bound to inform on him and arrest him should he do anything wrong. If this cannot be done can a respite be granted till one of us can see you or the Secretary of War?" (OR, II, V, 631).

Following receipt of Lincoln's note on May 19, Stanton caused *Special Orders No.* 223 to be issued, allowing Churchill "to reside at Louisville upon condition that he take the oath of allegiance to the Government of the United States and that the Hon. James Guthrie pledge himself to the officer commanding at Louisville that Colonel Churchill shall be of good behavior and do no act of hostility to the United States and communicate no information nor give any aid or comfort to the enemy. . . ." (*Ibid.,* pp. 663-64).

To Edward Bates[1]

Attorney General, please send me commissions according to the within.   A. LINCOLN

May 20, 1863

[1] AES, DNA RG 60, Papers of Attorney General, Appointments, Louisiana, Box 504. Lincoln's endorsement is written on a letter from Benjamin F. Flan-

ders and Michael Hahn, May 9, 1863, recommending appointment of Edward H. Durell, Rufus Waples, and James Graham, as U.S. district judge, attorney, and marshal, respectively, for the Eastern District of Louisiana. The appoint-ments were made accordingly.

To Edwin D. Morgan[1]

Hon. E. D. Morgan   Washington, D.C.,
New-York   May 20 1863

I presume the Commission of Hiatt has already gone forward, as the Sec. of the Treasury told me day-before yesterday he would send it forward. I wish the first time it is convenient you would call on me, as I feel sure I can give you some views in regard to this case which you do not think of   A. LINCOLN

[1] ALS, RPB. Senator-elect Morgan had telegraphed at 10 P.M. on May 19, "I hope you will not think it is asking too much to withhold the commission for Abrahm Hiatt until the friends of Depew can be heard." (DLC-RTL). Chauncey M. Depew, living at Peekskill, had actively supported Morgan for the Senate, but Abrahm Hyatt of Sing Sing, is listed in the *U.S. Official Register*, 1863, as assessor for the Tenth District in New York.

To William S. Rosecrans[1]

Major General Rosecrans   Executive Mansion, Washington,
Nashville, Tenn.   May 20, 1863. [9:50 A.M.]

Yours of yesterday in relation to Col. Haggard is received. I am anxious that you shall not misunderstand me. In no case have I in-tended to censure you, or to question your ability. In Col. Hag-gard's case I meant no more than to suggest that possibly you might have been mistaken, in a point that could be corrected. I frequently make mistakes myself, in the many things I am com-pelled to do hastily.   A. LINCOLN

[1] ALS, RPB. Rosecrans' telegram of May 19 is as follows: "The autograph letter of your Excellency dated May first . . . respecting the case of Col. David R. Haggard has just been handed me by the colonel. It seems to me. . . that my action . . . is not properly understood. My duty as comdr of troops is to see that they are kept at their maximum of efficiency . . . . officers exist only to effect this . . . . this duty is just recognized . . . by Genl Order Num-ber one hundred war Dept. of 1862 which requires . . . commanders to re-port all officers who by reason of ill health or other cause have been absent from duty over sixty days. This was Col. Haggard's case when I assumed the command of this Dept. but he was in ill health when I saw him. He continued in ill health & absent . . . more than sixty days & I reported the facts to the War Dept. . . . the War Dept. dismissed him instead of mustering him out . . . now the Col. appears here & has not a doubt of his health & physical ability to command his Regiment. . . . His former place has not as yet been filled. . . . I have no objection whatever to the revocation of the order where-

by he was mustered out. . . . I have thought it proper & due to you as well as to my official action to say this much in this case because the note of your Excellency seemed to imply that his being mustered out of the service was an official mistake of the Comdr. of this Dept. . . ." (DLC-RTL).

No further reference has been found to the case of Colonel David R. Haggard of the Fifth Kentucky Cavalry, and Lincoln's letter to Rosecrans of May 1 has not been located. See further Lincoln to Haggard, May 25, *infra*.

To Ambrose E. Burnside[1]

Major General Burnside   Washington City,
Cincinnati, Ohio.   May 21. 1863.

In the case of Thomas M. Campbell, convicted as a Spy, let execution of the sentence be respited until further order from me, he remaining in custody meanwhile.   A. LINCOLN

[1] ALS, RPB. Thomas T. Eckert added a postscript to Lincoln's message, "Please acknowledge receipt of the above telegram and time of delivery." Burnside replied at 4:30 P.M., "The Telegram in relation to Thos M. Campbell was received at ten (10) minutes past four (4) and will be obeyed" (DLC-RTL).

Thomas M. Campbell, captured on April 11, 1863, at Ruggles Mills, Kentucky, was tried by a military court at Cincinnati and sentenced to be hanged. He was not executed, but was held in close confinement on Johnson's Island, Ohio, until exchanged *circa* February, 1865. See Lincoln to Burnside, May 26, *infra*.

To William S. Rosecrans[1]

Major General Rosecrans   Washington City,
Murfreesboro, Tenn.   May 21. 1863 [4:45 P.M.]

For certain reasons it is thought best for Rev. Dr. Jaques not to come here. Present my respects to him, and ask him to write me fully on the subject he has in contemplation.   A. LINCOLN

[1] ALS, RPB. Rosecrans telegraphed Lincoln at 1:15 P.M., "The Rev. Dr Jaques Col of Seventy third (73) Illinois, a man of high character & great influence in the Methodist Church has proposed a mission to the South which in my judgment is worthy of being laid before you. Will you authorize me to send him to Washington for that purpose." (DLC-RTL).

On May 19, Colonel James F. Jaquess, a Methodist minister of Quincy, Illinois, wrote General James A. Garfield, proposing to go into Confederate territory to seek out members of the Methodist Church and others opposed to war and to effect terms for their return to allegiance which would be acceptable to the government. On May 23, Jaquess wrote Lincoln, assuring the president that his proposed mission could not fail. Both letters were carried to Washington by James R. Gilmore, who enclosed them with his own letter of May 27, requesting an interview on the proposed mission and other matters in Tennessee (DLC-Nicolay Papers). See further Lincoln's letter to Rosecrans, May 28, *infra*.

To Stephen A. Hurlbut[1]

Major General Hurlbut   Washington, D.C.,
Memphis Tenn.   May 22. 1863

We have news here in the Richmond newspapers of 20th. & 21st. including a despatch from Gen. Joe Johnson himself, that on 15th. or 16th. (a little confusion as to the day) Grant beat Pemberton & Loring[2] near Edwards' Station, at the end of a nine hours fight, driving Pemberton over the Big Black & cutting Loring off, & driving him South to Chrystal-Springs 25 miles below Jackson. Joe Johnson telegraphed all this, except about Loring, from his camp between Brownsville & Lexington, on the 18th. Another despatch indicates that Grant was moving against Johnson on the 18th.

A. LINCOLN

[1] ALS, RPB. Hurlbut replied on May 23:

"I forward the following, just received from Col. John A. Rawlins, assistant adjutant-general, rear of Vicksburg, 20th:

" 'The Army of the Tennessee landed at Bruinsburg on 30th April.

" 'On 1st May, fought battle of Port Gibson; defeated rebels under [John S.] Bowen, whose loss in killed, wounded, and prisoners was at least 1,500; loss in artillery, five pieces.

" 'On 12th May, at the battle of Raymond, rebels were defeated, with a loss of 800.

" 'On the 14th, defeated Joseph E. Johnston, captured Jackson, with loss to the enemy of 400, besides immense stores and manufactories, and seventeen pieces artillery.

" 'On the 16th, fought the bloody and decisive battle of Baker's Creek, in which the entire Vicksburg force, under [John C.] Pemberton, was defeated, with loss of twenty-nine pieces of artillery and 4,000 men.

" 'On the 17th, defeated same force at Big Black Bridge, with loss of 2,600 men and eleven pieces of artillery.

" 'On the 18th, invested Vicksburg closely. To-day General [Frederick] Steele carried the rifle-pits on the north of the city. The right of the army rests on the Mississippi above Vicksburg.'

"I learn further that there are from 15,000 to 20,000 men in Vicksburg, and that Pemberton lost nearly all his field artillery; that the cannonading at Vicksburg ceased about 3 p.m. of 20th. Grant has probably captured nearly all." (OR, I, XXIV, III, 344).   [2] William W. Loring.

Remarks to "The One-Legged Brigade"[1]

May 22, 1863

The President complimented the Chaplain, and said there was no need of a speech from him, as the men upon their crutches were orators; their very appearance spoke louder than tongues. As their Chaplain had alluded to the work he was at present very busy about, viz. in cleaning the devil out of Washington, the President hoped that when we could present that famous adversary at the

White House on his stumps, and therefore somewhat incapable of
further rebellion against constituted and divine authority, that we
would let him know. Whereupon the Chaplain informed the President that he would send him word when the funeral of that arch
rebel and great secessionist was to take place.

1 Washington *National Intelligencer*, May 25, 1863. Other papers give brief
mention of the visit to the White House of "The One-Legged Brigade," convalescent veterans at St. Elizabeth Hospital. The veterans were introduced by
their chaplain, the Reverend J. C. Richmond, in a short speech to which Lincoln replied.

To Joseph Holt[1]

Judge Advocate General   Executive Mansion,
My dear Sir   Washington, May 23. 1863.

Please send me, (if you have it) the record of the trial & conviction as a Spy, of William B. Compton, now in custody at Fort.
Mc.Henry. Yours truly   A. LINCOLN

1 ALS, owned by Carl Sandburg, Flat Rock, North Carolina. See Lincoln to
Schenck, May 27, *infra*.

To Edwin M. Stanton[1]

Hon. Sec. of War.   Executive Mansion,
My dear Sir   Washington, May 23. 1863.

In order to construct the Illinois Central Railroad, a large grant
of land was made by the United States to the State of Illinois,
which land was again given to the Railroad Company by the State,
in certain provisions of the Charter. By the U.S. grant, certain
previleges were attempted to be secured from the contemplated
Railroad to the U.S., and by the charter certain per centage of the
income of the road was to be from time to time paid to the State
of Illinois. At the beginning of the present war the Railroad did
certain carrying for the U.S. for which it claims pay; and, as I
understand, the U.S. claims that at least part of this the road was
bound to do without pay. Though attempts have been made to
settle the matter, it remains unsettled; meanwhile the Road refuses
to pay the per-centage to the State. This delay is working badly;
and I understand the delay exists because of there being no definite
decision whether the U.S. will settle it's own account with the
Railroad, or will allow the State to settle it, & account to the State
for it. If I had the leisure which I have not, I believe I could settle

it; but *prima facie* it appears to me we better settle the account ourselves, because that will save us all question as to whether the State deals fairly with us in the settlement of our account with a third party—the R.R.

I wish you would see Mr. Butler, late our State Treasurer, and see if something definite can not be done in the case. Yours truly

A. LINCOLN

[1] ALS-P, ISLA. Lincoln endorsed the envelope, "Please see Mr. Butler/May 23, 1863. A. Lincoln." An endorsement by Stanton referred the letter to the quartermaster general. Montgomery C. Meigs reported on May 27 (copy, IHi-Parsons Papers). On June 3 Meigs instructed the chief quartermaster Colonel Robert Allen of the Department of the West at St. Louis to settle all accounts with the railroad prior to May 3, 1862.

To Edwin M. Stanton[1]

May 23, 1863

There is a mistake somewhere in this case. By the accompanying copy of Gov. Curtin's letter, with my indorsement on it, it is seen that I removed the disability of Lt. Colonel Witherell, for the express purpose of allowing him to be appointed Lieut. Col. of the 82nd. Regt. & not, as the writer of this assumes, to allow him to be appointed to any regiment, other than the 82nd. Will the Sec. of War please have the matter corrected? or explain to me wherein the hitch is?

A. LINCOLN

May 23. 1863.

[1] AES, NHi. Lincoln's endorsement is written on the following letter from Assistant Adjutant General Thomas M. Vincent to John M. Wetherill, late major of the Eighty-second Pennsylvania Volunteers, May 13, 1863:

"Your application of date the 5th instant, in reference to your commission as Lieutenant Colonel of the 82d. Regiment Pennsylvania Volunteers, has been submitted to the Secretary of War and he directs me to inform you that you cannot be authorized to be mustered into that regiment.

"Your attention is invited to the telegram from this office of March 16. 1863, to the Governor of Pennsylvania, which removed the disability in your case, so far as any other regiment is concerned."

Wetherill was appointed lieutenant colonel of the Eighty-second Pennsylvania on June 20, 1863.

To Anson Stager[1]

Anson Stager   Washington, D.C.,
Cleveland, O.   May 24 1863 [10:40 P.M.]

Late last night Fuller telegraphed you, as you say, that "the stars and stripes float over Vicksburg, and the victory is complete"

Did he *know* what he said, or did he say it without knowing it? Your despatch of this afternoon throws doubt upon it.

A. LINCOLN

[1] ALS, RPB. Stager's telegram quoting from a telegram sent by William G. Fuller at Memphis on May 23 has not been located, but Stager's answer to Lincoln's query, received at 9:25 A.M. on May 25, reads: "Fullers message to his wife was no doubt based upon the hopeful feeling expressed in the despatches from Below and also at Head Quarters in Memphis. He would have sent me the information direct if it had been based upon later advices—that was my reason for holding for confirmation" (DLC-RTL).

To David R. Haggard[1]

Col. Haggard
Nashville. Tenn.

Executive Mansion,
Washington, May 25. 1863.

Your despatch to Green Adams has just been shown me. Gen. Rosecrans knows better than we can know here, who should be in charge of the (5th.) Fifth Cavalry.

A. LINCOLN

[1] ALS, RPB. See Lincoln to Rosecrans, May 20, *supra*. Haggard's despatch to Green Adams has not been located. The Fifth Kentucky Cavalry was at the time commanded by Lieutenant Colonel William T. Hoblitzell.

To Joseph Holt[1]

Judge Advocate General
My dear Sir

Executive Mansion,
Washington, May 25. 1863.

Please send me the record, if you have it, of the conviction of John R. Syles, of Ky, as a Spy. Yours truly

A. LINCOLN

[1] ALS, DLC-RTL. Lincoln's letter was returned on May 26 by the judge advocate general's office with an endorsement, "The record in the above case has not been received at this office." Lincoln undoubtedly misspelled the spy's name. On May 25, Halleck ordered General Burnside to suspend execution of John R. Lyle "till further orders" (OR, II, V, 696). See Lincoln to Burnside, May 26, *infra*.

To Richard Yates[1]

May 25, 1863

If the Governor of Illinois, in his discretion, see fit to reappoint Lieut. Gray to the place he was dismissed from, if it is still vacant, or to appoint him to any other Military Office, the disability now resting upon him to be so appointed, is hereby removed.

May 25, 1863.

A. LINCOLN

[1] Tracy, p. 224. Of the several lieutenants named Gray who are of record, none seems to have been dismissed so far as has been ascertained, and no further reference has been found to the case.

To Isaac N. Arnold[1]

Hon. I. N. Arnold.   Executive Mansion,
My dear Sir: Washington, May 26. 1863.

Your letter advising me to dismiss Gen. Halleck is received. If the public believe, as you say, that he has driven Fremont, Butler, and Sigel from the service, they believe what I know to be false; so that if I were to yield to it, it would only be to be instantly beset by some other demand based on another falsehood equally gross. You know yourself that Fremont was relieved at his own request, before Halleck could have had any thing to do with it—went out near the end of June, while Halleck only came in near the end of July. I know equally well that no wish of Halleck's had any thing to do with the removal of Butler or Sigel. Sigel, like Fremont, was relieved at his own request, pressed upon me almost constantly for six months, and upon complaints that could have been made as justly by almost any corps commander in the army, and more justly by some. So much for the way they got out. Now a word as to their not getting back. In the early Spring, Gen. Fremont sought active service again; and, as it seemed to me, sought it in a very good, and reasonable spirit. But he holds the highest rank in the Army, except McClellan, so that I could not well offer him a subordinate command. Was I to displace Hooker, or Hunter, or Rosecrans, or Grant, or Banks? If not, what was I to do? And similar to this, is the case of both the others. One month after Gen. Butler's return, I offered him a position in which I thought and still think, he could have done himself the highest credit, and the country the greatest service, but he declined it.[2] When Gen. Sigel was relieved, at his own request as I have said, of course I had to put another in command of his corps. Can I instantly thrust that other out to put him in again?

And now my good friend, let me turn your eyes upon another point. Whether Gen. Grant shall or shall not consummate the capture of Vicksburg, his campaign from the beginning of this month up to the twenty second day of it, is one of the most brilliant in the world. His corps commanders, & Division commanders, in part, are McClernand, McPherson,[3] Sherman, Steele, Hovey,[4] Blair, & Logan. And yet taking Gen. Grant & these seven of his generals, and you can scarcely name one of them that has not been constantly denounced and opposed by the same men who are now so anxious to get Halleck out, and Fremont & Butler & Sigel in. I believe no one of them went through the Senate easily, and certainly one failed to get through at all.[5] I am compelled to take a more impartial and unprejudiced view of things. Without claiming to be your superior, which I do not, my position enables me to understand my duty in all these matters better than you possibly can, and I hope you do not yet doubt my integrity. Your friend, as ever   A. LINCOLN

[1] ALS, ICHi. Isaac N. Arnold's letter of May 18 reads in part: "I desire as one of your old & true friends to respectfully suggest whether in view of the condition of military affairs . . . the office of *General in Chief* should not either be discontinued, or filled by a person other than Halleck. . . . The people generally believe that it is his personal hostility & prejudice that has driven from the public service, & keeps out of employment such men as Butler, Fremont, & Sigel. . . .

"Whether this opinion is right or wrong a change is needed to inspire confidence. . . ." (DLC-RTL).

[2] See Lincoln's letter to whom it may concern, February 11, *supra.*

[3] Major General James B. McPherson.

[4] Brigadier General Alvin P. Hovey of Indiana was a division commander under **Grant**.

[5] Lincoln's reference is not entirely clear. Of the men named all were confirmed by the Senate in March, 1863, except Sherman, McClernand, and Hovey. No one of these three, however, appears in the *Executive Journal* as being up for re-appointment or promotion at this time. It is possible that Lincoln was confusing Alvin P. Hovey with Colonel Charles E. Hovey of the Thirty-third Illinois Volunteers, whose appointment as brigadier general expired on March 4, 1863, without having had confirmation by the Senate.

To Ambrose E. Burnside[1]

Major General Burnside   Washington, D.C.,
Cincinnati, O.   May 26. 1863

   Your despatch about Campbell, Lyle & others received & postponement ordered by you, approved. I will consider & telegraph you again in a few days.   A. LINCOLN

[1] ALS, RPB. Burnside's despatch of May 26 is as follows: "The extension of time to [Thomas M.] Campbell and [John R.] Lyle in justice requires the same extension to the others condemned to be hung on Johnson's Island next Friday, and I have therefore ordered that the executions be postponed one week till I can hear more definitely from you." (OR, II, V, 707).

To William T. Otto[1]

Executive Mansion, Washington, May 26, 1863.

   The Acting Secretary of the Interior will transmit to me a *pro-tempore* commission for the appointment of Levi Bashford, of Wisconsin, to be Surveyor General of the U.S. for the Territory of Arizona.   A. LINCOLN

¹ ES, DNA NR RG 48, Applications, Surveyor General, Arizona, Box 1261. Lincoln's endorsement is on a letter from William T. Otto, May 26, 1863, submitting recommendations of Levi Bashford. Bashford's appointment was finally tabled by the Senate on July 4, 1864. He is listed as surveyor general, however, in the *U.S. Official Register* for 1863.

To Edwin M. Stanton¹

Let Isaac N. Phil[l]ips be appointed in place of William C. Carroll.   A LINCOLN
        May 26. 1863.

¹ AES, IHi. Lincoln's endorsement is written on a letter from James B. Fry to Stanton, May 26, 1863, recommending that William C. Carroll's appointment as provost marshal of the Thirteenth District of Illinois be revoked because Carroll was not a resident of the district.

To Edwin M. Stanton¹

Submitted to the Secretary of War, for his edification & consolation.   A. LINCOLN
        May 26. 1863.

¹ AES, MH. Lincoln's endorsement is written on an envelope addressed "President Lincoln/Washington D C."

To William A. Buckingham¹

Gov. Buckingham   Executive Mansion, Washington,
Hartford, Conn.   May 27. 1863. [2:50 P.M.]
    The execution of Warren Whitmarch is hereby respited or suspended, until further order from me, he to be held in safe custody meanwhile. On receiving this, notify me.   A. LINCOLN.

¹ ALS, RPB. Governor Buckingham's telegram, received at 9:45 A.M., is as follows:
    "Warren Whitmarch is condemned to be shot at New London on friday next for desertion.
    "I trust he will be reprieved until a full investigation can be made." (DLC-RTL).
    No record has been found of the name as spelled by Lincoln or Buckingham, but Warren Whitmarsh of Company C, First Connecticut Cavalry is listed as captured on June 8, 1862, at Cross Keys, Virginia, and discharged on November 15, 1864, at the expiration of his term (*Record of Connecticut Men in the War of the Rebellion*).

To Salmon P. Chase¹

                         Executive Mansion, May 27, 1863.
    My dear Sir: The office of second comptroller is vacant by the death of Mr. Cutts. Of course I wish your concurrence whenever I

shall fill it. I believe the only applicants—whose papers are now before me—are Augustin Chester, late of Connecticut, now of Chicago, and John M. Broadhead, of this city. I herewith inclose their papers to you. I believe they are both competent and worthy gentlemen. Yours truly, A. LINCOLN.

[1] NH, VIII, 283-84. Chase replied on May 29, "I send a commission for Mr. Brodhead. My choice between him and Mr. Chester who is also mentioned in your note . . . is determined by his great experience in the office & by the unanimous testimony of those who know him best to his superior capacity & diligence." (DLC-RTL).
   John M. Brodhead of New Hampshire and Washington, D.C., is listed in the *U.S. Official Register*, 1863, as successor to James M. Cutts, Sr.

To Joseph Hooker[1]

Washington, May 27, 1863– 11 p.m.
Major-General Hooker: Have you Richmond papers of this morning? If so, what news? A. LINCOLN.

[1] OR, I, XXV, II, 529. Hooker replied at 11:20 P.M., "I have received your telegram of 11 p.m.   Rumors, and reports of rumors indicate that important changes are being made by them. Nothing, however, so far as I know, is sufficiently developed to determine what these changes are. The Richmond paper of yesterday I have, but it contains no news. I will keep you fully advised." (*Ibid.*).

To William S. Rosecrans[1]

Major General Rosecrans. Washington City,
Murfreesboro, Tenn. May 27. 1863.
   Have you any thing from Grant? Where is Forrest's Head-Quarters? A. LINCOLN

[1] ALS, RPB. Rosecrans replied at 10:15 P.M., "According to our latest news, Forrest's headquarters were at Spring Hill yesterday, and moved to Riggs' cross-roads, 18 miles southwest of here, to-day. The latest from Grant we have is of the rebel dispatch last night, saying that Johnston had crossed Big Black north of him with 20,000 men. they were not jubilant at 2 o'clock to-day, when our provost-marshal was on their front, talking to Dr. [Benjamin F.] Avent Bragg's chief surgeon." (OR, I, XXIII, II, 366).

To Robert C. Schenck[1]

Major General Schenck Executive Mansion,
Baltimore, Md. Washington, May 27, 1863.
   Let the execution of William B. Compton be respited or suspended till further order from me, holding him in safe custody meanwhile. On receiving this, notify me. A. LINCOLN.

[1] ALS, RPB. See Lincoln to Holt, May 23, *supra*. No reply from Schenck has been located. Later references to William B. Compton in the *Official Records* indicate that he was still in confinement at Fort McHenry in January, 1865.

To John M. Schofield[1]

Executive Mansion,
Gen. J. M. Schofield   Washington, May 27. 1863.

My dear Sir: Having relieved Gen. Curtis and assigned you to the command of the Department of the Missouri—I think it may be of some advantage for me to state to you why I did it. I did not relieve Gen. Curtis because of any full conviction that he had done wrong by commission or omission. I did it because of a conviction in my mind that the Union men of Missouri, constituting, when united, a vast majority of the whole people, have entered into a pestilent factional quarrel among themselves, Gen. Curtis, perhaps not of choice, being the head of one faction, and Gov. Gamble that of the other. After months of labor to reconcile the difficulty, it seemed to grow worse and worse until I felt it my duty to break it up some how; and as I could not remove Gov. Gamble, I had to remove Gen. Curtis. Now that you are in the position, I wish you to undo nothing merely because Gen. Curtis or Gov. Gamble did it; but to exercise your own judgment, and do *right* for the public interest. Let your military measures be strong enough to repel the invader and keep the peace, and not so strong as to unnecessarily harrass and persecute the people. It is a difficult *role*, and so much greater will be the honor if you perform it well. If both factions, or neither, shall abuse you, you will probably be about right. Beware of being assailed by one, and praised by the other. Yours truly

A. Lincoln

[1] ADfS, DLC-RTL. The envelope in which the draft was filed bears Lincoln's endorsement "To Gen Schofield—May 27. 1863. & to Gen Curtis June 8. 1863." Schofield replied on June 1, "I have the honor to acknowledge the receipt of your letter . . . explaining the reasons which induced you to make a change in the command of this department, and your wish as to the principle which shall guide me. . . . I shall not fail to carry out your wishes to the fullest extent in my power, and shall be thankful for such instructions and advice as you may at any time be pleased to give me. The most serious difficulty I shall have to overcome will arise from the differences to which you allude between the factions into which the Union people are unfortunately divided. It shall be my highest aim, while keeping aloof from either faction, to reconcile their differences so far as my influence should extend, or at least to so conduct my administration as to give neither any just cause of complaint. . . ." (OR, I, XXII, II, 301).

See further Lincoln to Curtis, June 8, *infra*.

To Edwin M. Stanton[1]

May 27, 1863

Submitted to the Secretary of War, with the remark that while very probably Col. Woodroof is a very good man, I do not remember the matter he alludes to, or any promise of mine to him.

May 27. 1863.   A. LINCOLN

[1] AES, owned by Emanuel A. Gardiner, New York City. Lincoln's endorsement is written on a letter from William E. Woodruff, late colonel of the Second Kentucky Infantry, May 9, 1863, reminding the president of the "facts in my case" (see Lincoln to Stanton, June 5, 1862, *supra*), and proposing that he be appointed brigadier general to raise "an entirely new Command of *Mounted Infantry*, to operate on the flanks and in rear of the Enemy."

To Edwin M. Stanton[1]

I would be glad for Dr. Stipp to have the transfer within requested by Judge Davis.   A. LINCOLN

May 27, 1863

[1] AES, IHi. Lincoln's endorsement appears on a letter from David Davis, May 19, asking a transfer for medical inspector Dr. George Winfield Stipp who was suffering from diarrhea at Hilton Head, South Carolina. Stanton endorsed "The Adjt General will relieve Dr Stipp & direct him to report in writing for further orders." See further, Lincoln to Townsend, June 24, 1863, *infra*.

To Erastus Corning[1]

Hon. Erastus Corning   Executive Mansion,
Albany, N.Y.   Washington, May 28. 1863.

The letter of yourself & others dated the 19th. and inclosing the resolutions of a public meeting held at Albany on the 16th. was received night before last. I shall give the resolutions the consideration you ask, and shall try to find time, and make a respectful response. Your Obt. Servt.   A. LINCOLN

[1] ALS, RPB. Erastus Corning, wealthy iron manufacturer and Democrat, forwarded on May 19 a lengthy series of resolutions adopted by a public meeting in Albany, New York, on May 16, 1863. The resolutions are too long to quote in full, but may be found in the *American Annual Cyclopaedia*, 1863, pp. 799-800. In substance the resolutions pledged allegiance to the Union, but denounced "the recent assumption of a military commander to seize and try a citizen of Ohio, Clement L. Vallandigham, for no other reason than words addressed to a public meeting, in criticism of the course of the Administration, and in condemnation of the military orders of that general," and called upon the president to "be true to the Constitution" and "maintain the rights of the States and the liberties of the citizen. . . ." See Lincoln's reply of June 12, *infra*.

Memorandum: Appointment of Lawrence Kip[1]

Executive Mansion, Washington, May 28, 1863.

To-day Senator McDougal asks that 1st. Lieut. Lawrence Kip, now on Gen. Wool's Staff, may be a Brigadier General. The Senator makes this a personal request—almost—and I wish to oblige him.

[1] AD-P, ISLA. First Lieutenant Lawrence Kip had been brevetted captain (as of May 5, 1862), and major (as of July 1, 1862) for meritorious and distinguished service at Williamsburg and Fair Oaks. His appointment as major of Volunteers and aide-de-camp on General Sumner's staff, as of August 20, 1862, was confirmed by the Senate on March 11, 1863. No record has been found of his nomination as brigadier general.

To William S. Rosecrans[1]

Major General Rosecrans   Washington D.C.
Murfreesboro, Tenn.   May 28. 1863

I would not push you to any rashness; but I am very anxious that you do your utmost, short of rashness, to keep Bragg from getting off to help Johnston against Grant.   A. LINCOLN.

[1] ALS, RPB. Rosecrans' telegram acknowledging receipt of Lincoln's despatch was received May 29 at 1:25 A.M., "Dispatch rec'd. I will attend to it." (DLC-RTL).

To William S. Rosecrans[1]

Major General Rosecrans   Executive Mansion,
My dear Sir   Washington, May 28. 1863.

I have but a slight personal acquaintance with Col. Jaquess, though I know him very well by character. Such a mission as he proposes I think promises good, if it were free from difficulties, which I fear it can not be. First, he can not go with any government authority whatever. This is absolute and imperative. Secondly, if he goes without authority, he takes a great deal of personal risk—he may be condemned, and executed as a spy. If, for any reason, you think fit to give Col. Jaquess a Furlough, and any authority from me, for that object, is necessary, you hereby have it for any length of time you see fit. Yours very truly

A. LINCOLN.

[1] ALS copy, DLC-RTL. See Lincoln to Rosecrans, May 21, *supra*, and to Schenck, July 14, *infra*.

To Edwin M. Stanton[1]

Sec. of War, please see Mr. Garrison, about Mo. Railroad.
May 28. 1863.   A. LINCOLN

To Ambrose E. Burnside[1]

"Cypher"

Major General Burnside—   Washington, D.C.
Cincinnati, O.   May 29. 1863

Your despatch of to-day received. When I shall wish to supersede you I will let you know. All the cabinet regretted the necessity of arresting, for instance, Vallandigham, some perhaps, doubting, that there was a real necessity for it—but, being done, all were for seeing you through with it.   A LINCOLN

1 ALS, RPB. General Burnside telegraphed on May 29 at 12:40 P.M.:
"A messenger from Govr. Morton came to me this morning in reference to the arrest, by the military authorities of a citizen of Indiana. I understood from him that my action . . . was not approved by a single member of your Cabinet.

"This, taken in connection with your dispatch to me . . . approving of my course convinces me that my action here has been a source of embarrassment to you. . . . I should be glad to be relieved if the interest of the public service requires it, but at the same time I am willing to remain & assume the responsibility of carrying out the policy which has been inaugurated if it is approved." (DLC-RTL).

On May 30, Governor Morton wrote Lincoln a four-page letter protesting that Burnside's *General Order No. 38*, April 13, 1863, for violation of which Vallandigham had been arrested, had increased the extent and intensity of Democratic opposition to the war. Morton urged that, if military rule were needed for the Northwest, it should be instituted from the highest authority and not from department commanders, and expressed the opinion that state governments, aided by the federal government, should handle such problems. His state legislature, controlled by Democrats, had refused to appropriate funds for administration of the state. (DLC-RTL).

To Jesse K. Dubois and Others[1]

Executive Mansion, Washington, May 29. 1863.

Messrs Jesse K. Dubois
    O. M. Hatch   Charles W. Matheny
    John Williams   William F. Elkin
    Jacob Bunn   Francis Springer
    John Bunn   B. A. Watson
    George R. Weber.   Eliphalet Hawley &
    William Yates   James Campbell.
    S. M. Cullom.

Gentlemen Agree among yourselves upon any two of your own number, one of whom to be Quarter-Master, and the other to be Commissary, to serve at Springfield, Illinois, and send me their names, and I will appoint them. Yours truly   A. LINCOLN

¹ ALS-F, ISLA; ALS copy, DLC-RTL. Letters from William Yates (May 22); Jesse K. Dubois (May 23), endorsed in concurrence by William Yates, Charles W. Matheny, John W. Smith, John Armstrong, Benjamin A. Watson, Francis Springer, William F. Elkin, Gershom Jayne, and Pascal P. Enos; Jacob Bunn (May 25), Shelby M. Cullom (May 25), and Ozias M. Hatch (May 25)—all requested removal of Ninian W. Edwards, commissary, and William H. Bailhache, quartermaster, at Springfield, Illinois. Charges against the two men were that they had used their positions to amass personal fortunes and had made countless enemies for the administration. On June 22, George R. Weber was appointed commissary of subsistence with rank of captain to replace Edwards, and James Campbell was appointed assistant quartermaster with rank of captain to replace Bailhache. See Lincoln to Baker, June 15 and memorandum, June 22, *infra.*

To Andrew Johnson¹

Governor Andrew Johnson   Washington, D.C.
Louisville, Ky.   May 29. 1863.

    Gen. Burnside has been frequently informed lately that the Division under Gen. Getty can not be spared. I am sorry to have to tell you this, but [it] is true, and can not be helped.

                        A. LINCOLN

¹ ALS, RPB. Governor Johnson telegraphed on May 29 at 10:40 A.M., "It is believed that the third Division of ninth (9) Army Corps at Suffolk Genl [George W.] Getty comdg had better be added to Burnside's command. We hope this can be done as it will enable him to prosecute with success the expedition into East Tenn. . . . Genl Burnside is in high spirits & confident of being able to enter the State I have received much encouragement in getting up forces & think I shall succeed" (DLC-RTL).

To Edwin M. Stanton and Henry W. Halleck¹

Hon. Sec. of War. &   Executive Mansion,
Genl. in-Chief.   Washington, May 29. 1863.

    I concur with Gov. Curtin and Gen. Schenck that an increased Cavalry force upon & South of the Baltimore and Ohio Railroad, is very desireable. Please see them, and if you can devise an eligible mode of getting such force, let it be done. Yours truly

                        A. LINCOLN

¹ ALS, IHi. On May 18, General Schenck wrote Governor Curtin as follows:
"My conviction is briefly this: The only sure way to defend and guard the border is to keep all rebel forces out of West Virginia, or, rather, out of all the northern portion of Virginia, and this can only be done by a sufficient force of cavalry, to be kept south of the Baltimore and Ohio Railroad. The late rebel raid . . . should be a lesson. . . .
"Cavalry is, I repeat, needed; 10,000 well-mounted men would give more effective security than three times the number of infantry.

"I have represented time and again to the military authorities at Washington my want . . . but it occurs to me to endeavor to enlist your efforts also, as the Executive of your great State, so much concerned in the endeavor to have this command supplied with more of this arm of defense and aggression. Will you co-operate with me? . . ." (OR, I, XXV, II, 503).

Remarks to New York Committee[1]

May 30, 1863

The President declared that he would gladly receive into the service not ten thousand but ten times ten thousand colored troops; expressed his determination to protect all who enlisted, and said that he looked to them for essential service in finishing the war. He believed that the command of them afforded scope for the highest ambition, and he would with all his heart offer it to Gen. Fremont.

[1] New York *Tribune*, June 1, 1863. The members of the committee are not named, but are designated as "originating in Dr. Cheever's church, and endorsed by such men as Horace Greeley, George Opdyke, William Cullen Bryant, and Daniel S. Dickinson." Reverend George B. Cheever was pastor of the Church of the Puritans. The committee is reported as requesting that Lincoln "give a command to Gen. Fremont at some point where he can rally around him the colored men of the country." A three-page memorial dated May 28, 1863, presented by the committee and signed by Bryant, Greeley, Dickinson, and others, urged the assignment of Frémont to command 10,000 colored troops. (DLC-RTL). See Lincoln to Sumner, June 1, *infra*.

To Robert C. Schenck[1]

Private

Major Gen. Schenck   Executive Mansion,
Baltimore, Md.   Washington, May 31, 1863.

I have been requested to say, what I very truly can, that I esteem Gov. Francis Thomas, as an able, and very true man. I do not know that he agrees with me in everything—perhaps he does not; but he has given me evidence of sincere friendship, & as I think, of patriotism. Yours truly   A. LINCOLN

[1] ALS-P, ISLA. Representative Francis Thomas had served one term as governor of Maryland, 1841-1844.

Form Draft Order[1]

[June, 1863]
Executive Mansion,
Washington, D.C., ———, 1863.

I, Abraham Lincoln, President of the United States of America and Commander-in-Chief of the Army and Navy thereof, having

taken into consideration the number of volunteers and militia furnished by and from the several States, including the State of ——— , and the period of service of said volunteers and militia since the commencement of the present rebellion, in order to equalize the numbers among the districts of the said States, and having considered and allowed for the number already furnished as aforesaid, and the time of their services aforesaid, do hereby assign ——— as the first proportional part of the quota of troops to be furnished by the ——— district of the State of ——— , under this, the first call made by me on the State of ——— , under the act approved March 3, 1863, entitled, "An act for enrolling and calling out the national forces, and for other purposes," and, in pursuance of the act aforesaid, I order that a draft be made in the said ——— district of the State of ——— , for the number of men herein assigned to said district, and 50 per cent. in addition.

In witness whereof I have hereunto set my hand and caused the seal of the United States to be affixed. Done at the city of Washington this —— day of —— , in the year of our Lord one thousand eight hundred and sixty-three, and of the Independence of the United States the eighty-eighth.

¹ OR, III, V, 625. Numerous original signed copies of this printed order are extant. Each of these documents has the blanks properly filled in by a War Department clerk and bears Lincoln's full signature, "Abraham Lincoln." The earliest extant order of which we have record is that for the Seventeenth District of Pennsylvania, dated June 23, 1863, and the latest is that for the Second District of Minnesota, dated September 24, 1863. These signed documents have not been reproduced individually in the following pages.

² Although the printed form was obviously prepared for use after July 4, 1863, a scrupulous War Department clerk was careful to correct the printed text to "eighty-seventh" for at least some of the orders issued prior to July 4. Such a one is the order for the Seventh District of Pennsylvania, July 1, 1863 (DS, owned by Foreman M. Lebold, Chicago, Illinois).

To Edward Bates¹

June 1, 1863

As the Judge, Jury, Marshal, District Attorney & Post-Master General, join in asking a pardon in this case, I have concluded to grant it. The Attorney General will please make it out & send it to me.   A. LINCOLN

June 1. 1863.

¹ AES, DNA RG 204, U.S. Pardon Attorney, A 474. Lincoln's endorsement is written on a petition for pardon of Jacob Varner of West Virginia, sentenced to three years' imprisonment for robbing the mails. The petition, signed by the jurors in Varner's case, sets forth that Varner was "an ignorant man . . . the victim of designing politicians who deluded such as himself into the belief of the priority of State allegiance to that of the Government of the Country."

To Joseph Holt[1]

June 1, 1863

It appears that Martin Davis, of Co. G. 85th. N.Y. Vols. has been convicted of something, as he is applying to me for a pardon. Will the Judge Advocate General please send me the record?

June 1. 1863.   A LINCOLN

[1] AES, DLC-RTL. Lincoln's endorsement is written on a letter from William S. Briggs, Penn Yan, New York, May 18, 1863, introducing Ezekiel Clark, attorney for Private Martin Davis of the Eighty-fifth New York Volunteers, under sentence "for an offense committed against an officer." Holt endorsed, "The record in the above case has not been recvd, in this office." No further reference to this case has been found.

To Joseph Holt[1]

I can not interfere in this case.   A. LINCOLN

June 1. 1863

[1] AES, DNA WR RG 153, Judge Advocate General, Letters Received, No. 425. Lincoln's endorsement is written on the envelope containing petitions and letters in behalf of Thomas Lewis of Tennessee, sentenced to be sent out of the Department of the Tennessee for bribery of a U.S. detective.

To William H. Ludlow[1]

"Cypher"

Col. Ludlow   ·Executive Mansion,
Fort-Monroe.   Washington, June 1. 1863.

Richardson & Browne, correspondents of the Tribune, captured at Vicksburg, are detained at Richmond. Please ascertain why they are detained, & get them off if you can.   A. LINCOLN

[1] ALS, RPB. On May 26, Sydney H. Gay, editor of the New York *Tribune*, wrote Lincoln as follows:

"Two of the correspondents of The Tribune, Messrs. A. D. Richardson & Junius Browne, with a Mr. [Richard T.] Colburn of The World, were taken prisoners, not long ago, in an attempt to run by Vicksburg in a tug. They were . . . paroled . . . in due form, & sent forward to Richmond. There the World correspondent was permitted to pass on unmolested, doubtless, because he belonged to the World, while the Tribune men, in spite of the parole, were thrust into prison & are still detained there.

"A word of remonstrance from the Government on so flagrant a breach of faith, might, perhaps, right this wrong. . . ."

Lieutenant Colonel Ludlow, agent for exchange of prisoners, replied the same day that "Everything will be done that can be done to obtain the release of the parties named." (OR, II, V, 723). Later references in the *Official Records* show that Browne and Richardson were still imprisoned in January, 1865.

To William T. Otto[1]

June 1, 1863

I must repeat now in writing what I have told Mr. Kelly verbally, that the courts and not the President, must decide questions of land titles. There may be some questions in regard to pre-emptions, which by law, are to be decided through the Department, with appeal to me, and when such a case shall come regularly to me, I shall hear it. But I must now say, once for all, that mere vague assertions that the decisions of the Courts are fraudulent, with appeals to me to reverse them, can [not] be entertained.

June 1, 1863   A. LINCOLN.

[1] Edward Eberstadt & Sons, Catalog 129, April, 1951, No. 159. According to the catalog description, this communication is an endorsement on an appeal from George Fox Kelly, agent for California settlers. William T. Otto, acting secretary of Interior, wrote George F. Kelly on June 16, 1863:

"The affidavits which you have laid before the President, in which complaint is made against the action of the District Court for the Northern District of California in its approval of the survey of the land claim of Joaquin Carillo . . . the lines of which include . . . certain tracts . . . claimed by yourself and others as preemptors—have been referred to this Department.

"The President instructs me to state to you, that he cannot decide the questions which you submit, or any other relating to a contested title to land, where, as in the present instance, jurisdiction over the subject matter is visited by law in the Courts. The affidavits contain vague charges of fraud in certain judicial proceedings now concluded, but as the President has no appellate or supervisory power over them, it would, in his opinion, be improper for him to assume to take action, especially as the United States have no interest in the matter." (Copy, DLC-RTL).

To Edwin M. Stanton[1]

Sec. of War please inform me what there is of this case.

June 1. 1863   A. LINCOLN

[1] AES, owned by William Herzog, Chicago, Illinois. Lincoln's endorsement is written on a letter from Captain Franklin P. Ash, commissary of subsistence, Second Brigade, Second Division, Twelfth Army Corps, May 28, 1863, asking a hearing on his dismissal. Stanton endorsed "Referred to Major [Thomas M.] Vincent for Report." No further reference has been found.

To Charles Sumner[1]

Hon. Charles Sumner   Executive Mansion,
My dear Sir.   Washington, June 1. 1863.

In relation to the matter spoken of Saturday morning, and this morning, towit, the raising of colored troops in the North, with the understanding that they shall be commanded by Gen. Fremont, I have to say

That while it is very objectionable, as a general rule, to have troops raised on any special terms, such as to serve only under a particular commander, or only at a particular place or places, yet I would forego the objection in this case, upon a fair prospect that a large force of this sort could thereby be the more rapidly raised

That being raised, say to the number of ten thousand, I would very cheerfully send them to the field under Gen. Fremont, assigning him a Department, made or to be made, with such white force also as I might be able to put in.

That with the best wishes towards Gen. Fremont, I can not now give him a Department, because I have not spare troops to furnish a new Department; and I have not, as I think, justifiable ground to relieve the present commander of any old one.

In the raising of the colored troops, the same consent of Governors would have to be obtained as in case of white troops, and the government would make the same provision for them during organization, as for white troops.

It would not be a point with me whether Gen. Fremont should take charge of the organization, or take charge of the force only after the organization.

If you think fit to communicate this to Gen. Fremont you are at liberty to do so. Yours truly   A. LINCOLN

[1] ALS, DLC-RTL. See Lincoln's remarks to the New York Committee, May 30, *supra*. On June 9, Frémont wrote Sumner as follows: "I have delayed a few days my reply to your kind note. . . . I was pressingly reminded of your note by a visit from the committee which had called upon Mr. Lincoln & to which he had promised this letter to you. I beg you will say to the President that this movement does not, in the remotest way originate with me. On the contrary when the Committee called . . . I declined positively to enter into it, or to consent to having my name mentioned to the President in connection with it. . . . I disapproved the project of raising and sending to the field, colored troops in scattered and weak detachments. . . . I told them that if I had been placed in the Dept. which the President & Secretary arranged for me when I was last in Washington & in which I should have had a suitable field for this organization and white troops to protect it and ensure its success—I could have undertaken it & have undoubtedly organized a formidable force. But these views were mearly in answer to the committee and ended my relation to the subject. I beg you to say to the President that I have no design to embarrass him with creating a Dept. for me. . . . this whole business is as dangerous and difficult as it is important. . . . It demands . . . some officer of ability and judgment in whom the President would be willing to give the necessary powers. He must have power and the Presidents confidence—therefore I do not propose myself for this work. . . . Will the President realize that if this summer's campaigns are not successful the Confederacy is well nigh established? I think not. . . . But pray don't let him think that I am moving in any direction, or by any persons to get this command. Enclosed I return the

President's letter—which I have shown to no one. I informed the Committee that I had rec'd it through yourself but could not communicate its purport without the authority of the President. Will you please make my thanks to the President for his friendly expressions in my favor and accept my very warm thanks to yourself. . . ." (DLC-RTL).

To Ulysses S. Grant[1]

"Cypher"

Major Gen. Grant   Washington, D.C.,
Vicksburg, via Memphis.   June 2. 1863

Are you in communication with Gen. Banks? Is he coming towards you, or going further off? Is there, or has there been any thing to hinder his coming directly to you by water from Alexandria?   A. LINCOLN

[1] ALS, RPB. Grant telegraphed on June 8 that Banks, "has Port Hudson closely invested," and that he would forward by mail a letter from Banks of June 4 (DLC-RTL). Banks' letter of June 4 reads in part: "It seems to me that I have no other course than to carry my object here thus crippling the enemy, and to join you with my whole strength as soon as possible This I hope to accomplish in a few days. . . ." (*Ibid.*).

To Joseph Hooker[1]

Executive Mansion,
Major General Hooker: Washington, June 2, 1863.

It is said that Philip Margraff, in your army, is under sentence to be shot on Friday, the 5th instant, as a deserter. If this be so, please send me up the record of his case at once.   A. LINCOLN.

[1] Thirty-eighth Congress, Second Session, *Report of the Joint Committee on the Conduct of the War* (1865), I, 244. No reply from Hooker has been located. See Lincoln to Hooker, June 4, *infra*.

Reply to Members
of the Presbyterian General Assembly[1]

June 2, 1863

It has been my happiness to receive testimonies of a similar nature, from I believe, all denominations of Christians. They are all loyal, but perhaps not in the same degree, or in the same numbers; but I think they all claim to be loyal. This to me is most gratifying, because from the beginning I saw that the issues of our great struggle depended on the Divine interposition and favor. If we had that, all would be well. The proportions of this rebellion were not for a long time understood. I saw that it involved the greatest difficulties, and would call forth all the powers of the whole country. The end is not yet.

The point made in your paper is well taken as to "the Government" and the "administration" in whose hands are those interests. I fully appreciate its correctness and justice. In my administration I might have committed some errors. It would be, indeed, remarkable if I had not. I have acted according to my best judgment in every case. The views expressed by the Committee accord with my own; and on this principle "the Government" is to be supported though the administration may not in every case wisely act. As a pilot, I have used my best exertions to keep afloat our ship of State, and shall be glad to resign my trust at the appointed time to another pilot more skillful and successful than I may prove. In every case, and at all hazards, the Government must be perpetuated. Relying, as I do, upon the Almighty Power, and encouraged as I am by these resolutions which you have just read, with the support which I receive from Christian men, I shall not hesitate to use all the means at my control to secure the termination of this rebellion, and will hope for success.

I sincerely thank you for this interview, this pleasant mode of presentation, and the General Assembly for their patriotic support in these resolutions.

[1] Edward McPherson, *The Political History of the United States . . .* (1865), p. 471. Although McPherson's source seems to have been a newspaper report, no contemporary source of Lincoln's reply has been located. McPherson gives no date for the reply, and Nicolay and Hay supply "May [30?]" in error (NH, VIII, 287). The Washington *Evening Star*, June 2, 1863, and a Washington despatch of June 2 (New York *Tribune*, June 3) both reported that "A Committee of sixty-five from the General Assembly of the Presbyterian Church . . . waited upon the President this morning, and presented him with the resolutions of that body." Resolutions in support of the administration, adopted by the General Assembly on May 27, were read to the president by John A. Foote of Cleveland, Ohio, and were followed by Lincoln's reply. A copy of the lengthy resolutions clipped from a newspaper and provided with a holograph heading, is preserved in the Lincoln Papers.

To Edward Bates[1]

Hon. Attorney General   Executive Mansion,
My dear Sir   Washington, June 3, 1863.

It has been suggested to me, and readily adopted by, to tender the Judgeship of Florida, to Hon John A. Bingham of Ohio. Please send me a commission for him. Yours truly   A. LINCOLN

[1] ALS, DNA GE RG 60, Papers of Attorney General, Segregated Lincoln Material. Representative Bingham had not been re-elected to the Thirty-eighth Congress. Lincoln's proposal did not work out. See Lincoln to Bingham, August 4, *infra*.

Endorsement Concerning Henry W. DePuy[1]

June 3, 1863

Some time ago I said I was willing to appoint Mr. DePuy to an Indian Agency when there should be a vacancy; & I remember nothing coming to my knowledge since to change my mind in this respect.   A. LINCOLN

June 3. 1863.

[1] AES, ICHi. Lincoln's endorsement has been clipped from the document on which it was originally written. Henry W. DePuy's appointment as Indian agent on the Upper Missouri, made during the recess of the Senate, was submitted for confirmation under date of December 31, 1863, but was returned to the president on March 21, 1864, DePuy having declined the appointment. DePuy had served from 1861 to 1862 as agent of the Pawnee Agency until replaced by Benjamin F. Lushbaugh. See Lincoln to Caleb B. Smith, December 27, 1862, *supra*.

To Henry W. Halleck[1]

Will Gen. Halleck please glance over the within, & tell me whether there is anything in it which can be turned to account?

June 3. 1863.   A. LINCOLN

[1] AES, DLC-RTL. Lincoln's endorsement is written on an envelope containing papers submitted by Ambrose W. Thompson, June 2, 1863, proposing that immigrants and Negroes be organized into military units to work on the proposed Metropolitan Railroad of which Thompson was president and which was to be built from Washington to Pittsburgh. The proposal was that the government pay the troops for four months to work for the corporation eight hours, with two hours daily drill. Following this period the troops would be sent to regular duty, and the funds expended by the government would be repaid by the corporation when its railroad was in operation.

Halleck returned the papers on the same day with the following endorsement: "It has been found impossible to procure sufficient labor of enlisted men or 'contrabands' to complete the forts around Washington or at Harpers Ferry. I think that any emigrants or Negroes who are paid out of the public Treasury had better be employed on the forts rather than let out to work for corporations. Moreover, working on fortifications is a much better military training than working on Rail Roads."

To Joseph Holt[1]

Can the Judge Advocate General make any suggestion as to what should be done in this, or any similar case?   A LINCOLN

June 3. 1863.

[1] AES, owned by David L. Salisbury, Dunbar, West Virginia. This endorsement has been clipped from attendant papers, and no further reference has been found.

To Edward Bates[1]

Attorney General, please preserve. Judge Foot is cousin to the Admiral, & is vouched as an excellent man.   A. LINCOLN

June 4, 1863.

1 AES, The Rosenbach Company, Philadelphia and New York. Lincoln's endorsement is written on a letter from Samuel A. Foot, former Judge of the Court of Appeals of New York (1844-1852), offering himself for appointment as U.S. district judge for South Carolina until "the Government can find a suitable person, a citizen of that state, to take the position." No judges for South Carolina are listed in the *U.S. Official Register* for 1863 or 1865.

To Daniel Butterfield[1]

War Department,

Major General Butterfield: Washington, D.C., June 4, 1863.

The news you send me from the Richmond Sentinel of the 3d must be greatly if not wholly incorrect. The Thursday mentioned was the 28th, and we have dispatches here directly from Vicksburg of the 28th, 29th, 30th and 31st, and while they speak of the siege progressing, they speak of no assault or general fighting whatever, and in fact they so speak as to almost exclude the idea that there can have been any since Monday the 25th, which was not very heavy. Neither do they mention any demand made by Grant upon Pemberton for a surrender. They speak of our troops as being in good health, condition and spirits. Some of them do say that Banks has Port Hudson invested.   A. LINCOLN.

1 Tarbell (Appendix), p. 367. On June 4, General Butterfield telegraphed as follows: "Richmond Sentinel June 3d. says—Jackson June 1st. Grant demanded the surrender of Vicksburg on Thursday giving three days to Pemberton to consider the demand. Pemberton replied that he did not want 15 minutes & that his troops would die in the trenches before they would surrender. The federal troops are demoralized & refused to renew the attack on Saturday. The enemys Gunboats are firing hot shot at the City   the federal loss is estimated at 25,000 or 30,000. . . . Port Hudson is invested   Nothing in Enquirer of June 4." (DLC-RTL).

Endorsement
on Application of Richard Middleton[1]

June 4, 1863

I understand that Richard Middleton, named within, has an application before Col. Long,[2] for employment; and while I do not personally know him, the within names are so good and ample, that I do not hesitate to say I shall be very glad if he can get the employment.   A. LINCOLN

June 4, 1863

¹ AES, RPB. The endorsement has been cut off the attendant papers. See Lincoln to James Cooper and others, March 8, 1862, *supra*.
² Probably Stephen H. Long of the Corps of Engineers.

To Joseph Hooker¹

"Cypher"

Executive Mansion,
Major General Hooker Washington, June 4. 1863.

Let execution of sentences in the cases of Daily, Margraff, and Harrington, be respited till further order from me, they remaining in close custody meanwhile. A. LINCOLN

¹ ALS, owned by Edward C. Stone, Boston, Massachusetts. See Lincoln to Hooker, June 2, *supra*. On June 3, Alfred J. Bloor wrote Charles Sumner as follows: "Understanding you are with the President and not feeling it my duty to intrude again . . . I yet feel it to be my duty to Margraf—whose son is condemned to be shot to-morrow—to ask you . . . to urge upon the President, that, however desirable it may be to put an end to the lax discipline of the army, it is not best to commence with such an example as young Margrave—a German by birth—very young—and this his first offence—committed under a misunderstanding. He thought it an oppression that, enlisted, as he supposed, for 6 or 8 months, he should be required to serve for 3 years. . . . It is notorious among New-Yorkers that a regular system of deceit was practised by recruiting officers, through their verbal statements—the public papers and show bills posted all over the City—as in this case. . . . I trouble you with this because I understand you are interceding for one of the other men condemned. . . ." (DLC-RTL).
Privates Enos Daily, Philip Margraff, and Carlos Harrington of the One Hundred Forty-sixth New York Volunteers, were all sentenced to be shot for desertion. Hooker's telegram acknowledging receipt of Lincoln's order was received at 9:20 P.M., June 4 (DLC-RTL), but no further reference has been found.

To Edwin M. Stanton¹

Executive Mansion,
Hon. Secretary of War: Washington, D.C., June 4, 1863.

My dear Sir: I have received additional dispatches which, with former ones, induce me to believe we should revoke or suspend the order suspending the Chicago Times, and if you concur in opinion, please have it done. Yours, truly, A. LINCOLN.

¹ OR, III, III, 252. Edward D. Townsend promptly telegraphed Burnside a copy of Lincoln's letter and instructed him to revoke the order suspending publication of the Chicago *Times* (*ibid.*). On the same day Burnside issued an order revoking not only the suspension of the *Times* but also the suppression of the New York *World*, circulation of which had been prohibited in his department (*ibid.*, II, V, 741). Both papers had bitterly criticized Burnside and the administration for the arrest of Vallandigham.

To Joseph Hooker[1]

Washington, D.C., June 5, 1863.

Major-General Hooker: Would you like to have Capt. Treadwell Moore, now in California, to report to you for duty?

A. LINCOLN.

[1] Tarbell (Appendix), p. 367. Hooker telegraphed on the same day that he would "like to have Captain Moore ordered to this army." (DLC-RTL). On June 20, 1863, Tredwell Moore, West Point graduate in 1847, assumed quartermaster duties at Wheeling, West Virginia.

To Joseph Hooker[1]

Washington, D.C.,
June 5. 1863

Major General Hooker

Yours of to-day was received an hour ago. So much of professional military skill is requisite to answer it, that I have turned the task over to Gen. Halleck. He promises to perform it with his utmost care. I have but one idea which I think worth suggesting to you, and that is in case you find Lee coming to the North of the Rappahannock, I would by no means cross to the South of it. If he should leave a rear force at Fredericksburg, tempting you to fall upon it, it would fight in intrenchments, and have you at disadvantage, and so, man for man, worst you at that point, while his main force would in some way be getting an advantage of you Northward. In one word, I would not take any risk of being entangled upon the river, like an ox jumped half over a fence, and liable to be torn by dogs, front and rear, without a fair chance to gore one way or kick the other. If Lee would come to my side of the river, I would keep on the same side & fight him, or act on the defence, according as might be my estimate of his strength relatively to my own. But these are mere suggestions which I desire to be controlled by the judgment of yourself and Gen. Halleck.

A. LINCOLN

[1] ALS, IHi. Hooker's telegram of June 5, is as follows:

"Yesterday morning appearances indicated that during the night the Enemy had broken up a few of his camps and abandoned them. These changes were observed on the right of his line in the vicinity of Hamilton Crossing. So far as I was enabled to judge from all my means of information it was impossible for me to determine satisfactorily whether this movement had been merely a change of camps—the Enemy had moved in the direction of Richmond, or up the river, but taken in connection with the fact that some deserters came in from the divisions of [John B.] Hood and [George] Pickett I conclude that those divisions had been brought to the front from their late positions at Gordonsville and Taylorville and that this could be for no other purpose but to enable the Enemy to move up the river with a view to the execution of a movement similar to that of Lee's last year. He must either have it in mind to cross the Upper Potomac or to throw his army between mine and Washington. In case I am correct in my conjecture, to accomplish either he must have been greatly reinforced and, if making this movement, the fair presumption is that he has been by the troops from Charleston

"Of this I have no evidence farther than that furnished me by Gen Dix that they had come to Richmond

"This morning some more of their camps have disappeared. Their picket line along the river is preserved and as strong as ever. Gen Buford with three divisions of Cavalry and ten pieces of Artillery is on the Alexandria and Orange Rail Road and yesterday was along the river beyond Sulphur Springs and reports no Enemy. As I am liable to be called on to make a movement with the utmost promptitude I desire that I may be informed as early as practicable of the views of the Government concerning this Army. Under instructions from the Maj Genl Com'd'g the army dated Jany 31st. I am instructed to keep in view always the importance of covering Washington and Harpers Ferry either directly or by so operating as to be able to punish any force of the Enemy sent against them.

"In the event the Enemy should move, as I almost anticipate he will the head of his column will probably be headed towards the Potomac via Gordonsville or Culpepper while the rear will rest on Fredericksburg. After giving the subject my best reflections I am of opinion that it is my duty to pitch into his rear although in so doing the head of his column may reach Warrenton before I can return. Will it be within the spirit of my instructions to do so? In view of these contemplated movements of the Enemy I cannot too forcibly impress upon the mind of His Excellency The President the necessity of having one commander for all of the troops whose operations can have influence on those of Lee's army. Under the present system all independent commanders are in ignorance of the movements of the others at least such is my situation.

"I trust that I may not be considered in the way to this arrangement as it is a position I do not desire and only suggest it as I feel the necessity for concerted as well as vigorous action. It is necessary for me to say this much that my motive may not be misunderstood. . . ." (DLC-RTL).

Halleck's answer was telegraphed at 4:40 P.M., as follows:

"The President has directed me to reply to your telegram to him of . . . today. My instructions of January 31 . . . left you entirely free to act as circumstances, in your judgment, might require, with the simple injunction to keep in view the safety of Washington and Harper's Ferry. In regard to the contingency which you suppose may arise of General Lee's leaving a part of his forces in Fredericksburg, while, with the head of his column, he moves by Gordonsville or Culpeper toward the Potomac, it seems to me that such an operation would give you great advantages upon his flank to cut him in two, and fight his divided forces. Would it not be more advantageous to fight his movable column first, instead of first attacking his intrenchments, with your own forces separated by the Rappahannock? Moreover, you are aware that the troops under General Heintzelman are much less than the number recommended . . . for the defenses of Washington. Neither this capital nor Harper's Ferry could long hold out against a large force. They must depend for their security very much upon the co-operation of your army. It would, therefore, seem perilous to permit Lee's main force to move upon the Potomac while your army is attacking an intrenched position on the other side of the Rappahannock. Of course your movements must depend in a great measure upon those made by Lee. There is another contingency not altogether improbable— that Lee will seek to hold you in check with his main force, while a strong force will be detached for a raid into Maryland and Pennsylvania. The main force of the enemy in North Carolina have probably come north, but I think all available troops in South Carolina and Georgia have been sent to re-enforce Johnston in Mississippi. Such is the information here. General Heintzelman and General Dix are instructed to telegraph directly to you all the movements which they may ascertain or make. Directions have also been given to forward military information which may be received from General Schenck's command. Any movements you may suggest of troops in these commands will be ordered, if deemed practicable. Lee will probably move light and rapidly. Your movable force should be prepared to do the same.

"The foregoing views are approved by the President." (OR, I, XXVII, I, 31-32).

Anonymous Letter
to the Editor of the Washington *Chronicle*[1]

Executive Mansion,
Washington, June 6. 1863.

Editor of the Chronicle.

In your issue of this morning, you have an article on the "Chicago Times." Being an Illinoisian, I happen to know that much of the article is incorrect. As I remember, upon the repeal of the Missouri Compromise, the democratic newspapers at Chicago went over to the opposition. Thereupon the Times was established by the friends of the administration, Senator Douglas being the most prominent in establishing it. A man by the name of James Sheahan, from this city, was it's first, and only editor, nearly if not quite all the remainder of the Senator's life. On the political separation between Mr. Buchanan and Senator Douglas, the Times adhered to the Senator, and was the ablest paper in his support through his senatorial contest with Mr. Lincoln. Since the last Presidential election certainly, perhaps since Senator Douglas' death, Mr. Sheahan left the Times; and the Times since then, has been identical with the Times before then, in little more than the name.[2] The writer hereof is not well enough posted to say but that your article in other respects is correct.

[1] ADf, DLC-RTL. The article headed "THE CHICAGO TIMES" appeared in the *Daily Chronicle* for Saturday, June 6, 1863. Lincoln's anonymous letter, of which the above is obviously a first draft, appeared in the *Chronicle* on Sunday, June 7, considerably revised, or edited by the *Chronicle*, as follows:

"A correspondent corrects an error of date in the article in Saturday's CHRONICLE on the Chicago *Times*, and adds some items of interesting information. He says:

" 'Upon the repeal of the Missouri Compromise the democratic newspapers of Chicago went over to the Opposition. Thereupon the *Times* was established by the friends of the Administration, Senator Douglas being the most prominent in establishing it. Mr. James Sheahan, from this city, was its editor from its first foundation up to the election in 1860. On the political separation between Mr. Buchanan and Senator Douglas, the *Times* adhered to the Senator, and was the ablest paper in his support through his senatorial contest with Mr. Lincoln. During the last Presidential election Mr. Sheahan left the *Times*, which had been bought, as you state, by Mr. McCormick; and a man named McComas, a bitter pro-slavery man and a Virginian, became its editor. Sheahan for awhile edited the Springfield *Register,* and then went back to Chicago and established the *Post,* which he still conducts. From the period that the *Times* passed into its present hands it has borne little resemblance, but in name, to the *Times* which supported Senator Douglas in his contest with the corrupt and cowardly Administration of Mr. Buchanan. ILLINOISIAN.'"

2 Lincoln's recollection does not exactly fit the report in the Springfield *Illinois State Register,* September 1, 1860, which announced that James W. Sheahan, editor of the "late Chicago *Times*" was visiting Springfield for several months, and that readers of the *Register* would have "the assistance of his pen during the present canvass."

To Salmon P. Chase[1]

June 6, 1863

. . . see Mr. Powell, and do for him any thing that you may think is safe for the government to do.

1 Thomas Madigan, *Autograph Album,* October, 1935, No. 67. According to the catalog description this partial text is written on a card. Mr. Powell has not been identified.

To John A. Dix[1]

Major Gen. Dix   Washington, D.C.,
Fort-Monroe, Va.   June 6. 1863

By noticing the news you send from the Richmond Despatch of this morning you will see one of the very latest despatches says they have nothing reliable from Vicksburg since Sunday. Now, we here, have a despatch from there of Sunday, and others of almost every day preceding, since the investment; and while they show the siege progressing, they do not show any general fighting, since the 21st. and 22nd. We have nothing from Port-Hudson later than the 29th. when things looked reasonably well for us. I have thought this might be of some interest to you.   A. LINCOLN

1 ALS, RPB.

To Mrs. Elizabeth J. Grimsley[1]

Mrs. Elizabeth J. Grimsely   Washington, D.C.
Springfield, Illinois   June 6. 1863

Is your John ready to enter the Naval-School? If he is, telegraph me his full name.   A. LINCOLN

1 ALS, RPB. No reply has been located. John T. Grimsley, son of Harrison J. and Elizabeth J. Todd Grimsley, is not of record as appointed to the U.S. Naval Academy.

To Joseph Holt[1]

These papers reached me at 1. PM. June 6th. 1863.

[1] AE, DNA WR RG 153, Judge Advocate General, LL 422, John C. Schore (Schorr). Lincoln's endorsement is written on an envelope which contained papers in the case of John C. Shore, Company F, One Hundred Ninth Illinois Volunteers, sentenced to be shot for desertion. On recommendation of the judge advocate general the sentence was commuted to hard labor for one year. On August 31, 1864, Shore's sentence was extended to "discharge from the United States service, with forfeiture of all pay and allowances due, and imprisonment at the Dry Tortugas, Florida. . . ." (AGO *Special Orders No. 287*).

Order Assigning Daniel Tyler
to Middle Department[1]

War Department, Washington City, June 6, 1863.
Ordered, that Brig. Gen. D. Tyler be assigned to duty in the Middle Department, as senior brigadier in the Middle Department, without regard to priority in date of commission.

A. LINCOLN,
President of the United States

[1] OR, I, XXVII, III, 37. Lincoln's order was issued by Major General Robert Schenck, Headquarters Eighth Army Corps, Baltimore, June 8, 1863, *General Orders No. 37*. Schenck's *Special Orders No. 159*, June 13, sent Brigadier General Daniel Tyler to Harper's Ferry and Martinsburg, to "assume command of all forces, including brigade at Martinsburg, which can be sent to the support of Major-General Milroy, and cover the march of that general's forces to Harper's Ferry."

To Samuel R. Curtis[1]

Major General Curtis   Executive Mansion,
My dear Sir: Washington, June 8. 1863.
    I have scarcely supposed it possible that you would entirely understand my feelings and motives in making the late change of commander for the Department of the Missouri. I inclose you a copy of a letter which I recently addressed to Gen. Schofield, & which will explain the matter in part. It became almost a matter of personal self-defence to somehow break up the state of things in Missouri. I did not mean to cast any censure upon you, nor to indorse any of the charges made against you by others. With me the presumption is still in your favor that you are honest, capable, faithful, and patriotic. Yours very truly   A. LINCOLN.

[1] ALS, IHi; LS copy, DLC-RTL. See Lincoln to Schofield, May 27, *supra*. General Curtis wrote Lincoln on June 5, "While a little rest after two years care and toil may be very useful to me, I hope your Excellency will not hesitate to use my services on any occasions: and especially do not make me appear

as a special object of your displeasure, since as a faithful soldier and personal friend I have devoted myself to your support, and the cause of our unhappy country since the origin of our troubles." (DLC-RTL).

To John A. Dix[1]

Major Genl. Dix   Executive Mansion,
Fort-Monroe.   Washington, June 8. 1863.

We have despatches from Vicksburg of the 3rd. Siege progressing. No general fighting recently. All well. Nothing new from Port-Hudson.   A. LINCOLN

[1] ALS, RPB. Dix telegraphed at 3 P.M. in reply, "Steamer 'Cahawba' has just arrived from New Orleans with the 6th N.Y. Vols. Left on 2nd June Port Hudson was attacked on the (27th) twenty seventh. Gen Sherman was brought to New Orleans severely wounded and little hopes of his recovery. He was speechless when Col [William] Wilson saw him. . . ." (DLC-RTL).

The reports of General Sherman's condition were somewhat exaggerated.

To John A. Dix[1]

Major Gen. Dix.   Washington, D.C.,
Fort-Monroe   June 8 1863

The substance of the news sent of fight at Port-Hudson on the 27th. we have had here three or four days, and I supposed you had it also, when I said this morning "No news from Port-Hudson." We knew that Gen. Sherman was wounded; but, we hoped, not so dangerously as your despatch represents. We still have nothing of that Richmond newspaper story of Kirby Smith crossing & of Banks losing an arm.   A. LINCOLN

[1] ALS, RPB.

To Edwin M. Stanton[1]

June 8, 1863

Let Capt. Robert LeRoy, be appointed Assistant Adjutant General, with the rank of Captain, to report to Gen. Palmer, as within suggested by him.   A. LINCOLN
June 8. 1863.

[1] AES, IHi. Lincoln's endorsement is written on a letter from Brigadier General Innis N. Palmer, New York City, May 29, 1863:

"The enclosed is a copy of an endorsement made by His Excellency the President, on a communication of mine to the Adjutant General of the Army in relation to the case of Mr. Robert LeRoy, formerly Assistant Adjutant General of Volunteers. The original communication with endorsement having been forwarded to me at New Berne North Carolina, while I was on my way from that place to this [on] a short leave. Without waiting for these originals, I will respectfully state that His Excellency is in error in supposing that Mr. LeRoy was *dismissed*. His name was not sent in for confirmation by the Senate, as it was withdrawn at my request.

"In my communication to the Adjutant General I expressed a desire to see Mr. LeRoy restored to his position of Assistant Adjutant General of Volunteers which I suppose could only be done by a re-appointment. I know from personal observation that Mr. LeRoy has not relapsed into any kind of dissipation and I still hope that he may receive a reappointment. In my command—comprised of the 1st. Division of the 18th. Army Corps, are two Brigades neither of which has any regularly appointed Assistant Adjutant General of Volunteers and should Mr. LeRoy receive a reappointment and report to me I should assign him to duty with my command.

"All of which is respectfully submitted. . . ."

The copy of Lincoln's earlier endorsement is not with Palmer's letter, and no further reference to it has been found. On December 31, 1863, LeRoy was nominated assistant adjutant general with rank of captain, to date from June 8, 1863, and his appointment was confirmed by the Senate on March 8, 1864.

To John P. Hale[1]

Hon. John P. Hale
Dover N.H.

Executive Mansion,
Washington, June 9, 1863.

I believe it was upon your recommendation that B. B. Bunker was appointed Attorney for Nevada Territory. I am pressed to remove him on the ground that he does not attend to the office, nor, in fact, pass much time in the territory. Do you wish to say anything on the subject?   A. LINCOLN

[1] ALS, RPB. No reply has been located. Benjamin B. Bunker of New Hampshire, appointed U.S. attorney for Nevada Territory in 1861, was replaced by Theodore D. Edwards of Kentucky, who was confirmed by the Senate on January 20, 1864.

To Joseph Hooker[1]

Washington D.C.
June 9, 1863

Major Genl. Hooker

I am told there are fifty incendiary shells here at the Arsenal made to fit the 100 pdr. Parrott Gun now with you. If this be true, would you like to have the Shells sent to you?   A LINCOLN

[1] ALS, IHi. No answer from Hooker has been located, but Oliver S. Halsted telegraphed Lincoln on June 10, "I am with the Genl. forty nine shells are at the Arsenal—the Genl. has telegraphed an answer to your dispatch requesting that they be sent down." (DLC-RTL).

Halsted was probably Oliver S. Halsted, Jr., a lawyer of Newark, New Jersey, who was promoting the use of incendiary shells invented by his friend Alfred Berney. Letters in the Lincoln Papers from Halsted are signed "Jr." See further Lincoln's telegram to Hooker, June 12, *infra*.

To David Hunter[1]

Executive Mansion,
My Dear General   Washington, June 9, 1863.
   I find it still impossible to answer at length your communication received through Captain Kinzie. I am unwilling to detain him longer and have directed him to return to Hilton Head. I am very sincerely Your friend   A LINCOLN
   Maj. Gen. D. Hunter

[1] LS, CSmH. General Hunter wrote from Hilton Head, South Carolina, on May 22, sending the despatch by Captain Arthur M. Kinzie:
   "It is more than six weeks since the attack by the iron-clads upon Charleston; an attack in which from the nature of the plans of Admiral DuPont the Army had no active part. . . .
   "On the afternoon after the iron-clad attack on Fort Sumter the troops . . . were not only ready to cross Light-House Inlet, but were almost in the act . . . when they were recalled . . . by the announcement of Admiral DuPont that he had resolved to retire, and . . . we could expect no assistance from the Navy. . . .
   "A lodgment on Morris Island was thus made impossible for us. . . . the crossing which could have been effected in a couple of hours and with but little sacrifice six weeks ago will now involve . . . protracted operations and a very serious loss of life. . . .
   "I fear Admiral DuPont distrusts the iron-clads so much that he has resolved to do nothing with them this summer, and I therefore most earnestly beg you to liberate me from those orders to 'co-operate with the Navy' which now tie me down to share the admiral's inactivity. . . . Liberate me from this order . . . and I will immediately place a column of 10,000 . . . in the heart of Georgia. . . .
   "I deem this matter of so much importance and am so weary of inactivity that I send this letter by special steamer to Fortress Monroe, and have instructed the captain of the vessel to wait for your reply. . . ." (OR, I, XIV, 455-57). See Lincoln to Hunter, June 30, *infra*.

To Mary Todd Lincoln[1]

Mrs. Lincoln   Executive Mansion,
Philadelphia, Pa.   Washington, June 9. 1863.
   Think you better put "Tad's" pistol away. I had an ugly dream about him.   A. LINCOLN

[1] ALS, IHi. There is no reply to this telegram.

Endorsement Concerning James B. Caryl[1]

June 10, 1863
   I personally remember nothing about the case of Capt. Caryl, but if the Governor of New York, in his discretion, chooses to give him a military appointment, the disability resting upon Capt. Caryl is hereby removed, enabling the Governor to so appoint him.

1 Parke-Bernet Catalog 63, November 16-17, 1938, No. 182. According to the catalog description, Lincoln's endorsement is written on a letter from Edwin D. Morgan, June 8, 1863, asking removal of disability to hold a commission imposed on Captain James B. Caryl, Twenty-sixth New York Infantry, by court-martial conviction on charges of conduct subversive to military discipline. Caryl's offense consisted in writing a protest against the appointment of a major in his regiment, and tendering his resignation when facing the enemy. On July 9, Governor Seymour authorized Caryl to raise the Thirty-fifth Independent Battery of Artillery. The authorization was withdrawn on September 25, and the battery transferred to the Sixteenth New York Artillery where Captain Caryl served until honorably mustered out in August, 1865. His name is spelled "Caryle" in some sources.

To Joseph Hooker[1]

United States Military Telegraph

"Cypher"   War Department. Washington DC.

Major General Hooker   June 10. 1863. [6:40 P.M.]

Your long despatch of to-day is just received. If left to me, I would not go South of the Rappahannock, upon Lee's moving North of it. If you had Richmond invested to-day, you would not be able to take it in twenty days; meanwhile, your communications, and with them, your army would be ruined. I think *Lee's* Army, and not *Richmond*, is your true objective point. If he comes towards the Upper Potomac, follow on his flank, and on the inside track, shortening your lines, whilst he lengthens his. Fight him when oppertunity offers. If he stays where he is, fret him, and fret him.   A LINCOLN

1 ADfS, DLC-RTL. Hooker's telegram of June 10, 2:30 P.M., is as follows:
"General Pleasonton, by telegram . . . reports that he had an affair with the rebel cavalry yesterday near Brandy Station, which resulted in crippling him so much that he will have to abandon his contemplated raid into Maryland, which was to have started this morning.
"I am not so certain that the raid will be abandoned from this cause. It may delay the departure a few days. I shall leave the cavalry . . . where they are, near Bealeton, with instructions to resist the passage of the river by the enemy's forces. If to effect this he should bring up a considerable force of infantry, that will so much weaken him in my front that I have good reason to believe that I can throw a sufficient force over the river to compel the enemy to abandon his present position. If it should be the intention to send a heavy column of infantry to accompany the cavalry on the proposed raid, he can leave nothing behind to interpose any serious obstacle to my rapid advance on Richmond. I am not satisfied of his intention in this respect, but from certain movements in their corps I cannot regard it as altogether improbable. If it should be found to be the case, will it not promote the true interest of the cause for me to march to Richmond at once? From there all the disposable part of this army can be thrown to any threatened point north of the Potomac at short notice, and, until they can reach their destination, a sufficiency of troops can be collected to check, if not to stop, his invasion. If left to operate from my own judgment, with my present information, I do not hesitate to say that I should adopt this course as being the most speedy and certain mode of giving the

rebellion a mortal blow. I desire that you will give it your reflection. At present the enemy has one corps of infantry at Gordonsville, with the advance at Culpeper, with the manifest tendency of other corps to drift in that direction. I now have two bridges across the Rappahannock, ready to spring over the river below Fredericksburg, and it is this, I believe, that causes the enemy to hesitate in moving forward.

"Major-General Dix informs me that he intends moving two columns up James River to-morrow; but if organized to correspond in numbers to the troops as they have of late been posted, neither column will be successful. The one on the north side of the river will be too small, and on the south side, with his whole column, I question if Richmond can be taken at all, provided 2,000 or 3,000 men could be assembled to defend it. The columns should unite at City Point, or below, and move on the north bank of that river.

"From information, which I deem reliable, the only troops remaining in Richmond is the provost-guard, 1,500, and all the troops between here and there are brought well to the front.

"It would be of incalculable service to this army to be transferred to some more remote point from Washington and Alexandria. The stampedes in those towns, gotten up, no doubt, by people in the rebel interest, have their influence on my men, for many of them have no means of knowing whether they are with or without cause. They think there must be some fire when there is so much smoke."

On June 11, Halleck telegraphed Hooker, "The President has just referred to me your telegram and his reply of yesterday, with directions to say to you whether or not I agree with him. I do so fully." (OR, I, XXVII, I, 35).

To William H. Seward[1]

Regretting my forgetfulness. of course I will see Mr Molina to-morrow.

A. LINCOLN

June 10. 1863.

[1] Copy, DLC-RTL. The copy of Lincoln's note is on a copy of Seward's letter of June 10, 1863, calling the president's attention to the fact that he had failed to keep an appointment to see "Mr Molina," at twelve o'clock. Lincoln's caller may have been Luis Molina, minister from Nicaragua, or Cirilo Molina, confirmed on March 12, 1863, as U.S. consul to Cartagena, Spain.

To Edwin M. Stanton[1]

[c. June 10, 1863]

Let the recommendation of the Judge Advocate General be carried into effect as of the date of his new commission June 10. 1863

[1] Copy, DLC-RTL. The copy of Lincoln's endorsement is contained in a report from Thomas M. Vincent, assistant adjutant general, in reply to the president's request to Stanton for facts in the case of Colonel John C. Lemmon and other officers of the Tenth New York Cavalry, October 22, *infra*. Vincent's report quoted an earlier report dated August 25, 1863, from Judge Advocate General Holt, which quoted Lincoln's endorsement as it appeared on Holt's recommendation that Lemmon be re-mustered in spite of regulations which prohibited resigned officers from re-entering service except upon application of the governor who re-appointed them and upon a certificate from the surgeon

general. Lemmon had resigned on March 26, 1863, because of "continued ill health" while charges were being preferred against him in connection with the insubordination and mutiny of certain officers in his regiment. See Lincoln's communications to Stanton, October 22, *infra.*

To Lorenzo Thomas[1]

June 10 and 13, 1863

Will the Adjutant General please inform the bearer, Mr. Wood, what is the condition of L. W. Muzzey, as to being a Commissary of subsistence. Mr. Wood says he has, for a long time been acting as such, & supposing himself to have been appointed as such.

June 10. 1863.   A. LINCOLN

If the appointment within sought can be consistently made, let it be done.   A. LINCOLN

June. 13. 1863.

1 AES, owned by Gordon A. Block, Philadelphia, Pennsylvania. Lincoln's endorsements are written on a letter from General Robert Schenck, June 6, 1863, introducing David Wood of Boston, "who will explain the nature of his business." First Lieutenant Loring W. Muzzey, regimental quartermaster of the Twelfth Massachusetts Infantry, was appointed captain and commissary of subsistence March 21, 1864.

Introduction for Richard W. Thompson[1]

June 11, 1863

Col. R. W. Thompson is my friend, whom I would be glad to have obliged in any way not inconsistent with the public interest.

A. LINCOLN

1 Chicago Book and Art Auction Catalog 34, June 14-15, 1933, No. 496. On May 1, 1863, Richard W. Thompson had been appointed provost marshal of the Seventh District of Indiana.

To Jesus Jimenez[1]

June 11, 1863

Abraham Lincoln,
President of the United States of America,

To His Excellency
Señor Don Jesus Jimenez,
President of the Republic of Costa Rica.

Great and Good Friend: I have received the letter which you addressed to me on the 8th. ultimo, informing me of your Excellency's elevation to the Presidency of the Republic by the free suffrages of your fellow-citizens and offering to me assurances of your desire to cultivate the relations established between our respective Governments.

I congratulate your Excellency upon this token of the confidence of the People of Costa Rica in your sagacity and statesmanship, and feel satisfied that the trust conferred upon you will be discharged for the best interests of that Republic. It shall be my constant endeavor so to conduct the relations between our respective countries as to strengthen the good understanding which now happily subsists.

I pray your Excellency to accept the assurances of my earnest wishes for your personal happiness and for the prosperity of Costa Rica.

And so commending you to the care of the Almighty I remain Your Excellency's Good Friend,   ABRAHAM LINCOLN.

By the President:

WILLIAM H. SEWARD, Secretary of State.

Washington, June 11, 1863.

[1] Copy, DNA FS RG 59, Communications to Foreign Sovereigns and States, III, 209-10.

To Mary Todd Lincoln[1]

Mrs. Lincoln   Executive Mansion,
Philadelphia   Washington, June 11, 1863.

Your three despatches received. I am very well; and am glad to know that you & "Tad" are so.   A. LINCOLN

[1] ALS, IHi. The telegrams referred to have not been located.

To Erastus Corning and Others[1]

Executive Mansion
Hon. Erastus Corning & others   Washington [June 12][2] 1863.

Gentlemen   Your letter of May 19th. inclosing the resolutions of a public meeting held at Albany, N.Y. on the 16th. of the same month, was received several days ago.

[1] ADf, DLC-RTL; New York *Tribune*, June 15, 1863. The autograph draft in the Lincoln Papers lacks certain revisions which Lincoln must have made in the copy prepared for the press, as well as in the original letter sent to Corning, which has not been located. The draft has been followed, with Lincoln's significant emendations as they appear in the draft and those additional ones which appear in the text of the *Tribune* indicated in footnotes. The cover page of the draft bears Lincoln's endorsement, "Albany letter Manuscript & something about Proclamation." The other manuscript referred to has not been located.

The resolutions, as I understand them, are resolvable into two propositions—first, the expression of a purpose to sustain the cause of the Union, to secure peace through victory, and to support the administration in every constitutional, and lawful measure to suppress the rebellion; and secondly, a declaration of censure upon the administration for supposed unconstitutional action such as the making of military arrests.

And, from the two propositions a third is deduced, which is, that the gentlemen composing the meeting are resolved on doing their part to maintain our common government and country, despite the folly or wickedness, as they may conceive, of any administration. This position is eminently patriotic, and as such, I thank the meeting, and congratulate the nation for it. My own purpose is the same; so that the meeting and myself have a common object, and can have no difference, except in the choice of means or measures, for effecting that object.

And here I ought to close this paper, and would close it, if there were no apprehension that more injurious consequences, than any merely personal to myself, might follow the censures systematical-

---

On June 23, Corning acknowledged receipt of Lincoln's letter, "I have deemed it proper to hand your communication to the Committee who reported the Resolutions, for such action as in their judgment, the case may seem to demand. . . ." (DLC-RTL). On June 30, Corning and the committee conveyed their reply, which reads in part: ". . . We have carefully considered the grounds on which your pretensions to more than regal authority are claimed to rest; and if we do not misinterpret the misty and clouded forms of expression in which those pretensions are set forth, your meaning is that while the rights of the citizen are protected by the Constitution in time of peace, they are suspended or lost in time of war, or when invasion or rebellion exist. You do not, like many others in whose minds, reason and love of regulated liberty seem to be overthrown by the excitements of the hour, attempt to base this conclusion upon a supposed military necessity existing outside of and transcending the Constitution, a military necessity behind which the Constitution itself disappears in a total eclipse. We do not find this gigantic and monstrous heresy put forth in your plea for absolute power, but we do find another equally subversive of liberty and law, and quite as certainly tending to the establishment of despotism. Your claim to have found not outside, but within the Constitution, a principle or germ of arbitrary power, which in time of war expands at once into an absolute sovereignty, wielded by one man; so that liberty perishes, or is dependent on his will, his discretion or his caprice. This extraordinary doctrine, you claim to derive wholly from that clause of the Constitution, which, in case of invasion or rebellion, permits the writ of habeas corpus to be suspended. Upon this ground your whole argument is based.

"You must permit us, to say to you with all due respect, but with the earnestness demanded by the occasion, that the American people will never acquiese in this doctrine. . . ." (*Ibid.*).

2 The date is in Nicolay's handwriting. Welles' *Diary* on June 5 records that "The President read to-day a paper which he had prepared in reply to Erastus Corning and others. It has vigor and ability and with some corrections will be a strong paper."

ly cast upon me for doing what, in my view of duty, I could not forbear. The resolutions promise to support me in every constitutional and lawful measure to suppress the rebellion; and I have not knowingly employed, nor shall knowingly employ, any other. But the meeting, by their resolutions, assert and argue, that certain military arrests and proceedings following them for which I am ultimately responsible, are unconstitutional. I think they are not. The resolutions quote from the constitution, the definition of treason; and also the limiting safe-guards and guarrantees therein provided for the citizen, on trials for treason, and on his being held to answer for capital or otherwise infamous crimes, and, in criminal prossecutions, his right to a speedy and public trial by an impartial jury. They proceed to resolve "That these safe-guards of the rights of the citizen against the pretentions of arbitrary power, were intended more *especially* for his protection in times of civil commotion." And, apparantly, to demonstrate the proposition, the resolutions proceed "They were secured substantially to the English people, *after* years of protracted civil war, and were adopted into our constitution at the *close* of the revolution." Would not the demonstration have been better, if it could have been truly said that these safe-guards had been adopted, and applied *during* the civil wars and *during* our revolution, instead of *after* the one, and at the *close* of the other. I too am devotedly for them *after* civil war, and *before* civil war, and at all times "except when, in cases of Rebellion or Invasion, the public Safety may require" their suspension. The resolutions proceed to tell us that these safe-guards "have stood the test of seventysix years of trial, under our republican system, under circumstances which show that while they constitute the foundation of all free government, they are the elements of the enduring stability of the Republic." No one denies that they have so stood the test up to the beginning of the present rebellion if we except a certain matter [occurrence][3] at New-Orleans hereafter to be mentioned; nor does any one question that they will stand the same test much longer after the rebellion closes. But these provisions of the constitution have no application to the case we have in hand, because the arrests complained of were not made for treason—that is, not for *the* treason defined in the constitution, and upon the conviction of which, the punishment is death—; nor yet were they made to hold persons to answer for any capital, or otherwise infamous crimes; nor were the proceedings following, in any constitutional or legal sense, "criminal prossecutions." The arrests were made on totally different grounds,

[3] The *Tribune* gives "occurence."

and the proceedings following, accorded with the grounds of the arrests. Let us consider the real case with which we are dealing, and apply to it the parts of the constitution plainly made for such cases.[4]

Prior to my instalation here it had been inculcated that any State had a lawful right to secede from the national Union; and that it would be expedient to exercise the right, whenever the devotees of the doctrine should fail to elect a President to their own liking. I was elected contrary to their liking; and accordingly, so far as it was legally possible, they had taken seven states out of the Union, had seized many of the United States Forts, and had fired upon the United States' Flag, all before I was inaugerated; and, of course, before I had done any official act whatever. The rebellion, thus began soon ran into the present civil war;[5] and, in certain respects, it began on very unequal terms between the parties. The insurgents had been preparing for it more than thirty years, while the government had taken no steps to resist them. The former had carefully considered all the means which could be turned to their account. It undoubtedly was a well pondered reliance with them that in their own unrestricted effort to destroy Union, constitution, and law, all together, the government would, in great degree, be restrained by the same constitution and law, from arresting their progress. Their sympathizers pervaded all departments of the government, and nearly all communities of the people. From this material, under cover of "Liberty of speech" "Liberty of the press" and *"Habeas corpus"* they hoped to keep on foot amongst us a most efficient corps of spies, informers, supplyers, and aiders and abettors of their cause in a thousand ways. They knew that in times such as they were inaugerating, by the constitution itself, the "Habeas corpus" might be suspended; but they also knew they had friends who would make a question[6] as to *who* was to suspend it; meanwhile their spies and others might remain at large to help on their cause. Or if, as has happened, the executive should suspend the writ, without ruinous waste of time, instances of arresting innocent persons might occur, as are always likely to occur in such cases; and then a clamor[7] could be raised in regard to this, which might be, at least, of some service to the insurgent cause. It needed no very keen perception to discover

[4] The draft has the following sentence deleted at this point: "May I be indulged to submit a few general remarks upon this subject of arrests?"

[5] The first clause of this sentence, emended to the present reading in the draft, was originally as follows: "The present civil war soon followed;"

[6] "Make a question" is substituted in the draft for "raise a squabble."

[7] "Clamor" is substituted in the draft for "howl."

this part of the enemies' programme, so soon as by open hostilities their machinery was fairly put in motion. Yet, thoroughly imbued with a reverence for the guarranteed rights of individuals, I was slow to adopt the strong measures, which by degrees I have been forced to regard as being within the exceptions of the constitution, and as indispensable to the public Safety. Nothing is better known to history than that courts of justice are utterly incompetent to such cases. Civil courts are organized chiefly for trials of individuals, or, at most, a few individuals acting in concert; and this in quiet times, and on charges of crimes well defined in the law. Even in times of peace, bands of horse-thieves and robbers frequently grow too numerous and powerful for the ordinary courts of justice. But what comparison, in numbers, have such bands ever borne to the insurgent sympathizers even in many of the loyal states? Again, a jury[8] too frequently have at least one member, more ready to hang the panel than to hang the traitor. And yet again, he who dissuades one man from volunteering, or induces one soldier to desert, weakens the Union cause as much as he who kills a union soldier in battle. Yet this dissuasion, or inducement, may be so conducted as to be no defined crime of which any civil court would take cognizance.

Ours is a case of Rebellion—so called by the resolutions before me—in fact, a clear, flagrant, and gigantic case of Rebellion; and the provision of the constitution that "The previlege of the writ of Habeas Corpus shall not be suspended, unless when in cases of Rebellion or Invasion, the public Safety may require it" is *the* provision which specially applies to our present case. This provision plainly attests the understanding of those who made the constitution that ordinary courts of justice are inadequate to "cases of Rebellion"—attests their purpose that in such cases, men[9] may be held in custody whom the courts acting on ordinary rules, would discharge. Habeas Corpus, does not discharge men who are proved to be guilty of defined crime; and its suspension is allowed by the constitution on purpose that, men may be arrested and held, who can not be proved to be guilty of defined crime, "when, in cases of Rebellion or Invasion the public Safety may require it." This is precisely our present case—a case of Rebellion, wherein the public Safety does require the suspension. Indeed, arrests by process of

---

[8] This sentence, emended to the present reading in the draft, originally began as follows: "Again, a jury can scarcely be empannelled, that will not have at least. . . ."

[9] The remainder of this sentence, revised in the draft to the present reading, originally read as follows: "men might be held in custody in spite of the courts, and whom the courts if allowed, would release."

courts, and arrests in cases of rebellion, do not proceed altogether upon the same basis. The former is directed at the small per centage of ordinary and continuous perpetration of crime; while the latter is directed at sudden and extensive uprisings against the government, which, at most, will succeed or fail, in no great length of time. In the latter case, arrests are made, not so much for what has been done, as for what probably would be done. The latter is more for the preventive, and less for the vindictive, than the former. In such cases the purposes of men are much more easily understood, than in cases of ordinary crime. The man who stands by and says nothing, when the peril of his government is discussed, can not be misunderstood. If not hindered, he is sure to help the enemy. Much more, if he talks ambiguously—talks for his country with "buts" and "ifs" and "ands." Of how little value the constitutional provision I have quoted will be rendered, if arrests shall never be made until defined crimes shall have been committed, may be illustrated by a few notable examples. Gen. John C. Breckienridge, Gen. Robert E. Lee, Gen. Joseph E. Johnston, Gen. John B. Magruder, Gen. William B. Preston, Gen. Simon B. Buckner, and Comodore [Franklin] Buchanan, now occupying the very highest places in the rebel war service, were all within the power of the government since the rebellion began, and were nearly as well known to be traitors then as now. Unquestionably if we had seized and held them, the insurgent cause would be much weaker. But no one of them had then committed any crime defined in the law. Every one of them if arrested would have been discharged on Habeas Corpus, were the writ allowed to operate. In view of these and similar cases, I think the time not unlikely to come when I shall be blamed for having made too few arrests rather than too many.

By the third resolution the meeting indicate their opinion that military arrests may be constitutional in localities where rebellion actually exists; but that such arrests are unconstitutional in localities where rebellion, or insurrection, does not actually exist. They insist that such arrests shall not be made "outside of the lines of necessary military occupation, and the scenes of insurrection" In asmuch, however, as the constitution itself makes no such distinction, I am unable to believe that there is any such constitutional distinction. I concede that the class of arrests complained of, can be constitutional only when, in cases of Rebellion or Invasion, the public Safety may require them; and I insist that in such cases, they are constitutional *wherever* the public safety does require them—as well in places to which they may prevent the rebellion extending, as in those where it may be already prevailing—as well where they may restrain mischievous interference with the raising and supplying of armies, to suppress the rebellion, as where the rebellion may actually be—as well where they may restrain the enticing men out of the army, as where they would prevent mutiny in the army—equally constitutional at all places where they will conduce to the public Safety, as against the dangers of Rebellion or Invasion.

Take the particular case mentioned by the meeting. They assert [It is asserted][10] in substance that Mr. Vallandigham was by a military commander, seized and tried "for no other reason than words addressed to a public meeting, in criticism of the course of the administration, and in condemnation of the military orders of that general" Now, if there be no mistake about this—if this assertion is the truth and the whole truth—if there was no other reason for the arrest, then I concede that the arrest was wrong. But the arrest, as I understand, was made for a very different reason. Mr. Vallandigham avows his hostility to the war on the part of the Union; and his arrest was made because he was laboring, with some effect, to prevent the raising of troops, to encourage desertions from the army, and to leave the rebellion without an adequate military force to suppress it. He was not arrested because he was damaging the political prospects of the administration, or the personal interests of the commanding general; but because he was damaging the army, upon the existence, and vigor of which, the life of the nation depends. He was warring upon the military; and this gave the military constitutional jurisdiction to lay hands upon him. If Mr. Vallandigham was not damaging the military power of the country, then his arrest was made on mistake of fact, which I would be glad to correct, on reasonably satisfactory evidence.

I understand the meeting, whose resolutions I am considering, to be in favor of suppressing the rebellion by military force—by armies. Long experience has shown that armies can not be maintained unless desertion shall be punished by the severe penalty of death. The case requires, and the law and the constitution, sanction this punishment. Must I shoot a simple-minded soldier boy who deserts, while I must not touch a hair of a wiley agitator who induces him to desert? This is none the less injurious when effected by getting a father, or brother, or friend, into a public meeting, and there working upon his feelings, till he is persuaded to write the soldier boy, that he is fighting in a bad cause, for a wicked administration of a contemptable government, too weak to arrest

10 The *Tribune* reads "It is asserted."

and punish him if he shall desert. I think that in such a case, to silence the agitator, and save the boy, is not only constitutional, but, withal, a great mercy.[11]

If I be wrong on this question of constitutional power, my error lies in believing that certain proceedings are constitutional when, in cases of rebellion or Invasion, the public Safety requires them, which would not be constitutional when, in absence of rebellion or invasion, the public Safety does not require them—in other words, that the constitution is not in it's application in all respects the same, in cases of Rebellion or invasion, involving the public Safety, as it is in times of profound peace and public security. The constitution itself makes the distinction; and I can no more be persuaded that the government can constitutionally take no strong measure in time of rebellion, because it can be shown that the same could not be lawfully taken in time of peace, than I can be persuaded that a particular drug is not good medicine for a sick man, because it can be shown to not be good food for a well one. Nor am I able to appreciate the danger, apprehended by the meeting, that the American people will, by means of military arrests during the rebellion, lose the right of public discussion, the liberty of speech and the press, the law of evidence, trial by jury, and Habeas corpus, throughout the indefinite peaceful future which I trust lies before them, any more than I am able to believe that a man could contract so strong an appetite for emetics during temporary illness,[12] as to persist in feeding upon them through the remainder of his healthful life.

In giving the resolutions that earnest consideration which you request of me, I can not overlook the fact that the meeting speak as "Democrats." Nor can I, with full respect for their known intelligence, and the fairly presumed deliberation with which they prepared their resolutions, be permitted to suppose that this occurred by accident, or in any way other than that they preferred to designate themselves "democrats" rather than "American citizens." In this time of national peril I would have preferred to meet you upon a level one step higher than any party platform; because I am sure that from such more elevated position, we could do better battle for the country we all love, than we possibly can from those lower ones, where from the force of habit, the prejudices of the past, and selfish hopes of the future, we are sure to expend much of our ingenuity and strength, in finding fault with, and

11 An additional phrase is deleted in the draft, "and a great merit."

12 "During temporary illness" is substituted in the draft for "while temporarily sick."

aiming blows at each other. But since you have denied me this, I will yet be thankful, for the country's sake, that not all democrats have done so. He on whose discretionary judgment Mr. Vallandigham was arrested and tried, is a democrat, having no old party affinity with me; and the judge who rejected the constitutional view expressed in these resolutions, by refusing to discharge Mr. V. on Habeas Corpus, is a democrat of better days than these, having received his judicial mantle at the hands of President Jackson. And still more, of all those democrats who are nobly exposing their lives and shedding their blood on the battle-field, I have learned that many approve the course taken with Mr. V. while I have not heard of a single one condemning it. I can not assert that there are none such.

And[13] the name of President Jackson recalls a bit [an instance][14] of pertinent history. After the battle of New-Orleans, and while the fact that the treaty of peace had been concluded, was well known in the city, but before official knowledge of it had arrived, Gen. Jackson still maintained martial, or military law. Now, that it could be said the war was over, the clamor against martial law, which had existed from the first, grew more furious. Among other things a Mr. Louiallier[15] published a denunciatory newspaper article. Gen. Jackson arrested him. A lawyer by the name of Morel[16] procured the U.S. Judge Hall[17] to order a writ of Habeas Corpus to release Mr. Louaillier. Gen. Jackson arrested both the lawyer and the judge. A Mr. Hollander[18] ventured to say of some part of the matter that "it was a dirty trick." Gen. Jackson arrested him. When the officer undertook to serve the writ of Habeas Corpus, Gen. Jackson took it from him, and sent him away with a copy. Holding the judge in custody a few days, the general sent him beyond the limits of his encampment, and set him at liberty, with an order to remain till the ratification of peace should be regularly announced, or until the British should have left the Southern coast. A day or two more elapsed, the ratification of the treaty of peace was regularly announced, and the judge and others were fully liberated. A few days more, and the judge called Gen. Jackson into court and fined him a thousand dollars, for having arrested him and the others named. The general paid the fine, and there the matter rested for nearly thirty years, when congress refunded principal and interest. The late Senator Douglas, then in

[13] This paragraph and the next are autograph insertions in the draft.
[14] The *Tribune* reads "an instance."
[15] Louis Louaillier, member of the Louisiana legislature.
[16] Pierre L. Morel.   [17] Dominick A. Hall, U.S. district judge.
[18] Hollander was a New Orleans merchant.

the House of Representatives, took a leading part in the debate, in which the constitutional question was much discussed. I am not prepared to say whom the Journals would show to have voted for the measure.

It may be remarked: First, that we had the same constitution then, as now. Secondly, that we then had a case of Invasion, and that now we have a case of Rebellion, and: Thirdly, that the permanent right of the people to public discussion, the liberty of speech and the press, the trial by jury, the law of evidence, and the Habeas Corpus, suffered no detriment whatever by that conduct of Gen. Jackson, or it's subsequent approval by the American congress.

And yet, let me say that in my own discretion, I do not know whether I would have ordered the arrest of Mr. V. While I can not shift the responsibility from myself, I hold that, as a general rule, the commander in the field is the better judge of the necessity in any particular case. Of course I must practice a general directory and revisory power in the matter.

One of the resolutions expresses the opinion of the meeting that arbitrary arrests will have the effect to divide and distract those who should be united in suppressing the rebellion; and I am specifically called on to discharge Mr. Vallandigham. I regard this as, at least, a fair appeal to me, on the expediency of exercising a constitutional power which I think exists. In response to such appeal I have to say it gave me pain when I learned that Mr. V. had been arrested,—that is,[19] I was pained that there should have seemed to be a necessity for arresting him—and that it will afford me great pleasure to discharge him so soon as I can, by any means, believe the public safety will not suffer by it. I further say, that as the war progresses, it appears to me, opinion, and action, which were in great confusion at first, take shape, and fall into more regular channels; so that the necessity for arbitrary [strong][20] dealing with them gradually decreases. I have every reason to desire that it would cease altogether; and far from the least is my regard for the opinions and wishes of those who, like the meeting at Albany, declare their purpose to sustain the government in every constitutional and lawful measure to suppress the rebellion. Still,[21] I must continue to do so much as may seem to be required by the public safety.   A. LINCOLN.

[19] The clause set off by dashes appears in the *Tribune*, but is not in the draft.
[20] The *Tribune* has "strong" instead of "arbitrary."
[21] The last sentence and signature are from the *Tribune* and do not appear in the draft.

To Henry W. Halleck[1]

June 12, 1863

The within comes in answer to a proposition of mine to visit Gen. Hooker on tomorrow night (Saturday).

I have thought perhaps Gen. Halleck better see it.   A. LINCOLN

June 12. 1863.

[1] AES, DLC-RTL. Lincoln's endorsement is written on a telegram from General Hooker, 6:20 P.M., June 12, 1863: "If I am not very much mistaken I shall be constrained to move my Army on to the Alexandria and Orange Rail Road before that time. I have three (3) corps near there at this time. I presume that Gen Halleck showed you my dispatch of this morning. Also please see copy of my dispatch to Gen Dix of today."

See Lincoln's telegram to Hooker, *infra*.

To Joseph Holt[1]

June 12, 1863

[Lieut. Garretson]—forged a pass, or furlough.

If the Judge Advocate Genl upon examining this case shall be of opinion that Lt. Garretson can be relieved without detriment to the service, I shall be glad to do it. Will he please examine & report to me   A. LINCOLN

June 12. 1863.

[1] AES, DLC-RTL. Bracketed name is not in Lincoln's autograph. The endorsement is written on an envelope which bears a note in pencil, not Lincoln's, "altered the date of a furlough." As cataloged in the Lincoln Papers the envelope is incorrectly given the date January 12, 1864. Neither the papers of Lieutenant Garretson nor a reply from Holt has been located. Second Lieutenant John H. Garretson of the Twenty-first New Jersey Volunteers had been dismissed from the service on March 25, 1863. A petition signed by officers of his regiment, April 4, 1863, requested his reinstatement (DLC-RTL).

To Joseph Hooker[1]

Executive Mansion, June 12, 1863—2 p.m.

Major-General Hooker: If you can show me a trial of the incendiary shells on Saturday night, I will try to join you at 5 p.m. that day. Answer.   A. LINCOLN.

[1] OR, I, XXVII, I, 37. For Hooker's reply see Lincoln to Halleck, *supra*, note. At 9 P.M. Hooker telegraphed Lincoln again, "At the time of my reply to your telegram of to-day, I supposed that this was Thursday and not Friday. It will give me great pleasure to have the gun on exhibition at 5 p.m. to-morrow. I have some good targets in the shape of rebel camps which the gun will enfilade." (*Ibid.*).

To Erastus Corning[1]

Private

Hon. Erastus Corning   Executive Mansion,
My dear Sir   Washington, June 13, 1863.

Herewith I inclose you the promised response to the resolutions of the Albany meeting Your Obt. Servt.   A. LINCOLN

[1] ALS, WHi. This note accompanied the original letter to Corning and others of June 12, *supra*, which has not been located.

To Joseph Holt[1]

Judge Advocate General please examine & report on this case.
June 13. 1863.   A. LINCOLN

[1] AES, owned by John Davis, Jr., Topeka, Kansas. Lincoln's endorsement has been clipped from the attendant papers, and no further reference has been found.

To Joseph Hooker[1]

"Cypher"   Executive Mansion, Washington,
Major General Hooker   June. 13, 1863.

I was coming down this afternoon; but if you would prefer I should not, I shall blame you if you do not tell me so.

            A LINCOLN

[1] ALS, owned by R. E. Burdick, New York City. Hooker's reply was received at 1 P.M.: "It may be well not to come." (DLC-RTL). Lincoln seems to have departed, however, before Hooker's reply was received, and Stanton telegraphed Captain Colin B. Ferguson at Alexandria, "Stop the tug on which the president is and ask him to return." (DLC-RTL).

To Leopold[1]

           June 13, 1863

Abraham Lincoln,
President of the United States of America

To His Majesty, Leopold,
King of the Belgians.

Great and Good Friend: I have received through the minister of the United States accredited to Your Majesty, the award in the case of the claim of certain citizens of the United States upon the Government of the Republic of Chili, which by agreement between this Government and the Government of that Republic, was submitted to Your Majesty's arbitrament, a trust was accepted by Your Majesty. The confidence in Your Majesty's uprightness, impartiality and intelligence which led the parties interested to seek from Your Majesty a decision of the long pending controversy adverted to will, it is believed, be regarded by all the parties interested, as justified by the result. In this respect, I can speak with perfect assurance, at least on the part of this Government. I cannot omit to add an expression of my thanks for the pains which Your Majesty must have taken to reach a correct conclusion in so arduos a business, and my belief that Your Majesty's success in this instance will not be regarded as an unimportant proof of the wisdem which has characterized Your Majestys illustrious reign. And so I pray God to have Your Majesty in His safe and holy keeping

Written at the City of Washington the 13th. day of June Anno Domini 1863. Your Good Friend   ABRAHAM LINCOLN

By the President

WILLIAM H. SEWARD Secretary of State

[1] Copy, DNA FS RG 59, Communications to Foreign Sovereigns and States, III, 230-31. The convention with Chile of November 10, 1858, provided that the King of Belgium should act as arbiter in the claim to proceeds of the cargo of the U.S. brig *Macedonian*, consisting of silver in coin and bars, forcibly taken in 1821. On May 15, 1863, Leopold rendered his decision, awarding the U.S. $42,400

To Gideon Welles[1]

Sec. of Navy, please allow the bearer, Mr. Lyman, to take his new cannon into the Navy-Yard where I wish to see it fired next week.

June 13. 1863.   A. LINCOLN

[1] ALS, DNA WR RG 74, Navy Branch, Bureau of Ordnance, Inventions, Rifle and Smooth Bore, Letters Received 1862-1864. Lincoln's note was endorsed by Welles to the Chief of Ordnance and forwarded by Commander Henry A. Wise with an order to Lieutenant Commander William Mitchell to "mount and prepare for firing the accelerating gun of Mr. [Azel S.] Lyman in accordance with the request. . . ."

To Salmon P. Chase[1]

Executive Mansion, June 14, 1863.

Hon. Secretary of the Treasury.

Sir:—Your note of this morning is received. You will co-operate by the revenue cutters under your direction with the navy in arresting rebel depredations on American commerce and transportation and in capturing rebels engaged therein.

ABRAHAM LINCOLN.

¹ Lapsley, VI, 325. Chase wrote on June 14, requesting the authority granted by Lincoln in this letter, "in view of the intelligence just received of depredations by rebel cruisers on our Commerce & Navigation near the capes of Virginia." (DLC-RTL).

To Joseph Hooker¹

Washington, June 14, 1863 1.14 p.m.

Major-General Hooker: Do you consider it possible that 15,000 of Ewell's men can now be at Winchester?   A. LINCOLN.

¹ OR, I, XXVII, I, 38. General Alfred Pleasonton reported to Stanton on June 14, received 6:05 P.M., that a "negro states that he left Gaines' Cross-Roads last night, and the enemy's column passed there for Harper's Ferry on Friday morning [12th]. . . . Saw [Richard] Ewell . . . also [James] Longstreet and [Jubal A.] Early. . . . I believe this man's report." (OR, I, XXVII, III, 101). Hooker's reply to Lincoln of 7:10 P.M. merely referred to Pleasonton's report (OR, I, XXVII, I, 39).

To Joseph Hooker¹

Washington, June 14, 1863—5.50 p.m.

Major-General Hooker: So far as we can make out here, the enemy have Milroy surrounded at Winchester, and Tyler at Martinsburg. If they could hold out a few days, could you help them? If the head of Lee's army is at Martinsburg and the tail of it on the Plank road between Fredericksburg and Chancellorsville, the animal must be very slim somewhere. Could you not break him?

A. LINCOLN.

¹ OR, I, XXVII, I, 39.

To Joseph Hooker¹

Executive Mansion, Washington,

Major General Hooker.   June 14. *11.55 P.M.* 1863.

Yours of 11.30 just received. You have nearly all the elements for forming an opinion whether Winchester is surrounded that I have. I really fear—almost believe, it is. No communication has been had with it during the day, either at Martinsburg, or Harper's Ferry. At 7 P.M., we also lost communication with Martins-

burg. The enemy had also appeared there some hours before. At
9. PM. Harper's Ferry said the enemy was reported at Berryville
& Smithfield. If I could know that Longstreet and Ewell moved in
that direction so long ago as you stated in your last, then I should
feel sure that Winchester is strongly invested. It is quite certain
that a considerable force of the enemy is thereabout; and I fear it
is an overwhelming one, compared with Milroys. I am unable to
give any more certain opinion.   A. LINCOLN

¹ ALS-F, ISLA. Hooker proposed to Halleck in a telegram of 7 P.M., June 13,
that he transfer operations from the line of Aquia Creek to the Orange and
Alexandria Railroad (OR, I, XXVII, I, 38). His telegram to Lincoln of 11:15
P.M., June 14, is as follows: "Has anything further been heard from Winchester? Will the President allow me to inquire if it is his opinion that Winchester is surrounded by the rebel forces? I make this inquiry for the reason
that General [Isaac R.] Trimble was recently assigned, in orders, to the command of that district, and it is not known what command he had. . . . I do
not feel like making a move for an enemy until I am satisfied as to his
whereabouts. . . . With this feeling, unless otherwise directed, I feel it my
duty to execute the movement indicated on yesterday. . . ." (Ibid., pp. 39-40).

To Benjamin F. Kelley¹

Major-General Kelley,   Washington,
Harper's Ferry: June 14, 1863– 1.27 p.m.
     Are the forces at Winchester and Martinsburg making any ef-
fort to get to you?   A. LINCOLN.

¹ OR, I, XXVII, III, 108. Kelley replied, "Dispatch received. I am not advised that the forces at Winchester, under General Milroy, are falling back on
this place. The forces of my command at Martinsburg are ordered to fall back
on me, if assailed by overpowering numbers." (Ibid.).

To Robert C. Schenck¹

"Cypher"
Gen. Schenck   Washington, D.C.,
Baltimore   June 14 1863
     Get Milroy from Winchester to Harper's Ferry if possible. He
will be gobbled up, if he remains, if he is not already past salvation.   A. LINCOLN

¹ ALS, RPB. This telegram is misdated July 13, 1863, in Hertz, II, 901.
Schenck replied, "I am doing all I can to get Milroy back toward Harper's
Ferry on the railroad. He sent down a courier in the night to say that, if he
could not fall back, he could sustain himself, and hold his position five days,
but I have no force to support him. The rebels appear to have pushed on beyond him rapidly and impetuously, and are reported approaching Martinsburg." (OR, I, XXVII, II, 174).

To Daniel Tyler[1]

"Cypher"

Gen. Tyler—   Washington, D.C.,
Martinsburg.   June 14 1863

Is Milroy invested, so that he can not fall back to Harper's
Ferry?   A. LINCOLN

[1] ALS, RPB. Tyler replied at 3 P.M., "General Milroy is in a tight place. If
he gets out, it will be by good luck and hard fighting. Not a straggler from
his army is yet in; it is neck or nothing. We are besieged here; have had a
little skirmish. I imagine our rebel friends are waiting for grub and artillery."
(OR, XXVII, II, 174).

To Daniel Tyler[1]

"*Cypher*"

Gen. Tyler   Washington, D.C.,
Martinsburg.   June 14 1863

If you are beseiged, how do you despatch me? Why did you not
leave, before being besieged?   A. LINCOLN

[1] ALS, RPB. No reply has been located, but Tyler fell back on Harper's
Ferry.

To Edward L. Baker[1]

E. L. Baker, Esq   Executive Mansion,
Dear Sir   Washington, June 15, 1863.

Not to exceed two hours after you left me I received a letter from
Springfield, renewing the pressure upon me in the matter we
talked of; and, in fact, leaving me no alternative but to make some
change there. I can say but little beyond what I then said to you.
The appeal to me in behalf of Mr. Edwards and Mr. Bailhasche,[2]
for a hearing, does not meet the case. No formal charges are preferred against them, so far as I know; nor do I expect any will be
made; or, if made, will be substantiated. I certainly do not suppose
Mr. Edwards has, at this time of his life, given up his old habits,
and turned dishonest; and while I have not known Mr. Bailhasche
so long, I have no more affirmative reason to suspect him. The
trouble with me is of a different character. Springfield is my home,
and there, more than elsewhere, are my life-long friends. These,
for now nearly two years, have been harrassing me because of Mr.
E. & Mr. B. I think Mr. E. & Mr. B. without dishonesty on the
other hand, could have saved me from this, if they had cared to do

so. They have seemed to think that if they could keep their official record dryly correct, to say the least, it was not any difference how much they might provoke my friends, and harrass me. If this is too strong a statement of the case, still the result has been the same to me; and, as a *misfortune* merely, I think I have already borne a fair share of it.

In what I may do, I shall try to so shape it, as to not seem to mean more than is really intended. Your Obt. Servt.

A. LINCOLN.

¹ ALS (copy?), DLC-RTL. See Lincoln to Jesse K. Dubois and others, May 29, *supra*. On June 18, Ninian W. Edwards wrote Edward Bates, and at "the *advice of Judge Davis* of the Supreme Court" enclosed a letter to Lincoln with the comment, "*I am anxious to do what you and he may think best*." To Lincoln, Edwards wrote as follows: "Mr Baker has shown me your letter of the 15th. It pains me very much to hear that I give you any trouble. I know that I have not only kept my record correct, but I have taken *extraordinary* pains to avoid giving any cause for complaint. . . . When I asked an office from you . . . I needed it very much. I can now do without it. I don't wish to embarrass you. If I am removed from here it will be said that there is good cause for it. Under my present orders I can keep my office at Chicago . . . or rather than give you further trouble I will resign. I will do what you think best. . . ." (DLC-RTL). See Lincoln's memorandum, June 22, *infra*.
² William H. Bailhache.

To Joseph Hooker¹

Major General Hooker   Washington City,
Fairfax Station.   June 15. 8 ½ P.M. 1863

The facts are now known here that Winchester and Martinsburg were both besieged yesterday; the troops from Martinsburg have got into Harper's Ferry without loss; those from Winchester, are also in, having lost, in killed, wounded and missing, about one third of their number. Of course the enemy holds both places; and I think the report is authentic that he is crossing the Potomac at Williamsburg. We have not heard of his yet appearing at Harper's Ferry, or on the river anywhere below. I would like to hear from you.   A. LINCOLN

¹ ALS-P, ISLA. Hooker acknowledged receipt of Lincoln's telegram as follows: "Your telegram of 8.30 p.m. received. It seems to disclose the intentions of the enemy to make an invasion, and, if so, it is not in my power to prevent it. I can, however, make an effort to check him until he has concentrated all his forces. I may possibly be able to prevent the junction, and commence the movement during to-morrow. On so short reflection, I am not prepared to say this is the wisest move, nor do I know that my opinion on this subject is wanted. A. P. Hill moved up toward Culpeper this morning, indicating his intention to re-enforce their forces on the Upper Potomac." (OR, I, XXVII, I, 43).

At 10 P.M. Hooker telegraphed Lincoln again: "With regard to the enemy, your dispatch is more conclusive than any I have received. I now feel that invasion is his settled purpose. . . . It is an act of desperation on his part, no matter in what force he moves. It will kill copperheadism in the North. I do not know that my opinion as to the duty of this army in the case is wanted; if it should be, you know that I will be happy to give it. I have heard nothing of the movements of the enemy to-day. . . . I have only heard that all of A.P. Hill's forces moved up the river this morning, in the direction of Culpeper. If it should be determined for me to make a movement in pursuit, which I am not prepared to recommend at this time, I may possibly be able to move some corps to-morrow, and can reach the point of the enemy's crossing in advance of A.P. Hill. . . . If they are moving toward Maryland, I can better fight them there than make a running fight. If they come up in front of Washington, I can threaten and cut their communications, and Dix can be re-enforced from the south to act on their rear. . . ." (*Ibid.*, pp. 43-44).

To Mary Todd Lincoln[1]

Mrs. Lincoln   June 15, 1863.
Philadelphia, Pa.

Tolerably well. Have not rode out much yet, but have at last got new tires on the carriage wheels, & perhaps, shall ride out soon.   A. LINCOLN

[1] ALS, IHi. No communication from Mrs. Lincoln has been located.

Proclamation Calling for 100,000 Militia[1]

June 15, 1863
By the President of the United States of America.

A Proclamation.

Whereas the armed insurrectionary combinations now existing in several of the States are threatening to make inroads into the States of Maryland, Western Virginia, Pennsylvania and Ohio, requiring immediately an additional military force for the service of the United States;

Now, therefore, I, Abraham Lincoln, President of the United States and Commander-in-Chief of the Army and Navy thereof and of the Militia of the several States when called into actual service, do, hereby, call into the service of the United States, one hundred thousand militia from the States following, namely—from the State of Maryland ten thousand, from the State of Pennsylvania, fifty thousand, from the State of Ohio, thirty thousand, from the State of West Virginia, ten thousand, to be mustered into the service of the United States forthwith and to serve for the period of six months from the date of such muster into said service, unless sooner discharged; to be mustered in as infantry, artillery and cavalry, in proportions which will be made known through the

War Department, which Department will also designate the several places of rendezvous. These militia to be organized according to the rules and regulations of the volunteer service and such orders as may hereafter be issued. The States aforesaid will be respectively credited under the enrolment act for the militia services rendered under this proclamation.

In testimony whereof, I have hereunto set my hand and caused the seal of the United States to be affixed.

Done at the City of Washington this fifteenth day of June, in the year of our Lord one thousand eight hundred and [L.S.] sixty-three, and of the Independence of the United States the eighty seventh. ABRAHAM LINCOLN

By the President:

WILLIAM H. SEWARD Secretary of State.

[1] DS, DNA FS RG 11, Proclamations. With the official copy is the draft in Seward's handwriting with corrections by Stanton.

To Daniel Tyler[1]

Gen. Tyler,   War Department Washington City,
Harper's Ferry.   June 15. 8/45. P.M 1863.

It would be useful, if we could tell Hooker, about what number of the enemy is about Winchester and all North of it—also what troops they are. I will be obliged, if you will ascertain as nearly as you can, and inform me.   A. LINCOLN

[1] ALS, NN. No reply has been located, but Tyler telegraphed Hooker on June 17, "The only rebel force of any amount that I am satisfied of was at Williamsport at 6 o'clock last evening. I think, allowing for exaggerations, there might be 7,000 or 8,000 men of all arms at Williamsport. . . ." (OR, I, XXVII, II, 23).

To Edward Bates[1]

June 16, 1863

I sought and obtained an interview with the District Attorney in regard to this case, and thereupon concluded to remit the fines in this, and the case of the brother convicted at the same time, leaving the costs, and imprisonment, undisturbed. Will the Attorney General please prepare the proper paper?   A. LINCOLN

June 16. 1863.

[1] AES, DNA RG 204, Pardon Attorney, A 476. Lincoln's endorsement is written on a petition signed by Elizabeth Knowles, June 16, 1863, in behalf of

her son John Knowles, sentenced to ten days' imprisonment and a fine of one hundred and fifty dollars for assault and battery against "one Noble," who purportedly insulted Knowles' sister.

To Horace Binney, Jr.[1]

Horace Binney, Jr   Washington, D.C.,
Philadelphia   June 16. 1863

I sent Gen. Cadwallader, some hours ago, to the Sec. of War, & Gen. in-chief, with the question you ask. I have not heard the result.   A. LINCOLN

[1] ALS, RPB. A telegram signed by Horace Binney and others, June 16, 1863, asked whether Major General George Cadwalader could be "sent to Phila with orders to organize a force under the present head of this Dept for the present emergency." (DLC-RTL). Cadwalader was assigned to command of troops at Philadelphia.

To William S. Bliss[1]

Col. Wm. S. Bliss.   Executive Mansion,
New-York Hotel   Washington, June 16 1863.

Your despatch, asking whether I will accept "the loyal Brigade of the North" is received. I never heard of that Brigade, by name, and do not know where it is; yet presuming that it is in New-York, I say I will gladly accept it, if tendered by and with the consent and approbation of the Governor of that State—otherwise not.
                             A. LINCOLN

[1] ALS, RPB. On June 16, William S. Bliss telegraphed Lincoln as follows: "Will you accept the loyal brigade of the North I have four thousand three hundred men which are now ready. I did intend to take a thousand men from each New England state to place at your disposal. I try to serve my country My family do not expect any money from this government I will show you the signatures of all the bank officers of this city Reply immediately." No reference has been found indicating either acceptance of the brigade or service by Bliss.

To Augustin Chester[1]

The reports which I have, from the Judge Advocate General, are adverse to Capt Riley and Lieut. Pike   A. LINCOLN
June 16. 1863

[1] AES, ICHi. Lincoln's endorsement is written on a letter from Augustin Chester, Washington, June 15, 1863, transmitting "letters of Hon I. N. Arnold in behalf of Capt. Riley. I ask that you will enclose to me the decision in his case & that of Lieut Pike. . . ." The officers referred to were probably Captain Lawrence Riley and First Lieutenant Edgar M. Pike of the One Hundred Twenty-seventh Illinois, dismissed on March 13, 1863, dismissal later modified to honorable discharge.

To Joseph Holt[1]

Sentence remitted & accused ordered to be discharged.
June 16, 1863   A. LINCOLN

[1] AES, DNA WR 153, Judge Advocate General, MM 220. Lincoln's endorsement is written on the papers of Private John Beiser, Company E, Thirty-second Indiana Volunteers, sentenced to be shot for desertion, but reported by medical examiners to be insane.

To Joseph Hooker[1]

Washington, D.C.,
Major General Hooker: June 16, 1863.
    Your despatches of last night and this morning are just received. I shall have General Halleck to answer them carefully. Meanwhile, I can only say that, as I understand, Heintzelman commands here in this District; that what troops, or very nearly what number, are at Harper's Ferry I do not know, though I do know that Tyler is in command there. Your idea to send your cavalry to this side of the river may be right—probably is; still, it pains me a little that it looks like defensive merely, and seems to abandon the fair chance now presented of breaking the enemy's long and necessarily slim line, stretched now from the Rappahannock to Pennsylvania.   A. LINCOLN.

[1] Thirty-eighth Congress, Second Session, *Report of the Joint Committee on the Conduct of the War* (1865), I, 266. Hooker's telegram from Fairfax Station, June 15, received at 1:15 A.M. on the 16th, is as follows: "I have received your despatch of this evening. The army of the Potomac is in this vicinity, except-ing the 2d and 6th corps, and, as they are marching in rear of all the trains, they will not be up before some time during to-morrow. Perhaps the 2d corps will not be here until some time to-morrow night. The 1st and 11th corps were first to arrive on this line, but I have not yet learned whether they have drawn their supplies in readiness to march to-morrow morning or not. As soon as they are provided, they, as well as the others, will be put *en route.* I have been informed that the enemy nowhere crossed the Rappahannock on our withdrawal from it. But General Hill's troops moved up the river in the direc-tion of Culpeper this morning, for the purpose of, I conclude, re-enforcing Longstreet and Ewell, wherever they may be. I request that I may be informed what troops there are at Harper's Ferry, and who is in command of them, and also who is in command in this district." (*Ibid.,* p. 265).
    Hooker's later telegram, received at 8:35 A.M., is as follows: "It appears to me . . . that nearly all of the cavalry of the army of the Potomac should at once be sent into Maryland by the most direct route. General Stahl has an abundance to perform all cavalry duty that will be required south of the Po-tomac. I merely make this suggestion. If any considerable body of the enemy's infantry should be thrown across the Potomac, they will probably take the direction of his advance pickets, and, in that event, it seems to me that a heavy column of ours should be thrown as speedily as possible to cross the river at Harper's Ferry, while another should be thrown over the most direct line

covering Baltimore and Philadelphia. I only speak with reference to this army, as I know nothing of the location or numbers of troops at the disposal of the government elsewhere." (*Ibid.*).

To Joseph Hooker[1]

(*Private.*)

Executive Mansion, Washington, D.C., June 16, 1863.

My dear General: I send you this by the hand of Captain Dahlgren.[2] Your despatch of 11:30 A.M. to-day is just received. When you say I have long been aware that you do not enjoy the confidence of the major-general commanding, you state the case much too strongly.

You do not lack his confidence in any degree to do you any harm. On seeing him, after telegraphing you this morning, I found him more nearly agreeing with you than I was myself. Surely you do not mean to understand that I am withholding my confidence from you when I happen to express an opinion (certainly never discourteously) differing from one of your own.

I believe Halleck is dissatisfied with you to this extent only, that he knows that you write and telegraph ("report," as he calls it) to me. I think he is wrong to find fault with this; but I do not think he withholds any support from you on account of it. If you and he would use the same frankness to one another, and to me, that I use to both of you, there would be no difficulty. I need and must have the professional skill of both, and yet these suspicions tend to deprive me of both.

I believe you are aware that since you took command of the army I have not believed you had any chance to effect anything till now. As it looks to me, Lee's now returning toward Harper's Ferry gives you back the chance that I thought McClellan lost last fall. Quite possibly I was wrong both then and now; but, in the great responsibility resting upon me, I cannot be entirely silent. Now, all I ask is that you will be in such mood that we can get into our action the best cordial judgment of yourself and General Halleck, with my poor mite added, if indeed he and you shall think it entitled to any consideration at all. Yours as ever,

A. LINCOLN.

1 NH, VIII, 320-21. Hooker's telegram of 11 A.M., received at 11:30, is as follows:

"Please accept my suggestions in regard to what should be done in the spirit with which they were given.

"They were suggestions merely, for I have not the data necessary to form an enlightened opinion in the case. Upon general principles, I thought those were the movements to make. You have long been aware Mr President that I have not enjoyed the confidence of the Major General Commanding the Army & I can assure you so long as this continues we may look in vain for success. Especially as future operations will require our relations to be more dependent upon each other than heretofore.

"It may be possible now to move to prevent a junction of A P Hills Corps with those of Ewell & Longstreet.

"If so please let instructions to that effect be given me. As will appear to you the chances for my doing this are much smaller than when I was on the Rappahannock for if he should hold the passes stoutly he can cause delay. You may depend upon it we can never discover the whereabouts of the enemy or divine his intentions so long as he fills the country with a cloud of cavalry. We must break through that to find him." (DLC-RTL).

2 Ulric Dahlgren.

To Joseph Hooker[1]

Executive Mansion, Washington,
Major General Hooker.   June 16. 1863. [10 P.M.]

To remove all misunderstanding, I now place you in the strict military relation to Gen. Halleck, of a commander of one of the armies, to the General-in-Chief of all the armies. I have not intended differently; but as it seems to be differently understood, I shall direct him to give you orders, and you to obey them.

A. LINCOLN

[1] ALS, NN. The time of this telegram is taken from the *Official Records* (I, XXVII, I, 47). Lincoln had received at 9:50 the following telegram from Hooker:

"My orders are out to march at 3 o'clock to-morrow morning. It will be likely to be one of vigor and power. I am prepared to move without communications with any place for ten days. I hope to reach my objective point before the arrival of Hill's corps, should it be moving in that direction. If I do not know this fact, I will shortly, but of information to the north of the Potomac I really have nothing.

"I wish that it might be made the duty of some person in the telegraph office in Washington to keep me informed of the enemy's movements in Maryland." (*Ibid.*).

Throughout the day the exchange of telegrams between Hooker and Halleck up to this time had indicated beyond question that Hooker and Halleck did not understand either the military situation or their respective relations to each other.

To Frederick Kapp and Others[1]

Frederick Kapp & others   Washington, D.C.,
New-York   June 16. 1863

The Governor of New-York promises to send us troops; and if he wishes the assistance of Gen. Fremont & Gen. Sigel, one or both, he can have it. If he does not wish them, it would but breed confusion for us to set them to work independently of him.

A. LINCOLN

¹ ALS, RPB. Friedrich (Frederick) Kapp, Sigismund Kaufmann, and Charles Kessman telegraphed on June 16: "In the present emergency will you allow Genls Fremont & Sigel to issue a call for volunteers to march at once to the defence of Pennsylvania & the Nation." (DLC-RTL).

To Mary Todd Lincoln¹

Mrs. Lincoln   Washington City, D.C.
Philadelphia.   June 16. 1863

It is a matter of choice with yourself whether you come home. There is no reason why you should not, that did not exist when you went away. As bearing on the question of your coming home, I do not think the raid into Pennsylvania amounts to anything at all   A. LINCOLN

¹ ALS, IHi. No communication from Mrs. Lincoln has been located.

To Thomas F. Meagher¹

Gen. T. Francis Meagher   Washington, D.C.,
New-York.   June 16, 1863

Your despatch received. Shall be very glad for you to raise 3000 Irish troops, if done by the consent of, and in concert with, Governor Seymour.   A. LINCOLN

¹ ALS, RPB. General Meagher had resigned on May 14, 1863. His despatch offering to raise 3,000 Irish soldiers was received at 5:30 P.M. (DLC-RTL). No further reference has been found.

To Daniel Tyler¹

Gen. Tyler,   Washington, D.C.,
Harper's Ferry.   June 16. 5/35 P.M. 1863

Please answer as soon as you can the following inquiries, which Gen. Hooker makes.   A. LINCOLN

¹ ALS, RPB. Lincoln forwarded to Tyler a telegram from Hooker to Halleck received at 4:50 P.M., as follows: "Please inform me whether our forces at Harper's Ferry are in the town or on the heights, and, if the latter, whether we hold Bolivar, Loudon, or Maryland Heights . . . ; what bridges at Harper's Ferry, and where; from what direction is the enemy making his attack? . . ." (OR, I, XXVII, I, 46).

Tyler's reply received at 9:40 P.M. is in part as follows: "We have not been attacked at Harper's Ferry. We are threatened from the direction of Charlestown. . . . We hold Maryland Heights strongly; Bolivar Heights with a less force." (OR, I, XXVII, III, 159).

To Edward Bates[1]

Hon. Attorney General   Executive Mansion,
Sir: Washington, June 17, 1863.

I have concluded to tender to Richard S. Cox Esq, of this District, the appointment for codifying the laws of the District, under the 17th. & 18th. sections of the act of Congress entitled "An act to reorganize the Courts in the District of Columbia, and for other purposes" Approved March 3. 1863. Please prepare & send me a proper paper to sign for that object. Yours truly   A. LINCOLN

[1] ALS, DNA GE RG 60, Papers of Attorney General, Segregated Lincoln Material. The *U.S. Official Register*, 1863, lists Richard S. Coxe as commissioner for revising and codifying the laws of the District of Columbia.

To Joseph Hooker[1]

         Washington, D.C.,
Majr. Genl. Hooker   June 17. 1863

Mr. Eckert, Superintendent in the Telegraph Office, assures me that he has sent, and will send you everything, that comes to the office.   A. LINCOLN

[1] ALS, owned by Edward C. Stone, Boston, Massachusetts. Hooker had telegraphed Lincoln on the 16th and Halleck on the 17th of his need for "correct information concerning the enemy on the north side of the Potomac." (OR, I, XXVII, I, 48).

Memorandum about Israel D. Andrews[1]

Executive Mansion, Washington, June 17. 1863.

Mr. Israel D. Andrews appeals to me, saying he is suffering injury by something I have said of him. I really know very little of Mr. Andrews. As well as I can remember, I was called on by one or two persons, asking me to give him, or aid him in getting some public employment; and, as a reason for declining I stated that I had a very unfavorable opinion of him, chiefly because I had been informed that, in connection with some former service of his to the government, he had presented an enormous, and unjustifiable claim, which I understood he was still pressing the government to pay. I certainly did not pretend to know anything of the matter personally; and I say now, I do not personally know anything which should detract from Mr. Andrews' character

A LINCOLN

[1] ADS, DLC-RTL. Israel D. Andrews had been agent of the United States for drawing up a reciprocity trade treaty with Great Britain, approved June 5, 1854. An appropriation act of June 12, 1858 (Section 16) authorized the secretary of state to "adjust . . . the accounts of I. D. Andrews . . . for expenses

and disbursements in connection with the Reciprocity Treaty, and that the same be paid according to said adjustment."

To Edwin M. Stanton[1]

Sec. of War, please respond to this.   A. LINCOLN

June 17. 1863.

[1] AES, NHi. Lincoln's endorsement is written on a received telegram from General Burnside, June 17, 1863, "The twenty seventh (27) Regt New Jersey Vols whose time expires on the 19. inst has been ordered home by me from the interior of Kentucky. They are now here. They are willing to volunteer their services during the present emergency & I have ordered them to report to Gen Brooks at Pittsburg Do you approve of the acceptance."

The Twenty-seventh New Jersey remained in the vicinity of Pittsburgh and Harrisburg, Pennsylvania, for ten days before proceeding to Newark, where it was mustered out of service on July 2.

To A. Dingman[1]

Gen. A. Dingman   Washington, D.C.,

Belleville, C.W.   June 18. 1863

Thanks for your offer of the fifteenth battalion. I do not think Washington is in danger.   A. LINCOLN

[1] ALS, RPB. A telegram signed "A. Dingman, Brig. Genl. Vols. Canada," from Belleville, C. W. [Ontario], was received in cipher from New York on June 18, as follows: "If Washington is in danger the fifteenth battalion is at your service to drive Lee back to Richmond. Hurrah for the Union—answer." (DLC-RTL).

To Joseph Holt[1]

June 18, 1863

Sentence mitigated to a severe reprimand, in accordance with the Judge Advocate General's recommendation, to be published in General Orders by the War Department.   A. LINCOLN

June 18, 1863.

[1] ES, DNA WR RG 153, Judge Advocate General, MM 575. On April 22, 1863, Surgeon Alfred Wynkoop was sentenced to dismissal by a court-martial for communicating information concerning troop movements to William Pollock of Virginia, known to be friendly to the enemy. AGO *General Orders No. 281*, August 11, 1863, remitted the sentence with a reprimand as follows: "The President, in reviewing the record, is willing to believe there was less intentional criminality than there was indiscretion in the conduct of Surgeon Wynkoop; but he does not find any excuse for so grave an offence in the fact that the information conveyed by him was not proved to have been put to an improper use. Surgeon Wynkoop was visiting professionally a family residing near the rebel lines, when he conversed with them in reference to the movements of the United States troops. An officer who justly appreciates his military obligations would require no reminder that such indiscretion, admitting it to be nothing worse, is reprehensible in the highest degree, and might have caused serious disaster to the Army.

"In order that Surgeon Wynkoop may have an opportunity to justify the opinion of the members of the Court as to his loyalty, and to retrieve what he has lost in the estimation of his fellow officers by reason of his culpable disregard of the confidential trust belonging to his official position, the President directs that his sentence be remitted with this reprimand."

To James K. Moorhead[1]

"Cypher"

Hon. J. K. Moorehead   Washington City,
Pittsburgh, Penn.   June 18. 1863.

If Gen. Brooks, now in command at Pittsburgh, finds any person or persons, injuriously affecting his military operations, he is authorized to arrest him, or them, at once, if the case is urgent; if not urgent, let him communicate the particulars to me. Gen. Brooks is the man to now manage this matter at Pittsburgh. Please show this to him.   A. LINCOLN.

[1] ALS, RPB. A telegram from Representative James K. Moorhead and other citizens of Pittsburgh, June 17, 1863, requested that Major General William T. H. Brooks be authorized to declare martial law (DLC-RTL).

To Edwin M. Stanton[1]

Hon. Sec. of War   Executive Mansion,
My dear Sir.   Washington, June 18. 1863.

Could you, without too much trouble, have sent to me a statement of the case of John Steele, who, it seems, has been banished to Canada. Yours truly   A. LINCOLN

[1] ALS, DLC-RTL. On June 24, General Edward R. S. Canby returned Lincoln's letter together with a statement of Judge Advocate Levi C. Turner summarizing the case of John Steele, native of Canada and resident of the U.S., arrested for fraud and treasonable practices while employed as a detective by the provost marshal and released on his own request to return to Canada (DLC-RTL).

To Joshua Tevis[1]

Joshua Tevis, Esq   Executive Mansion,
U.S. Attorney   Washington,
Frankfort, Ky.   June 18. 1863.

A Mr. Buckner is here, showing a record, and asking to be discharged from a suit in Scire-Facias, as bail for one Thompson. Unless the record shown me is defectively made out, I think it can be successfully defended against. Please examine the case carefully; and if you shall be of opinion it can not be sustained, dismiss it, and relieve me from all trouble about it. Please answer.

                    A. LINCOLN

[1] ALS, RPB. Joshua Tevis telegraphed from Louisville on June 20, "Your dispatch of eighteenth . . . inst. to me at Frankfort just received I will examine record in Scire Facias against Buckler Cant you get rid of Buckler by suggesting that the Attorney General has decided that you have no power to remit in case of France." (DLC-RTL).

No further reference has been found, and the confusion of names has not been clarified.

To David Tod[1]

"Cypher"

Gov. D. Tod.
Columbus, O.

Executive Mansion,
Washington, June 18, 1863.

Yours received. I deeply regret that you were not re-nominated —not that I have ought against Mr. Brough. On the contrary, like yourself, I say, hurrah, for him. A. LINCOLN

[1] ALS, RPB. Governor Tod lost his re-nomination to John Brough, also a railroad executive, 216 to 193 votes, less on national issues than on local considerations involving Brough's advocacy of a scheme for consolidation of east-west railroad lines, to which Tod was cool. Tod telegraphed Lincoln on June 18, "The opponents of the administration will attempt to attribute my defeat to the advocacy of the leading measures of your administration. Do not for a moment believe it. Personal considerations alone was the cause of my defeat. No man in Ohio will do more to secure the triumphant election of the ticket nominated than I will" (DLC-RTL).

To Joseph Holt[1]

June 19, 1863

Sentence in this case commuted to imprisonment at hard labor for the term of one year. A. LINCOLN

[1] AES, DNA WR RG 153, Judge Advocate General, MM 333. Lincoln's endorsement is written on the papers of Samuel D. Crumb, drummer in the Eighty-ninth New York Volunteers, sentenced to be shot for desertion.

To E. E. Malhiot, Bradish Johnson, and Thomas Cottman[1]

Messrs E. E. Malhiot,
Bradish Johnson, &
Thomas Cottman

Executive Mansion,
Washington,
June 19, 1863.

Gentlemen   Your letter, which follows, has been received, and considered.

"To His Excellency Abraham Lincoln
President of the United States:

The undersigned, a committee appointed by the Planters of the State of Louisiana, respectfully represent, that they have been

delegated to seek of the General Government a full recognition of all the rights of the State, as they existed previous to the passage of an act of secession, upon the principle of the existence of the State Constitution unimpaired, and no legal act having transpired that could in any way deprive them of the advantages conferred by that Constitution. Under this constitution the State wishes to return to its full allegiance, in the enjoyment of all rights and privileges exercised by the other states under the Federal Constitution. With the view of accomplishing the desired object, we farther request that your Excellency will as Commander-in-chief of the Army of the United States direct the military Governor of Louisiana to order an election in conformity with the constitution and laws of the State, on the first Monday of November next, for all State and Federal Officers.

"With high consideration and respect we have the honor to subscribe ourselves Your Obt Servts.　　　　E. E. MALHIOT

BRADISH JOHNSON

THOMAS COTTMAN."

Since receiving the letter, reliable information has reached me that a respectable portion of the Louisiana people, desire to amend their State constitution, and contemplate holding a convention for that object. This fact alone, as it seems to me, is a sufficient reason why the general government should not give the committal you seek, to the existing State constitution. I may add that, while I do not perceive how such committal could facilitate our military operations in Louisiana, I really apprehend it might be so used as to embarrass them.

As to an election to be held next November, there is abundant time, without any order, or proclamation from me just now. The people of Louisiana shall not lack an oppertunity of a fair election for both Federal and State officers, by want of anything within my power to give them. Your Obt. Servt.　　　　A. LINCOLN

¹ ADfS and LS copy, DLC-RTL. The original letter from Malhiot, Johnson, and Cottman is undated, but it was presented to Lincoln prior to Monday, June 15. On June 18, Thomas Cottman wrote Lincoln as follows: "My colleagues have departed leaving me to receive the response that your Excellency was kind enough to promise us for Monday last. I hope it will not be regarded as impertinent to ask attention to the matter at earliest convenience. . . ." (DLC-RTL). The meeting of planters at New Orleans, which appointed the committee to present Lincoln with their request, was held on May 1, at the St. Charles Hotel, and the letter was probably delivered by the committee prior to June 1. On June 6, Michael Hahn wrote Lincoln, "The Union people of this State (except, of course, office-holders) are all in favor of a re-organization of a loyal State government. The only question on which they are divided is as to whether a new Constitution should be made, or the old Constitution of 1852 adhered to. Those in favor of a Convention and a new Constitution are

the more radical or free-soil Union men. . . . Others, whose interests are in . . . slavery . . . are strongly opposed . . . and are satisfied with the Constitution of 1852, which unjustly gives the country parishes a very large preponderance over the City in the number of members of the legislature. . . ." (DLC-RTL).

Memorandum[1]

[June 19, 1863]

If the military force of the rebellion were already out of the way, so that the people of Louisiana could now practically enter upon the enjoyment of their rights under the present State and National Constitutions, your request would stand before me in a different aspect.

[1] AD, DLC-RTL. Written on a slip of paper filed with the draft and copy of Lincoln to Malhiot and others, *supra*, this memorandum was probably a sentence intended for inclusion in the letter, but rejected. It restates substantially a draft by Seward which is also filed with the other papers, as follows: "In whatever I may do or say on the subject at the present time, I cannot ignore the fact that in view of military operations outside of the state of Louisiana the presence of the land and naval forces of the United States in that now loyal state cannot yet be discontinued."

To Joseph Hooker[1]

Washington, June 21, 1863– 9 a.m.

Major-General Hooker: Operator at Leesburg just now tells us that firing commenced about 7 this morning in direction from here of Aldie's Gap and Middleburg; has continued all day, and has receded from him, and is apparently now about White Plains; was very heavy this morning, but lighter now.   A. LINCOLN.

[1] OR, I, XXVII, I, 54.

To John M. Schofield[1]

Gen. Schofield.   Washington D.C.
St. Louis, Mo   June 21. 1863.

I write you to-day in answer to your despatch of yesterday. If you can not await the arrival by mail, telegraph me again.

A. LINCOLN

[1] ALS, RPB. General Schofield's telegram of June 20 is as follows: "The action of the Missouri state convention upon the question of Emancipation will depend very much upon whether they can be assured that the action will be sustained by the General Government & the people protected in their slave property during the short time that slavery is permitted to exist. Am I authorized in any manner directly or indirectly to pledge such support & protection? This question is of such vital importance to the peace of Missouri that I deem it my duty to lay it before your Excellency." (DLC-RTL).

See Lincoln's letter to Schofield, June 22, *infra*.

Assignment of Stephen J. Field[1]

Executive Mansion, Washington, June 22, 1863.

Whereas the act of Congress approved the 3d day of March, A.D. 1863, entitled "An act to provide circuit courts for the districts of California and Oregon, and for other purposes," authorized the appointment of one additional associate justice of the Supreme Court of the United States, and provided that the districts of California and Oregon should constitute the tenth circuit and that the other circuits should remain as then constituted by law; and

Whereas Stephen J. Field was appointed the said additional associate justice of the Supreme Court since the last adjournment of said court, and consequently he was not allotted to the said circuit according to the fifth section of the act of Congress entitled "An act to amend the judicial system of the United States," approved the 29th day of April, 1802:

Now I, Abraham Lincoln, President of the United States, under the authority of said section, do allot the said associate justice, Stephen J. Field, to the said tenth circuit.

Attest: ABRAHAM LINCOLN.
Titian J. Coffey
Attorney-General ad interim.

[1] James D. Richardson, ed., *Messages and Papers of the Presidents*, VI, 175. Stephen J. Field, chief justice of the California Supreme Court, was nominated associate justice of the U.S. Supreme Court on March 6 and confirmed by the Senate on March 10, 1863.

To Joseph Hooker[1]

Washington, June 22, 1863.

Major-General Hooker: Operator at Leesburg just now says:

"I heard very little firing this a.m. about daylight, but it seems to have stopped now. It was in about the same direction as yesterday, but farther off."   A. LINCOLN.

[1] OR, I, XXVII, I, 55.

Memorandum[1]

June 22, 1863

Appointments within recommended, made this 22nd. June 1863.

[1] AES, DLC-RTL. Lincoln's endorsement is written on a letter from Jesse K. Dubois and others, June 4, 1863, in reply to Lincoln's letter of May 29, *supra*. The letter recommended appointment of George R. Weber as commissary and James Campbell as quartermaster.

To John M. Schofield[1]

Gen. John M. Schofield.   Executive Mansion,
My dear Sir: Washington, June 22, 1863.

Your despatch, asking in substance, whether, in case Missouri shall adopt gradual emancipation, the general government will protect slave owners in that species of property during the short time it shall be permitted by the State to exist within it, has been received. Desirous as I am, that emancipation shall be adopted by Missouri, and believing as I do, that *gradual* can be made better than *immediate* for both black and white, except when military necessity changes the case, my impulse is to say that such protection would be given. I can not know exactly what shape an act of emancipation may take. If the period from the initiation to the final end, should be comparatively short, and the act should prevent persons being sold, during that period, into more lasting slavery, the whole would be easier. I do not wish to pledge the general government to the affirmative support of even temporary slavery, beyond what can be fairly claimed under the constitution. I suppose, however, this is not desired; but that it is desired for the Military force of the United States, while in Missouri, to not be used in subverting the temporarily reserved legal rights in slaves during the progress of emancipation. This I would desire also. I have very earnestly urged the slave-states to adopt emancipation; and it ought to be, and is an object with me not to overthrow, or thwart what any of them may in good faith do, to that end.

You are therefore authorized to act in the spirit of this letter, in conjunction with what may appear to be the military necessities of your Department.

Although this letter will become public at some time, it is not intended to be made so now. Yours truly   A. LINCOLN

1 ALS copy, DLC-RTL. See Lincoln to Schofield June 21, *supra.* The Missouri Constitutional Convention summoned by Governor Gamble's proclamation of April 15, 1863, to meet on June 15, adopted an ordinance abolishing those provisions of the Missouri Constitution which restricted the legislature's power over slavery and providing a plan for gradual emancipation.

To Edwin M. Stanton[1]

Hon. Sec. of War   Executive Mansion,
My dear Sir   Washington, June 22, 1863.

Do you not remember the french officer, Col. Duffie, whom we saw at Gen. McDowell's Head Quarters near Fredericksburg, last May a year ago? I rem[em]ber he was then well spoken of. On the night of the 17th. Ist. he was surrounded by Stuart's cavalry near Millersburg, and cut his way out with proportionate heavy loss to his then small command. Please see and hear him. I think you have strong recommendations on file in his behalf. Yours truly

A. LINCOLN

[1] ALS-P, ISLA. Colonel Alfred N. Duffie, First Rhode Island Cavalry, was appointed brigadier general on June 23, 1863.

To Joseph Holt[1]

[c. June 23, 1863]

Sentence commuted to imprisonment at hard labor during the war.

A. LINCOLN

[1] AES, DNA WR RG 153, Judge Advocate General, MM 763. Lincoln's endorsement is written on the papers of Private James G. Lyon, Fifth Vermont Volunteers, sentenced to be shot for cowardice and absence without leave.

To Edwin M. Stanton[1]

Executive Mansion, Washington, D.C., June 23, 1863.

My dear Sir: You remember that Hon. W. D. Kelley and others are engaged in raising or trying to raise some colored regiments in Philadelphia. The bearer of this, Wilton M. Herpert [Milton L. Hupert?], is a friend of Judge Kelley as appears by the letter of the latter. He is a private in the 112th Penn. and has been disappointed in a reasonable expectation of one of the smaller offices. He now wants to be a Lieutenant in one of the colored regiments. If Judge Kelley will say in writing he wishes to so have him, I am willing for him to be discharged from his present position and be so appointed. If you approve, so endorse and let him carry this letter to Kelley. Yours truly, A. LINCOLN.

[1] NH, VIII, 331. No further reference has been located. The roster of the One Hundred Twelfth Pennsylvania lists no soldier of the name Wilton M. Herpert, but Private Milton L. Hupert of Battery A is listed as deserting on August 8, 1863.

To Stewart Van Vliet[1]

Major Van Vliet.   Washington, D.C.,
New. York   June 23 1863

Have you any idea what the news is, in the despatches of Gen. Banks to Gen. Halleck?   A. LINCOLN

[1] ALS, RPB. No reply has been located, and Lincoln's reference to despatches from Banks to Halleck remains unexplained. Since Major Van Vliet was quartermaster at New York, it may be inferred that the despatches were sent by boat to New York care of the quartermaster.

To Darius N. Couch[1]

Major Genl. Couch   June 24. 1863.
Harrisburg, Pa.

Have you any reports of the enemy moving into Pennsylvania?
and if any, what?   A. LINCOLN

[1]ALS, RPB. This telegram is misdated June 23 in the *Complete Works*
(VIII, 332). General Couch, in command of the Department of the Susquehanna, replied at 9:30 A.M.: "Rebel cavalry are this side of Chambersburg.
Scouts from Gettysburg report 7,000 at Greencastle. Deserters say A. P. Hill
and Longstreet are across the Potomac; 40,000.

"Ten deserters in at McConnellsburg from Ewell's forces, say the latter is at
Greencastle, with 30,000 men and thirty pieces of artillery. Two lieutenants
taken prisoners say that Lee's headquarters are at Millwood, 12 miles from
Winchester." (OR, I, XXVII, III, 295).

A copy of Couch's telegram in the Lincoln Papers is endorsed by Lincoln
"Please forward this to Gen. Hooker/A. Lincoln/June 24. 1863." and by
Thomas T. Eckert "This was forwarded to Gen Hooker at 12.25 P.M."

To John A. Dix[1]

Major Genl. Dix   Washington
York Town, Va   June 24– 1863 [9 P.M.]

We have a despatch from Gen. Grant of the 19th. Dont think
Kirby Smith took Miliken's Bend since, allowing time to get the
news to Joe Johnston & from him to Richmond. But it is not absolutely impossible. Also have news from Banks to the 16th. I think.
He had not run away then, nor thought of it.   A LINCOLN

[1] ALS-P, ISLA. The telegram is written in pencil. The time appears to have
been written as given in brackets, but was erased and "905 P.M." written in
the upper left-hand corner, presumably by the clerk. No communication from
General Dix has been located to which this seems to be a reply. Grant's despatch to Halleck of June 19 reported his removal of General John A. Mc-
Clernand "for his publication of a congratulatory address calculated to create
dissension and ill-feeling in the army. I should have relieved him long since
for general unfitness for his position." (OR, I, XXIV, I, 43).

To Joseph Holt[1]

                                                        June 24, 1863
Let Capt. Eagan be dishonorably dismissed the service in accordance with the recommendation of the Judge Advocate General.
                                                        A. LINCOLN

[1] ES, DNA WR RG 153, Judge Advocate General, MM 268. Lincoln's endorsement is written on the papers of William P. Eagan, Twenty-third Kentucky
Volunteers, dismissed for cowardice.

To Edwin M. Stanton[1]

Sec. of War, please see the bearer, Mr. Lucky, who is introduced
by the Sec. of State.   A. LINCOLN
    June 24. 1863.

[1] AES, NHi. Lincoln's endorsement is written on the envelope of a letter from
Seward, June 22, 1863, introducing T. B. Luckey of New York. First Lieutenant Theron B. Luckey of the One Hundred Forty-third New York Infantry
had been discharged on May 24, 1863.

To Edward D. Townsend[1]

Dr. Stipp is my old personal friend, and I shall be very glad if he
can, consistently with the public service, be assigned as he desires.
    June 24, 1863.   A. LINCOLN

[1] AES, owned by R. E. Burdick, New York City. See Lincoln to Joseph
R. Smith, October 6, 1862, *supra*. Lincoln's endorsement is written on a letter
from Medical Inspector George Winfield Stipp to Townsend, June 22, 1863,
asking that "in consideration of my bad health . . . I may be assigned for
duty, to the Department of Ohio, for a few months, in the hope & belief that
a change of climate, water and diet, will aid materially, in restoring to me a
measure of former health." Townsend referred the letter to Surgeon General
Hammond, who recommended a leave of absence instead of the transfer, and
on June 25 Townsend directed that a leave be granted. Lieutenant Colonel
Stipp was assigned as medical inspector of the Department of the Gulf on December 19, 1863 (OR, I, XXVI, I, 867).

To Edward Bates[1]

Let a pardon be granted in this case on the ground that the party
was used by the government as a witness, & testified fairly.
    June 25, 1863.   A. LINCOLN

[1] AES, DNA RG 204, U.S. Pardon Attorney, A 455. Lincoln's endorsement
is written on a letter from U.S. District Attorney Richard H. Dana, Jr., to
lawyer Milton Andros, Boston, June 23, 1863, concerning the pardon application of Samuel P. Skinner, convicted of fitting out a slave ship.

To Salmon P. Chase[1]

                                     Executive Mansion, Washington,
Hon. Secretary of Treasury: June 25, 1863.
    My Dear Sir: Hon. William Kellogg will tell you plainly what
he wants; and I wish him obliged so far as you can consistently do
it. Please strain a point for him, if you do not have to strain it too
far. Yours truly,   A. LINCOLN.

[1] Robert B. Warden, *Account of the Private Life and Public Services of
Salmon Portland Chase* (1874), p. 530. See Lincoln to Kellogg, June 29, *infra*.

To John J. Peck[1]

Gen. Peck   Washington, D.C.,
Suffolk, Va   June 25, 1863

Col. Derrom,[2] of the 25th. N-J. Vols, now mustered out, says there is a man in your hands, under conviction for desertion, who formerly belonged to the above named regiment, and whose name is Templeton—Isaac F. Templeton, I believe. The Colonel & others appeal to me for him. Please telegraph to me what is the condition of the case, & if he has not been executed send me the record of the trial & conviction.   A LINCOLN

1 ALS, RPB. Brigadier General Michael Corcoran replied to Lincoln's telegram at 3 P.M., "Isaac Templeton . . . has not yet been executed. The proceedings were reviewed by Maj Genl Dix and the record is in his hands. I will advise him that you wish it sent to you. Genl Peck is absent" (DLC-RTL).
  See Lincoln to Holt, June 26, *infra*.   2 Andrew Derrom.

To Henry W. Slocum[1]

Major General Slocum   Washington, D.C.,
Leesburg, Va.   June 25 1863

Was *William Gruvier* Co. A. 46th. Penn, one of the men executed as a deserter last Friday?   A. LINCOLN

1 ALS, RPB. No reply has been located, but the roster of the Forty-sixth Pennsylvania lists William Gruver, enlisted September 2, 1861; deserted June 4, 1863, and executed at Leesburg, Virginia, June 19, 1863.

To Robert K. Stone[1]

Dr. Stone   Executive Mansion,
My dear Sir   Washington, June 25, 1863.

Herewith is the note of Mrs. Stone to Mrs. L. You percieve I have put an endorsement upon it. By presenting the note and endorsement to the Sec. of War, he will oblige Mrs. S. as she requests. He already understands the case. Yours truly   A. LINCOLN

1 ALS-P, ISLA. The enclosed letter with endorsement has not been located.

To Ambrose E. Burnside[1]

"Cypher"

Major Gen. Burnside   Washington,
Cincinnati, O.   June 26. 1863.

What is the case of *"Willie Waller"* at Maysville, Kentucky?
                                                   A LINCOLN

¹ ALS, RPB. On June 11, 1863, Montgomery Blair enclosed a letter from Harrison Blanton, Frankfort, Kentucky, June 8, requesting mitigation of the sentence of William Waller, whom Blair described as "a kinsman of my mothers . . . & of my fathers," and added "I can not imagine that he would do any thing deserving other punishment than ordinary rebels. . . . I hope you will order his execution to be suspended till the case can be looked into." (DLC-RTL).

William Waller had been convicted as a spy and sentenced to be hanged. The court recommended clemency, and Burnside telegraphed Lincoln on June 27, recommending commutation to imprisonment for duration of the war. On June 30 Lincoln endorsed Burnside's telegram, "Let the sentence be commuted as Gen. Burnside recommends. The name is Willie Waller. A. LINCOLN." (DNA WR RG 153, Judge Advocate General, MM 315).

To Joseph Holt¹

June 26, 1863

Sentence commuted to imprisonment at hard labor during the remainder of the war, in some military prison.　　　A. LINCOLN

¹ ES, DNA WR RG 153, Judge Advocate General, MM 356. Lincoln's endorsement is written on the papers of Private Andrew Brower, New York Battery, Fifth Corps, Army of the Potomac, sentenced to be shot for mutiny.

To Joseph Holt¹

June 26, 1863

Sentence commuted to loss of six months pay in accordance with the recommendation of Maj. Genl. Rosecrans.　　　A. LINCOLN

¹ ES, DNA WR RG 153, Judge Advocate General, MM 355. Lincoln's endorsement is written on the papers of Private John H. Clark, Eighty-sixth Indiana Volunteers, sentenced to be shot for desertion.

To Joseph Holt¹

June 26, 1863

Sentence commuted to confinement at hard labor on government works during the war.　　　A. LINCOLN

¹ ES, DNA WR RG 153, Judge Advocate General, MM 350. Lincoln's endorsement is written on the papers of Private George Felsinger, One Hundred Fortieth New York Volunteers, sentenced to be shot for violence to a superior officer.

To Joseph Holt¹

June 26, 1863

Sentence commuted to imprisonment at hard labor for one year.
A. LINCOLN

[1] ES, DNA WR RG 153, Judge Advocate General, MM 354. Lincoln's endorsement is written on the papers of Private Patrick McLaughlin, Twenty-ninth Pennsylvania Volunteers, sentenced to be shot for drunkenness on duty and insubordination.

To Joseph Holt[1]

June 26, 1863

Sentence commuted to imprisonment at hard labor during the war in accordance with the recommendation of the Judge Advocate General.   A. LINCOLN

[1] ES, DNA WR RG 153, Judge Advocate General, MM 349. Lincoln's endorsement is written on the papers of Private Henry H. Moore, Twentieth Maine Volunteers, sentenced to be shot for disobedience and insubordination. AGO *Special Orders No. 135*, April 2, 1864, ordered that Private Moore be released from confinement and returned to duty with his regiment.

To Joseph Holt[1]

June 26, 1863

Sentence commuted to forfeiture of six months pay in accordance with the recommendation of Maj. Genl. Rosecrans.
                                                        A. LINCOLN

[1] ES, DNA WR RG 153, Judge Advocate General, MM 348. Lincoln's endorsement is written on the papers of Private George Strathdee, One Hundredth Illinois Volunteers, sentenced to be shot for sleeping on post.

To Joseph Holt[1]

June 26, 1863

Judge Advocate General please send me the record mentioned within.   A. LINCOLN

[1] AES, DNA WR RG 153, Judge Advocate General, MM 366. See Lincoln to Peck, June 25, *supra*. No record has been found of the final disposition of the case of Isaac F. Templeton.

To Joseph Hooker[1]

Washington,

Major-General Hooker: June 27, 1863– 8 a.m.

It did not come from the newspapers, nor did I believe it, but I wished to be entirely sure it was a falsehood.   A. LINCOLN.

[1] OR, I, XXVII, I, 58. The circumstances surrounding this telegram are not entirely clear. At 6 P.M. on June 26, Hooker telegraphed Major Thomas T. Eckert of the telegraph office, "Dispatch received. My compliments to the President, and inform him that I had not that honor." (*Ibid*). A footnote in the source comments that the despatch referred to could not be found. At 8 P.M.

the same evening, Hooker telegraphed Lincoln, "You need not believe any more than you choose of what is published in the Associated Press dispatches concerning this army tomorrow. Was it from the newspapers that you received a report, or an idea, that I was in Washington last night?" (*Ibid.*).

To Edwin M. Stanton[1]

I think the Secretary of War better let them have the clothes.
June 28 [27], 1863.   A. LINCOLN

[1] AES, NHi. Lincoln's endorsement, apparently misdated, is written on a telegram from Simon Cameron, June 27, 1863, recommending that uniforms be furnished to all men called into state service by Governor Curtin's proclamation of that date. Stanton telegraphed Cameron at 3:10 P.M. on June 27, "The President has referred your telegram of this date to me . . . . Instructions have been given to the Quartermaster-General to furnish uniforms to State troops upon the requisition of the Governor of the State. You are aware that officers in the field can only issue clothing to persons in the United States service, and that for State troops such supplies should be called for by the State Executive. . . ." (OR, I, XXVII, III, 365).

To Jeremiah T. Boyle[1]

Gen. J. T. Boyle   Executive Mansion
Cincinnati, O.   Washington D.C. June 28, 1863
There is nothing going on in Kentucky on the subject of which you telegraph, except an enrolment. Before anything is done beyond this, I will take care to understand the case better than I now do.   A. LINCOLN

[1] ALS, RPB. See the same telegram to Burnside, *infra*. The date seems first to have been written "27" by Lincoln and changed to "28." General Boyle telegraphed Lincoln on June 26, calling attention to his telegram of June 25 to James B. Fry, which reads in part: "There are only four thousand one hundred and thirty (4130) free male negroes in the state—one eighth ($\frac{1}{8}$) of them is a fair estimate of those between the ages eighteen and forty-five (45) giving less than seven hundred. If you gain these you will lose more than ten thousand—you will revolutionize the State and do infinite & unconceivable harm, and am sure this all wrong, and there is not an honest loyal man in the state in favor of it—and will meet with decided opposition for the peace and quiet of the Country. I beg you will change your order on subject. I request that you confer with President Lincoln on the subject and show him this telegram" (DLC-RTL).

To Ambrose E. Burnside[1]

Major Gen. Burnside   Executive Mansion,
Cincinnati, O.   Washington, June 28 1863. [9 A.M.]
There is nothing going on in Kentucky on the subject of which you telegraph, except an enrolment. Before anything is done beyond this, I will take care to understand the case better than I now do.   A. LINCOLN

1 ALS, RPB. See the same telegram to Boyle, *supra*. The time of despatch is not in Lincoln's autograph. Burnside telegraphed Lincoln on June 26, "I am satisfied from my knowledge of Ky that it would be very unwise to enrol the free negroes of that State It would not add materially to our strength and I assure you it would cause much trouble I sincerely hope this embarassment to the interests of the public service will not be placed in our way Please answer at once."

For Burnside's reply, see Lincoln to Stanton, June 28, *infra*.

To Darius N. Couch[1]

Major Gen. Couch   Washington City, D.C.
Harrisburgh. Pa.   June 28– 3/40 P.M. 1863

What news now? What are the enemy firing at four miles from your works?   A. LINCOLN

1 ALS, RPB. General Couch replied from Harrisburg, Pennsylvania, at 7:40 P.M.:

"They have not up to this time made any show of attack in force. They are burning bridges on the Northern Central road.

"I may have lost 400 men in the vicinity of York and Gettysburg. Probably 15,000 men within a short distance of my front." (OR, I, XXVII, III, 385).

To Robert C. Schenck[1]

Major Gen. Schenck   Washington, D.C.,
Baltimore, Md   June 28 1863

Every place in the Naval School subject [to] my appointment, is full, and I have one unredeemed promise of more than half a year's standing.   A. LINCOLN

1 ALS, RPB. On June 13, General Schenck telegraphed Lincoln, "I see appointment of Midshipmen at large announced in papers today. I trust mine for my brother Lieut. Schencks orphan son is not too late. . . ." (DLC-RTL). On June 28, Schenck telegraphed again, "I am very sorry that I can get no reply to my application for an appointment at large at the Naval Academy for the Son of my deceased Brother Lieut. Schenck who died in the service." (*Ibid.*).

To Edwin M. Stanton[1]

I really think the within is worth considering.
June 28. 1863.   A. LINCOLN

1 AES, NHi. Lincoln's endorsement is written on a telegram from General Ambrose E. Burnside, June 27 (in reply to Lincoln's telegram of June 27, *supra*) as follows:

"Your dispatch of this date is received. The enrolment of the free negroes properly belonging to the State will not yield one thousand men subject to draft. If draft is required in Kentucky the number required from this class will not be over three hundred (300) for this small number we will lose a much larger number of good white volunteers & give the secret enemies of the Government a weapon to use against it. If there was any principle of right involved in it I would say carry it out but the people are ready & willing to stand the draft if necessary from the white population There will not be half the trouble in the State of Kentucky there will be in Indiana Ohio & Illinois. The enrolment of these negroes is what the loyal people fear will do the harm We not only need all these for labor which we draft at our pleasure but we draft slaves for labor continually & if any of the free negroes wishes to join the colored Regiments now forming in this Dept they are at liberty to do so. I was just about issuing an order drafting all the free able bodied negroes in the State for labor on a military road. I sincerely hope the enrolment may be stopped. Kentucky is in good order now."

To Matthew Birchard and Others[1]

Washington, D.C. June 29,[2] 1863

Messrs M. Birchard   David A Houk   Geo. Bliss   T. W. Bartley W. J. Gordon   Jno. O'Neill   C. A. White   W. E. Finck Alexander Long   J. W White   Geo. H. Pendleton   Geo L. Converse   Warren P. Noble   Jas. R. Morris   W. A. Hutchins   Abner L. Backus   J. F. McKinney   F. C. Le Blond   Louis Schaefer

Gentlemen: The resolutions of the Ohio Democratic State convention which you present me, together with your introductory and closing remarks, being in position and argument, mainly the

[1] ADf, DLC-RTL. Following the delegation's arrival in Washington on the evening of June 24, Secretary Chase wrote Lincoln the next day, "to suggest that what is said to them or replied to them should be only in writing." (DLC-RTL). They were given an interview on the 25th, at which Lincoln suggested that they present their request in writing. The letter from the delegation on June 26, presenting resolutions adopted by the Democratic state convention at Columbus on June 11, considerably abridged, is as follows:

"Resolved

"1st. That the will of the people is the foundation of all free government. That to give effect to this will, free thought, free speech and a free press are absolutely indispensable. . . .

"2d. That it is an inherent and constitutional right of the people to discuss all measures of their government, and to approve or disapprove. . . .

"3d. That these and all other rights, guaranteed to them by their constitutions, are their rights in time of war as well as in time of peace. . . .

"4th. That we now say . . . calmly, and firmly, that we will not surrender these rights, nor submit to their forcible violation. We will obey the laws ourselves and all others must obey them.

"5th. That Ohio will adhere to the Constitution and the Union as the best, it may be the last hope of popular freedom. . . .

"6th. That we will earnestly support every constitutional measure tending to preserve the Union. . . .

"7. That the arrest, imprisonment, pretended trial, and actual banishment of Clement L. Vallandigham . . . we regard as a palpable violation of the . . . Constitution. . . .

"8th. That Clement L Vallandigham was at the time of his arrest, a prominent candidate for nomination by the Democratic party of Ohio for the office of Governor of the State; that the Democratic party was fully competent to decide whether he was a fit man for that nomination; and that the attempt to deprive them of that right by his arrest and banishment was an unmerited imputation upon their intelligence and loyalty, as well as a violation of the Constitution.

"9th. That we respectfully and most earnestly call upon the President of the United States to restore Clement L. Vallandigham to his home in Ohio. . . .

"The undersigned. . . . do not call upon your Excellency as Suppliants praying the revocation of the order . . . as a favor, but by the authority of a Convention representing a majority of the Citizens of . . . Ohio. They respectfully ask it as a right due to an American Citizen in whose personal injury, the Sovereignty and dignity of the people of Ohio as a free State have been offended. . . .

"You are reported to have used in a public communication on this subject, the following language 'It gave me pain when I learned that Mr. Vallandigham had been ˄rrested—that is I was pained that there should have seemed to be a necessity for arresting him, and that it will afford me great pleasure to discharge him so soon as I can by any means believe the public safety will not suffer by it.[']

"The undersigned assure your Excellency . . . that the public safety will be far more endangered by continuing Mr. Vallandigham in exile than by releasing him. . . .

"If a man . . . beleives that from the inherent nature of the federal compact, the war . . . cannot be used as a means of restoring the Union . . . but would inevitably result in the final destruction of both the constitution and the Union, is he not to be allowed the right . . . to appeal to the judgment of the people, for a change of policy, by the constitutional remedy of the ballot box?

"During the war with Mexico many of the political opponents of the Administration . . . thought it their duty to denounce and oppose the war . . . with equal reason it might have been said of them, that their discussions before the people were calculated to discourage enlistments, 'to prevent the raising of troops' & to induce desertions. . . .

"When gentlemen of high standing . . . including your Excellency opposed in discussions before the people, the policy of the Mexican War, were they 'warring upon the Military' & did this 'give the Military constitutional jurisdiction to lay hands upon them?' . . .

"The undersigned are unable to agree with you in the opinion you have expressed that the constitution is different in time of insurrection or invasion from what it is, in time of peace & public security. The constitution provides for no limitations upon . . . the guaranties of personal liberty, except as to the writ of habeas corpus. . . . Expunge from the constitution this limitation upon the power of Congress to suspend the writ of habeas corpus and yet the other guaranties of personal liberty would remain unchanged. . . . Does your Excellency wish to have it understood that you hold, that the rights of every man throughout this vast country are subject to be annulled whenever you may say that you consider the public safety requires it, in time of insurrection or invasion? . . .

"The people of Ohio, are willing to co-operate zealously with you in every effort warranted by the Constitution to restore the Union . . . but they cannot consent to abandon those fundamental principles of civil liberty, which are essential to their existence as a free people. In their name we ask, that by a revocation of the order of his banishment, Mr. Vallandigham, may be restored to the enjoyment of those rights of which they believe, he has been unconstitutionally deprived." (*Ibid.*).

2 Lincoln's date "28" changed by Nicolay to "29."

same as the resolutions of the Democratic meeting at Albany, New-York, I refer you to my response to the latter, as meeting most of the points in the former. This response you evidently used in preparing your remarks, and I desire no more than that it be used with accuracy. In a single reading of your remarks I only discovered one inaccuracy in matter which I suppose you took from that paper. It is when you say "The undersigned are unable to agree with you in the opinion you have expressed that the constitution is different in time of insurrection or invasion from what it is in time of peace & public security." A recurrence to the paper will show you that I have not expressed the opinion you suppose. I expressed the opinion that the constitution is different, *in its application* in cases of Rebellion or Invasion, involving the Public Safety, from what it is in times of profound peace and public security; and this opinion I adhere to, simply because, by the constitution itself, things may be done in the one case which may not be done in the other.

I dislike to waste a word on a merely personal point; but I must respectfully assure you that you will find yourselves at fault should you ever seek for evidence to prove your assumption that I "opposed, in discussions before the people, the policy of the Mexican war."

You say "Expunge from the constitution this limitation upon the power of congress to suspend the writ of Habeas corpus, and yet the other guarranties of personal liberty would remain unchanged" Doubless if this clause of the constitution, improperly called, as I think, a limitation upon the power of congress, were expunged, the other guarranties would remain the same; but the question is, not how those guarranties would stand, with that clause *out* of the constitution, but how they stand with that clause remaining in it—in cases of Rebellion or Invasion, involving the public Safety. If the liberty could be indulged, of expunging that clause letter & spirit, I really think the constitutional argument would be with you. My general view on this question was stated in the Albany response, and hence I do not state it now. I only add that, as seems to me, the benefit of the writ of Habeas corpus, is the great means through which the guarranties of personal liberty are conserved, and made available in the last resort; and coroborative of this view, is the fact that Mr. V. in the very case in question, under the advice of able lawyers, saw not where else to go but to the Habeas Corpus. But by the constitution the benefit of the writ of Habeas corpus itself may be suspended when in cases of Rebellion or Invasion the public Safety may require it.

You ask, in substance, whether I really claim that I may over-ride all the guarrantied rights of individuals, on the plea of con-serving the public safety—when I may choose to say the public safety requires it. This question, divested of the phraseology calcu-lated to represent me as struggling for an arbitrary personal pre-rogative, is either simply a question *who* shall decide, or an affirmation that *nobody* shall decide, what the public safety does require, in cases of Rebellion or Invasion. The constitution con-templates the question as likely to occur for decision, but it does not expressly declare who is to decide it. By necessary implication, when Rebellion or Invasion comes, the decision is to be made, from time to time; and I think the man whom, for the time, the people have, under the constitution, made the commander-in-chief, of their Army and Navy, is the man who holds the power, and bears the responsibility of making it. If he uses the power justly, the same people will probably justify him; if he abuses it, he is in their hands, to be dealt with by all the modes they have reserved to themselves in the constitution.

The[3] earnestness with which you insist that persons can only, in times of rebellion, be lawfully dealt with, in accordance with the rules for criminal trials and punishments in times of peace, induces me to add a word to what I said on that point, in the Al-bany response. You claim that men may, if they choose, embarrass those whose duty it is, to combat a giant rebellion, and then be dealt with in turn, only as if there was no rebellion. The consti-tution itself rejects this view. The military arrests and detentions, which have been made, including those of Mr. V. which are not different in principle from the others, have been for *prevention,* and not for *punishment*—as injunctions to stay injury, as proceed-ings to keep the peace—and hence, like proceedings in such cases, and for like reasons, they have not been accompanied with indict-ments, or trials by juries, nor, in a single case by any punishment whatever, beyond what is purely incidental to the prevention. The original sentence of imprisonment in Mr. V.'s case, was to prevent injury to the Military service only, and the modification of it was made as a less disagreeable mode to him, of securing the same pre-vention.

I am unable to perceive an insult to Ohio in the case of Mr. V. Quite surely nothing of the sort was or is intended. I was wholly unaware that Mr. V. was at the time of his arrest[4] a candidate for the democratic nomination for Governor until so informed by your

[3] This paragraph is an autograph insertion in the draft.
[4] "At the time of his arrest," inserted in Nicolay's autograph.

reading to me the resolutions of the convention. I am grateful to the State of Ohio for many things, especially for the brave soldiers and officers she has given in the present national trial, to[5] the armies of the Union.

You claim, as I understand, that according to my own position in the Albany response, Mr. V. should be released; and this because, as you claim, he has not damaged the military service, by discouraging enlistments, encouraging desertions, or otherwise; and that if he had, he should have been turned over to the civil authorities under recent acts of congress. I certainly do not *know* that Mr. V. has specifically, and by direct language, advised against enlistments, and in favor of desertion, and resistance to drafting. We all know that combinations, armed in some instances, to resist the arrest of deserters, began several months ago; that more recently the like has appeared in resistance to the enrolment preparatory to a draft; and that quite a number of assassinations have occurred from the same animus. These had to be met by military force, and this again has led to bloodshed and death. And now under a sense of responsibility more weighty and enduring than any which is merely official, I solemnly declare my belief that this hindrance, of the military, including maiming and murder, is due to the course in which Mr. V. has been engaged, in a greater degree than to any other cause; and is due to him personally, in a greater degree than to any other one man. These things have been notorious, known to all, and of course known to Mr. V. Perhaps I would not be wrong to say they originated with his special friends and adhereants. With perfect knowledge of them, he has frequently, if not constantly made speeches, in congress, and before popular assemblies; and if it can be shown that, with these things staring him, in the face, he has ever uttered a word of rebuke, or counsel against them, it will be a fact greatly in his favor with me, and one of which, as yet I, am totally ignorant. When it is known that that [*sic*] the whole burthen of his speeches has been to stir up men against the prossecution of the war, and that in the midst of resistance to it, he has not been known, in any instance, to counsel against such resistance, it is next to impossible to repel the inference that he has counselled directly in favor of it. With all this before their eyes the convention you represent have nominated Mr. V. for Governor of Ohio; and both they and you, have declared the purpose to sustain the national Union by all constitu-

---

[5] "To the armies of the Union" inserted in Nicolay's hand, and the following phrase deleted: "and very especially for giving birth to Generals Rosecrans and Grant."

tional means. But, of course, they and you, in common, reserve to yourselves to decide what are constitutional means; and, unlike the Albany meeting, you omit to state, or intimate, that in your opinion, an army is a constitutional means of saving the Union against a rebellion; or even to intimate that you are conscious of an existing rebellion being in progress with the avowed object of destroying that very Union. At the same time your nominee for Governor, in whose behalf you appeal, is known to you, and to the world, to declare against the use of an army to suppress the rebellion. Your own attitude, therefore, encourages desertion, resistance to the draft and the like, because it teaches those who incline to desert, and to escape the draft, to believe it is your purpose to protect them, and to hope that you will become strong enough to do so. After a short personal intercourse with you gentlemen of the committee, I can not say I think you desire this effect to follow your attitude; but I assure you that both friends and enemies of the Union look upon it in this light. It is a substantial hope, and by consequence, a real strength to the enemy. If it is a false hope, and one which you would willingly dispel, I will make the way exceedingly easy. I send you duplicates of this letter, in order that you, or a majority of you, may if you choose, indorse your names upon one of them, and return it thus indorsed to me, with the understanding that those signing, are thereby committed to the following propositions, and to nothing else.

1   That there is now a rebellion in the United States, the object and tendency of which is to destroy the national Union; and that in your opinion, an army and navy are constitutional means for suppressing that rebellion.

2.   That no one of you will do any thing which in his own judgment, will tend to hinder the increase, or favor the decrease, or lessen the efficiency of the army or navy, while engaged in the effort to suppress that rebellion; and,

3.   That each of you will, in his sphere, do all he can to have the officers, soldiers, and seamen of the army and navy, while engaged in the effort to suppress the rebellion, paid, fed, clad, and otherwise well provided and supported.

And with the further understanding that upon receiving the letter and names thus indorsed, I will cause them to be published, which publication shall be within itself, a revocation of the order in relation to Mr. V.[6]

[6] On July 1 the delegation replied, ". . . In the conclusion of your communication, you propose, that, if a majority of the Committee shall affix their signatures to a duplicate copy of it, which you have furnished, they shall stand

It will not escape observation that I consent to the release of Mr. V. upon terms, not embracing any pledge from him, or from others as to what he will, or will not do. I do this because he is not present to speak for himself, or to authorize others to speak for him; and because I should expect that on his returning, he would not put himself practically in antagonism with the position of his friends. But I do it chiefly because I thereby preval on other influential gentlemen of Ohio to so define their position, as to be of immense value to the Army—thus more than compensating for the consequences of any mistake in allowing Mr. V. to return; and so that, on the whole, the public safety will not have suffered by it. Still, in regard to Mr. V. and all others, I must hereafter as heretofore, do so much as the public safety may seem to require. I[7] have the honor to be respectfully yours, &c.,   A. LINCOLN.

---

committed to three propositions, therein at length set forth; that he will publish the names thus signed, and that this publication shall operate as a revocation of the order of banishment. The Committee cannot refrain from the expression of their surprise, that the President should make the fate of Mr. Vallandigham depend upon the opinion of this Committee, upon these propositions. If the arrest and banishment were legal and were deserved,—if the President exercised a power clearly delegated, under circumstances which warranted its exercise, the order ought not to be revoked, merely because the Committee hold or express opinions accordant with those of the President. . . . The opinion of the undersigned, touching the questions involved in these propositions, are well known, have been many times publicly expressed, and are sufficiently manifested in the resolutions of the Convention, which they represent, and they cannot suppose that the President expects, that they will seek the discharge of Mr. Vallandigham, by a pledge, implying not only an imputation upon their own *sincerity* and *fidelity* as Citizens of the United States, but also carrying with it by implication a concession of the *legality* of his arrest, trial and banishment, —against which, they . . . have solemnly protested. And while they have asked the revocation of the order . . . not as *a favor*, but as *a right* due to the people of Ohio, . . . they do not do this, nor does Mr. Vallandigham desire it, at any sacrifice of their dignity and self respect. The idea, that such a pledge, as that asked . . . would secure the public safety sufficiently to compensate for any mistake of the President in discharging Mr. Vallandigham, is, in their opinion, a mere evasion of the grave questions involved in this discussion, and of a direct answer to their demand. And this is made especially apparent by the fact, that this pledge is asked in [a] communication which concludes with an intimation of a disposition on the part of the President to repeat the acts complained of.

"The undersigned, therefore, having fully discharged the duty enjoined upon them, leave the responsibility with the President." (*Ibid.*)

[7] The concluding sentence and signature are not in the draft, but appear in the New York *Tribune*, July 9, 1863, and other contemporary printed sources. Neither of the two original copies of this letter, which Lincoln specifies that he sent the delegation, has been located.

To William Kellogg[1]

Hon. Wm. Kellogg.   Executive Mansion,
My dear Sir: Washington, June 29. 1863.

I have received, and read, your pencil note. I think you do not know how embarrassing your request is. Few things are so troublesome to the government as the fierceness with which the profits of trading in cotten are sought. The temptation is so great that nearly every body wishes to be in it; and when in, the question of profit controls all, regardless of whether the cotten seller is loyal or rebel, or whether he is paid in corn-meal or gun-powder. The officers of the army, in numerous instances, are believed to connive and share the profits, and thus the army itself is diverted from fighting the rebels to speculating in cotten; and steam-boats and wagons in the pay of the government, are set to gathering and carrying cotten, and the soldiers to loading cotten-trains and guarding them.

The matter deeply affects the Treasury and War Departments, and has been discussed again and again in the cabinet. What can, and what can not be done, has, for the time been settled, and it seems to me I can not safely break over it. I know it is thought that one case is not much, but how can I favor one and deny another. One case can not be kept a secret. The authority given would be utterly ineffectual until it is shown; and when shown, every body knows of it. The administration would do for you as much as for any other man; and I personally would do some more than for most others; but really I can not involve myself and the Government as this would do. Yours as ever   A. LINCOLN

[1] ADfS, DLC-RTL. See Lincoln to Chase, June 25, *supra.* Kellogg's note of June 29 is as follows:

"The reply of Mr. Chase to me on reading your note and hearing my proposition was 'It can not be done Sir' an iceburg would be as a furnace compared to your Sec of the Treasury.

"Mr. Lincoln—I very much desire that Mr. A[mos] C Babcock be permitted to take to and sell ordinary articles of commerce at Helena, Arkansas—not 'contraband of war' and to buy of loyal men cotton & other productions—at that place and Fryers Point Miss. & transport northward. If in your judgment there is nothing wrong in this *I do think* the administration should grant me this much

"I do not know of any consideration that would induce me again to ask a favour of Mr Chase. If I can not get this of the Commander in Chief—of the armies—I can not get it at all I dislike to trouble you but will ask you to consider the matter. . . .

"If this can not be done, will the govt. permit certain persons *loyal men* who have raised and own cotton who may be named to ship *themselves* their cotton to St Louis or other points. This would *answer* my purpose" (DLC-RTL).

A later but undated note, also in pencil, is as follows: "I sent you a note by Mr Nicolay. Will you say whether any thing can be done. if I can not see you please write your answer on a card so that I can get it from your attendant at 4 oclock. . . ." (*Ibid.*).

To Robert H. Milroy[1]

Major General Milroy   Executive Mansion,
My dear Sir: Washington, June 29. 1863.

Your letters to Mr. Blair[3] and to myself, are handed to me by him. I have never doubted your courage and devotion to the cause. But you have just lost a Division, and *prima facie* the fault is upon you; and while that remains unchanged, for me to put you in command again, is to justly subject me to the charge of having put you there on purpose to have you lose another. If I knew facts sufficient to satisfy me that you were not in fault, or error, the case would be different. But the facts I do know, while they are not at all conclusive, and I hope they may never prove so, tend the other way.

First, I have scarcely seen anything from you at any time, that did not contain imputations against your superiors, and a chafing against acting the part they had assigned you. You have constantly urged the idea that you were persecuted because you did not come from West-Point, and you repeat it in these letters. This, my dear general, is I fear, the rock on which you have split.

In the Winchester case, you were under General Schenck, and he under Gen. Halleck. I know by Gen. Hallecks order-book, that he, on the 11th. of June advised Gen. Schenck to call you in from Winchester to Harper's Ferry; and I have been told, but do not know, that Gen. Schenck gave you the order accordingly, on the same day—and I have been told, but do not know, that on receiving it, instead of obeying it, you sent by mail a written protest against obeying it, which did not reach him until you were actually beleagered at Winchester. I say I do not know this. You hate West-Point generally, and General Halleck particularly; but I do know that it is not his fault that you were at Winchester on the 13th. 14th. and morning of the 15th.—the days of your disaster. If Gen. Schenck gave the order on the 11th. as Gen. Halleck advised, it was an easy matter for you to have been off at least on the 12th. The case is inevitably between Gen. Schenck & you. Neither Gen. Halleck, nor any one else, so far as I know, required you to stay and fight 60,000, with 6,000, as you insinuate. I know Gen. Halleck, through Gen. Schenck required you to get away, & that in abundant time for you to have done it. Gen. Schenck is not a West-Pointer & has no prejudice against you on that score.
Yours very truly   A. LINCOLN

[1] ALS, DLC; LS copy, DLC-RTL. The original autograph letter has Milroy's endorsement at the end of the letter as follows: "Old Abe is mistaken.

[308]

Schenck never gave me Hallocks said order. But mearly ordered me to send off (back) all surpluss stores &c. but in the mean time to hold my position till further orders. I sent off all surpluss stores held my position, but got no *further orders* becaus I was surrounded & telegraf wires cut."

On June 28 Milroy wrote John P. Usher, from Baltimore, "I ask you as a friend in Gods name, to go with it [enclosed letter] to the President at once, & try to procure my release from the grasp of an incompetent unprincipled tyrant." The letter to Lincoln is in part as follows: "I had no orders to evacuate Winchester, I was told to get ready. . . . Myself and brother officers felt sure that Hooker would occupy the whole of Lee's army, & I felt entirely able for all the Rebel forces in the Valley. . . . And the salvation of the Baltimore & Ohio Rail road depending wholly upon our holding . . . and mistaking the advance of Lee's Army by way of Front Royal, for a feint by a few hundred cavalry . . . I held on at Winchester until I was surrounded by a force of about 60,000. . . .

"I love my country & the Union dearer than life, and God knows that every faculty of my soul & body has been devoted to its salvation. . . . I have never asked a leave of absence & have not been absent from my command a single day or night . . . until two days ago, I was suspended from command and placed in arrest by order of General Halleck, like a common fellon.

"I may have erred in judgment in remaining too long at Winchester . . . but without disobeying any orders or being guilty of any crime, I am deprived of command & made a prisoner. . . . Halleck hates me without cause . . . with the blind unreasoning hatred of an Indian & I can ask or expect nothing but injustice from him, and I respectfully ask you sir, as a friend of our country, to suspend my arrest if only temporarily, during the present terrible crisis, and give me something to do, if it is only the command of a company in active service. If permitted I would freely resign my present commission, & take any command, or go into the ranks as a private, rather than remain idle at this critical period.

"After the crisis is passed, & my country is saved, Halleck may have me tried to his hearts content and hang me if he can." (DLC-RTL).

The records show that on June 11, Schenck relayed to Lieutenant Colonel Donn Piatt from Martinsburg, Halleck's instructions to withdraw to Harper's Ferry, and that Piatt's telegram relaying the order was received by Milroy at midnight on the same day. Milroy thereupon telegraphed Schenck that he had the place well protected and hated to give it up, and Schenck replied at 1 A.M. on June 12, "Lieutenant-Colonel Piatt . . . misunderstood me, and somewhat exceeded his instructions. You will make all the required preparations for withdrawing, but hold your position in the meantime. Be ready for movement, but await further orders. . . ." (OR, I, XXVII, II, 49-50).

On the night of June 12, Milroy telegraphed Schenck of the approach of the enemy and asked whether to abandon his position or not. Schenck's reply ordering Milroy to fall back to Harper's Ferry was not received because the wires had been cut by the enemy. (*Ibid.*, 50-52).

2 In John Hay's autograph on the original.

3 The autograph letter has "Blair" corrected to "Usher" by Milroy.

To Edwin M. Stanton[1]

June 29, 1863

The Sec. of War will please let him be discharged.

1 Copy, DNA WR RG 107, Secretary of War, Letters Received, P 39, Irregular Book 5. The copy of Lincoln's endorsement is preserved as a notation in the register concerning a letter from Archbishop John J. Hughes asking discharge of M. C. Byrnes, imprisoned for using disloyal language.

To Darius N. Couch[1]

Major Gen. Couch   Washington D.C.
Harrisburg, Penn.   June 30. 1863 3/25 PM

I judge by absence of news that the enemy is not crossing, or pressing up to the Susquehannah. Please tell me what you know of his movements.   A LINCOLN

[1] ALS, RPB. A telegram from Couch received at 2:20 P.M. is in the Lincoln Papers, but apparently had not been seen by Lincoln at the time he telegraphed. It is as follows: "Part of the rebel force has left the Vicinity of Carlisle with fifty pieces of artillery, and massed towards Shippensburg. This looks like concentrating a portion of their troops down the Cumberland valley. Eight thousand of their men left York and went towards Carlisle this morning" (DLC-RTL).

At 9 P.M. Couch replied to Lincoln's telegram, "The rebel infantry force left Carlisle early this morning, on the Baltimore pike. Cavalry still on this side of that town. Early, with 8,000, left York this morning; went westerly or northwesterly. Rebels at York and Carlisle yesterday a good deal agitated about some news they had received. I telegraphed news to General Meade, care of the Secretary of War." (OR, I, XXVII, III, 434).

To David Hunter[1]

                              Executive Mansion,
My Dear General   Washington, 30 June, 1863.

I have just received your letter dated the 25th of June.

I assure you, and you may feel authorized in stating, that the recent change of commanders in the Department of the South was made for no reasons which convey any imputation upon your known energy, efficiency and patriotism; but for causes which seemed to me sufficient, while they were in no degree incompatible with the respect and esteem in which I have always held you, as a man and an officer.

I cannot, by giving my consent to a publication of whose details I know nothing, assume the responsibility of whatever you may write. In this matter your own sense of military propriety must be your guide, and the regulations of the service your rule of conduct. I am very truly Your friend   A. LINCOLN
   Major General Hunter

[1] LS, CSmH. This letter is misdated June 30, 1862, by Hertz (II, 870-71). Hunter had been relieved of his command of the Department of the South on June 3, 1863. On June 25, he wrote Lincoln from Princeton, New Jersey:

"You cannot fail to be aware that my removal from command of the Dept. of the South, has been all but universally regarded as a censure on my conduct. . . .

"Satisfied and well knowing that I acted throughout in strict obedience to orders, and that my record when .published will prove an ample vindication of my course,—I now respectfully request . . . liberty to make such publication of official documents and records as may be necessary to set me right in the eyes of my friends and in the justice of history. . . .

"Knowing how greatly your time is occupied, I shall regard your not answering this note as giving me the liberty I ask for, and will act accordingly. . . ." (DLC-RTL).

Hunter served on courts of inquiry until he assumed command of the Department of West Virginia on May 19, 1864.

To Alexander K. McClure[1]

A. K. McClure   Washington City,
Philadelphia   June 30 1863

Do we gain anything by opening one leak to stop another? Do we gain any thing by quieting one clamor, merely to open another, and probably a larger one?   A. LINCOLN

[1] ALS, RPB. McClure's telegram received at 11:05 A.M. is as follows:

"Have been twenty-four hours hoping to hasten the organization of troops. It seems impossible to do so to an extent at all commensurate with the emergency. Our people are paralyzed for want of confidence and leadership, and, unless they can be inspired with hope, we shall fail to do anything worthy of our State or Government. I am fully persuaded that to call McClellan to a command here would be the best thing that could be done. He could rally troops from Pennsylvania, and I am well assured that New York and New Jersey would also respond to his call with great alacrity. With his efficiency in organizing men, and the confidence he would inspire, early and effective relief might be afforded us, and great service rendered to the Army of the Potomac.

"Unless we are in some way rescued from the hopelessness now prevailing, we shall have practically an inefficient conscription, and be powerless to help either ourselves or the National Government.

"After free consultation with trusted friends of the Administration, I hesitate not to urge that McClellan be called here. He can render us and you the best service, and in the present crisis no other consideration should prevail. Without military success we can have no political success, no matter who commands. In this request I reflect what seems to be an imperative necessity rather than any preference of my own." (OR, I, XXVII, III, 436).

To Joel Parker[1]

Gov. Parker   Executive Mansion,
Trenton, N.J.   Washington, June 30, 1863.

Your despatch of yesterday received. I really think the attitude of the enemies' army in Pennsylvania, presents us the best opportunity we have had since the war began. I think you will not see the foe in New-Jersey. I beg you to be assured that no one out of my position can know so well as if he were in it, the difficulties and involvements of replacing Gen. McClellan in command—and this aside from any imputations upon him.

Please accept my sincere thanks for what you have done, and are doing to get troops forward.   A. LINCOLN

[1] ALS, RPB. Governor Parker's telegram of June 29 is as follows:
"The people of New Jersey are apprehensive that the invasion of the enemy may extend to her soil. We think that the enemy should be driven from Pennsylvania. There is now certainly great apathy under such fearful circumstances. That apathy should be removed. The people of New Jersey want McClellan at the head of the Army of the Potomac. If that cannot be done, then we ask that he may be put at the head of the New Jersey, New York, and Pennsylvania troops now in Pennsylvania, defending these Middle States from invasion. If either appointment be made, the people would rise *en masse*.
"I feel it my duty, respectfully, to communicate this state of feeling to you."
(OR, I, XXVII, III, 409).

To Edwin M. Stanton and Henry W. Halleck[1]

Submitted to the Sec. of War & Gen-in-chief, with my consent to the proposition.   A. LINCOLN
June 30. 1863.

[1] AES, NHi. Lincoln's endorsement is written on a telegram from Waldo Hutchins, Prosper M. Wetmore, and James Wadsworth of New York, June 30, asking that General William B. Franklin be detailed for duty because "our citizens generally have great confidence in the military capacity of Genl Franklin." Franklin had been awaiting orders since January 24, 1863, but was assigned to the Department of the Gulf as of June 27.

Appointment of William H. Jones[1]

Washington, July 1st. 1863
Wm. Hemphill Jones, is hereby appointed to discharge the duties of First Comptroller of the Treasury, during the absence of R. W. Tayler, the Comptroller.   ABRAHAM LINCOLN

[1] DS-P, ISLA. William H. Jones is listed in the *U.S. Official Register*, 1863, as chief clerk under Robert W. Tayler, first comptroller of the Treasury.

To Benjamin B. French[1]

Major B. B. French.   Executive Mansion
My dear Sir: Washington, July 1st. 1863.
I have just been to the Secretary of War with Dr. Stewart's case. He says that scarsely any case has been so fully heard on both sides, and that he is not clearer of the correctness of any decision made. Of course I can over rule his decision if I will, but I cannot well administer the War Department independent of the Secretary

of War. Besides on a one sided presentation made to me as this is, I have no confidence that my decision would be more correct than the one already made. Yours truly,   A. LINCOLN

1 Copy, DLC-Benjamin F. Wade Papers. Surgeon William D. Stewart had been dismissed for being absent without leave. On July 9, Lincoln revoked the special order of dismissal and reinstated Surgeon Stewart (DNA RG 130, White House Office, Register of U.S. Army Court-Martial Cases).

To Edwin M. Stanton[1]

Hon. Sec. of War.   Executive Mansion,
My dear Sir: Washington, July 2. 1863.
    I wish you would allow the Republican (my paper as you jokingly call it), to be paid for advertising. The non-payment is made a source of trouble to me. Yours truly   A. LINCOLN

1 ALS, NHi. No reply has been located. The *U.S. Official Register*, 1863, shows the *National Republican* to have received from the War Department payments for advertising as follows: Secretary's Office, $428.75; Quartermaster General's Office, $8.00; Surgeon General's Office, $51.13; Ordnance Office, $21.88.

To Ambrose E. Burnside[1]

                War Department, Washington, D.C.,
Major-General Burnside, Cincinnati, Ohio: July 3, 1863.
    Private Downey, of the Twentieth or Twenty-sixth Kentucky Infantry, is said to have been sentenced to be shot for desertion to-day. If so, respite the execution until I can see the record.
                            A. LINCOLN.

1 Tarbell (Appendix), p. 374. No reply has been located. On August 5, 1863, Private John Downey, Company G, Twenty-sixth Kentucky Volunteers, was pardoned by the president and ordered to return to duty (AGO *General Orders No. 272*).

To William A. Hammond[1]

                            July 3, 1863
Submitted to the Surgeon General, with the request that he will report to me any contemplated action of his in the premises & his reasons.   A. LINCOLN
    July 3. 1863

1 AES, DLC-RTL. Lincoln's endorsement is written on a letter from Henry Hopkins, John A. Bowman, Chauncey B. Thomas, Thomas G. Carver, and Rodney Gage, chaplains of the army hospitals in Alexandria, Virginia, July 3,

1863, protesting the proposed reduction of the number of chaplains to one per division. On July 7 Hammond returned the letter with a lengthy endorsement disapproving the request on the basis that under the proposed reduction each chaplain would have to minister to approximately six hundred men, which "is no greater than that [number] embraced commonly in a parochial charge."

To Robert T. Lincoln[1]

Robert T. Lincoln Esq.   Executive Mansion,
Cambridge Mass.   Washington, July 3rd. 1863.
    Dont be uneasy. Your mother very slightly hurt by her fall.
                                                      A. L.

         Please send at once

[1] D, RPB. The telegram is not in Lincoln's handwriting. On the morning of July 2, while riding from the Soldiers' Home to the Executive Mansion, Mrs. Lincoln fell from the carriage during a runaway (New York *Times*, July 3, 1863).

Announcement of News From Gettysburg[1]

                          Washington City, July 4, 10.A.M. 1863
The President announces to the country that news from the Army of the Potomac, up to 10 P.M. of the 3rd. is such as to cover that Army with the highest honor, to promise a great success to the cause of the Union, and to claim the condolence of all for the many gallant fallen. And that for this, he especially desires that on this day, He whose will, not ours, should ever be done, be everywhere remembered and reverenced with profoundest gratitude.   ABRAHAM LINCOLN

[1] ADS, RPB. The announcement was a "press release" sent by telegraph from the War Department.

To Samuel P. Lee[1]

Rr. Adml.   Navy Department
        S. P. Lee.   Washington, D.C. July [4] 1863
    Your despatch transmitting a note from Mr. Alexander H. Stephens has been received. You will not permit Mr. Stephens to proceed to Washington, or to pass the blockade. He does not make known the subjects to which the communication in writing from Mr. Davis relates, which he bears, and seeks to deliver in person

to the President, and upon which he desires to confer. Those subjects can only be Military, or not Military, or partly both. Whatever may be military will be readily received, if offered through
the well understood Military channel. Of course nothing else, will
be received by the President, when offered, as in this case, in terms
assuming the independence of the so-called Confederate States; and
anything will be received and carefully considered by him, when
offered by any influential person or persons, in terms not assuming the independence of the so-called Confederate States.

1 ADf, DLC-RTL. This draft of a telegram was not sent, being replaced by
the brief communication *infra*. Rear Admiral Lee telegraphed Secretary Welles
from Fort Monroe at 4:30 P.M., July 4 (DLC-RTL):
"The following communication is just received from Mr Stephens who is on
the flag of truce boat anchored above. I shall inform Mr Stephens that I await
your instructions before giving him an answer.
" 'Confederate States Str. "Torpedo"
" 'In James' River July 4 1863
" 'Sir: As military commissioner, I am the bearer of a communication in writing from Jefferson Davis Commander-in-Chief of the land and Naval forces of
the Confederate States to Abraham Lincoln Comd'r-in-Chief of the land & Naval
forces of the United States.
" 'Hon Robert Ould, Confederate States' Agent of Exchange, accompanies me
as Secretary.
" 'For the purpose of delivering the communication in person and conferring
upon the subjects to which it relates, I desire to proceed directly to Washington
in the Steamer "Torpedo" Commanded by Lieut. Hunter Davidson of the Confederate States' Navy. No person being on board but the Hon. Mr Ould, myself
& the boat's officers & crew. Yours most respectfully
" 'ALEXANDER H. STEPHENS' "
"S. P. LEE
"Act'g. Rr. Adml."

Welles' *Diary* for July 4 records his reception of the telegram as follows:
"Received this evening a dispatch from Admiral Lee, stating he had a communication from A. H. Stephens, who wishes to go to Washington with a com-
panion as military commissioner from Jefferson Davis . . . and desires permission to pass the blockade. . . . Showed the dispatch to Blair, whom I met.
He made no comment. Saw Stanton directly after, who swore and growled in-
dignantly. The President was at the Soldiers' Home and not expected for an
hour or two. Consulted Seward, who was emphatic against having anything to
do with Stephens or Davis. Did not see the President till late. In the mean time
Stanton and others had seen him, and made known their feelings and views.
The President treats the subject as not very serious nor very important, and
proposes to take it up to-morrow."
On July 5 Welles' *Diary* records the cabinet meeting at 11 A.M. as follows:
"The principal topic was the mission of Alexander H. Stephens. The President
read a letter from Colonel [William H.] Ludlow . . . to Secretary Stanton,
stating that Stephens had made a communication to Admiral Lee, which the
Admiral had sent to the Secretary of the Navy. After reading them, the President said he was at first disposed to put this matter aside without many words,
or much thought, but a night's reflection and some remarks yesterday had modified his views. While he was opposed to having Stephens and his vessel come
here, he thought it would be well to send some one—perhaps go himself—to
Fortress Monroe. Both Seward and Stanton were startled when this remark

was made. Seward did not think it advisable the President should go, nor any one else. . . . The most he . . . would do would be to allow Stephens to forward any communication through General Dix. . . . Stanton was earnest and emphatic against having anything to do with Stephens, or Jeff Davis, or their communication. Chase was decided against having any intercourse with them. Blair took a different view. . . . I propose to take some notice of his application, and, unless the President objects, send an answer as follows to Admiral Lee:—

" 'The object of the communication borne by Mr. Stephens is not stated or intimated. It is not expedient from this indefinite information that you should permit that gentleman to pass the blockade. . . .' . . . The President said my letter did not dispose of the communication which Stephens bore. I told him the dispatch did not exclude it. . . ."

On July 2, Jefferson Davis had enclosed two copies of a communication addressed to Lincoln with the following instructions to Alexander H. Stephens:

"Having accepted your patriotic offer to proceed as a military commissioner under flag of truce to Washington, you will receive here with your letters of authority to the Commander-in-Chief of the Army and Navy of the United States. This letter is signed by me as Commander-in-Chief of the Confederate land and naval forces.

"You will perceive from the terms of the letter that it is so worded as to avoid any political difficulties in its reception. Intended exclusively as one of those communications between belligerents which public law recognizes as necessary and proper between hostile forces, care has been taken to give no pretext for refusing to receive it on the ground that it would involve a tacit recognition of the independence of the Confederacy. . . . Your mission is simply one of humanity and has no political aspect. If objection is made to receiving your letter on the ground that it is not addressed to Abraham Lincoln as President . . . then you will present the duplicate letter, which is addressed to him as President and signed by me as President. To this latter objection may be made on the ground that I am not recognized to be President of the Confederacy. In this event you will decline any further attempt to confer on the subject of your mission, as such conference is admissible only on the footing of perfect equality. . . ." (OR, II, VI, 74-75).

Davis' communication to Lincoln, abridged, is as follows:

"Numerous difficulties . . . have arisen in relation to the execution of the cartel of exchange . . . and the commissioners of the exchange of prisoners have been unable to adjust their differences. . . . I believe that I have just ground of complaint against the officers and forces under your command for breach of trust of the cartel, and being myself ready to execute it at all times in good faith I am not justified in doubting the existence of the same disposition on your part. In addition to this matter I have to complain of the conduct of your officers . . . in many parts of the country who violate all the rules of war by carrying on hostilities . . . against non-combatants, aged men, women and children. . . .

"Still again others of your officers . . . have recently taken the lives of prisoners . . . by asserting a right to treat as spies the military officers and enlisted men under my command who may penetrate into States recognized by us as our allies . . . against the United States, but claimed by the latter as having refused to engage in such warfare. . . . I have . . . refrained from the exercise of . . . retaliation because of its obvious tendency to lead to war of indiscriminate massacre on both sides. . . .

"With the view . . . of making one last solemn attempt to avert such calamities . . . I have selected the bearer of this letter, the Hon. Alexander H. Stephens, as a military commissioner to proceed to your headquarters under flag of truce, there to confer and agree on the subjects above mentioned. . . ." (Ibid., 75-76).

To Samuel P. Lee[1]

War Department, Washington, D.C., July 4, 1863.
Rear-Admiral S. P. Lee: The request of A. H. Stephens is inadmissible. The customary agents and channels are adequate for all needful communication and conference between the United States forces and the insurgents. A. LINCOLN.

[1] NH, IX, 16. The editors include this telegram as reproduced by Nicolay and Hay. In the absence of the original, it is not certain that Lincoln composed or signed it, and that it was prepared on July 4 may be questioned. As printed in the *Official Records* (II, VI, 84), over the signature of Gideon Welles, the text of this telegram is dated July 6, and Welles' *Diary* on this date records:
"There was a special Cabinet-meeting at 9 A.M. on the subject of A. H. Stephens's mission. Seward came prepared with a brief telegram, which the President had advised, to the effect that Stephens's request to come to W. was inadmissible, but any military communication should be made through the prescribed military channel. A copy of this answer was to be sent to the military officer . . . at Fortress Monroe by the Secretary of War, and the Secretary of the Navy was to send a copy to Admiral Lee. The President directed Mr. Seward to go to the telegraph office and see that they were correctly transmitted. . . ."

To Robert C. Schenck[1]

Major Gen. Schenck. Washington, D.C.,
Baltimore Md July 4. 9./20 1863

Your despatches about negro regiment are not uninteresting or unnoticed by us, but we have not been quite ready to respond. You will have an answer to-morrow. A. LINCOLN

[1] ALS, RPB. General Schenck had telegraphed Lincoln on June 30 that he had "four thousand able bodied Negroes at work on fortifications. . . . I sent papers ten days ago urging and recommending a proposition to create from among them a regt. of Sappers & Miners." (DLC-RTL). On July 4, Schenck telegraphed again (received 8:40 P.M.), "to suggest that somebody . . . be authorized to accept the services of . . . these blacks, who are now willing to be enrolled. . . ." (OR, I, XXVII, III, 528). On July 6, Secretary Stanton telegraphed Schenck, "The chief of Bureau for Organizing Colored Troops will issue an order for organizing a regiment in your department. . . ." (OR, III, III, 470-71).

To William H. French[1]

Major Genl. French Washington, D.C.,
Frederick Town, Md. July 5. 1863

I see your despatch about destruction of Pontoons. Can not the enemy ford the river? A. LINCOLN

[1] ALS, RPB. Major General French reported to Halleck on July 4 that an expedition sent out by his command had destroyed the pontoon bridge over the Potomac at Williamsport (OR, I, XXVII, III, 524). At 9:15 P.M. on July 5, French reported to Halleck that "Five hundred wagons (rebel), guarded by

about 150 infantry, 150 cavalry, three pieces of . . . artillery, and from 3,000 to 5,000 head of cattle passed through Hagerstown last night. . . . Could not cross the ford at Williamsport, the river being too high. . . ." (*Ibid.*).

To Henry W. Halleck[1]

Soldiers' Home,

[Washington,] July 6, 1863– 7 p.m.

Major-General Halleck: I left the telegraph office a good deal dissatisfied. You know I did not like the phrase, in Orders, No. 68, I believe, "Drive the invaders from our soil." Since that, I see a dispatch from General French, saying the enemy is crossing his wounded over the river in flats, without saying why he does not stop it, or even intimating a thought that it ought to be stopped. Still later, another dispatch from General Pleasonton, by direction of General Meade, to General French, stating that the main army is halted because it is believed the rebels are concentrating "on the road toward Hagerstown, beyond Fairfield," and is not to move until it is ascertained that the rebels intend to evacuate Cumberland Valley.

These things all appear to me to be connected with a purpose to cover Baltimore and Washington, and to get the enemy across the river again without a further collision, and they do not appear connected with a purpose to prevent his crossing and to destroy him. I do fear the former purpose is acted upon and the latter is rejected.

If you are satisfied the latter purpose is entertained and is judiciously pursued, I am content. If you are not so satisfied, please look to it. Yours, truly,   A. LINCOLN.

[1] OR, I, XXVII, III, 567. Major General George G. Meade's *General Orders No. 68*, July 4, 1863, after thanking his army for defeating "an enemy, superior in numbers, and flushed with the pride of a successful invasion," continued as follows: "Our task is not yet accomplished, and the commanding general looks to the army for greater efforts to drive from our soil every vestige of the presence of the invader. . . ." General Alfred Pleasonton telegraphed General William H. French at 11 A.M. on July 6, "Major-General Meade desires me to say, in consequence of a large body of the enemy being concentrated on the road toward Hagerstown, beyond Fairfield, he has suspended his operations for the present. Indications go to show that he intends evacuating the Cumberland Valley, but it is not yet positively ascertained. Until so ascertained, the general does not feel justified in leaving here and moving down toward you."

"[The enemy is very much crippled. The general is under no apprehension of their attacking you, provided your cavalry keep a good lookout, and are kept well out to your front and flanks.]" (OR, I, XXVII, III, 559). The brackets are in the source, and a footnote explains: "The clause in brackets does not appear in the telegram as received 4 p.m. at the War Department." Had Lincoln seen the omitted paragraph, he would probably have been even more displeased at Meade's obvious intent to let Lee withdraw.

To Jesse K. Dubois and Others[1]

J. K. Dubois & others   Washington, D.C.
Springfield, Ills.   July 7. 1863

An appointment of Chesley at Danville had already been made and gone forward, for Enrolment Comr. of 7th. Dist. when your Despatch arrived.   A. LINCOLN

[1] ALS, RPB. The dispatch from Dubois and others has not been located. On June 29, Samuel Frazier was appointed enrollment commissioner at Danville, Illinois. There is no record of Chesley's appointment. R. V. Chesley was a harness maker at Danville.

To Henry W. Halleck[1]

Major-General Halleck: [July 7, 1863]

We have certain information that Vicksburg surrendered to General Grant on the 4th of July. Now, if General Meade can complete his work, so gloriously prosecuted thus far, by the literal or substantial destruction of Lee's army, the rebellion will be over. Yours, truly,   A. LINCOLN.

[1] OR, I, XXVII, I, 83. In the source Lincoln's note to Halleck is introduced in a telegram from Halleck to Meade of July 7 as follows: "I have received from the President the following note, which I respectfully communicate."

On July 8 at 12:30 P.M., Halleck again prodded Meade, but gently: "There is reliable information that the enemy is crossing at Williamsport. The opportunity to attack his divided forces should not be lost. The President is urgent and anxious that your army should move against him by forced marches." (OR, I, XXVII, III, 605).

Response to a Serenade[1]

                                         July 7, 1863

Fellow-citizens: I am very glad indeed to see you to-night, and yet I will not say I thank you for this call, but I do most sincerely thank Almighty God for the occasion on which you have called. [Cheers.] How long ago is it?—eighty odd years—since on the Fourth of July for the first time in the history of the world a nation by its representatives, assembled and declared as a self-evident truth that "all men are created equal." [Cheers.] That was the birthday of the United States of America. Since then the Fourth of July has had several peculiar recognitions. The two most distinguished men in the framing and support of the Declaration were Thomas Jefferson and John Adams—the one having penned it and the other sustained it the most forcibly in debate—the only two of the fifty-five who sustained [signed?][2] it being elected

President of the United States. Precisely fifty years after they put their hands to the paper it pleased Almighty God to take both from the stage of action. This was indeed an extraordinary and remarkable event in our history. Another President, five years after, was called from this stage of existence on the same day and month of the year; and now, on this last Fourth of July just passed, when we have a gigantic Rebellion, at the bottom of which is an effort to overthrow the principle that all men were [are?][3] created equal, we have the surrender of a most powerful position and army on that very day, [cheers] and not only so, but in a succession of battles in Pennsylvania, near to us, through three days, so rapidly fought that they might be called one great battle on the 1st, 2d and 3d of the month of July; and on the 4th the cohorts of those who opposed the declaration that all men are created equal, "turned tail" and run. [Long and continued cheers.] Gentlemen, this is a glorious theme, and the occasion for a speech, but I am not prepared to make one worthy of the occasion. I would like to speak in terms of praise due to the many brave officers and soldiers who have fought in the cause of the Union and liberties of the country from the beginning of the war. There[4] are trying occasions, not only[5] in success, but for the want of success. I dislike to mention the name of one single officer lest I might do wrong to those I might forget. Recent events bring up glorious names, and particularly prominent ones, but these I will not mention. Having said this much, I will now take the music.

[1] New York *Tribune, Herald,* and *Times,* July 8, 1863. Brackets are in the *Tribune* except as otherwise noted. Typographical errors in the sources have been corrected, and important variants have been indicated in the succeeding notes.

[2] This clause is given by Nicolay and Hay as follows: "who signed it that were elected Presidents of the United States" (NH, IX, 20).

[3] "Are" (*ibid.,* 21).   [4] "These" in *Times.*   [5] "Daily" in *Tribune.*

To Gideon Welles[1]

Hon. Sec. of the Navy   Executive Mansion,
My dear Sir   Washington, July 7, 1863.

The gentlemen named in the attached resolution, have presented it to me this morning. It explains itself. Please carefully consider the subject, and do the best in regard to it which you can consistently with the general public service. Yours truly

A. LINCOLN

[1] ALS, DNA WR NB RG 45, Executive Letters, No. 22. The attached newspaper clipping reads: "*Resolved,* That Hon. Hannibal Hamlin, Vice-President of the United States, and our two Senators in Congress, be requested to repair

immediately to Washington, for the purpose of urging upon the President the importance and necessity of placing along the coast a sufficient naval and military force to protect the commerce of the country from piratical depredations of the rebels, and to have the same accomplished in such manner as shall be most efficient and expeditious." Welles' *Diary* records on July 8, 1863, "I yesterday informed Vice-President Hamlin and the Maine Senators we should try to keep a couple of steamers and two sailing-vessels cruising off New England during the fishing season; that we could not furnish a gunboat to every place; that the shore defenses belonged properly to the War Department, etc. They on the whole seemed satisfied."

To Frederick F. Low[1]

Hon. F. F. Low.
San Francisco. Cal.

Washington, D.C.,
July 8 1863

There is no doubt that Gen. Meade, now commanding the Army of the Potomac, beat Lee, at Gettysburg, Pa. at the end of a three days battle; and that the latter is now crossing the Potomac at Williamsport, over the swolen stream & with poor means of crossing, and closely pressed by Meade. We also have despatches rendering it entirely certain that Vicksburg surrendered to Gen. Grant on the glorious old 4th.   A. LINCOLN

[1] ALS, RPB. Frederick F. Low, collector of the Port of San Francisco and Republican nominee for governor of California, had telegraphed Stanton on July 7, "Give me result in Pennsylvania as far as consistent. Our citizens very anxious." (OR, I, L, II, 513).

To E. Delafield Smith[1]

E. Delafield Smith
New-York

Washington, D.C.,
July 8 1863

Your kind despatch, on behalf of self and friends, is gratefully received.

Capture of Vicksburg confirmed by despatch from Gen. Grant himself.   A. LINCOLN

[1] ALS, RPB. Smith had telegraphed congratulations at 10:50 A.M. (DLC-RTL).

To Lorenzo Thomas[1]

Gen. Thomas
Harrisburg, Penn.

Washington, D.C.,
July 8 1863

Your despatch of this morning to the Sec. of War is before me. The forces you speak of, will be of no immagineable service, if they

can not go forward with a little more expedition. Lee is now passing the Potomac faster than the forces you mention are passing Carlyle. Forces now beyon[d] Carlyle, to be joined by regiments still at Harrisburg, and the united force again to join Pierce somewhere, and the whole to move down the Cumberland Valley, will, in my unprofessional opinion, be quite as likely to capture the Man-in-the-Moon, as any part of Lee's Army   A. LINCOLN

[1] ALS, RPB. A telegram from Lorenzo Thomas to Stanton was received at 10:45 A.M.: "General [Charles] Yates, with three regiments and a battery of artillery . . . is beyond Carlisle. He will be joined by two regiments, ready to move from this place. This force can make a junction with [Lewis B.] Pierce, and move down the Cumberland Valley on the enemy's rear. Four regiments are nearly ready at Reading. These will also be pushed forward. We have no definite information this morning of the enemy's movements or position." (OR, I, XXVII, III, 612).

Upon receiving Lincoln's telegram, Thomas telegraphed Stanton, "Telegram of the President received. It is a slow business to organize militia and put them in march. I am afraid the President supposed the troops in advance were to delay until those behind came up, but not so, as the orders are to press forward. . . ." (*Ibid.*).

To Leonard Swett and Frederick F. Low[1]

Hon. Leonard Swett, &   Washington City, D.C.
Hon. F. F Low.   July 9. 1863
San Francisco, Cal.

Consult together, and do not have a riot, or great difficulty about delivering possession   A. LINCOLN

[1] ALS, RPB. See Lincoln's order to Charles W. Rand, May 8, *supra*. When Leonard Swett reached California with Lincoln's order to Rand, Frederick F. Low telegraphed his superior Salmon P. Chase on July 8, "Orders are here for taking possession of Almaden mine by military force the result of such a move will be terrible. The secessionists will seize upon it as a pretext for a general uprising I fear   See the President at once & have Genl Wright instructed by telegraph to withdraw action   a delay of one day in the order may be fatal." (DLC-RTL). See further Lincoln to Swett, July 15, *infra*.

To Daniel E. Sickles[1]

My dear General,   Washington, July 10, 1863.

I understand you are troubled with some report that the 3rd Corps has sustained a disaster, or repulse. I can only say that I have watched closely, and believe I have seen all the despatches at the Military Telegraph Office up to a half hour ago, one from Ingalls, with the Army, reaching here since this morning, and I have

heard of no such disaster or repulse. I add that I do not believe
there has been any such. Yours truly,   A. LINCOLN.
   Maj. Gen. Sickles.

¹ Thomas F. Madigan, *A Catalogue of Lincolniana* (1929), No. 45. No correspondence connected with this communication has been found. General Sickles
was in command of the Third Corps at Gettysburg, where he was severely
wounded and underwent amputation of a leg.

To Jesse K. Dubois¹

Hon. J. K. Dubois   Washington City, D.C.
Springfield, Ills—   July 11 1863
   It is certain that after three days fighting at Gettysburg, Lee
withdrew and made for the Potomac; that he found the river so
swollen as to prevent his crossing, that he is still this side near
Hagerstown and Williamsport, preparing to defend himself; and
that Meade is close upon him preparing to attack him, heavy skirmishing having occurred nearly all day yesterday. I am more than
satisfied with what has happened North of the Potomac so far, and
am anxious and hopeful for what is to come.   A. LINCOLN

¹ ALS, RPB. Jesse K. Dubois' telegram received at 9:30 P.M. on July 10 asked,
"Is all right for us against rebel Lee?" (DLC-RTL).

To Robert T. Lincoln¹

R. T. Lincoln   Executive Mansion,
New-York Fifth Ave. Hotel   Washington, July 11 1863.
        Come to Washington   A. LINCOLN

¹ ALS, IHi. No communication relating to this telegram has been discovered.

To Robert C. Schenck¹

Major General Schenck   Washington City, D.C.
Baltimore, Md   July 11. 1863
   How many rebel prisoners, captured within Maryland &
Pennsylvania, have reached Baltimore within this month of July?
                                          A. LINCOLN

¹ ALS, RPB. General Schenck replied at 5:30 P.M., "Have received in this
month of July at Fort McHenry six thousand one hundred and forty two (6142)
prisoners of war captured in Maryland and Pennsylvania" (DLC-RTL). At
12:30 A.M. on July 12, Schenck telegraphed again, "Add to the number of

Prisoners I reported . . . six hundred & fifty three, more received at Fort Delaware by way of Philadelphia Those in hospitals here are not included."
(*Ibid.*).

To Edwin M. Stanton[1]

Executive Mansion, Washington,
Hon. Secretary of War.   July 11, 1863.

Please allow the bearer Mr. D. M. Leatherman, to take with him from the prison at Alton, Ill., his brother, J. A. Leatherman to his home at Memphis, Tenn. upon the honor of both that he will remain at Memphis, until further permission to leave. The latter resides near Murfreesboro, and was arrested and sent away by Gen. Rosecrans police for disloyalty. He has not been in the army. His brother who will take charge of him, is abundantly vouched as a Union man and honorable gentleman, by Gen. Hurlbut and many others. Yours truly,   A. LINCOLN.

[1] Hertz, II, 901. No correspondence connected with this communication has been located, but see Lincoln's memorandum, April 17, *supra*.

To Edwin M. Stanton[1]

I submit the within to the Sec. of War for action, with an impression, that the suggestion of Gen. Cameron may be right.
July 11. 1863.   A. LINCOLN

[1] AES, NHi. Lincoln's endorsement is written on a telegram from Simon Cameron, received at 10:30 A.M. on July 11, recommending that Confederate General Isaac R. Trimble, wounded at Gettysburg and ordered to Baltimore to be paroled, should be confined as a prisoner of war at Harrisburg or Pittsburgh: "From his knowledge of the Railroads in Penna Maryland & Delaware he is a dangerous man. He burned the bridges between Phila & Balto in the beginning of the rebellion. Within the last ten days he directed and superintended the burning of the bridges between Balto & Columbia and York and Harrisburg He resided in Balto for twenty five years & is in close connection with all the rebel sympathizers in that city. He is now living in comfort at the house of a rebel sympathizer in this town while some of our wounded soldiers are still unattended." See Lincoln to Schenck, July 12, *infra*.

To George Wright[1]

July 11, 1863
I desire military protection, when needed, to be given to Arazona, so far as it can be given consistently with the general military service   A. LINCOLN
July 11. 1863.

[1] AES, IHi. Lincoln's endorsement is written on the bottom of a letter from General Edward R. S. Canby, July 10, 1863, introducing Governor John A. Gurley of Arizona and instructing Brigadier General George Wright, commanding the Department of the Pacific at San Francisco, to furnish Gurley "with an escort and such other facilities as may be necessary."

To Robert C. Schenck[1]

"Cypher"

Major Genl. Schenck   Washington, D.C.,
Baltimore, Md.   July 12 1863

You seem to misunderstand the nature of the objection to Gen. Tremble's going to Baltimore. His going there is opposed to prevent his meeting his traitorous associates there.   A LINCOLN

[1] ALS, RPB. Upon receiving Stanton's instructions in regard to General Trimble (Lincoln to Stanton, July 11, *supra*), Schenck replied at 11 A.M. on July 12 that Trimble was still at Gettysburg:

"I do not know why Messrs. Cameron and Moorhead think it dangerous for Trimble to be brought here. The distance is less than to either Philadelphia or Pittsburg, and as to any just exasperation of loyal Baltimore citizens, he need have no fear that he will not be protected even at the scene of his traitorous and scoundrel acts.

"The fact is he intended, and it was arranged at Gettysburg, that he should come here until it was found that he would have to fare like other prisoners, and not be treated with special consideration. Gettysburg is not in my department." (OR, II, VI, 107-108).

Schenck replied to Lincoln's telegram at 11 P.M., "With due respect to Messrs. Cameron and Moorhead, I must say that I do not think there is a city in the Union where Trimble would be as little likely to get a chance for intercourse with traitorous associates as in Baltimore. He has constantly been favored with opportunities at Gettysburg, whch he could not have had here." (OR, I, XXVII, III, 663).

General Trimble was later transferred to Baltimore, whence he was sent to Johnson's Island to remain until March, 1865.

To Henry T. Blow[1]

War Department, Washington, July 13, 1863.

Hon. H. T. Blow, St. Louis, Mo.: I saw your dispatch to the Secretary of War. The publication of a letter without the leave of the writer or the receiver I think cannot be justified, but in this case I do not think it of sufficient consequence to justify an arrest; and again, the arrest being, through a parole, merely nominal, does not deserve the importance sought to be attached to it. Cannot this small matter be dropped on both sides without further difficulty?

A. LINCOLN.

[1] OR, I, XXII, II, 366. On July 13 Henry T. Blow telegraphed his protest against General Schofield's arrest of William McKee, editor of the *Missouri Democrat*. See Lincoln to Schofield, *infra*.

To Ulysses S. Grant[1]

Major General Grant   Executive Mansion,
My dear General   Washington, July 13, 1863.

I do not remember that you and I ever met personally. I write this now as a grateful acknowledgment for the almost inestimable service you have done the country. I wish to say a word further. When you first reached the vicinity of Vicksburg, I thought you should do, what you finally did—march the troops across the neck, run the batteries with the transports, and thus go below; and I never had any faith, except a general hope that you knew better than I, that the Yazoo Pass expedition, and the like, could succeed. When you got below, and took Port-Gibson, Grand Gulf, and vicinity, I thought you should go down the river and join Gen. Banks; and when you turned Northward East of the Big Black, I feared it was a mistake. I now wish to make the personal acknowledgment that you were right, and I was wrong.   Yours very truly

A. LINCOLN

[1] ALS, PHi. General Grant did not acknowledge receipt of this letter until August 23 when he replied to Lincoln's letter of August 9, *infra*.

To John M. Schofield[1]

Gen. Schofield   Washington City, D.C.
St. Louis, Mo.   [July 13] 1863

I regret to learn of the arrest of the Democrat editor. I fear this loses you the middle position I desired you to occupy. I have not learned which of the two letters I wrote you, it was that the Democrat published; but I care very little for the publication of any letter I have written. Please spare me the trouble this is likely to bring   A. LINCOLN

[1] ALS, RPB. The bracketed portion of the date is not in Lincoln's handwriting. On July 14 General Schofield replied that he feared Lincoln had been misinformed as to the circumstances of William McKee's arrest and summarized the case as follows: "While I was temporarily absent from Saint Louis your letter of May 27 appeared in the Democrat. I regard this letter as official and confidential. The publication of it, with my knowledge or consent, would have been a gross breach of your confidence. . . . If obtained by the connivance of one of my subordinates . . . a like breach of trust had been committed. If a copy of the letter had been sent by you to General Curtis, and this found its way to the press without his or your authority, a serious offense had been committed by some one. In either case it was my . . . duty to ascertain who had been guilty of so great a breach of trust. . . . I then sent . . . a verbal request to Mr. McKee to call and explain. . . . Mr. McKee paid no attention. . . . After waiting several days, I caused one of my staff officers, a personal friend of Mr. McKee, to repeat the request in writing. This Mr. McKee also treated with

contempt. . . . After waiting several days longer, I ordered Mr. McKee to be arrested and brought before the provost-marshal-general, and required to give the desired information. Mr. McKee stated that the letter did not come to him from my office, but he was unwilling to say from whom it did come, and asked ten days' time in which to make his reply. This request was granted. Mr. McKee's arrest was merely nominal, he simply giving his verbal parole that he would report at the end of ten days. It is now sought, I presume, to get your order suspending further proceedings . . . and thus screen the guilty party. Mr. McKee declares his own innocence, saying he came by the letter honestly, but he is unwilling to inform me who the guilty party is. It seems probable from all I can learn that Mr. McKee obtained the letter . . . through some friend of General Curtis, to whom, I presume, you sent a copy of it, and not through the infidelity of some person under my command, as at first appeared. If this is true, I am very willing to stop proceedings in the matter if you will express your willingness to overlook the offense committed in the publication of the letter, or in giving it to the press for publication, and to pardon the offender without knowing who he may be. . . ." (OR, I, XXII, II, 373-74).

See further Lincoln to Schofield, July 20, *infra*.

To Robert T. Lincoln[1]

Robt. T. Lincoln
New-York. 5th. Av. Hotel—
Why do I hear no more of you?

Washington, D.C.,
July 14 1863
A. LINCOLN

[1] ALS, IHi. No correspondence has been located in connection with this telegram, but Robert was en route to Washington.

To George G. Meade[1]

Major General Meade

Executive Mansion,
Washington, July 14, 1863.

I have just seen your despatch to Gen. Halleck, asking to be relieved of your command, because of a supposed censure of mine. I am very—*very*—grateful to you for the magnificient success you gave the cause of the country at Gettysburg; and I am sorry now to be the author of the slightest pain to you. But I was in such deep distress myself that I could not restrain some expression of it. I had been oppressed nearly ever since the battles at Gettysburg, by what appeared to be evidences that yourself, and Gen. Couch, and Gen. Smith,[2] were not seeking a collision with the enemy, but were trying to get him across the river without another battle. What these evidences were, if you please, I hope to tell you at some time, when we shall both feel better. The case, summarily stated is this. You fought and beat the enemy at Gettysburg; and, of course, to say the least, his loss was as great as yours. He retreated; and you did not, as it seemed to me, pressingly pursue him; but a flood in the river detained him, till, by slow degrees, you were again upon him. You had at least twenty thousand veteran troops directly with you, and as many more raw ones within supporting distance, all in addition to those who fought with you at Gettysburg; while it was not possible that he had received a single recruit; and yet you stood and let the flood run down, bridges be built, and the enemy move away at his leisure, without attacking him. And Couch and Smith! The latter left Carlisle in time, upon all ordinary calculation, to have aided you in the last battle at Gettysburg; but he did not arrive. At the end of more than ten days, I believe twelve, under constant urging, he reached Hagerstown from Carlisle, which is not an inch over fiftyfive miles, if so much. And Couch's movement was very little different.

Again, my dear general, I do not believe you appreciate the magnitude of the misfortune involved in Lee's escape. He was within your easy grasp, and to have closed upon him would, in connection with our other late successes, have ended the war. As it is, the war will be prolonged indefinitely. If you could not safely attack Lee last monday, how can you possibly do so South of the river, when you can take with you very few more than two thirds of the force you then had in hand? It would be unreasonable to expect, and I do not expect you can now effect much. Your golden opportunity is gone, and I am distressed immeasureably because of it.

I beg you will not consider this a prossecution, or persecution of yourself. As you had learned that I was dissatisfied, I have thought it best to kindly tell you why.

¹ AL, DLC-RTL. The envelope containing this letter bears Lincoln's endorsement "To Gen. Meade, never sent, or signed." Halleck telegraphed Meade at 1 P.M. on July 14, "The enemy should be pursued and cut up, wherever he may have gone. This pursuit may or may not be upon the rear or flank, as circumstances may require. The inner flank toward Washington presents the greatest advantages. Supply yourself from the country as far as possible. I cannot advise details, as I do not know where Lee's army is, nor where your pontoon bridges are. I need hardly say to you that the escape of Lee's army without another battle has created great dissatisfaction in the mind of the President, and it will require an active and energetic pursuit on your part to remove the impression that it has not been sufficiently active heretofore." (OR, I, XXVII, I, 92).

Meade replied at 2:30 P.M., "Having performed my duty conscientiously and to the best of my ability, the censure of the President conveyed in your dispatch of 1 p.m. this day, is, in my judgment, so undeserved that I feel compelled most respectfully to ask to be immediately relieved from the command of this army." (Ibid., p. 93).

Halleck replied at 4:30 P.M., "My telegram, stating the disappointment of the President at the escape of Lee's army, was not intended as a censure, but as a stimulus to an active pursuit. It is not deemed a sufficient cause for your application to be relieved." (Ibid., pp. 93-94).

Under date of July 14, John Hay's Diary records Lincoln's depression over Meade's despatches, and on July 15 adds that Robert Todd Lincoln "says the

Tycoon is grieved silently but deeply about the escape of Lee. He said, 'If I had gone up there, I could have whipped them myself.' I know he had that idea." ² Darius N. Couch and William F. Smith.

To Robert C. Schenck[1]

"Cypher"

Majr. Genl. Schenck   Washington D.C.
Baltimore, Md.   July 14. 1863

Mr. Jaquess is a very worthy gentleman; but I can have nothing to do, directly, or indirectly, with the matter he has in view.

A. LINCOLN

[1] ALS, RPB. General Schenck telegraphed Lincoln on July 13 that Colonel James F. Jaquess "desires me to send him on to Fortress Monroe Shall I do so He says you understand." (DLC-RTL). Colonel Jaquess was pursuing his proposed peace mission (see Lincoln to Rosecrans, May 21, *supra*). Schenck allowed him to go to Fortress Monroe, where he boarded a flag of truce boat and entered the Confederate lines. On July 22, Jaquess wrote Lincoln from Baltimore:

"I have obtained *valuable* information, and proposals for *peace* through the channel I proposed. *Unofficial*, but from men of character and great influence in the south, residents there.

"Would it be *consistent*—for me to communicate them to you? If so; how? By *Telegraph-Mail* or in person? Latter greatly preferred if through propper. I am moving strictly private. I await your ans." (*Ibid.*)

So far as is known, Lincoln did not reply.

To James O. Broadhead[1]

J. O. Brodhead   Washington City,
St. Louis, Mo   July 15. 1863

The *effect* on political position, of McKee's arrest, will not be relieved any, by it's not having been made with that *purpose*

A. LINCOLN

[1] ALS, RPB. See Lincoln to Schofield, July 13, *supra*. Broadhead telegraphed Lincoln on July 14, "Be assured that, whatever you may have heard, the arrest of McKee had nothing whatever to do with his political position. This can be fully and satisfactorily explained." (OR, II, VI, 115).

To Simon Cameron[1]

"Cypher"

Hon. Simon Cameron   Washington City,
Harrisburg, Penn.   July 15, 1863.

Your despatch of yesterday received. Lee was already across the river when you sent it. I would give much to be relieved of the impression that Meade, Couch, Smith and all, since the battle at Gettysburg, have striven only to get Lee over the river without another fight. Please tell me, if you know, who was the one corps commander who was for fighting, in the council of War on Sunday-night.   A. LINCOLN

¹ ALS, RPB. Cameron telegraphed on July 14, "I left the Army of the Potomac yesterday believing that the decision of Genl Meades Council of war on Sunday night not to attack the rebels would allow them to escape. His army is in fine spirits & eager for battle. They will win if they get a chance. Genl Couch has a fine army between Carlisle & Green Castle but will move no further south without orders under the strong belief that his duty is to guard the Susquehanna. In my opinion the Susquehanna needs no guard. I have urged him from the beginning to join Meade. I hope in God that you will put forth your authority & order every man in arms between the Susquehanna & the Potomac to unite with Meade so that he may have no reason for delay in giving battle before the falling of the flood allows Lee to escape." (DLC-RTL).

No reply from Cameron has been located. Meade's despatch to Halleck of 5 P.M., July 13, specifies that "five out of six" of his corps commanders "were unqualifiedly opposed" to making an attack (OR, I, XXVII, I, 91), but does not name the general who favored it—possibly Major General Oliver O. Howard, or Brigadier General James S. Wadsworth, temporarily in command of the First Corps during the illness of Brigadier General John Newton, whom Meade had placed in command of the First Corps at Gettysburg. The later reports appearing in the press do not entirely agree with Meade's statement that only one Corps commander favored an attack, although Meade may not have considered Wadsworth a corps commander in view of his temporary assignment. See Lincoln to Howard, July 21, *infra*.

Endorsement on Letter of James R. Gilmore to Zebulon B. Vance¹

[July 15? 1863]

This letter has been written in my presence, has been read by me, and has my entire approval.   A. L.

¹ James R. Gilmore, *Personal Recollections of Abraham Lincoln and the Civil War* (1898), p. 216. This endorsement is misdated 1864 in Lapsley (VI, 358). Although Gilmore does not give the exact date, preceding and succeeding dates in his narrative indicate mid-July, 1863. According to Gilmore, Lincoln endorsed the following letter immediately after reading it:

"My dear Sir:—My former business partner, Mr. Frederic Kidder, of Boston, has forwarded to me a letter he has recently received from his brother, Edward Kidder, of Wilmington, in which he (Edward Kidder) says that he has had an interview with you in which you expressed an anxiety for any peace compatible with honor; that you regard slavery as already dead, and the establishment of the Confederacy as hopeless; and that you should exert all your influence to bring about any reunion that would admit the South on terms of perfect equality with the North.

"On receipt of this letter I lost no time in laying it before the President of the United States, who expressed great gratification at hearing such sentiments from you, one of the most influential and honored of the Southern governors, and he desires me to say that he fully shares your anxiety for the restoration of peace between the States, and for a reunion of all the States on the basis of the abolition of slavery,—the bone we are fighting over,—and the full reinstatement of every Confederate citizen in all the rights of citizenship in our common country. These points conceded, the President authorizes me to say that he will be glad to receive overtures from any man, or body of men, who have authority to control the armies of the Confederacy; and that he and the United States Congress will be found very liberal on all collateral points that may come up in the settlement.

"His views on the collateral points that may naturally arise, the President desires me to say he will communicate to you through me if you should suggest the personal interview that Mr. Edward Kidder recommends in his letter to his brother. In that case you will please forward to me, through Mr. Kidder, your official permit, as Governor of North Carolina, to enter and leave the State, and to remain in it in safety during the pendency of these negotiations, which, I suppose, should be conducted in entire secrecy until they assume an official character. With high consideration, I am. . . ." (*Ibid.*, 215-16).

Gilmore's account of subsequent events should be consulted in the source.

To Robert A. Maxwell[1]

Robert A. Maxwell   Washington, D.C.,
  1032. Chestnut St. Phil.   July 15 1863
Your despatch of to-day is received, but I do not understand it.

                               A. LINCOLN

[1] ALS, RPB. Maxwell's telegram, received at 2:35 P.M., is as follows: "Albert Gallatin Thorp informed me that Seymour is well controlled beyond safe limits—why hesitate" (DLC-RTL).

An undated letter from Maxwell is apparently in reply to Lincoln's telegram:

"My friend Albert Gallatin Thorp a zealous Republican, a large property owner in New York a connexion of Mr Vanderbilt and intimate with conttrolling friends of Gov Seymour stated to me that, in deprecating the dangerous issues which Seymour was presenting in the last election, he was assured that he need not feel disturbed that they had perfect control of Seymour intimating that he should not go further than the U.S. Government would let him.

"The whole country is observing with interest the course of the Administration in dealing with the New York conscription. If not proceeded with, say by an officer of known determination such as General Butler with military and *naval* forces to support him, the Union goes up in a blaze of State Rights. An exhibition of resolution will insure Seymours submission, the execution of the draft elsewhere and the avoidance of foreign intervention   I stated the views of Mr Thorp to a gentleman who went to Washington this morning but fearing he might not obtain an interview during his brief stay I dispatched the telegram that led to these particulars in answer to your dispatch. I would further refer you to the continuation of my 'Rough Notes' that I mailed you this morning."

"Rough Notes for the President

"Execute the draft regardless of Seymours hired rioters or abandon it everywhere. If you enforce it in New York the democrats have nothing left to stand on. If you suspend it there and execute it elsewhere dissatisfaction will destroy the Administration party.

"Ask Swinton of the New York Times who are the tardy generals in Rosecrans army.

"Ask Sympher of the N.Y. Tribune who are the tardy generals in Meade's army. Meade and Wise married sisters. Wellington could not purchase success in Spain till government sent him $1,000,000.

"Ask administration papers to send you their army correspondents from time to time for examination as to causes of delays."

Proclamation of Thanksgiving[1]

July 15, 1863

By the President of the United States of America.

A Proclamation.

It has pleased Almighty God to hearken to the supplications and prayers of an afflicted people, and to vouchsafe to the army and the navy of the United States victories on land and on the sea so signal and so effective as to furnish reasonable grounds for augmented confidence that the Union of these States will be maintained, their constitution preserved, and their peace and prosperity permanently restored. But these victories have been accorded not without sacrifices of life, limb, health and liberty incurred by brave, loyal and patriotic citizens. Domestic affliction in every part of the country follows in the train of these fearful bereavements. It is meet and right to recognize and confess the presence of the Almighty Father and the power of His Hand equally in these triumphs and in these sorrows:

Now, therefore, be it known that I do set apart Thursday the 6th. day of August next, to be observed as a day for National Thanksgiving, Praise and Prayer, and I invite the People of the United States to assemble on that occasion in their customary places of worship, and in the forms approved by their own consciences, render the homage due to the Divine Majesty, for the wonderful things he has done in the Nation's behalf, and invoke the influence of His Holy Spirit to subdue the anger, which has produced, and so long sustained a needless and cruel rebellion, to change the hearts of the insurgents, to guide the counsels of the Government with wisdom adequate to so great a national emergency, and to visit with tender care and consolation throughout the length and breadth of our land all those who, through the vicissitudes of marches, voyages, battles and sieges, have been brought to suffer in mind, body or estate, and finally to lead the whole nation, through the paths of repentance and submission to the Divine Will, back to the perfect enjoyment of Union and fraternal peace.

In witness whereof, I have hereunto set my hand and caused the seal of the United States to be affixed.

JULY 15, 1863

Done at the city of Washington, this fifteenth day of July, in
the year of our Lord one thousand eight hundred and
[L.S.] sixty-three, and of the Independence of the United
States of America the eighty-eighth.

By the President: ABRAHAM LINCOLN
WILLIAM H. SEWARD, Secretary of State.

[1] DS, DNA FS RG 11, Proclamations.

To Leonard Swett[1]

Hon. L. Swett.   Washington City,
San Francisco, Cal.   July 15. 1863

Many persons are telegraphing me from California, begging
me, for the peace, of the State, to suspend the military enforcement
of the writ of possession, in the Almedan case, while you are the
single one who urges the contrary. You know I would like to oblige
you, but it seems to me my duty, in this case, is the other way.

A. LINCOLN

[1] ALS, RPB. See Lincoln to Swett and Low, July 9, *supra*. On July 13, Halleck had telegraphed Frederick Billings, attorney for the New Almaden Mine:
"The order for a military occupation of New Almaden was surreptitiously
obtained. The Secretary of War has directed General Wright to suspend operations, to restore everything as he found it, and to obey no orders which do not
come through the proper channels." (OR, I, L, II, 522).

On July 14, Swett sent Lincoln three telegrams as follows:
"Abraham Lincoln, President United States:
"After full consultation with owner and attorney at mine, it was determined
no actual resistance should be offered. In a short time I would have had peace-
able possession, but when your dispatch came the marshal was telegraphed that
you had ordered to wait. Your order can yet be executed. If you determine to
do it, telegraph me giving discretion, and I will be responsible for consequences.
If you do not think best to execute the order let the Attorney-General authorize me by telegraph to obtain an injunction and receiver. In my opinion the
injunction had better be applied for. The Government owes it to its own dignity to do one of these things. I have offered the company the same terms proposed by the Quicksilver Company, and they positively refuse to do anything.
LEONARD SWETT. (Sent to Secretary of Interior.)" (*Ibid.*, p. 523).

"To Abraham Lincoln President US For Secretary of Interior—
"The Almaden Company realize more than a million of dollars annually.
They have no recognized miners claim, for a miners claim is a certain number
of feet allowed by local law—contrary to mining laws, they claim a large tract
of land. If Government had not yielded there would have been acquiescence, but having yielded one step the Almaden Company are striving by
every conceivable means to make Government abandon property. Their position now is that the mine is government land and because of that fact the Govt
should do nothing either by the order or the courts. If this deliberate attempt to
drive the Government from its rights succeeds, it will be quoted as a precedent
in future and will breed great mischief. The mandate of the Supreme Court
should be sent here, and the Govt by an injunction ought to save the fund aris-

ing from the Mine, until the termination of the suit, when Congress may dispose of it as it pleases. LEONARD SWETT." (DLC-RTL).

"His Excellency Abraham Lincoln, President United States:
"General Halleck has telegraphed the following dispatch, which has been published here [copying Halleck to Billings, July 13.] LEONARD SWETT." (OR, I, L, II, 523).
See further Lincoln to Low, August 17, *infra*.

To Edwin M. Stanton[1]

I shall be glad for this promotion to be made, so soon as it can be consistently.   A. LINCOLN
   July 16, 1863.

[1] AES, owned by Theodore S. Charrney, Chicago, Illinois. Lincoln's endorsement is written on a copy of an undated letter from Governor Joel Parker of New Jersey, recommending that Brigadier General Gershom Mott be made a major general. Mott was not promoted until a year later. See Lincoln to Stanton, August 11, 1864, *infra*.

To James H. Lane[1]

Hon J. H. Lane;   Executive Mansion,
My dear Sir: Washington, July 17, 1863.
   Gov. Carney has not asked to [have][2] Gen. Blunt removed, or interfered with in his Military operations. He has asked that he, the Governor, be allowed to commission officers for troops raised in Kansas, as other governors of loyal states do; and I think he is right in this. He has asked that Gen. Blunt shall not take persons charged with civil crimes, out of the hands of the courts, and turn them over to mobs to be hung;[3] and I think he is right in this also. He has asked that Gen. Ewing's Department be extended to include all Kansas; and I have not determined whether this is right or not.[4]
Yours truly   A. LINCOLN

[1] Copy, DLC-RTL. Senator Lane wrote Lincoln on July 17: "I am pained to learn that an effort is now being made to get you to interfere in the personal quarrel going on between Gov Carney & Maj Genl Blunt. That charges have been preferred by the Gov. against Maj Genl Blunt and an application made for his removal. Genl Blunt is now at the head of his army in the field bravely battling the enemies of his country. While thus employed this effort is made. I desire to file with you this my earnest but respectful protest against any interference with Genl Blunt until his campaign against the enemy is finished. When I ask that he may have the opportunity of confronting his accusers all of which is respectfully submitted." (DLC-RTL).
In the margin of Lane's letter is an endorsement, "I concur A C Wilder M.C." See further Lincoln to Carney, July 21, *infra*.
[2] Brackets are in the source.
[3] On May 18, 1863, "A ruffian and thief named Sterling was hung by the citizens of Atchison. On the 23d, about 300 men from the country went into

Atchison, took Mooney and Brewer, two other members of the gang, and hung them." (A. C. Wilder, *Annals of Kansas*, p. 347).

4 Brigadier General Thomas Ewing, Jr., was in command of the District of the Border, including northern counties of Kansas and border counties of Missouri, with headquarters at Kansas City, Missouri. General James G. Blunt was in command of the District of the Frontier, including Southern Kansas, Western Arkansas and the Indian Territory.

To Edwin M. Stanton[1]

Hon. Secretary of War: Executive Mansion,
My dear Sir: Washington, July 17. 1863.

It is proper, on principle, that the Governor of Kansas, should stand on the same ground as other loyal governors, in giving original commissions, and in filling vacancies, for troops raised in his state; and I wish him to be so placed at once, unless you know some substantial reason to the contrary   Yours very truly

A. LINCOLN.

1 ALS, DLC-Stanton Papers. See Lincoln to Lane, *supra*, and Lincoln to Carney July 21, *infra*.

To Joseph Holt[1]

Let him fight instead of being shot   A LINCOLN
July 18. 1863.

1 AES, DNA WR RG 153, Judge Advocate General, MM 304. Lincoln's endorsement is written on the papers of Private Michael Delany, Company K, First Colorado Cavalry, sentenced to be shot for desertion.

To Joseph Holt[1]

Sentence commuted according to the recommendation of Gen. Wool.   A. LINCOLN
July 18, 1863

1 AES, DNA WR RG 153, Judge Advocate General, MM 404. Lincoln's endorsement is written on the papers in the case of Private Francis Dew (age 16), Company G, Second Massachusetts Cavalry, sentenced to be shot on charges of mutiny. General Wool had without authority commuted the sentence to imprisonment and hard labor for the duration of the war.

To Joseph Holt[1]

July 18, 1863
Sentence commuted to forfeiture of pay for three months

A. LINCOLN

1 AES, DNA WR RG 153, Judge Advocate General, MM 364. Lincoln's endorsement is written on the papers of Second Lieutenant Jacob Garcy, Com-

pany A, Eighty-second Pennsylvania Volunteers, sentenced to dismissal for disobedience of orders and conduct prejudicial to military discipline, with recommendation of mercy for previous good character and bravery.

To Joseph Holt[1]

Sentence commuted to forfeiture of pay for one month

July 18, 1863   A. LINCOLN

[1] AES, DNA WR RG 153, Judge Advocate General, MM 540. Lincoln's endorsement is written on the papers of Second Lieutenant Charles B. Leathe, Fortieth Massachusetts Volunteers, sentenced to dismissal for being absent without leave.

To Joseph Holt[1]

Sentence commuted to loss of one months pay   A. LINCOLN

July 18. 1863

[1] AES, DNA WR RG 153, Judge Advocate General, MM 544. Lincoln's endorsement is written on the papers of Colonel G. L. Prescott, Thirty-second Massachusetts Volunteers, dismissed for overstaying leave.

To Joseph Holt[1]

Sentence as to dismissal approved, remainder disapproved.

July 18. 1863   A. LINCOLN

[1] AES, DNA WR RG 153, Judge Advocate General, MM 571. Lincoln's endorsement is written on the papers of Captain Charles Roescher, Second Artillery, One Hundred Twelfth Pennsylvania Volunteers, sentenced for breach of arrest and desertion, to forfeit all pay, dishonorable dismissal, and imprisonment for one year at hard labor.

To Joseph Holt[1]

Sentence commuted to loss of pay for one month   A. LINCOLN

July 18, 1863

[1] AES, DNA WR RG 153, Judge Advocate General, MM 273. Lincoln's endorsement is written on the papers of Captain James Saunders, Sixty-ninth New York Volunteers, dismissed for conduct unbecoming an officer and gentleman.

To Joseph Holt[1]

July 18, 1863

Lieut. Scott is hereby dismissed the service.   A. LINCOLN

[1] ES, DNA WR RG 153, Judge Advocate General, MM 358. Lincoln's endorsement is written on the papers of Second Lieutenant Alpheus Scott, Company L, Sixth Iowa Cavalry, dismissed for drunkenness.

To Joseph Holt[1]

Sentence commuted to loss of one months pay.   A. LINCOLN
July 18, 1863

[1] AES, DNA WR RG 153, Judge Advocate General, MM 546. Lincoln's endorsement is written on the papers of Lieutenant Colonel Luther J. Stephenson, Thirty-second Massachusetts Volunteers, dismissed for overstaying leave.

To Oliver P. Morton[1]

Gov. O. P. Morton   Washington DC.
Indianapolis.   July 18. 1863.
What do you remember about the case of John O. Brown, convicted of mutinous conduct & sentenced to death? What do you desire about it?   A. LINCOLN

[1] ALS, RPB. See Lincoln's order of April 1, *supra*. Governor Morton replied on July 20, "My recollection in case of Jno O Brown is that he was released Unconditionally pardoned & discharged from the service   I asked that he be pardoned" (DLC-RTL).

To Joseph Holt[1]

July 20, 1863
Let Major Gilmer be dismissed, as recommended by Gen. Heintzleman.   A. LINCOLN

[1] AES, DNA WR RG 153, Judge Advocate General, MM 376. Lincoln's endorsement is written on the papers of Major Joseph Gilmer, Eighteenth Pennsylvania Cavalry, cashiered for drunkenness.

To Joseph Holt[1]

Sentence disapproved, & prisoner to be held & treated as a prisoner of War.   A. LINCOLN
July 20. 1863.

[1] AES, DNA WR RG 153, Judge Advocate General, MM 543. Lincoln's endorsement is written on the papers of Private John W. Irwin (Irving), Company A, Ninth Virginia Cavalry, CSA, sentenced to be hanged as a spy.

To Joel Parker[1]

His Excellency   Executive Mansion,
Joel Parker   Washington,
Gov. of New-Jersey.   July 20. 1863.
Dear Sir   Yours of the 15th. has been received, and considered by the Secretary of War and myself. I was pained to be informed this morning by the Provost-Marshal-General that New-Jersey is now behind twelve thousand irrespective of the draft. I did not

have time to ascertain by what rule this was made out; and I shall be very glad if it shall, by any means, prove to be incorrect. He also tells me, that 8000 will be about the quota of New-Jersey on the first draft; and the Sec. of War says the first draft in that State would not be made for some time in any event. As every man obtained otherwise lessens the draft so much, and this may supersede it altogether, I hope you will push forward your volunteer regiments as fast as possible. It is a very delicate matter to postpone the draft in one State, because of the argument it furnishes others to have postponements also. If we could have a *reason* in, one case, which would be good if presented, in all cases, we could act upon it.

I will thank you therefore to inform me if you can, by what day, at the earliest, you can promise to have ready to be mustered into the U.S. service, the 8000, men. If you can make a reliable promise (I mean one which you can rely on yourself) of this sort, it will be of great value, if the day is not too remote.

I beg you to be assured I wish to avoid the difficulties you dread, as much as yourself. Your Obt. Servt.   A Lincoln

¹ ALS (copy), DLC-RTL. Governor Parker wrote Lincoln on July 15:

"A few weeks since authority was given me . . . to raise new regiments in this state and also to recruit for the old regiments. . . . When I asked for authority to raise these troops, I did it, not only for the purpose of adding to the strength of the Union Army, but also to give the people an opportunity to avoid the draft.

". . . I understand that no draft has yet been ordered in New Jersey, and the object of this communication is to request that it will not be ordered. . . . If New Jersey can raise the men required of her, by the volunteer system, I take it for granted you do not desire to execute the draft. . . . I deem it my duty to state to you that there is a deep rooted hostility . . . to . . . the conscription act, which is liable to lead to popular outbreak if it be enforced. . . ." (*Ibid.*).

See further Lincoln to Parker, July 25, *infra*.

To John M. Schofield¹

Executive Mansion,
My Dear General   Washington, July 20th, 1863.

I have received and read your letter of the 14th of July.

I think the suggestion you make, of discontinuing proceedings against Mr. McKee, a very proper one. While I admit that there is an apparent impropriety in the publication of the letter mentioned without my consent or yours, it is still a case where no evil could result, and which I am entirely willing to overlook. Yours truly
To Gen Schofield   A. Lincoln

¹ Copy, DLC-RTL. See Lincoln to Schofield, July 13, *supra*.

To Edwin M. Stanton[1]

[c. July 20, 1863]

Secretary of War—Please see Mr. R. Green of Troy, N.Y.

A. LINCOLN

[1] Troy, New York, *Times*, February 9, 1909. According to the source, Lincoln gave this note to Robert Green of Troy, who sought to recover the remains of Lieutenant Colonel James M. Green, Forty-eighth New York Infantry, killed in the assault on Fort Wagner, South Carolina, July 18, 1863.

To Thomas Carney[1]

His Excellency Gov. Thos. Carney   Executive Mansion,
Topeka, Kansas.   Washington, July 21. 1863.

Yours dated Pittsburgh, the 19 Inst. is received. The day after you were with me I wrote a note to the Sec. of War, asking him to place you on the same ground, with all other governors of loyal States as to the appointment of military officers. In reply to this he verbally told me, when I next met him, that he had never placed you on any other ground—that the forces in regard to which you and Gen. Blunt have a controversy, were raised on special authority from the War Department, given before you were governor, and that the officers were commissioned by him (the Sec. of War) according to the original authority; and that he never had required you to commission officers nominated by Gen. Blunt. The like of this has been done in some other States, as I remember. As to leaving no part of Kansas in Blunt's Department, the thing should not be hastily done. He, with his command, is now in the field South of Kansas; and while I do not know how much what you now desire, might interfere with his supplies, it is very certain that he can not now be interfering with you.

It is my purpose to take care that he shall not any more, take persons charged with civil crimes, out of the custody of the courts and turn them over to mobs to be hanged. Your Obt. Servt.

A. LINCOLN

[1] ALS, IHi. See Lincoln's letters to Stanton and to Lane, July 17, *supra*. Carney's letter of July 19 is as follows:

"I called to see you on Saturday morning last, and was informed . . . that you would see me at 4 o'clk. I . . . waited until half past 5 . . . but did not have the pleas[ur]e of an interview with you, therefore, hope I shall be pardoned for again calling your attention to the papers submitted . . . by me, in which the people of . . . Kansas, naturally feel a deep interest in, because the State of Kansas has never yet been treated as other loyal States. . . .

"You will remember that I asked that Kansas be placed under one military commander instead of two, as is now the case. . . . I gave you my reasons fully . . . why I wished Maj Genl Blunt's military authority to be absolutely suspended in the State. . . . I also asked that all orders from the War Department, that Maj Genl. Blunt shall name the officers for me as the Govr. of Kansas to commission be revoked. . . . Please inform me your decision [sic] . . . addressed to me at Topeka . . . where I am now on my way." (DLC-RTL). See further Lincoln's letter to Blunt, August 18, *infra*.

To Salmon P. Chase[1]

July 21, 1863

I know most of the gentlemen named within to be good and worthy gentlemen, and I shall be glad if the Secretary of the Treasury will see and hear one of them, Mr. Butler who will present this   A. LINCOLN

July 21. 1863

[1] Copy, IHi-Nicolay and Hay Papers. The copy of Lincoln's endorsement is with a copy of the following: "The name of the firm who desire to do a legitimate trade in the south, within our lines, is H. E. Bridge & Co, and is composed of the following named parties Hon Hudson E. Bridge of St. Louis Mo., James L. Lamb of Springfield Ill., Henry Hening & Woodruff of St. Louis Mo., W. T. Hecox of Chicago Ill. Hon W. Butler of Springfield Ill. We wish to get letters from Mr. Chase and others high in authority, to Mr. [William P.] Mellen and other special agents of the Treasury Department recommending us as good loyal men and entitled to all the privileges of trade granted to the most worthy. We desire also to know when the St. Francis and other tributaries of the Mis River will be opened to trade, and if we, as a company can depend upon being protected in any and all of our property that we may have in the States of Tennessee, Arkansas and Mississippi until such time as trade is regularly opened, and that we then be allowed to bring out all such property."

To Joseph Holt[1]

Let the sentence of Sergeant Sutton be remitted   A. LINCOLN

July 21. 1863

[1] AES, DNA WR RG 153, Judge Advocate General, MM 484. Lincoln's endorsement is written on the papers of Sergeant Robert Sutton, Company G, First Regiment, South Carolina Volunteers, sentenced to be hanged for mutiny.

To Charles E. Hovey[1]

Gen Chas. E. Hovey.   Executive Mansion
Dear Sir: Washington July 21, 1863

I distinctly say that I will nominate you as a Brig. Genl. of Volunteers, if you will furnish me with Maj Gen W. T. Shermans written request to do so Yours Truly   A. LINCOLN

[1] Copy, DLC-RTL. Colonel Charles E. Hovey, Thirty-third Illinois Infantry, was appointed brigadier general of Volunteers September 5, 1862, but his appointment expired March 4, 1863. Although strongly recommended by a letter from General William T. Sherman, August 3, 1863, Hovey's nomination was not confirmed by the Senate, and he entered law practice in Washington, D.C.

To Oliver O. Howard[1]

Executive Mansion,
My dear General Howard   Washington, July 21. 1863.

Your letter of the 18th. is received. I was deeply mortified by the escape of Lee across the Potomac, because the substantial destruction of his army would have ended the war, and because I believed, such destruction was perfectly easy—believed that Gen. Meade and his noble army had expended all the skill, and toil, and blood, up to the ripe harvest, and then let the crop go to waste. Perhaps my mortification was heightened because I had always believed—making my belief a hobby possibly—that the main rebel army going North of the Potomac, could never return, if well attended to; and because I was so greatly flattered in this belief, by the operations at Gettysburg. A few days having passed, I am now profoundly grateful for what was done, without criticism for what was not done. Gen. Meade has my confidence as a brave and skillful officer, and a true man. Yours very truly   A. LINCOLN

[1] ADfS, DLC-RTL. General Howard's letter of July 18, marked "Unofficial" by Howard, reads:

"Having noticed in the newspapers certain statements bearing upon the battles [*sic*] of Gettysburg and subsequent operations which I deem calculated to convey a wrong impression to your mind, I wish to submit a few statements. The successful issue of the battle of Gettysburg was due mainly to the energetic operations of our present commanding General prior to the engagement and to the manner in which he handled his troops on the field. The reserves have never before during the war been thrown in at just the right moment. . . . Moreover I have never seen a more hearty co-operation on the part of General officers as since General Meade took the command.

"As to not attacking the enemy prior to leaving his stronghold beyond the Antietam it is by no means certain that the repulse of Gettysburg might not have been turned upon us; at any rate the Commanding General was in favor of an immediate attack but with the evident difficulties in our way the uncertainty of a success and the strong conviction of our best military minds against the risk, I must say, that I think the General acted wisely.

"As to my request to make a reconnaissance on the morning of the 14th which the papers state was refused; the facts are, that the General had required me to reconnoitre the evening before and give my opinion as to the practicability of making a lodgement on the enemy's left, and his answer to my subsequent request was, that the movements he had already ordered would subserve the same purpose.

"We have, if I may be allowed to say it, a Commanding General in whom all the officers, with whom I have come in contact, express complete confidence. I have said this much because of the censure and of the misrepresentations which have grown out of the escape of Lee's army." (DLC-RTL).

Howard doubtless referred to a Washington dispatch of July 17, entitled "The Escape of Lee's Army," appearing in the New York *Tribune* of July 18, stating: "The President sent two dispatches to Gen. Meade a day or two before the escape of the enemy across the river, in both of which he urged the necessity of an immediate attack. In one of these dispatches he said he thought all the appearances indicated that no other occasion would speedily arise offering circumstances so favorable to us and so unfavorable to the enemy. He therefore wished a battle to be delivered at once. In the council of war which decided against attacking Gen. Lee, at a time when subsequent disclosures have shown only two-thirds of his army, perhaps forty thousand men would have been in line to receive our soldiers flushed with victory, the other third having already crossed, the Generals who pronounced against the attack were [John] Sedgwick, [George] Sykes, [William H.] French, [Alexander] Hays and [Henry W.] Slocum. Those in favor of attack were Generals Meade, Howard, Pleasonton, and [James S.] Wadsworth, temporarily commanding the First Corps, (Gen. John Newton being sick), with Generals [Andrew A.] Humphreys and [Gouverneur K.] Warren, of Gen. Meade's staff. The last named made a powerful speech, in which he showed the necessity of immediate movement. Gen. Wadsworth also, adding his voice to his vote, insisted with all his might that there was the occasion to destroy Lee's army."

To William H. Seward[1]

Hon. Sec. of State   Executive Mansion,
My dear Sir.   Washington, July 21. 1863.

I supose you can easily lay your hands upon copies of the Instructions of the Sec. of the Navy, on the subject we have in hand, & if you can please send them over to me. Yours truly

A. LINCOLN

[1] ALS, NAuE. See Lincoln to Welles, July 25, *infra*.

To Edwin M. Stanton[1]

Hon. Sec. of War   Executive Mansion,
My dear Sir: Washington, July 21, 1863.

I desire that a renewed and vigorous effort be made to raise colored forces along the shores of the Missippi.

Please consult the General-in-Chief; and if it is perceived that any acceleration of the matter can be effected, let it be done.

I think the evidence is nearly conclusive that Gen. Thomas is one of the best, if not the very best, instruments for this service. Yours truly   A. LINCOLN.

[1] ALS, DLC-Stanton Papers. See Lincoln to Grant, August 9, *infra*, concerning Lorenzo Thomas' mission to raise colored troops along the Mississippi.

To Edwin M. Stanton and Gideon Welles[1]

July 21, 1863
I desire that the bill for the late instalments of the new powder be paid by the Sec. of War & Sec. of Navy on the same principle and at the same rate as former ones have been paid.

July 21st. 1863.   A. LINCOLN.

1 Copy, DNA WR NB RG 74, Bureau of Ordnance, Diller's Powder, Letters
Received, 1862-1863. The copy of Lincoln's endorsement is on the back of a copy
of a bill rendered July 20, 1863, by Isaac R. Diller for "1000 pounds of Experi-
mental Powder made by direction of the President @ $2.—per pound.——
$2000.00," and approved July 21 by James M. Ripley as chief of ordnance, "for
one thousand dollars to be paid at the Frankfort Arsenal, and of the appropriation for the 'Purchase of Gun Powder and Lead.'" The inference is that the
Army and Navy shared equally in the payments. See Lincoln to Diller, December 15, 1862, *supra*, and Lincoln's memorandum of instructions for testing Diller's powder, November 2, 1863, *infra*.

To Gideon Welles[1]

Hon. Secretary of the Navy   Executive Mansion,
My dear Sir: Washington, July 21. 1863.

If you conveniently can send copies of all your general instructions to Naval commanders, for me to read and return, I shall be
obliged. Yours as ever   A. LINCOLN

1 ALS-P, ISLA. See Lincoln to Welles, July 25, *infra*.

To Isaac Newton[1]

July 22, 1863

I know not what the law is as to compensation of the Chief Chem-
est for the Agricultural Department; but I certainly think $2500,
per year, is, on general principles, a moderate compensation for
the services of one having Dr. Wetherill's high scientific reputation.
July 22. 1863.   A. LINCOLN

1 AES, InLTHi. See Lincoln to Newton, August 5, *infra*. The appropriations
act of February 25, 1863, set aside $90,000 to establish and equip a laboratory
and to pay the salary of the chemist for the Department of Agriculture, but
did not stipulate the salary. The appropriations act of June 25, 1864 allowed
$2,000 per annum for the salary of the chief chemist.

To John M. Schofield[1]

Major General Schofield   Executive Mansion, Washington,
St. Louis, Mo.   July 22. 1863. [10:45 A.M.]

The following despatch has been placed in my hands. Please look
to the subject of it.   A. LINCOLN.

Lexington, Mo., July 21, 1863.

Hon. S. C. Pomeroy: Under Orders, No. 63, the sheriff is arresting slaves of rebels inside our lines, and returning them in great
numbers. Can he do it? Answer.   GOULD.[2]

¹ ALS, RPB; OR, I, XXII, II, 386. The "following despatch" is not with the autograph telegram but is reproduced as printed in the *Official Records*. The time of sending written on Lincoln's telegram is in hand of the telegraph operator. Schofield's reply was received at 8 P.M.: "Your dispatch relative to arrest of slaves of rebels is received. I will attend to the matter immediately." (DLC-RTL). ² Unidentified.

To William M. Cooper¹

Mr. Wm. M. Cooper   Executive Mansion
My dear Sir: Washington July 23, 1863

I have no doubt that what you did was done with the most worthy motives; and I therefore regret that you were treated with harsh language in regard to it. Still, I have as little doubt, that the interference of outsiders, generally does more harm than good. It breeds confusion, and with it, delays and neglect.

You are conscious of having meant well, and therefore you should care no more about it. Yours truly   A. LINCOLN

¹ ALS, PHi. This communication is written on the back of a letter from William M. Cooper, president of Cooper Shop Volunteer Refreshment Saloon, Philadelphia, July 22, 1863. Cooper set forth that he had written Surgeon General Hammond on the 17th of July, "stating to him a large number of wounded soldiers had past through our city to N. York and I had taken the responsibility of having a number taking to our hospital, and cared for in a proper manner. . . . With others I thought I was doing an act of kindness. . . ." Cooper included a transcript of the reply from the Surgeon General's Office which denounced Cooper's "outrage committed upon U.S. Soldiers" and promised that "the Surgeon Genl. will take steps to prevent the sick and wounded soldiers being again put in position where their sense of discipline and duty . . . must be destroyed. . . ."

To Hamilton R. Gamble¹

His Excellency   Executive Mansion,
H. R. Gamble   Washington, July 23, 1863.

Sir   My Private Secretary has just brought me a letter saying it is a very *"cross"* one from you, about mine to Gen. Schofield, recently published in the Democrat. As I am trying to preserve my own temper, by avoiding irritants, so far as practicable, I have declined to read the cross letter. I think fit to say, however, that when I wrote the letter to Gen. Schofield, I was totally unconscious of any malice, or disrespect towards you, or of using any expression which should offend you, if seen by you. I have not seen the document in the Democrat, and therefore can not say whether it is a correct copy. Your Obt. Servt.   A. LINCOLN.

¹ ADfS, DLC-RTL. See Lincoln's letters to Schofield, May 27, July 13 and 20, *supra*. Governor Gamble's "cross" letter of July 13 is as follows:

"Your letter to Major General Schofield of the 27th of May was published in the newspapers of this city on the 27th of June last and but for my engagements in the State Convention in aiding in the passage of an ordinance of emancipation, and other pressing official duties I would sooner have attended to that most extraordinary publication.

"As a paper written by the President . . . concerning the Governor of a loyal state it is a most remarkable production and its publication is a most wanton and unmerited insult. . . . I have borne in silence the attacks . . . by newspaper writers, but when the President . . . in an official communication undertakes to characterise me, the Governor of a loyal state, as the head of a faction in that state, an answer is demanded. . . .

"I take leave to say . . . that the language of your letter . . . is in my judgment unbecoming your position. . . . But there is in your accusation . . . this further wrong, that the charge is not true. . . .

"I have earnestly desired that the military might be restrained from all wanton violence and cruelty. . . . When my views of the policy necessary to the restoration of peace and civil government have been disregarded, I have caused the facts to be made known to you in order that you might apply the remedy. . . . If making to you the proper representation of facts constituted me the head of a faction then I have been such; but if I was performing a simple duty to you, upon whom rests the ultimate responsibility for the government of the military, then my conduct was necessary for the country, and just to you, and furnished no ground for your attack upon me. . . .

"Mr President, I have disapproved of acts of your administration, but I have carefully abstained from denouncing you . . . and this because there is nothing of a 'factional' spirit in me. . . .

"You can then judge sir how grossly offensive the language of your letter is, when you say 'as' (that is, *because*) 'I could not remove Gov Gamble I had to remove General Curtis' distinctly intimating that you would have removed me if you could. . . .

"Occupying the position which I reluctantly accepted at the call of my State . . . I am obliged to say to you that your insult published over the land was most undeserved, and in our relations most unbecoming your station.

"I will not address this to you through the newspapers as I would be justified in doing at once after the publication of your letter, but will leave its publication for future consideration." (DLC-RTL).

To Robert C. Schenck[1]

Private

Major General Schenck   Executive Mansion,
My dear Sir: Washington, July 23, 1863.

Returning to the Executive Room yesterday, I was mortified to find you were gone, leaving no word of explanation. I went down stairs, as I understood, on a perfect understanding with you that you would remain till my return. I got this impression distinctly from "Edward"[2] whom I believe you know. Possibly I misunderstood him. I had been very unwell in the morning, and had scarcely tasted food during the day, till the time you saw me go down. I beg you will not believe I have treated you with intentional discourtesy. Yours as ever   A. LINCOLN

¹ ALS, owned by Roy A. Heymann, Philadelphia, Pennsylvania. Schenck answered on July 25:

"I did not for a moment suppose there was any discourtesy intended me. But I left your ante-room without waiting longer, because I was hurried by the approach of the hour when I was to take a little dinner with a friend, & get ready for the train by which I was to return to Baltimore. I left this explanation with Edward, who seems to have failed a little in making either of us clearly understood by the other

"I *do* want to see you for a few minutes; I will call the next time I can find leisure to go over." (DLC-RTL).

² Edward McManus (Burke?) doorkeeper and messenger at the White House

To Montgomery Blair¹

Hon. Post-Master-General   Executive Mansion,
Sir: Washington, July 24, 1863.

Yesterday little indorsements of mine went to you in two cases of Post-Masterships sought for widows whose husbands have fallen in the battles of this war. These cases occurring on the same day, brought me to reflect more attentively than I had before done, as to what is fairly due from us here, in the dispensing of patronage, towards the men who, by fighting our battles, bear the chief burthen of saving our country. My conclusion is that, other claims and qualifications being equal, they have the better right; and this is especially applicable to the disabled soldier, and the deceased soldier's family. Your Obt. Servt.   A. LINCOLN

¹ADfS, DLC-RTL. This letter is misdated July 27, 1863, in Hertz, II, 902. The endorsements to which Lincoln refers have not been located, but one of them was certainly concerned with the appointment of the widow of Lieutenant Colonel Melancthon Smith, Forty-fifth Illinois Infantry, killed at Vicksburg. Smith's position as postmaster at Rockford, Illinois, had been filled during his absence by Mrs. Smith as acting deputy postmaster. The New York *Tribune* and other papers on July 29, 1863, carried the story of Mrs. Smith's appointment, together with the text of Lincoln's letter to Blair of July 24.

To Ambrose E. Burnside¹

Major Genl. Burnside   Washington, D.C.,
Cincinnati, O.   July 24. 1863

What, if anything further do you hear from John Morgan?
                                   A. LINCOLN

¹ ALS, RPB. Burnside's reply, received at 11:55 P.M., reported "conflicting reports as to whereabouts" of a Confederate raid led by John Hunt Morgan: "One report places him with[in] ten miles of Cadiz Junction & the other between Antrim & Hendricsburg Shackleford close after him & we will try to have forces in his front whichever report is correct" (DLC-RTL). At 8 A.M. on July 25, Burnside telegraphed again, "I can answer your dispatch now

more fully Morgan was four miles from Cadiz at six (6) oclock moving towards the River with our people pursuing him closely & skirmishing with
him   This information is from Genl Brooks who is at Steubenville I have
requested to use the two bodies of Cavalry which I sent from here by Rail
Road to Bellair & Cadiz Junction & I hope he will capture him They have
both been ordered to close in on Morgan by Rail" (*ibid.*).

To Joseph Holt[1]

July 24, 1863

Let execution of the persons within named be suspended until Gen.
Meade can act upon the cases, who will dispose of them according
to his judgment & discretion.   A. LINCOLN

July 24. 1863.

[1]AES, DNA WR RG 153, Judge Advocate General, MM 545. Lincoln's endorsement is written on a group of six court-martial cases of men sentenced
to be shot for desertion. See Lincoln to Meade, July 30, *infra*. On July 31,
Lincoln approved General Meade's recommendation of mercy for the sentenced
men.

To Joel Parker[1]

His Excellency   Executive Mansion,
Gov. Joel Parker,   Washington, July 25. 1863.

Sir. Yours of the 21st. is received; and I have taken time, and
considered and discussed the subject with the Secretary of War, and
Provost-Marshall General, in order, if possible, to make you a more
favorable answer than I finally find myself able to do. It is a vital
point with us to not have a special stipulation with the Governor
of any one State, because it would breed trouble in many, if not
all other states; and my idea was, when I wrote you, as it still is,
to get a point of time, to which we could wait, on the reason that
we were not ready ourselves to proceed, and which might enable
you to raise the quota of your state, in whole, or in large part, without the draft. The points of time you fix, are much further off than
I had hoped. We might have got along in the way I have indicated
for twenty, or possibly thirty days. As it stands, the best I can say
is, that every volunteer you will present us within thirty days from
this date, fit and ready to be mustered into the United States service, on the usual terms, shall be, pro-tanto– an abatement of your
quota of the draft. That quota I can now state at eight thousand,
seven hundred and eighty three, (8783). No draft from New
Jersey, other than for the above quota, will be made before an
additional draft, common to the States, shall be required; and I
may add, that if we get well through with this draft, I entertain a

strong hope that any further one may never be needed. This expression of hope, however, must not be construed into a promise.

As to conducting the draft by Townships. I find it would require such a waste of labor already done, and such an additional amount of it, and such a loss of time, as to make it, I fear, inadmissible. Your Obt. Servt.   A. LINCOLN

(Copy.)

P.S. Since writing the above getting additional information, I am enabled to say that the draft may be made in sub-districts, as the enrollment has been made, or is in process of making. This will amount practically to drafting by townships as the enrollment subdistricts, are generally about the extent of townships   AL

[1] ADf and copy, DLC-RTL. The draft is dated July 24, but the copy is dated July 25, and endorsed by Lincoln "To Gov. Parker—July 25, 1863." The draft shows considerable revision in handwriting not Lincoln's. The copy does not follow the draft in all details and must have been made from Lincoln's final version. The text above follows the copy rather than the draft.

On July 21, Governor Parker had replied to Lincoln's letter of the 20th (*supra*):

"I feel quite confident that I can raise the 8000 men in sixty days, and I entertain little or no doubt that the men can be had in 90 days at the furthest.

"You speak . . . of New Jersey being behind 12000 men irrespective of those now ordered. . . . I can only say that New Jersey has sent in her own regiments more than the state has been required or authorized by the General Government to send. My only reason, however for alluding to this matter now is that I may be assured that if the 8000 men are raised in the time fixed upon, there will be no draft; that is, of course, none until a new call is made. No draft for the 12000.

"It would aid me very much . . . if I could assure the several Townships of the state that if any Township raised its quota, no draft would be made from such township. . . . All I desire on this point is that you will say that if a draft should be deemed to become necessary it should be conducted by Townships, if it is feasible so to do. The matters I desire information on are:

1.— Whether the time named in which to raise the 8000 men is satisfactory?
2.— Am I to understand, then no draft is contemplated for the 12000 men?
3.   If feasible, and if you should [find?] a draft to become necessary can it be made by Townships?" (DLC-RTL).

To Gideon Welles[1]

Hon. Secretary of the Navy: Executive Mansion, Washington,
Sir: July 25, 1863.

Certain matters have come to my notice, and considered by me, which induce me to believe, that it will conduce to the public interest for you to add to the general instructions given to our Naval Commanders, in relation to contraband trade, propositions substantially as follows, to wit:

"1st. You will avoid the reality, and as far as possible, the appearance, of using any neutral port, to watch neutral vessels, and then to dart out and seize them on their departure.

"Note—Complaint is made that this has been practiced at the Port of St. Thomas, which practice, if it exist, is disapproved, and must cease.

"2nd. You will not, in any case, detain the crew of a captured neutral vessel, or any other subject, of a neutral power on board such vessel, as prisoners of war, or otherwise, except the small number necessary as witnesses in the prize court.

"Note—The practice here forbidden is also charged to exist, which, if true, is disapproved, and must cease."

My dear Sir, it is not intended to be insinuated that you have been remiss in the performance of the arduous and responsible duties of your Department, which I take pleasure in affirming has, in your hands, been conducted with admirable success. Yet while your subordinates are, almost of necessity, brought into angry collision with the subjects of foreign States, the representatives of those States and yourself do not come into immediate contact, for the purpose of keeping the peace, in spite of such collisions. At that point there is an ultimate, and heavy responsibility upon me.

What I propose is in strict accordance with international law, and is therefore unobjectionable; while if it do no other good, it will contribute to sustain a considerable portion of the present British Ministry in their places, who, if displaced, are sure to be replaced by others more unfavorable to us. Your Obt. Servt.

ABRAHAM LINCOLN

1 LS, DNA WR NB RG 45, Executive Letters, No. 83. On August 12, Welles' *Diary* records the receipt of this letter as follows:

"August 12, Wednesday. The President addressed me a letter, directing additional instructions and of a more explicit character to our naval officers in relation to their conduct at neutral ports. In doing this, the President takes occasion to compliment the administration of the Navy in terms most commendatory and gratifying.

"The proposed instructions are in language almost identical with certain letters which have passed between Mr. Seward and Lord Lyons, which the former submitted to me and requested me to adopt. My answer was not what the Secretary and Minister had agreed between themselves should be my policy and action. The President has therefore been privately interviewed and persuaded to write me,—an unusual course with him and which he was evidently reluctant to do. He earnestly desires to keep on terms of peace with England and, as he says to me in his letter, to sustain the present Ministry, which the Secretary of State assures him is a difficult matter, requiring all his dexterity and ability,—hence constant derogatory concessions.

"In all of this Mr. Seward's subservient policy, or want of a policy, is perceptible. He has no convictions, no fixed principles, no rule of action, but is governed and moved by impulse, fancied expediency, and temporary circumstances. We injure neither ourselves nor Great Britain by an honest and firm maintenance of our rights, but Mr. Seward is in constant trepidation lest the

Navy Department or some naval officer shall embroil us in a war, or make trouble with England. Lord Lyons is cool and sagacious, and is well aware of our *premier's* infirmities, who in his fears yields everything almost before it is asked. . . ." See further Lincoln to Seward, August 10, *infra*.

To Ambrose E. Burnside[1]

Major General Burnside   Washington, D.C.,
Cincinnati, O   July 27 1863

Let me explain. In Gen. Grant's first despatch after the fall of Vicksburg, he said, among other things, he would send the Ninth Corps to you. Thinking it would be pleasant to you, I asked the Secretary of War to telegraph you the news. For some reason, never mentioned to us by Gen. Grant, they have not been sent, though we have seen out-side intimations that they took part in the expedition against Jackson. Gen. Grant is a copious worker, and fighter, but a very meagre writer, or telegrapher. No doubt he changed his purpose in regard to the Ninth Corps, for some sufficient reason, but has forgotten to notify us of it.   A. LINCOLN

[1] ALS, RPB. On June 4, the Ninth Corps was sent to reinforce Grant at Vicksburg, and after Vicksburg the corps took part in the campaign against Jackson, Mississippi. Halleck notified Burnside, 11:20 A.M., July 25, that "whether the Ninth Corps will be returned to your department or sent to General Rosecrans will depend upon the enemy's movements." (OR, I, XXIII, II, 558). On July 31, Grant ordered the corps returned to its former command at Cincinnati.

To George G. Meade[1]

Private   Executive Mansion,
Major General Meade: Washington, July 27, 1863.

I have not thrown Gen. Hooker away; and therefore I would like to know whether, it would be agreeable to you, all things considered, for him to take a corps under you, if he himself is willing to do so. Write me, in perfect freedom, with the assurance that I will not subject you to any embarrassment, by making your letter, or its contents, known to any one. I wish to know your wishes before I decide whether to break the subject to him. Do not lean a hair's breadth against your own feelings, or your judgment of the public service, on the idea of gratifying me. Yours truly

A. LINCOLN

[1] ALS, NHi; ADfS, DLC-RTL. Meade replied on July 30, "Your favor of the 27th was only last evening received. In reply I have no hesitation in saying, that if Genl. Hooker is willing to take a command under me, I shall be very glad to have the benefit of his services. I saw the other day Genl. [Gilman] Marston, who broached this subject to me, & I authorised him to say to you what I have written above." (DLC-RTL).

Memorandum:
Appointment of Arthur H. Grimshaw[1]

Executive Mansion, Washington, July 27. 1863.

To-day, my friend Jackson Grimshaw, and asks that his brother, Arthur H. Grimshaw, Col. of the 4th. Delaware Vols. may be a Brig-General.   A. LINCOLN

[1] ADS, owned by Charles W. Olsen, Chicago, Illinois. Arthur H. Grimshaw is listed in the *U.S. Official Register*, 1863, as postmaster at Wilmington, Delaware.

To Edwin M. Stanton[1]

Hon. Sec. of War: Executive Mansion,
My dear Sir: Washington, July 27, 1863.

Col. Charles F. Havelock has been mustered out of our service, as I suppose, in strict accordance with law, and the routine of the Department. With an imperfect understanding of this, he is deeply mortified by us, whose cause, I think, he has made some sacrifices to try to serve. Considering who he is, how he came here, and the apparantly abrupt, and, to Europeans, unusual mode of his dismissal, I think the order of dismissal as to him, better be revoked—allowing him his pay. If a reason is asked, place it on the ground of my order. Yours truly   A. LINCOLN

[1] ALS, owned by Eli Moschcowitz, New York City. Charles F. Havelock was an English officer appointed assistant aide-de-camp to McClellan on November 23, 1861. Instead of being mustered out, he was permitted to resign as of July 31, 1863.

To Edwin M. Stanton[1]

July 27, 1863

Will the Sec. of War please glance over these papers, and inform me on what ground Dr. Phillips' nomination was withheld from the Senate, and what objection there is, if any, to his re-appointment?   A. LINCOLN

July 27. 1863.

[1] AES, DLC-RTL. Lincoln's endorsement is written on a letter from Assistant Adjutant General James A. Hardie to Assistant Surgeon James Phillips, April 23, 1863, informing him that his commission expired on March 4, and that his name was not submitted to the Senate for reappointment. On July 28, Stanton endorsed in reply: "Dr. Phillips was appointed in the place of Dr [James] King who was expected to be retired. It happened that Dr King was not retired and therefore the nomination fell. Dr Phillips is not reappointed because he is not a citizen of the United States but is believed to be a British

subject. As the subjects of Great Britain claim under the sanction of their government exemptions from Military Service it is not deemed expedient to appoint them to offices and open a door to the interference of their Government in case they should be displeased at any time with action of their military superiors."

To Edwin M. Stanton[1]

Secretary of War please see & hear Mr. Ordway, of New-Hampshire. A. LINCOLN
July 27. 1863.

[1] ALS, New York Avenue Presbyterian Church, Washington, D.C. Nehemiah G. Ordway, chairman of the Republican Central Committee of New Hampshire, was in Washington "in relation to the subject of the equalization of the draft" in New Hampshire (OR, III, III, 808), and according to a letter from Hiram Rollins to Lincoln, July 14, 1863, to obtain a brigadier generalship for Colonel Walter Harriman of the Eleventh New Hampshire Infantry (DLC-RTL).

To Edwin M. Stanton[1]

Let this appointment be made if no substantial reason to the contrary is known. A. LINCOLN
July 27, 1863.

[1] AES, IHi. Lincoln's endorsement is written on a letter of Brigadier General William W. Orme to Stanton, Vicksburg, July 10, 1863, recommending appointment of Captain John L. Routt, Company E, Ninety-fourth Illinois Volunteers, as assistant quartermaster. Routt was appointed assistant quartermaster on July 28, 1863.

To Edwin M. Stanton and Henry W. Halleck[1]

[c. July 27, 1863]

I think the general object of the within is a very important one, while I can not speak as to particulars. I hope the Secretary of War & General-in-Chief will give it an attentive consideration.

As the rebellion grows weaker, it will run more & more into guarrillaism, thus increasing the need for such a force as proposed A. LINCOLN

[1] AES, NHi. Lincoln's endorsement is written on the back of a letter from General William S. Rosecrans, dated Winchester, Tennessee, July 27, 1863, recommending the formation of a new mounted force to be enlisted by General Lovell H. Rousseau. The proposal was further advocated by General Rousseau in a letter to Stanton, August 7, 1863, but Halleck disapproved the proposal on August 10: "I fully appreciate the importance of increasing the cavalry force of the army, but I see no advantages in this project over the usual plan of enlisting. . . . It greatly increases the number of officers, already out of pro-

portion to the men. Moreover, it carries on its face the idea of a special organization for a special purpose and with a special commander. . . ." (OR, I, XXIII, II, 599). See Lincoln to Stanton, August 17, *infra*.

To Mary Todd Lincoln[1]

Mrs. A. Lincoln
New-York.

Washington,
July 28 1863

Bob went to Fort-Monroe & only got back to-day. Will start to you at 11. AM to-morrow. All well

A. LINCOLN

1 ALS, RPB. This telegram is written in pencil on a slip of lined paper pasted on the bottom of the following telegram from Mrs. Lincoln, received from New York at 6 P.M. on July 28, addressed to Edward McManus, doorkeeper and messenger at the White House: "Did Robert leave this morning for New York. I hope the President is well   Answer this immediately."

To Edwin M. Stanton[1]

Hon Secretary of War
My dear Sir:

Executive Mansion
Washington July 28 1863

A young son of the Senator Brown of Mississippi, not yet twenty, as I understand, was wounded, and made a prisoner at Gettysburg. His mother is sister [of] Mrs P. R. Fendall, of this city. Mr Fendall, on behalf of himself and family, asks that he and they may have charge of the boy, to cure him up, being responsible [for] his person and good behavior. Would it not be rather a grateful and graceful thing to let them have him? Yours truly   A LINCOLN

1 Copy, DLC-RTL. Brackets are in the source. In the Lincoln Papers there is a letter dated July 18, 1863, from Mary L. Fendall to Mrs. Stephen P. Lee, whom she addresses, "Dear Cousin": "The various reports we heard of the great suffering of the wounded at Gettysburg . . . made me so anxious concerning the fate of Robert . . . I decided to go & see for myself. . . . Everything in Gettysburg is in the utmost confusion. No provisions of any kind can be obtained & the atmosphere of the whole town is absolutely stifling. . . . If it is quite impossible for us to bring Robert home, don't you think we might get him transferred to a Hospital in this city where we could give him the care he so sorely needs. . . ."
No further correspondence concerning the case has been found. Captain Robert Y. Brown of the Eighteenth Mississippi, CSA, a son of Albert G. Brown, was exchanged and re-entered the Confederate Army in June, 1864.

To Edward Bates[1]

Attorney General please have a pardon made out in this case.
July 29, 1863

A. LINCOLN

1 AES, DNA RG 204, U.S. Pardon Attorney, A 400. Lincoln's endorsement is written on a letter from Robert F. Paine, Cleveland, Ohio, June 23, 1863, asking pardon for Amos Burden, convicted of forging land claims.

To Henry W. Halleck[1]

Executive Mansion,
Major General Halleck: Washington, July 29, 1863.

Seeing Gen. Meade's despatch of yesterday to yourself, causes, me to fear that he supposes the government here is demanding of him to bring on a general engagement with Lee as soon as possible. I am claiming no such thing of him. In fact, my judgment is against it; which judgment, of course, I will yield if yours and his are the contrary. If he could not safely engage Lee at Williamsport, it seems absurd to suppose he can safely engage him now, when he has scarcely more than two thirds of the force he had at Williamsport, while it must be, that Lee has been re-inforced. True, I desired Gen. Meade to pursue Lee across the Potomac, hoping, as has proved true, that he would thereby clear the Baltimore and Ohio Railroad, and get some advantages by harrassing him on his retreat. These being past, I am unwilling he should now get into a general engagement on the impression that we here are pressing him; and I shall be glad for you to so inform him, unless your own judgment is against it. Yours truly A. LINCOLN.

[1] ADfS, DLC-RTL; LS, IHi. General Meade telegraphed Halleck at 3 P.M. on July 28:

"I am making every effort to prepare this army for an advance. . . . I am in hopes to commence the movement to-morrow, when I shall first throw over a cavalry force to feel for the enemy, and cross the infantry as fast as possible. . . .

"No reliable intelligence of the position of the enemy has been obtained. He pickets the Rappahannock from Fredericksburg to Rappahannock Station. These pickets, however, seem to be mere 'lookouts,' to warn him of my approach.

"Contradictory reports . . . place the main body, some at Gordonsville, others say at Staunton and Charlottesville, and some assert the retreat has been extended to Richmond. My own expectation is that he will be found behind the line of the Rapidan. . . .

"P.S. 4 p.m.—A scout just returned . . . reports the enemy have repaired the railroad bridge across the Rapidan, and are using the road to Culpeper Court-House; that Lee has been re-enforced by D. H. Hill, reported with 10,000 men, and that he intends to make a stand at Culpeper or in its vicinity." (OR, I, XXVII, I, 103-104).

At 10 A.M., Halleck communicated Lincoln's note to Meade (*ibid.*, p. 105).

To Edwin M. Stanton[1]

Hon. Sec. of War: Executive Mansion,
Sir: Washington, July 29, 1863

Can we not renew the effort to organize a force to go to Western Texas? Please consult with the General-in-Chief on the subject. If the Governor of New-Jersey shall furnish any new regiments, might not they be put into such an expedition. Please think of it. I believe no local object is now more desirable. Yours truly

A. LINCOLN

¹ ALS-P, ISLA; copy, DNA RG 108, HQA, Letters Received, Box 63, No. 705. The occasion for this note is indicated by the entry in Welles' *Diary* on July 31, 1863: "Seward wished me to meet him and the President . . . to consider the subject of the immediate occupation of some portion of Texas. . . . The European combination, or concerted understanding, against us begins to be developed and appreciated. The use of the Rio Grande to evade the blockade, and the establishment of regular lines of steamers to Matamoros did not disturb some of our people, but certain movements and recent givings-out of the French have alarmed Seward, who says Louis Napoleon is making an effort to get Texas. . . ."

To Edwin M. Stanton¹

Executive Mansion,
Hon. Secretary of War.   Washington, D.C. July 29, 1863.

Dear Sir: I understand the Gov. of New Hampshire is anxious in regard to trouble about the draft, and desires that the 5th N.H. should be sent home on that account. The regiment is now here, going down the Potomac, somewhere, and contains, as I hear, only 115 men. Yours truly,   A. LINCOLN

¹ Tracy, p. 228. The Fifth New Hampshire was ordered to Point Lookout, Maryland, on July 26, but its destination was changed to Concord, New Hampshire, where it reported at draft rendezvous on August 3 (Otis F. R. Waite, *New Hampshire in the Great Rebellion*, p. 288).

To Edwin M. Stanton¹

Sec. of War, please respond, & give him the "Inquiry"
July 29. 1863.   A. LINCOLN

¹ AES, DNA WR RG 108, HQA, Letters Received, 703 (formerly P 115). Lincoln's endorsement is written on a telegram from General Robert H. Milroy, July 29, 1863, "I have been here in arrest over one month Will you permit me to come to Washington[?]" Further endorsements conclude with an unsigned order to "Col. Townsend to issue the order for a Ct of Inquiry to meet in this city."

To John P. Usher¹

Send me an appointment according to the above   A. LINCOLN
July 29. 1863.

¹ AES, DNA NR RG 48, Applications, Indian Agencies, Miscellaneous, Box 1269. Lincoln's endorsement is written on a memorandum in an unidentified

hand, "Henry W DePuy to be an Indian agent for the Indians on the Upper Mo. and the country ajacent thereto." See Lincoln's endorsement of June 3, *supra.*

To Francis P. Blair, Sr.[1]

Hon. F. P. Blair   Executive Mansion,
My dear Sir   Washington, July 30, 1863.

Yours of to-day with inclosure is received. Yesterday I commenced trying to get up an expedition for Texas. I shall do the best I can. Meantime I would like to know who is the great man Alexander, that talks so oracularly about "if the president keeps his word" and Banks not having "capacity to run an omnibus on Broadway." How has this Alexander's immense light been obscured hitherto? Yours truly   A. LINCOLN

[1] ADfS, DLC-RTL. Francis P. Blair, Sr., enclosed in a letter of July 30 the following from William Alexander, New York City, July 28, 1863:

"As there is now a chance to get some relief for the union men of Texas, (that is if the President, who promised that an expedition should be sent there as soon as Vicksburg should be taken, keeps his word,) I must trouble you again on the subject. It is all important that, as a preliminary move, Texas should be taken from the paralysing rule of Banks, and made into a separate military District or Department. Banks is an incapable as well as an incurable. He has not the capacity to run an omnibus on Broadway. So long as Texas is in his Department I shall remain absent. Now I should prefer to have a separate Department created, to consist solely of Texas, and to have Frank sent out to Western Texas to command it. I am here as the secret agent of the leading union men of western Texas, and am anxious to do anything in my power to bring it about that Frank should at once be sent there to take command. . . ." (DLC-RTL).

Blair replied on August 1 to Lincoln's query concerning Alexander: "He is, I understand, a Texan of talent, a lawyer, one of the first Union men driven out & made the agent of like sufferers. . . ." (*Ibid.*).

To George G. Meade[1]

                         Executive Mansion,
Major-General Meade: Washington, July 30, 1863.

Please suspend execution of Peter Schalowsky, Company B, Forty-fifth New York Regiment Volunteers, till further order and send me record of his conviction.   A. LINCOLN.

[1] Tarbell (Appendix), p. 376. General Meade answered on the same day: "The execution of the sentence in the case of private 'Peter Schalowsky' of Company 'B' 45th Regt New York vols was suspended until further orders on the 28th inst. The record of the court martial in the case was forwarded for your action on the same date." (DLC-RTL).

Private Peter Schalowsky was one of several soldiers condemned to death whose execution was ordered suspended by Lincoln (see Lincoln to Holt, July 24, *supra*), and on July 31, remitted in accordance with Meade's recommendation.

Order of Retaliation[1]

Executive Mansion, Washington D.C July 30. 1863

It is the duty of every government to give protection to its citizens, of whatever class, color, or condition, and especially to those who are duly organized as soldiers in the public service. The law of nations and the usages and customs of war as carried on by civilized powers, permit no distinction as to color in the treatment of prisoners of war as public enemies. To sell or enslave any captured person, on account of his color, and for no offence against the laws of war, is a relapse into barbarism and a crime against the civilization of the age.

The government of the United States will give the same protection to all its soldiers, and if the enemy shall sell or enslave anyone because of his color, the offense shall be punished by retaliation upon the enemy's prisoners in our possession.

It is therefore ordered that for every soldier of the United States killed in violation of the laws of war, a rebel soldier shall be executed; and for every one enslaved by the enemy or sold into slavery, a rebel soldier shall be placed at hard labor on the public works and continued at such labor until the other shall be released and receive the treatment due to a prisoner of war

ABRAHAM LINCOLN

[1] DS, DNA WR RG 94, Adjutant General, Letters Received, P 518. This order, drafted by the War Department and signed by Lincoln, was issued by the Adjutant General's Office on July 31, 1863, as *General Orders No. 252.*

To Frederick VII[1]

July 31, 1863

Abraham Lincoln
President of the United States of America.

To His Majesty Frederick VII.
    King of Denmark

Great and Good Friend: I have received the letter which Your Majesty was pleased to address to me on the 7th instant conveying the melancholy tidings of the demise on the 29th ultimo of His Royal Hig[h]ness the Hereditary Prince Frederick Ferdinand, of Denmark, Your Majesty's beloved Uncle.

I participate in the grief occasioned by this sad event, and offer to Your Majesty and to Your Majesty's Royal Family my sincere condolence

May God have Your Majesty always in His safe and holy keeping Your Good Friend ABRAHAM LINCOLN.

Washington, 31st. July. 1863.

By the President

WILLIAM H. SEWARD Secretary of State.

¹ Copy, DNA FS RG 59, Communications to Foreign Sovereigns and States, III, 225.

To Stephen A. Hurlbut¹

Executive Mansion,

My dear General Hurlbut: Washington, July 31, 1863.

Your letter by Mr. Dana was duly received. I now learn that your resignation has reached the War Department. I also learn that an active command has been assigned you by Gen. Grant. The Secretary of War and Gen. Halleck are very partial to you, as you know I also am. We all wish you to re-consider the question of resigning; not that we would wish to retain you greatly against your wish and interest, but that your decision may be at least a very well considered one.

I understand that Senator Sebastian² of Arkansas thinks of offering to resume his place in the Senate. Of course the Senate, and not I, would decide whether to admit or reject him. Still I should feel great interest in the question. It may be so presented as to be one of the very greatest national importance; and it may be otherwise so presented, as to be of no more than temporary personal consequence to him.

The emancipation proclamation applies to Arkansas. I think it is valid in law, and will be so held by the courts. I think I shall not retract or repudiate it. Those who shall have tasted actual freedom I believe can never be slaves, or quasi slaves again. For the rest, I believe some plan, substantially being gradual emancipation, would be better for both white and black. The Missouri plan, recently adopted, I do not object to on account of the time for *ending* the institution; but I am sorry the *beginning* should have been postponed for seven years, leaving all that time to agitate for the repeal of the whole thing. It should begin at once, giving at least the new-born, a vested interest in freedom, which could not be taken away. If Senator Sebastian could come with something of this sort from Arkansas, I at least should take great interest in his case; and I believe a single individual will have scarcely done the world so great a service. See him, if you can, and read this to him; but charge him to not make it public for the present. Write me again.

Yours very truly.   A. LINCOLN

1 ADfS, DLC-RTL. Charles A. Dana, who had been on an inspection tour under special instructions from the War Department, brought a letter from General Stephen A. Hurlbut dated July 10, as follows:

"I take the liberty of writing this unofficial letter by Mr. Dana now on his way to Washington, that you may more fully understand the reasons of my resignation which will soon reach you.

"I believe the war as war is practically over. . . . My duties and responsibilities for the last six months have been peculiarly trying. . . . Yet . . . this and much more I would freely undergo did I believe it necessary.

"You are aware that I am very comfortably poor, in fact dependent on my profession.

"I am rapidly losing the faculty of practice and when I return unless it is done soon, shall be but a fourth rate lawyer. . . .

"It is from no disgust at the service—from no difficulties with my superiors. . . . I urgently therefore request that my resignation now passing through official channels may be accepted. . . .

"You will believe that I am perfectly sincere in this—and you too will believe that from the midst of an unbounded corruption, and with the largest opportunities for private gain, I come out of this place with clean hands. . . ." (DLC-RTL).

Hurlbut's resignation was not accepted.

2 On July 20, B. W. Sharp wrote Lincoln from Memphis that William K. Sebastian "former (and present Senator Elect from the State of Ark) senator from the state of Ark . . . informed me that it is his intention upon the next meeting of Congress to be present & claim his seat. . . . The leading men of the state are desirous that he should take this course; I believe Judge S. to be a consistent Union man. . . ." (DLC-RTL). On September 8, Hurlbut wrote Lincoln "I have seen Mr. Sebastian and shown him your letter. . . . I doubt if Sebastian has nerve enough, to accept the necessities of the times. . . ." (*Ibid.*).

To Samuel W. Moulton[1]

Executive Mansion,

My Dear Sir   Washington, July 31, 1863.

There has been a good deal of complaint against you by your superior officers of the Provost Marshal General's Department and your removal has been strongly urged on the ground of "persistent disobedience of orders and neglect of duty." Firmly convinced as I am of the patriotism of your motives, I am unwilling to do anything in your case which may seem unnecessarily harsh, or at variance with the feelings of personal respect and esteem, with which I have always regarded you. I consider your services in your district valuable, and should be sorry to lose them. It is unnecessary for me to state however, that when differences of opinion arise between officers of the Government, the ranking officer must be obeyed. You of course recognize as clearly as I do the importance of this rule. I hope you will conclude to go on in your present position under the regulations of the Department. I wish you would write to me. I am very truly your friend and Obt Servt

[A. LINCOLN]

[1] Df, DLC-RTL. The draft is in John Hay's handwriting. Samuel W. Moulton, enrollment commissioner for the Tenth District of Illinois at Shelbyville, tendered his resignation on August 11, 1863:

"Your very kind favor of the 31st Ultimo was missent & was not received until to day.

"I regret very much that my superior officers have had cause to complain of my seeming neglect of duty. I confess that I have not been constantly at my post on account of sickness in my family & some matters of business that I could not possibly neglect. . . . My heart is in the work & . . . I want to act honorably. . . . Would it not be better for me to resign & have another appointed who can better discharge his duty by more constant attendance. . . .

"I therefore . . . enclose . . . my resignation. . . ." (*Ibid.*).

To James S. Rollins[1]

Private   Executive Mansion,
Hon. James S. Rollins   Washington, August, 1863

Yours in reference to Gen. Sterling Price, is received. If he voluntarily returns and takes the oath of allegiance to the United States before the next meeting of Congress, I will pardon him, if you shall then wish me to do so. Yours truly   A. Lincoln

[1] ALS-F, Kansas City, Missouri, *Star*, October 20, 1929. On July 26, 1863, Representative James S. Rollins wrote Lincoln from Columbia, Missouri:

"Major Genl Sterling Price is no smarter than he ought to be, or he never would have been caught in this rebellion. . . .

"He started out a Union man, and I have every reason to believe, his vanity and his ignorance, induced him to drift into the whirlpool of treason.

"Now that the State of Missouri is about fixed—I am inclined to the opinion, that Price would be glad to quit—lay down his arms, and come home. . . . Rest assured (altho' I have no respect for the intellect or the intelligence of the man) it would be a great point gained to get him back. Can't you offer him a free pardon if he will return? If you will say so—I'll try and induce some of his particular friends—to go and have an interview with him. . . .

"We are *convalescent* in Missouri (All safe for the Union The 'Nigger' about played out), and would be well in a short time, if we could just get clear of the reckless Dutch, and Radical Doctors!" (DLC-RTL).

To George Stoneman[1]

                                                  Executive Mansion,
Gen. Stoneman.   Washington, Aug. 1863.

I am appealed to in behalf of E. S. Doty, Co. A. 1st. Vermont Cavalry, whose friends do not know where he is but fear he has been executed, or is under sentence of death, somewhere, as a deserter. Records in these cases do not necessarily come, & in this case, none is here. Please ascertain, & inform me if you can, how the case stands. Yours truly   A. Lincoln

[1] ALS, OClWHi. Private Ezra S. Doty is listed on the roster of his regiment as "missing in action July 3, 1863." No reply from General Stoneman has been found.

To Hiram Barney[1]

Hon. Hiram Barney   Executive Mansion,
My dear Sir: Washington, August 1, 1863.

The bearer of this tells me he resides in your City, and has so resided for many years; that he has served for us in this war three months; that he has a son now a Colonel in the service under Gen. Corcoran, which son has served ever since the commencement of the war; that he also has a brother & a first cousin in the war. His name is Patrick Murphy, and he now seeks employment in the Custom-House. I shall be glad if you can find it for him. Yours truly   A LINCOLN

[1] ALS, RPAB. The *U.S. Official Register*, 1863, lists Patrick Murphy as "Night Inspector" in the New York Custom House at an annual salary of $730.

Endorsement Concerning William T. Smithson[1]

August 1, 1863

The bearer of this says that William T. Smithson is imprisoned at the "Old Capitol" and has been indicted indicted [*sic*] in the District Court for treason. He asks to be turned over to the Civil Court according to a recent Act of Congress. Please consider the case & dispose of it according to law.   A. LINCOLN

Aug. 1, 1863.

[1] AES, The Rosenbach Company, Philadelphia and New York. Lincoln's endorsement is written on the back of a letter from Grant Goodrich, July 6, 1863, introducing J. G. Hamilton, "a loyal man & true patriot," whose brother-in-law, William T. Smithson, had been imprisoned. The document carries another endorsement in unidentified handwriting as follows: "Please see 'Statutes at Large' 1863; Chapter LXXXI, Sections 2 & 3—pages 755 & 756." Smithson had been arrested early in the war and released upon his oath. In May 1863 he was again imprisoned for his dealings in Confederate securities.

To Horatio Seymour[1]

"Cypher"   Washington, D.C.,
His Excellency Gov. Seymour   Aug. 1. 1863
Albany, N.Y.

By what day may I expect your communication to reach me? Are you anxious about any part, except the City & vicinity?
                                                     A. LINCOLN

[1] ALS, RPB. On August 1, Governor Seymour telegraphed Provost Marshal General James B. Fry, "Mr. Waterbury told me on his return from Washington that the Draft would not be made in New York and Brooklyn without some

notice being given to me. I see it is stated in some of the Journals that it will [be] made at once. I trust this is not so. I have in preparation a letter to the President which will reach him next week probably on Tuesday next" (DLC-RTL).

On August 3 Seymour replied to Lincoln's telegram, "My letter will reach you on Wednesday. I wish all drafts delayed, particularly in New York & Brooklyn." (*Ibid.*). See further Lincoln to Seymour, August 7, *infra*.

To John G. Foster[1]

Executive Mansion, Washington, August 3, 1863.

Major General Foster, or whoever may be in command of the Military Department, with Head Quarters at Fort-Monroe, Va.

If Dr. Wright, on trial at Norfolk, has been, or shall be convicted, send me a transcript of his trial and conviction, and do not let execution be done upon him, until my further order.

A. LINCOLN

[1] ALS, RPB. General Foster's reply was received at 5:33 P.M.: "Your orders will be strictly obeyed The trial is concluded. Gen [James] Naglee informs me that the proceedings findings & sentence have been forwarded to you for your revision and approval." (DLC-RTL). Dr. David M. Wright of Norfolk, Virginia, shot and killed Second Lieutenant Anson L. Sanborn of the First U.S. Colored Volunteers, who was marching at the head of his company on Main Street in Norfolk, July 11, 1863. Convicted of murder, Wright was executed on October 23. See further Lincoln to Foster, August 28, and to John P. Gray, September 10 and 13, *infra*.

Memorandum:
Appointment of George T. Harris[1]

As soon as I consistently can, I wish to oblige Bishop McIlvaine
Aug. 3. 1863.   A. LINCOLN

[1] AES, DNA WR RG 94, U.S. Military Academy 1863, Box 81, No. 82. Lincoln's endorsement is written on a letter from Salmon P. Chase, July 3, 1863, enclosing two letters from Bishop Charles P. McIlvaine recommending appointment of George T. Harris to West Point. See also Lincoln's memorandum of October 24, 1862, *supra*.

To Edwin M. Stanton[1]

I believe the subject mentioned within deserves attention. Does the Sec. of War know to whom, or where, to refer it? A. LINCOLN
Aug. 3. 1863.

[1] AES, IHi. Lincoln's endorsement appears on a letter from A. J. Hardee, Washington, July 21, 1863:
"Allow me to ask your consideration in behalf of the contrabands employed repairing Roads in and around Washington.

"They experience much suffering from the delay in receiving their wages due them for some time past. All of them are very much in want of clothing and almost every necessary of life. A number of them have families depending on them who must suffer very much unless they receive the pay due them speedily

"They have worked faithfully an have suffered uncomplainingly. Satisfied that if their condition was represented to your Excelency that from your known kindness of Heart that you would take some action to relieve their necessities."

Other endorsements indicate that the letter was referred to Major General Samuel P. Heintzelman, commander of the Department of Washington.

To James H. Van Alen[1]

Executive Mansion,
My dear General   Washington, August 3, 1863.
Your letter, without date, announcing your resignation, has been on my table some considerable time. I hope it may be a sufficient appology for not replying sooner, that it was not a business letter, requiring prompt attention; particularly as I am closely pressed with business matters. I am grateful for the Military service you have performed, which has been valuable to the country and honorable to yourself; and I regret the illness which has compelled you to discontinue it. I trust that illness, may speedily be superseded by renewed health, if, indeed, it has not already been. Since you wrote, as you anticipated, Port-Hudson has fallen. By that, and our other sucesses, I am greatly encouraged; still, we must not flag in our efforts, till the end shall be more clearly in view than it yet is   Yours truly   A. LINCOLN

[1] ALS-P, ISLA. Colonel James H. Van Alen of the Third New York Cavalry resigned on July 14, 1863. His undated letter to Lincoln cites "continued illness which forbids . . . my return . . . to . . . the field. . . ." and concludes with "my earnest hope that your Administration will be signalized by the complete restoration . . . of the peaceful authority of the Government." (DLC-RTL).

To John A. Bingham[1]

Hon. John A. Bingham   Executive Mansion
Cadiz, Ohio.   Washington D.C. Aug. 4. 1863
It is indispensable for us to have a judge at Key-West, as soon as possible. Please inform me whether you will go.   A. LINCOLN

[1] ALS, RPB. John A. Bingham replied on August 5: "I have the honor . . . to say . . . that I cannot *immediately* accept and enter upon the duties of the office . . . at Key West, and therefore feel constrained to say that if . . . the public interests require that the office should be filled at once, I respectfully decline the appointment so kindly tendered me. . . ." (DLC-RTL). The *U.S. Official Register*, 1863, lists William W. Lawrence of Ohio as judge of the U.S. District Court at Key West, Florida.

Memorandum:
Appointment of Charles J. Hoyt[1]

August 4, 1863

The within recommendations seem ample; but as they do not allude to the reason of Major Hoyt's rejection by the Senate, they do not cover the whole ground. If any Senator will say to me in writing that he fully understands what caused his rejection, & that things are so changed that he now believes Major Hoyt would be confirmed, I should be disposed to re-nominate him & would do so if the service should then be in need of additional forces in the Pay Master Department.   A. LINCOLN.

August 4, 1863.

[1] Hertz, II, 904. The appointment of Charles J. Hoyt of New York as an additional paymaster was rejected by the Senate on February 27, 1863. Reappointed as of September 29, he again failed of Senate confirmation and resigned April 28, 1864. A letter from Thomas P. May, Louisiana Republican and editor of the New Orleans *Times*, May 2, 1863, introduced Major Charles J. Hoyt with the following comment: "I merely wish to state that a loyal Planter of Louisiana heartily endorses him in opposition to malignant secession influences which I believe have been brought to bear against him in order to secure his removal as Paymaster in this Department. . . ." (DLC-RTL).

Memorandum: Pardon of Abraham Lower[1]

Executive Mansion, Washington, August 4, 1863.

Let Abraham Lower, 72nd Regiment Pa Vols, now under arrest in Philadelphia for desertion be pardoned and discharged from the military service of the United States.   A. LINCOLN

[1] DS, owned by Charles W. Olsen, Chicago, Illinois. Sergeant Abraham Lower, Company A, was discharged by special order on August 5, 1863.

To Nathaniel P. Banks[1]

Executive Mansion, Washington,

My dear General Banks   August 5, 1863.

Being a poor correspondent is the only apology I offer for not having sooner tendered my thanks for your very successful, and very valuable military operations this year. The final stroke in opening the Mississippi never should, and I think never will, be forgotten.

Recent events in Mexico, I think, render early action in Texas more important than ever. I expect, however, the General-in-Chief, will address you more fully upon this subject.[2]

Governor Boutwell read me to-day that part of your letter to him, which relates to Louisiana affairs. While I very well know

what I would be glad for Louisiana to do, it is quite a different thing for me to assume direction of the matter. I would be glad for her to make a new Constitution recognizing the emancipation proclamation, and adopting emancipation in those parts of the state to which the proclamation does not apply. And while she is at it, I think it would not be objectionable for her to adopt some practical system by which the two races could gradually live themselves out of their old relation to each other, and both come out better prepared for the new. Education for young blacks should be included in the plan. After all, the power, or element, of "contract" may be sufficient for this probationary period; and, by it's simplicity, and flexibility, may be the better.

As an anti-slavery man I have a motive to desire emancipation, which pro-slavery men do not have; but even they have strong enough reason to thus place themselves again under the shield of the Union; and to thus perpetually hedge against the recurrence of the scenes through which we are now passing.

Gov. Shepley has informed me that Mr. Durant is now taking a registry, with a view to the election of a Constitutional convention in Louisiana. This, to me, appears proper. If such convention were to ask my views, I could present little else than what I now say to you. I think the thing should be pushed forward, so that if possible, it's mature work may reach here by the meeting of Congress.

For my own part I think I shall not, in any event, retract the emancipation proclamation; nor, as executive, ever return to slavery any person who is free by the terms of that proclamation, or by any of the acts of Congress.

If Louisiana shall send members to Congress, their admission to seats will depend, as you know, upon the respective Houses, and not upon the President.

If these views can be of any advantage in giving shape, and impetus, to action there, I shall be glad for you to use them prudently for that object. Of course you will confer with intelligent and trusty citizens of the State, among whom I would suggest Messrs. Flanders, Hahn, and Durant; and to each of whom I now think I may send copies of this letter. Still it is perhaps better to not make the letter generally public. Yours very truly

A. LINCOLN

[Endorsement]

Copies sent to Messrs. Flanders, Hahn & Durant, each indorsed as follows.

The within is a copy of a letter to Gen. Banks. Please observe my directions to him. Do not mention the paragraph about Mexico.

Aug. 6. 1863.   A. LINCOLN

[1] ALS, IHi; copy and AES, DLC-RTL. The endorsement as printed at the end of the letter is written on the copy preserved in the Lincoln Papers. See Lincoln to Flanders, August 6, *infra*. Banks' letter to George S. Boutwell has not been located.

On September 5, Banks acknowledged receipt of Lincoln's letter:

"It gives me pleasure to acknowledge the receipt of your letter relating to the re-organization of Government in the State of Louisiana—and to say that I shall not only execute your orders, but that I cordially concur in your views. . . .

"The expedition ordered by the department of war for the re-establishment of the American Flag in Texas is now nearly ready. The advance sailed for the Sabine Pass at midnight the 4th instant. My purpose is to move upon the Sabine Lake, marching to Beaumont, thence to Liberty Houston and Galveston. Galveston will fall by a movement in its rear. In possession of Galveston and Houston the whole state is in our possession. . . . All depends on the movement upon the Sabine which sailed last night under command of Major General Franklin. . . . The Sabine is the weak and the key point of Texas for assault. From thence, if safely landed we can secure every position to the Rio Grande. Let me say that if we land safely your utmost expectations will be realized. . . ." (DLC-RTL).

[2] Halleck telegraphed Banks at 12:30 P.M., August 6, "There are important reasons why our flag should be restored in some point of Texas with the least possible delay. Do this by land at Galveston, at Indianola, or at any other point you may deem preferable. . . ." (OR, I, XXVI, I, 672).

To the Cincinnati *Gazette*[1]

"Cypher"   Washington, D.C.,
Cincinnati Gazette: August 5. 1863
    Please send me your present posting as to Kentucky election.

                                                               A. LINCOLN

[1] ALS, RPB. Richard Smith's reply for the *Gazette* was received at 10:45 P.M.: "The union state ticket is elected by a very large majority over twenty thousand. . . . official reports come in slowly now that the general result is ascertained & conceded by all parties to be great union triumph. Legislature decided union majority. . . . Congressional indications are the whole delegation is union. . . . Green Clay Smith . . . was elected over [John W.] Menzies against the opposition of the whole Ky press. . . . Brutus Clay . . . has two thousand majority. . . " (DLC-RTL).

Memorandum:
Appointment of William F. Smith[1]

William F. Smith, City of New-York. Born April 12. 1846. His mother very much desires his appointment to West Point.

August. 5. 1863   A. LINCOLN

1 AES, DNA WR RG 94, U.S. Military Academy, 1864, Box 83, No. 425. Lincoln's endorsement is written on a recommendation signed by Smith's teacher George S. Parker. William F. Smith entered West Point in 1865 and graduated in 1869.

To Isaac Newton[1]

Commissioner of Agriculture	Executive Mansion,
Sir:	Washington, Aug. 5, 1863.

About a year ago Capt. Isaac R. Diller came to me with a proposition in regard to a new compound of gunpowder, the ingredients and mode of compounding, being a secret. It promised important advantages, which would be very valuable, if the promise were made good. But he did not wish to give the government the secret; nor did the government wish to buy it, without a test of it's value. For this object, the manufacture of a quantity of it became indispensable; and this again required the service of a good Chemist. Dr. Charles M. Wetherill, Chemist in your Department, was an acquaintance of Capt. Diller, and was sought by him to aid in the manufacturing of the powder. As I remember I requested you to allow him to do so, which you did. A small quantity was manufactured, and proved so far satisfactory that Capt. now, Admiral Dahlgren advised the making a larger quantity so as to test it for artillery use. I consented, and procured the Secretary of War and Secretary of the Navy, to advance, from time [to time], sums amounting in the whole to five thousand dollars, from funds under their discretionary control. Dr. Wetherill's service was again required, and again obtained, perhaps, so far as you are concerned, at my request. At the time, nothing was said, or thought of, so far as I remember, as to his receiving his salary at your Department, while engaged at the powder. Now, being brought to my mind, it seems reasonable he should receive his salary for that time, which he tells is refused. The manufacturer of the powder has required the building a good deal of expensive machinery, leaving the five thousand dollar fund no reliance for Dr. Wetherell. In fact, I suppose Capt. Diller thought the government was furnishing Dr. Wetherell, as one of it's officers, to make the experiment.

Dr. Wetherell presents another question, which is as to the amount of his permanent or general Salary. I see that the law fixes the salaries of a class to which the chemist belongs "corresponding to the salaries of similar officers in other Departments" and I do not see that the law assigns me any duty or discretion about it. All I can do is to give a sort of legal opinion, that his salary should be fixed according to the law. I do wish these questions could be settled, without further difficulty. I do not know what has been fixed as the salary of similar officers in other Departments; but I suppose this can not be hard to ascertain. Yours truly

A. LINCOLN

[1] ALS, CtSoP. See Lincoln to Diller, December 15, 1862, and to Newton, July 22, 1863, *supra;* also Lincoln to Diller, November 7, 1863, *infra.*

To Benjamin F. Flanders[1]

Hon B. F. Flanders.   August 6, 1863

The within is a copy of a letter to Gen. Banks. Please observe my direction to him. Do not mention the paragraph about Mexico.

Aug. 6. 1863.   A. LINCOLN

[1] AES, LU-Flanders Papers. Lincoln's endorsement is written on the back of a copy of his letter to Nathaniel P. Banks, August 5, *supra.* The original copies supposedly sent to Michael Hahn and Thomas J. Durant have not been located. See Lincoln to Banks, November 5, *infra.*

To Joseph Gilmore[1]

Executive Mansion,
Joseph A. Gilmore, Gov. N.H.   Washington Aug. 7, 1863.

My dear Governor Gilmore: I thank you very heartily for your kind invitation to visit Concord, and especially for the exceedingly cordial terms in which you have conveyed it. I very much regret that I cannot at present accept it. I am by no means certain that I can leave Washington at all this summer. *The exacting nature of my official duties renders it exceedingly improbable.* I assure you however that I am none the less sincerely grateful for your kind intentions and for the expressions of personal good will contained in your letter. I am very truly yours,   A. LINCOLN.

[1] Tracy, p. 229. This letter is also in Hertz, II, 940, but without date. A footnote in the source states that the letter is in John Hay's handwriting, signed by Lincoln. Governor Gilmore wrote on August 4, 1863, "I see from the public prints that you are intending to spend a few weeks among the Mountains of New Hampshire. May we not have the privilege of welcoming you to our state capital? . . . I have no desire to subject you to . . . speeches or parading you over our dusty streets in the broiling sun. But if you were to let me know . . . a day or two before your arrival that you would spend a night at least at my house, the people . . . would give you a spontaneous & informal ovation which would do your soul good. . . ." (DLC-RTL).

To William H. Seward[1]

Sir,   Executive Mansion August 7. 1863.

I hereby direct that the sum of $20.000.– appropriated by the 10th Section of an act of Congress approved 3d March 1863, for expenses of carrying into effect the habeas corpus act of the same date, be placed on the books of the Treasury and held subject to your control.   ABRAHAM LINCOLN

Hon: William H. Seward.
Secretary of State

1 LS, DNA FI RG 56, General Records of the Treasury Department, Series AB, 1863, Letters from Executive Officers, Part I, Vol. I, p. 2.

To Horatio Seymour[1]

His Excellency Gov. Seymour.   Washington, D.C.,
Albany. N.Y.   Aug. 7 1863

I send by first mail a letter, of which I now telegraph a copy.
                                                                      A. LINCOLN

1 ALS, RPB.

To Horatio Seymour[1]

His Excellency Horatio Seymour   Executive Mansion,
Governor of New-York   Washington, August 7, 1863.

Your communication of the 3rd. Inst. has been received, and attentively considered.

I can not consent to suspend the draft in New-York, as you request, because, among other reasons, *time* is too important.

By the figures you send, which I presume are correct, the twelve Districts represented fall into two classes of eight, and four respectively. The disparity of the quotas for the draft, in these two classes is certainly very striking, being the difference between an average of 2200 in one class, and 4864 in the other. Assuming that the Districts are equal, one to another, in entire population, as required by the plan on which they were made, this disparity is such as to require attention. Much of it, however, I suppose will be accounted for by the fact that so many more persons fit for soldiers, are in the city than are in the country, who have too recently arrived from other parts of the United States and from Europe to be either included in the Census of 1860, or to have voted in 1862. Still, making due allowance for this, I am yet unwilling to stand upon it as an entirely sufficient explanation of the great disparity.

I shall direct the draft to proceed in all the Districts, drawing however, at first, from each of the four Districts, towit: the second, fourth, sixth, and eighth, only 2200, being the average quota of the other class. After this drawing, these four Districts, and also the seventeenth and twentyninth, shall be carefully re-enrolled, and, if you please, agents of yours may witness every step of the process. Any deficiency which may appear by the new enrollment will be supplied by a special draft for that object, allowing due credit for volunteers who may be obtained from these Districts respectively, during the interval. And at all points, so far as consistent, with practical convenience, due credits will be given for volunteers; and your Excellency shall be notified of the time fixed for commencing a draft in each District.

I do not object to abide a decision of the United States Supreme Court, or of the judges thereof, on the constitutionality of the draft law. In fact, I should be willing to facilitate the obtaining of it; but I can not consent to lose the *time* while it is being obtained. We are contending with an enemy who, as I understand, drives every able bodied man he can reach, into his ranks, very much as a butcher drives bullocks into a slaughter-pen. No time is wasted, no argument is used. This produces an army which will soon turn upon our now victorious soldiers already in the field, if they shall not be sustained by recruits, as they should be. It produces an army with a rapidity not to be matched on our side, if we first waste time to re-experiment with the volunteer system, already deemed by congress, and palpably, in fact, so far exhausted, as to be inadequate; and then more time, to obtain a court decision, as to whether a law is constitutional, which requires a part of those not now in the service, to go to the aid of those who are already in it; and still more time, to determine with absolute certainty, that we get those, who are to go, in the precisely legal proportion, to those who are not to go.

My purpose is to be, in my action, just and constitutional; and yet practical, in performing the important duty, with which I am charged, of maintaining the unity, and the free principles of our common country. Your Obt. Servt.   A. LINCOLN.

[1] ADfS, DLC-RTL; LS, RPB; LS, THaroL. Governor Seymour's long letter of August 3, 1863, gave a resumé of the draft riots of July 13-19 in New York City, and protested that "the quotas now demanded from the Congressional districts in New York and Kings County are glaringly unjust. . . . I ask that the draft may be suspended in this State, as has been done elsewhere, until we shall learn the results of recruiting which is now actively going on. . . ." Seymour also proposed that the constitutionality of the draft act should be judged by the courts before the law was executed (OR, III, III, 612-19).

To Edwin M. Stanton[1]

Sir,   Executive Mansion August 7. 1863.

I hereby direct that the sum of $80,000.–appropriated by the 10th. section of an act of Congress approved 3d March 1863, for

expenses of carrying into effect the habeas corpus act of the same
date, be placed on the books of the Treasury and held subject to
your control. ABRAHAM LINCOLN

Hon. E. M. Stanton
Secretary of War.

¹ LS, DNA FI RG 56, General Records of the Treasury Department, Series
AB, 1863, Letters from Executive Officers, Part I, Vol. I, p. 3.

To John G. Foster¹

Executive Mansion, August 8, 1863.

General Foster: This will be handed you by Governor Peirpoint
of Virginia.

He goes, among other things, seeking to adjust a difficulty at
Norfolk and Portsmouth. It seems there is a large number of families in Portsmouth who are destitute and whose natural supporters
are in the rebel army or have been killed in it. These destitute
families must live somehow, and it seems the city authorities on
one side, and our military on the other, are in ruinous conflict
about the mode of providing.

Governor Peirpoint is a good man, and if you will place him in
conference and amicable relations with the military authority in
the vicinity, I do not doubt that much good will come of it. Please
do it. Yours truly, A. LINCOLN.

¹ NH, IX, 62-63. The controversy was over an ordinance passed by the city
council of Portsmouth, Virginia, on July 13, by which the mayor, Daniel Col-
lins, was authorized to collect rents for all property owned by citizens who
refused to take the oath of allegiance, the proceeds to be used to relieve destitute families. General Henry M. Naglee refused to use the military to enforce
the ordinance, on the ground that proceeds thus collected by the provost marshal
should remain in government custody as reimbursement for federal expenditures in taking care of the destitute. Naglee reported to Foster on August 15
that he refused to follow Peirpoint's suggestion that he confiscate property of
all who refused to take the oath, but that he would keep possession of all
property of those within rebel lines actively engaged in the rebellion and use
the proceeds to help the needy (OR, I, XXIX, II, 54-58).

To Mary Todd Lincoln¹

Executive Mansion, Washington, August 8, 1863.

My dear Wife. All as well as usual, and no particular trouble any
way. I put the money into the Treasury at five per cent, with the
previlege of withdrawing it any time upon thirty days' notice. I
suppose you are glad to learn this. Tell dear Tad, poor "Nanny
Goat," is lost; and Mrs. Cuthbert & I are in distress about it. The

day you left Nanny was found resting herself, and chewing her little cud, on the middle of Tad's bed. But now she's gone! The gardener kept complaining that she destroyed the flowers, till it was concluded to bring her down to the White House. This was done, and the second day she had disappeared, and has not been heard of since. This is the last we know of poor "Nanny"

The weather continues dry, and excessively warm here.

Nothing very important occurring. The election in Kentucky has gone very strongly right. Old Mr. Wickliffe[2] got ugly, as you know, ran for Governor, and is terribly beaten. Upon Mr. Crittendens death, Brutus Clay, Cassius' brother, was put on the track for Congress, and is largely elected. Mr. Menzies,[3] who, as we thought, behaved very badly last session of Congress, is largely beaten in the District opposite Cincinnati, by Green Clay Smith, Cassius Clay's nephew. But enough. Affectionately   A. LINCOLN

[1] ALS, DLC-RTL. The unaddressed envelope with the letter is endorsed by Lincoln "Letter about 'Nanny goat.'" The remarkable story of how so rare a domestic letter should have been preserved in the Lincoln Papers is told in a letter from D. P. Bacon, postmaster at LeRoy, Genesee County, New York, to Lincoln, April 25, 1864:

"When in the Army of the Potomac a few weeks ago, I met a young man, who in the course of conversation remarked that he had an original letter of the President. Expressing a desire to see it. he complied & produced the enclosed. On a further request that he would allow me to retain it, he assented. And what under other circumstances I should have greatly prized (an original letter of the Prest), a *private & domestic* one like this, all the 'proprieties' seemed to forbid that I should retain. On my return through Washington I thought to have returned it, but being presented . . . at one of your public receptions (the only occasion of seeing you), the opportunity was not favorable. I therefore now enclose it,—trusting that after so long & adventurous a journey it may reach its original source. Had it been a *fragment* of the original Emancipation Proclamation, or the Syracuse letter [Albany letter to Erastus Corning?] it would not probably have *thus* found its way back to the author.

"I will only remark that I know nothing of the circumstances by which it came into the possession of the party who delivered it to me. His only answer to my inquiry on the subject was the vague one, 'it was picked up in the Army.' It is evident from its *soiled* condition that it has had a 'career.'

"Hoping that you will pardon this intrusion I remain. . . ." (DLC-RTL).

The mystery of how the letter came into a soldier's possession remains unexplained.   [2] Charles A. Wickliffe.   [3] John W. Menzies.

To Edwin M. Stanton[1]

Executive Mansion,

Hon. Sec. of War   Washington, August 8. 1863.

Please look over the accompanying note addressed to Gen. Meade, and send it to him, unless you perceive some objection. Yours truly   A. LINCOLN

1 ALS, NHi. The "accompanying note addressed to Gen. Meade" has not been located, but Meade's reply of August 12 is as follows: "Your note of the Eighth inst. in relation to Col. M. D. Hardin 12th Pa Reserves has just reached me & I have given a leave for ten . . . days to that officer." (DLC-RTL). See Lincoln's endorsement concerning Colonel Martin D. Hardin's leave of absence, August 15, *infra*.

To John M. Fleming and Robert Morrow[1]

Messrs Jno. M. Fleming &   Executive Mansion,
    Ro. Morrow.   Washington, August 9, 1863.

Gentlemen: The petition of which you were the bearers, has just been handed me. Your cards and notes had come to me on two or three successive days before; and I knew then, as well as I do now, after reading the petition, what your mission was. I knew it was the same true, and painful story, which Gov. Johnson, Mr. Maynard, Dr. Clements and others have been telling me for more than two years. I also knew that meeting you could do no good; because I have all the while done, and shall continue to do the best for you I could, and can. I do as much for East Tennessee as I would, or could, if my own home, and family were in Knoxville. The difficulties of getting a Union army into that region, and of keeping it there, are so apparant,—so obvious—that none can fail to see them, unless it may be those who are driven mad and blind by their sufferings. Start by whatever route they may, their lines of supply are broken before they get half way. A small force, sufficient to beat the enemy now there, would be of no value, because the enemy would re-inforce to meet them, until we should have to give back, or accumulate so large a force, as to be very difficult to supply, and as to ruin us entirely if a great disaster should befal it. I know you are too much distressed to be argued with; and therefore I do not attempt it at length. You know I am not indifferent to your troubles; else I should not, more than a year and a half ago, have made the effort I did to have a Railroad built on purpose to relieve you. The Secretary of War, Gen. Halleck, Gen. Burnside, and Gen. Rosecrans are all engaged now in an effort to relieve your section. But remember, you will probably thwart them if you make this public.

1 ADf, DLC-RTL. In addition to the draft there is in the Lincoln Papers what appears to be the letter, copied by Hay, which was to have been signed and sent. An endorsement on the envelope of a letter from Fleming and Morrow, August 8, 1863, enclosing a "petition from the loyal people of East Tennessee," is as follows: "Also the President's answer—which I do not think was sent R. T. Lincoln May 13- 65." Fleming and Morrow, citizens of Knoxville, Tennessee, wrote Lincoln on August 8 as follows:

"We have the honor to enclose . . . the copy of a petition, from the loyal people of East Tennessee. For now five days we have unsuccessfully sought an opportunity to deliver it . . . in person. . . . Finding it necessary to return this evening we have but the one resort left—that of submitting the document to your Excellency. . . . Our people . . . driven almost to desperation . . . having so long waited in vain . . . for protection from the Government . . . have, as the final resort, appealed directly to Your Excellency. . . ." (DLC-RTL).

To Ulysses S. Grant[1]

Executive Mansion,
My dear General Grant:　　　　Washington, August 9, 1863.

I see by a despatch of yours that you incline quite strongly towards an expedition against Mobile. This would appear tempting to me also, were it not that in view of recent events in Mexico, I am greatly impressed with the importance of re-establishing the national authority in Western Texas as soon as possible. I am not making an order, however. That I leave, for the present at least, to the General-in-Chief.

A word upon another subject. Gen. Thomas has gone again to the Mississippi Valley, with the view of raising colored troops. I have no reason to doubt that you are doing what you reasonably can upon the same subject. I believe it is a resource which, if vigorously applied now, will soon close the contest. It works doubly, weakening the enemy and strengthening us. We were not fully ripe for it until the river was opened. Now, I think at least a hundred thousand can, and ought to be rapidly organized along it's shores, relieving all the white troops to serve elsewhere.

Mr. Dana understands you as believing that the emancipation proclamation has helped some in your military operations. I am very glad if this is so. Did you receive a short letter from me, dated the 13th. of July? Yours very truly　　A. LINCOLN.

[1] ALS, ICHi; ADfS, DLC-RTL. General Grant's despatch to Halleck of July 24, responding to Halleck's of July 11 that he was "exceedingly anxious about General Banks' command" (OR, I, XXIV, III, 497), reported, "I have sent Banks one division, numbering full 4,000 effective men. . . . My troops are very much exhausted, and entirely unfit for any present duty requiring much marching. But, by selecting, any duty of immediate pressing importance could be done. It seems to me that Mobile is the point deserving the most immediate attention. . . . (ibid., pp. 546-47). At Cairo, Illinois, on August 23, Grant replied to Lincoln's letter:

"Your letter of the 9th inst. reached me at Vicksburg just as I was about starting for this place. Your letter of the 13th of July was also duly received.

"After the fall of Vicksburg I did incline very much to an immediate move on Mobile. I believed then the place could be taken with but little effort, and . . . we would have . . . a base to opperate from . . . as would make them abandon entirely the states bound . . . by the Miss. I see however the importance of a movement into Texas just at this time.

"I have reinforced Gen. Banks with the 13th Army Corps. . . .

"I have given the subject of arming the negro my hearty support. This, with the emancipation . . . is the heavyest blow yet given the Confederacy. . . .

"There has been great difficulty in getting able bodied negroes to fill up the colored regiments in consequence of the rebel cavalry running off all that class to Georgia and Texas. . . . I am . . . moving a Brigade of Cavalry . . . to Vicksburg . . . which will . . . facilitate materially the *recruiting service*.

"Gen. [Lorenzo] Thomas is now with me and you may rely on it I will give him all the aid in my power. . . ." (DLC-RTL).

To Mrs. Rachel S. Evans[1]

Executive Mansion,

Dear Madam Washington, August 10, 1863.

I thank you very cordially for the beautifully-finished Cushion, received, through your courtesy, today. But grateful as I am, it must be your greatest satisfaction to reflect that the brave soldiers who reap the benefit of your compassionate kindness and liberality, are this day more grateful still. I am very truly Your Obt. Servt

Mrs. Rachel S. Evans   A. LINCOLN
N.E. Cor. 11th & Vine

[1] LS, PHi. The letter is in John Hay's handwriting, signed by Lincoln. On the draft of this letter preserved in the Lincoln Papers, also in Hay's hand, the deleted name of the person addressed appears to be "Mrs. Hutter," (see similar letter of the same date addressed to Mrs. Hutter, *infra*). Mrs. Evans' note accompanying the cushion, July 9, 1863, is as follows: "Will please accept the accompanying Sofa Cushion, which was purchased by subscription, from the table of 'The Penn Relief Association for Sick and Wounded Soldiers,' at the Grand Floral Fair recently held in this city." (DLC-RTL).

To Mrs. Hutter, Misses Lager, and Miss Claghorn[1]

Executive Mansion, Washington, August 10, 1863.

Permit me to return my grateful acknowledgements to the fair manufacturer and generous donors of the beautiful present which accompanies their note of the 20th July. If anything could enhance to me the value of this representation of our national ensign, so elegantly executed and so gracefully bestowed, it would be the consideration that its price has been devoted to the comfort and restoration of those heroic men, who have suffered and bled in our flag's defense. We never should, and I am sure, never shall be niggard of gratitude and benefaction to the soldiers who have en-

dured toil, privations and wounds, that the nation may live. Yours very truly
  A. LINCOLN.
  To Mrs Hutter
  Misses Lager
  Miss Claghorn

[1] LS, The Rosenbach Company, Philadelphia and New York; Df, DLC-RTL. The lower left-hand corner of the letter bearing the names of the persons addressed has been torn away, but the draft preserves the names. Both draft and letter are in John Hay's handwriting. The letter of July 20 accompanying the present has not been located. Mrs. Elizabeth E. Hutter was president of the Northern Home for Friendless Children and Associated Institute for Soldiers' and Sailors' Orphans, at Philadelphia. Mrs. John W. and James L. Claghorn were members of the board of directors. The "Misses Lager" have not been identified.

Memorandum:
Appointment of Robert J. Sperry[1]

August 10, 1863

At this date, I am under obligation to give the first appointment to the Naval School in my power, to John T. Grimsley, of Illinois, and no other commital must supersede this obligation. After saying this much, I add that I would be glad for the boy within named, to have another chance, if at all consistent with the service.

Aug. 10. 1863.
  A. LINCOLN

[1] AES, ICHi. Lincoln's endorsement is written on the back of a letter from Gideon Welles to Robert J. Sperry, January 8, 1863, dismissing Sperry from the Naval Academy "for insubordination, neglect of studies and having in your possession a most obscene book." John T. Grimsley was appointed (see Lincoln's telegram to Mrs. Grimsley, August 24, *infra*), but there is no record of his entrance. Robert J. Sperry is listed as mate in the Navy, May 13, 1864.

Memorandum Concerning Alexander C. Sands[1]

August 10, 1863

After the report mentioned, was made, this case, including the report, was brought before me; and upon quite full hearing & consideration, my conclusion was that Mr. Sands is probably a rather disagreeable man, and that these charges made to get rid of him, are frivolous. Such is my present impression.
  A. LINCOLN
  Aug. 10. 1863

[1] AES, DLC-RTL. Lincoln's endorsement is written on a letter from Joseph H. Geiger, clerk of the U.S. District Court for Southern Ohio, July 30, 1863, complaining that Alexander C. Sands, U.S. marshal for Southern Ohio, had not been removed from office on charges preferred by Geiger.

To William S. Rosecrans[1]

My Dear General Rosecrans   Washington, August 10, 1863.

Yours of the 1st was received two days ago. I think you must have inferred more than Gen Halleck has intended, as to any dissatisfaction of mine with you. I am sure you, as a reasonable man, would not have been wounded, could you have heard all my words and seen all my thoughts, in regard to you. I have not abated in my kind feeling for and confidence in you. I have seen most of your despatches to General Halleck—probably all of them. After Grant invested Vicksburg, I was very anxious lest Johnston should overwhelm him from the outside, and when it appeared certain that part of Bragg's force had gone, and was going to Johnston, it did seem to me, it was the exactly proper time for you to attack Bragg with what force he had left. In all kindness, let me say, it so seems to me yet. Finding from your despatches to General Halleck that your judgement was different, and being very anxious for Grant, I, on one occasion told Gen. Halleck, I thought he should direct you to decide at once, to immediately attack Bragg or to stand on the defensive, and send part of your force to Grant. He replied he had already so directed, in substance. Soon after, despatches from Grant abated my anxiety for him, and in proportion abated my anxiety about any movement of yours. When afterwards, however, I saw a despatch of yours arguing that the right time for you to attack Bragg was not before but would be after the fall of Vicksburg, it impressed me very strangely; and I think I so stated to the Secretary of War and General Halleck. It seemed no other than the proposition that you could better fight Bragg *when* Johnston should be at liberty to return and assist him, than you could *before* he could so return to his assistance.

Since Grant has been entirely relieved by the fall of Vicksburg, by which Johnston is also relieved, it has seemed to me that your chance for a stroke, has been considerably diminished, and I have not been pressing you directly or indirectly. True, I am very anxious for East Tennessee to be occupied by us; but I see and appreciate the difficulties you mention. The question occurs, Can the thing be done at all? Does preparation advance at all? Do you not consume supplies as fast as you get them forward? Have you more animals today than you had at the battle of Stone River? and yet have not more been furnished you since then than your entire present stock? I ask the same questions as to your mounted force.

Do not misunderstand. I am not casting blame upon you. I

rather think, by great exertion, you can get to East Tennessee. But a very important question is, "Can you stay there?" I make no order in the case—that I leave to General Halleck and yourself.

And now, be assured once more, that I think of you in all kindness and confidence: and that I am not watching you with an evil-eye. Yours very truly

¹ Copy, DLC-RTL. Halleck's despatches to Rosecrans on July 24 and 25 continued to urge the importance of a movement on General Braxton Bragg's army at Chattanooga before Bragg could be reinforced by General Joseph E. Johnston: "There is great disappointment felt here at the slowness of your advance. Unless you can move more rapidly, your whole campaign will prove a failure. . . ." (OR, XXIII, II, 552). On August 1, Rosecrans replied to Halleck, explaining the difficulties of terrain and supply which confronted his army (*ibid.*, p. 585), and also wrote Lincoln to the same effect, with the observation that "Genl. Hallecks dispatches imply that you not only feel solicitude for the advance of this Army but dissatisfaction at its supposed inactivity." (DLC-RTL).

To Robert C. Schenck¹

[c. August 10, 1863]

The officer in command in Baltimore is hereby directed to take no further steps in the case of the Rev'd Peyton Harrison until further order from me.   A. LINCOLN.

¹ Alexander B. Hagner, *A Personal Narrative of the Acquaintance of My Father and Myself with Each of the Presidents of the United States* (Washington, D.C., 1915), p. 47. According to the source Lincoln's order was written on a card and given to Alexander B. Hagner of Annapolis, Maryland, who had called in behalf of his wife's uncle, the Reverend Peyton Harrison of Baltimore, under arrest on charges of disloyal conduct. Although Hagner's account does not give the specific date of Lincoln's order, the letter of Reverend Phineas D. Gurley, August 10, 1863, introduced Hagner "on behalf of the Rev. Peyton Harrison, an excellent and venerable minister of the Old School Pres. church who is now under arrest. . . ." (DLC-RTL).

To William H. Seward¹

Hon. Secretary of State.   August 10, 1863

I have for a good while had this particular question under consideration; and my judgment [is] that the within, substantially, should be the answer to Lord Lyons.   A. LINCOLN

August 10, 1863.

¹ AES, RPB. Lincoln's endorsement has been removed from the attendant document. It seems probable that Lincoln's letter to Welles, July 25, *supra*, was not delivered until shortly before August 12, as indicated by the entry

in Welles' *Diary* under that date. If so, it may be inferred that Lincoln on August 10 transmitted to Seward the substance of his instructions to Welles, to be incorporated in a reply to Lord Lyons. Secretary Welles pursued the matter further in a letter to Lincoln dated September 30, 1863:

"Since the interview with you some weeks since in relation to certain proposed instructions to our Naval Officers, I have, as suggested, given the subject careful and thorough investigation, and am fully satisfied that neither in British law nor British practice is there any authority or precedent for such instructions. As Her Majesty's representative has introduced the subject, I have embodied what I believe to be the law and usage on the several points, in a distinct paper, which can, if you think proper, be submitted to Lord Lyons, and, if I have in that document done injustice, in any respect, to British authority and British usage, or misapprehended or misstated international law, I shall be happy to be corrected.

"Permit me in this connection to express my surprise and regret that the British Minister should so persistently insist on interfering in matters that belong to the Prize Courts, and on which he should not be heard from diplomatically, as were Great Britain in our case and we in hers, the American Minister in London would not be heard diplomatically, until judicial remedies have been exhausted. His right to be heard in the Court of Prize, according to its rules of procedure, and in the proper cases, is unquestioned. If the Court, after its appellate jurisdiction is fully exhausted, should fail to do justice in any case, then undoubtedly, and not till then, diplomacy may properly come in. But I do not understand by what authority Her Majesty's Minister intervenes at all, even in the Prize Courts by suggestion, or before you, in cases where the violation of territorial immunities of neutral powers, other than Great Britain is in question. If our Naval Offi[c]ers violate the Sovereignty, or the neutrality, or the municipal regulations of a neutral State, we are, first in our prize courts, and then diplomatically, amenable for that violation to the Neutral State itself, and not to Great Britain, even though the act of violation has been perpetrated there by us upon a British vessel. There is no principal of international law better settled than this, and I respectfully insist that no one but the Sovereign of the neutral territory which is violated, has the slightest right to allege, or suggest such violation even in our prize courts and much less diplomatically.

"As regards persons on board of captured neutral vessels, the best rule of law is that they shall be sent in as witnesses; the requirement of law is that some be sent in; and if the Captor fails to send them all in, he so fails at his peril of not sending enough; and if he sends them all in, all being neutral, no one has the right any where to complain of him, provided only that he had probable cause for capturing the ship. But in the war in which we are now engaged, it must be remembered that no inconsiderable portion of the persons captured on some of the vessels claiming to be neutral, are rebels. It is impossible for the captor to decide, who or how many, are rebels. It certainly is not advisable to go counter to the rule so framed by all the courts nor to release captured rebel prisoners.

"I am not unaware of your strong desire to conciliate Great Britain and to make all reasonable concessions to preserve friendly relations with her. In this feeling I cordially participate. But my earnest conviction is that we shall best command the respect, which insures peace, by firmly but not offensively maintaining our rights; and in no way can amicable relations with Great Britain, and all others, be so surely maintained as by our claiming only what is right, by surrendering nothing that is clearly and indispensably our own, and by referring always the question of what our just rights are to those tribunals of Prize, which are instituted by the consent of nations to adjudge these points under the law of nations and in the interests of peace, by reason of the acknowledged inability of diplomacy, even in the most skilful hands, to deal

satisfactorily before hand with these complicated questions as they arise."
(DLC-RTL).

Further reference has not been discovered, and final disposition of the matter
has not been ascertained.

To Edwin M. Stanton[1]

Hon. Sec. of War   Executive Mansion,
Sir: Washington, Aug. 10. 1863.

I have not heard of any charges being filed against Gen. J. A.
McClernand. Are there any? Yours truly   A. LINCOLN

[1] ALS, DLC-RTL. On the bottom of the letter is the following endorsement:
"I do not know of any charges against General McClernand. General Grant
has made a report which I have not seen & know nothing of its contents
                                          "EDWIN M STANTON"
An accompanying page bears the following note from Halleck to whom this
communication had been referred:
"There are no formal charges against Major Genl McClernand. Genl Grant
has reported his reasons for removing him from command."
John A. McClernand wrote Lincoln on August 3:
"According to news-paper account it is the purpose of my enemy's, at this
late day, to attempt to gloss [?] the more than mortal injury they have done
me, by bringing me before a court martial. If so; let me, as an American . . .
more jealous of my honor than of my life, appeal to you to see that I am fairly
dealt by—that I am not held up before the country for months in the character
of an alleged culprit, as an excuse for withholding from me a command. . . ."
(DLC-RTL).
Grant had removed McClernand for publishing *General Orders No. 72*, May
30, 1863, in the Memphis *Evening Bulletin* of June 13, in which McClernand
praised his Thirteenth Corps and insinuated that in the unsuccessful assault on
the Vicksburg fortifications of May 22, he was not supported by Sherman's Fifteenth Corps and McPherson's Seventeenth Corps. McClernand failed to submit
the order to Grant before issuing it to the press, as was required by regulations.
On June 18 Grant removed McClernand, and on June 26 transmitted the papers
in the case to Lorenzo Thomas with the comment: "A disposition and earnest
desire on my part to do the most I could with the means at my command,
without interference with the assignments to command which the President
alone was authorized to make, made me tolerate General McClernand long
after I thought the good of the service demanded his removal. It was only when
almost the entire army under my command seemed to demand it that he was
relieved. . . ." (OR, I, XXIV, I, 158-59). See further Lincoln to McClernand,
August 12, *infra*.

Check[1]

No. 52   Washington, D.C. Aug. 11   1863
                    RIGGS & CO.
Pay to   Colored man, with one leg.   *or bearer*
   Five . . . . *Dollars*
   $5/00.   A. LINCOLN
[1] DS-F, ISLA.

To George G. Meade[1]

Executive Mansion, Washington,

My dear General Meade　　　　　　　　August 11, 1863.

Yesterday week I made known to Gen. Hooker our brief correspondence in regard to him. He seemed gratified with the kind spirit
manifested by both of us; but said he was busy preparing a report,
and would consider.

Yesterday he called again and said he would accept the offer if
it was still open; would go at once if you desire; but would prefer
waiting till the first of September, unless there was to be a battle,
or you desired him to come sooner. I told him I would write you.
Please answer. Yours very truly　　　　　　　A. LINCOLN

1 ALS, NHi. Meade replied on August 12:
"You seem to think, or rather such is the inference left on my mind, that I
have made an offer to Genl. Hooker & that I desire his assignment to this army.
Now in the frankness, which has marked your letters, permit me to say, this
is a mis-apprehension on your part. My position is purely one of acquiescence.
I wrote you, that if you desired Genl. Hooker to have a command under me
I should not object, but you will pardon me, if I call to your recollection, that
the proposition originated with yourself that the offer when made was yours
and that I have neither entertained nor expressed any desire upon the subject." (DLC-RTL).

To Horatio Seymour[1]

His Excellency　　　　　　　　　　Executive Mansion
Horatio Seymour　　　　　　　　　　　Washington
Governor of New-York.　　　　　　　August 11 1863

Yours of the 8th. with Judge Advocate General Waterbury's report, was received to-day. Asking you to remember that I consider
time as being very important, both to the general cause of the
country, and to the soldiers already in the field, I beg to remind
you that I waited, at your request, from the 1st till the 6th. Inst.
to receive your communication dated the 3rd. In view of it's great
length, and the known time, and apparant care, taken in it's preparation, I did not doubt that it contained your full case as you desired to present it. It contained figures for twelve Districts, omitting the other nineteen, as I supposed, because you found nothing
to complain of, as to them. I answered accordingly. In doing so, I
laid down the principle to which I purpose adhering—which is, to
proceed with the draft, at the same time employing infallible
means to avoid any great wrongs. With the communication received to-day, you send figures for twenty eight Districts, includ-

ing the twelve sent before, and still omitting three, from which I suppose the enrolments are not yet received. In looking over this fuller list of twenty eight Districts, I find that the quotas for six-teen of them are above 2000 and below 2700, while, of the rest, six are above 2700 and six are below 2000. Applying the principle to these new facts, the 5th. and 7th. Districts must be added to the four in which the quotas have already been reduced to 2200 for the first draft; and, with these, four others must be added to those to be re-enrolled.

The corrected case will then stand:

The quotas of the 2nd. 4th. 5th. 6th. 7th. & 8th. Districts fixed at 2200. for the first draft.

The Provost-Marshal-General informs me that the drawing is already completed in 16th. 17th. 18th. 22nd. 24th. 26th. 27th. 28th. 29th. & 30th. Districts.

In the others, except the three outstanding, the drawing will be made upon the quotas as now fixed.

After the first draft, the 2nd. 4th. 5th. 6th. 7th. 8th. 16th. 17th. 21st. 25th. 29th & 31st. Districts[2] will be re-enrolled for the purpose, and in the manner stated in my letter of the 7th. Inst. The same principle will be applied to the now outstanding Districts when they shall come in. No part of my former letter is repudiated, by reason of not being restated in this, or for any other cause. Your Obt. Servt.   A. LINCOLN

[1] ADfS, DLC-RTL; LS, RPB. On August 8, Governor Seymour replied to Lincoln's communication of August 7, *supra*: ". . . I regret your refusal to comply with my request to have the draft in this State suspended until it can be ascertained if the enrollments are made in accordance with the laws. . . . I now send you a full report, made to me by Judge-Advocate-General [Nelson J.] Waterbury. . . . You will see by the report . . . that there is no theory which can explain or justify the enrollments in this State. . . ." (OR, III, III, 639-40). Waterbury's report may be found in the same source, pp. 640-51.

[2] "Districts" inserted by John Hay.

To Edwin M. Stanton[1]

Sec. of War, please give Gen. Logan the extended leave asked for, unless you know a good reason to the contrary.   A. LINCOLN
      Aug. 11. 1863.

[1] AES, DLC-Stanton Papers. Lincoln's endorsement is written on a telegram from Jesse K. Dubois, August 10, 1863, asking an extension of leave for Gen-eral John A. Logan. A letter from William P. Dole to John P. Usher, August 9, 1863, explains what Logan was doing: "I have just seen & conversed with Genl. Logan He is doing much good to our cause here in Ill. His leave . . . only

lasts 10 or 12 days more See the President and if it is at all consistent . . .
get the Leave extended 20 or 30 days longer that he may visit portions of our
state. Genl. Logan sd. to me that if he had the leave he would do the work but
did not like to ask for the leave himself. . . . Logan calls things by their right
names and his speeches will do a world of good in this state as showing the
spirit & temper of the army. . . ." (DLC-RTL).

To John A. McClernand[1]

Major General McClernand: Executive Mansion,
My dear Sir: Washington, August 12, 1863.

Our friend, William G. Greene, has just presented a kind letter
in regard to yourself, addressed to me by our other friends, Yates,
Hatch, and Dubois. I doubt whether your present position is more
painful to you than to myself. Grateful for the patriotic stand so
early taken by you in this life-and-death struggle of the nation, I
have done whatever has appeared practicable to advance you and
the public interest together. No charges, with a view to a trial, have
been preferred against you by any one; nor do I suppose any will
be. All there is, so far as I have heard, is Gen. Grant's statement
of his reasons for relieving you. And even this I have not seen or
sought to see; because it is a case, as appears to me, in which I
could do nothing without doing harm. Gen. Grant and yourself
have been conspicuous in our most important successes; and for me
to interfere, and thus magnify a breach between you, could not
but be of evil effect. Better leave it where the law of the case has
placed it. For me to force you back upon Gen. Grant, would be
forcing him to resign. I can not give you a new command, because
we have no forces except such as already have commanders. I am
constantly pressed by those who *scold* before they *think*, or without
thinking at all, to give commands respectively to Fremont, McClellan, Butler, Sigel, Curtis, Hunter, Hooker, and perhaps others;
when, all else out of the way, I have no commands to give them.
This is now your case, which, as I have before said, pains me, not
less than it does you.

My belief is that the permanent estimate of what a general does
in the field, is fixed by the "cloud of witnesses" who have been
with him in the field; and that relying on these, he who has the
right needs not to fear. Your friend as ever   A. LINCOLN

1 ALS, IHi. See Lincoln to Stanton, August 10, *supra.* William G. Greene,
Lincoln's old friend of New Salem days, was a prominent Union Democrat.
The letter of August 6 which he brought from Governor Yates, Hatch and
Dubois, explained that "there is a deep and general feeling of regret; nay dissat-
isfaction at the dismissal of Gen'l McClernand from his late command. . . . His

name is indissolubly blended with . . . the great military actions and events occuring in the South West. . . . The popular verdict is irreversibly in his favor as a General. . . ." (DLC-RTL).

On August 24, McClernand replied to Lincoln's letter of August 12:

"Your kind favor, by the hand of Mr. Green, is received. Please accept my grateful acknowledgments for the friendly assurances it contains. If my humble efforts in behalf of the country have in any degree, met your approbation I am rejoiced. I only regret that I am debarred the privilege of continuing them in the same form.

"Feeling that I have done my duty I shrink from no charges that Genl. Grant may prefer. On the contrary . . . I challenged investigation both of his and my conduct. . . . I only ask . . . for an impartial court. Such investigation would bring to light . . . many things, both military and personal, which are unwritten or unheeded. . . ." (DLC-RTL).

On September 14, Stanton replied to McClernand's letter of September 5 in which he repeated his request for a court of inquiry:

"Your letter of the 5th instant has been submitted to the President, who directs me to say that a court of inquiry embracing any one of the subjects specified in that letter would necessarily withdraw from the field many officers whose presence with their commands is absolutely indispensable to the service, and whose absence might cause irreparable injury to the success of operations now in active progress. For these reasons he declines at present your applications, but if hereafter it can be done without prejudice to the service, he will, in view of your anxiety upon the subject, order a court." (OR, I, XXIV, I, 169).

On January 14, 1864, McClernand wrote Lincoln, enclosing a copy of his resignation as major general, "an office which for more than six months past, has neither afforded me an opportunity to combat the rebellion, nor to defend myself against the proscription and calumnies of . . . Maj. Genl. U. S. Grant." (DLC-RTL).

To Edwin M. Stanton[1]

Executive Mansion, Washington, August 12, [1863].

Hon. Secretary of War: Mrs. Baird tells me that she is a widow; that her two sons and only support joined the army, where one of them still is; that her other son, Isaac P. Baird, is a private in the Seventy-second Pennsylvania Volunteers—Baxter's Fire Zouaves, Company K; that he is now under guard with his regiment on a charge of desertion; that he was under arrest for desertion, so that he could not take the benefit of returning under the proclamation on that subject. Please have it ascertained if this is correct, and if it is, let him be discharged from arrest and go to duty. I think, too, he should have his pay for duty actually performed. Loss of pay falls so hard upon poor families. Yours truly,   A. LINCOLN.

[1] NH, VII, 309-10. This letter is misdated by Nicolay and Hay "August 12, 1862." AGO *Special Orders No. 462*, October 15, 1863, ordered that "By direction of the President, so much of the sentence awarded Private Isaac P. Baird, Company 'K', 72d Pennsylvania Volunteers, as relates to the forfeiture of ten dollars of his monthly pay for the balance of his term of service, is hereby remitted." See further, Lincoln to Stanton, March 1, 1864, *infra*.

To Edwin M. Stanton[1]

August 12, 1863

Thinking there may be some importance in recalling this subject, which seems to have not been before the Sec. of War, I submit this to him   A. LINCOLN

Augt. 12. 1863.

[1] AES, owned by Dale Carnegie, New York City. Lincoln's endorsement has been clipped from an envelope, and the reference has not been identified.

To Gideon Welles[1]

Will the Secretary of the Navy please send me the record of conviction in this case & any other information in his power.?

Augt. 12. 1863.   A LINCOLN

[1] AES, DNA RG 204, U.S. Pardon Attorney, A 439. Lincoln's endorsement is written on an envelope containing papers in the case of James Dillon of New York, convicted of mutiny. A further unsigned endorsement, not Lincoln's, indicates that the ship involved was "not in the naval service and was most probably a merchant vessel." A third endorsement referred the request to the Department of State. See Lincoln to Bates, September 28, *infra*.

To Joseph Holt[1]

Judge Advocate General: Executive Mansion,
Dear Sir;   Washington, August 13. 1863.

Major Alexander Montgomery, who has been dismissed from the Regular Army, is now with me, and denies the charges upon which he was dismissed, and which he says he now, for the first time, has officially heard. As the principal charge, can be given the appearance at least of being merely personally offensive to me, and as he denies it, I think he should have a Court-Martial, rather than to abide my arbitrary dismissal.

Please give him the Court-Martial if he desires it. Yours truly
       A. LINCOLN

[1] ALS, IHi. Major Alexander Montgomery, quartermaster at Pittsburgh, Pennsylvania, was dismissed on July 18, 1863, and reinstated on June 14, 1864. Letters from Montgomery Blair (August 5, 1863), Simon Cameron (August 10, 1863), and several others, requested his reinstatement (DLC-RTL).

To Mrs. Elizabeth J. Grimsley[1]

Executive Mansion, Washington, August 14, 1863.

My dear Cousin Lizzie   I have, by the law, two classes of appointments to make to the Naval-School—ten of each, to the year.

The first class, according to the law, must be of families of the meritorious Naval-Officers; while the other class does not have such restriction. You see at once that if I have a vacancy in the first class, I can not appoint Johnny to it; and I have intended for months, and still intend, to appoint him to the very first vacancy I can get in the other class   Yours very truly   A. LINCOLN

[1] ALS, CSmH. See Lincoln's memorandum concerning appointment of Robert J. Sperry, August 10, *supra.*

To Edwin M. Stanton[1]

August 14, 1863

The subscribers of this letter are most worthy & reliable gentlemen. They ask three things.

1st. That the City of Rock-Island, which is on the main land, Illinois side, may have consent of the U.S. to build a bridge across the Slough to Rock-Island, which Island belongs to the U.S.

2nd. That Capt. Ben. Harper be appointed Post-Quarter-Master; and William Baily Military Storekeeper.

3rd. That the Island be not thrown into a Military Department lying West of the River.

I submit the whole to the Secretary of War.   A. LINCOLN
Aug. 14. 1863.

[1] AES, IHi. Lincoln's endorsement is written on the back of a letter from Ira O. Wilkinson and Thomas J. Buford, August 12, 1863. An endorsement by Halleck dated August 20 is partly torn off but the concluding portion is as follows:

". . . to another dept has never, to my knowledge been contemplated.

"Permission to build a private bridge on public land is not recommended.

"I have no knowledge of Messrs Harper & Baily and therefore cannot recommend them."

Neither Captain Benjamin Harper nor William Baily is listed in federal service.

To Robert Anderson[1]

Executive Mansion, Washington,
My dear General Anderson   August 15, 1863.

I have been through the War Department this morning looking up your case. Section 20 of "An act providing for the better Organization of the Military Establishment" Approved August 3, 1861, seems to leave no discretion to President, Secretary of War, General-in-Chief, or any one else.[2] The General-in-Chief, however says that, if agreeable to you, he will give you command of Fort-

Adams (I think) at New-Port, R.I. by which your pay will be the same as if this law did not exist. I advise you to try it, at all events. Gen. Halleck says it will require substantially no labor, or thought, whatever. Please telegraph whether you conclude to try it.

And now, my dear General allow me to assure you that we here are all your sincere friends. Very truly   A LINCOLN

[1] ALS, RPB. General Robert Anderson, in ill health, had been awaiting orders since October 8, 1861. He was assigned to command of Fort Adams on August 19, 1863, but was retired on October 27 for disability.

[2] Section 20 provided that officers "absent from appropriate duties for a period exceeding six months, either with or without leave, shall not receive the allowances for servants, forage, fuel, quarters & transportation of baggage, either in kind or in commutation."

Draft of a Communication to Stephen A. Hurlbut[1]

Executive Mansion,
Washington, [c. August 15?] 186[3]

The within discusses a difficult subject—the most difficult with which we have to deal. The able bodied male contrabands are already employed by the Army. But the rest are in confusion and destitution. They better be set to digging their subsistence out of the ground. If there are plantations near you, on either side of the river, which are abandoned by their owners, first put as many contrabands on such, as they will hold—that is, as can draw subsistence from them. If some still remain, get loyal men, of character in the vicinity, to take them temporarily on wages, to be paid to the contrabands themselves—such men obliging themselves to not let the contrabands be kidnapped, or forcibly carried away. Of course, if any voluntarily make arrangements to work for their living, you will not hinder them. It is thought best to leave details to your discretion subject to the provisions of the acts of Congress & the orders of the War Department.

By direction of the President.

[1] AD, DLC-Nicolay Papers. On August 15, General Stephen A. Hurlbut wrote Lincoln enclosing a letter of his to S. B. Walker, August 10, 1863, in which he gave his personal views concerning the conditions under which Mississippi could return to the Union. Hurlbut designated the letter as a communication to be presented before a reconstruction meeting in Mississippi and expressed the hope that it would meet Lincoln's approval. His comment on the relation of former masters and slaves is as follows: "So far . . . as the U. States are concerned the relation of master and slave does not exist in Mississippi . . . . and soon the banks of the Great River will bristle with the bayonets of colored Regiments taken from the former slaves of the soil.

"Let this war continue six months and a very heavy proportion of the able

bodied negroes of the Insurrectionary States will be in arms. . . ." (DLC-RTL).
If Lincoln's draft became a letter or order, the original has not been located.

Draft of Proclamation[1]

[August 15, 1863?]
By the President of the United States of America:

A Proclamation.

Whereas, in the judgment of the President, it is necessary to use
the military force in the State of New York in order to suppress
existing unlawful combinations against the enforcement of the
laws of the United States;

Therefore, I, Abraham Lincoln, President of the United States,
do hereby command all persons acting against the enforcement of
said laws, to disperse, and return peaceably to their respective
abodes, by, and before   o'clock   M. of this day.

In witness whereof, I have hereunto set my hand, and caused the
seal of the United States to be affixed.

Done at the City of Washington this   day of August, in the
year of our Lord one thousand eight hundred and sixty
(Seal)   three, and of the Independence of the United States of
America the eighty-eighth.   ABRAHAM LINCOLN
By the President:
WILLIAM H. SEWARD Secretary of State.

[1] DS, NAuE. This proclamation was never issued, but see note to Lincoln's
letter to Horatio Seymour, *infra*.

Extension of Leave for Francis P. Blair, Jr.[1]

The leave of absence for Major General Frank P. Blair Jr. and Staff
is extended to the first day of October next   A. LINCOLN
August 15. 1863.

[1] AES, RPB. Lincoln's endorsement is written on Blair's leave of absence
"for twenty days," July 26, 1863.

Extension of Leave for Martin D. Hardin[1]

This leave of absence, as to Col. M. D. Hardin, is extended to the
first of September next.   A. LINCOLN
Aug. 15. 1863

[1] AES, ICHi. Lincoln's endorsement is written on Hardin's leave of absence
"for 10 days." See Lincoln to Stanton, August 8, *supra*.

To John G. Foster[1]

Major Genl. Foster   Washington, D.C.,
Fort-Monroe, Va   Aug. 15 1863

I think you are right in placing "little reliance in the report"; still the question is so interesting that I would like to know if the Capt. of the Hudson gave any particulars—how he got his news, and the like. Please answer.   A LINCOLN

[1] ALS, RPB. General Foster telegraphed Lincoln at 6:10 P.M. on August 13: "The Capt of the Hudson did not give any particulars. The two steamers passed going in opposite directions. . . . The Hudson hailed in passing saying— 'Have you heard the news. Charleston is taken.' The steamers being by this time past each other nothing further was heard. The Hudson disappeared steering southward. . . . The circumstance induces the belief that the news is not reliable. The Hudson was paddle wheel steamer . . . with New York on her stern indicating *that* as the Port from which she hailed" (DLC-RTL).

To Edward S. Sanford[1]

                                          Executive Mansion,
To   Sanford.   Washington, [August 15], 186[3]
      Major General of Militia for the State of New York.

Whereas by reason of unlawful combinations against the authority of the government of the United States, it has become impracticable, in my judgment to enforce, by the ordinary course of judicial proceedings, the laws of the United States, within
                                          therefore I,
Abraham Lincoln, President of the United States, do call forth yourself and your command, as part of the Militia of the State of New-York, to aid in suppressing said combinations and opposition to said laws; and I do order and direct that, for this object, you report forthwith to Major General John A. Dix.

                                      ABRAHAM LINCOLN

[1] ADfS, DLC-Stanton Papers; DS-P, ISLA. See footnote, Lincoln to Seymour, *infra.*

To Horatio Seymour[1]

His Excellency   Executive Mansion,
Horatio Seymour   Washington,
Governor of the State of New-York.   [August 15,] 1863

Whereas, by reason of unlawful combinations against the authority of the Government of the United States, it has become impracticable, in my judgment, to enforce, by the ordinary course of judicial proceedings, the laws of the United States, within

therefore: I, Abraham Lincoln, President of the United States, do call forth the Militia of the State of New-York, to aid in suppressing said combinations and opposition to said laws. And I do respectfully request, and direct that, for this purpose, your Excellency do forthwith order Major General Sanford, with his command, to report for orders to Major General John A. Dix.

ABRAHAM LINCOLN

[1] DS, IHi. See the similar undated order to Major General Edward S. Sanford, *supra*.

On July 30 Major General John A. Dix inquired of Governor Seymour "whether the military power of the State may be relied on to enforce the execution of the [draft] law in case of forcible resistance to it. I am very anxious that there should be perfect harmony between the Federal Government and that of the State of New York, and if, under your authority to see the laws faithfully executed, I can feel assured . . . I need not ask the War Department to put at my disposal . . . troops in the service of the United States. . . ." (OR, III, III, 592). Failing to receive a reply, on August 12, Dix requested 10,000 federal troops and suggested the propriety of the president's calling out the state militia (*ibid.*, pp. 672-74).

On August 15 Seymour answered Dix's letter of July 30, and Dix replied on August 18 as follows:

"I did not receive until last evening your letter of the 15th instant. [A footnote in the source designates the letter as 'not found.'] Immediately on my arrival in this city on the 18th ultimo I called upon you with General Canby, and in a subsequent interview with you at my headquarters I expressed the wish that the draft in this state should be executed without the employment of the troops in the service of the United States. In a letter addressed to you on the 30th I renewed more formally the expression of this wish. . . . In the same spirit, when some of the provost-marshals in the interior applied to me for aid against threatened violence, I referred them to you. . . . It was my earnest wish that the Federal arm should neither be seen nor felt. . . . Not having received an answer from you, I applied to the Secretary of War on the 14th instant for a force adequate to the object. The call was promptly responded to and I shall be ready to meet all opposition to the draft. I trust, however, that your determination, of which your letter advises me, to 'call into requisition the military power, if need be, to put down violations of good order, riotous proceedings, and disturbances of the public peace, as infractions of the laws of this State,' will render it unnecessary to use the troops. . . ." (*Ibid.*, p. 690).

Under date of August 15 (according to John Hay's *Diary*, on the night of August 14) Stanton wrote Dix as follows:

"Enclosed herewith I send you by the hands of Colonel Fry—

"1. A Proclamation by the President to be used by you in case of any necessity arising for the employment of military force to overcome unlawful combinations against the authority of the General Government in executing the Act of Congress to enroll and call out the National force. Of this necessity you are authorized to be judge, and if it arises, you will fill up the blanks and promulgate the Proclamation. The original with the Great Seal remains with the Archives of the Government in the State Department.

"2. A call upon the Governor of New York by the President, notifying him to issue orders to Major General Sanford (Charles W.) [*sic*]. The use of this paper is left to your discretion. It has occurred to the President that it may be proper and servicable to put upon Governor Seymour a call for assistance, and let him render it or shoulder the responsibility of refusing. It is not supposed that this call is essential to the authority of the President, or that the assent or obedience of Governor Seymour affects the right or power of the President to issue an order to General Sanford directly. But it may be an expedient courtesy of which you are to judge and which you should have the means of employing if you think proper.

"A blank is left for you to fill up with the State of New York, or any specific districts, as the case may require, and also a blank for date to be filled.

"3. An order by the President upon General Sanford to report to you.

"The date and also the blank for state or specific districts are to be filled up.

"You will be apprised by the Provost Marshal General what reinforcements will be sent forward. He will confer with you. Any further aid or direction you may require, will on notice, be given you if in the power of the Government. . . ." (Copy, DLC-Stanton Papers).

With Governor Seymour's co-operation, however, Dix found issuance of the proclamation and communications to Sanford and Seymour unnecessary. The draft commenced on August 19, with relative quiet.

To Horatio Seymour[1]

Governor Seymour   Executive Mansion,
New-York: Washington, August 16, 1863.

Your despatch of this morning is just received; and, I, fear I do not perfectly understand it.

My view of, the principle is that every soldier obtained voluntarily, leaves one less to be obtained by draft. The only difficulty is, in applying the principle properly. Looking to *time,* as heretofore I am unwilling to give up a drafted man *now,* even for the *certainty,* much less for the mere *chance,* of getting a volunteer *hereafter.*

Again, *after* the draft in any District would it not make trouble to take any drafted man out and put a volunteer in; for how shall it be determined, which drafted man is to have, the previlege of thus going out, to the exclusion of all the others?

And even *before* the draft in any District the quota must be fixed; and the draft might be postponed indefinitely, if every time a volunteer is offered the officers must stop and reconstruct the quota. At least I fear there might be this difficulty; but, at all events let credits for volunteers be given up to the last moment, which will not produce confusion or delay.

That, the principle of giving credits for volunteers shall be applied by Districts seems fair and proper, though I do not know how far, by present statistics, it is practicable. When, for any cause, a fair credit is not given at one time, it should be given as soon thereafter as practicable.

My purpose is to be just and fair; and yet to not lose time.

A. LINCOLN

[1] ALS, RPB. Governor Seymour telegraphed at 9:30 A.M. on August 16: "In view of the uncertainty as to the quotas which may be required from the several Congressional districts . . . there is a doubt by many as to whether volunteers now recruited will be available to reduce the quotas as they may be ultimately adjusted. This doubt interferes with the recruiting of volunteers. I therefore request that volunteers heretofore recruited and mustered . . . shall be accepted as substitutes for such conscripts residing in the same Congressional districts, whether now drawn or heretofore drawn, as may be designated by the State authorities. I am satisfied that such an arrangement will secure immediately a large number of volunteers." (OR, III, III, 681).

To Edwin M. Stanton[1]

Hon. Sec. of War   Executive Mansion
Sir: Washington, Aug. 16, 1863.

It seems that George W. McGuire, and David Bell, have been tried and condemned to be shot by a Military commission, at St. Louis, Mo, of which commission, Gen. W. K. Strong was the head. If a transcript of the record is at your control, please send it to me.
Yours truly   A. LINCOLN

[1] ALS, DLC-RTL. Stanton endorsed the letter referring it to Assistant Adjutant General Townsend, and Townsend referred it to Judge Advocate General Holt, who endorsed, August 17, "The records in the within named cases have not been received at this office." See Lincoln to Strong, August 17, and to Schofield, August 22, *infra*.

To James H. Hackett[1]

                                              Executive Mansion,
My dear Sir: Washington, August 17, 1863.

Months ago I should have acknowledged the receipt of your book, and accompanying kind note; and I now have to beg your pardon for not having done so.

For one of my age, I have seen very little of the drama. The first presentation of Falstaff I ever saw was yours here, last winter or spring. Perhaps the best compliment I can pay is to say, as I truly can, I am very anxious to see it again. Some of Shakspeare's plays I have never read; while others I have gone over perhaps as frequently as any unprofessional reader. Among the latter are Lear, Richard Third, Henry Eighth, Hamlet, and especially Macbeth. I think nothing equals Macbeth. It is wonderful. Unlike you gentlemen of the profession, I think the soliloquy in Hamlet commencing "O, my offence is rank" surpasses that commencing "To be, or not to be." But pardon this small attempt at criticism. I should like to hear you pronounce the opening speech of Richard the Third. Will you not soon visit Washington again? If you do, please call and let me make your personal acquaintance. Yours truly   A. LINCOLN.

James H. Hackett, Esq.

¹ ALS, owned by Alfred W. Stern, Chicago, Illinois. On March 20, James H. Hackett sent Lincoln a copy of his recently published *Notes and Comments upon Certain Plays and Actors of Shakespeare, with Criticisms and Correspondence* (New York, 1863), accompanied by a letter reading in part as follows:

"Your Excellency favored me last Friday eveng. 13th inst. by a spontaneous visit to the Washington theatre to witness my personation of the Falstaff of King Henry IV, and I would respectfully ask your acceptance of a volume which I have recently published and the concluding portion of which refers particularly to the remarkable points of that renowned character. . . .

"I . . . venture to hope that at your . . . leisure you may find therein some agreeable relaxation from your cares of State. . . ." (DLC-RTL).

Upon receiving Lincoln's letter, Hackett issued a broadside printing entitled "A Letter from President Lincoln to Mr. Hackett," which bore the notice "Printed not for publication but for private distribution only, and its convenient perusal by personal friends." Seized upon by political enemies, the letter thus distributed was soon carried in the newspapers with sarcastic comments on the president's lack of critical sense. For Hackett's apology, see note to Lincoln's letter of November 2, *infra*.

To Andrew Johnson¹

Gov. Johnson   Washington D.C
Nashville, Tenn.   Aug. 17. 1863

The appointment of Col. Gillem to be a Brigadier general has been ordered.   A. LINCOLN

¹ ALS, RPB. On August 16 Governor Johnson telegraphed Lincoln, "We are succeeding in raising Tennessee forces. There are more than two brigades of Tennesseeans at Carthage and Nashville. When I was in Washington last spring I urged the appointment of A. C. Gillem, of the Regular Army, commanding First Middle Tennessee, as brigadier-general of volunteers . . . [see Lincoln to Stanton, November 19, 1862, *supra*] I earnestly recommend his appointment to fill the vacancy caused by Governor [William B.] Campbell's resignation. General Rosecrans desires that this appointment should be made." (OR, I, XXX, III, 54).

To Frederick F. Low¹

Hon. F. F. Lowe.   Washington D.C.
San Francisco, Cal.   August 17. 1863

There seems to be considerable misunderstanding about the recent movement to take possession of the New-Almedan mine. It had no reference to any other mines or miners. In regard to mines and miners generaly, no change of policy by the government has been decided on, or even thought of, so far as I know. The New-Almedan mine was peculiar in this, that its occupants claimed to be the legal owners of it, on a Mexican grant, and went into court on the claim. The case found it's way into the Supreme Court of the United States; and last term, in and by that court, the claim of the occupants was decided to be utterly fraudulent. Thereupon it was considered the duty of the government, by the Secretary of the Interior, the Attorney General, and myself, to take possession of the premises; and the Attorney General carefully made out the Writ, and I signed it. It was not obtained surreptitiously, although I suppose Gen. Halleck thought it had been, when he telegraphed, simply because he thought possession was about being taken by a Military order—while he knew no such order had passed through his hands, as General-in-Chief.

The Writ was suspended, upon urgent representations from California, simply to keep the peace. It never had any direct or indirect reference to any mine, place, or person, except the New-Almedan mine, and the persons connected with it.

A. LINCOLN.

[1] ALS, RPB. See Lincoln to Swett and Low, July 9, *supra*, and to Swett, August 29, *infra*.

To Edwin M. Stanton[1]

August 17, 1863

The writer of the within is reliable. Dr. Chipley has a son at Camp Chase, captured in the Confed. Army, who is now only in his eighteenth year. I think the Sec. of War may safely bail him to his father, who is unquestionably loyal.   A. LINCOLN

Aug. 17. 1863.

[1] AES, RPB. Lincoln's endorsement is written on a letter from Dr. Theodore S. Bell, president of the Kentucky Branch of the U.S. Sanitary Commission, August 6, 1863, introducing "the bearer of this, Dr Wm S. Chipley, of Lexington, Ky . . . one of the most perfect specimens of a pure, unadulterated, *un-kinky* Kentucky Union man that I could send you. . . ." The letter is endorsed also by Stanton, who referred it to Major General Ethan A. Hitchcock, commissioner for exchange of prisoners, and by Hitchcock, recommending that "the son, C. Chipley, be discharged upon taking the oath of allegiance." Privately Chipley had been with John H. Morgan's raid in Ohio and was captured on July 20.

To Edwin M. Stanton[1]

Sec. of War please see Gen. Rousseau, at once.

Aug. 17. 1863   A. LINCOLN

[1] AES, RPB. See Lincoln to Stanton and Halleck, July 27, *supra*. Lincoln's endorsement is written on the following draft of an order, not in Lincoln's handwriting:

"That full power & authority is hereby given to Major General Rousseau, with the consent and approbation of Major General Rosecrans, to mount his own

Division, and such other Regiments or Brigades in the army of the Dept of the Cumberland as may be deemed expedient, on mules or horses, armed with Sharp's or Spencer's rifle, and that the Ordnance Bureau & the Quarter Masters Dept. are authorized and required, respectively, to supply, on the requisition of Major Genl. Rousseau, approved by Major Genl Rosecrans, the necessary number of mules or horses, and arms, for that purpose."

To Frederick P. Stanton[1]

Dear Sir   August 17, 1863

I think there is no occasion for changing the Order in the Court of Inquiry case of which we spoke this morning. The main point is to put in all your evidence, and have it duly reported and entered so that, at the end, I can see it. Unless you have difficulty (which I do not anticipate) about getting your evidence in, I think you have no occasion to appeal to me. Yours truly   A. LINCOLN

[1] Stan. V. Henkels Catalog 1343, January 17, 1924, No. 369. No further reference has been found.

To William K. Strong[1]

Gen. W. K. Strong   Washington, D.C
St. Louis, Mo.   Aug. 17. 1863

Please send me a transcript of the record in the case McGuire & Bell, under sentence of death by a Commission of which you were the head.   A LINCOLN

[1] ALS, RPB. See Lincoln to Stanton, August 16, *supra*, and to Schofield, August 22, *infra*.

To Edward Bates[1]

I believe Mr. North has already been appointed Judge, but if not, I think it may be done at once.   A LINCOLN
     Aug. 18. 1863

[1] AES, DNA GE RG 60, Papers of Attorney General, Segregated Lincoln Material. Lincoln's endorsement is written on a telegram from Frederick F. Low, San Francisco, August 18, 1863, asking appointment of John W. North of Nevada as associate justice for Nevada Territory in place of Gordon N. Mott, resigned. North received the appointment.

To James G. Blunt[1]

               Executive Mansion,
Major General Blunt: Washington, August 18, 1863.

Yours of July 31st is received. Governor Carney did leave some papers with me concerning you; but they made no great impression upon me; and I believe they are not altogether such as you seem to think. As I am not proposing to act upon them, I do not now take the time to re-examine them.

I regret to find you denouncing so many persons as liars, scoundrels, fools, thieves, and persecutors of yourself. Your military position looks critical, but did any body *force* you into it? Have you been *ordered* to confront and fight ten thousand men, with three thousand men? The Government cannot make men; and it is very easy, when a man has been given the highest commission, for him to turn on those who gave it and vilify them for not giving him a command according to his rank.

My appointment of you first as a Brigadier, and then as a Major General, was evidence of my appreciation of your service; and I have not since marked but one thing in connection with you, with which to be dissatisfied. The sending a military order twenty five miles outside of your lines, and all military lines, to take men charged with no offence against the military, out of the hands of the courts, to be turned over to a mob to be hanged, can find no precedent or principle to justify it.[2] Judge Lynch sometimes takes jurisdiction of cases which prove too strong for the courts; but this is the first case within my knowledge, wherein the court being able to maintain jurisdiction against Judge Lynch, the military has come to the assistance of the latter. I take the facts of this case as you state them yourself, and not from any report of Governor Carney, or other person. Yours truly   A LINCOLN

[1] LS (copy?), DLC-RTL. See Lincoln to Lane, July 17, and to Carney, July 21, *supra*. On July 31, General Blunt wrote Lincoln:

"I have learned . . . that Thomas Carney, Governor of Kansas, has recently filed with you charges against myself. . . . Justice . . . demands that these charges should be investigated. . . . I know that he never intended that there should be an investigation . . . but expected to . . . get rid of me upon his own representation. . . . I have denounced him publicly as a thief and a liar. . . . I have no hesitation in saying that a greater thief and corrupt villain than Thomas Carney does not live, and all that he lacks to make him a finished scoundrel is his stupidity and want of brains. . . . He has furthermore been aided in his crusade against me by the commanding general of this department . . . a general inferior to me in grade and rank, who enjoys a reputation among the soldiers of the west for cowardice and imbecility. . . .

"My private grievances shall not interfere with the public interest. If the good of the cause requires it I will command 500 negroes, and my present command is not much more—a gay command for a major-general. . . . I have made repeated application for re-enforcements . . . . the enemy . . . are at least 12,000 strong . . . and are offering battle. I have not more than 3,000 effective men. . . . I am well convinced that there has been a determined purpose . . . to sacrifice this command by withholding re-enforcements in order . . . to get rid of me. . . ." (OR, I, LIII, 565-67).

Blunt was relieved of his command at Fort Smith, Arkansas, by *General Orders No. 118*, Headquarters Department of the Missouri, October 19, 1863 (OR, I, XXII, II, 666).

2 Blunt's reply on September 24 said of this point in Lincoln's letter, "In regard to the matter of hanging certain men in Atchison, and which you remark is the only act of mine with which you have been dissatisfied, I think you must have misunderstood the fact when you state that I 'went twenty-five miles outside of my lines, or any other military lines.' Atchison is in Kansas and Kansas was under my military rule and under my command. The courts were not competent to try offenders, and the civil law could not be executed. . . . Murderers and thieves had inaugurated a reign of terror . . . and the people looked to me, and to me alone, for protection. I had not troops sufficient to protect them in all parts of the State, and when the honest people themselves resolved to take matters into their own hands and protect themselves, I did give my consent that they should deal with them as their crimes deserved. The effect of the hanging at Atchison was salutary, and the condition of affairs in Kansas since the command passed from my hands has convinced me . . . that the hangings stopped too soon. . . ." (OR, I, LIII, 573).

To Salmon P. Chase[1]

August 18, 1863

Sec. of Treasury, please see this Lady who says she is wife of a preacher who is in the war as a Captain in the 126th. N.Y. She wants employment.   A. LINCOLN

Aug. 18. 1863

1 ALS, PHi. The lady has not been identified.

To Joseph Holt[1]

This Report first reached me, August 18, 1863.

A. LINCOLN

1 AES, owned by C. Norton Owen, Glencoe, Illinois. Lincoln's endorsement is written on the review and record of twenty-seven cases of officers investigated for improper use of their authority in dealing in cotton, as reported to the judge advocate general by a court of inquiry presided over by General Irvin McDowell.

To Benjamin B. French[1]

Col. B. B. French   Executive Mansion,
Dear Sir: Washington, Aug. 19, 1863.

I have just seen the Secretary of War who says he will return to the Trustees their own building now in the control of the Surgeon General.   A. LINCOLN

1 Copy, ISLA. On August 19, Colonel French wrote Lincoln:
"The War Department having taken possession of the school house of the First District of Washington for the purpose of converting it into a *Medical Museum*, the Trustees of the Public Schools were left without any place for the schools. They applied to me for leave to occupy Franklin Square *temporarily* for the erection of school houses. That square is owned by the U.S. & . . .

I called on you, made known my business, & stated the facts. . . . The conversation ended by your saying, emphatically, 'Do as you think best in the matter'. . . . I replied, 'then I shall grant the privilege with your sanction.' . . . .

"An appropriation was made by the City Council for the building, and it was commenced, when a guard of soldiers was sent by order, I learn, of the Secy. of War, and the building stopped by force. . . .

"I most respectfully request, that you will take such measures as will result in granting the small boon that has been asked and once supposed to be granted. . . ." (DLC-RTL).

To Edwin M. Stanton[1]

Hon. Sec. of War   Executive Mansion,
Dear Sir: Washington, August 19, 1863.

The bearer of this, Judge Colt, of Mo, introduced to me by the Attorney General, tells me [he] has a Step-son—Singleton Wilson —who ran away into the rebel army, then under seventeen, and still under nineteen, and who is now a prisoner at Camp-Morton, Indiana. He now wants to take the oath of allegiance, and go home with the Judge, and the Judge desires the same.

May it not be safely done? Yours truly   A. LINCOLN

[1] ALS, DLC-RTL. James B. Colt's letter to William Hoffman, commissary general of prisoners, August 18, 1863, requesting the release of Singleton Wilson, bears Hoffman's endorsement referring the letter to Stanton, Stanton's endorsement referring it to General Ethan A. Hitchcock, and Hitchcock's endorsement of disapproval (DLC-RTL). On the bottom of Lincoln's letter Stanton wrote the following endorsement:

"The Secretary of War respectfully reports that in his opinion the release within requested upon the terms stated, should not be granted. He has been over two years voluntarily in the rebel service. He is a young gentleman of education obtained membership in a military organization under pretext of serving the government, has ever since and until his capture at Vicksburg borne arms against the government and is believed to be an officer of an organization that has been distinguished for active & relentless hostility against the United States. If such offences are to be taken out of the general rule of captives of war what should not be? He stands good at least for the release of one Union soldier from bondage. I am unwilling that our soldiers should lose that chance for the sake of favoring one who is so deep in this war and in crime against this government For this reason as well as those assigned by General Hitchcock I advise against any mitigation of the laws of war in his favor."

See further Lincoln to Bates, August 20, *infra*.

To Edward Bates[1]

August 20, 1863

Attorney General, please read & return to me as the report I get on the case he sent me Judge Colt—at the case presented to me by Judge Colt, coming with an introduction from Atty. Genl.

Aug. 20. 1863   A. LINCOLN

1 AES, DLC-RTL. Lincoln's somewhat incoherent endorsement is written on the back of his letter to Stanton concerning Singleton Wilson, August 19, *supra*. Bates replied on August 26, "I have nothing to say against the views of the case taken by Genl. Hitchcock & the Secretary of War." (DLC-RTL).

To James C. Conkling[1]

Hon. James C. Conkling   Washington, D.C.,
Springfield, Illinois   August 20 1863
     Your letter of the 14th. is received. I think I will go, or send a letter—probably the latter.   A. LINCOLN

1 ALS, RPB. James C. Conkling wrote Lincoln on August 14:
"The unconditional union men of all parties in our State are to hold a Grand Mass Meeting at Springfield on the 3rd day of September next. It would be gratifying to the many thousands who will be present . . . if you would also meet with them. It is stated in the public papers that you will visit the White Mountains and perhaps you can make it convenient to extend your trip to Illinois. . . .
"We intend to make the most imposing demonstration that has ever been held in the Northwest. . . . I know that nothing could add more to the interest of the occasion than your presence
"Can you not give us a favorable reply. . . ." (DLC-RTL).
See Lincoln to Conkling, August 26, *infra*.

To Andrew J. Hamilton[1]

Gen. A. J. Hamilton, (of Texas)   Washington, D.C.,
New-York—   August 20 1863
     Telegraph me the name of a boy, or young man, whom you would like to have appointed to West-Point.   A. LINCOLN

1 ALS, RPB. No reply has been found.

To Edwin M. Stanton[1]

Hon. Sec. of War   Executive Mansion,
    Dear Sir: Washington, Aug. 20, 1863.
     Since leaving the Telegraph office it has occurred to me that it might be well to have Gen. Lockwood send down to us, the two men he mentions as just arrived from Fredericksburg. Yours truly   A. LINCOLN

1 ALS, CSmH. Brigadier General Henry H. Lockwood telegraphed General Meade from Harper's Ferry at 1:25 P.M., "A gentleman of the highest respectability . . . has ridden into town to report information just received from Fredericksburg by two men from that place, one a Unionist, the other a secessionist. These men agree in reporting Lee's army very much disorganized;

has received no re-enforcements; has lost largely by desertion, and that he will not make a stand this side of Richmond, and is even now preparing to retreat. This is his object in maneuvering to his right, &c." (OR, I, XXIX, II, 80).

To Joseph Holt[1]

August 21, 1863

Judge Advocate General, please get all the papers, and report upon this case, with reference to the *law*, & the *animus* of Capt. Paige in the case.   A. LINCOLN

August 21. 1863

[1] AES, ORB. Lincoln's endorsement has been clipped from attendant papers. The register of letters received by the secretary of War lists the document, however, as the case of W. W. Paige dismissed for alleged fraud against the government for use and risk of a horse (DNA WR RG 107, P 207).

To George G. Meade[1]

Major General Meade   Executive Mansion,
Warrenton, Va   Washington, Aug. 21, 1863.

At this late moment I am appealed to in behalf of William Thompson of Co. K. 3rd. Maryland Volunteers, in 12th. Army Corps said to be at Kelly's Ford, under sentence to be shot to-day as a deserter. He is represented to me to be very young, with symptoms of insanity. Please postpone the execution till further order   A. LINCOLN

[1] ALS, owned by Edward C. Stone, Boston, Mass. General Meade replied the same day, "Your despatch of 9.50 rec'd. Upon representations made . . . by his Corps commander, I yesterday suspended for one week, the execution of . . . John Thompson, of Company 'K' 3d. Maryland Volunteers. . . .
"In compliance with your instructions, I will at once direct that the execution . . . be suspended until further orders from you." (DLC-RTL).
Lincoln is in error as to Thompson's first name. *General Orders No. 77*, Headquarters of the Army of the Potomac, August 19, 1863, orders execution of John Thompson of Company K, Third Maryland Volunteers. The roster of the regiment, however, carries John Thompson as "dishonorably" discharged as of February 28, 1863.

To Edwin M. Stanton[1]

Sec. of War, please see this Pittsburgh boy. He is very young, and I shall be satisfied with whatever you do with him

Aug. 21. 1863.   A. LINCOLN

[1] ALS-F, ISLA. No further reference has been found.

To Edwin M. Stanton[1]

Hon. Secretary of War: Executive Mansion,
My dear Sir: Washington, August 21. 1863.

In the autumn of 1861, certain persons in armed rebellion, against the United States, within the counties of Acomac and Northampton, laid down their arms upon certain terms then proposed to them by Genl. Dix, in and by a certain procla[ma]tion. It is now said that these persons or some of them, are about to be forced into the military lines of the existing rebellion, unless they will take an oath prescribed to them since, and not included in, Gen. Dix' proclamation referred to. Now, my judgment is that no one of these men should be forced from his home, who has not broken faith with the government, according to the terms fixed by Gen. Dix and these men. It is bad faith in the government to force new terms upon such as have kept faith with it. At least so it seems to me.

[1] ADf, DLC-RTL. See Lincoln's communications to Stanton on September 1, *infra.*

To Whom It May Concern[1]

Executive Mansion, Washington, D.C.,
To whom it may concern: August 21, 1863.

To-day I am called upon by a committee of colored ministers of the Gospel, who express a wish to go within our military lines and minister to their brethren there. The object is a worthy one, and I shall be glad for all facilities to be afforded them which may not be inconsistent with or a hindrance to our military operations.

A. LINCOLN.

[1] Washington *Morning Chronicle*, August 26, 1863. A committee of Negro Baptist ministers appointed by the American Baptist Missionary Convention in session at the First Colored Baptist Church interviewed the president to present the request. "The President then made some interesting remarks, after which he presented the chairman" with the letter (*ibid.*).

To Green Adams[1]

Hon. Green Adams   Executive Mansion,
My dear Sir   Washington, Aug 22, 1863

I see by the papers that with nine counties still out Bramlette has over 50,000 majority. I wish you would ascertain for me the aggregate vote he has received. I wish to see whether it will be a clear majority of the largest vote ever cast in Kentucky. The Presidential vote of 1860 which I suppose to be the largest, was 146,216 and 73,109 would be a clear majority of it. Yours truly

A LINCOLN

1 ALS, owned by John S. Adams, Sr., Wayne, Pennsylvania. No reply from Green Adams has been found.

To John M. Schofield[1]

Gen. Schofield   Washington, D.C.
St. Louis, Mo.   Aug. 22. 1863

Please send me, if you can, a transcript of the record in the case of McGuire & Bell, convicted of Murder by a Military Commission. I telegraphed Gen. Strong for it, but he does not answer.

A. LINCOLN

1 ALS, RPB. See Lincoln to Stanton, August 16, and to Strong, August 17, *supra*. General Schofield replied on August 25, "The records in the cases of McGuire & Bell were sent to the Judge Advocate General Washn on the 17th of June" (DLC-RTL).
The records in the case have not been found. On August 31, Colonel John F. Philips of the Seventh Cavalry, Missouri State Militia, wrote Lincoln about the case. David Bell, a sergeant in Company B of Philips' regiment, and one McGuire, were convicted of the murder of William Major, a citizen of Pettis County, Missouri. On furlough at the time, Bell was drunk and blamed the murder on McGuire (DLC-RTL).

To Daniel E. Sickles[1]

Major General Sickles   Washington D.C.
My Dear Sir   August 22. 1863

Your note and brief, about the California Land Claim, are received. The question presented is a property question, with which I do not think I should meddle as a volunteer. It will save me labor, therefore, if you will first point me to the law which assigns any duty to the President in the case. This done, next send me a reference to the treaty, and all the statutory law which bears upon the case. Yours truly   A LINCOLN

1 Copy, DLC-RTL. General Sickles, recuperating at Saratoga Springs, New York, wrote Lincoln on August 15, 1863, concerning the case of the Panoche Grande, California, Land Grant, in which Sickles had an interest. On October 23, Sickles submitted a further statement of facts and legal authorities, "relied upon to establish the right of myself and associates, owners of the Estate known as the Panoche Grande, to a patent from the United States. . . ." (DLC-RTL).

To Joseph P. Taylor[1]

Commissary General please see Hon. J. O. Norton & oblige him if possible.   A. LINCOLN

Aug. 22, 1863.

Let Edward L. Gooding, recommended within, be appointed a Commissary of Subsistence.   A. LINCOLN

Aug. 22, 1863.

[1] AES, IHi. These endorsements have been clipped from the attendant papers. Edward L. Gooding of Chicago, Illinois, was appointed captain and commissary of subsistence of Volunteers on August 22, 1863.

To Mrs. Elizabeth J. Grimsley[1]

Mrs. Elizabeth J. Grimsley   Washington, D.C.,
Springfield, Illinois.   August 24, 1863
   I mail the papers to you to-day appointing Johnny to the Naval-School.   A. LINCOLN

[1] ALS, RPB. See Lincoln's memorandum concerning appointment of Robert J. Sperry, August 10, and Lincoln to Mrs. Grimsley, August 14, *supra.*

Memorandum: Appointment of Edward Sherer[1]

[August 24, 1863]

Edward Sherer, 20 last March, wishes to go to West-Point.

[1] AE, DNA WR RG 94, U.S. Military Academy 1864, Box 83. No. 414. Lincoln's endorsement is written on an envelope filed with the papers of Edward Sherer. No record of Sherer's appointment has been found.

Memorandum Concerning Illinois Claims[1]

[August 24, 1863]

Under that provision of the United States Constitution which requires the President to take care that the Laws be faithfully executed, I am requested to cause a sum of money to be paid from the Treasury of the United States to the State of Illinois.

By the sixth Section of the Illinois enabling act, approved April 18, 1818, it was among other things, provided that two per cent of the net proceeds of the sales of the United States lands, within Illinois, and which should be sold after the 1st. day of January 1819, should be disbursed under the direction of Congress in making roads leading to the State—this under a condition that the State should not tax the lands sold within five years of the day of sale.

Illinois closed with these terms; and they became matter of compact. The money now claimed by Illinois is sought to be legally derived from this two per cent fund.

1806–	$ 30.000–	2 per ct. fund	
1810–	60.000–	" " " "	Ohio
1811–	50.000.	" " " "	fund
1812–	30.000.	" " " "	
1815–	100.000	" " " "	
1818	{ 52.984.62		
	{ 260.000		
1825–	150.000	2 per ct fund	{ O
1827–	30.000		{ In
1829	100.000		{ Ills.
" "	50.000		{ Mo.
" "	100.000		
1831	244.915		
1834 { O	200.000		
{ In–	150.000		
{ Ills. –	100.000		
Pen	300.000.		
1835–	300.000		
" "	346.186–	East of Ohio	
1836	600.000–	" "	
1838	450.000		

[1] AD, DLC-RTL. See Lincoln to James M. Edmunds, February 9, *supra*, and the communications to Morris and Usher, *infra*.

To Isaac N. Morris[1]

I sent your case to the Secretary of the Interior yesterday, and have not yet heard of it. A. LINCOLN.

August 24, 1863.

[1] *Illinois Reports* (1865), I, 226. See Lincoln's memorandum, *supra*, and letter to Usher, *infra*. Morris acknowledged Lincoln's note on August 25: "I hardly know how I am to understand your note. Must I infer from it that I am refered to the Interior Department or must I wait upon your Excellency until you hear from it? When may I expect a definite answer?" (DLC-RTL). See Lincoln's reply, August 26, *infra*.

To John P. Usher[1]

Executive Mansion, August 24, 1863.

Sir: By the within you see the claim of Illinois for the two per cent. on sales of public lands is again presented.

My view of the case is not changed. I believe the law is with the State; and yet I think it is ungracious to be pressing the claim at this time of national trouble.

Nevertheless, I have to ask that you will determine what is your duty according to the law, and then do it. Yours truly,

A. LINCOLN.

¹ NH, IX, 91. See Lincoln's memorandum and letter to Morris, *supra*. A different version of this letter to Usher appears in *Illinois Reports* (1865) I, 312, as follows:

"Hon. Interior Secretary:

"Illinois has again presented her claim for the two per cent. I do not think it very gracious in her to do so at this time of our National troubles. My opinion of the law has undergone no change. I think the law is with the State. I therefore desire you to take up the case and act upon it as you may think the law is.

"A. LINCOLN."

Note for Mrs. Brannon¹

August 25, 1863

Please see Mrs. Brannon.

¹ *The Collector*, January, 1928, No. 9891. No further reference has been found.

Order for Clearance of Vessels Bound for New Orleans¹

Executive Mansion,
Ordered.   Washington, August 25 1863

1st. That clearances issued by the Treasury Department for vessels or merchandize bound for the port of New-Orleans for the military necessities of the Department cert[i]fied by Brigadier General Shepley the Military Governor of Louisiana, shall be allowed to enter said port.

2nd. That vessels and domestic produce from New-Orleans permitted by the Military Governor of Louisiana at New-Orleans for the military purpose of his Department, shall on his permit be allowed to pass from said port to its destination to any port not blockaded by the United States.   ABRAHAM LINCOLN

¹ DS, MeHi.

To Edwin M. Stanton¹

[August 25, 1863]

The little short act on page 804 of the large new volume was shown to me by Mr. Bingham of Ohio, as being the one, in con-

nection with the other laws therein referred to, which works the
result. I have not tracked up the other laws. A. LINCOLN.

¹ NH, IX, 92. Lincoln's endorsement is on a note from Stanton of this date:
"Please give me the reference to the act of Congress in relation to the election
of members of the House, which you have mentioned to me on one or two occa-
sions. I cannot find the act." (*Ibid.*, pp. 91-92).
The act referred to was presumably "An Act to regulate the Duties of the
Clerk of the House of Representatives in preparing for the Organization of the
House," approved March 3, 1863 (*U.S. Statutes at Large*, XII, 804).

To James C. Conkling¹

Hon. James C. Conkling   Executive Mansion,
My Dear Sir.   Washington, August 26, 1863.

Your letter inviting me to attend a mass-meeting of unconditional Union-men, to be held at the Capital of Illinois, on the 3d
day of September, has been received.

It would be very agreeable to me, to thus meet my old friends,
at my own home; but I can not, just now, be absent from here,
so long as a visit there, would require.

The meeting is to be of all those who maintain unconditional
devotion to the Union; and I am sure my old political friends will
thank me for tendering, as I do, the nation's gratitude to those
other noble men, whom no partizan malice, or partizan hope, can
make false to the nation's life.

There² are those who are dissatisfied with me. To such I would
say: You desire peace; and you blame me that we do not have it.³
But how can we attain it? There are but three conceivable ways.
First, to suppress the rebellion by force of arms. This, I am trying
to do. Are you for it? If you are, so far we are agreed. If you are
not for it, a second way is, to give up the Union. I am against this.

¹ LS, IHi; ADf and ADfS, DLC-RTL. The present text follows the letter sent
to Conkling, which was copied by a clerk from the final draft and corrected and
signed by Lincoln. An insertion sent later by telegraph and significant dele-
tions and emendations in the preliminary and final drafts are indicated in the
succeeding footnotes.
² The second page of Lincoln's final draft begins with this paragraph, the
first page having been revised from a non-extant first page of the preliminary
draft. The second page of the preliminary draft, however, preserves at this point
the last few lines of the introduction as Lincoln first wrote it, to wit:
". . . Grandfathers employed to establish it? and our own fathers have already employed once to maintain it? Are we degenerate?—Unworthy sons
of noblest sires?
"But, say some of you, we know for what our sires fought; what fight we for
now? So far as it is for me to answer I have told you many times. I will repeat
in another form. You desire peace. . . ." etc.
³ The preliminary draft has the additional sentence: "I desire it also."

Are you for it? If you are, you should say so plainly. If you are not for *force*, nor yet for *dissolution*, there only remains some imaginable *compromise*. I do not believe any compromise, embracing the maintenance of the Union, is now possible. All I learn, leads to a directly opposite belief. The strength of the rebellion, is its military—its army. That army dominates all the country, and all the people, within its range. Any offer of terms made by any man or men within that range, in opposition to that army, is simply nothing for the present; because such man or men, have no power whatever to enforce their side of a compromise, if one were made with them. To[4] illustrate—Suppose refugees from the South, and peace men of the North, get together in convention, and frame and proclaim a compromise embracing a restoration of the Union; in what way can that compromise be used to keep Lee's army out of Pennsylvania? Meade's army can keep Lee's army out of Pennsylvania; and, I think, can ultimately drive it out of existence. But no paper compromise, to which the controllers of Lee's army are not agreed, can, at all, affect that army. In an effort at such compromise we should waste time, which the enemy would improve to our disadvantage; and that would be all. A compromise, to be effective, must be made either with those who control the rebel army, or[5] with the people first liberated from the domination of that army, by the success of our own army. Now allow me to assure you, that no word or intimation, from that rebel army, or from any of the men controlling it, in relation to any peace compromise, has ever come to my knowledge or belief. All charges and insinuations to the contrary, are[6] deceptive and groundless. And I promise you, that if any such proposition shall hereafter come, it shall not be rejected, and kept a secret from you. I freely acknowledge myself the servant of the people, according to the bond of service—the United States constitution; and that, as such, I am responsible to them.

But, to be plain, you are dissatisfied with me about the negro. Quite likely there is a difference of opinion between you and myself upon that subject. I certainly wish that all men[7] could be free, while I suppose you do not. Yet I have neither adopted, nor proposed any measure, which is not consistent with even your view, provided you are for the Union. I suggested compensated eman-

[4] This and the succeeding three sentences are not in the preliminary draft.

[5] The preliminary draft has, "or with the people first liberated from it's domination, by its first having been vanquished by our enemies."

[6] The final draft is emended to the present reading from "are utter humbuggery and falsehood."

[7] "Everywhere" deleted at this point in preliminary draft.

cipation; to which you replied you wished not to be taxed to buy negroes. But I had not asked you to be taxed to buy negroes, except in such way, as to save you from greater taxation to save the Union exclusively by other means.

You dislike the emancipation proclamation; and, perhaps, would have it retracted. You say it is unconstitutional—I think differently. I think the constitution invests its commander-in-chief, with the law of war, in time of war. The most that can be said, if so much, is, that slaves are property. Is there—has there ever been— any question that by the law of war, property, both of enemies and friends, may be taken when needed? And is it not needed whenever taking it, helps us, or hurts the enemy? Armies, the world over, destroy enemies' property when they can not use it; and even destroy their own to keep it from the enemy. Civilized belligerents do all[8] in their power to help themselves, or hurt the enemy, except a few things regarded as barbarous or cruel. Among the exceptions are the massacre of vanquished foes, and non-combatants, male and female.

But the proclamation, as law, either is valid, or is not valid. If[9] it is not valid, it needs no retraction. If it is valid, it can not be retracted, any more than the dead can be brought to life. Some of you profess to think its retraction would operate favorably[10] for the Union. Why better *after* the retraction, than *before* the issue? There was more than a year and a half of trial to suppress the rebellion before the proclamation issued, the last one hundred days of which passed under an explicit notice that it was coming, unless averted by those in revolt, returning to their allegiance. The war has certainly progressed as favorably for us, since the issue of the proclamation as before.[11] I[12] know as fully as one can know the opinions of others, that some of the commanders of our armies in the field who have given us our most important successes, believe the eman-

[8] "Everything" emended to "all" in preliminary draft.

[9] The next two sentences in the preliminary draft read: "If it is not so valid, the courts will hold accordingly, and men of your views will not be hurt by it. If it is valid, it can no more be effectually retracted, than a judge can retract a judgment after its final rendering."

[10] "Work wonders" changed to "work favorably" in preliminary draft and to "operate favorably" in the final draft.

[11] An additional sentence appearing in the preliminary draft at this point was omitted in the final draft and in the letter sent: "Some generals in the field, not originally partial to to [sic] the proclamation, now think it has been of service to them."

[12] The remainder of this paragraph was inserted by means of a telegram which Lincoln sent to Conkling on August 31 (*infra*). The text of the letter sent is marked by the parenthetical "*Here insert Telegram*," probably inserted by Conkling.

cipation policy, and the use of colored troops, constitute the heaviest blow yet dealt to the rebellion; and that, at least one of those important successes, could not have been achieved when it was, but for the aid of black soldiers. Among the commanders holding these views are some who have never had any affinity with what is called abolitionism, or with republican party politics; but who hold them purely as military opinions. I submit these opinions as being entitled to some weight against the objections, often urged, that emancipation, and arming the blacks, are unwise as military measures, and were not adopted, as such, in good faith.

You say you will not fight to free negroes. Some[13] of them seem willing to fight for you; but, no matter. Fight you, then, exclusively to save the Union. I issued the proclamation on purpose to aid you in saving the Union. Whenever you shall have conquered all resistance to the Union, if I shall urge you to continue fighting, it will be an apt time, then, for you to declare you will not fight to free negroes.

I thought that in your struggle for the Union, to whatever extent the negroes should cease helping the enemy, to that extent it weakened the enemy in his resistance to you. Do you think differently? I thought that whatever negroes can be got to do as soldiers, leaves just so much less for white soldiers to do, in saving the Union. Does it appear otherwise to you? But negroes, like other people, act[14] upon motives. Why should they do any thing for us, if we will do nothing for them? If they stake their lives for us, they must be prompted by the strongest motive—even the promise of freedom. And the promise being made, must be kept.[15]

The signs look better. The Father of Waters again goes unvexed to the sea. Thanks to the great North-West for it. Nor yet wholly to them. Three hundred miles up, they met New-England, Empire, Key-Stone, and Jersey, hewing their way right and left. The Sunny South too, in more colors than one, also lent a hand. On the spot, their part of the history was jotted down in black and white. The job was a great national one; and let none be banned who bore an honorable part in it. And while those who have cleared the great river may well be proud, even that is not all. It is hard to say that anything has been more bravely, and well done, than at Antietam, Murfreesboro, Gettysburg, and on many fields of lesser note. Nor must Uncle Sam's Web-feet be forgotten. At all the watery margins they have been present. Not only on the deep sea,

13 This sentence does not appear in the preliminary draft.
14 The preliminary draft reads "are creatures of motives."
15 The preliminary draft ends at this point.

the broad bay, and the rapid river, but also up the narrow muddy bayou, and wherever the ground was a little damp, they have been, and made their tracks. Thanks to all. For the great republic—for the principle it lives by, and keeps alive—for man's vast future,— thanks to all.

Peace does not appear so distant as it did. I hope it will come soon, and come to stay; and so come as to be worth the keeping in all future time. It will then have been proved that, among free men, there can be no successful appeal from the ballot to the bullet; and that they who take such appeal are sure to lose their case, and pay the cost. And then, there will be some black men who can remember that, with silent tongue, and clenched teeth, and steady eye, and well-poised[16] bayonet, they have helped mankind on to this great consummation; while, I fear, there will be some white ones, unable to forget that, with malignant heart, and deceitful speech, they have strove to hinder it.

Still let us not be over-sanguine of a speedy final triumph. Let us be quite sober. Let us diligently apply the means, never doubting that a just God, in his own good time, will give us the rightful result. Yours very truly   A. LINCOLN.

[16] "Well-borne" changed to "well-poised" in the letter sent.

Fragment[1]

[c. August 26, 1863?]

Suppose those now in rebellion should say: "We cease fighting: re-establish the national authority amongst us—customs, courts, mails, land-offices,—all as before the rebellion—we claiming to send members to both branches of Congress, as of yore, and to hold our slaves according to our State laws, notwithstanding anything or all things which has occurred during the rebellion." I probably should answer: "It will be difficult to justify in reason, or to maintain in fact, a war on one side, which shall have ceased on the other. You began the war, and you can end it. If questions remain, let them be solved by peaceful means—by courts, and votes. This war is an appeal, by you, from the ballot to the sword; and a great object with me has been to teach the futility of such appeal—to teach that what is decided by the ballot, can not be reversed by the sword— to teach that there can be no successful appeal from a fair election, but to the next election. Whether persons sent to congress, will be admitted to seats is, by the constitution, left to each House to decide, the President having nothing to do with it. Yet the question can not be one of indifference to me. I shall dread, and I think we all should dread, to see the 'the disturbing element' so brought back into the government, as to make probable a renewal of the terrible scenes through which we are now passing. During my continuance here, the government will return no person to slavery who is free according to the proclamation, or to any of the acts of congress, unless such return shall be held to be a legal duty, by the proper court of final resort, in which case I will promptly act as may then appear to be my personal duty. ["]

Congress has left to me very large powers to remit forfeitures and personal penalties; and I should exercise these to the greatest extent which might seem consistent with the future public safety. I have thus told you, once more, so far as it is for me to say, what you are fighting for. The prospects of the Union have greatly improved recently; still, let us not be over-sanguine of a speedy final triumph. Let us diligently apply the means, never doubting that a just God, in his own good time, will give us the rightful result.

1 AD, DLC-RTL. The date supplied to this two-page manuscript in the Lincoln Papers has been retained for want of a better assignment, and is based on the following endorsement written by Robert Todd Lincoln on the back of the second page: "This was probably written at the time of the Springd Letter, but not incorporated with it—& never published."

Although the contents of the fragment are apropos of circumstances in August, 1863, it should be noted that they are hardly less apropos of August, 1864 (see Lincoln's letter to Charles D. Robinson, August 17, 1864, *infra*), and might well have expressed Lincoln's point of view at any one of numerous dates.

Memorandum: Appointment of Howard North[1]

Col. Alexander, of Engineers, desires Howard North appointed to West-Point—no kin—father lives in Conn.   A. LINCOLN

Aug. 26. 1863

1 AES, DNA WR RG 94, U.S. Military Academy, 1864, Box 83, No. 364. Lincoln's endorsement is written on a visiting card attached to a letter from Colonel Barton S. Alexander, August 24, 1863, recommending Howard North. No record of North's appointment has been found.

To Isaac N. Morris[1]

Hon. I. N. Morris   Executive Mansion,
Dear Sir: Washington, August 26, 1863.

Your note, asking what you were to understand, was received yesterday. Monday morning, I sent the papers to the Secretary of the Interior, with an indorsement that my impression of the law was not changed, and that I desired him to take up the case and do his duty according to his view of the law. Yesterday I said the same thing to him verbally.

Now, my understanding is that the law has not assigned me, specifically, any duty in the case, but has assigned it to the Secretary of the Interior. It may be my general duty to direct him to act; which I have performed. When he shall have acted, if his action is not satisfactory, there may, or may not, be an appeal to me. It is a point I have not examined; but if then it be shown that the law gives such appeal, I shall not hesitate to entertain it when presented. Yours truly   A LINCOLN

1 ALS, owned by Edward C. Stone, Boston, Massachusetts. See Lincoln's memorandum and the letters to Morris and to Usher, August 24, *supra.* Morris acknowledged receipt of Lincoln's note of August 26 on the same day: "Your letter of this date has just been placed in my hands by your private Secretary. It is all I expected you now to say—full, complete and just in its spirit and sentiments. In behalf of Illinois I return you her greatful thanks for it." (DLC-RTL).

To Edwin M. Stanton[1]

Hon. Secretary of War,   Executive Mansion,
Sir.   Washington, D.C. Aug. 26, 1863.

In my correspondence with Gov. Seymour in relation to the draft, I have said to him, substantially, that credits shall be given for volunteers up to the latest moment, before drawing in any district, that can be done without producing confusion or delay. In order to do this, let our mustering officers in New-York, and elsewhere, be at once instructed that whenever they muster into our service any number of volunteers, to at once make return to the War Department, both by telegraph and mail, the date of the muster, the number mustered, and the Congressional or enrolment District, or Districts, of their residences, giving the number separately for each District. Keep these returns diligently posted, and by them give full credit on the quotas, if possible, on the last day before the draft begins in any District.

Again, I have informed Governor Seymour that he shall be notified of the time when the draft is to commence in each District in his State. This is equally proper for all the States. In order to carry it out, I propose that so soon as the day for commencing the draft in any District is definitely determined, the Governor of the

State, including the District, be notified thereof, both by telegraph and mail, in form, about as follows:

> . . . .
> 1863
> Governor of . . . .
> . . . .
> You are notified that the draft will commence in the . . . . District, at . . . . on the . . . . day of . . . . 1863, at . . . . A.M. of said day. Please acknowledge receipt of this, by telegraph and mail.
> . . . .
> . . . .

This notice may be given by the Provost-Marshall-General here, the sub-Provost-Marshall-Generals in the States, or perhaps by the District Provost-Marshalls.

Whenever we shall have so far proceeded in New York as to make the re-enrolments specially promised there, practicable, I wish that also to go forward; and I wish Governor Seymour notified of it; so that, if he choose, he can place agents of his, with ours, to see the work fairly done. Yours truly   A LINCOLN

[1] LS copy, DLC-RTL. See Lincoln to Seymour, August 27, *infra.* Seymour's letter to Lincoln, August 21, 1863, reiterated his objections to the execution of the draft, and among numerous particulars stated that "On Monday of this week—the 17th instant—I learned, through the public journals, that a draft would be made on Wednesday, the 19th instant, in the Sixth District of New York. This was the first notice I received of that proceeding." (OR, III, III, 703). Footnotes to this sentence as printed in the source give James B. Fry's statements that "On the 12th I notified him that orders were issued to resume the draft for quotas, as designated in the President's letter [Lincoln to Seymour, August 11, *supra*]. . . . On the 16th I wrote from New York City and told him the drawing would begin on Wednesday, 19th instant." (*Ibid.*).

To Edwin M. Stanton[1]

Sec. of War, please see & hear the bearer.
Aug. 26, 1863   A. LINCOLN

[1] AES, DNA WR RG 94, U.S. Military Academy, 1863, Box 82, No. 170. Lincoln's endorsement is written on a letter from Assistant Adjutant General David C. Wager, August 26, 1863, requesting that "the name of Barnet Wager of New York may be added to the list of appointments of cadets to West Point in place of Charles Hoskin whose name . . . has been withdrawn." Stanton endorsed, "Approved & Apt ordered." Barnet Wager entered West Point in 1863 and graduated in 1867.

To Edward Bates[1]

Hon. Attorney General.   War Department
Dear Sir   Washington City, Aug. 27 1863
    Please make out and send for my signature, a formal pardon
according to the letter with my little endorsement on it which will
be shown you by Gen. Green Clay Smith. Yours truly

                                          A. LINCOLN

William Duke is hereby pardoned for all offences herein confessed
by him, up to the time of his taking the oath and giving bond.
    Aug. 27. 1863.   A. LINCOLN.

    [1] ALS and AES, owned by William C. and Otto Madlener, Chicago, Illinois.
The envelope is endorsed by Lincoln, "Please see Gen. Green Clay Smith. A.
Lincoln," and the accompanying letter from William Duke to his brother-in-
law, Green Clay Smith, August 20, 1863, is endorsed by Lincoln as above.
Duke's letter sets forth that although he had "in a state of excitement" accepted
a Confederate commission in September, 1862, he had within a few days recognized his error and taken an oath of allegiance. Smith endorsed Duke's letter
with the request that a final pardon be granted to Duke.

To James C. Conkling[1]

Private   War Department Washington City, D.C.
My dear Conkling   Aug. 27 1863.
    I can not leave here now. Herewith is a letter instead. You are
one of the best public readers. I have but one suggestion. Read it
very slowly.
    And now God bless you, and all good Union-men. Yours as ever
                                            A. LINCOLN

    [1] ALS, IHi. See Lincoln's letter of August 26, *supra*, which was enclosed with
this on August 27.

To George G. Meade[1]

Major General Meade   Washington, D.C.,
Warrenton Va   August 27 1863
    Walter, Rainese, Faline, Lae, & Kuhne appeal to me for mercy,
without giving any ground for it whatever. I understand these are
very flagrant cases, and that you deem their punishment as being
indispensable to the service. If I am not mistaken in this, please let
them know at once that their appeal is denied.   A. LINCOLN

    [1] ALS, owned by Alden S. Condict, New York City. Lincoln received the
following telegram on August 26 at 4:45 P.M.: "We the undersigned sentenced
to suffer death for desertion on Saturday next, humbly beg that you exercise

your authority to commute our sentence, to imprisonment, & hard labor, for any term of years, you may see fit, as we each have wives & children, depending upon us. Charles Walter, John Rainese, John Faline, Emile Lae & George Kuhne." (DLC-RTL).

At 9:30 A.M. on August 27, General Meade replied to Lincoln's telegram: "Walter, Rionese, Faline, Lae and Kuhn were to have been executed yesterday. Their execution was postponed by my order till Saturday the 29th that time might be given to procure the services of a Roman Catholic Priest to assist them in preparing for death. They are substitute conscripts who enlisted for the purpose of deserting after receiving the bounty, and being the first of this class whose cases came before me, I believed that humanity the safety of this Army, and the most vital interests of the Country, required their prompt execution as an example. . . . In view of these circumstances I shall therefore inform them their appeal to you is denied." (DLC-RTL).

Charles Walter (alias C. Zene), John Rainese (alias George Rionese), John Falene (or "Faline," "Folaney" as listed on the roster, and alias Geacinto Lerchize), Emile Lae (or "Lai," alias E. Duffie), and George Kuhne (or "Kuhn," alias G. Weik)—all recruits in the One Hundred Eighteenth Pennsylvania Volunteers—were executed on August 29, 1863.

To John M. Schofield[1]

Gen. Schofield   Washington, D.C.,
St. Louis, Mo.   Aug. 27 1863

I have just received the despatch which follows, from two very influential citizens of Kansas, whose names I omit. The severe blow they have received, naturally enough makes them intemperate, even without there being any just cause for blame. Please do your utmost to give them future security, and to punish their invaders.   A. LINCOLN

[1] ALS, RPB. The despatch which Lincoln forwarded was received from Representative Abel C. Wilder and Senator James H. Lane on August 26 at 8:45 P.M., and read: "The result of the massacre at Lawrence having excited feelings amongst our people, which makes a collision between them & the military probable, the imbecility & incapacity of Schofield is most deplorable. Our people unanimously demand the removal of Schofield, whose policy has opened Kansas to invasion & butchery" (DLC-RTL).

On August 28, General Schofield replied to Lincoln as follows:
"Since the capture of Vicksburg a considerable portion of the rebel army in the Mississippi Valley has disbanded, and large numbers of men have come back to Missouri . . . some . . . under instructions to carry on a guerrilla warfare, and others, men of the worst character, become marauders on their own account. . . .

"Under instructions from the rebel authorities, as I am informed and believe, considerable bands, called 'Border Guards,' were organized in the counties of Missouri bordering on Kansas, for the ostensible purpose of protecting those counties from inroads from Kansas, and preventing slaves of rebels from escaping from Missouri into Kansas. . . .

"Upon the representation of General Ewing and others . . . I became satisfied there could be no cure for the evil short of the removal from those counties of all slaves entitled to their freedom, and of the families of all men known to belong to these bands, and others who were known to sympathize with them.

Accordingly I directed General Ewing to adopt and carry out the policy he had indicated, warning him, however, of the retaliation which might be attempted. . . .

"Almost immediately after it became known that such policy had been adopted, [William C.] Quantrill secretly assembled from several of the border counties of Missouri about 300 of his men. They met at a preconcerted place . . . near the Kansas line, at about sunset, and immediately marched for Lawrence, which place they reached at daylight the next morning. They sacked and burned the town and murdered the citizens in the most barbarous manner.

"It is easy to see that any unguarded town in a country where such a number of outlaws can be assembled is liable to a similar fate, if the villains are willing to risk the retribution which must follow. . . .

"I am officially informed that a large meeting has been held at Leavenworth, in which a resolution was adopted to the effect that the people would assemble at a certain place on the border, on the 8th of September, for the purpose of entering Missouri to search for their stolen property. Efforts have been made by the mayor of Leavenworth to get possession of the ferry at that place for the purpose of crossing armed parties of citizens into Northern Missouri.

"I have strong reasons for believing that the authors of the telegram to you are among those who introduced and obtained the adoption of the Leavenworth resolution, and who are endeavoring to organize a force for the purpose of general retaliation upon Missouri. Those who so deplore my 'imbecility and incapacity' are the very men who are endeavoring to bring about a collision between the people of Kansas and the troops under General Ewing's command. I have not the 'capacity' to see the wisdom or justice of permitting an irresponsible mob to enter Missouri for the purpose of retaliation even for so grievous a wrong as that which Lawrence has suffered.

"I have increased the force upon the border . . . and no effort will be spared to punish the invaders of Kansas and to prevent such acts in future. . . ." (OR, I, XXII, II, 482-84).

To Horatio Seymour[1]

His Excellency   Executive Mansion
Horatio Seymour,   Washington, D.C.
Governor of New-York   Aug. 27. 1863

Yours of the 21st. with exhibits, was received on the 24th. In the midst of pressing duties, I have been unable to answer sooner. In the mean time the Provost-Marshal General has had access to yours, and has addressed a communication in relation [to] it, to the Secretary of War, a copy of which communication, I herewith inclose to you.[2]

Independently of this, I addressed a letter, on the same subject, to the Secretary of War, a copy of which I also inclose to you.[3] The Secretary has sent my letter to the Provost-Marshal-General, with direction that he adopt and follow the course therein pointed out. It will, of course, over-rule any conflicting view of the Provost Marshal-General, if there be such. Yours very truly

A. LINCOLN—

"over"

P.S. I do not mean to say that if the Provost-Marshal General can find it practicable to give credits by sub-districts, I over-rule him in that. On the contrary I shall be glad of it; but I will not take the risk of over-burthening him, by ordering him to do it.

A. L.

¹ ADfS, DLC-RTL. Governor Seymour's letter of August 21, 1863, together with enclosures and answers to the questions raised, is too long and complicated for quotation here, but may be found in the *Official Records* (III, III, 703-706).

² See *Official Records* (III, III, 728-29). Lincoln's marginal endorsement on the draft reads, "No copy of P.M.G. letter kept by me."

³See Lincoln to Stanton, August 26, *supra.*

To Francis C. Sherman and Samuel S. Hayes¹

"Cypher"

F. C. Sherman, Mayor, &　　　　　　　　　Executive Mansion
S. S. Hayes, Comptroller.　　　　　　　　Washington, D.C.
Chicago, Illinois　　　　　　　　　　　　Aug. 27, 1863.

Yours of the 24th. in relation to the draft, is received. It seems to me the Government here will be overwhelmed, if it undertakes to conduct these matters with the authorities of cities and counties —that they must be conducted with the Governors of States, who will, of course, represent the cities and counties. Meanwhile you need not to be uneasy until you again hear from here.

A. LINCOLN

¹ ALS, RPB. Sherman and Hayes telegraphed Lincoln on August 24 to protest the unfairness of the draft in Chicago. The telegram, with James B. Fry's inserted comments reproduced in brackets, is as follows:

"The Common Council Chicago on the tenth inst appropriated one hundred & twenty thousand (120000) dollars to be expended in procuring volunteers to take the place of poor men with families who might be drafted from Chicago. They appointed a committee of eleven including the undersigned to take charge of the business and specially authorized them to correspond & confer with any of the Federal authorities ["They should confer with the Governor as we cannot correspond direct with all the civil authorities J B FRY"] in relation to the fairness of the conscription—the acceptance of said Volunteers in lieu of drafted men and such other matters as might pertain to the efficient performance of their duties under the ordinance. A sub committee appointed to wait on the boards of enrolment reported that they were informed by the board that the number of names enrolled for this city was over twenty eight thousand (28000) while the entire vote of the city was twenty thousand three hundred & forty seven (20347) That they (the sub committee) believed the enrolment contained forty percent or eight thousand (8000) more names than could have been legally entered ["I don't see how the vote of the city can control the question of the legality of the Enrolment. If a man didn't choose to vote does it follow from that that it is illegal to enrol him? No such cause of exemption is provided in the law JBF"] & requested of the board permission to take a copy of the corrected consolidated list in order to canvass it & suggest corrections—that the request was refused on the ground among others that the list had been sealed up and the board did not feel authorized to unseal it without authority from Washington There upon the committee adopted the following Resolution.

" 'Resolved that a sub committee to be composed of the Mayor & Comptroller be & is hereby appointed to obtain from the President . . . or other proper authority permission for the committee to take copies of the corrected consolidated enrolment list of this District which embraces the City, now on file in the office of the board of Enrolment of this District & such other documents & papers as will enable this committee to ascertain the correctness or incorrectness of said list & all other matters pertaining to the draft in this city.' ["I don't think we should undertake to prove to every squad of men who choose to assemble & appoint a '*committee*' that we are right. We have opened correspondence with the Governors in regard to everything which affects their States or any part of the same & we are prepared to give the Governors anything they deem necessary for the welfare of the States or any part of them."]

"The undersigned accordingly represent that the desire of the committee & the City authorities is not to impede in any way the execution of the Conscription Law but only to secure Justice and prevent unfairness in its operation upon the people of Chicago ["I don't think the people of Chicago have any reason to anticipate injustice or unfairness J B FRY"]—to properly administer the funds and perform the duties committed to them & incidentally to preserve the public peace. They desire to take a copy of said list for examination the same having never been published that they may urge such corrections as are important & time will permit & they Respectfully request you Mr President to authorize & direct the sealed consolidated list for the Chicago District on file in the enrolment office here to be unsealed and permission given the conscription war fund committee to take a copy of the same at the expense of the City." (DLC-RTL).

To Abel C. Wilder and James H. Lane[1]

Hon. A. C. Wilder, & Hon. J. H. Lane   Washington, D.C.,
Leavenworth, Kansas.   Aug: 27 1863

    Notice of your *demand* for the removal of Gen. Schofield, is hereby acknowledged.   A. LINCOLN

[1] ALS, RPB. For the telegram from Wilder and Lane, see note to Lincoln's telegram to Schofield, *supra.*

To Samuel W. Crawford[1]

Gen. Crawford   Executive Mansion Washington D.C.
Rappahannock-Station Va.   Aug. 28. 1863

    I regret that I can not be present to witness the presentation of a Sword by the gallant Pennsylvania Reserve Corps, to one so worthy to receive it as Gen. Meade.   A. LINCOLN.

[1] ALS, RPB. Brigadier General Samuel W. Crawford wrote Lincoln on August 20: "The honor of your company is requested at the presentation of a sword to Major General Meade, by the Officers of the Penna. Res. Corps, at the Head Quarters near Rappahannock Station, on Friday, the 28th inst; at 5 o'clock." (DLC-RTL).

To John G. Foster[1]

Major Gen. Foster   Washington, D.C.,
Fort-Monroe, Va   August 28, 1863

Please notify, if you can, Senator Bowden, Mr. Segar, and Mr. Chandler, all, or any of them, that I now have the record in Dr. Wright's case, and am ready to hear them. When you shall have got the notice to them, please let me know.   A. LINCOLN

[1] ALS, RPB. See Lincoln to Foster, August 3, *supra*. Lemuel J. Bowden of Norfolk requested on August 7 that "so soon as the record in the case of Dr. D. M. Wright . . . shall be laid before you, you will telegraph the Hon. L. H. Chandler and myself, fixing some day when we may appear before you and present the mass of testimony which has been taken to prove the insanity of Doctor Wright. . . ." (OR, II, VI, 187).

General Foster replied at 11:20 A.M. on August 28, "I have notified Mr Chandler of your wishes & he will start for Washington this evening. I have also sent notice to Senator Bowden Mr Segar is not here but is understood to be in Washington. . . ."

To Joseph Holt[1]

Judge Advocate General, please if you can, to get the record and report on this case to me.   A. LINCOLN

Aug. 28. 1863.

[1] AES, DNA WR RG 153, Judge Advocate General, NN 111. Lincoln's endorsement is written on the papers in the case of Captain Joseph M. Bushfield, Company H, Second Virginia Volunteers, dismissed for conduct unbecoming an officer and gentleman. See Lincoln to Holt, February 9 and March 31, 1864, *infra*.

To Edwin M. Stanton[1]

I know not whether the service will admit of this. If it will, of course I have no objection.   A. LINCOLN

Aug. 28. 1863.

[1] AES, DNA WR RG 107, Secretary of War, Letters Received, B 1063. Lincoln's endorsement is written on a letter from Brigham Buswell, August 26, 1863, requesting permission as a disabled soldier to sell stationery to the army.

To Edwin M. Stanton and Henry W. Halleck[1]

August 28, 1863

It is represented that Col. Wm. Mayer, named within, was the most efficient officer in suppressing the late New-York riots. He

[419]

wishes to be a Brigadier General. I submit his case to the Sec. of War & General in-Chief.   A. LINCOLN

Aug. 28. 1863

[1] AES, owned by R. E. Burdick, New York City. Lincoln's endorsement has been removed from the attendant papers. No record has been found of William Mayer's appointment.

To Salmon P. Chase[1]

Hon. Sec. of the Treasury. Please see Mr. Erskine who wishes a brief interview in relation to U.S. bonds   A. LINCOLN.

August 29. 1863

[1] Copy, IHi-Nicolay and Hay Papers. Erskine has not been identified.

To Ben Field[1]

Ben. Field, Esq   Executive Mansion,
Syracuse, N. Y.   Washington, August 29, 1863.

I send you by mail to-day, a copy of the Springfield letter.

A. LINCOLN

[1] ALS, RPB. Ben Field, secretary of the Union State Committee of New York telegraphed on August 26, "The Young men of this State hold a mass convention at Syracuse September third & they desire your excellency to send them the same address you send to Springfield. We think it will do great good & hope you may comply   Answer" (DLC-RTL).

To Ben Field[1]

Ben. Field, Esq   Executive Mansion,
My dear Sir   Washington, August 29, 1863.

Herewith is a copy of the Springfield letter, as requested. Do not let it become public until your meeting shall have come off—or, perhaps I should say "come on"   Your Obt. Servt

A LINCOLN

[1] ALS, Lincoln Memorial Shrine, Redlands, California. The enclosed copy of the letter to James C. Conkling, August 26, is no longer with this letter.

To William A. Hammond[1]

If the Surgeon General knows of a vacancy, to which Mr. Maddux, could be appointed, please indorse it below and return to me.

Aug. 29. 1863.   A. LINCOLN

[1] AES, IHi. Lincoln's endorsement is written on a letter from Thomas H. Hicks, August 24, 1863, introducing "the Revd. J. B. Maddux" who wished ap-

pointment as hospital chaplain at Chester, Pennsylvania. Surgeon General Hammond endorsed "Respectfully returned to His Excellency the President. There are no vacancies except one in St. Louis, Mo."

To Joseph Holt[1]

Judge Advocate General, please examine these, & any other papers accessable to you, pertaining to the case, and report to me.

Aug. 29, 1863.   A. LINCOLN

[1] AES, DNA WR RG 153, Judge Advocate General, LL 717. Lincoln's endorsement is written on the papers in the case of J. H. Townsend, arrested for treason and sentenced to $1,000 fine and imprisonment for one year at hard labor. On April 27, 1864, Lincoln endorsed again:

"Application denied   A. LINCOLN."

To Mary Todd Lincoln[1]

Mrs. A. Lincoln.   Executive Mansion,
Manchester, N. H.   Washington D.C. Aug. 29, 1863

All quite well. Fort-Sumpter is *certainly* battered down, and utterly useless to the enemy, and it is *believed* here, but not entirely certain, that both Sumpter and Fort-Wagner, are occupied by our forces. It is also certain that Gen. Gilmore has thrown some shot into the City of Charleston.   A. LINCOLN

[1] ALS, IHi. No reply from Mrs. Lincoln has been located. On August 24, 1863, Brigadier General Quincy A. Gillmore reported to Halleck: "I have the honor to report the practical demolition of Fort Sumter as the result of our seven days' bombardment of that work. . . ." (OR, I, XXVIII, I, 598).

Recommendation for Nelson L. Crist[1]

August 29, 1863

This man wants employment, and I shall be glad if it can be given him.   A. LINCOLN

[1] American Art Association Anderson Galleries Catalog 3781, October 30, 1929, No. 93. According to the catalog description, Lincoln's note was written on the back of Private Nelson L. Crist's discharge for disability from the Twelfth Illinois Volunteers.

To Edwin M. Stanton[1]

Executive Mansion,
Hon. Secretary of War:—   Washington, Aug. 29, 1863.

Dr. Brown, the embalmer, who has so long gone with our Armies, says he is now prevented in consequence of the loss of a

paper. I suppose he should be given another, unless there be some reason to the contrary unknown to me. Yours truly

A. LINCOLN

[1] Tracy, pp. 231-32. No further reference has been found. Charles D. Brown was the embalmer who prepared "Willie" Lincoln for burial, in February, 1862, and, in 1865, Abraham Lincoln.

To Edwin M. Stanton[1]

August 29, 1863

I am appealed to, for the release of Robert Howard and Junius B. Alexander, now prisoners of war at Fort Delaware. They are both privates, and the latter only eighteen years of age as represented to me. They wish to take the oath, give bond, and be discharged. Has any rule been established that meets the case? Sec. of War please see the bearer.

[1] Parke-Bernet Catalog 63, November 16-17, 1938, No. 183. No further reference has been found.

To Leonard Swett[1]

Hon. L. Swett   Washington D.C.
San Francisco, Cal.   Aug. 29. 1863

If the government's rights are reserved, the government will be satisfied; and, at all events, it will consider.   A. LINCOLN

[1] ALS, RPB. See Lincoln to Low, August 17, *supra*. On August 29, Swett telegraphed Lincoln, "Have compromised subject to approval, and under advice of Governor of this State and other leading men. The rights and interests of the Government have been respected. Shall return in September, and as the case is complicated would like to have opinion suspended until I can personally explain. You will then be satisfied with my action. I congratulate you on the great victories." (OR, I, L, II, 596).

To Gideon Welles[1]

Secretary of the Navy please see & hear the bearer.

Aug. 29, 1863.   A. LINCOLN

[1] Stan. V. Henkels Catalog 1342, January 4, 1924, No. 48a. According to the catalog description Lincoln's endorsement is written on the back of a letter from Andrew G. Curtin concerning A. J. Salsbury (Salisbury?). No further reference has been found.

To James C. Conkling[1]

Hon. James C. Conkling   Executive Mansion,
Springfield, Illinois   Washington, August 31. 1863.

In my letter of the 26th.[2] insert between the sentence ending "since the issue of the emancipation proclamation, as before" and the next, commencing "You say you will not fight &c" what follows below my signature hereto—   A. LINCOLN.

"I know as fully as one can know the opinions of others, that some of the commanders of our armies in the field who have given us our most important successes, believe the emancipation policy, and the use of colored troops, constitute the heaviest blow yet dealt to the rebellion; and that, at least one of those important successes, could not have been achieved when it was, but for the aid of black soldiers. Among the commanders holding these views are some who have never had any affinity with what is called abolitionism, or with republican party politics;[3] but who hold them purely as military opinions. I submit these opinions as being entitled to some weight against the objections, often urged, that emancipation; and arming the blacks, are unwise as military measures, and were not adopted as such, in good faith."

[1] ALS, RPB; LS copy, DLC-RTL; received copy, IHi. See Lincoln's letter to Conkling, August 26, *supra*, n. 9.
[2] The received copy reads "26 Inst. the" instead of "26th. insert between the."   [3] The received copy reads "policies" instead of "politics."

To Henry W. Halleck[1]

August 31, 1863

It is not improbable that retaliation for the recent great outrage at Lawrence, in Kansas, may extend to indiscriminate slaughter on the Missouri border, unless averted by very judicious action. I shall be obliged if the general-in-chief can make any suggestions to General Schofield upon the subject.   A. LINCOLN.

[1] OR, I, XXII, II, 488. Lincoln's endorsement is on a memorial signed by Austin A. King, Richard C. Vaughn, and Abraham Comingo, August 27, 1863, praying that those counties of Western Missouri attached to the District of the Border under command of General Thomas Ewing, Jr., be placed under the control of the Central District of Missouri, and urging a firm military policy to prevent retaliation from Kansas. (*Ibid.*, 485-88).

Halleck telegraphed General Schofield on September 2: "You will please report whether measures are being taken to prevent hostile collisions on the Kansas border; also whether General Ewing's order to depopulate certain counties in Missouri has been approved or disapproved by you." (*Ibid.*, p. 505).

Schofield replied from Leavenworth City, Kansas, at 8 P.M.: "Your dispatch is just received. I came here to prevent the trouble you refer to. Shall go to Kansas City to-morrow, and remain on the border until the difficulty is over. I believe I can prevent any collision. As yet I have neither approved nor disapproved General Ewing's order. I think it must be modified, but will not do it until I see him." *(Ibid.,* p. 506).

To Atwood G. Hobson[1]

Col. A. G. Hobson   Washington, D.C.,
Bowling Green, Kentucky   August 31 1863

I have telegraphed Lt. Col. Lauck, at Munfordsville, to suspend the execution of Coleman and Johns, until further order from here.

A. LINCOLN

[1] ALS, RPB. Atwood G. Hobson was provost marshal for the Third District of Kentucky, and James F. Lauck was lieutenant colonel of the Thirty-third Kentucky Infantry. No further reference to the cases of Thomas E. Coleman and Charles Johns has been found.

To James F. Lauck[1]

Lieut. Colonel Lauck   Washington, D.C.,
Munfordsville, Kentucky.   August 31 1863

Let the execution of Thomas E. Coleman, and Charles Johns, be suspended until further order from here. Acknowledge receipt of this.   A. LINCOLN

[1] ALS, RPB. Lieutenant Colonel Lauck replied at 8:30 P.M., "Your telegraph of today received." (DLC-RTL).

To William S. Rosecrans[1]

Executive Mansion, Washington,
My dear General Rosecrans   August 31. 1863.

Yours of the 22nd. was received yesterday. When I wrote you before, I did [not][2] intend, nor do I now, to engage in an argument with you on military questions. You had informed me you were impressed, through Gen. Halleck, that I was dissatisfied with you; and I could not bluntly deny that I was, without unjustly implicating him. I therefore concluded to tell you the plain truth, being satisfied the matter would thus appear much smaller than it would if seen by mere glimpses. I repeat that my appreciation of you has not abated. I can never forget, whilst I remember anything, that about the end of last year, and beginning of this, you gave us a hard earned victory which, had there been a defeat instead, the nation could scarcely have lived over. Neither can I forget the check you so opportunely gave to a dangerous sentiment which was spreading in the North. Yours as ever

A. LINCOLN.

1 ADfS, DLC-RTL. On August 22, Rosecrans replied to Lincoln's communication of August 10, *supra:*

"Permit me to assure you that I am not and have not been touched with any of that official pride which desires to have its own way. It has been a principle and a characteristic of my life to take advice and learn both from superiors and inferiors. When great interests are confided to my care this principle becomes even more imperative.

"On the question of moving against Bragg every division and corps commander gave his written opinion adversely to an immediate or early move. . . .

"But I am sure when you consider we have but a single line of rail road from Louisville—that we are three hundred miles from that base that we have crossed by three days march the formidable barrier of the Cumberland mountains that we have in front a swift river from five to eight hundred yards wide and seventy miles of mountains in front of us to reach the fertile regions of northern Georgia you see that few armies have been called upon to attempt a more arduous campaign.

"Thanking you for your kindness may I ask you when impulsive men suppose me querrulous to believe I am only straight forward and in earnest and that you may always rely upon my using my utmost efforts to do what is best for our country and the lives and honor of the soldiers of my command, I remain very respectfully. . . ." (DLC-RTL).

2 Bracketed insertion in the manuscript, but not in Lincoln's hand.

To Henry B. Wilson and Others[1]

H. B. Wilson, & others
Camden, N. J.

Washington D.C.
Aug. 31. 1863

Will grant you an interview, on Wednesday, or sooner.

A. LINCOLN

1 ALS, RPB. A telegram from Henry B. Wilson and others, received at 11 P.M. on August 31, is as follows: "The republican committee on the P.O. for the city of Camden respectfully request that you will not make any appointment till you see Mr [James M.] Scovel who represents the views of the people of Camden. Will you grant us an interview on Wednesday or sooner" (DLC-RTL). Samuel Andrews is listed as postmaster at Camden, New Jersey, in the *U.S. Official Register*, 1863.

To Edward Bates[1]

September 1, 1863

Whereas it is represented to me that there is an indictment pending, against William Stephens (who writes his name W. N. Stephens) of which the within is a substantial copy; and that said Stephens, since the finding of said indictment, did, in good faith, under a certain proclamation, or order of

tendering indemnity upon certain terms, return to his

[425]

allegiance to the United States. Now, therefore the said William Stephens, alias William N. Stephens, may offer to plead this paper in the court, wherein said indictment is pending, with the additional allegation that he shall have maintained his allegiance to the United States, up to the time of pleading, and, if received, he shall prove the allegations true, then he is fully pardoned for all matters charged in the indictment. Or, if the Court refuse to receive the plea, or hear the proof being offered as aforesaid, then he, the said William Stephens, alias William N. Stephens, if [is] fully pardoned for all matters charged in the indictment.

Sept. 1. 1863. ABRAHAM LINCOLN

[1] AES, DNA RG 204, U.S. Pardon Attorney, A 482. Lincoln's endorsement is written on a copy of the indictment for treason of William Stephens at the February, 1863, term of the U.S. Circuit Court, Louisville, Kentucky. See Lincoln's letter to Bates, September 2, *infra*.

To Joseph Holt[1]

Judge Advocate General
Sir:

Executive Mansion,
Washington, Sept. 1, 1863.

I am told that Carbery Lay, a Captain in the 12th. Regular Infantry has been dismissed by a Court-Martial. Please get the record, and examine the case & report to me. Yours truly

A. LINCOLN

[1] ALS, owned by Charles W. Olsen, Chicago, Illinois. No reply has been discovered. Captain Joseph Carbery Lay was cashiered on July 21, 1862, for being drunk on duty and breach of arrest. Reappointed a second lieutenant in the Seventeenth Infantry on October 30, 1863, he served until he resigned as first lieutenant on September 12, 1864.

Recommendation[1]

I do not know the bearer; but he says he has served in the war, is disabled & now wants employment. I shall be glad if he can get it.

Sep. 1. 1863. A. LINCOLN

[1] ALS, MnSM.

To Edwin M. Stanton[1]

Secretary of War, please hand me a full report of this case.

Sep. 1, 1863. A. LINCOLN

[1] AES, DLC-RTL. Lincoln's endorsement is written on a letter from Representative Robert H. Duell, August 31, 1863, asking an investigation of the case

of William H. Gray, late corporal of Company D, Twenty-seventh New York Volunteers, arrested and confined in the Old Capitol Prison. Numerous other endorsements represent the reports of authorities, to the effect that Gray was a "Sharper," with a carpetbag filled with *card photographs, fancy pictures and songs,*" who had obtained a pass "for the purpose of seeing sick brother" allegedly in the Army of the Potomac.

To Edwin M. Stanton[1]

Hon. Sec. of War   Executive Mansion,
My dear Sir: Washington, Sep 1, 1863.

I am now informed, contrary to my impression when I last talked with you, that the order compelling the four hundred on Eastern Shore of Virginia to take the oath or be sent away, is about being carried into execution. As this, and also the assessment for damage done to, and at the light house, are very strong measures, and as I have to bear the responsibility of them, I wish them suspended till I can at least be better satisfied of their propriety than I now am. Yours truly   A. LINCOLN.

[1] ALS-P, ISLA. See Lincoln to Stanton, August 21, *supra;* also to Segar, September 5, and to Schenck, September 6, *infra.* A thirty-page report submitted on September 10, 1863, by Major Henry Z. Hayner, aide-de-camp on General Schenck's staff, indicates that the difficulties on the Eastern Shore of Virginia were twofold. Several hundred citizens formerly in the "39th Rebel Regiment" had accepted amnesty offered by General Dix on the simple provision that they lay down their arms. Later, upon being required by Schenck to take an oath of allegiance, or (1) to be regarded as prisoners of war and put up for exchange, or (2) to be sent beyond Union lines; they objected to the oath on grounds of conscience, regarding themselves as still bound by their oath of allegiance to the Confederacy. The second phase of the difficulty concerned the destruction of a lighthouse by unknown persons. Two hundred and twenty-one residents of Northampton were assessed $20,000 on the grounds that the community was responsible, and collections were made from one hundred and sixty-one, over their violent protests. Hayner's report indicates that the order suspending the oath and assessments were received in a spirit of triumph over the government (DLC-RTL).

To Edwin M. Stanton[1]

Hon. Secretary of War   Executive Mansion,
Dear Sir   Washington, Sept. 1, 1863.

I am quite satisfied that it will be good policy for us to suspend until further order, the collection of the assessment levied to indemnify the government for destruction and spoliation of property at and about the Light-House on Smith Island, Virginia. Please let an order be made accordingly. Yours truly   A. LINCOLN

[1] ALS, RPB. See note to Lincoln's communication, *supra.*

To Edwin M. Stanton[1]

[September 1, 1863]

Mr. Speed wishes to see the Sec. of War, concerning the appointment of a cadet, on recommendation of Gen. Rosecrans. Please see him.   A. LINCOLN

[1] AES, DNA WR RG 94, U.S. Military Academy, 1863, Box 81, No. 44. Lincoln's endorsement is written on a card attached to a letter of Edward Davis to William S. Rosecrans, September 1, 1863, requesting assistance in obtaining appointment to West Point. Whether the letter was carried by Joshua F. Speed or James Speed is uncertain. Second Lieutenant Edward Davis of the Fifth Kentucky Cavalry resigned his commission on November 2, 1863, upon entering West Point, where he graduated in 1867.

To Edward Bates[1]

Executive Mansion,
Hon. Attorney General.   Washington Sept. 2, 1863.

Satisfactory evidence having been produced to me that William A. [N.?] Stephens of Shelby county, Kentucky, is under an indictment for treason in the Circuit Court of the United States for the District of Kentucky; and that said Stephens, under a certain proclamation tendering upon certain terms, did, on or about the fifth day of June, 1863, and since the finding of said indictment, take the oath of allegiance to the United States, and give bond with security accordingly, I do hereby pardon him for the offense charged in the indictment, and for all similar offenses up to the said fifth of June, 1863.

Please make out a pardon accordingly.   A. LINCOLN.

[1] Tracy, p. 232. See Lincoln to Bates, September 1, supra.

To Salmon P. Chase[1]

Hon. S. P. Chase.   Executive Mansion,
My dear Sir: Washington, September 2. 1863.

Knowing your great anxiety that the emancipation proclamation shall now be applied to certain parts of Virginia and Louisiana which were exempted from it last January, I state briefly what appear to me to be difficulties in the way of such a step. The original proclamation has no constitutional or legal justification, except as a military measure. The exemptions were made because the military necessity did not apply to the exempted localities. Nor does that necessity apply to them now any more than it did then. If I take the step must I not do so, without the argument of mili-

[428]

tary necessity, and so, without any argument, except the one that I think the measure politically expedient, and morally right? Would I not thus give up all footing upon constitution or law? Would I not thus be in the boundless field of absolutism? Could this pass unnoticed, or unresisted? Could it fail to be perceived that without any further stretch, I might do the same in Delaware, Maryland, Kentucky, Tennessee, and Missouri; and even change any law in any state? Would not many of our own friends shrink away appalled? Would it not lose us the elections, and with them, the very cause we seek to advance?

1 ADf, DLC-RTL. No correspondence from Chase in this connection has been located.

To William H. Seward[1]

Please Telegraph Dr. Gray asking him whether he could come and serve the government one month more or less, & how soon.

Sept. 2. 1863.   A. LINCOLN

1 AES, NAuE. Lincoln's endorsement is written on a note from Seward, September 2, 1863, as follows:

"Dr Nicholl's surroundings are so disloyal as to shake public confidence in himself. Dr Gray of Utica occurs to me as a very proper person."

Dr. Nicholl has not been identified. See further Lincoln's letter to John P. Gray, September 10, *infra*.

To Edwin M. Stanton[1]

Hon. Sec. of War   Executive Mansion,
Dear Sir   Washington, Sept. 2. 1863.

This woman says her husband and two sons are in the war; that the youngest son W. J. Klaproth, is a private in Co. D, of 143rd. Pennsylvania, volunteers, was wounded, made a prisoner & paroled at Gettysburg, and is now at Center-Street hospital, New-Jersey; and that he was under eighteen when he entered the service without the consent of his father or herself. She says she is destitute, and she asks that he may be discharged   If she makes satisfactory proof of the above let it be done.   A. LINCOLN

1 ALS, owned by Charles W. Olsen, Chicago, Illinois. A letter from Marcus L. Ward, Newark, New Jersey, August 31, 1863, introduced "Mrs. Dorcas Klaprath a respectable woman residing in this city. She visits Washington in the hope of securing the discharge . . . of her son William J. Klaprath of 143rd Reg N.J. Vols." (DLC-RTL). The roster of the One Hundred Forty-third Pennsylvania lists William J. Klasprath as "Discharged by special order—date unknown," but no record of the name as given by Ward or by Lincoln has been found.

To Timothy P. Andrews[1]

Pay Master General

My dear Sir

Executive Mansion,

Washington, Sept. 3, 1863.

Please see and hear Major Mallett, and oblige him so far as you consistently can, in the place he may be assigned to duty. Yours truly

A. LINCOLN

[1] ALS, owned by J. Coleman Scal, New York City. Edward J. Mallett of New York City was appointed additional paymaster of Volunteers, August 12, 1863, and assigned to duty in New York City.

To James C. Conkling[1]

Hon. James C. Conkling

Springfield, Illinois:

Executive Mansion,

Washington, Sept. 3, 1863.

I am mortified this morning to find the letter to you, botched up, in the Eastern papers, telegraphed from Chicago. How did this happen?

A. LINCOLN

[1] ALS, RPB. Conkling replied on September 4:

"Your telegram of 3 inst was received by me at the Fair Grounds during the progress of our Mass Meeting and I had no opportunity of replying immediately

"In order that the St Louis Chicago and Springfield papers might publish your Letter simultaneously and at the earliest period after the meeting, so as to gratify the intense anxiety which existed with regard to your views, copies were sent to the two former places with strict injunctions not to permit it to be published before the meeting or make any improper use of it But it appears that a part of it was telegraphed from Chicago to New York contrary to my express directions. I do not know what particular individual is chargeable with this breach of faith, but I presume it was some one connected with the Chicago Tribune. I was very much mortified at the occurrence, but hope that no prejudicial results have been experienced as the whole letter was published the next day" (DLC-RTL).

John W. Forney wrote Lincoln on September 3:

"The appearance of your letter in the Chronicle of this morning may surprise, but cannot, I hope, offend you, when I tell you it came to us from [Lewis A.] Gobright, of the Associated Press, and was received and published during my absence, and appears in most if not all of the other daily papers of the country. Even the Intelligencer of this morning has an abstract of it. To-morrow we will republish it, accompanied by a strong editorial endorsement. I make this explanation in justice to myself, after our conversation yesterday." (*Ibid.*).

Endorsement[1]

Two despatches. Telegraph.   A. LINCOLN

September 3, 1863.

[1] Stan. V. Henkels Catalog 1430, April 24, 1929, No. 85. According to the catalog description, Lincoln's endorsement is written on despatches which were to be telegraphed.

To D. M. Leatherman[1]

D. M. Leatherman, Esq   Executive Mansion,
Sir   Washington, Sep. 3. 1863.
    I see your card on my table. I would be glad to oblige all, but it is impossible. I suppose I understand your business at this time. It is about some property claimed by a woman in or near Memphis, under a deed from her husband who is in the rebel service, and which claim has been passed upon once or twice already. The impropriety of bringing such cases to me, is obvious to any one who will consider that I could not properly act on any case without understanding it, and that I have neither the means nor time, to obtain such understanding. Yours &c.   A. LINCOLN

[1] ALS, owned by Paul Leatherman, Hot Springs, Arkansas. See Lincoln's memorandum of April 17, *supra*. No further reference to this case has been found.

To Mary Todd Lincoln[1]

Mrs. A. Lincoln.   Washington, D.C.
Manchester, Vermont.   Sept. 3. 1863.
    The Secretary of War tells me he has telegraphed Gen. Doubleday to await further orders. We are all well, and have nothing new.
                                                        A. LINCOLN

[1] ALS, IHi. No correspondence from Mrs. Lincoln has been found which would explain this letter, but it may be inferred that she had interceded in some manner for General Abner Doubleday, who had been removed from command by Meade's *Special Orders No. 181*, July 5, 1863 (OR, I, XXVII, III, 543). Doubleday was not returned to duty until December, 1863, when he was assigned to duty on court-martials and commissions.

To Edwin M. Stanton[1]

Sec. of War, please see the bearer a moment.
Sept. 3. 1863.   A. LINCOLN

[1] ALS, owned by John F. Reed, Upper Darby, Pennsylvania. The bearer has not been identified.

To Edwin M. Stanton[1]

Hon. Sec. of War.   Executive Mansion,
My dear Sir: Washington, Sep. 3. 1863
    Please have made and sent to me a statement of the case of Capt. Samuel Ford, of Co. A. 5. Md. Regt. now in Carroll prison. Yours truly   A. LINCOLN

[1] ALS, DLC-RTL. This letter was returned with endorsements showing that Captain Samuel Ford of the Fifth Maryland Volunteers was charged with permitting persons "under his command and employ, as detectives, to examine and improperly & unlawfully take & retain from the person and possession of Mrs. Lucy Ann Baggott the sum of $160," and that he also had allowed "two young Ladies [Misses E. L. and S. M. Adams], in the same manner to be relieved of $310." Tried before a court-martial on September 17, Ford was acquitted and released from arrest (AGO *General Orders No. 343*, October 19, 1863).

To Gideon Welles[1]

Submitted to the Secretary of the Navy, with request that Lieut. Riell be heard.   A. LINCOLN
    Sept. 3 1863

[1] Copy, DLC-RTL. Lincoln's endorsement was written on papers asking for promotion of Lieutenant Robert Riell, copies of which were enclosed by Riell in a letter to Lincoln dated April 5, 1864. Lieutenant Riell is listed as retired September 29, 1864.

Order Concerning Export of War Materiel[1]

Executive Mansion   Washington City, Sept. 4th., 1863.
    Ordered, That the Executive Order, dated November 21st., 1862, prohibiting the exportation from the United States of arms, ammunition or munitions of war, under which the commandants of Departments were, by Order of the Secretary of War, dated May 13, 1863, directed to prohibit the purchase and sale for exportation from the United States of all horses and mules within their respective commands, and to take and appropriate to the use of the United States any horses, mules and live stock designed for exportation, be so far modified that any arms heretofore imported into the United States may be re-exported to the place of original shipment, and that any live stock raised in any State or Territory bounded by the Pacific Ocean may be exported from any port of such State or Territory.   ABRAHAM LINCOLN

[1] DS, DNA FI RG 56, General Records of Treasury Department, Series AB, 1863, Letters from Executive Officers, I, 4.

To Montgomery C. Meigs[1]

Q. M. General.   Executive Mansion,
My dear Sir   Washington, Sept. 5. 1863.
    This introduces C. Vanderbilt Jr. son of the Comodore. He comes with a business proposition to you. Please give him a fair & re-

spectful hearing, and oblige him if consistent with the service.
Yours truly   A. LINCOLN

1 ALS-F, ISLA. Cornelius Vanderbilt, Jr. brought a letter of introduction from
Schuyler Colfax, September 2, 1863 (DLC-Nicolay Papers). No further reference has been discovered.

Memorandum:
Appointment of Daniel Applegate[1]

I would like for Mr. Bates to be obliged.   A. LINCOLN
Sep. 5, 1863

1 AES, DNA WR RG 94, U.S. Military Academy, 1863, Box 82, No. 184.
Lincoln's endorsement is written on a letter of Jesse Applegate, Yoncalla,
Oregon, to Edward Bates, July 22, 1863, asking his help in obtaining appoint-
ment of a son, Daniel Applegate, to West Point. There is no record of Daniel
Applegate's appointment.

Memorandum:
Appointment of Thornton A. Jenkins[1]

If there is a vacancy, not committed, let this young man be appointed.   A. LINCOLN
Sep. 5, 1863

1 AES, DNA WR RG 94, U.S. Military Academy, 1864, Box 83, No. 309.
Lincoln's endorsement is written on a letter from Thornton A. Jenkins, Washington, D.C., September 5, 1863, endorsed with recommendations by Gustavus
V. Fox and Edward D. Townsend, asking appointment to West Point. There is
no record of his appointment.

Memorandum Concerning William E. Morgan[1]

September 5 and 18, 1863

I know nothing of this particular case. I have said a great many
times, that all whose services we receive, should be paid,—but I do
not know, nor have I the time to enquire, whether this claim can
be lawfully paid or not. If it can, let it be done.
Sep. 5. 1863.   A. LINCOLN

I can not properly say more than I have said above.
Sep. 18. 1863.   A. LINCOLN

1 AES, PHC. Lincoln's endorsements are written on a letter of Second Lieutenant William E. Morgan, Company D, First District of Columbia Infantry, to
Assistant Adjutant General Thomas M. Vincent, August 28, 1863, asking an
endorsement which will enable him to collect back pay.

To Joseph Segar[1]

Hon. Joseph Segar: Washington, D.C.,
Fort-Monroe—Va   Sept. 5 1863

I have just seen your despatch to the Secretary of War, who is absent. I also send a despatch from Major Hayner of the 3rd. showing that he had notice of my order, and stating that the people were jubilant over it, as a victory over the government extorted by fear, and that he had already collected about four thousand of the money. If he has proceeded since I shall hold him accountable for his contumacy. On the contrary no dollar shall be refunded by my order, until it shall appear that my act in the case has been accepted in the right spirit.   A. LINCOLN

[1] ALS, RPB. See Lincoln's communications to Stanton, September 1, *supra*. On September 6, Segar telegraphed Lincoln in reply, "If the people of Northampton have exhibited the spirit charged upon them I shall most certainly, though their representative, abandon them to their fate, but I have reliable information directly the reverse of what has been telegraphed by Maj Hayner. There was, as was most natural, rejoicing among the people but in no spirit of taunt or triumph over the Government that has been so kind to them, but joy over the relief your justice and kindness have given them from an unjust and degrading tax. Towards yourself there is but one feeling and that of gratitude and respect for your just and generous intervening they will so make it appear" (DLC-RTL).

To Mary Todd Lincoln[1]

Mrs. A Lincoln   Washington, D.C.,
Manchester, Vermont   Sep. 6. 1863

All well, and no news, except that Gen. Burnside has Knoxville, Tennessee.   A. LINCOLN

[1] ALS, IHi.

To Robert C. Schenck[1]

Major Genl. Schenck.   Washington, D.C.,
Baltimore.   Sep. 6. 1863

The Secretary of War is absent. Please direct or order that the collection of the Light-House be suspended, and that the money already collected be held, both till further order

A. LINCOLN

[1] ALS, RPB. See Lincoln to Segar, September 5, *supra*. On September 8, Schenck telegraphed Lincoln:
"I beg you to see & hear Major Hayner of my staff, who is the bearer of this note. He is the Officer who was sent to the Eastern Shore of Virginia to superintend the assessment & collection of the tax for destruction of the light house,

& to administer the oath of allegiance to certain persons there. He has just returned from this duty, because of your orders suspending further action.

"I am perfectly satisfied that the policy I was pursuing, under direction, & with approval, of the Secretary of War, was the true policy, for the Union cause in that portion of my Department. I am just as sure that the representations which have been made to you to induce you to change that policy are in many respects incorrect, & founded on motives lower than an unselfish & thorough devotion to the government.

"Maj. Hayner is a man to be relied on." (DLC-RTL).

To Francis C. Sherman and Samuel S. Hayes[1]

F. C. Sherman & S. S. Hayes   Washington D.C.
Chicago, Illinois.   Sep. 6. 1863

Yours of Aug. 29 just received. I suppose it was intended by Congress that this government should execute the Act in question, without dependence upon any other government, State, City, or County. It is, however, within the range of practical convenience, to confer with the Governors of States, while it would go quite beyond that range, to have correspondence on the subject with counties and cities. They are too numerous. As instances, I have correspondence with Governor Seymour, but none with Mayor Opdycke—with Gov. Curtin, but none with Mayor Henry.

A LINCOLN

1 ALS, RPB. This letter is misdated September 7, 1863, by Nicolay and Hay (IX, 112). On August 29, Sherman and Hayes replied to Lincoln's communication of August 27, *supra*:

"We are in receipt of your dispatch dated August 27th, in answer to our communication of the 24th. inst.

"We have not been able to discover in the act of Congress, known as the Conscription act, or in the practice of the Government under it, any such clear and distinct recognition of state authority, as to authorise the impression that such an application as that which we had the honor to make on behalf and at the request of the Committee of the Common Council, would create confusion unless first submitted to the Governor of the State.

"The enrollment list is a record of the names of the persons reported to be liable, in demand of the Government, to be called directly into the field to undergo the hardships and dangers of military service. It would seem reasonable that such a record should be kept open for public inspection in the district for which it was made. . . .

"We are however contented to apply to the State authorities. . . ." (DLC-RTL).

Upon being denied access to the consolidated enrollment list by Lieutenant Colonel James Oakes, assistant provost marshal general for Illinois, Sherman and Hayes wrote Lincoln again on September 17:

". . . What we seek is . . . information, clear and definite, of each and all of the names as they stand on the list from which the draft will be made. We wish to know who have been enrolled, who have been omitted, and who have been enrolled more than once. That knowledge we cannot obtain from the original lists. It can only be had from the corrected or final enrollment, which is now sealed up.

[435]

"Our object is to secure equal rights to this community, and especially to protect the ignorant and poor from injustice and oppression, to bring such cases, if we find any, to the attention of the Government for correction, and thereby to promote harmony, and mutual reliance, and concert of action between all classes of the people in doing whatever may be necessary and right to suppress the rebellion, and preserve our constitutional system—amidst the trials to which it is exposed.

"We have not yet surrendered the hope that further reflection may lead you to order a compliance with our request. We venture to add . . . that in our humble judgment a general order of the same nature, applicable to all the districts in the United States would tend greatly to strengthen the confidence of the people in the Government, and to promote the public good." (DLC-RTL).

To Edwin M. Stanton[1]

Hon. Secretary of War   Washington, D.C.,
Bedford, Pa.   Sept. 6 1863

Burnside has Kingston, & Knoxville, and drove the enemy across the river at Loudon, the enemy destroying the bridge there. Captured some stores & one or two trains. Very little fighting—few wounded and none killed. No other news of consequence

               A. LINCOLN

[1] ALS, RPB. The news which Lincoln relayed to Stanton had been telegraphed by Burnside to Halleck on September 3 and received at 12 P.M. on September 5 (OR, I, XXX, III, 333).

Pass for Louis Bargdorf[1]

The bearer is one of my Messengers, & should be passed in to & out of the Department.   A. LINCOLN

 Sep. 7. 1863.

[1] ADS, owned by Richard F. Lufkin, Boston, Massachusetts. Lincoln's note is written on a card issued to Louis Bargdorf, White House messenger. The U.S. Official Register, 1863, lists "Louis Baigdorf, Doorkeeper at President's House."

To Edwin M. Stanton[1]

        Executive Mansion, Washington,
Honorable Secretary of War.   September 7, 1863.

My dear Sir: This lady says her husband, Theophilus Brown, and his brother, George E. Brown, are in the Old Capitol Prison as prisoners of war, that they were conscripted into the rebel army, and were never for the rebel cause, and are now willing to do anything reasonable to be at liberty. This may be true, and if true they should be liberated. Please take hold of the case, and do what may seem proper in it. Yours truly, A. LINCOLN.

[436]

1 Leslie J. Perry, "Appeals to Lincoln's Clemency," *The Century Magazine*, LI (December, 1895), 254. No further reference to these prisoners has been found.

To George G. Meade[1]

Major-General Meade,   Executive Mansion,
Warrenton, Va.:   Washington, September 9, 1863.

It would be a generous thing to give General Wheaton a leave of absence for ten or fifteen days, and if you can do so without injury to the service, please do it.   A. LINCOLN.

1 Tarbell (Appendix), p. 381. Meade replied at once, "Gen. Wheaton, has made no application for a leave of absence. There will be no difficulty in his obtaining one, when he does apply." (DLC-RTL). See Lincoln to Wheaton, September 10, *infra*.

To Edwin M. Stanton[1]

September 9, 1863

Mrs. Harvey wishes the Hospital to be named for her late husband. . . .

1 *American Book Prices Current*, XXXIV, Walpole Galleries, March 14, 1918, No. 407. According to an article in *The Wisconsin Magazine of History*, March, 1918, I, 245-46, giving the recollections of Mrs. Cordelia A. P. Harvey, widow of Governor Lewis Harvey of Wisconsin, Lincoln wrote a card "requesting the Secretary of War to name the hospital 'Harvey Hospital,' in memory of my husband." This account also reproduces an endorsement written by Lincoln on a letter from Senator James R. Doolittle introducing Mrs. Harvey: "Admit Mrs. Harvey at once; listen to what she says; she is a lady of intelligence and talks sense. A. LINCOLN." The date of the endorsement is not given, but the context of the article implies that it was written the previous day, September 8, 1863.

To John P. Gray[1]

Dr. John P. Gray   Executive Mansion,
Sir,   Washington, September 10th. 1863.

Dr. David M. Wright is in military custody at Norfolk, Virginia, having been, by a military commission, tried for murder, and sentenced to death, his execution awaiting the order of the Major General in command of that Military Department, or of the President of the United States. The record is before me; and a question is made as to the sanity of the accused. You will please proceed to the Military Department whose head-quarters are at Fort-Monroe, and take in writing all evidence which may be offered on behalf of Dr. Wright and against him, and any, in addition, which you may find within your reach, and deem pertinent;

all said evidence to be directed to the question of Dr. Wright's sanity or insanity, and not to any other questions; you to preside, with power to exclude evidence which shall appear to you clearly not pertinent to the question.

When the taking of the evidence shall be closed, you will report the same to me, together with your own conclusions, as to Dr. Wright's sanity, both at the time of the homocide, and the time of your examination. On reaching Fort-Monroe, you will present this letter to the officer then commanding that Department, and deliver to him a copy of the same; upon which he is hereby directed to notify Hon. L. J. Bowden, and Hon. L. H. Chandler, of the same; to designate some suitable person in his command to appear for the government, as Judge Advocate or Prossecuting Attorney; to provide for the attendance of all such witnesses before you as may be desired by either party, or by yourself, and who may be within convenient reach of you; to furnish you a suitable place, or places for conducting the examination; and to render you such other reasonable assistance in the premises as you may require. If you deem it proper, you will examine Dr. Wright personally, and you may, in your discretion, require him to be present during the whole, or any part, of the taking of the evidence. The Military are hereby charged to see that an escape does not occur. Yours truly.

A. LINCOLN

[1] LS (copy?), DLC-RTL; ALS-F (partial), ISLA. See Lincoln to Foster, August 3 and August 28, and to Seward, September 2, *supra*.

Memorandum Concerning Frederick Moelich[1]

September 10, 1863

I can not listen to a man's own story, unsupported by any evidence, who has been convicted of violating the law; because that would put an end to all law.   A. LINCOLN

Sep. 10. 1863.

[1] AES, DLC-RTL. Lincoln's endorsement is written on a letter from Frederick Moelich, proprietor of a restaurant at 289 B Street in Washington, August 10, 1863. Moelich protested his innocence of selling liquor to soldiers, for which he had been fined.

To Edwin M. Stanton[1]

September 10, 1863

The bearer is Dr. Gray who is to go to Norfolk for us.

[1] Anderson Galleries, Catalog 2324, February 27, 1929, No. 251. This partial text is all that is available. See Lincoln's letter to Gray, *supra*.

[438]

To Frank Wheaton[1]

Gen. Wheaton   Washington D.C
Army of Potomac.   Sep. 10. 1863

Yesterday, at the instance of Mr. Blair, senr. I telegraphed Gen.
Meade asking him to grant you a leave of absence, to which he
replied that you had not applied for such leave, and that you can
have it when you do apply. I suppose it is proper for you to know
this.   A. LINCOLN

1 ALS, RPB. See Lincoln to Meade, September 9, *supra*. Brigadier General
Frank Wheaton was in command of the Third Brigade, Third Division, Sixth
Corps, Army of the Potomac.

To Ambrose E. Burnside[1]

Cypher
Major General Burnside   Washington, D.C.
Cumberland Gap: Sep. 11. 1863

Yours received. A thousand thanks for the late sucesses you
have given us.

We can not allow you to resign until things shall be a little more
settled in East-Tennessee. If then, purely on your own account,
you wish to resign, we will not further refuse you
                                                  A. LINCOLN

1 ALS, RPB. Burnside telegraphed Lincoln on September 10: "You will remember that I some time ago told you that I wished to retire to private life.
The rebellion now seems pretty well checked & the work I am doing can no
doubt be as well or better performed by some one else so that I can now conscientiously ask to be allowed to resign if you think the good of service will
permit. I shall be here tomorrow & will be glad to get an answer   I look upon
East Tennessee as one of the most loyal sections of the U.S." (DLC-RTL).
He replied to Lincoln's despatch on September 17: "Thank you for your dispatch & I desire to stay as long as you think necessary but am very anxious to
look after my private affairs as soon as the public service will allow." (*Ibid*).

To Hannibal Hamlin[1]

Vice-President Hamlin   Washington D.C.
Bangor, Maine   Sep. 11. 1863

Your letter of Aug. 22nd., to be presented by your son Cyrus
is on my table; but I have not seen him, or know of his being here
recently.   A. LINCOLN

1 ALS, RPB. Hamlin wrote on August 22:
"This note will be handed you by my son Cyrus who is command[er] of
the 3d Reg. of Colored troops in La. Genl Ullmanns Brigade.

[439]

"He goes to Washington to submit to you and the Secy of War the difficulties and embarrassment under which the Brig has suffered. . . ." (DLC-RTL).

To Andrew Johnson[1]

Private

Hon. Andrew Johnson: Executive Mansion,
My dear Sir: Washington, September 11, 1863.

All Tennessee is now clear of armed insurrectionists. You need not to be reminded that it is the nick of time for re-inaugerating[2] a loyal State government. Not a moment should be lost. You, and the co-operating friends there, can better judge of the ways and means, than can be judged by any here. I only offer a few suggestions. The re-inaugeration[3] must not be such as to give control of the State, and it's representation in Congress, to the enemies of the Union, driving it's friends there into political exile. The whole struggle for Tennessee will have been profitless to both State and Nation, if it so ends that Gov. Johnson is put down, and Gov. Harris is put up. It must not be so. You must have it otherwise. Let the reconstruction be the work of such men only as can be trusted for the Union. Exclude all others, and trust that your government, so organized, will be recognized here, as being the one of republican form, to be guarranteed to the state, and to be protected against invasion and domestic violence.

It is something on the question of *time*, to remember that it can not be known who is next to occupy the position I now hold, nor what he will do.

I see that you have declared in favor of emancipation in Tennessee, for which, may God bless you. Get emancipation into your new State government—Constitution—and there will be no such word as fail for your case.

The raising of colored troops I think will greatly help every way.
Yours very truly   A. LINCOLN

[1] ALS, NNP; LS copy, DLC-RTL. Governor Johnson telegraphed his reply on September 17: "I have just read your letter which gives me pleasure & encouragement. It remind me of calling your attention while in Washington the 4th Section of the constitution & the propriety under that section of authorizing the military govt to exercise all power necessary & proper to secure to the people of Tennessee a republican form of govt you will perhaps remember that I showed you a paper which was drawn up containing the whole proposition which you endorsed & referred to the Secy of War Such authority emanating from the Prest under the clause above referred would exert much influence on the public mind here. I desire it—directed from the President. I have taken decided ground for Emancipation for immediate emancipation from gradual emancipation Now is the time for settlement of this question Hence

I am for immediate emancipation." (DLC-RTL). See further, Lincoln to Johnson, September 18, *infra*.

2 "Re-inaugerating" emended to "re-inaugurating" by someone other than Lincoln.

3 "Re-inaugeration" emended to "re-inauguration" by someone other than Lincoln.

To George G. Meade[1]

Major-General Meade,   Executive Mansion,
Warrenton, Va.:   Washington, September 11, 1863.

It is represented to me that Thomas Edds, in your army, is under sentence of death for desertion, to be executed next Monday. It is also said his supposed desertion is comprised in an absence commencing with his falling behind last winter, being captured and paroled by the enemy, and then going home. If this be near the truth, please suspend the execution till further order and send me the record of the trial.   A. LINCOLN.

1 Tarbell (Appendix), p. 382. No reply to this telegram has been found, but see Lincoln to Meade, September 12, *infra*.

To Edwin M. Stanton[1]

Hon Sec. of War   Executive Mansion
Sir   Washington September 11th. 1863

The father Lieut A. S. Eddy, a personal acquaintance of mine, is here saying his son has been in arrest for several months.

Genl. Orme, in the West has more than once asked to have the Lieut. on his Staff.

Please have the case looked up, and let us see if there is not a better use to put him to, than, keeping him in arrest. I have reason to believe, he is a gallant young officer   Yours truly
     A. LINCOLN

1 Copy, DNA WR RG 153, Judge Advocate General, MM 187. See Lincoln's endorsements to Holt, May 12 and 17, *supra*. On September 28, Stanton transmitted to Lincoln a copy of the report in Adelbert S. Eddy's case (DLC-RTL). No further reference has been found.

To John W. Geary[1]

Gen. Geary   Executive Mansion,
Kellys Ford   Washington, Sep. 12, 1863.

Please tell me what you know, or believe as to the conduct and disposition of E. Jacquelin Smith, residing near Salem on the Mannassas Gap Railroad.   A. LINCOLN

[1] ALS, RPB. "Kelly's Ford" is not in Lincoln's handwriting, and may have been inserted by the telegrapher. Montgomery Blair wrote Lincoln on September 11, 1863, "The bearer of this Mrs E. J. Smith is a relative of mine from Fauquier Co. Va. Her husband is confined in the Old Capitol for no offense save that he lives in the 'belt of desolation' & refuses to take the oath of allegiance, and his only reason for this refusal is that the Govt has not heretofore protected the people of his neighborhood. He has been a consistent Union man— is a man of Education a lawyer formerly but of late years ceased to practice his profession. Was an intimate friend of Scott & is well known to Geary & others of our officers who have been stationed in that county." (DLC-RTL).

General Geary replied to Lincoln at 12 M., September 13, "In reply to your telegram I have the honor to state that 'Edward Jaquelin Smith' from near Salem was a warm secessionist disposed to aid the rebel cause to the extent of his ability. He plotting and his son William T. Smith executing. This son was arrested by me upon May 28th. 1862. and sent to Washington . . . as a noted spy and bearer of dispatches for the rebels with proofs of his being a dangerous man." (DLC-RTL).

A second despatch from Geary received on September 15 is as follows: "I have a telegram from Mrs E. B. Smith relative to her husband My telegraph of Sept 12th referred to E. Jacquline Smith of Fauquier County. E. Jacqulin Smith of Clark County is also a warm secessionist & abettor of the rebel cause. His son William gave (8) horses to the rebel cavalry early in the war. Both families were similarly disposed I have the honor to offer this as explanatory of any distinction that may be made between the two." (DLC-RTL).

To Joseph Holt[1]

The Recommendation of Gen. Rosecrans is approved and sentence commuted as suggested   A. LINCOLN

Sept. 12, 1863

[1] ES, DNA WR RG 153, Judge Advocate General, MM 378. Lincoln's endorsement is written on the papers in the case of Captain William W. Woodbury, Second Minnesota Volunteers, dismissed for disloyal language, insubordination, drunkenness, and misapplication of company funds. In view of irregularity of proceedings of the trial, Rosecrans recommended commutation to loss of pay for three months.

To George G. Meade[1]

Washington, D.C., September 12, 1863.

Major-General Meade, Warrenton, Va.:

The name is "Thomas Edds" not "Eddies" as in your dispatch. The papers left with me do not designate the regiment to which he belongs. The man who gave me the papers, I do not know how to find again. He only told me that Edds is in the Army of the Potomac, and that he fell out of the ranks during Burnsides' mud march last winter. If I get further information I will telegraph again.   A. LINCOLN.

[1] Tarbell (Appendix), p. 382. Meade replied the same day, "There is no man of the name of 'Edds' under sentence of death. Twelve men are sentenced to be

executed next Friday Sept 18th but no case approximates either in date or circumstances to the one you specify" (DLC-RTL). Thomas Edds has not been identified.

To Josiah Quincy[1]

Executive Mansion, September 12, 1863.

Dear and honored Sir: Allow me to express the personal gratification I feel at the receipt of your very kind letter of the 7th of September, and to thank you most cordially for its wise and earnest words of counsel.

Believe me, my dear sir, to be very respectfully and sincerely your friend and servant,   A. LINCOLN.

1 NH, IX, 118. On September 7 Josiah Quincy of Quincy, Massachusetts, former congressman and president of Harvard University, wrote Lincoln a letter expressing "gratification & my gratitude for your letter to the Illinois Convention. . . ." (DLC-RTL).

To Edwin M. Stanton[1]

September 12, 1863
Let the re-appointment be made.

1 AE, DNA WR RG 94, U.S. Military Academy, 1862, Box 81, No. 284. Lincoln's endorsement is written on a telegram from Lieutenant Colonel Alexander H. Bowman, West Point, New York, to Montgomery Blair, September 9, 1863, that the board recommends re-appointment of Samuel M. Swigert. Swigert was appointed to West Point on September 29, 1863, and graduated in June, 1868.

To John P. Gray[1]

Dr. John P. Gray.   Executive Mansion,
Norfolk, Va.   Washington, Sept. 13, 1863.

The names of those whose affidavits are left with me on the question of Dr. Wrights sanity are as follow:

Mrs. Jane C. Bolsom   Mrs. Elizabeth Rooks.
Mrs. M. E. Smiley   Dr. E. D. Granier
Moses Hudgin   Thomas K. Murray.
J. D. Ghislin, Jr.   William J. Holmes
Felix Logue   Miss Margaret E. Wigeon.
Robert B. Tunstall, M.D.   Mrs. Emily S. Frost.

A. LINCOLN

1 ALS, RPB. See Lincoln to Gray, September 10, supra.

To William H. H. Scott[1]

Dr. Wm. H. H. Scott   Executive Mansion,
Danville, Illinois   Washington, Sep. 13. 1863.

Your niece, Mrs. Kate Sharp, can now have no difficulty in going
to Knoxville, Tennessee, as that place is within our Military lines.

A. LINCOLN

[1] ALS, RPB. William H. H. Scott wrote Lincoln on August 21, 1863, that his
niece "Mrs Kate Sharp of Louisville Kentucky a widow has since her husband
deceased become involved in a law suit in which her entire estate is complicated
and finds that important witnesses to the successful defence of her suit are
within the Rebel lines. . . . Having failed in her application in Kentucky I
earnestly beg as a personal favor to myself as well as to a most excellant
woman if not inconsistent with the public interest you would grant her a pass
throug[h] our lines to Knoxvill[e] Tennessee & to return to Kentucky. . . ."
(DLC-RTL). A letter from Mrs. Kate Sharpe, written from Frankfort, Kentucky, September 19, is also in the Lincoln Papers.

Opinion on the Draft[1]

[September 14?] 1863

It is at all times proper that misunderstanding between the public
and the public servant should be avoided; and this is far more im-

[1] AD, DLC-RTL. Nicolay and Hay date this document "August [15?] 1863"
(NH, IX, 74), but a bracketed date on the first page of the manuscript reads
"[Aug 30?] 1863." From the contents it may be inferred that Lincoln intended
to use the piece either as a public address or as part of a communication. An
endorsement by Robert Todd Lincoln written on the back of the last page of
the manuscript reads: "This Mss. was probably written at the time of the
Sprd. Letter of Aug– 63—but not incorporated with it & never published." The
reference is, of course, to Lincoln's letter to James C. Conkling, August 26,
supra, but it would seem more probable that Lincoln contemplated issuance of
his sentiments on the draft to counteract the numerous efforts to block enforcement of the law. Gideon Welles refers to such a paper as having been prepared
by the president on September 14, but abandoned in favor of the proclamation
of September 15, *infra*, suspending habeas corpus with respect to persons taken
by the draft. Welles' *Diary* records the Cabinet discussion:

"September 14, Monday. The President called a special Cabinet council this
morning at eleven. The course pursued by certain judges is, he says, defeating
the draft. They are discharging the drafted men rapidly under *habeas corpus*,
and he is determined to put a stop to these factious and mischievous proceedings
if he has the authority. The Secretary of State and Attorney-General have each
been consulted and declare they have no doubt of his authority. Mr. Blair was
satisfied the President had the legal power, but whether the measure proposed,
which is an order from the President directing the provost marshals to disregard the writ, or to make return that the persons to be discharged was held by
authority of the President, was perhaps not the best process [see draft of order,
September 17, *infra*]. Mr. Chase feared civil war would be inaugurated if the
privilege of the writ of *habeas corpus* was suspended. Mr. Usher had doubts
and uncertainties.

"The President was very determined, and intimated that he would not only

portant now, than in times of peace and tranquility. I therefore address you without searching for a precedent upon which to do so. Some of you are sincerely devoted to the republican institutions, and territorial integrity of our country, and yet are opposed to what is called the draft, or conscription.

At the beginning of the war, and ever since, a variety of motives pressing, some in one direction and some in the other, would be presented to the mind of each man physically fit for a soldier, upon the combined effect of which motives, he would, or would not, voluntarily enter the service. Among these motives would be patriotism, political bias, ambition, personal courage, love of adventure, want of employment, and convenience, or the opposites of some of these. We already have, and have had in the service, as appears, substantially all that can be obtained upon this voluntary weighing of motives. And yet we must somehow obtain more, or relinquish the original object of the contest, together with all the blood and treasure already expended in the effort to secure it. To meet this necessity the law for the draft has been enacted. You who do not wish to be soldiers, do not like this law. This is natural; nor does it imply want of patriotism. Nothing can be so just, and necessary, as to make us like it, if it is disagreeable to us. We are prone, too, to find false arguments with which to excuse ourselves for opposing such disagreeable things. In this case those who desire the rebellion to succeed, and others who seek reward in a dif-

---

enforce the law, but if Judge Lowry [Chief Justice Walter H. Lowrie, Supreme Court of Pennsylvania] and others continued to interfere and interrupt the draft he would send them after Vallandigham. As considerable discussion had taken place, he was prepared to act, though willing to listen to, and, if mistaken, to defer to, others. Up to this point neither Mr. Stanton or myself had taken part in the discussion, though Stanton had undoubtedly expressed his opinion and prompted the proposed action.

"I remarked that the subject was not new to me, . . . I had as high regard and reverence for that writ as any one, but it seemed to me there should be some way to prevent its abuse. A factious and evil-minded judge . . . could embarrass the Government, could delay the departure of a vessel . . . could stop armies on the march. . . .

"The President said he would prepare and submit a paper at an adjourned meeting for criticism to-morrow at 9 A.M.

"September 15, Tuesday. The President read the paper which he had drawn up. Mr. Chase proposed as a preferable course that the President should, pursuant to the act of the 3rd of March last, suspend by proclamation the privilege of the writ of *habeas corpus* on military questions. This proposition . . . met with favor from all, and the Council adjourned to 1 P.M. for Mr. Seward to prepare a proclamation. On meeting . . . the draft which Mr. Seward had prepared was criticized and after some modifications was ordered to be recopied and carried into effect. All came into the arrangement cordially after Stanton read the reports of sundry provost marshals and others detailing the schemes practiced for defeating the draft. . . ."

ferent way, are very active in accomodating us with this class of arguments. They tell us the law is unconstitutional. It is the first instance, I believe, in which the power of congress to do a thing has ever been questioned, in a case when the power is given by the constitution in express terms. Whether a power can be implied, when it is not expressed, has often been the subject of controversy; but this is the first case in which the degree of effrontery has been ventured upon, of denying a power which is plainly and distinctly written down in the constitution. The constitution declares that "The congress shall have power . . . To raise and support armies; but no appropriation of money to that use shall be for a longer term than two years." The whole scope of the conscription act is "to raise and support armies." There is nothing else in it. It makes no appropriation of money; and hence the money clause just quoted, is not touched by it. The case simply is the constitution provides that the congress shall have power to raise and support armies; and, by this act, the congress has exercised the power to raise and support armies. This is the whole of it. It is a law made in litteral pursuance of this part of the United States Constitution; and another part of the same constitution declares that "This constitution, and the laws made in pursuance thereof . . . shall be the supreme law of the land, and the judges in every state shall be bound thereby, anything in the constitution or laws of any state to the contrary notwithstanding."

Do you admit that the power is given to raise and support armies, and yet insist that by this act congress has not exercised the power in a constitutional mode?—has not done the thing, in the right way? Who is to judge of this? The constitution gives congress the power, but it does not prescribe the mode, or expressly declare who shall prescribe it. In such case congress must prescribe the mode, or relinquish the power. There is no alternative. Congress could not exercise the power to do the thing, if it had not the power of providing a way to do it, when no way is provided by the constitution for doing it. In fact congress would not have the power to raise and support armies, if even by the constitution, it were left to the option of any other, or others, to give or withhold the only mode of doing it. If the constitution had prescribed a mode, congress could and must follow that mode; but as it is, the mode necessarily goes to congress, with the power expressly given. The power is given fully, completely, unconditionally. It is not a power to raise armies *if* State authorities consent; nor *if* the men to compose the armies are entirely willing; but it is a power to raise and support armies given to congress by the constitution, without an if.

It is clear that a constitutional law may not be expedient or proper. Such would be a law to raise armies when no armies were needed. But this is not such. The republican institutions, and territorial integrity of our country can not be maintained without the further raising and supporting of armies. There can be no army without men. Men can be had only voluntarily, or involuntarily. We have ceased to obtain them voluntarily; and to obtain them involuntarily, is the draft—the conscription. If you dispute the fact, and declare that men can still be had voluntarily in sufficient numbers prove the assertion by yourselves volunteering in such numbers, and I shall gladly give up the draft. Or if not a sufficient number, but any one of you will volunteer, he for his single self, will escape all the horrors of the draft; and will thereby do only what each one of at least a million of his manly brethren have already done. Their toil and blood have been given as much for you as for themselves. Shall it all be lost rather than you too, will bear your part?

I do not say that all who would avoid serving in the war, are unpatriotic; but I do think every patriot should willingly take his chance under a law made with great care in order to secure entire fairness. This law was considered, discussed, modified, and amended, by congress, at great length, and with much labor; and was finally passed, by both branches, with a near approach to unanimity. At last, it may not be exactly such as any one man out of congress, or even in congress, would have made it. It has been said, and I believe truly, that the constitution itself is not altogether such as any one of it's framers would have preferred. It was the joint work of all; and certainly the better that it was so.

Much complaint is made of that provision of the conscription law which allows a drafted man to substitute three hundred dollars for himself; while, as I believe, none is made of that provision which allows him to substitute another man for himself. Nor is the three hundred dollar provision objected to for unconstitutionality; but for inequality—for favoring the rich against the poor. The substitution of men is the provision if any, which favors the rich to the exclusion of the poor. But this being a provision in accordance with an old and well known practice, in the raising of armies, is not objected to. There would have been great objection if that provision had been omitted. And yet being in, the money provision really modifies the inequality which the other introduces. It allows men to escape the service, who are too poor to escape but for it. Without the money provision, competition among the more wealthy might, and probably would, raise the price of substitutes above three hundred dollars, thus leaving the man who could raise only three hundred dollars, no escape from personal service. True, by the law as it is, the man who can not raise so much as three hundred dollars, nor obtain a personal substitute for less, can not escape; but he can come quite as near escaping as he could if the money provision were not in the law. To put it another way, is an unobjectionable law which allows only the man to escape who can pay a thousand dollars, made objectionable by adding a provision that any one may escape who can pay the smaller sum of three hundred dollars? This is the exact difference at this point between the present law and all former draft laws. It is true that by this law a some what larger number will escape than could under a law allowing personal substitutes only; but each additional man thus escaping will be [a] poorer man than could have escaped by the law in the other form. The money provision enlarges the class of exempts from actual service simply by admitting poorer men into it. How, then can this money provision be a wrong to the poor man? The inequality complained of pertains in greater degree to the substitution of men, and is really modified and lessened by the money provision. The inequality could only be perfectly cured by sweeping both provisions away. This being a great innovation, would probably leave the law more distasteful than it now is.

The principle of the draft, which simply is involuntary, or enforced service, is not new. It has been practiced in all ages of the world. It was well known to the framers of our constitution as one of the modes of raising armies, at the time they placed in that instrument the provision that "the congress shall have power to raise and support armies." It has been used, just before, in establishing our independence; and it was also used under the constitution in 1812. Wherein is the peculiar hardship now? Shall we shrink from the necessary means to maintain our free government, which our grand-fathers employed to establish it, and our own fathers have already employed once to maintain it? Are we degenerate? Has the manhood of our race run out?

Again, a law may be both constitutional and expedient, and yet may be administered in an unjust and unfair way. This law belongs to a class, which class is composed of those laws whose object is to distribute burthens or benefits on the principle of equality. No one of these laws can ever be practically administered with that exactness which can be conceived of in the mind. A tax law, the principle of which is that each owner shall pay in proproportion [*sic*] to the value of his property, will be a dead letter, if no one can be compelled to pay until it can be shown that every other one will pay in precisely the same proportion according to value; nay even, it will be a dead letter, if no one can be compelled to pay until it is certain that every other one will pay at all—even in unequal proportion. Again the United States House of representatives is constituted on the principle that each member is sent by the same number of people that each other one is sent by; and yet in practice no two of the whole number, much less the whole number, are ever sent by precisely the same number of constituents. The Districts can not be made precisely equal in population at first, and if they could, they would become unequal in a single day, and much more so in the ten years, which the Districts, once made, are to continue. They can not be re-modelled every day; nor, without too much expence and labor, even every year.

This sort of difficulty applies in full force, to the practical administration of the draft law. In fact the difficulty is greater in the case of the draft law. First, it starts with all the inequality of the congressional Districts; but these are based on entire population, while the draft is based upon those only who are fit for soldiers, and such may not bear the same proportion to the whole in one District, that they do in another. Again, the facts must be ascertained, and credit given, for the unequal numbers of soldiers which have already gone from the several Districts. In all these points errors will occur in spite of the utmost fidelity. The government is bound to administer the law with such an approach to exactness as is usual in analagous cases, and as entire good faith and fidelity will reach. If so great departures as to be inconsistent with such good faith and fidelity, or great departures occurring in any way, be pointed out, they shall be corrected; and any agent shown to have caused such departures intentionally, shall be dismissed.

With these views, and on these principles, I feel bound to tell you it is my purpose to see the draft law faithfully executed.

To James G. Blaine[1]

J. G. Blaine   Washington, D.C.,
Augusta, Maine   Sept. 15, 1863

Thanks both for the good news you send, and for the sending of it.   A. LINCOLN

[1] ALS, RPB. James G. Blaine, chairman of the Maine Union Committee, telegraphed on September 14: "Maine sustains your administration by a majority of 15000." (DLC-RTL). On September 15 he telegraphed again: "Fuller returns magnify our victory. Indications now are that we have carried every County in the State. Elected every Senator Secured seven eighths (⅞) of the Representatives and rolled up a Majority of twenty thousand (20 000) out of a total vote of one hundred thousand (100 000)" (*ibid.*).

To Jesse K. Dubois and Ozias M. Hatch[1]

"Cypher"

Hon. J. K. Dubois &
Hon. O. M. Hatch

Executive Mansion,
Washington, Sept. 15, 1863.

What nation do you desire Gen. Allen to be made Quarter-Master-General of? This nation already has a Quarter-Master-General.

A. LINCOLN.

[1] ALS, RPB. This telegram is misdated September 13 in Nicolay and Hay (IX, 119) and Tarbell (Appendix), p. 382. A Washington despatch appearing in the New York *Times* on September 3, 1863, erroneously announced the removal of Montgomery C. Meigs as quartermaster general and William A. Hammond as surgeon general. On September 12 Dubois and Hatch telegraphed Lincoln recommending that Brigadier General Robert Allen be appointed to Meigs' place. See further, Lincoln to Hatch and Dubois, September 22, *infra*.

To Henry W. Halleck[1]

Major General Halleck:

Executive Mansion,
Washington, Sept. 15. 1863.

If I did not misunderstand Gen. Meade's last despatch, he posts you on facts as well as he can, and desires your views and those of the government, as to what he shall do. My opinion is that he should move upon Lee at once in manner of general attack, leaving to developements, whether he will make it a real attack. I think this would develope Lee's real condition and purposes better than the cavalry alone can do. Of course my opinion is not to control you and Gen. Meade. Yours truly

A. LINCOLN

[1] ALS, IHi. Meade's despatch to Halleck of 4 P.M. is as follows:
"The latest intelligence . . . is to 10 a.m., when General Pleasonton reports that the enemy have increased their forces, both infantry and artillery, at the several crossing places threatened by our cavalry. The enemy have likewise a force of infantry and artillery on this side of the Rapidan . . . evidently to defend and dispute the possession of the bridge. . . . General [Gouverneur K.] Warren remains at Culpeper, to which point our trains run, and the telegraph is being opened to Mitchell's Station, the rebels having left their line intact. Two scouts have arrived from below, having been some 5 miles south of Chancellorsville. They confirm the report of the departure of Longstreet's corps, but heard nothing of Ewell's or Hill's corps leaving.
"Your telegram of 11 a.m. this day has been received. I have given orders to concentrate and mass the different corps at the several crossing places on the Rappahannock, but shall await your letter before making any further movement." (OR, I, XXIX, II, 186).
Halleck replied, "After preparing my telegram to you this morning, I received a note from the President, of which I send you a copy. I do not understand this note as materially differing from my dispatch. The main objects are to threaten Lee's position, to ascertain more certainly the actual condition of affairs in his army, and, if possible, to cut off some portion of it by a sudden

raid. . . . And especially every effort should be made to ascertain if any considerable forces have gone by the Valley Railroad toward East Tennessee. . . ."
(*Ibid.*, pp. 186-87).

Proclamation Suspending Writ of Habeas Corpus[1]

September 15, 1863
By the President of the United States of America.

A Proclamation.

Whereas the Constitution of the United States has ordained that the privilege of the Writ of Habeas Corpus shall not be suspended unless when in cases of rebellion or invasion the public safety may require it, And whereas a rebellion was existing on the third day of March, 1863, which rebellion is still existing; and whereas by a statute which was approved on that day, it was enacted by the Senate and House of Representatives of the United States in Congress assembled, that, during the present insurrection, the President of the United States, whenever, in his judgment, the Public safety may require, is authorized to suspend the privilege of the Writ of Habeas Corpus in any case throughout the United States or any part thereof; and whereas in the judgment of the President the public safety does require that the privilege of the said writ shall now be suspended throughout the United States in the cases where, by the authority of the President of the United States, military, naval and civil officers of the United States or any of them hold persons under their command or in their custody either as prisoners of war, spies, or aiders or abettors of the enemy; or officers, soldiers or seamen enrolled or drafted or mustered or enlisted in or belonging to the land or naval forces of the United States or as deserters therefrom or otherwise amenable to military law, or the Rules and Articles of War or the rules or regulations prescribed for the military or naval services by authority of the President of the United States or for resisting a draft or for any other offence against the military or naval service. Now, therefore, I, Abraham Lincoln, President of the United States, do hereby proclaim and make known to all whom it may concern, that the privilege of the Writ of Habeas Corpus is suspended throughout the United States in the several cases before mentioned, and that this suspension will continue throughout the duration of the said rebellion, or until this proclamation shall, by a subsequent one to be issued by the President of the United States, be modified or revoked. And I do hereby require all magistrates, attorneys and other civil officers within the United States, and all officers and others in the military and naval services of the United States, to take distinct notice of this suspension, and to give it full effect, and all citizens of the United States to conduct and govern themselves accordingly and in conformity with the Constitution of the United States and the laws of Congress in such case made and provided.

In testimony whereof, I have hereunto set my hand, and caused the Seal of the United States to be affixed, this Fifteenth day of September, in the year of our Lord one thousand eight [L.S.]   hundred and sixty three and of the Independence of the United States of America the Eighty-eighth.

By the President: ABRAHAM LINCOLN
    WILLIAM H. SEWARD, Secretary of State.

1 DS, DNA FS RG 11, Proclamations. See Lincoln's opinion on the draft, September 14, *supra.*

To Edwin M. Stanton[1]

Hon. Sec. of War   Executive Mansion,
Dear Sir: Washington, Sep. 15. 1863.

The bearer of this, Mrs. Craddock, tells me she has a nephew—Edwin Selvage—who was in the rebel service, made a prisoner, and is now at Fort-Delaware; that he has two brothers in the Union Army, is yet under twenty one years of age; and wishes to take the oath of allegiance and be discharged. Upon reasonable proof of all this, let him take the oath and be discharged. Yours truly
                                                    A. LINCOLN

1 ALS, IHi. Mrs. Craddock and Edwin Selvage have not been identified.

To Edwin M. Stanton[1]

Hon. Sec. of War   Executive Mansion,
My dear Sir   Washington, Sep. 15, 1863.

It seems that E. Jaquelin Smith, and George Mason, are in the Old Capital Prison. The two cases have no connection; but I would like to have a statement, of each case. Yours truly   A. LINCOLN

1 ALS, NN. Endorsements on the letter are as follows: "Make a copy & refer it to Gen [John H.] Martindale for report." "Attended to and copy sent G.E.S." See Lincoln to Geary, September 12, *supra.*

To Edwin M. Stanton[1]

September 15 and 17, 1863

The within are very good recommendations; and if it can be, consistently with the rules of the service, arranged at the Adjutant

General's Office to give the applicant, a Staff-appointment, such as he desires, I am quite satisfied to have it done. I submit the case to the Secretary of War.   A. LINCOLN

Sep. 15. 1863.

I can say just as much as the above, & no more, in favor of Major Seeley being appointed a Pay-Master.   A. LINCOLN

Sep. 17. 1863.

[1] AES, RPB. Lincoln's endorsements are written on a letter from Charles W. Sandford and others, September 9, 1863, recommending appointment of "Major Aaron Seeley, now of the Tenth New York National Guard, who desires again to enter the Service of the United States." Seeley had served with the Tenth New York Infantry from September 10, 1861 to June 15, 1862, and as captain and assistant aide-de-camp, June 21 to December 29, 1862. There is no record of his appointment in 1863, but he was appointed lieutenant colonel of the Twenty-fifth New York Cavalry as of September 8, 1864.

Instructions to Tax Commissioners in South Carolina[1]

September 16, 1863

To the Hon: Abraham D. Smith, Hon: William E. Wording, and Hon: William Henry Brisbane, Tax Commissioners for the District of South Carolina:

Whereas, you were duly appointed a Board of Tax Commissioners, for the District of South Carolina, wherein by reason of insurrection and rebellion, the civil authority of the Government of the United States, has been and continues to be obstructed, so that the provisions of the act entitled "An act to provide increased revenue from imports, to pay interest on the public debt, and for "other purposes," approved August. 5. 1861, could not be peaceably executed; and

Whereas, heretofore, to wit, in the months of February and March of the present year, you as Commissioners aforesaid caused certain lots and parcels of land situated in the Parish of St. Helena in said State, to be sold for the direct taxes, unpaid and charged on the same: and

Whereas, at said sale you struck off to the United States, divers of said lots and parcels of land at certain sums, equal in each case, to at least the tax penalty and costs, and ten per cent interest on said tax charged on each lot or parcel of land respectively; pursuant to public notice therefore given; and

Whereas, the owners of said lots and parcels of land so struck

[1] DS, DNA FI RG 58, Direct Tax Commission of South Carolina.

off to the United States, have abandoned the same, and have not paid the taxes thereon, nor redeemed them, and

Whereas, you have represented to me that you are satisfied that the said owners have left the said lots and parcels of land to engage in and abet the said rebellion.

Now therefore, these presents, witness that I, Abraham Lincoln, President of the United States, pursuant to the provisions of the Act of Congress, entitled, "An act for the collection of direct taxes in insurrectionary districts within the United States and for other purposes" approved on the 7th day of June A.D. 1862, and the amendments thereto, approved on the Sixth day of February A.D. 1863, have issued and hereby do issue these my instructions and directions to you, as the board of Tax Commissioners aforesaid, in the manner and form following, that is to say:

First. You will cause the said lands, except such as in these instructions are particularly excepted or provided for, to be surveyed and subdivided and sold at public sale, in parcels not to exceed three hundred and twenty acres to any one purchaser, after giving due notice thereof for sixty days, as upon the sale of other public lands of the United States, and to issue a certificate therefor. Such lands to be sold on the terms prescribed in the eleventh section of the act entitled "An act for the collection of direct taxes, in insurrectionary districts, within the United States, and for other purposes," and of the act amendatory of the same, approved the sixth day of February A.D. 1863.

Second. If upon such sale, any person serving in the army or navy or marine corps, shall become a purchaser, and shall pay one fourth part of the purchase money pursuant to the provisions of the said eleventh section of the said act of congress, the said Commissioners shall issue a certificate for the said tract or parcel of land so purchased, subject nevertheless to the payment of the residue of the purchase money in three years from the date of said sale, either in money or in certificates of indebtedness of the United States, and subject also to the condition that he, his heirs or assigns shall commit no waste upon the premises sold: and in case he or they shall fail to pay the residue of the said purchase money, within the time limited for the payment, thereof, or shall at any time prior to the full payment of the purchase money in cash or in certificates of indebtedness as aforesaid, with interest, if any, due upon the same, together with costs, commit any waste, it shall and may be lawful for said Commissioners, or their successors in office, to enter upon the said premises and to sell the same for the payment of the purchase money due the United States, returning the over-plus, if any there shall be, to the said purchaser, his heirs or assigns holding the said land, which conditions shall be fully set out in the certificate of the commissioners.

You will cause the plantations on St. Helena Island & known as Lands End, and the Ben. Chaplin place to be laid off and divided into town lots of such size as you may judge proper, not exceeding five acres each, and you will proceed to sell all said lots not needed or selected for Government purposes at public sale, for cash. Or if to any person or persons serving in the army or navy or marine corps, on the terms provided in the 11th section of the act of congress hereinbefore mentioned, and subject to the conditions stated in these instructions in case of sales to such person or persons serving as aforesaid. Prior to making sale of said lots, you will cause the corners of the same to be permanently marked and duplicate plots or drafts of said lots to be made, describing them accurately by metes and bounds thereof, or other definite description, and you will cause said copies to be duly authenticated under your hands, one whereof you will transmit to the office of the Secretary of the Treasury to be filed therein.

There are excepted from these instructions to sell parts of the following tracts of land which are reserved for the use of the United States, for war, military, naval, revenue and police purposes:

On St. Helena Island, Eddings Point, St. Helenaville, St. Helenaville Co., pine land, Lands End, and the Ben Chaplin place.

On Coosaw Island, Coosaw.

On Ladies Island, White Hall and Laurel Bay.

On Port Royal Island, the Hermitage, the Cottage, the Old Fort, The Farm, Pigeon Point, the Campbell place, the Bell place, Magnolia, and the Middleton Stewart place; and On Parrys Island, the Means place.

Also, on Hunting Island, and on Phillips Island the woodland tracts deemed necessary for the use of the United States.

And you will cause the said parts, so reserved as aforesaid, to be surveyed, and duplicate plots and drafts of the same to be made, describing the same by metes and bounds, or other definite description; one of which plots or drafts, duly authenticated under your hands, you will cause to be filed in the office of the Secretary of the Treasury.

You will set apart for school purposes in a convenient form for use as a farm or farms, one or more tracts, (which are hereby excepted from the operation of said instructions to sell) a part or parts of the said land so purchased in (and) by you and belonging to the United States as aforesaid, not exceeding 160 acres in

each, and including such dwelling house or houses and out buildings, as may be upon either of the following named plantations, on
St. Helena Island—The Oaks, Indian Hill, The Thomas James
Tripp place, Cedar Grove, the McTurens lands, Frogmore, the
Frank Prichard place, the Oliver Tripp place, the Wallace place,
and Eddings Point, and the whole of the Thomas B. Chaplin place,
the Grove, and the Baker place. On Coosaw Island, Coosaw, On Ladies Island—Orange Grove, White Hall, the James Chaplin place,
including the Saxby Chaplin lot, Pleasant Point, the John Johnson
place, Springfield, the Williams place and the Capers place; On
Port Royal Island—the Cottage, the Old Fort, Swamp Place, Halfway House, Gray Hill, the the [sic] Middleton Stuart place, Oak
Mulligan, Little Baynard, the Rhett Place, Laurel Bay and the
Thompson place, and on Parry's Island—the Fuller place and the
Means place.

You will cause the parts of the said tracts and parcels of land
so set apart as aforesaid to be surveyed and accurately described
by metes and bounds or other definite description, and the corners thereof, to be permanently marked, and duplicate plots and
drafts of the same to be made and duly authenticated under your
hands, one copy of which you will cause to be filed in the office of
the Secretary of the Treasury.

The lands so set apart you will let and lease for such terms not
exceeding five years, and on such conditions as you may deem
eligible, reserving the rents and issues thereof to yourselves and
your successors in office, and you will take receive and collect such
rents and issues and appropriate and apply the same to the education of colored youths, and of such poor white persons, being mi-
nors, as may by themselves, parents, guardians, or next friends,
apply for the benefit thereof, and you are authorized to establish
such schools, and to direct the tuition of such branches of learning
as you in your judgment shall deem most eligible, subject nevertheless to the general direction and control of the Secretary of the
Treasury.

And there is also excepted and reserved out of and from the
said lands so purchased by the United States, and directed to be
sold as aforesaid, all parts of the following tracts of land not otherwise appropriated, to wit: On St. Helena Island, the Oaks, Oakland,
Indian Hill, Eddings point, The Thomas James Tripp place, Cedar
Grove, The Hamilton Tripp place, the McTurens lands, Hope
place, Woodstock, Frogmore, the Frank Prichard place, the Jane
Prichard place, the Scott place, the Oliver Tripp place[,] the
Wallace place, the Fendon place. On Coosaw Island, Coosaw and

Corn Island; On Ladies' Island, Orange Grove, the Hazel Farm, White Hall, the James Chaplin place, Pleasant Point, the John Johnson place, Springfield, Laurel Bay, the Williams place, and the Capers place. On Port Royal Island—the Farm, the Old Fort, Polly's Grove, the Bell place, the Campbell place, the Swamp place, Halfway House, Grays Hill, Magnolia, the Middleton Stuart place, Oak Mulligan, the John F Chaplin place, Oakland, Little Baynard, Jericho, the Oswald place, the Ellis place, the Rhett place, and Laurel Bay, and on Parry's Island, the Fuller place, the Elliott place No 1. The Elliott place No. 2[,] the El[l]iott place No. 3, and the Means place

And you will cause the same to be surveyed and to be particularly described by metes and bounds or other definite description, and to be divided into lots and parcels not exceeding twenty acres each, corners of which you will cause to be permanently designated by stones planted, or by marked trees or other suitable monuments. In case of irregularity in the boundaries of tracts or plantations, between those which have been or may be selected for specific purposes, and those which are not so selected, you will not be strictly limited to such boundaries but may conform the division to the general lines of the new survey.

And you will cause accurate plots or drafts of the surveys to be made, exhibiting the said subdivisions of twenty acres each, duly authenticated under your hands, one whereof shall be filed in the office of the Secretary of the Treasury.

You are further directed to issue certificates for the said lots and parcels of land to the heads of families of the African race, one only to each, preferring such as by their good conduct, meritorious services or exemplary character, will be examples of moral propriety and industry to those of the same race, for the charitable purpose of providing homes for such heads of families and their families respectively, so as to give them an interest in the soil, and to form an industrial settlement of worthy persons of said race, they the said heads of families paying to the Commissioners such sum not less than $1.25 per acre as the said commissioners shall designate and determine as proper to be charged for the said lands, in view of the charitable purposes aforesaid.

And you are further instructed to announce in your advertisement of the sale of said lands so directed to be sold as aforesaid, that the same will be set up for sale at $1.25 an acre each, and that the same will not be sold unless the bids advance beyond that price.

Where any tracts or lots of land have erected thereon dwelling houses, barns or other out houses, you will appraise the same at what you deem the cash value thereof, and in case the said lots or tracts of land on which the said buildings are erected shall fail when offered for sale as aforesaid to be bid up to a sum equal to one third part of the appraised value thereof, you will cause the same to be withdrawn from sale, and to be readvertised and again offered for sale as soon as conveniently practicable on the same conditions as are stated in these instructions.

In order to enable you so to protect the interests of the United States, you will in your written conditions of sale reserve a single bid to be publicly made by the Commissioners or by their authority of such a sum as you may deem eligible not less than one third of the appraised value.

In case on a third attempt, you shall fail to sell such lands as may be offered for sale as aforesaid, or any of them, after again advertising them as above directed, you will sell them to the highest bidder, if the Secretary of the Treasury shall so direct, upon report to him of your proceedings.

You will keep a book or books, in which you will enter or cause to be entered, full descriptions of the said lands so to be surveyed as aforesaid, with a draft or plot of each survey, exhibiting the subdivisions, if any, and you shall also make an entry therein of each tract and lot sold, with the name of the purchaser, and the sum for which the same may be sold, the date of the sale, and the date of the issuing of the certificates to the purchasers, and you shall also particularly describe and set out in said book the tracts reserved for the use of the United States for military, naval, revenue and police purposes, and the tract or tracts also set apart for school purposes, and you will make an entry of each tract for which a certificate shall be given to any colored citizen, being the head of a family as aforesaid, together with the name of such head of family and the sum of money with which he shall be charged for any lot for which a certificate shall be given him and the date of the issue of such certificate, and you will cause transcripts of said book or books duly verified by you, to be filed in the office of the Secretary of the Treasury, and when your commission shall expire you shall cause said book or books to be filed in said office.

You will also sell at public sale after giving notice as aforesaid, all the lots and buildings in the town of Beaufort and State aforesaid struck off to the United States, at such sale and not redeemed. Prior to making such sale you will appraise the said lots and buildings at their cash value, and in case any of the same on being offered for sale shall not be bid to one third of the appraised value, you will cause the same to be with-drawn from sale, and upon being advertised to be again offered for sale, and if after being so advertised and offered a third time for sale, it shall fail to be bid to one fifth of its appraised value, you will sell the same to the highest bidder, if on report of your proceedings to the Secretary of the Treasury, he shall deem it eligible so to do. The conditions of sale in each case shall be the same as those above stated in relation to the plantations or tracts of land to be sold pursuant to these instructions.

In your conditions of sale of the said town of Beaufort, you are authorized to protect the interests of the United States by reserving a bid on each or any of the said lots or buildings, to be made by the Commissioners or by some one by their authority, to be publicly made, for such sum as you may deem proper. Witness, my hand, this 16th. day of September AD. 1863. ABRAHAM LINCOLN

To George G. Meade[1]

Major General Meade   Executive Mansion,
Warrenton, Va   Washington, Sep. 16, 1863.
    Is Albert Jones, of Co. K. 3rd. Maryland volunteers, to be shot on Friday next? If so, please state to me the general features of the case.   A. LINCOLN

[1] ALS, owned by R. E. Burdick, New York City. No reply has been discovered, but see Lincoln to Meade, September 17, *infra*.

To William H. Seward[1]

This was presented some time last November. Will the Sec. of State please prepare a suitable answer to it?   A. LINCOLN
    Sep. 16. 1863.

[1] AES, NAuE. Lincoln's endorsement appears on a pamphlet, *Minutes of the Twenty-fifth Annual Session of the Synod of Pennsylvania, with an Appendix, A.D., 1862.* The session was held at Wilmington, Delaware, October 21-23, 1862.

To Mrs. Joshua F. Speed[1]

Mrs. J. F. Speed   Washington, DC.
Louisville, Ky.   Sep. 16. 1863
    Mr. Holman will not be jostled from his place, with my knowledge and consent   A. LINCOLN

[1] ALS, RPB. No correspondence in relation to this matter has been located. Holman has not been identified.

To Salmon P. Chase[1]

Sec. of Treasury. Please see Mr. Church and Mr. Farwell, very respectable gentlemen of Illinois.　　　　　　　A. LINCOLN

Sept. 17. 1863

[1] Copy, IHi-Nicolay and Hay Papers. The gentlemen from Illinois have not been positively identified, but may have been Charles B. Farwell of Chicago and Lawrence S. Church of Woodstock, Illinois.

Draft of Order Concerning
Writ of Habeas Corpus[1]

[September 17, 1863]

Please order each Military officer of the United States, that, whenever he shall have in his custody any person, by the authority of the United States and any writ of *habeas corpus* shall be served upon him, commanding him to produce such person before any court or judge, he, the said Military officer, make known to the court or judge issuing such writ, by a proper return thereto, that he holds such person by the authority of the President of the United States, acting as the Commander-in-Chief, of the Army of the United States in time of actual rebellion and war against the United States; and that, thereupon he do not produce such person according said writ, but that he deal with him according to the orders of his military superiors; and that, having made known to such court or judge, the cause of holding said person as aforesaid, if said court or judge, shall issue any process for his, said officer's, arrest, he refuse obedience thereto; and that, in case there shall be any attempt, to take such person from the custody of such officer, or to arrest such officer, he resist such attempt, calling to his aid any force that may be necessary to make such resistance effectual.

[1] ADf, DNA WR RG 110, Provost Marshal General's Bureau, II, H 319 (1863). The substance of this draft was covered in AGO *General Orders No. 315*, September 17, 1863, and *Circular No. 85*, Provost Marshal General's Office of the same date (OR, III, III, 818). See also note to Lincoln's opinion on the draft, September 14, *supra*.

To George G. Meade[1]

Major-General Meade,　　　　　Executive Mansion, Washington,
Headquarters Army of Potomac:　　　September 17, 1863.

Yours in relation to Albert Jones is received. I am appealed to in behalf of Richard M. Abrams of Company A, Sixth New Jersey Volunteers, by Governor Parker, Attorney-General Freelinghoysen,[2] Governor Newell, Hon. Mr. Middleton,[3] M.C., of the

[460]

district and the marshal who arrested him. I am also appealed to in behalf of Joseph S. Smith, of Company A, Eleventh New Jersey Volunteers, by Governor Parker, Attorney-General Freelinghoysen, and Hon. Marcus C. Ward.[4] Please state the circumstances of their cases to me.   A. LINCOLN.

[1] Tarbell (Appendix), p. 384. See Lincoln to Meade, September 16, *supra*. Meade's reply has not been located. The roster of Company K, Third Maryland Volunteers, lists Albert Jones as "killed, September 18, 1863." Richard M. Abrahams is listed on the roster as dishonorably discharged at Fort Jefferson, Florida, June 12, 1864, and released from confinement July 3, 1865. Joseph S. Smith is listed as transferred to Company A, Twelfth New Jersey Volunteers, returned to duty May 20, 1865, and mustered out July 15, 1865.

[2] Frederick T. Frelinghuysen.   [3] George Middleton.

[4] Marcus L. Ward, governor of New Jersey, 1865-1869.

Memorandum: Appointment of John Pitman, Jr.[1]

I have quite a strong desire for young Pitman to be appointed.

Sep. 17. 1863.   A. LINCOLN

[1] AES, DNA WR RG 94, U.S. Military Academy, 1862, Box 81, No. 239. Lincoln's endorsement is written on a letter from Israel C. Woodruff to John Hay, September 17, 1863, "In reply to your note . . . to Gen Totten, you are informed that John Pitman of R.I. has not been appointed a Cadet. . . ." Second Lieutenant John T. Pitman, Jr. of the Eleventh Rhode Island Infantry was appointed to West Point, September 29, 1863, and graduated June 17, 1867.

Recommendation[1]

September 17, 1863

This lady says she has a mother but no father living; that she has two brothers, both in the Army. She wants employment, and I shall be glad if any of the Departments or Bureaus can give it to her.   A. LINCOLN

Sep. 17. 1863.

[1] ADS, The Rosenbach Company, Philadelphia and New York. The lady has not been identified.

To Robert C. Schenck[1]

Major General Schenck   Executive Mansion,
Baltimore, Md.   Washington, Sep. 17, 1863.

Major Haynor left here several days ago, under a promise to put down in writing, in detail, the facts in relation to the misconduct of the people on the Eastern Shore of Virginia. He has not returned. Please send him over.   A. LINCOLN

[1] ALS, RPB. Schenck replied at 2 P.M., "Major Hayner has prepared the writing you requested & will go to you with it tomorrow." (DLC-RTL). The

following day he telegraphed, "Maj Hayner was accidentally prevented from going to Washington in this mornings train Will be there in the early train tomorrow morning." (*Ibid.*) For a summary of Hayner's report of September 10, see note to Lincoln's communication to Stanton, September 1, *supra.*

To Edwin M. Stanton[1]

Washington, Sept. 17, 1863

A lady called as the wife of John S. Struthers, a Captain in the 13th Peny. Vol. Cavalry, and urges that he may be allowed to resign. She has not a resignation with her. If she had, I would be for accepting it, on the general principle, that we are rapidly getting an over proportion of officers. Yours truly,

A. LINCOLN

[1] Ritter-Hopson Catalog 51, December 19, 1933, No. 212 B. According to the catalog description, this communication is an autograph letter signed. Captain John S. Struthers was discharged on a surgeon's certificate, July 9, 1864.

To Mrs. Hannah Armstrong[1]

Mrs. Hannah Armstrong   Washington,
Petersburg, Illinois.   Sep. 18. 1863

I have just ordered the discharge of your boy William, as you say, now at Louisville, Ky.   A. LINCOLN.

[1] ALS, RPB. No correspondence from Hannah Armstrong has been found. The roster of Company C, Eighty-fifth Illinois Volunteers lists William Armstrong as "Discharged at Louisville, Ky. by order of the President." According to tradition, the son of Jack and Hannah Armstrong, William ("Duff") Armstrong, whom Lincoln had successfully defended in a famous murder trial in 1858, was ill with rheumatism and unable to obtain a discharge; whereupon his mother asked a friend, "Uncle Jakey" Garber, to write a letter for her asking the president to obtain William's discharge (*Journal of the Illinois State Historical Society*, XIV, 266).

To Andrew Johnson[1]

"Cypher"

Hon. Andrew Johnson   Executive Mansion,
Nashville, Tenn.   Washington, Sept. 18, 1863.

Despatch of yesterday just received. I shall try to find the paper you mention, and carefully consider it. In the mean time let me urge that you do your utmost to get every man you can, black and white, under arms at the very earliest moment, to guard roads, bridges and trains, allowing all the better trained soldiers to go forward to Rosecrans. Of course I mean for you to act in co-operation with, and not independently of, the military authorities.

A. LINCOLN

1 ALS, RPB. This telegram is misdated September 8, 1863, by Nicolay and Hay (IX, 113). For Johnson's despatch of September 17, see note to Lincoln's letter of September 11, *supra.* See also Lincoln to Stanton, infra.

Memorandum:
Appointment of Joseph J. Gillespie[1]

I would like for my friend Gillespie to be obliged in this matter whenever it can be done.   A. LINCOLN

Sep. 18. 1863

1 AES, DNA WR RG 94, U.S. Military Academy, 1861, Box 78, No. 326. Lincoln's endorsement is written on a note from Joseph Gillespie, September 18, 1863, "I respectfully recommend Joseph J. Gillespie of Madison County Ills. for a cadetship . . . at West Point." No record of the appointment of Gillespie's nephew has been found.

To Isaac N. Morris[1]

Hon. I. N. Morris.   Executive Mansion,
Sir   Washington, Sep. 18, 1863.

Please carefully put the argument in writing, with reference to authorities, in the matter intended to show that the law gives an appeal to me, in the case referred to. When that is ready to be presented, I will try to give you the personal interview about Illinois matters generally. Yours truly   A. LINCOLN

1 ALS-P, ISLA; LS copy, DLC-RTL. See Lincoln's letter to Morris of August 26, *supra.* Morris wrote Lincoln on September 18:
"In your letter to me under date of the 26th ult you say, in refering to the business of Illinois, then pending before the Secretary of the Interior, when he shall have acted, if his action is not satisfactory, there may or may not be an appeal to me. It is a point I have not considered, but if . . . the law gives such appeal, I shall not hesitate to entertain it. . . . The action of the Interior Secretary not being satisfactory I am now ready to make the showing you refer to. I have also some general views to present which, I am sure, you will not be averse to hearing as you cannot but feel an interest in all that pertains to Illinois. I desire an audience in her behalf, and if, after I shall have presented the facts, you should think she has no rights which you have power to enforce so let it be. . . ."
"P.S.: The Hon Reverdy Johnson will assist in the argument and will be oblige if you will state when you will hear us. Tomorrow morning at ten o'clock would suit us for the interview. Will it suit yours. . . ." (DLC-RTL).

Order Concerning Lewis H. Cox,
Alias John M. Dillon[1]

Executive Mansion, Washington, Sep. 18th. 1863.
It is represented to me that Lewis H. Cox, Quarter-master Sergeant in the 8th. Pennsylvania Cavalry, being in hospital at Baltimore,

recently, was induced to go to Philadelphia, and receive pay, and enter, as a substitute, in Co. D. in the 111th. Pennsylvania Volunteers, under the name of John M. Dillon; and, without being arrested, or detected, has himself confessed his fault, and expressed his wish to atone for it, in the best way he can, to his father, who calls on me. Now, in case he shall faithfully perform his whole duty, according to his enlistment in the said 111th. Pennsylvania Regiment, upon that condition he is fully pardoned for the offense aforesaid. A. LINCOLN

[Endorsement]

Thinking it was better to have this young man for three years, than to shoot him, or even to have him for the remaining one year in the old regiment, I gave his father the paper, of which the within is a copy. I send it to the Department, in order that a proper note, or entry may be made on the roll of the 8th. Penn. Cavalry.

Sep. 18. 1863 A LINCOLN

[1] DS and AES, owned by Charles W. Olsen, Chicago, Illinois. A letter from Andrew G. Curtin, September 17, 1863, requested the president's "kind interposition in behalf of the young gentleman whose father will present this. From letters which he will exhibit . . . it is evident that his son has fallen a victim to . . . a professional substitute-broker. . . ." (DLC-RTL). The roster of the Eighth Pennsylvania Cavalry lists Lewis H. Cox as "Not accounted for." The roster of the One Hundred Eleventh Pennsylvania Volunteers lists John M. Dillon as mustered on August 26, 1863, and mustered out with Company D on July 19, 1865.

Recommendation for H. Littlefield[1]

September 18, 1863

I personally know H. Littlefield to be a true and reliable man.

A. LINCOLN

[1] Metropolitan Art Association Catalog, January 14, 1914, No. 503. According to the catalog description this is an autograph note signed. It is possible that H. Littlefield was John H. Littlefield, formerly a student in the Lincoln & Herndon law office.

To Clark M. Smith[1]

C. M. Smith, Esq Washington D.C.
Springfield, Illinois Sep. 18. 1863.

Why not name him for the General you fancy most? This is my suggestion. A. LINCOLN

[1] ALS, RPB. No communication from Smith has been found. His son, named Allen Hall Smith, was born on September 16, 1863. The only likely candidate

for "the General you fancy most," as suggested by Lincoln, would seem to be Brigadier General Robert Allen of Springfield, Illinois, concerning whom see Lincoln to Hatch and Dubois, September 22, *infra*.

To Edwin M. Stanton[1]

Hon. Sec. of War.   Executive Mansion,
Sir: Washington, Sept. 18, 1863.

Gov. Johnson, of Tenn. in his despatch, mentions a paper which he says he drew up, on re-organization, which I indorsed in some way, & which I understand him to suppose is on file in your Department. If it is there, please send me a copy of it. Yours truly
                                                    A. LINCOLN

[1] ALS, IHi. See Lincoln's communication to Johnson, *supra*. Johnson's paper to which Lincoln referred is reproduced in the note to Lincoln's endorsement to Stanton, April 25, *supra*.

To Edwin M. Stanton[1]

Hon. Sec. of War   Executive Mansion,
Sir: Washington, Sept. 18. 1863.

Please cause a statement to be made to me in regard to the Mustering out of service of Col. George P. Ihrie, who was upon Gen. Grant's Staff. Yours truly   A. LINCOLN

[1] ALS, NN. Stanton replied on September 19:
"In obedience to the requirement of your note of yesterday I have the honor to state as follows, Colonel George P. Ihrie was appointed an additional aid de camp upon the staff of Major General Halleck through a misapprehension as to that officer's wishes with regard to the appointment. Gen'l Halleck however declined to take him upon his staff; and he was then assigned to Gen'l Grant, who became dissatisfied with him and dismissed him from his head quarters.

"After being some months unemployed, and the War Department having no employment for him, he was, in the same way, with other officers similarly situated, under a provision of law requiring the discharge of super numerary additional aides de camp, mustered out of service." (DLC-RTL).

To Nathaniel P. Banks[1]

Major General Banks   Executive Mansion,
My dear Sir: Washington, Sept. 19, 1863.

In strong hope that you have the old flag flying in Texas by this time, we are about sending Gen [Andrew J.][2] Hamilton to act as Military Governor there. I believe you know him; but it can do no harm for me to say I really believe him to be a man of worth and ability; and one who, by his acquaintance there, can scarcely fail to be efficient in re-inaugurating the National authority. He has suffered so long and painful an exile from his home and family that I feel a deep sympathy for him; and I scarcely need say I am sure he has received, and will receive the same from you. Yours very truly   A. LINCOLN

1 ALS, CSmH. On December 4, General Banks acknowledged receipt of this letter:

"Your letter . . . was presented to me by General Hamilton the 13th October. It gave me pleasure to assure him of my desire to comply with your instructions, and to assist him in the performance of his official duties. . . . I gave him an outline of my purposes . . . but advised him to remain in New Orleans until the practicability of re-establishing the flag . . . in Texas could be determined. . . .

"Advised of our success . . . he . . . left New Orleans . . . and met me . . . on the 25th November. . . . I advised him to make his headquarters at Brownsville. . . . He adopted this course, and sailed for Brownsville on the 26th of November. . . ." (OR, I, XXVI, I, 832).

2 Lincoln left a blank for insertion of Hamilton's first name.

To Hughey Gallagher[1]

Hughey Gallagher   Washington, D.C.,
Philadelphia, Pa.   Sept. 19 1863

I know nothing as to John Gallagher. The law does not require this class of cases to come before me, and they do not come, unless brought by the friends of the condemned.   A LINCOLN

1 ALS, RPB. A telegram from Hughey Gallagher received at 12:20 P.M. simply asked, "Is John Gallagher to be shot Answer please." (DLC-RTL). John Gallagher, alias Jacob Watson, Company H, Fourth New Jersey Volunteers, was sentenced to be shot for desertion, September 18, 1863. Reprieved, he deserted again while on furlough in April, 1865.

To Henry W. Halleck[1]

                                            Executive Mansion
Major General Halleck: Washington, Sept. 19. 1863.

By Gen. Meade's despatch to you of yesterday it appears that he desires your views and those of the government, as to whether he shall advance upon the enemy. I am not prepared to order, or even advise an advance in this case, wherein I know so little of particulars, and wherein he, in the field, thinks the risk is so great, and the promise of advantage so small. And yet the case presents matter for very serious consideration in another aspect. These two armies confront each other across a small river, substantially midway between the two Capitals, each defending it's own Capital, and menacing the other. Gen. Meade estimates the enemies infantry in front of him at not less than forty thousand. Suppose we add fifty per cent to this, for cavalry, artillery, and extra duty men stretching as far as Richmond, making the whole force of the enemy sixty thousand. Gen. Meade, as shown by the returns, has with him, and between him and Washington, of the same classes of well men, over ninety thousand. Neither can bring the whole of his men into a battle; but each can bring as large a per centage in as the other. For a battle, then, Gen. Meade has three men to Gen. Lee's two. Yet, it having been determined that choosing ground, and standing on the defensive, gives so great advantage that the three can not safely attack the two, the three are left simply standing on the defensive also. If the enemies sixty thousand are sufficient to keep our ninety thousand away from Richmond, why, by the same rule, may not forty thousand of ours keep their sixty thousand away from Washington, leaving us fifty thousand to put to some other use? Having practically come to the mere defensive, it seems to be no economy at all to employ twice as many men for that object as are needed. With no object, certainly, to misle[a]d myself, I can perceive no fault in this statement, unless we admit we are not the equal of the enemy man for man. I hope you will consider it.

To avoid misunderstanding, let me say that to attempt to fight the enemy slowly back into his intrenchments at Richmond, and there to capture him, is an idea I have been trying to repudiate for quite a year. My judgment is so clear against it, that I would scarcely allow the attempt to be made, if the general in command should desire to make it. My last attempt upon Richmond was to get McClellan, when he was nearer there than the enemy was, to run in ahead of him. Since then I have constantly desired the Army of the Potomac, to make Lee's army, and not Richmond, it's objective point. If our army can not fall upon the enemy and hurt him where he is, it is plain to me it can gain nothing by attempting to follow him over a succession of intrenched lines into a fortified city. Yours truly   A. LINCOLN

[1] ADfS, DLC-RTL; LS, IHi. Meade's despatch to Halleck of 3 P.M., September 18, is as follows:

"I have reached such a position that I do not feel justified in making a further advance without some more positive authority than was contained in your last letter enclosing one from the President. If I apprehend rightly the views of the President and yourself it was to the effect that I might advance on Lee and threaten him with an attack and not permit him to cross the Rapidan without giving him battle. After accomplishing this my feint might be converted into a real attack if the development of the movement and subsequent information justified the same. It is precisely this question which now embarrasses me and which I desire to be advised upon. The situation is simply this—Lee in command of Ewells and Hills Corps estimated at not less than forty thousand Infantry occupies the south bank of the Rapidan with every available point covered with artillery and prepared to dispute the passage. The character of the south bank and its command forbids any attempt being made till Morton's ford is reached which is some ten miles below the Railroad. At this place the command is on this side and I think a passage can be forced but it would undoubtedly result in a considerable sacrifice and would also most certainly involve a general engagement immediately on crossing. Presuming for the discussion that the crossing was effected and the Enemy overcome he would probably fall back on Gordonsville, as I suppose his policy is to check and retard my advance as long and where he can. I do not deem it necessary to discuss the contingencies of a failure as they will of course present themselves to your mind. The whole question however in my judgement hangs upon the advantages to be gained and the course to be pursued in event of success. I am not in condition to follow Lee to Richmond and will be less so after being weakened by a severe battle. The only thing I could do would be to change my base to the Fredericksburg Rail Road and after taking a position in front of that place await an increase of force. The men I should have to sacrifice in the operation would be sufficient to secure the longer line of communication I now have. In fine I can get a battle out of Lee under very disadvantageous circumstances which may render his inferior force my superior and which is not likely to result in any very decided advantage, even in case I should be victorious. In this view I am reluctant to run the risks involved without the positive sanction of the Government. If any demonstration on the Peninsula were practicable or a force could threaten an advance on the Fredericksburg Road Lee would I think retire from my front but I take it for granted, either of these contingencies is out of the question.

"I send this by an aide-de-camp who will bring your reply." (DLC-RTL).

To Andrew Johnson[1]

Private

Hon. Andrew Johnson.   Executive Mansion
My dear Sir: Washington, D C. Sept. 19. 1863

Herewith I send you a paper, substantially the same as the one, drawn up by yourself,[2] and mentioned in your despatch, but slightly changed in two particulars. First, yours was so drawn as that I authorized you to carry into effect the fourth Section &c. whereas I so modify it as to authorize you to so act as to require the United States to carry into effect that Section. Secondly, you had a clause committing me, in some sort to the State constitution of Tennessee, which I feared might embarrass you in making a new constitution if you desire. So I dropped that clause. Yours very truly   A LINCOLN

[1] ADfS, DLC-RTL; LS, NNP.
[2] See the note to Lincoln's endorsement to Stanton, April 25, *supra.*

To Andrew Johnson[1]

Executive Mansion
Washington D.C.

Hon. Andrew Johnson
Military Governor of Tennessee
Sept. 19. 1863.

In addition to the matters contained in the orders and instructions given you by the Secretary of War,[2] you are hereby authorized to exercise such powers as may be necessary and proper to enable the loyal people of Tennessee to present such a republican form of State government, as will entitle the State to the guaranty of the United States therefor, and to be protected under such State government, by the United States against invasion and domestic violence, all according to the fourth Section of the fourth Article of the constitution of the United States.   ABRAHAM LINCOLN

[1] ADfS, DLC-RTL; LS, NNP. This letter was sent as an enclosure with the preceding letter.   [2] See OR, III, III, 115, 122-23.

To Mary Todd Lincoln[1]

Mrs. A. Lincoln
New-York.
Washington, D.C.,
Sep. 20 1863

I neither see nor hear anything of sickness here now; though there may be much without my knowing it. I wish you to stay, or come just as is most agreeable to yourself.   A. LINCOLN.

[1] ALS, IHi. No communication from Mrs. Lincoln has been found.

Recommendation for Mr. Hall[1]

September 20, 1863

I personally know Mr. Hall to be a very worthy and deserving man; and if a man is to be taken from so distant a locality as Springfield, a more proper man than Mr. Hall cannot be found.
A. LINCOLN.

[1] *The Flying Quill*, January-February, 1951, No. 9. Of several residents of Springfield, Illinois, by the name of "Hall," the bearer of this note has not been positively identified.

To Ambrose E. Burnside[1]

"Cypher"
Gen. Burnside
Knoxville, Tenn
Washington City,
Sep. 21. 2.AM 1863

Go to Rosecrans with your force, without a moments delay.
A. LINCOLN

[469]

¹ ALS, RPB. See Lincoln to Rosecrans, *infra*. Burnside's reply from Carters Station, Tennessee, was received at 11:30 A.M. on September 23:

"Your despatch of the twenty first is recd & the order shall be obeyed at once Every available man shall be concentrated at the point you direct & with as little delay as possible We hold this road effectually to this point & have driven the enemy within a few miles of Virginia & probably into Virginia. I am now waiting for reports from the front so that I can definitely report to you the position of our advance. One of our cavalry Brigades had a sharp fight yesterday at Blountsville in which the enemy were beaten & dispersed. I will telegraph the particulars this evening or tomorrow. The main body of the troops are now moving in the direction your order indicates. The bridge at this place is burned & I suppose the one over the Holston at Union Station is also burned. That is the extreme point that I was ordered by Genl Halleck to hold. I leave for Knoxville very soon & will try to telegraph you from there early tomorrow morning. Nearly forty miles of the distance has to be made on horse back owing to the burning of some small bridge between Greenville & Jonesboro which I hope to have repaired very soon. I shall leave force enough in this neighborhood to, in all probability, hold the Section until the citizens can be armed. The entire country is Union up to the line of the Watauga River. Sylvan County is intensely rebellious. I hoped to have been able to have accomplished one very important piece of work within forty eight hours but the receipt of your order will delay it but I do not for a moment doubt the wisdom of the order You may be sure I will use all possible dispatch in carrying it out. The news from Rosecrans is rather discouraging but I sincerely hope and believe that he will be able to hold his position until such reinforcements as you have ordered to him can arrive. Our cavalry under Genl. Shackelford, has been continually in contact with the enemy driving them all the time. Col [James P. T.] Carter's Brigade has been moving along line of Rail Road and Col [John W.] Foster has been on the flank. He whipped the enemy very handsomely both at Blountsville & Bristol. We have thus far captured but four (4) pieces of Artillery and but few prisoners. I hope direct Telegraphic communication will be open with you tomorrow" (DLC-RTL).

To Ambrose E. Burnside¹

Gen. Burnside   Washington, D.C.,
Greenville, Tenn.   Sept 21, 1863 [11 A.M.]

If you are to do any good to Rosecrans it will not do to waste time with Jonesboro. It is already too late to do the most good that might have been done, but I hope it will still do some good. Please do not lose a moment.   A. LINCOLN

¹ ALS, RPB. This second telegram to Burnside was probably sent because Lincoln's attention was called to Burnside's telegram to Halleck on September 17, received on the 19th, which stated "I go to Greeneville to-night. Dispositions for attacking the enemy at Jonesborough made." (OR, I, XXX, III, 718).

To Henry W. Halleck¹

                                                Executive Mansion
Major General Halleck   Washington, D.C. Sep. 21. 1863

I think it very important for Gen. Rosecrans to hold his position, at or about Chattanooga, because, if held from that place to

Cleveland, both inclusive, it keeps all Tennessee clear of the enemy, and also breaks one of his most important Railroad lines. To prevent these consequences, is so vital to his cause, that he can not give up the effort to dislodge us from the position, thus bringing him to us, and saving us the labor, expence, and hazard of going further to find him; and also giving us the advantage of choosing our own ground, and preparing it, to fight him upon. The details must of course be left to Gen. Rosecrans, while we must furnish him the means to the utmost of our ability. If you concur, I think he would better be informed, that we are not pushing him beyond this position; and that, in fact, our judgment is rather against his going beyond it. If he can only maintain this position, without more, the rebellion can only eke out a short and feeble existence, as an animal sometimes may with a thorn in its vitals. Yours truly

A. LINCOLN

[1] ADfS, DLC-RTL. The envelope is endorsed by Lincoln "To Gen. Halleck, for Gen. Rosecrans. Sep. 21. 1863." Halleck replied, "It is respectfully submitted that the within instructions, given ten days ago, conform to those suggested in the President's letter of this morning." (OR, I, XXX, I, 148). Halleck enclosed his despatch to Rosecrans of September 11, 1:35 P.M.: "General Burnside telegraphs from Cumberland Gap that he holds all East Tennessee above Loudon, and also the gaps of the North Carolina mountains. A cavalry force is moving toward Athens to connect with you. After holding the mountain passes on the west, and Dalton, or some other point on the railroad, to prevent the return of Bragg's army, it will be decided whether your army shall move farther south into Georgia and Alabama. It is reported here by deserters that a part of Bragg's army is re-enforcing Lee. It is important that the truth of this should be ascertained as early as possible." Halleck also enclosed his despatch to Burnside of September 11, 2 P.M.: "I congratulate you on your successes. Hold the gaps of the North Carolina mountains, the line of the Holston River, or some point, if there be one, to prevent access from Virginia and connect with General Rosecrans, at least with your cavalry. The Secretary of War directs that you raise all the volunteers you can in East Tennessee. Select the officers, and if not commissioned by Governor Johnson they will be by the President. If you have not arms and equipments at your disposal telegraph for them. How is the supply of forage and provisions in East Tennessee? General Rosecrans will occupy Dalton, or some point on the railroad, to close all access from Atlanta, and also the mountain passes on the west. This being done it will be determined whether the movable forces shall advance into Georgia and Alabama, or into the Valley of Virginia and North Carolina." (*Ibid.*, pp. 148-49).

To Mary Todd Lincoln[1]

Mrs. A Lincoln   Washington, D.C.,
Fifth Avenue Hotel New-York   Sept. 21. 1863

The air is so clear and cool, and apparantly healthy, that I would be glad for you to come. Nothing very particular, but I would be glad [to] see you and Tad.   A LINCOLN

1 ALS, IHi. Mrs. Lincoln telegraphed the White House doorman, Edward Mc-
Manus, on September 21, 1863: "Go to Col. McCullum [Daniel C. McCallum,
director of military railroads] and ask him to send the green car on to Phila-
delphia for me and make arrangements for a special car from New York to
Philadelphia. Send me a reply immediately." (Katherine Helm, *Mary, Wife of
Lincoln,* pp. 214-15).

To George G. Meade[1]

Major General Meade   Washington, D.C.,
Army of Potomac   Sep. 21. 1863

I am appealed to in behalf John H. Williams Co. D. 4 Regt. Md
Vols, 1 Corps who is said to be under sentence of death to be executed on the 25th. for desertion. The appeal is made on the ground
of unsoundness of mind. Please give me briefly the facts and your
views   A. LINCOLN

1 ALS-P, ISLA. No reply has been found. The roster of Co. D, Fourth Maryland Volunteers, lists no John H. Williams, but Charles W. Williams who was
sentenced to be shot for desertion (Army of the Potomac, *General Orders No.
91,* September 17, 1863) is listed with the notation "Died, September 25, 1863."

To Francis H. Peirpoint[1]

Governor Pierpoint   Washington, D.C.,
Alexandria, Va.   Sep. 21. 1863

I would be glad to have your opinion whether it would be good
policy to refund the money collected from the people of East Virginia, as indemnity for the Light-House depredation. I believe you
once gave me your opinion on the point, but I am not entirely sure.
Please answer.   A. LINCOLN.

1 ALS, RPB. No reply has been discovered.

To William S. Rosecrans[1]

Major Gen. Rosecrans   Washington, D.C.,
Chattanooga Tenn.   Sep 21. 12.35 AM 1863

Be of good cheer. We have unabated confidence in you, and in
your soldiers and officers. In the main you must be the judge as to
what is to be done. If I were to suggest, I would say, save your
army, by taking strong positions, until Burnside joins you, when I
hope you can turn the tide. I think you had better send a courier
to Burnside to hurry him up. We can not reach him by Telegraph.
We suppose some force is going to you from Corinth, but for want

of communication, we do not know how they are getting along. We shall do our utmost to assist you. Send us your present posting.[2]

A. LINCOLN

[1] ALS, RPB. Rosecrans telegraphed from Chattanooga at 8 P.M. on September 19, "We have just concluded a terrific days fighting and have another in prospect for tomorrow. The Enemy attempted to turn our left, but his design was anticipated and a sufficient force placed there to render his attempt abortive. The battle ground was densely wooded and its surface irregular and difficult. We could make but little use of our artillery. The number of our killed is inconsiderable, that of our wounded very heavy. The enemy was greatly our superior in number. Among our prisoners are men from some thirty regiments. We have taken ten cannon and lost seven. The Army is in excellent condition and spirits and by the blessing of Providence the defeat of the Enemy will be total tomorrow." (DLC-RTL).

[2] This sentence, written in pencil, is not in Lincoln's handwriting.

To Ozias M. Hatch and Jesse K. Dubois[1]

Hon O. M. Hatch & Hon. J. K. Dubois: Executive Mansion,
Springfield, Ills. Washington, Sep. 22, 1863.

Your letter is just received. The particular form of my despatch was jocular, which I supposed you gentlemen knew me well enough to understand. Gen. Allen is considered here as a very faithful and capable officer; and one who would be at least thought of for Quarter-Master-General if that office were vacant A. LINCOLN.

[1] ALS, RPB. On September 16, Hatch and Dubois replied to Lincoln's telegram of September 15, *supra:*

"Your despatch was received last evening. Before telegraphing you last saturday the following despatch was received here, to wit:

" 'To Gov. Yates. St Louis Sept 12th. 1863

" 'There is to be a new Quarter Master General will you go for me, if so telegraph the President and get the State officers to do the same.

" 'ROBT. ALLEN
" 'Brig General'

"Governor Yates was absent, and supposing that General Allen *knew what he said*, and as we have always understood him to be a faithful officer and believing him competent to discharge the duties of the office, and as *he* had treated us in Illinois with *some* consideration—we telegraphed you.

"We profess to be your friends and have no desire to embarrass you, or annoy you—and in all instances, when we have had occasion to write, or telegraph you,—we have done it from the best of motives, and according to the light before us at the time. We trust the same spirit governs you—though we confess your despatch read harshly to us." (DLC-RTL).

To Herman Kretz[1]

Military Officer in Command Executive Mansion,
at Cumberland, Md. Washington, Sep. 22. 1863.

It is represented to me that one Dennis McCarty, is at Cumberland under sentence of death, but that the time is not yet fixed for his execution. Please answer, telling me whether this statement is correct, and also if an order shall come to you for his execution, notify me of it at once by telegraph.   A. LINCOLN.

¹ ALS, RPB. Major Herman Kretz commanding at Cumberland, replied on September 27, 1863, "I have recd orders from the Commanding Genl of this department to turn over to his regt private Dennis McCarty of—'B' Co 23d. Ill Vols Infy. for execution, said execution to take place on the 16th. day of October 1863" (DLC-RTL). See further, Lincoln to Kretz, October 15, *infra*.

To Mary Todd Lincoln¹

Mrs. A. Lincoln.   Executive Mansion, Washington,
Fifth Avenue House New-York.   Sep. 22, 1863.

Did you receive my despatch of yesterday? Mrs. Cuthbert did not correctly understand me. I directed her to tell you to use your own pleasure whether to stay or come; and I did not say it is sickly & that you should on no account come. So far as I see or know, it was never healthier, and I really wish to see you. Answer this on receipt.   A LINCOLN

¹ ALS, IHi. Mrs. Lincoln replied on the same day: "Your telegram received. Did you not receive my reply? I have telegraphed Col. McCullum [McCallum] to have the car ready at the earliest possible moment. Have a very bad cold and am anxious to return home as you may suppose. Taddie is well." (Katherine Helm, *Mary, Wife of Lincoln*, p. 215).

To William S. Rosecrans¹

"Cypher"

Major General Rosecrans   Washington, D.C.,
Chattanooga, Tenn.   Sep. 22. 1863 [8:30 A.M.]

We have not a word here as to the whereabouts or condition of your Army, up to a later point than Sunset Sunday the 20th. Your despatches to me of 9. A.M. and to Gen. Halleck of 2. PM. yesterday tell us nothing later on those points. Please relieve my anxiety as to the position & condition of your army up to the latest moment.   A. LINCOLN

¹ ALS, RPB. Rosecrans' telegram from Chattanooga, Tennessee, 5 P.M., September 20, is as follows:

"We have met with a serious disaster, extent not yet ascertained. Enemy overwhelmed us, drove our right, pierced our centre, and scattered them. Thomas who had seven divisions remained intact at last news. [Gordon] Granger with two brigades had gone to support Thomas on the left. Every available reserve was used. . . . Burnside will be notified the state of things at once and you will be informed. Troops from Charleston, Florida, Virginia and all along the seaboard are found among the prisoners. It seems that every available man was thrown against us." (DLC-RTL).

His telegram of 9 A.M., September 21, is as follows:

"After two days of the severest fighting I ever witnessed our right and centre were beaten. The left held its position until sunset. Our loss is heavy and our troops worn down. The Enemy received heavy reinforcements Saturday night. Every man of ours was in action Sunday & all but one Brigade on Saturday. Our wounded large compared with the killed. We took prisoners from two divisions of Longstreet. We have no certainty of holding our position here. If Burnside could come immediately it would be well, otherwise he may not be able to join us unless he comes on west side of river." (DLC-RTL).

He replied to Lincoln's telegram at 5:40 P.M.:

"Have dispatched daily (Mr. [Charles A.] Dana oftener) to the War Department. I trust you will receive those dispatches. We are now in Chattanooga in line of battle, the enemy threatening our whole front; have pushed to our picket line. Whether they will attack to-day uncertain. General Burnside will be too late to help us. We are about 30,000 brave and determined men; but our fate is in the hands of God, in whom I hope." (OR, I, XXX, I, 161).

To Thomas Daines[1]

Thomas Daines   Executive Mansion,
Indianapolis, Ia.   Washington, Sep. 23. 1863.

Forward your petition, and record of trial immediately. There is time for them to reach [me] before the 1st. of next month.

A. LINCOLN

[1] ALS, RPB. A petition sent by J. N. Birch set forth that Private Adam K. Daines, Company E, Sixty-third Indiana Volunteers, sentenced to be shot for desertion, was "ignorant and illiterate" and had been obviously influenced by others (DLC-RTL). See further, Lincoln's telegram to Willcox, September 29, *infra.*

To Robert A. Maxwell[1]

"Cypher"

Robert A. Maxwell   Executive Mansion,
New-York   Washington, Sep. 23. 1863.

I hasten to say that in the State of information we have here, nothing could be more ungraceful than to indulge any suspicion towards Gen. Thomas. It is doubtful whether his heroism and skill exhibited last sunday afternoon, has ever been surpassed in the world.

A. LINCOLN

[1] ALS, IHi. Lincoln received a telegram from Maxwell at 1:31 P.M. on September 23, "Will Buells testamentous Executor Geo Thomas ever let Rosecrans succeed? Is Bragg dumb enough to punish Thomas severely and disgraceingly?" (DLC-RTL).

The story of Lincoln's reply, which was never sent, is related by Charles A. Tinker, cipher clerk in the War Department, in a letter to General George H. Thomas, May 27, 1867:

"I have had in my possession since the day it was written a telegram penned by our late loved President. Its history is this:—

"Robert A. Maxwell, A Quixotic individual resident of Philadelphia, has, during the war and since, humored a propensity for addressing numerous

dictatorial and sensational despatches to the President, his cabinet and prominent officers of the Government. By those who are familiar with his character
no consideration is accorded to these despatches. On receipt of one of these
despatches—a copy of which I enclose also—President Lincoln came to the Department and handed me his reply marked 'cypher.' He lingered in the Office
while I was preparing it for transmission and when nearly ready he remarked,
'I guess on the whole, Mr Tinker, you need not send that—I will pay no attention to the crazy fellow.' I put it into my pocket and have preserved it as a
precious autograph, hoping sometime to be honored with an opportunity to
present it to you in person to whom I feel it justly belongs, a priceless tribute
to a noble hero whose dauntless courage on that fatal day saved the Army of
the Cumberland
"It gives me profound pleasure to hereby make the presentation." (ALS,
IHi).

To Montgomery C. Meigs[1]

I am quite willing to concur in any promotion of Capt. McClure
which can be consistently made at the War Department.

Sept. 23, 1863.   A. LINCOLN.

[1] Copy, DNA WR RG 92, Quartermaster General, P 117, B 221. The copy
of Lincoln's endorsement is on a copy of Nathaniel P. Banks' letter to Montgomery C. Meigs, September 12, 1863, transmitting a report from Captain John
W. McClure, assistant quartermaster in the Department of the Gulf, and recommending his promotion. McClure was brevetted major as of March 13, 1865.

To William S. Rosecrans[1]

Major Gen. Rosecrans   Washington, D.C.,
Chattanooga, Tenn.   Sep. 23 1863

Below is Bragg's despatch,[2] as found [in] the Richmond papers.
You see he does not claim so many prisoners or captured guns, as
you were inclined to concede. He also confesses to heavy loss. An[3]
exchanged General of ours leaving Richmond yesterday says two
of Longstreets Divisions, & his entire Artillery, and two of Picketts
brigades, and Wies'[4] legion, have gone to Tennessee. He mentions
no other.   A. LINCOLN

[1] ALS, RPB.
[2] The autograph telegram does not preserve the text of General Bragg's
despatch to Samuel Cooper, which is printed with the telegram in the *Official
Records* (I, XXX, III, 791):

"(Via Ringgold, 21st)
"General Cooper, Adjutant-General: Chickamauga River, September 20.
"After two days' hard fighting we have driven the enemy, after a desperate
resistance, from several positions, and now hold the field; but he still confronts
us. The losses are heavy on both sides, especially in our officers. We have taken
over twenty pieces of artillery and some 2,500 prisoners. BRAXTON BRAGG."
[3] The remainder of the telegram is written in the margin, to the right of
where the Bragg despatch must have been pasted.   [4] Henry A. Wise.

To Edwin M. Stanton[1]

Hon. Secretary of War, please have the Judge Advocate General
examine & report upon this case.   A. LINCOLN
   Sep. 23. 1863.

[1] AES, IHi. Lincoln's endorsement appears on a fragment of a letter from
Mrs. Josephine Campbell, requesting that her brother William T. Godwin
(Goodwin) of Philadelphia be restored to his rank as first lieutenant:
"He served through all the campaign in Virginia, down to the last Battle
before Richmond. He went from a sick couch to join those battles. He was in
twenty one engagements.
"He was then sick with Typhoid fever. By permission of the surgion in charge
of the Hospital at Newark I took him home & nursed him. While there, and yet
sick, he was summarily dismissed from the service.
"He is now drafted as a private and among the conscripts in Pa."
Additional endorsements referred the case to Assistant Adjutant General
James A. Hardie, who endorsed on September 26: "Respectfully referred to
John Hay Esq. There are probably important papers in this case, believed to
be not a meritorious one, which are momentarily mislaid. They will be sent as
soon as found."
William T. Goodwin (or Godwin) was appointed second lieutenant in the
Tenth U.S. Infantry on May 15, 1861. No record of his reappointment has been
found.

To Edward Bates[1]

Attorney General please make out a pardon in this case.
   Sept. 24, 1863   A. LINCOLN

[1] AES, DNA RG 204, U.S. Pardon Attorney, A 485. Lincoln's endorsement is
written on a petition for pardon of Robert Welsh, convicted of passing counter-
feit money.

To Andrew G. Curtin[1]

His Excellency A. G. Curtin   Executive Mansion,
My dear Sir: Washington, Sep. 24, 1863.
   The Secretary of War tells me the claims for draft expences of
last year, have been paid, except a few of questionable fairness;
and that the appropriation, the amount of which I think he says
was fixed by yourself, has been almost entirely expended. The
reasonable requests you speak of we are complying with as nearly
as we can. Yours very truly   A. LINCOLN

[1] ALS-P, ISLA. Governor Curtin wrote Lincoln on September 18:
". . . The failure to pay the expences of the draft made in this State in
1862 is doing me great injury and may if not corrected controul the result of
the election. It is hard that I should suffer personally but for the Governm't
it is suicide. There is no antagonism and I am assured that the accounts . . .
are just. . . .

[477]

"I leave tonight and will be engaged every day until the election. We can carry the election but it will require constant effort and I earnestly ask that the reasonable requests of our State committee meet a ready compliance from your surroundings. . . ." (DLC-RTL).

To Mary Todd Lincoln[1]

Mrs. A. Lincoln,   Washington, D.C.,
Fifth Avenue Hotel New York—   Sep. 24 1863

We now have a tolerably accurate summing up of the late battle between Rosecrans and Bragg. The result is that we are worsted, if at all, only in the fact that we, after the main fighting was over, yielded the ground, thus leaving considerable of our artillery and wounded to fall into the enemies' hands, for which we got nothing in turn. We lost, in general officers, one killed, and three or four wounded, all Brigadiers; while according to rebel accounts, which we have, they lost six killed, and eight wounded. Of the killed, one Major Genl. and five Brigadiers, including your brother-in-law, Helm;[2] and of the wounded, three Major Generals, and five Brigadiers. This list may be reduced two in number, by correction of confusion in names. At 11/40 A.M. yesterday Gen. Rosecrans tele-graph[ed] from Chattanooga "We hold this point, and I can not be dislodged, except by very superior numbers, and after a great battle" A despatch leaving there after night yesterday says, "No fight to-day"   A. LINCOLN.

[1] ALS, IHi.   [2] Confederate Brigadier General Ben Hardin Helm.

To George G. Meade[1]

Major-General Meade,   Executive Mansion,
Army of Potomac: Washington, September 24, 1863.

I am appealed to in favor of a private (name not remembered) in Company D, First Regiment New Jersey Volunteers, in Sixth Corps, who is said to be under sentence to be shot to-morrow. Please give me briefly the facts of the case, including his age and your opinion on it.   A. LINCOLN.

P.S. Also give me a like statement in the case of Daniel Sullivan, of Thirteenth Regiment of Massachusetts Volunteers, First Army Corps.   A. LINCOLN.

[1] Tarbell (Appendix), p. 386. No reply has been located. Private Daniel Sullivan of Company E, Thirteenth Massachusetts, drafted and mustered August 4, 1863, was sentenced to be shot for desertion. His sentence was commuted to imprisonment for six months (AGO General Orders No. 512, 1863). See Lincoln's communications to McCallum and to Meade, September 25, infra.

[478]

Proclamation Opening the Port of Alexandria, Virginia[1]

September 24, 1863

By the President of the United States of America:

A Proclamation.

Whereas, in my Proclamation of the twenty-seventh of April, 1861, the ports of the States of Virginia and North Carolina, were, for reasons therein set forth, placed under blockade; and whereas the port of Alexandria, Virginia, has since been blockaded; but as the blockade of said port may now be safely relaxed with advantage to the interests of commerce:

Now, therefore, be it known, that I, Abraham Lincoln, President of the United States, pursuant to the authority in me vested by the fifth section of the act of Congress, approved on the 13th of July, 1861, entitled "An act further to provide for the collection of duties on imports, and for other purposes," do hereby declare that the blockade of the said port of Alexandria, shall so far cease and determine, from and after this date, that commercial intercourse with said port, except as to persons, things, and information contraband of war, may, from this date, be carried on, subject to the laws of the United States, and to the limitations and in pursuance of the regulations which are prescribed by the Secretary of the Treasury in his order which is appended to my proclamation of the 12th. of May, 1862.

In witness whereof, I have hereunto set my hand and caused the Seal of the United States to be affixed.

Done at the City of Washington, this Twenty-fourth day of September, in the year of our Lord one thousand eight [L.S.] hundred and sixty-three, and of the Independence of the United States the Eighty-eighth.

By the President: ABRAHAM LINCOLN
    WILLIAM H. SEWARD, Secretary of State.

[1] DS, DNA FS RG 11, Proclamations.

Recommendation for Belle Garcia[1]

I personally know nothing of this young lady, but upon Senator Hale's statement, I very cheerfully join in his recommendation.

Sep. 24. 1863.   A. LINCOLN

[1] AES, CSmH. Lincoln's endorsement is written on the bottom of a recommendation by Senator John P. Hale, as follows: "The Bearer Belle Garcia is a

very good girl, whom I have known for a long time, and is deserving of patronage. I earnestly commend her to the patronage of any one in any Department of the Government who may have any work to give to a deserving young girl."

To William S. Rosecrans[1]

Major General Rosecrans   Washington, D.C.,
Chattanooga, Tenn.   Sept. 24. 10 A.M. 1863

Last night we received the rebel accounts, through Richmond papers, of your late battle. They give Major Genl. Hood, as mortally wounded,[2] and Brigaders Preston Smith, Woolford, Walthall, Helm, of Ky, and Deshler killed;[3] and Major Generals Preston, Cleburne and Greeg,[4] and Brig. Generals Benning, Adams, Bunn, Brown, and John Helm, wounded.[5] By confusion, the two Helms may be the same man, and Bunn and Brown may be the same man. With Burnside, Sherman, and from elsewhere, we shall get to you, from forty to sixty thousand additional men.

A. LINCOLN

[1] ALS, RPB.   [2] John B. Hood lost a leg at Chickamauga, but survived.
[3] Of these only Preston Smith, Ben Hardin Helm, and James Deshler were killed; William T. Wofford and Edward C. Walthall survived.
[4] William Preston, Patrick R. Cleburne, and John Gregg were not killed.
[5] Henry L. Benning was not killed and no generals by the other names have been identified as killed.

To Edwin M. Stanton[1]

September 24, 1863

I shall be personally obliged if the Sec. of War can find a place at West Point, for George W. Miller, named within, at once or very soon.   A. LINCOLN.

Sept. 24, 1863
Care of Hon. P. G. Watson.

[1] ALS, owned by Miss Alvera Miller, Oakland, California. No record of George W. Miller's appointment has been found.

To Ambrose E. Burnside[1]

Office U.S. Military Telegraph,
War Department, Washington, D.C.,
Major General Burnside   Sep. 25. 1863

Yours of the 23rd. is just received, and it makes me doubt whether I am awake or dreaming. I have been struggling for ten days, first through Gen. Halleck, and then directly, to get you to go to assist Gen. Rosecrans in an extremity, and you have repeatedly declared you would do it, and yet you steadily move the contrary way. On the 19th. you telegraph once from Knoxville, and twice from Greenville, acknowledging receipt of order, and saying you will hurry support to Rosecrans. On the 20th. you telegraph again from Knoxville, saying you will do all you can, and are hurrying troops to Rosecrans. On the 21st. you telegraph from Morristown, saying you will hurry support to Rosecrans; and now your despatch of the 23rd. comes in from Carter's Station, still farther away from Rosecrans, still saying you will assist him, but giving no account of any progress made towards assisting him

You came in upon the Tennessee River at Kingston, Loudon, and Knoxville; and what bridges or the want of them upon the Holston, can have to do in getting the troops towards Rosecrans at Chattanooga is incomprehensible. They were already many miles nearer Chattanooga than any part of the Holston river is, and on the right side of it. If they are now on the wrong side of it, they can only have got so by going from the direction of Chattanooga, and that too, since you have assured us you would move to Chattanooga; while it would seem too, that they could re-cross the Holston, by whatever means they crossed it going East.

1 ADf, DLC-RTL. Lincoln endorsed the back of the second page "Not sent." For Burnside's telegram of September 23, see footnote, Lincoln to Burnside, September 21, *supra*.

To Salmon P. Chase[1]

September 25, 1863

Within is a claim for the price of 1100 bales of cotten, alledged to have been delivered to the agents of the government & converted into money Will the Sec. of the Treasury please examine the claim?   A. LINCOLN

Ser. 25. 1863.

1 AES, DNA RG 56, Treasury Department, Cotton and Captured Property Records, No. 19763. Lincoln's endorsement is written on a letter from Reverdy Johnson, September 19, 1863, enclosing a letter from Mrs. Mary Duncan, "the Lady you honored with an interview yesterday," relative to cotton claimed by her husband. No further reference has been found.

To Daniel C. McCallum[1]

Gen. McCallum.   Washington, D.C.,
Alexandria, Va   Sep. 25. 1863

I have sent to Gen. Meade, by telegraph, to suspend the execution of Daniel Sullivan, of Co. E, 13. Mass. which was to to [*sic*] be to-day; but understanding there is an interruption on the line, may I beg you to send this to him, by the quickest mode in your power?　　　　　　　　　　　　　　　　　　　A. LINCOLN

¹ ALS, RPB. Colonel (not General) Daniel C. McCallum was military director and superintendent of railroads at Alexandria. See Lincoln to Meade, *infra*.

To George G. Meade[1]

Major General Meade　　　　　　　　　　Washington, D.C.,
Army of Potomac　　　　　　　　　　　　　Sep. 25. 1863
　Owing to the press in behalf of Daniel Sullivan, Co. E. 13 Mass. and the doubt, though small, which you express of his guilty intention, I have concluded to say, let his execution be suspended till further order, & copy of record sent me.　　　　　A. LINCOLN.

¹ ALS, IHi. See Lincoln to Meade, September 24, *supra*.

To Robert C. Schenck[1]

Major General Schenck　　　　　　　　　Washington, D.C.,
Baltimore, Md.　　　　　　　　　　　　　　Sep. 25 1863
　Please send Major Hayner over now.　　A LINCOLN

¹ ALS, RPB.

To George G. Meade[1]

Major General Meade　　　　　　　　　　Executive Mansion,
Army of the Potomac　　　　　　　Washington, Sep. 26. 1863.
　I am appealed to in behalf of Adam Wolf, private in Co. H. 13th. Mass. Regt. Please answer as you have done in other cases.
　　　　　　　　　　　　　　　　　　　　　A. LINCOLN

¹ ALS, IHi. No reply has been located. Army of the Potomac, *General Orders No. 93*, September 27, 1863, gives Meade's endorsement on the case of Adam Wolfe, convicted of treason, that the "proceedings are disapproved, the evidence being entirely insufficient to sustain the finding. Private *Adam Wolfe* . . . will be released from custody and returned to duty."

Memorandum Concerning Henry M. Naglee[1]

September 26, 1863
A curious coincidence occured in the relieving of Gen Negley [Naglee]—towit, that the Secretarys order relieving him, and

Gen. Foster's request to have him relieved were simultaneous, & independent of each other. I do not know what Foster's reason was; but I understand Stantons to be that Negley was disinclined to raise colored troops, and he, S, wanted some one there who would take to it more heartily.   A. LINCOLN

Sep. 26. 1863.

1 ADS, IHi. Lincoln obviously confused the name of General Henry M. Naglee with that of General James S. Negley who was with Rosecrans at Chattanooga. AGO *Special Orders No. 422*, September 21, 1863, relieved General Henry M. Naglee from duty under General John G. Foster in the Department of Virginia and North Carolina, and ordered him to report to General Meade as soon as relieved by General James Barnes (OR, I, XXIX, II, 219).

To Gideon Welles[1]

Hon. Sec. of Navy, please see the bearer, Mrs. Peters.

Sept. 26, 1863.   A. LINCOLN

1 Anderson Galleries Catalog 1786, December 17, 1923, No. 54. Mrs. Peters has not been identified.

To Ambrose E. Burnside[1]

Major General Burnside   Washington, D.C.,
Knoxville, Tenn.   Sep. 27 1863

Your despatch just received. My order to you meant simply that you should save Rosecrans from being crushed out, believing if he lost his position, you could not hold East Tennessee in any event; and that if he held his position, East Tennessee was substantially safe in any event. This despatch is in no sense an order. Gen. Halleck will answer you fully.   A LINCOLN

1 ALS, RPB. Burnside's telegram to Lincoln was received at 6 P.M.: "I have just telegraphed General Halleck very fully, asking an explanation of your order, and anxiously await a reply." (OR, I, XXX, III, 904.).

His despatch to Halleck received at 6:30 P.M. is as follows:

"Does the President's order requiring me to move with my force intend the evacuation of that portion of East Tennessee held by me, or do you desire sufficient force left here to hold the line of the railroad? . . . .

"You . . . speak of my delay. I have made no delay. I was ordered to move into East Tennessee. . . . I was then ordered to hold the railroad to the crossing of the Holston River, and the gaps of the mountains leading into North Carolina, and to recruit all the men possible. . . . I made dispositions to carry out these orders which necessarily scattered my forces. . . . Had we commenced moving to General Rosecrans by detail down the north side of the Tennessee River, as we were directed, the cavalry . . . of the enemy would have destroyed our trains and prevented any possibility of an effective junction with Rosecrans. . . . If I can be allowed to move down the south side of the river, keeping a force between the enemy and our depots here . . . I feel quite sure we can do Rosecrans some good. . . . In order to satisfy you of our disposition to aid General Rosecrans, if you desire the evacuation of East Tennessee, we can do it at once, but I must say that I think the move would be very unwise. . . ." (*Ibid.*, pp. 904-905).

To Ambrose E. Burnside[1]

Major General Rosecrans [Burnside].   Washington, D.C.,
Knoxville, Tenn.   Sep. 27 1863

It was suggested to you, not ordered, that you should move to Rosecrans on the North side of the river, because it was believed the enemy would not permit you to join him if you should move on the South side. Hold your present positions, and send Rosecrans what you can spare, in the quickest and safest way. In the mean time, hold the remainder as nearly in readiness to go to him as you can consistently with the duty it is to perform while it remains. East Tennesse can be no more than temporarily lost, so long as Chattanooga is firmly held.   A LINCOLN

[1] ALS, RPB. Lincoln's error in addressing Rosecrans was corrected in the War Department and endorsed: "Intended for Maj Gen Burnside and was sent to him." Halleck telegraphed Burnside at 8:30 P.M.: "Your orders before leaving Kentucky and frequently repeated since, were to connect your right with General Rosecrans' left, so that, if the enemy concentrated on one, the other would be able to assist. . . . Telegram after telegram has been sent to you to go to his [Rosecrans'] assistance with all your available force, you being the judge of what troops it was necessary . . . to leave in East Tennessee. . . . The substance of all telegrams from the President and from me is, you must go to General Rosecrans' assistance, with all your available force, by such route as . . . you may deem most practicable. The orders are very plain, and you cannot mistake their purport. It only remains for you to execute them. . . . The President has just shown me his telegram, which is added, and in which I fully concur." (OR, I, XXX, III, 906).

To Horatio Ames[1]

Mr. Horatio Ames   Executive Mansion, Washington,
Falls Village[2] Connecticut   September 28, 1863.

If you will, on or before the first day of March 1864,[3] within the state of Connecticut, or at any point nearer this city, produce fifteen guns, each of capacity to carry a missile of at least one hundred pounds weight, and notify me thereof, I will cause some person or persons to examine and test said guns; and if, upon such examination and test, it shall be the opinion of such person or persons, that said guns, or any of them, are, on the whole better guns, than any of like calibre heretofore, or now, in use in the

United States, I will on account of the United States, accept said guns, or so many thereof as shall be so favorably reported on, and advise that you be paid for all so accepted, at the rate of Eighty five cents per pound, avoirdupois weight, of said guns so accepted; it being understood that I have no public money at my control, with which I could make such payment absolutely. Yours &c.

A. LINCOLN.

1 DfS, DLC-RTL. The draft is in the handwriting of John Hay with close and signature and insertions, as noted, in Lincoln's autograph. See further, Lincoln to Butler, September 13, 1864, and Lincoln's order of August 21, 1864, *infra.*   2 "Falls Village" inserted by Lincoln.
3 "March" and "4" inserted by Lincoln.

Memorandum[1]

[September 28, 1863]

If Horatio Ames will make ten wrought iron guns after his method, which shall answer satisfactorily such tests as I shall order, I will see that he gets paid $1 per pound for each gun.

A. LINCOLN.

1 Hertz, II, 917. The date has been supplied by the editors on the basis of Lincoln's letter to Ames, *supra.*

To Edward Bates[1]

Attorney General please send me the papers by my Messenger.
Sep. 28. 1863   A. LINCOLN

1 AES, DNA RG 204, U.S. Pardon Attorney, A 439. See Lincoln to Welles, August 12, *supra.* Lincoln's endorsement is written on the back of a memorandum, filed with the papers of James Dillon: "The Pardon clerk (Attorney General's office) cannot let papers in pardon-cases go out of his hands without a written order from the President." See Lincoln's memorandum of September 30, *infra.*

To Ambrose E. Burnside[1]

Major General Burnside   Washington, D.C.,
Knoxville, Tenn.   Sept. 28, 8. AM. 1863
You can perhaps communicate with Gen. Rosecrans more rapidly by sending telegrams to him at Chattanooga. Think of it. I send a like despatch to him.   A. LINCOLN

1 ALS, RPB.

To William S. Rosecrans[1]

Major General Rosecrans   Washington, D.C.,
Chattanooga, Tenn.   Sep. 28. 8.A.M. 1863
    You can, perhaps, communicate with Gen. Burnside more
rapidly by sending telegrams directly to him at Knoxville. Think
of it. I send a like despatch to him.   A LINCOLN

[1] ALS, RPB.

To William S. Rosecrans[1]

                                 Executive Mansion,
My Dear General Rosecrans   Washington, September 28, 1863.
    We are sending you two small corps, one under General How-
ard, and one under General Slocum, and the whole under General
Hooker. Unfortunately the relations between Generals Hooker and
Slocum are not such as to promise good, if their present relative
positions remain. Therefore let me beg,—almost enjoin upon you—
that on their reaching you, you will make a transposition by which
Gen. Slocum with his corps, may pass from under the command of
Gen. Hooker, and Gen. Hooker, in turn, receive some other equal
force. It is important for this to be done, though we could not well
arrange it here. Please do it. Yours very truly   A. LINCOLN

   [1] Copy, DLC-RTL. On September 25, General Henry W. Slocum telegraphed
Lincoln, "I have just been informed that I have again been placed under command of Maj Gen Jos. Hooker. My opinion of Gen Hooker both as an Officer
& a gentleman is too well known to make it necessary for me to refer to it in
this communication. The public service cannot be promoted by placing under
his command an Officer who has so little confidence in his ability as I have.
Our relations are such that it would be degrading in me to accept any position
under him. I have the honor therefore to respectfully tender the resignation
of my commission as Maj Genl of volunteers" (DLC-RTL).
   On October 12 Hooker telegraphed Lincoln from Stevenson, Alabama, suggesting that "Gen'l Slocum may be tendered a command in Missouri, or somewhere else" (DLC-RTL), and on October 13 Rosecrans replied to Lincoln's
communication of September 28, that any attempt to mingle his troops with
"Potomac troops by placing them under Potomac Generals would kindle a
flame . . . where, by care, and judgement, we shall soon have only a spirit
of courageous emulation." (*Ibid.*). Slocum remained with the Eleventh and
Twelfth Corps until April 4, 1864, when he was placed in command of the
District of Vicksburg, Mississippi, under William T. Sherman's command
(AGO *General Orders No. 144*, April 4, 1864).

Reply to Sons of Temperance[1]

                               September 29, 1863
    As a matter of course, it will not be possible for me to make a
response coextensive with the address which you have presented to

me. If I were better known than I am, you would not need to be told that in the advocacy of the cause of temperance you have a friend and sympathizer in me. [Applause.]

When I was a young man, long ago, before the Sons of Temperance as an organization, had an existence, I in an humble way, made temperance speeches, [applause] and I think I may say that to this day I have never, by my example, belied what I then said. [Loud applause.]

In regard to the suggestions which you make for the purpose of the advancement of the cause of temperance in the army, I cannot make particular responses to them at this time. To prevent intemperance in the army is even a part of the articles of war. It is part of the law of the land—and was so, I presume, long ago—to dismiss officers for drunkenness. I am not sure that consistently with the public service, more can be done than has been done. All, therefore, that I can promise you is, (if you will be pleased to furnish me with a copy of your address) to have it submitted to the proper Department[2] and have it considered, whether it contains any suggestions which will improve the cause of temperance and repress the cause of drunkenness in the army any better than it is already done. I can promise no more than that.

I think that the reasonable men of the world have long since agreed that intemperance is one of the greatest, if not the very greatest of all evils amongst mankind. That is not a matter of dispute, I believe. That the disease exists, and that it is a very great one is agreed upon by all.

The mode of cure is one about which there may be differences of opinion. You have suggested that in an army—our army—drunkenness is a great evil, and one which, while it exists to a very great extent, we cannot expect to overcome so entirely as to leave [have?] such successes in our arms as we might have without it. This undoubtedly is true, and while it is, perhaps, rather a bad source to derive comfort from, nevertheless, in a hard struggle, I do not know but what it is some consolation to be aware that there is some intemperance on the other side, too, and that they have no right to beat us in physical combat on that ground. [Laughter and applause.]

But I have already said more than I expected to be able to say when I began, and if you please to hand me a copy of your address it shall be considered. I thank you very heartily, gentlemen, for this call, and for bringing with you these very many pretty ladies.[3]

1 Washington *National Republican*, September 29, and *National Intelligencer*, September 30, 1863. Celebrating the twenty-first anniversary of their organiza-

tion on September 29, the Sons of Temperance marched in a long parade to the White House, where a committee headed by R. G. Greene presented a lengthy address, a copy of which had been sent to Lincoln by Greene on September 26 (DLC-RTL).   2 See Lincoln to Stanton, September 30, *infra.*

3 John Hay's *Diary* records on September 29 a somewhat less politic view: "Today came to the Executive Mansion an assembly of cold-water men & cold-water women to make a temperance speech at the Tycoon & receive a response. They filed into the East Room looking blue & thin in the keen autumnal air. . . . Three blue-skinned damsels did Love, Purity, & Fidelity in Red, White & Blue gowns. A few invalid soldiers stumped along in the dismal procession. They made a long speech at the Tycoon in which they called Intemperance the cause of our defeats. He could not see it, as the rebels drink more & worse whisky than we do. . . ."

To Orlando B. Willcox[1]

Officer in command at   Executive Mansion
Indianapolis, Ia.   Washington, D.C. Sep. 29. 1863
    Please suspend execution of Adam Daines till further order from me.   A. LINCOLN

1 ALS, RPB. See Lincoln to Thomas Daines, September 23, *supra.*

To Francis S. Corkran[1]

Hon. Francis S. Corkaron   Executive Mansion,
Baltimore, Md.   Washington, Sep. 30. 1863.
    Mrs. L. is now at home & would be pleased to see you any time. If the grape time has not passed away, she would be pleased to join in the enterprize you mentioned. Yours truly
                                                        A. LINCOLN.

1 ALS-F, ISLA. No correspondence related to this letter has been located.

Memorandum Concerning James Dillon[1]

                                                September 30, 1863
I find the papers presented for the pardon of James Dillon, has nothing from the Judge, Jury, or Attorney who tried him, and no record of the trial, containing the evidence upon which he was convicted. Unless something more definite is presented, I will have to dismiss the application.   A. LINCOLN
    Sep. 30. 1863.

1 ADS, DNA RG 204, U.S. Pardon Attorney, A 439. See Lincoln to Welles, August 12, and to Bates, September 28, *supra.* Lincoln's memorandum is writ-

ten on both sides of a visiting card filed with papers in Dillon's case. The jacket notation indicates that Dillon was pardoned by order of the president on November 7, 1863.

To John M. Schofield[1]

Gen. Schofield   Executive Mansion.
St. Louis, Mo—   Washington, DC. Sep. 30. 1863
Following despatch just received:

Union Men Driven Out of Missouri.[2]
Leavenworth, Sept. 29.—Governor Gamble having authorized Colonel Moss,[3] of Liberty, Mo., to arm the men in Platte and Clinton counties, he has armed mostly the returned Rebel soldiers and men under bonds. Moss' men are now driving the Union men out of Missouri. Over one hundred families crossed the river to-day. Many of the wives of our Union soldiers have been compelled to leave. Four or five Union men have been murdered by Colonel Moss' men.

Please look to this; and if true, in whole or part put a stop to it.
A. LINCOLN

[1] ALS, RPB. On October 2, Schofield replied to Lincoln's telegram, "I find . . . that the report from Leavenworth . . . is a gross misrepresentation and exaggeration. A few men who claim to be loyal, but who have been engaged in murder, robbery, and arson, have been driven out. . . . It is a base attempt of my enemies to influence your action." (OR, I, XXII, II, 591).

[2] The despatch is in the form of a newspaper clipping pasted on the autograph telegram.   [3] James H. Moss.

To Edwin M. Stanton[1]

September 30, 1863
This Address was presented to me yesterday by the "Sons of Temperance" and I promised to submit to the War Department, in order that the suggestions therein, as to the Army, may be considered, and adopted if thought to be expedient   A. LINCOLN
Sep. 30. 1863.

[1] AES, IHi. Lincoln's endorsement is written on a sheet of paper accompanying the address presented by the Sons of Temperance on September 29. No reference has been found to action by the War Department on the request presented in the address as follows:
"1. That the officers under you shall, as far as consistent with the public service, extend all needed facilities for the organization of Divisions of our Order in the army.
"2. That soldiers in regiments and hospitals may have facilities for attending the evening meetings of the Divisions composed of citizens.
"3. That suitable rooms be prepared in the hospitals for the meetings of the soldier Divisions. Such a room as would be suitable for this object is required

for other, and perhaps more important purposes. Every hospital needs a place for public worship on the Sabbath. The same place could be used for prayer and social meetings, and for a library and reading room."

To Edwin M. Stanton[1]

The Secretary of War:
Dear Sir

Executive Mansion,
Washington, September 30, 1863.

I believe Col. Halpine to be a most capable and deserving officer, and hope that his request may be granted if it can be, consistently with the interests of the service. Your Obt. Servt.   A. LINCOLN

[1] LS (copy?), DLC-Nicolay Papers. The letter is in John Hay's handwriting signed by Lincoln. On September 19, 1863, Charles G. Halpine ("Miles O'Reilly") wrote Lincoln as follows:

"The subscriber was appointed Asst. Adjt. Genl. of Vols. with the rank of Major on the 5th of Sept. 1861. . . .

"Since his appointment as Major and Asst. Adjt. Genl., he has served as A.A.G. and Chief of Staff to General Hunter. . . .

"In November, last, the subscriber was appointed Asst. Adjt. Genl. of the 10th Army Corps, Dept of the South, with the rank of Lieut. Colonel, in which capacity he served until the 1st of last July, when he was relieved at his own request and on medical certificate showing that he had lost the sight of one eye in the service, and . . . the remaining eye . . . would be certainly destroyed by a further exposure to . . . the climate . . . of the South.

"On being so relieved, your Subscriber was returned to duty with the rank of Major and assigned to Gen. Dix. . . . To this lowering of his rank he would beg . . . to call your attention—more especially in view of the fact that he has reason to believe that his name has been frequently brought before your Excellency . . . for promotion to . . . Brigadier. For this promotion . . . he has no desire; but he does beg of you to relieve him from the apparent stigma of being reduced in his grade. . . ." (DLC-RTL).

Halpine was brevetted lieutenant colonel as of June 5, 1864.

To Edwin M. Stanton[1]

September 30, 1863

I personally know Col. McConnell, named within, to be a sterling man; and I shall be obliged if he can be mustered in by special order.

[1] Copy, DNA WR RG 107, Register, Secretary of War, Letters Received, P 171. The copy of Lincoln's endorsement preserved as a notation on the register indicates that the endorsement was written on a letter from Governor Yates requesting that Colonel John McConnell, Fifth Illinois Cavalry, be mustered from the day he reported. The letter and endorsement have not been found. McConnell wrote Lincoln on October 2:

"I presented Gov. Yates letter with your endorsement to Mr. Stanton, requesting an Order for me to be mustered as Colonel of the 5th Regiment of Illinois Cavalry.

"Mr. Stanton thinks he cannot grant the Order but sent the letter to Maj. T. M. Vincent for information. Maj. Vincent informed me yesterday that he thinks I cannot be mustered." (DLC-RTL).

Appointment of Springer Harbaugh[1]

Executive Mansion, Washington, October   , 1863.
By virtue of the authority conferred upon me, by the first section of the act of Congress of the United States being the act entitled "An act to aid in the construction of a RailRoad and Telegraph Line from the Missouri River to the Pacific Ocean, and to secure to the Government the use of the same for Postal Military and other purposes" approved July 1st 1862, Springer Harbaugh of Pennsylvania is hereby appointed a Director, on the part of the Government of the United States, of the Union and Pacific RailRoad Company.   ABRAHAM LINCOLN

[1] DS, Union Pacific Railroad Company, Omaha, Nebraska. This document is in John Hay's handwriting, signed by Lincoln.

To Augustus W. Bradford[1]

Gov. Bradford   Washington City, D.C.
Baltimore, Md.   Oct. 1. 1863.
Please be here in person at 12.M. Saturday to fix up definitely in writing, the matter about which Mr. Johnson & Gov. Hicks brings a communication from you.   A. LINCOLN

Please repeat to Anapolis.   A L.

[1] ALS, RPB. The telegram received at Annapolis is in the Maryland Hall of Records at Annapolis. Governor Bradford replied the same day, "I will wait on your Excellency Saturday at 12." The occasion of the conference was a long letter from Bradford dated September 28, complaining of the enlistment of Negroes in Maryland, which was brought to the president by Reverdy Johnson and former governor Thomas H. Hicks. The principal grievance was that slaves of loyal Marylanders were being enlisted along with other Negroes. Bradford's letter bears Lincoln's endorsement "Submitted to the Secretary of War. Oct. 1, 1863. A. LINCOLN." (DLC-RTL). See also Lincoln to Tyler, *infra*.

To George G. Meade[1]

Executive Mansion,
Major-General Meade: October 1, 1863.
Let respite of ten days be granted to Herman Barber, alias E. W. Von Heinecke, sentenced to be shot to-morrow for desertion.
                                                    A. LINCOLN.

Major Eckert:
Send by telegraph at once.

[491]

1 Tarbell (Appendix), p. 389. No reply has been located. Army of the Potomac, *General Orders No. 90*, September 17, 1863, announced sentence of Herman Barber, alias Edmund Von Heinicke, Company D, Ninetieth Pennsylvania Volunteers, to be shot for desertion on September 25, 1863. Presumably Lincoln's telegram refers to the same man. The roster of Company D lists Barber as "Deserted—April 24, 1864."

To John M. Schofield[1]

Executive Mansion
Gen. John M. Schofield   Washington, D.C. Oct. 1. 1863.

There is no organized military force in avowed opposition to the general government, now in Missouri; and if any such shall reappear, your duty in regard to it will be too plain to require any special instruction. Still the condition of things, both there and elsewhere, is such as to render it indispensable to maintain for a time, the United States Military establishment in that State, as well as to rely upon it for a fair contribution of support to that establishment generally.

Your immediate duty, in regard to Missouri, now is to advance the efficiency of that establishment, and to so use it, as far as practicable, to compel the excited people there to leave one another alone.

Under your recent order, which I have approved, you will only arrest individuals, and suppress assemblies, or newspapers, when they may be working *palpable* injury[2] to the Military in your charge; and, in no other case will you interfere with the expression of opinion in any form, or allow it to be interfered with violently by others. In this, you have a discretion to exercise with great caution, calmness, and forbearance.

With the matters of removing the inhabitants of certain counties *en masse;* and of removing certain individuals from time to time, who are supposed to be mischievous, I am not now interfering, but am leaving to your own discretion

Nor am I interfering with what may still seem to you to be necessary restrictions upon trade and intercourse.

I think proper, however, to enjoin upon you the following:

Allow no part of the Military under your command, to be engaged in either returning fugitive slaves, or in forcing, or enticing slaves from their homes; and, so far as practicable, enforce the same forbearance upon the people.

Report to me[3] your opinion upon the availibility for good, of the enrolled militia of the State.

Allow no one to enlist colored troops, except upon orders from you, or from here through you.

Allow no one to assume the functions of confiscating property, under the law of congress, or other wise, except upon orders from here.

At elections, see that those, and only those are allowed to vote, who are entitled to do so, by the laws of Missouri, including as of those laws, the restriction laid by the Missouri convention upon those who may have participated in the rebellion.

So far as practicable you will, by means of your military force, expel guerrillas, marauders, and murderers, and all who are known to harbor, aid, or abet them. But, in like manner, you will repress assumptions of unauthorized individuals to perform the same service; because under pretence of doing this, they become marauders and murderers themselves. To now restore peace, let the military obey orders; and those not of the military, leave each other alone; thus not breaking the peace themselves.

In giving the above directions, it is not intended to restrain you in other expedient and necessary matters not falling within their range. Your Obt. Servt. A LINCOLN

[1] ADfS, DLC-RTL. The occasion for this communication was Lincoln's interview on September 30 with a delegation of Missouri and Kansas Union men whose demands are fully answered in Lincoln's letter to Charles D. Drake and others, October 5, *infra*. On October 19, Schofield enclosed a copy of Lincoln's letter of October 1, with comment, to Brigadier General John B. Sanborn, sent to relieve John McNeil as commander of Southwestern Missouri: "I cannot do more or better than to commend these instructions to your careful consideration, as setting forth the principles by which you are to be guided in the discharge of the most delicate duties which will devolve upon you. . . . " (OR, I, XXII, II, 666). [2] Lincoln deleted "mischief" and substituted "injury."

[3] This sentence is revised to the present reading in the draft, but originally stood as follows: "Report to me the status and action, of the enrolled militia. It must be either under United States orders, or be without United States support, and without the proclamation in regard to *Habeas Corpus*." On October 20, Schofield replied that the militia had done good service but recommended that its service be dispensed with as fast as it was possible to replace militia with troops raised for general service (*ibid.*, pp. 666-68).

To Thomas A. Scott[1]

Thomas A. Scott
Louisville, Ky

Washington, D.C.,
Oct. 1. 4/20 P.M. 1863.

Tell me how things have advanced, so far as you know.

A LINCOLN

[1] ALS, RPB. Thomas A. Scott, who had resigned as assistant secretary of war on June 1, 1862, was called back from his job as first vice-president of

the Pennsylvania Railroad to supervise transport of the Eleventh and Twelfth Corps to Rosecrans at Chattanooga (see Lincoln to Rosecrans, September 28, *supra*). Scott replied at 9 P.M.:

"In reply to your inquiry, will say, have sent south fifteen trains [,] troops with nine thousand four hundred seventy men from East, and thirteen hundred forty from Cairo. Total—ten thousand eight hundred ten, and one battery of artillery.

"Ten trains had passed Nashville up to nine thirty (9.30) AM this morning, and all of them are at Bridgeport [Alabama] before this hour. Every thing that has reached this point has gone forward. We are hoping to get another battery and about sixteen hundred men by midnight. Will ship them before daylight could handle them more rapidly, if Eastern roads could let us have them.

"Genl Hooker left at eight this morning. Genl Howard at four thirty (4 30) PM. Eleventh Corps all gone, and part of Twelfth."

To Erastus B. Tyler[1]

Gen. Tyler   Washington, D.C.,
Baltimore.   Oct. 1. 1863

Take care of colored troops in your charge; but do nothing further about that branch of affairs until further orders. Particularly do nothing about Gen. Vickers of Kent county.   A. LINCOLN.

Send a copy to Col. Birney.   A.L.

[1] ALS, RPB. See Lincoln to Bradford, *supra*. William Birney, Colonel of the Second U.S. Colored Troops and mustering officer at Baltimore, telegraphed Lorenzo Thomas on October 13 that upon receipt of Lincoln's telegram he had ceased raising colored troops. Concerning Major General George Vickers of the Maryland Militia, Birney commented: "The part of the order relating to General Vickers was probably sent me from wrong information, as I had no knowledge of the general, or any intention of taking action in regard to him. . . . I have made inquiry since and find that the general in question was formerly a noisy constitutional Union man, but has recently, and on the slave question, become a virulent enemy of the Government and associate with known secessionists; that he proposed to two secessionists to raise a mob at Chestertown and burn the small Government steamer employed for the transportation of recruits for the U.S. colored troops; and that he was busy and officious in advising masters of slaves to offer armed resistance to the recruiting officers." (OR, III, III, 881-82).

To John P. Usher[1]

Hon. Sec. of Interior   Executive Mansion,
Sir: Washington, Oct. 1. 1863.

I suppose ——— Edmunds better be appointed Governor of Dakota. Get the name, and send it with this to the Sec. of State.
Yours truly   A. LINCOLN

¹ ALS-P, ISLA. Newton Edmunds, chief clerk in the surveyor general's office for Dakota Territory, was appointed governor to succeed William Jayne, who had been elected delegate to congress.

To John M. Schofield¹

Gen. Schofield St. Louis, Mo.

Washington, D.C., Oct. 2 1863

I have just seen your despatch to Gen. Halleck about Gen. Blunt. If possible, you better allow me to get through with a certain matter here, before adding to the difficulty of it. Meantime telegraph me the particulars of Gen. Blunt's case.   A. LINCOLN

¹ ALS, RPB. See Lincoln to Blunt, August 18, *supra.* On October 1 Schofield telegraphed Halleck, "I am compelled to relieve . . . Blunt from his command. I would send Brigadier-General McNeil to take his place, but have no competent officer to relieve . . . McNeil. . . ." (OR, I, XXII, II, 586). A telegram from Schofield to Lincoln, dated October 1, 1 P.M., received October 1, 4:45 P.M., must have been despatched on October 2 rather than October 1, as follows: "I will send the papers in Gen Blunts case and defer action until I know your pleasure regarding it. I desire if possible to diminish and not to increase your difficulty this was one reason why I informed Gen Halleck what I thought it necessary to do." (DLC-RTL; also OR, I, XXII, II, 589).

On October 19, Schofield's *General Orders No. 118,* sent John B. Sanborn to relieve John McNeil, ordered McNeil to relieve Blunt at Fort Smith, Arkansas, and ordered Blunt to return to Fort Leavenworth and report to Schofield by letter.

To Edward Bates¹

Hon. Attorney General. My dear Sir:

Executive Mansion, Washington, Oct. 3, 1863.

Whenever there shall be a vacancy of a Judgeship in any of the territories, I will thank you to remind [me] of the name of *Martin P. Sweet,* of Illinois. Yours truly   A. LINCOLN

¹ ALS, DNA GE RG 60, Papers of Attorney General, Segregated Lincoln Material. There is no record of Sweet's appointment.

To William Birney¹

Col. Birney Baltimore, Md.

Washington, D.C., Oct. 3. 1863

Please give me, as near as you can, the number of *slaves* you have recruited in Maryland. Of course, the number is not to include the free colored.   A. LINCOLN

¹ ALS, RPB. See Lincoln's communications to Bradford and to Tyler, October 1, *supra.* Colonel Birney replied at 8 P.M., "Yours just received. Between 1250 and 1300 as near as I can judge." (DLC-RTL).

To George G. Meade[1]

Major-General Meade,   Executive Mansion,
Army of Potomac: Washington, D.C., October 3, 1863.

Have you a man in jeopardy as a deserter by the name William
T. Evers, private in Company D, Brooklyn Fourteenth State Militia, or Eighty-fourth Volunteers? If you have please send me the
facts and conditions of his case.   A. LINCOLN.

[1] Tarbell (Appendix), p. 389. Meade replied the same day, "Private Wm. T.
Evers Brooklyn 14th State militia 84th New York Vols. is being tried by a
Division Court martial   proceedings not yet recd here." (DLC-RTL). The
roster of Company D lists Evers as dishonorably discharged on May 25, 1864.

Proclamation of Thanksgiving[1]

October 3, 1863
By the President of the United States of America.

A Proclamation.

The year that is drawing towards its close, has been filled with
the blessings of fruitful fields and healthful skies. To these bounties,
which are so constantly enjoyed that we are prone to forget the
source from which they come, others have been added, which are
of so extraordinary a nature, that they cannot fail to penetrate
and soften even the heart which is habitually insensible to the ever
watchful providence of Almighty God. In the midst of a civil war
of unequalled magnitude and severity, which has sometimes
seemed to foreign States to invite and to provoke their aggression,
peace has been preserved with all nations, order has been maintained, the laws have been respected and obeyed, and harmony
has prevailed everywhere except in the theatre of military conflict;
while that theatre has been greatly contracted by the advancing
armies and navies of the Union. Needful diversions of wealth and
of strength from the fields of peaceful industry to the national defence, have not arrested the plough, the shuttle or the ship; the axe
has enlarged the borders of our settlements, and the mines, as well
of iron and coal as of the precious metals, have yielded even more
abundantly than heretofore. Population has steadily increased, notwithstanding the waste that has been made in the camp, the siege
and the battle-field; and the country, rejoicing in the consciousness
of augmented strength and vigor, is permitted to expect continuance of years with large increase of freedom. No human counsel
hath devised nor hath any mortal hand worked out these great
things. They are the gracious gifts of the Most High God, who,

while dealing with us in anger for our sins, hath nevertheless remembered mercy. It has seemed to me fit and proper that they should be solemnly, reverently and gratefully acknowledged as with one heart and one voice by the whole American People. I do therefore invite my fellow citizens in every part of the United States, and also those who are at sea and those who are sojourning in foreign lands, to set apart and observe the last Thursday of November next, as a day of Thanksgiving and Praise to our beneficent Father who dwelleth in the Heavens. And I recommend to them that while offering up the ascriptions justly due to Him for such singular deliverances and blessings, they do also, with humble penitence for our national perverseness and disobedience, commend to His tender care all those who have become widows, orphans, mourners or sufferers in the lamentable civil strife in which we are unavoidably engaged, and fervently implore the interposition of the Almighty Hand to heal the wounds of the nation and to restore it as soon as may be consistent with the Divine purposes to the full enjoyment of peace, harmony, tranquillity and Union.

In testimony whereof, I have hereunto set my hand and caused the Seal of the United States to be affixed.

Done at the City of Washington, this Third day of October, in the year of our Lord one thousand eight hundred and [L.S.] sixty-three, and of the Independence of the United States the Eighty-eighth.   ABRAHAM LINCOLN

By the President:

WILLIAM H. SEWARD, Secretary of State.

[1] DS, DNA FS RG 11, Proclamations. On September 28, 1863, Sara Josepha Hale wrote Lincoln "as Editress of the 'Lady's Book,' to request a few minutes of your precious time, while laying before you a subject of deep interest . . . even to the President of our Republic. . . . This subject is to have the *day of our annual Thanksgiving made a National and fixed Union Festival*. . . ." (DLC-RTL).

The original draft of this proclamation has not been located, but a letter from John G. Nicolay to John Hay from New York, April 1, 1864, relates that "the Mss. of the President's Thanksgiving Proclamation, which was written by Seward and is in his handwriting" had been sent by the State Department to Leavitt Hunt "to be sold at the Fair." (DLC-Nicolay Papers).

To John P. Usher[1]

Sec. of Interior, please see, hear, & oblige of [*sic*] you can my friend T. J. Carter.   A. LINCOLN

Oct. 3. 1863

[1] ALS, ORB. Timothy J. Carter was a civil engineer associated with the Great Western Railroad at Springfield, Illinois. See Lincoln's communication to whom it may concern, October 5, *infra*.

To George G. Meade[1]

Major General Meade,   Washington, D.C.,
Army of Potomac   Oct. 4 1863

I am appealed to in behalf of Daniel Hanson, of 97th. New-York, said to be under sentence of death for desertion. Please inform me as usual.   A. LINCOLN

[1] ALS, owned by R. E. Burdick, New York City. No reply from Meade has been located, but see Lincoln to Meade, October 15, *infra*.

To William S. Rosecrans[1]

Major General Rosecrans: Washington, D.C.,
Chattanooga, Tenn.   Oct 4. 1863

Yours of yesterday received. If we can hold Chattanooga, and East Tennessee, I think the rebellion must dwindle and die. I think you and Burnside can do this; and hence doing so is your main object. Of course, to greatly damage, or destroy, the enemy in your front would be a greater object, because it would include the former, and more; but it is not so certainly within your power. I understand the main body of the enemy is very near you—so near that you could "board at home" so to speak, and menace or attack him any day. Would not the doing of this, be your best mode of counteracting his raids on your communications? But this is not an order. I intend doing something like what you suggest, whenever the case shall appear ripe enough to have it accepted in the true understanding, rather than as a confession of weakness and fear.   A. LINCOLN

[1] ALS, RPB. Rosecrans' telegram of October 3 is as follows: "If we can maintain this position in such strength that the enemy are obliged to abandon their position, and the Elections in the great States go favorably, would it not be well to offer a general amnesty to all officers and soldiers in the Rebellion? It would give us moral strength and weaken them very much." (DLC-RTL).

To John M. Schofield[1]

Gen. Schofield   Washington, D.C.,
St. Louis, Mo.   Oct. 4 1863

I think you will not have just cause to complain of my action.   A. LINCOLN.

[1] ALS, RPB. Schofield telegraphed on October 3: "I have just read the address presented to you by the Radical Delegation from Missouri So far as it refers to me, it is not only untrue in spirit but most of it is literally false. If an

answer or explanation from me is on any account desirable I shall be glad to make it." (DLC-RTL). See Lincoln to Charles D. Drake and others, October 5, *infra*.

To Charles D. Drake and Others[1]

Hon. Charles D. Drake &   Executive Mansion
others, Committee   Washington D.C. Oct. 5. 1863

Gentlemen   Your original address, presented on the 30th. ultimo, and the four supplementary ones, presented on the 3rd. inst. have been carefully considered.

I hope you will regard the other duties claiming my attention, together with the great length and importance of these documents as constituting a sufficient apology for my not having responded sooner.

These papers, framed for a common object, consist of the things

[1] ADfS, DLC-RTL. On September 30 delegations from Missouri and Kansas headed by Charles D. Drake waited upon the president to present a lengthy "address" alluding to various Radical conventions throughout Missouri which culminated in a state convention meeting in Jefferson City from which the delegation headed by Drake was appointed to visit Washington. All these conventions sustained the administration in the Emancipation Proclamation and the employment of Negro troops, but demanded immediate rather than gradual emancipation in Missouri, arraigned Governor Gamble, and demanded restoration of military control in Missouri. The substance of the nineteen-page "address" is so specifically covered in Lincoln's reply as to require no additional quotations.

Following presentation of the address, the conference continued for several hours. Lincoln's remarks as reported in the New York *Tribune* on October 1 are as follows:

"The President promised to consider carefully all the points urged, but left his auditory in doubt as to his intentions. He assured the delegation that he believed them to be the true friends of the Administration, whether the other 'set,' not using the word 'faction' this time, was so or not. As for Gen. Schofield, the President said that he had no reason to be dissatisfied with him, since he had not only obeyed orders, but had done so with unusual promptitude, had reënforced Grant, and sent troops elsewhere, when ordered to do so, without objection or delay. Thereupon Mr. Lincoln was asked whether, if he were satisfied that the removal of Schofield were the wish of the loyal people of Missouri and Kansas, he would remove him? The President answered that this circumstance, if proved beyond question, would go a great way with him. Of Gen. Butler, Mr. Lincoln said not a word. In the course of the interview, he remarked to the delegations, that their 'set' was a little too fast for his policy, which favored gradual, rather than immediate emancipation in Missouri." A more complete report of this conference is given in John Hay's *Diary* and may be found in *Abraham Lincoln: A History* (VIII, 215-19).

Although the draft of Lincoln's reply is dated October 5, according to a Washington despatch of October 15 the communication was not sent until October 14: "The President's reply to the address of the Missouri delegation, which was mailed to the Hon. C. D. Drake, Chairman . . . at St. Louis yesterday, will be published or not at the option of that gentleman. . . ." (New York *Tribune*, October 17, 1863).

demanded, and the reasons for demanding them. The things demanded are:

First: That General Schofield shall be relieved, and General Butler be appointed, as commander of the Military Department of Missouri.

Second: That the system of Enrolled Militia in Missouri may be broken up, and national forces be substituted for it, and

Third: That at elections, persons may not be allowed to vote who are not entitled by law to do so.

Among the reasons given, enough of suffering and wrong to Union men is certainly, and I suppose truly stated. Yet the whole case, as presented, fails to convince me, that Gen. Schofield, or the Enrolled Militia, is responsible for that suffering and wrong. The whole can be explained on a more charitable, and, as I think, a more rational hypothesis. We are in civil war. In such cases there always is a main question; but in this case that question is a perplexing compound—Union and Slavery. It thus becomes a question not of two sides merely, but of at least four sides, even among those who are for the Union, saying nothing of those who are against it. Thus, those who are for the Union *with*, but not *without* slavery—those for it *without*, but not *with*—those for it *with* or *without*, but prefer it *with*—and those for it *with* or *without*, but prefer it *without*. Among these again, is a subdivision of those who are for *gradual* but not for *immediate*, and those who are for *immediate*, but not for *gradual* extinction of slavery. It is easy to conceive that all these shades of opinion, and even more, may be sincerely entertained by honest and truthful men. Yet, all being for the Union, by reason of these differences, each will prefer a different way of sustaining the Union. At once sincerity is questioned, and motives are assailed. Actual war coming, blood grows hot, and blood is spilled. Thought is forced from old channels into confusion. Deception breeds and thrives. Confidence dies, and universal suspicion reigns. Each man feels an impulse to kill his neighbor, lest he be first killed by him. Revenge and retaliation follow. And all this, as before said, may be among honest men only. But this is not all. Every foul bird comes abroad, and every dirty reptile rises up. These add crime to confusion. Strong measures, deemed indispensable but harsh at best, such men make worse by mal-administration. Murders for old grudges, and murders for pelf, proceed under any cloak that will best cover for the ocasion. These causes amply account for what has occurred in Missouri, without ascribing it to the weakness, or wickedness of any general. The newspaper files, those chroniclers of current events, will show that the evils now complained of were quite as prevalent under Fremont, Hunter, Halleck, and Curtis, as under Schofield. If the former had greater force opposed to them, they also had greater force with which to meet it. When the organized rebel army left the state, the main federal force had to go also, leaving the Department commander at home relatively no stronger than before. Without disparaging any, I affirm with confidence that no commander of that Department has, in proportion to his means, done better than Gen. Schofield.

The first specific charge against Gen. Schofield is that the Enrolled Militia was placed under his command, whereas it had not been placed under the command of Gen. Curtis. The fact I believe is true; but you do not point out, nor can I conceive, how that did, or could injure loyal men, or the Union cause.

You charge that upon Gen. Curtis being superseded by Gen. Schofield, Franklin A. Dick was superseded by James O. Brodhead, as Provost Marshal-General. No very specific showing is made as to how this did, or could injure the Union cause. It recalls, however, the condition of things, as presented to me, which led to a change of commander for that Department.

To restrain contraband intelligence and trade, a system of searches, seizures, permits, and passes, had been introduced, I think, by Gen. Fremont. When Gen. Halleck came, he found, and continued this system, and added an order applicable to some parts of the State, to levy and collect contributions from noted rebels, to compensate losses, and relieve destitution caused by the rebellion. The action of Gen. Fremont and Gen. Halleck, as stated, constituted a sort of system, which Gen. Curtis found in full operation when he took command of the Department. That there was a necessity for something of the sort was clear; but that it could only be justified by stern necessity, and that it was liable to great abuse in administration, was equally clear. Agents to execute it, contrary to the great Prayer, were led into temptation. Some might, while others would not resist that temptation. It was not possible to hold any to a very strict accountability; and those yielding to the temptation, would sell permits and passes to those who would pay most, and most readily for them; and would seize property, and collect levies in the aptest way to fill their own pockets. Money being the object, the man having money, whether loyal or disloyal, would be a victim. This practice doubtless existed to some extent, and it was a real additional evil, that it could be and was, plausably charged to exist in greater extent than it did.

When Gen. Curtis took command of the Department, Mr. Dick,

against whom I never knew anything to allege, had general charge of this system. A controversy in regard to it rapidly grew into almost unmanageable proportions. One side ignored the *necessity*, and magnified the evils of the system; while the other ignored the evils, and magnified the necessity; and each bitterly assailed the motives of the other. I could not fail to see that the controversy enlarged in the same proportion as the professed Union-men there distinctly took sides in two opposing political parties. I exhausted my wits, and very nearly my patience also, in efforts to convince both that the evils they charged on each other, were inherent in the case, and could not be cured by giving either party a victory over the other.

Plainly the irritating system was not to be perpetual; and it was plausably urged that it could be modified at once with advantage. The case could scarcely be worse, and whether it could be made better, could only be determined by a trial. In this view, and not to ban, or brand, Gen. Curtis, or to give a victory to any party, I made the change of commander for the Department. I now learn that soon after this change, Mr. Dick was removed, and that Mr. Brodhead, a gentleman of no less good character, was put in the place. The mere fact of this change is more distinctly complained of, than is any conduct of the new officer, or other consequence, of the change.

I gave the new commander no instructions as to the administration of the system mentioned, beyond what is contained in the private letter, afterwards surreptitiously published, in which I directed him to act solely for the public good, and independently of both parties. Neither anything you have presented me, nor anything I have otherwise learned, has convinced me that he has been unfaithful to this charge.

Imbecility is urged as one cause for removing Gen. Schofield; and the late massacre at Lawrence, Kansas, is pressed as evidence of that imbecility. To my mind that fact scarcely tends to prove the proposition. That massacre is only an example, of what Grierson,[2] John Morgan, and many others, might have repeatedly done, on their respective raids, had they chose to incur the personal hazard, and possessed the fiendish hearts to do it.

The charge is made that Gen. Schofield, on purpose to protect the Lawrence murderers, would not allow them to be pursued into Missouri. While no punishment could be too sudden, or too severe for those murderers, I am well satisfied that the preventing of the threatened remedial raid into Missouri, was the only safe way to

[2] Benjamin H. Grierson.

avoid an indiscriminate massacre there, including probably more innocent than guilty. Instead of condemning, I therefore approve what I understand Gen. Schofield did in that respect.

The charges that Gen. Schofield has purposely withheld protection from loyal people, and purposely facilitated the objects of the disloyal, are altogether beyond my power of belief. I do not arraign the veracity of gentlemen as to the facts complained of; but I do more than question the judgment which would infer that those facts occurred in accordance with the *purposes* of Gen. Schofield.

With my present views I must decline to remove Gen. Schofield. In this I decide nothing against Gen. Butler. I sincerely wish it were convenient to assign him a suitable command.

In order to meet some existing evils I have addressed a letter of instructions to Gen. Schofield, a copy of which I inclose to you.

As to the "Enrolled Militia" I shall endeavor to ascertain, better than I now know, what is it's exact value.

Let me say now, however, that your proposal to substitute national force for the "Enrolled Militia" implies that in your judgment the latter is doing something which needs to be done; and if so, the proposition to throw that force away, and to supply its place by bringing other forces from the field where they are urgently needed seems to me very extraordinary. Whence shall they come? Shall they be withdrawn from Banks, or Grant, or Steele, or Rosecrans? Few things have been so grateful to my anxious feeling as when, in June last, the local force in Missouri aided Gen. Schofield to so promptly send a large general force to the relief of Gen. Grant, then investing Vicksburg, and menaced from without by Gen. Johnston. Was this all wrong? Should the Enrolled Militia then have been broken up, and Gen. Herron[3] kept from Grant, to police Missouri? So far from finding cause to object, I confess to a sympathy for whatever relieves our general force in Missouri, and allows it to serve elsewhere. I therefore, as at present advised, can not attempt the destruction of the Enrolled Militia of Missouri. I may add that the force being under the national military control, it is also within the proclamation in regard to the *Habeas Corpus*.

I concur in the propriety of your request in regard to elections, and have, as you see, directed Gen. Schofield accordingly.

I do not feel justified to enter upon the broad field you present in regard to the political differences between radicals and conservatives. From time to time I have done and said what appeared to me proper to do and say. The public knows it all. It obliges nobody to follow me, and I trust it obliges me to follow nobody. The

[3] Francis J. Herron.

radicals and conservatives, each agree with me in some things, and disagree in others. I could wish both to agree with me in all things; for then they would agree with each other, and would be too strong for any foe from any quarter. They, however, choose to do otherwise, and I do not question their right. I too shall do what seems to be my duty. I hold whoever commands in Missouri, or elsewhere, responsible to me, and not to either radicals or conservatives. It is my duty to hear all; but at last, I must, within my sphere, judge what to do, and what to forbear. Your Obt. Servt.

A. LINCOLN.

To George G. Meade[1]

Major Gen. Meade   Washington, D.C.,
Army of Potomac.   Oct. 5 1863

Yesterday I inquired of you about Daniel Hanson, private in 97. New-York, said to be under sentence of death for desertion. I fear you did not receive the despatch. Please answer.

A. LINCOLN

[1] ALS, IHi. See Lincoln to Meade, October 15, *infra.*

To Edwin M. Stanton[1]

October 5, 1863

Sec. of War, please have the facts of this case reported to me.

A. LINCOLN

[1] AES, DNA WR RG 107, Secretary of War, Letters Received, P 168. Lincoln's endorsement is written on a letter from Sarah M. Ulrich, September 21, 1863, asking release of her husband William, imprisoned in Old Capitol on suspicion of fraud. No further reference has been found.

To Whom It May Concern[1]

Executive Mansion,
Whom it may concern.   Washington, Oct. 5th, 1863.

Unless something now unknown, and unexpected, shall come to my knowledge, tending to change my purpose, I shall, at the proper time, appoint Timothy J. Carter, one of the two directors, to be appointed by the President, according to a provision in the first Section of the act of Congress, Entitled "An act to aid in the construction of a Railroad and Telegraph Line from the Missouri

River to the Pacific Ocean, and to secure to the Government the use of the same for Postal, Military and other purposes," Approved July 1, 1862.   ABRAHAM LINCOLN

1 DS, DLC-RTL. See Lincoln to Usher, October 3, *supra*, and to Carter, October 29, *infra*.

Approval of Sentence
in Case of David M. Wright[1]

October 7, 1863

Upon the presentation of the record in this case and the examination thereof, aided by the report thereon of the Judge-Advocate-General, and on full hearing of counsel for the accused, being satisfied that no proper question remained open except as to the insanity of the accused, I caused a very full examination to be made on that question, upon a great amount of evidence, including all offered by counsel of accused, by an expert of high reputation in that professional department, who thereon reports to me, as his opinion, that the accused Dr. David M. Wright, was not insane prior to or on the 11th day of July, 1863, the date of the homicide of Lieutenant Sanborn; that he has not been insane since, and is not insane now (October 7, 1863). I therefore approve the finding and sentence of the military commission, and direct that the major-general in command of the department including the place of trial, and wherein the convict is now in custody, appoint time and place and carry said sentence into execution.

ABRAHAM LINCOLN.

1 OR, II, VI, 360. Wright was sentenced to death by hanging, and General Foster set October 16 as the date, but see Lincoln's communication to Foster, October 15, *infra*.

To Andrew Johnson[1]

Governor Johnson   Washington, D.C.,
Nashville, Tenn   Oct. 7. 1863
    What news have you from Rosecrans' Army, or in that direction beyond Nashville?   A. LINCOLN

1 ALS, RPB. Governor Johnson replied to Lincoln's telegram (received at 8:45 P.M.): "Nothing definite from the front. Our hopes are strong that all will come out right, the damage on the R.R. is being rapidly repaired. Telegraph wire will be up tonight. Chattanooga must be held." (DLC-RTL).

To George G. Meade[1]

Major General Mead°   Washington, D.C.,
Army of Potomac   Oct. 8. 1863
    I am appealed to in behalf of August Blittersdorf, at Mitchells Station, Va. to be shot to-morrow, as a deserter. I am unwilling for any boy under eighteen to be shot; and his father affirms that he is yet under sixteen.
    Please answer. His Regt. or Co. not given me.

                                   A LINCOLN

    [1] ALS, IHi. No reply from Meade or other communications about Blittersdorf have been found, and there seems to be no record of the name in the *General Orders*, Army of the Potomac, but see Lincoln to Meade, October 15, *infra*.

To George G. Meade[1]

Major General Meade   Executive Mansion,
Army of Potomac   Washington, Oct. 8, 1863.
    The boy telegraphs from Mitchell's Station, Va. The father thinks he is in the 119th. Penn. Vols. The father signs the name "Blittersdorf" I can tell no more.   A. LINCOLN

    [1] ALS, IHi. See Lincoln to Meade, October 15, *infra*.

To George G. Meade[1]

Major General Meade   Washington, D.C.,
Army of Potomac   Oct. 8 1863
    I am appealed to in behalf of John Murphy, to be shot to-morrow. His Mother says he is but seventeen. Please answer.

                                   A. LINCOLN

    [1] ALS, owned by R. E. Burdick, New York City. No reply from Meade has been located. Army of the Potomac, *General Orders No. 93*, October 2, 1863, announced sentence of John Murphy, unassigned recruit, One Hundred Nineteenth Pennsylvania Volunteers, to be shot October 9 for desertion. See Lincoln to Meade, October 12, *infra*.

To George G. Meade[1]

If there is any reason to believe that this boy was under eighteen when he deserted, suspend his execution until further order.
    Oct. 8. 1863.   A. LINCOLN
    To Major Gen. Meade

1 AES, DNA RG 153, Judge Advocate General, MM 1041. Lincoln's endorsement is written on the jacket of papers in the case of William F. Weeks, Company K, Fifty-ninth New York Volunteers, sentenced to be shot for desertion. No further reference has been located.

To John P. Usher[1]

Hon. Sec. of Interior   Executive Mansion
Sir: Washington City, D.C. Oct. 8. 1863
    Please send me an appointment for Daniel W. Wilder of Kansas, as Surveyor General, in place of Mark W. Delahay, resigned.
                                   A. LINCOLN

1 ALS-P, ISLA. Following the death of Archibald Williams on September 21, 1863, Mark W. Delahay was appointed to succeed him as judge of the U.S. District Court for Kansas, and Wilder replaced Delahay as surveyor general.

To William H. Seward[1]

Hon. Sec. of State   Executive Mansion,
My dear Sir   Washington, Oct. 9, 1863.
    To-day Mrs. Galez[2] calls to make interest for Mr. Frederick Wippermann, now Consul at Galatz, in Moldavia. She wishes him to be transfered to Hamburg, as a matter of preference; but, at all events, wishes him sent to some more agreeable place than that where he now is. If you can conveniently find a way to oblige Mrs. Galez, I shall be glad. Yours truly.   A. LINCOLN.

1 ALS, NAuE. James H. Anderson of Ohio is listed in the *U.S. Official Register* both for 1863 and 1865 as consul at Hamburg. Frederick Wippermann is listed as consul at Galatza in 1863 but is replaced by Oscar Malmros of Minnesota in 1865. No record has been found of a later appointment for Wippermann.
2 Lincoln wrote "Mrs. Gales," but in both instances seems to have tried to change the final "s" to "z." She has not been identified.

To Edwin M. Stanton[1]

                                Executive Mansion,
Hon. Secretary of War   Washington, Oct. 9, 1863.
    Sir—Mrs. Thomas G. Clemsin is a daughter of the late Hon. John C. Calhoun, and is now residing near Bladensburg in Maryland.
    She understands that her son, Calhoun Clemsin, is now a prisoner of War to us at "Johnsons Island["]; and she asks the previ-

lege merely of visiting him. With your approbation, I consent for her to go. Yours truly   A. LINCOLN

[1] ALS, owned by William H. Townsend, Lexington, Kentucky. No further reference has been located.

To Whom It May Concern[1]

Executive Mansion,
To whom it may concern   Washington, October 9, 1863.

In pursuance of a Resolution of the Senate and Assembly of the State of New-York, in the words following, towit:

Resolved, That the Governor be and hereby is empowered and requested to invite the President of the United States to select and detail a competent engineer in behalf and at the expense of the General Government, to consult with the engineers so to be appointed by the Canal Board, in respect to the surveys mentioned in the preceding resolution, and as to the mode of constructing the work so as most effectually to promote the national interests.[2]

and in response to the invitation of the Governor of said State of New-York, made in virtue of said Resolution, I do hereby select and detail Charles B. Stuart, of Geneva, in said State,[3] to perform the duties contemplated in and by said resolution, it being understood by said Stuart that he is to rely upon an appropriation hereafter to be made by congress, for any compensation he may receive.

ABRAHAM LINCOLN

[1] ADfS, DLC-RTL. On October 5, Governor Horatio Seymour enclosed a copy of the joint resolution and requested the president to "select and detail a competent engineer for the purpose. . . ." (DLC-RTL). On October 6 Seymour wrote again, "I understand that Col. Charles B. Stewart, late Engineer in Chief of the United States Navy, has been, or will be recommended to you as a fit person to be designated for this duty, in which I heartily concur, believing him to be abundantly qualified and eminently fitted by experience and knowledge of our public works, for the position." (*Ibid.*). On October 8, Stuart wrote from Willard's Hotel, enclosing recommendations from Edwin D. Morgan and Millard Fillmore: "Governor Morgan advised me to remain in the City until you could act upon my application, in view of the *limited* time allowed for making the surveys & report for the action of Congress." (*Ibid.*).
[2] The resolution is in the form of a printed clipping.
[3] "Of Geneva, in said State," inserted in a different handwriting.

Commutation of Sentence[1]

October 10, 1863

The Report of the Judge Advocate General is approved & as in the state of the pleadings & in the absence of proof the court was not warranted in finding the prisoner guilty of desertion, & as he has confessed himself guilty of absence without leave only, it is ordered that the death sentence be commuted to confinement at hard labor for six-months from this date.   A LINCOLN

Oct. 10. 1863

[1] DS, ORB. The signature and date are in Lincoln's autograph. Since this document has been removed from the papers with which it was originally filed, there is no clue to the case.

To George G. Meade[1]

Major General Meade   Washington, D.C.,
Army of Potomac   Oct. 10 1863
   Am interested with your despatch of noon. How is it now?
                                                A. LINCOLN

[1] ALS, IHi. Meade's noon telegram to Halleck had reported that "Every indication would lead to the conclusion that the enemy's cavalry attacking me are supported by a large force of infantry, and there are some reasons to believe there is a movement into the Shenandoah Valley. . . . I am quite positive no troops have left Lee's army for the West. . . ." (OR, I, XXIX, II, 278).

He replied to Lincoln at 8:30 A.M., October 11: "I am falling back to the Rappahannock. The enemy are either, moving to my right and rear or moving down on my flank. I cannot tell which as their movements are not developed. I am prepared for either contingency." (DLC-RTL).

To Edwin M. Stanton[1]

October 10, 1863

I think these papers are sufficient to take the case of Lieut. Thomson out of the general run. The strong recommendation of Gens. Meade, Pleasonton & others, together with the almost unanimous wish of the officers of the 5th Cavalry, to have him appointed, I think fully justify his appointment. Sec. of War, please see him.

Oct. 10, 1863   A. LINCOLN

[1] AES, owned by Mrs. Andrew Jackson, New York City. No record of promotion for First Lieutenant Clifford Thomson, First New York Cavalry, has been discovered. Mustered out on June 25, 1865, he was appointed Major of the Fifth Colored Cavalry on June 26.

To George G. Meade[1]

Major-General Meade,   War Department, Washington, D.C.,
Army of Potomac: October 11, 1863—9.50 A.M.
           How is it now?   A. LINCOLN.

[1] Tarbell (Appendix), p. 390. No reply has been found.

To George G. Meade[1]

Major General Meade   Washington City,
Army of Potomac   Oct. 12. 9.A.M. 1863

What news this morning? A despatch from Rosecrans, leaving him at 7/30 PM. yesterday, says "Rebel rumors that head of Ewells column reached Dalton yesterday"

I send this for what it is worth.   A. LINCOLN

[1] ALS, IHi. Meade's reply was received at 1:10 P.M.:
"We took yesterday some fifty prisoners. . . . There is no doubt but that up to yesterday the whole of Hill's and Ewell's Corps' were here, and some say reinforced by . . . troops from Richmond.

"Lee never would have made the movements he has, leaving a strong position, if he was weakened by the detachment of any portion of Ewell's and Hill's Corps" (DLC-RTL).

To George G. Meade[1]

Major General Meade   Executive Mansion,
Army of Potomac   Washington, Oct. 12, 1863.

The father and mother of John Murphy of the 119th. Pennsylvania Vols. have filed their own affidavits that he was born June 22, 1846; and also the affidavits of three other persons who all swear that they remember the circumstance of his birth and that it was in the year 1846, though they do not remember the particular day. I therefore, on account of his tender age, have concluded to pardon him, and to leave it to yourself whether to discharge him, or continue him in the service.   A. LINCOLN

[1] ALS, NN. See Lincoln to Meade, October 8, *supra*. The roster of the One Hundred Nineteenth Pennsylvania Volunteers lists John Murphy as "deserted May 29, 1864."

To William S. Rosecrans[1]

Major General Rosecrans   Washington, D.C.,
Chattanooga, Tenn.   Oct. 12. 8/35 A.M. 1863

As I understand, Burnside is menaced from the East, and so can not go to you without surrendering East Tennessee. I now think the enemy will not attack Chattanooga; and I think you have to look out for his making a concentrated drive at Burnside. You and Burnside now have him by the throat, and he must break your hold, or perish. I therefore think you better to try to hold the river up to Kingston, leaving Burnside to what is above there. Sherman *is* coming to you, though gaps in the telegraph prevent

our knowing how far he is advanced. He and Hooker will so support you on the West & North-West, as to enable you to look East
& North East. This is not an order. Gen. Halleck will give his
views.   A LINCOLN

1 ALS, RPB. Rosecrans telegraphed at 3 P.M., "Line from here to Kingston
is long; our side is barren mountain; rebel side has railroad. Our danger is
subsistence. We cannot bring up Hooker to cover our left against a crossing
above us, for want of means to transport provisions and horse-feed. Enemy's
side of valley full of corn. Every exertion will be made to hold what we have
and gain more, after which we must put our trust in God, who never fails
those who truly trust." (OR, I, XXX, IV, 306-307).

To Mrs. Alice C. Smith[1]

Mrs Alice C. Smith   Executive Mansion,
Boston Mass.   Washington, Oct. 12th. 1863.
    Dear Madame, I shall have to acknowledge very briefly your
letter informing me of the prosperity of your little boy whom you
so kindly named after me. You may rest assured that my little
namesake has my best wishes that he may grow to be a good man
and a good citizen. Yours Very Truly   A. LINCOLN

1 LS, RPB. Mrs. Smith's letter has not been located.

To Gideon Welles[1]

If this appointment can be consistently made, I shall be glad.
    Oct. 12. 1863.   A. LINCOLN

1 AES, owned by Alexander W. Armour, Princeton, New Jersey. Lincoln's
endorsement is written on a letter of George D. Morgan (cousin and business
partner of Edwin D. Morgan) to Gideon Welles, September 26, 1863, recommending his cousin N. D. Morgan's son, William Morgan, for appointment to
the Naval Academy. William G. Morgan was appointed, but later resigned.

To Clinton B. Fisk[1]

Gen'l Clinton B. Fisk,   Executive Mansion, Washington.
Pilot Knob, Mo.   October 13, 1863.
    My Dear Gen'l:— I have received and read, with great satisfac-
tion, your letter of the 8th inst.   It is so full of *charity and good
will,* I wish I had time to more than thank you for it. Very truly
yours,   A. LINCOLN.

1 Osborn H. Oldroyd, *The Lincoln Memorial: Album-Immortelles,* p. 446.
General Fisk's letter of October 8 has not been found. See Lincoln to Fisk,
October 29, *infra.*

To I. Wayne McVeagh[1]

McVeigh.   Executive Mansion,
Philadelphia   Washington, Oct. 13. 1863.

The enemy some days ago made a movement, apparantly to turn Gen. Meades right. This led to a manoevering of the two armies, and to pretty heavy skirmishing on Saturday, Sunday, and Monday. We have frequent despatches from Gen. Meade, and up to ten o'clock last night, nothing had happened giving either side any marked advantage. Our army reported to be in excellent condition. The telegraph is open to Gen. Meade's camp this morning, but we have not troubled him for a despatch.

                                                    A. LINCOLN

[1] ALS, RPB. Isaac Wayne McVeagh, chairman of the Pennsylvania Union Committee, acknowledged Lincoln's telegram the same day: "Am thankful for your kind thoughtfulness. God is good, in delaying Lees advance until it is harmless to the cause here. McClellans letter for Woodward cannot harm us much now. All the indications are cheering. Will advise you later in afternoon. May I hope to hear from you again." (DLC-RTL). By 10:45 P.M., McVeagh telegraphed again, "Everything most cheering but no definite returns yet." (*Ibid.*).

To James K. Moorhead[1]

Hon. J. K. Moorehead   Executive Mansion,
Pittsburg, Penn.   Washington, Oct. 13, 1863.

    Not unless you think it necessary.   A. LINCOLN

[1] ALS, RPB. Lincoln's telegram to McVeagh, *supra*, was presumably sent to Moorhead as well. At 12:15 P.M. Moorhead telegraphed, "Shall I publish despatchs. Allegheny County good for eight thousand (8000)." (DLC-RTL). On October 15 Moorhead telegraphed again:

"I thank you for the despatch on Election day, immediately after I telegraphed you with regard to its publication, I found a bulletin on the streets giving an account of Meade's defeat. I at once published yours to counteract it, without using your name.

"Let me congratulate you on the glorious result in Ohio & Penna, who now declare for .1 *Lincoln* in 1864." (*Ibid.*).

Note[1]

Wants to be Chaplain of Invalid Corps in Washington.
Oct. 13, 1863.   A. LINCOLN.

[1] American Art Association Anderson Galleries Catalog 4389, April 18-19, 1938, No. 244.

To Andrew G. Curtin[1]

Gov. Curtin   Washington, D.C.,
Harrisburg, Penn.   [October 14,] 186[3]
           How does it stand.   A. LINCOLN

[1] ALS, RPB. Governor Curtin's reply was received at 8:45 P.M.: "My majority cannot vary much from 20,000" (DLC-RTL).

To I. Wayne McVeagh[1]

Wayne McVeigh   Washington, D.C.,
Philadelphia.   Oct. 14. 3/35. 1863
        How does it stand now?   A. LINCOLN

[1] ALS, RPB. McVeagh's reply was received at 6:15 P.M., "Everything continues to look well. Curtin is certainly elected by a decided majority say fifteen to twenty thousand (20 000)" (DLC-RTL).

To Edwin M. Stanton[1]

October 14, 1863

My impulse would be to say "Let Charles O. Roby, take the oath and be discharged["]; yet I do not so say, not knowing what valid objection there may be, known at the War Department. Mr. Foster who presents this, was a M.C from New-York several years ago, and afterwards a resident of Virginia, as he states. He is vouched to me as a respectable & worthy gentleman. I submit the case to the Sec. of War.   A. LINCOLN
     Oct. 14. 1863.

[1] AES, owned by E. Channing Coolidge, Chicago, Illinois. Lincoln's endorsement is written on a letter from A. Lawrence Foster, September 23, 1863, enclosing an affidavit of Charles Roby, Fairfax County, Virginia, which sets forth the circumstances under which his son Charles O. Roby, captured at Gettysburg, was forced into the Confederate Army, and asks for his release. Roby was released by order of Secretary Stanton on taking the oath.

To Thurlow Weed[1]

Hon. Thurlow Weed   Executive Mansion,
My dear Sir: Washington, Oct 14, 1863.

I have been brought to fear recently that somehow, by commission or omission, I have caused you some degree of pain. I have never entertained an unkind feeling or a disparaging thought towards you; and if I have said or done anything which has been construed into such unkindness or disparagement, it has been misconstrued. I am sure if we could meet we would not part with any unpleasant impression on either side. Yours as ever

A. LINCOLN

[1] ALS-P, ISLA; ADfS, DLC-RTL. Weed replied on October 18:

"Amid your great and constant responsibilities I regret that you should have been annoyed by any small grief of mine.

"It is not, however, pleasant to be misunderstood. I certainly was pained to learn that you regarded my controversy with the N.Y. Tribune as a *personal* quarrel with Mr Greeley, in which both were damaging our cause.

"If, a year or more since, when ultra Abolition was rampant, I had not throttled it, rescuing Republican organizations from its Incendiary influences, the North would have been fatally divided, and your power to serve the Country as fatally paralized. But if, by this time, your experience of the 'Horse Leech' exactions of that spirit is either profitable or pleasant, I must have erred in endeavoring to 'cut its claws, and draw its teeth.'

"My 'quarrels' are in no sense *personal*. I am without personal objects or interests. I have done something in my day towards Electing Presidents and Governors, none of whom have found me an expensive Partizan. Possibly some Gentlemen in Power may have derived advantage and found relief in a Friend, without 'Axes' of any kind to 'Grind.'

"I have confided unwaveringly, in your Integrity and Patriotism, from the begining of this Rebellion, the certainty and magnitude of which I foresaw; and I have earnestly and faithfully laboured to uphold your Administration.

"But I am consuming too much of your time. Dismiss me from your thoughts, or if you remember me at all, remember that I do not desert those in power who are faithful to their Country, or permit personal griefs, real or imaginary, to interfere with the discharge of any duty. If you will carry our Country safely through its great Trial—and I know you will if you can—I will serve, honor and bless you—with all my strength and my whole heart, as long as Life is given to me." (DLC-RTL).

Endorsement[1]

I perceive no reason why the within recommendation of Gen. Grant shall not be followed.   A. LINCOLN

Oct. 15, 1863

[1] William D. Morley Catalog, November 17, 1941, No. 176. According to the catalog description, Lincoln's endorsement is written on a letter of General Grant to the commanding officer at Indianapolis, Indiana, asking for discharge of a Confederate prisoner "whose father has been a staunch and unflinching Union man from the first to last . . . and his son went into the service solely for the purpose of saving his family."

To John G. Foster[1]

Major General Foster   Washington, D.C.,
Fort-Monroe, Va   Oct. 15 1863

Postpone the execution of Dr. Wright to Friday the 23rd. Inst. (October). This is intended for his preparation and is final.

A. LINCOLN

[1] ALS, RPB. See Lincoln's approval of sentence in the Wright case, October 7, *supra*, and telegram to Foster, October 17, *infra*.

To James W. Grimes[1]

Hon. James W. Grimes   Washington City,
Burlington, Iowa.   Oct. 15. 1863

Thanks for your Iowa election news. I suppose you know that Pennsylvania and Ohio are all right. Gov. Morton telegraphs that county[2] elections in Indiana have gone largely in the same direction   A. LINCOLN.

1 ALS, RPB. Grimes telegraphed on October 14: "As ever Iowa is erect. We have swept the state overwhelmingly. We could not have asked for more." (DLC-RTL). Governor David Tod of Ohio also telegraphed on October 14: "God be praised our majority on the home vote cannot be less than 30,000 Advise Sec'y Stanton" (ibid.). Governor Morton's telegram of October 14 reported, "Returns from county election in Indiana show an enormous union gain keeping pace with that in Ohio" (ibid.).

2 Lincoln deleted "little vacancy filling" and substituted "county."

To Herman Kretz[1]

Major Herman Krettz   Executive Mansion,
Cumberland, Md.   Washington, Oct. 15, 1863.

Suspend execution of Dennis McCarty till further order from here. If McCarty has been removed send this to the officer where he is.   A LINCOLN

1 ALS, RPB. See Lincoln to Kretz, September 22, supra, and to Joseph Holt, February 10, 1864, infra.

To George G. Meade[1]

Major-General Meade,   Executive Mansion,
Army of Potomac: Washington, October 15, 1863.

On the 4th instant you telegraphed me that Private Daniel Hanson, of Ninety-seventh New York Volunteers, had not yet been tried. When he shall be, please notify me of the result, with a brief statement of his case, if he be convicted. Gustave Blittersdorf, whom you say is enlisted in the One hundred and nineteenth Pennsylvania Volunteers, as William Fox, is proven to me to be only fifteen years old last January. I pardon him, and you will discharge him or put him in the ranks at your discretion.[2] Mathias Brown, of Nineteenth Pennsylvania Volunteers, is proven to me to be eighteen last May, and his friends say he is convicted on an enlistment and for a desertion, both before that time.[3] If this last be true he is pardoned, to be kept or discharged as you please.

[515]

If not true suspend his execution and report the facts of his case.
Did you receive my dispatch of 12th pardoning John Murphy?

A. LINCOLN.

1 Tarbell (Appendix), p. 392. No reply has been located.
2 The roster of Company E, One Hundred Nineteenth Pennsylvania Volunteers lists William Fox as drafted on August 31, 1863, and transferred to Company E, Eighty-second Pennsylvania Volunteers on June 4, 1865.
3 See Lincoln to Meade, October 29, *infra*.

To Montgomery C. Meigs[1]

Executive Mansion,
Quarter-Master-General   Washington, Oct. 15, 1863.

Some time ago I felt constrained to have Captain William H. Bailhasch relieved from duty at Springfield, Illinois. This was not because of a loss of confidence in him, but because of a different matter not now necessary to be explained. I now understand that Capt. Potter would like to have Capt. B. assigned to him, and that this would be agreeable also to Capt. B.   Supposing this to be true, I shall be very glad of the arrangement. Yours truly

A. LINCOLN

1 ALS, IHi. Meigs endorsed "Request the adjt Genl to order Capt B to report to Capt Potter as an asst in the discharge of his duties. . . ." See Lincoln to Dubois and others, May 29, *supra.* Captain Joseph A. Potter, chief quartermaster at Chicago, wrote Edward L. Baker at Springfield, Illinois, on September 28, 1863, that he "would really like to have him [Bailhache] ordered to report to me *here in Chicago*" (DLC-RTL), but Bailhache was ordered to act temporarily as chief quartermaster of the Twenty-third Corps in Burnside's command (Mrs. Ada Bailhache to Lincoln, October 8, 1863, DLC-RTL).

To Edwin M. Stanton[1]

October 15, 1863

This lady, Abigail C. Berea, had a husband and three sons in the war, and has been a nurse herself, without pay, during nearly the whole war. Her husband was killed at Gettysburg, and one of her sons also has died in the service. One other son she is willing to leave in the service where he still is, but the youngest, James H. Benjamin, private in Co. K. 104 N.Y. vols. and who is in poor health, she asks to have discharged. Let it be done.

October 15th, 1863.   A. LINCOLN.

1 William D. Morley Catalog, January 28, 1944, No. 83. According to the catalog description Lincoln's endorsement is written on a letter from the Treasury Department. No further reference has been found.

To Lyman B. Todd[1]

L. B. Todd   Washington, D.C.,
Lexington Ky   October 15th. 1863
I send the following pass to your care   A. LINCOLN

"Washington D.C.
"To whom it may concern   Oct 15th. 63
    Allow Mrs Robert S. Todd, widow, to go south and bring her daughter, Mrs Genl B. Hardin Helm, with her children, North to Kentucky.   *"signed"*   A. LINCOLN"

[1] LS, RPB. This telegram has been reproduced as nearly as possible to the original but requires some description because of emendations made by the War Department in the effort to make the copy received at Lexington more suitable. Lincoln's autograph signature to the first portion was deleted but replaced. Quotation marks and the date line were added to the second part and *"signed"* inserted before Lincoln's second autograph signature. No communication from Lyman B. Todd requesting the pass has been located, but a letter from E. M. Bruce, Madison, Georgia, October 6, 1863, reads as follows:

"At the instance of Mrs. E. T. Helm it becomes my painful duty to announce to you the death of General Ben. Hardin Helm—your Brother-in-law. . . . Mrs. Helm is crushed by the blow—almost broken hearted—, and desires to return to her mother and friends in Kentucky—indeed, this is a necessity as you must be aware that her means are very small, and expenses of living in the South much more than in the United States—she is now at my home in this place—, and it will afford me pleasure to minister to her wants and comfort so long as it may be agreeable for her to remain under my roof; mean time she asks that you order the War department to send her a pass to enter the Federal truce Boat at City Point—and would suggest that you send *triplicates*, say, one to me here, one to care Col Wm Preston Johnston, Richmond, and one to Mrs. Helm here by different Boats.

"Would also be obliged if you would send at the same time a pass for Mrs. Bruce and her sister—Mrs Hutchinson—to accompany Mrs. Helm, to Kentucky, their father having recently died leaving mother in a very desolate condition. . . ." (DLC-RTL).

On October 11, John L. Helm, Elizabethtown, wrote to Mrs. Robert S. Todd, Lexington, Kentucky: "It is due to you that I announce the death of my son. He fell in the battle south of Chattanooga I have unquestionable information. He was buried at Atlanta. It is probable Emilie was there. Could you through friends or by your own relationship secure for Emilie a passport home. . . . I am totally at a loss to know how to begin. Could you or one of your daughters write to Mrs. Lincoln and through her secure a pass?" (Katherine Helm, *Mary, Wife of Lincoln*, p. 219).

See further, Lincoln to Todd, October 31, *infra*.

To Salmon P. Chase[1]

Hon. S. P. Chase   Executive Mansion Washington D.C.
Cincinnati & Columbus O.   Oct. 16. 1863
    If Judge Lawrence can not go to Key West at once, I shall have to appoint another.   A. LINCOLN

To Thomas C. Durant¹

T. C. Durant, New York:

Washington, D.C.,
October 16, 1863.

I remember receiving nothing from you of the 10th, and I do not comprehend your dispatch of to-day. In fact I do not remember, if I ever knew who you are, and I have very little conception as to what you are telegraphing about.   A. LINCOLN.

¹ Tarbell (Appendix), p. 393. Thomas C. Durant of the Union Pacific Railroad telegraphed on October 16: "On tenth inst I addressed you requesting an order from War Dept on Comds of Posts in Rocky Mountains near Cheyenne & Bridgers Passes for escort & provisions required by a party of Engrs. to be used in case of necessity Will you please decide whether such order can be given or not that I may make arrangements accordingly. Brigham Young telegraphs me he provides for Engrs running line from Salt Lake East to meet ours going west. This is important." (DLC-RTL). See further, Lincoln to Durant, October 18, *infra*.

To Henry W. Halleck¹

Major General Halleck

Executive Mansion,
Washington, Oct. 16. 1863.

I do not believe Lee can have over sixty thousand effective men. Longstreet's corps would not be sent away, to bring an equal force back upon the same road; and there is no other direction for them to have come from. Doubtless, in making the present movement Lee gathered in all available scraps, and added them to Hills & Ewell's corps; but that is all. And he made the movement in the belief that *four* corps had left Gen. Meade; and Gen. Meade's apparantly avoiding a collision with him has confirmed him in that belief. If Gen. Meade can now attack him on a field no worse than equal for us, and will do so with all the skill and courage, which he, his officers and men possess, the honor will be his if he succeeds, and the blame may be mine if he fails. Yours truly,

A. LINCOLN

¹ ALS, ORB. Halleck forwarded a copy of this communication to Meade, who replied the same day, "I have to acknowledge the receipt of your communication . . . by the hands of Colonel [Richard D.] Cutts, aide-de-camp, inclosing one from the President, and have to say in reply, that it has been my intention to attack the enemy, if I can find him on a field no more than equal for

us, and that I have only delayed doing so from the difficulty of ascertaining his exact position, and the fear that in endeavoring to do so my communications might be jeopardized." (OR, I, XXIX, II, 333).

To George G. Meade[1]

Major-General Meade,   Executive Mansion,
Army of Potomac: Washington, October 16, 1863.

Have you in custody for desertion a man by the name of Jacob Schwarz, a Swiss? If so please send a short statement of his case. Neither his company, regiment or corps is given me.

A. LINCOLN.

[1] Tarbell (Appendix), p. 393. Meade's reply was received at 4:50 P.M.: "Nothing is known here in relation to a man by name Jacob Schwarz, charged with desertion. Should the record in his case reach here, I will inform you of the facts in the case, and will suspend action until your orders are received." (DLC-RTL). The record in the case of Private Jacob Schwartz, Company E, Thirteenth Massachusetts Volunteers, sentenced on September 28, 1863, shows that Meade recommended commutation of sentence, and the president returned the papers to the Judge Advocate General without recommendation on April 16, 1864 (DNA WR RG 153, Judge Advocate General, MM 838).

To Montgomery C. Meigs[1]

October 16, 1863

Please see Mrs. Hutter, who has given most of her time to the soldiers, during the war, and who wishes to present an invention of hers for the soldier's comfort, which she would like to have introduced into the service. . . . I certainly would prefer having it over my ears in cold weather, to their being naked.

[1] American Art Association Anderson Galleries Catalog 4346, November 11-12, 1937, No. 278. According to the catalog description, this is the partial text of an autograph letter signed. Mrs. Elizabeth E. Hutter had designed some earmuffs. See further, Lincoln to Meigs, October 17, *infra.*

To Officers of the Union Pacific Railroad[1]

To the officers of   Executive Mansion,
The Pacific Railroad   Washington, Oct 16, 1863.

Richard P. Morgan, bearer of this, is my personal acquaintance and friend, whom I would like to have obliged in any reasonable way. I became acquainted with him, while he was acting as a Railroad Civil Engineer, and I knew him long enough and well enough

in this capacity to believe him to be both competent and faithful.
Yours &c   A. LINCOLN

₁ ALS-P, ISLA. No further reference has been located.

To Edwin M. Stanton[1]

Executive Mansion Washington Oct. 16, 1863
Today Mrs. Elizabeth J. Platt calls and states that she is a
widow, and at the beginning of the war had two sons only, both
whom entered the army, and the eldest was mortally wounded at
Gettysburgh, and afterwards died; that the younger Edwin F.
Platt, of Co. F. 7 New Jersey Vols. was made a prisoner at same
battle, but by parole or exchange is now at Annapolis Md. She
says he was under sixteen when he entered the service and is now
only a trifle over eighteen and is in feeble health. She says he and
his brother were in all the battles of their Regiment.

She now asks his discharge and if Hon. Daniel S. Gregory will
say in writing on this sheet, that he personally knows Mrs. Platt
and that he fully believes this statement, I will allow the discharge
upon the papers so indorsed being presented to me.

A. LINCOLN

Let Edwin F. Platt, named in my note on the other half of this
sheet, be discharged.   A. LINCOLN
    Oct. 21, 1863

₁ Copy, ISLA. On Lincoln's note Daniel S. Gregory endorsed:
"The representation of Mrs. Platt as set forth in the accompanying statement is correct, excepting one particular which the President mis-understood,
but it does not detract from the merits of the case. She has another son, now
in France. Her husband I knew personally as a worthy man whose funeral
I attended six years ago, and the family have been residents in this place more
than a quarter of a century.   D. S. GREGORY
    "Jersey City, Oct. 20, 1863"
The roster of Company F, Seventh New Jersey Volunteers lists Charles F.
Platt, died July 24, 1863, at Jersey City, of wounds received at Gettysburg, and
Edwin F. Platt, discharged for disability, November 2, 1863.

To Thomas W. Sweney[1]

Thomas W. Sweney   Washington, D.C.,
Continental.   Oct. 16 1863
Philadelphia.
    Tad is teasing me to have you forward his pistol to him.
                                              A LINCOLN

[1] ALS, RPB. See Lincoln's telegram to Mrs. Lincoln, June 9, *supra.* Thomas W. Sweney, assessor of Internal Revenue at Philadelphia, was apparently a particular friend of young "Tad" Lincoln and purveyed to him playthings of various sorts.

To Gideon Welles[1]

Submitted to the Secretary of the Navy, to go on file with other papers in relation to Captn. Diller's new gunpowder.

Oct. 16, 1863   A. LINCOLN.

[1] Copy, DNA WR RG 74, Navy Branch, Bureau of Ordnance, Diller's Powder, Letters Received, 1862-1863. The copy of Lincoln's endorsement is with a copy of a letter of Lieutenant Commander William N. Jeffers to Isaac R. Diller, October 12, 1863, as follows:

"Having been detailed by the Bureau of Ordnance, in conjunction with Major Laidley, U.S.A., to experiment with the material submitted by you as a substitute for common Gunpowder, I have been strongly impressed with its prospective value, and the results of experiments with the several specimens presented by you.

"As at first submitted, it was in too fine a state to be with safety and convenience transported; it was, therefore, made imperative that it should be grained. The small quantity submitted in that state appears to satisfy all the required conditions. If it retains its original properties, while conforming to these requirements, I think it will prove valuable. At any rate, the successful results already obtained, in my opinion, warrant a continuation of these experiments, and the manufacture of at least 500 lbs. that a definite opinion may be formed, after experiments of a more extended character than those hitherto made."

See Lincoln to Diller, December 15, 1862, *supra;* also his letter to Wise, October 21, and memorandum of November 2, 1863, *infra.*

Authorization for James A. Hardie[1]

October 17, 1863

Lt. Col. James Hardie is authorized to perform the duties of Secretary of War during the temporary absence of the Secretary and Assistant Secretary.

[1] Anderson Galleries Catalog 1245, November 8, 1916, No. 211. According to the catalog description this text is from a signed document.

To Ambrose E. Burnside[1]

Major General Burnside   Washington, D.C.,
Knoxville, Tenn.   Oct. 17 1863

I am greatly interested to know how many new troops of all sorts you have raised in Tennessee. Please inform me.

A. LINCOLN

[1] ALS, RPB. Burnside replied on October 22: "Your dispatch received. We have already over three thousand in the three year service & half armed. About twenty five hundred home guards many more recruits could have been had for the three years' service but for the want of clothing & camp equipage. We have not means of bringing those things with us & since our arrival we have not been able to accumulate them by transportation from Kentucky. Our command is now & have been ever since our arrival on half rations of everything except fresh beef. We have no rations of beans rice pickles &c in fact no small stores but sugar coffee & salt, but the command is remarkably happy cheerful & willing . . . . the country thus far has supplied an abundance of forage. We are suffering considerably for want of shoes & clothing & horse shoes. I have told Gen Halleck fully as to our position. A road has been surveyed from Clinton to the mouth of Big South Fork on the Cumberland from which point are transported supplies. After the Cumberland River becomes navigable . . . we will commence work on it. . . . I have already made arrangements to build the RR. bridge at that place. . . ." (DLC-RTL).

To Simon Cameron[1]

Hon. Simon Cameron   Washington, D.C.,
Harrisburg, Penn.   Oct. 17 1863

I forgot to notify you that your despatch of day-before-yesterday was duly received and immediately attended to in the best way we could think of.   A. LINCOLN

[1] ALS, RPB. Cameron's telegram received at 10:55 A.M. on October 15 is as follows: "Our majority in the Senate depends upon the release of Major White. He was captured with Milroys command and an especial exchange ought to be made for him. He is now in Libby Prison." State Senator Major Harry White of the Sixty-seventh Pennsylvania Infantry had been captured at Winchester with a large portion of General Milroy's command. Although efforts to make an exchange for White were initiated immediately, he remained in Confederate hands until September 29, 1864.

To John G. Foster[1]

Major General Foster   Washington, D.C.,
Fort-Monroe, Va   Oct. 17. 1863

It would be useless for Mrs. Dr. Wright to come here. The subject is a very painful one, but the case is settled.

                         A LINCOLN

[1] ALS, RPB. See Lincoln's approval of Wright's sentence, October 7, *supra.* Foster telegraphed at 2:30 P.M. on October 17: "The Hon. Mr. Chandler has made application for permission for Mr William Talbot & Mrs Dr Wright to proceed to Washington for the purpose of having an interview with you in behalf of her husband who is sentenced to be executed. My rules are not to allow any one to leave the Dept who are not willing to take the oath of allegiance but as you have postponed the execution one week I feel it my duty to forward the application to you for your decision." (DLC-RTL).

To Montgomery C. Meigs[1]

Executive Mansion,

Quarter-Master-General   Washington, Oct. 17, 1863.

If, upon your judgment, you favor the introducing to the service, to any extent, the invention of Mrs. Hutter, for protection of Soldiers' ears, this may be taken as my order for you to do so. Yours &c.   A. LINCOLN

[1] ALS, owned by Edward C. Stone, Boston, Massachusetts. See Lincoln to Meigs, October 16, *supra*.

Proclamation Calling for 300,000 Volunteers[1]

October 17, 1863

By the President of the United States of America.

A Proclamation.

Whereas, The term of service of a part of the Volunteer forces of the United States will expire during the coming year, and whereas, in addition to the men raised by the present draft, it is deemed expedient to call out three hundred thousand volunteers to serve for three years or the war, not however exceeding three years.

Now, therefore, I, Abraham Lincoln, President of the United States and Commander in Chief of the Army and Navy thereof, and of the Militia of the several States, when called into actual service, do issue this my Proclamation, calling upon the Governors of the different States to raise and have enlisted into the United States service, for the various companies and Regiments in the field from their respective States, their quotas of three hundred thousand men.

I further proclaim, that all volunteers thus called out and duly enlisted, shall receive advance pay, premium and bounty as heretofore communicated to the Governors of States by the War Department through the Provost Marshal General's Office by special letters.

I further proclaim, that all volunteers received under this call, as well as all others not heretofore credited, shall be duly credited on and deducted from the quotas established for the next draft.

I further proclaim, that if any State shall fail to raise the quota assigned to it by the War Department under this call, then a draft

for the deficiency in said quota shall be made on said State or on the Districts of said State for their due proportion of said quota; and the said draft shall commence on the fifth day of January, 1864.

And I further proclaim, that nothing in this Proclamation shall interfere with existing orders, or those which may be issued for the present draft in the States where it is now in progress or where it has not yet commenced.

The quotas of the States and districts will be assigned by the War Department, through the Provost Marshal General's office, due regard being had for the men heretofore furnished whether by volunteering or drafting, and the recruiting will be conducted in accordance with such instructions as have been or may be issued by that Department.

In issuing this Proclamation, I address myself not only to the Governors of the several States, but also to the good and loyal people thereof, invoking them to lend their willing, cheerful and effective aid to the measures thus adopted, with a view to reinforce our victorious armies now in the field and bring our needful military operations to a prosperous end, thus closing forever the fountains of sedition and civil war.

In witness whereof, I have hereunto set my hand and caused the seal of the United States to be affixed.

Done at the City of Washington, this Seventeenth day of October, in the year of our Lord one thousand eight [L.S.] hundred and sixty-three, and of the Independence of the United States the eighty-eighth.

By the President: ABRAHAM LINCOLN.
WILLIAM H. SEWARD, Secretary of State.

[1] DS, DNA FS RG 11, Proclamations.

To Henry W. Slocum[1]

Major Gen. Slocum   Executive Mansion,
Stevenson, Alabama.   Washington, Oct. 17, 1863.

Please have a medical examination made of William Brown, private in Co. C, 5th. Connecticut Vols. and report the result to me.

A. LINCOLN

[1] ALS, RPB. No reply has been located. Private William Brown of Hartford, Connecticut, mustered on September 1, and promoted to Corporal on October 16, 1863, served until discharged on August 5, 1865.

To William B. Thomas[1]

Hon. Wm. B. Thomas   Executive Mansion
Philadelphia, Pa   Washington, D.C. Oct. 17. 1863
   I am grateful for your offer of 10,000 men; but, as at present advised, I do not consider that Washington is in danger, or that there
is any emergency requiring 60. or 90. day men.

                                           A. LINCOLN

[1] ALS, RPB. William B. Thomas telegraphed Stanton on October 17, "It appears by the papers Lee is menacing Washington. I could organize I think a
large force, perhaps 10,000, in a short time in this city for a campaign of 60
or 90 days if desirable." (DLC-RTL).

To John Williams and Nathaniel G. Taylor[1]

John Williams & N. G. Taylor.   Washington, D.C.,
Knoxville, Tenn.   Oct. 17 1863
   You do not estimate the holding of East Tennessee more highly
than I do. There is no *absolute* purpose of withdrawing our forces
from it; and only a *contingent* one to withdraw them *temporarily*,
for the purpose of not losing the position *permanently*. I am in
great hope of not finding it necessary to withdraw them at all—
particularly if you raise new troops rapidly for us there.

                                           A. LINCOLN

[1] ALS, RPB. John Williams and Nathaniel G. Taylor telegraphed on October
15: "In the name of Christianity & humanity, in the name of God and Liberty,
for the sake of their chives and children & every thing they hold sacred & dear
on earth the loyal people of Tennessee appeal to you & implore you not to
abandon them again to the merciless dominion of the Rebels by a withdrawal
of the U.S. forces from upper East Tenn." (DLC-RTL).

To Thomas C. Durant[1]

T. C. Durant.   Washington City, DC.
New-York.   Oct. 18 1863
   As I do with others, so I will try to see you when you come.

                                           A. LINCOLN

[1] ALS, RPB. See Lincoln to Durant, October 16, *supra*. Durant telegraphed
Lincoln on October 17:
   "I sent duplicate of letters of tenth 10th by mail which will explain telegram.
On Tuesday will furnish you with documents relative to union pacific R Road
& my connection there. Can you give me an audience on that day? I refer to
John A. Dix Thurlow Weed & John J. Cisco as to who I am." (DLC-RTL).
   His letter of the same date reads: "Enclosed find copy of letters sent you on
the 10th inst. Four Corps of Engineers are now at work surveying between the

Missouri River and Salt Lake. As the board of Directors for the Union Pacific R R Co have not been elected, I am, in order to gain time furnishing money to pay for these surveys. The order asked for will only be used in case of necessity." (*Ibid.*).

The enclosures were copies of Durant's letter of October 10 and a letter from George T. M. Davis with which Durant's letter had originally been enclosed.

To Edward Bates[1]

Attorney General please make out and send me a pardon in this case.   A. LINCOLN
Oct. 19, 1863

[1] AES, DNA RG 204, U.S. Pardon Attorney, A 490. Lincoln's endorsement is written on a petition for pardon of William S. Leavell, Jefferson County, Kentucky, October 15, 1863, sentenced for treason.

To Montgomery Blair[1]

Post-Master General, read & return.
Oct. 19, 1863   A. LINCOLN

[1] AES, DLC-RTL. Lincoln's endorsement is written on a letter from judges of the U.S. Court of Claims, James Hughes, Joseph Casey, and Ebenezer Peck, October 16, 1863, enclosing a newspaper clipping of a letter from assistant solicitor of the Court of Claims, John D. McPherson, to Jefferson Davis, in which McPherson suggested plans for the South to obtain guarantees from the North. The letter was purported to have been found in captured correspondence. The judges expressed their willingness for McPherson to be replaced in view of his disloyalty.

To Hamilton R. Gamble[1]

His Excellency Hamilton R. Gamble   Executive Mansion.
Governor of Missouri.   Washington D.C. Oct. 19. 1863

Yours of the 1st. Inst. was duly received; and I have delayed so long to answer it, because of other pressing duties; because it did not appear to me that the domestic violence you apprehend, was very imminent; and because, if it were so imminent, my direction to Gen. Schofield embraces very nearly the extent of my power to repress it. Being instructed to repress all violence, of course he will, so far as in his power, repress any which may be offered to the State government.

At the beginning of our present troubles, the regularly installed State officers of Missouri, taking sides with the rebellion, were forced to give way to the provisional State government, at the head of which you stand and which was placed in authority, as I understood, by the unanamous action and acquiescence, of the Union people of the State. I have seen no occasion to make a distinction against that provisional government because of it's not having been chosen and inaugurated in the usual way. Nor have I seen any cause to suspect it of unfaithfulness to the Union. So far as I have yet considered, I am as ready, on a proper case made, to give the State the constitutional protection against invasion and domestic violence, under the provisional government, as I would be if it were under a government installed in the ordinary manner. I have not thought of making a distinction.

In your proclamation of the 12th. Inst. you state the proposition substantially, that no objection can be made to any change in the State government, which the people may desire to make, so far as the end can be effected by means conforming to the constitution and laws through the expression of the popular will; but that such change should not be effected by violence. I concur in this; and, I may add, that it makes precisely the distinction I wish to keep in view. In the absence of such violence, or imminent danger thereof, it is not proper for the national executive to interfere; and I am unwilling, by any formal, action, to show an appearance of belief that there is such imminent danger, before I really believe there is. I might thereby, to some extent, bear false witness.

You tell me "a party has sprung up in Missouri, which openly and loudly proclaims the purpose to overturn the provisional government by violence." Does the party so proclaim, or is it only that, some members of the party so proclaim? If I mistake not, the party alluded to recently held a State convention, and adopted resolutions. Did they, therein declare violence against the provisional State government? No party can be justly held responsible for what individual members of it may say or do.

Nothing in this letter is written with reference to any State which may have maintained within it, no State government professedly loyal to the United States. Your Obt. Servt.

A. LINCOLN

[1] ADfS, DLC-RTL. Governor Gamble wrote on October 1: "Since I have undertaken the administration of the State . . . there has been an unhesitating compliance with every call of the Federal authorities, and I have exhausted the resources of the State in maintaining the supremacy of the Federal Government.

"There has been no attempt to evade or violate any law of the United States. Notwithstanding . . . a party has sprung up in Missouri which openly and loudly proclaims the purpose to overturn the Provisional Government by violence. . . .

"While it is the duty of the Federal Government under the Constitution to protect each state from domestic violence, it is clearly the duty of the . . . Government to discountenance every combination of men who conspire to overthrow the State Government. . . .

"I therefore demand . . . that you shall order the General commanding this department to maintain . . . the integrity of the State Government, and to suppress in its incipiency every combination designed to subvert its authority. . . ." (DLC-RTL).

To William S. Rosecrans[1]

Major General Rosecrans
Chattanooga, Tenn.

Washington, D.C.,
Oct. 19. 1863

There has been no battle recently at Bul-Run. I suppose what you have heard a rumor of was not a general battle, but an "Affair" at Bristow-Station, on the Railroad a few miles beyond Manassas-Ju[n]ction towards the Rappahannock, on Wednesday the 14th. It began by an attack of the enemy upon Gen. Warren, and ended in the enemy being repulsed, with a loss of four cannon & from four to seven hundred prisoners.   A. LINCOLN

[1] ALS, RPB. The communication from Rosecrans to which Lincoln seems to have been replying has not been located.

To Edwin M. Stanton[1]

October 19, 1863

Let Col. Lucius Fairchild, of Wisconsin, be appointed a Brigadier General of Volunteers. You will find the Christian name on file.

[1] *The Collector*, June, 1944, No. 670. According to the description in the source this item is an autograph letter signed. Candidate for secretary of state for Wisconsin on the Union ticket, Colonel Lucius Fairchild of the Second Wisconsin Volunteers was appointed brigadier general on October 19, 1863, and resigned on November 2.

To Edwin M. Stanton[1]

I agree with Mr. Kellogg that William Casey is a proper man, if such an agent is to be appointed.   A. LINCOLN
Oct. 19, 1863

[1] AES, DNA WR RG 107, Secretary of War, Personnel Appointments, Box 21. Lincoln's endorsement is written on a letter from Francis W. Kellogg, U.S. congressman from Michigan, October 12, 1863, recommending William Casey of Kentucky as superintendent of abandoned plantations. No further reference has been found.

To Ambrose E. Burnside and
Jeremiah T. Boyle[1]

Major General Burnside &
Brig. Gen. J. T. Boyle
Louisville Ky

Executive Mansion,
Washington,
October 20, 1863.

Let execution of sentence of Lee W. Long be suspended until further order.

A. LINCOLN

[1] LS, RPB. Confederate Major Lee W. Long, sentenced to be shot on October 30, 1863, had been a quartermaster under General Kirby Smith but had resigned to return to Kentucky. "Whilst here trying to settle some business affairs he was taken prisoner, tried by a military commission . . . & condemned for 'being secretly within the lines in violation of Genl Burnside's order.'" (Letter of R. D. Spalding, October 2, 1863, enclosed by Kathie Todd to Lincoln, October 15). See Lincoln's telegram to Commander at Evansville, Indiana, October 22, and to Boyle, October 25, *infra*.

To Donn C. Piatt[1]

(Cypher)

Col. Donn Piatt,
Baltimore, Md.:

War Department,
Washington, D.C., October 20, 1863.

If the young men seem to know anything of importance, send them over.

A. LINCOLN.

[1] Tarbell (Appendix), p. 394. Lieutenant Colonel Piatt, Schenck's chief of staff at Baltimore, telegraphed on October 20, "Two young men very intelligent & reliable are here from Richmond which place they left last Tuesday. Shall I send them to you." (DLC-RTL). A letter from Piatt of the same date introduced the "young men I telegraphed about" without giving their names. (*Ibid.*).

Reply to Maryland Slaveholders[1]

October 21, 1863

. . . the President asserted, first, that he did not know by what authority the force in question had been sent there, and accordingly he directed Mr. Watson (Acting Secretary of War in the absence of Mr. Stanton on a visit to the army) to communicate with Gen. Schenck upon that point. He then added, in substance, that he thought that negroes might be recruited in Maryland by consent of masters, as they had been in the Army of the Cumberland, but he did not wish to effect the object in any rude or ungentlemanly manner. The President said he had promised Governor Bradford, Mr. Reverdy Johnson, and others that the enlistment of negroes should not take place under ninety days. He thought he

[529]

would order the withdrawal of the negro troops now upon the Patuxent.

¹ Washington *National Intelligencer*, October 23, 1863, quoting the Washington correspondent of the Baltimore *Sun*, October 22. See Lincoln to Schenck, *infra*.

To Robert C. Schenck¹

Major General Schenck   Executive Mansion
Baltimore, Md   Washington, D.C. Oct² 21. 1863

A delegation is here saying that our armed colored troops are at many if not all the landings on the Patuxent river, and by their presence, with arms in their hands, are frightening quiet people, and producing great confusion. Have they been sent there by any order? and if so, for what reason?   A. LINCOLN

¹ ALS, RPB. General Schenck replied at 6:45 P.M.:
"The delegation from St. Mary's County have grossly misrepresented matters. Col. [William] Birney went under my orders to look for the site of a camp of instruction and rendezvous for colored troops. See his report, this day forwarded to the Adjutant General. He took with him a recruiting squad, who were stationed, each with an officer at Mill Stone, Spencers, Saint Leonards, Dukes, Forest Grove & Benedict landings on the Patuxent. They are under special instructions, good discipline and have harmed no one.

"The only disorder or violence has been that two secessionists, named Southeron [John H. Sothoron and son] have killed second Lieut. White [Eben White, Seventh U.S. Colored Troops] at Benedict, but we hope to arrest the murderers. The officer was a white man. The only danger of confusion must be from the citizens, not the soldiers—but Col. Birney himself visited all the landings, talked with the citizens, and the only apprehension they expressed was that their slaves might leave them. It is a neighborhood of rabid secessionists. I beg that the President will not intervene and thus embolden them."
(DLC-RTL).   ² "Oct" inserted, perhaps by telegraph operator.

To Henry A. Wise¹

Executive Mansion,
Capt. H. A. Wise   Washington,
Chef. Ord. Bureau Navy Department   Oct. 21, 1863.

In relation to the new-powder, of Capt. Diller, please act upon the statements contained in the letters of Major Laidley, and Lieut. commanding Jeffers to Capt. Diller, sent by me, & now on file with you, the same as if the statements were contained in formal reports, and this shall be your justification therefor. Yours truly
A. LINCOLN

¹ ALS, DNA WR RG 74, Navy Branch, Bureau of Ordnance, Diller's Powder, Letters Received, 1862-1863. See Lincoln to Welles, October 16, *supra*, and

Lincoln's memorandum of November 2, *infra*. Major Theodore T. S. Laidley was in command of the Frankfort (Pennsylvania) Arsenal. Lieutenant Commander William N. Jeffers was in the Navy Ordnance Bureau.

To Commander at Evansville, Indiana[1]

Military Commander at   Washington, D.C.,
Evansville, Indiana   Oct. 22. 1863

A certain Major Long—I believe Lee W. Long—is, by sentence of Court Martial, or Military commission, to be executed soon—on the 30th. Inst. I think,—at Evansville. I have directed execution of the sentence to be suspended till further order. Please act accordingly.   A. LINCOLN.

[1] ALS, RPB. See Lincoln to Burnside and Boyle, October 20, *supra*. No reply has been found, but see Lincoln to Boyle, October 25, *infra*.

To William P. Mellen[1]

If Mr. Mellen can consistently oblige Mr. Sweeney, I shall be glad; but I would not have him do it otherwise.   A. LINCOLN
Oct. 22. 1863.

[1] AES-P, ISLA. Lincoln's endorsement is written on the back of the following letter from Joseph J. Lewis, commissioner of Internal Revenue, to Colonel Thomas W. Sweney "or Gustave Gumpert Esq," October 21, 1863:

"I presented to day the accompanying letter of the President to Mr Secretary Chase. He considered that under the regulations of the department the whole matter was in the hands of Mr Mellon, supervising special agent; and that nothing that he could write could be of more avail than what the President had already written.

"I have no doubt that Mr Chase's view of the subject is correct and that Mr Mellon will regard the expression of the Presidents wishes as equivalent to a command within the limits of his legal authority."

The "accompanying letter of the President to Mr Secretary Chase" has not been found, and the matter under discussion has not been determined.

Remarks to New School Presbyterians[1]

October 22, 1863

It has been stated that he had a heavy responsibility resting upon him. He felt it when he considered the great territory of the country—the large population, with the institutions which have grown up—liberty and religion to be maintained. He could only do his duty by the assistance of God and the means which He has supplied, of which the reverend gentlemen around him were noble examples. If God be with us, we will succeed; if not, we will fail.

[1] Washington *National Republican*, October 22, 1863. The New School Presbyterian Synod, meeting in Washington, called on the president to convey their sentiments of loyalty.

To Robert C. Schenck[1]

Major General Schenck   Executive Mansion,
Baltimore, Md.   Washington, Oct. 22, 1863.

Please come over here. The fact of one of our officers being killed on the Patuxent, is a specimen of what I would avoid. It seems to me we could send white men to recruit better than to send negroes, and thus inaugerate homicides on punctillio. Please come over.

A. LINCOLN.

[1] ALS, RPB. General Schenck's reply was received at 4:05 P.M.: "I will be with you by 10 Oclock tomorrow AM. We had discovered this man Sothern engaged in raising & sending off recruits to the rebel army & were about to send to arrest him when this murder was reported." (DLC-RTL).

To Edwin M. Stanton[1]

October 22, 1863

Let the boy, Samuel B. Bristow, named within take the oath of allegiance, be discharged; and go with his father. He is at Camp Douglas.   A. LINCOLN

Oct. 22. 1863.

[1] AES, CCamStJ. Lincoln's endorsement is written on a letter from General Jeremiah T. Boyle, October 16, 1863, written at the request of Reverend J. H. Bristow, chaplain of the Fifth Kentucky Infantry, who wished release of his "wayward son, eighteen years of age, who joined Morgan last year during their raid into Kentucky. . . ."

To Edwin M. Stanton[1]

Hon. Sec. of War   Executive Mansion,
Sir: Washington, Oct. 22. 1863.

I have so many appeals made to me by so very respectable people, in behalf of nearly a dozen Captains and Lieutenants of the 10th. New-York Cavalry, who have been summarily dismissed, that I will thank you to have these cases thoroughly re-investigated, and the facts reported to me. Yours truly

A. LINCOLN

[1] ALS, DLC-RTL. See Lincoln to Stanton, June 10, *supra*. Lincoln's letter was returned on November 6, 1863, together with a report from Joseph Holt on "The cases of Col. Lemmon & other officers of the 10th N.Y. Cav. Oct. 22, 1863."

The report indicated that several of the officers had been restored and that four were regarded unfavorably. Of the four reported unfavorably, Captain John Ordner was restored to rank on February 6, 1864, and killed in action on June 11; Captain Wilkinson W. Paige was restored to rank on March 28, 1864, and killed in action on June 24. Two failed to be restored—Henry Fields and Henry S. Pratt. Colonel John C. Lemmon who had resigned because of "continued ill health" on March 26 had been recommissioned on June 11, 1863, but was never mustered again. (DLC-RTL). The dismissal of the officers grew out of insubordination and near mutiny at Elmira, New York, in April, 1863.

To Edwin M. Stanton[1]

Hon. Sec. of War.   Executive Mansion,
Sir: Washington, Oct. 22, 1863.

I am told that one John C. Lemmon, had been commissioned Colonel of the 10th. New-York Cavalry by Gov. Seymour; that he was refused at the War Department, to be mustered in, perhaps because the regiment was not full enough, that I have ordered him to be mustered in when the regiment shall be full. I am also told that at the time I made the order, Gov. Seymour had recanted, and sent a request that he should not be mustered. Please inform me whether papers on file show these facts, and, in fact, what the papers do show in the case. Yours truly   A. LINCOLN

[1] ALS, DLC-RTL. See Lincoln to Stanton, *supra.*

To Lorenzo Thomas[1]

Executive Mansion, Washington,
To the Adjutant-General: October 23d, 1863.
Please grant such request as Col. Huidekoper may make.
                                    A. LINCOLN

[1] Henry S. Huidekoper, *Personal Notes and Reminiscences of Lincoln* (1896), p. 12. According to the source, Lincoln gave this note when Lieutenant Colonel Henry S. Huidekoper told him that he was on his way "to the War Department, to ask for light duty at Philadelphia for a month or two, until I should be strong enough to return to the regiment." Huidekoper had lost an arm at Gettysburg.

To George H. Boker[1]

George H. Boker Esq   Executive Mansion,
Secretary   Washington, October 24, 1863.

My Dear Sir   It is with heartfelt gratification that I acknowledge the receipt of your communication of the 30th of September, and the accompanying medal, by which I am made an honorary member of the Union League of Philadelphia.

[533]

I shall always bear with me the consciousness of having endeavored to do my duty in the trying times through which we are passing, and the generous approval of a portion of my fellow-citizens so intelligent and so patriotic as those composing your Association, assures me that I have not wholly failed. I could not ask, and no one could merit, a better reward.

Be kind enough, sir, to convey to the gentlemen whom you represent, the assurance of the grateful appreciation with which I accept the honor you have conferred upon me. I am very sincerely Your Obedient Servant   A. LINCOLN

[1] LS, Union League Club, Philadelphia, Pennsylvania. The letter is in John Hay's handwriting, signed by Lincoln. This letter is misdated by Nicolay and Hay, October 26, 1863 (IX, 181-82), due to the fact that Hay's draft (DLC-RTL) was misdated. Boker's letter of September 30 has not been located.

To Henry W. Halleck[1]

Executive Mansion

Major General Halleck.   Washington, Oct 24, 63.

Taking all our information together I think it probable that Ewell's corps has started for East Tennessee by way of Abingdon, marching last Monday, say, from Meade's front directly to the Railroad at Charlottesville. First, the object of Lee's recent movement against Meade, his destruction of the Alexandria & Orange Rail road, and subsequent withdrawal, without more, not otherwise apparent, would be explained by this hypothesis. Secondly, the direct statement of Sharpe's man that Ewell has gone to Tennessee. Thirdly, the Irishman's statement that he has *not* gone through Richmond; and his further statement of an appeal made to the people at Richmond to go and protect their salt, which could only refer to the works near Abingdon. Fourthly, Graham's[2] statement from Martinsburg that Imboden[3] is in retreat for Harrisonburg. This last matches with the idea that Lee has retained his cavalry, sending Imboden, and perhaps other scraps, to join Ewell.

Upon this probability, what is to be done? If you have a plan matured, I have nothing to say. If you have not, then I suggest that with all possible expedition the Army of the Potomac get ready to attack Lee; and that, in the mean time, a raid shall, at all hazzards, break the Railroad at or near Lynchburg, Yours truly

A. LINCOLN.

[1] Copy, DLC-RTL. On October 23, General Meade forwarded to Halleck by telegraph a despatch which he had received from Colonel George H. Sharpe, deputy provost marshal at Alexandria, Virginia, as follows:
"Our men returned this morning. The old man says that Ewell's Corps went

to Tennessee last Monday. He did not have time to go to the army himself but yesterday he saw a man from Fredericksburg who had gone up to Culpepper on Monday as claimant to get certificates for damages done to his property, & citizens around Fredericksburg. These certificates were to come from Officers in Ewell's Corps. The claimant returned to Fredericksburg on Tuesday & said that he was unable to complete his business because Ewell's Corps had left for Tennessee on Monday.

"This is the authority & the old man thinks it straight.

"The old man also says that he is quite sure no troops have come to Lee's army, that it is reported that the Division at Petersburg has gone to reinforce Bragg & that the main body of the enemy lies at Culpepper with some troops thrown over the Rapidan. The people about Fredericksburg report that Lee's late advance upon Meade's front has turned out disastrous, & that A. P. Hill is in arrest for the failure. On the other hand one man brought with them, an Irish refugee from Richmond, who says he left there Wednesday morning at 7 o'clock, that up to that time Ewell's Corps had not passed through. That on Saturday evening last Gov [William] Smith addressed the citizens of Richmond urging the Home Co's. to go to protect the Salt works. He did not hear where but very few went; that Mr Davis returned from Bragg's army on Monday last & addressed the citizens the same evening, assuring them of success in the West. . . ." (DLC-RTL).

Halleck telegraphed Meade at 11 A.M. on October 24, "The President desires that you will prepare to attack Lee's army, and, at all hazards, make a cavalry raid, to break the railroad at or near Lynchburg, and such other places as may be practicable. . . . I send herewith a copy of the President's letter, just received." (OR, I, XXIX, II, 375).

Meade replied at 2 P.M., "Your telegram . . . received. The information given by Colonel Sharpe's dispatch is disproved by two deserters just in, who report Ewell's corps in my immediate front. . . . From all the information I can get, Lee's army is now between the Rappahannock and the Rapidan, principally at Stevensburg, Brandy, and Jefferson. . . . I shall make every preparation with the utmost expedition to advance, and in the meantime select a cavalry command, and arrange the details for the raid ordered." (*Ibid.*, 376-77).

2 Probably Michael Graham, a secret service agent.
3 Confederate General John D. Imboden.

Remarks to Baltimore Presbyterian Synod: Two Versions[1]

October 24, 1863

I can only say in this case, as in so many others, that I am profoundly grateful for the respect given in every variety of form in which it can be given from the religious bodies of the country. I saw, upon taking my position here, that I was going to have an administration, if an administration at all, of extraordinary difficulty. It was, without exception, a time of the greatest difficulty that this country ever saw. I was early brought to a living reflection that nothing in my power whatever, in others to rely upon, would succeed without the direct assistance of the Almighty, but all must fail.

I have often wished that I was a more devout man than I am.

[535]

Nevertheless, amid the greatest difficulties of my Administration, when I could not see any other resort, I would place my whole reliance in God, knowing that all would go well, and that He would decide for the right.

I thank you, gentlemen, in the name of the religious bodies which you represent, and in the name of the Common Father, for this expression of your respect. I cannot say more.

Gentlemen of the Baltimore Synod: I can only say that in this case, as in many others, I am profoundly grateful for the support given me in every field of labor in which it can be given, and which has ever been extended to me by the religious community of the country. I saw before taking my position here that I was to have an administration, if it could be called such, of extraordinary difficulty, and it seems to me that it was ever present with me as an extraordinary matter that in the time of the greatest difficulty that this country had ever experienced, or was likely to experience, the man who, at the least of it, gave poor promise of ability, was brought out for duty at that time. I was early brought to the living reflection that there was nothing in the arms of this man, however there might be in others, to rely upon for such difficulties, and that without the direct assistance of the Almighty I was certain of failing. I sincerely wish that I was a more devoted man than I am. Sometimes in my difficulties I have been driven to the last resort to say God is still my only hope. It is still all the world to me.

I again say that I thank you in the name of the religious people of the country generally, and in the name of our common Father of returning you my thanks for the encouraging and most unanimous support that has been constantly given me. I know not that I can say more.

1 Washington *National Republican*, October 24, 1863, and *National Intelligencer*, October 26, 1863. Both versions are in substance the same, but show enough variation to make collation impossible. Other papers repeated one or the other of the versions here reproduced. The Baltimore Presbyterian Synod (Old School) repaired to the White House at 2 P.M., and were presented by the Reverend Dr. Phineas D. Gurley, pastor of the New York Avenue Presbyterian Church, which was attended by President and Mrs. Lincoln. Lincoln replied to the brief "respects" extended by the Moderator, Dr. Septimus Tustin.

To Edwin M. Stanton[1]

Hon. Sec. of War.   Executive Mansion,
Sir: Washington, Oct. 24, 1863.

It is said to me that *Slaughter Bradford* is in the Old Capitol prison, as is believed, because he was met upon the road by our troops, as they came from Culpepper ten days ago, when, if left alone, he might have met the enemy and given information. If this is true he should be liberated.

What is known about the case?   A. LINCOLN

1 ALS, IHi. No further reference has been located.

To Edwin M. Stanton[1]

Executive Mansion October 24, 1863
Respectfully referred to the Secretary of War for the consideration of the Bureau of Cavalry   A. LINCOLN.

1 ES, DNA WR RG 107, Secretary of War, Letters Received, P 182. The endorsement is in John Hay's handwriting, signed by Lincoln, on a letter from J. S. Schenck, October 17, 1863, submitting a plan for making condemned government horses useful. General George Stoneman, chief of cavalry, endorsed on October 31 that "It is hoped . . . that the establishment of the Cavly Bureau will . . . obviate the necessity of entering into any such extensive arrangements. . . ."

To Jeremiah T. Boyle[1]

Gen. J. T. Boyle   Executive Mansion
Louisville, Ky.   Washington D.C. Oct. 25. 1863.

Let the order suspending the execution of Long, apply also to the case of Woolfolk.   A. LINCOLN

1 ALS, RPB. See Lincoln to Burnside and Boyle, October 20, *supra*. General Boyle telegraphed on October 23, "George Woolfolk was tried & condemned for same offence at same time with Lee W. Long execution of whose sentence was indefinitely suspended by you What shall be done in case of Woolfolk, letter on the subject was addressed to Adjt Genl, October tenth (10) 1863." George Woolfolk was a private in the Confederate Army, condemned at the same time with Long. His sentence was remitted upon his taking the oath of allegiance (New York *Tribune*, November 4, 1863).

To Salmon P. Chase[1]

Executive Mansion, Washington,
Hon. Secretary of Treasury: October 26, 1863.

My Dear Sir: The writer of the accompanying letter is one of Mrs. L[incoln]'s numerous cousins. He is a grandson of Millikin's Bend, near Vicksburg—that is, a grandson of the man who gave name to Millikin's Bend. His father was a brother to Mrs. L's mother. I know not a thing about his loyalty beyond what he says. Supposing he is loyal, can any of his requests be granted? and, if any, which of them? Yours truly,   A. LINCOLN.

1 Robert B. Warden, *Account of the Private Life and Public Services of Salmon Portland Chase* (1874), pp. 554-55. Neither "the accompanying letter" nor any reply from Chase has been located. John Parker, son of James P. Parker of Lexington, Kentucky (who married the daughter of General Milliken), was the person referred to.

To James M. Cutts, Jr.[1]

Capt. James M. Cutts.

Executive Mansion,
Washington, Oct 26, 1863.

Although what I am now to say is to be, in form, a reprimand, it is not intended to add a pang to what you have already suffered upon the subject to which it relates. You have too much of life yet before you, and have shown too much of promise as an officer, for your future to be lightly surrendered. You were convicted of two offences. One of them, not of great enormity, and yet greatly to be avoided, I feel sure you are in no danger of repeating. The other you are not so well assured against. The advice of a father to his son "Beware of entrance to a quarrel, but being in, bear it that the opposed may beware of thee," is good, and yet not the best. Quarrel not at all. No man resolved to make the most of himself, can spare time for personal contention. Still less can he afford to take all the consequences, including the vitiating of his temper, and the loss of self-control. Yield larger things to which you can show no more than equal right; and yield lesser ones, though clearly your own. Better give your path to a dog, than be bitten by him in contesting for the right. Even killing the dog would not cure the bite.

In the mood indicated deal henceforth with your fellow men, and especially with your brother officers; and even the unpleasant events you are passing from will not have been profitless to you.

1 ADf, DLC-RTL. This reprimand may have been delivered to Captain Cutts in a personal interview. Never published by Nicolay and Hay for obvious reasons, a portion was, however, incorporated in their footnote to Lincoln's letter to William G. Anderson, October 31, 1840, as an unidentified bit of advice "given many years afterward to a young officer condemned to be court-martialed for quarreling" (NH, I, 152).

The court-martial trial on June 30, 1863, of Captain James Madison Cutts, Jr., brother of Stephen A. Douglas' second wife, on the charge of "conduct unbecoming an officer and a gentleman," involved three subordinate specifications: (1) that Cutts had used unbecoming language in addressing Captain Charles G. Hutton, aide-de-camp to General Burnside, when Hutton attempted to take over Cutts' desk; (2) that Cutts had sent a written communication to Major William Cutting derogatory to the accomplishments of Captain Hutton as an officer; and (3) that the said *"James M. Cutts . . .* did, on or about the 10th day of April, 1863, while occupying room No. 79, Burnet House, Cincinnati, Ohio, on the afternoon of said day, attempt to look through the key-hole of room No. 80 of said house, occupied by a gentleman and his wife; and did, in the evening of said day, at about half past eleven o'clock, after said lady had retired to her room, and while her husband was in the corridor below, said lady being at the time partly undressed, previous to retiring, take a valise or portmanteau from his room and . . . placing himself thereon, did look through the Venetian blind or transom light in or over the door into said room and at said lady while undressing. . . ." (AGO *General Orders No. 330*, October 8, 1863). To the first and second specifications Cutts pleaded not guilty; to the third, he acknowledged the facts "with deep regret," and pleaded guilty. The court found him guilty on all three specifications and sentenced him to be dismissed from the service.

In connection with this episode, John Hay's *Diary* on July 18 records Lincoln's humorous remark that Cutts "should be elevated to the peerage for it with the title of Count Peeper." Lincoln's pun and allusion were probably suggested by the name of the Swedish minister, Edward Count Piper.

Tried before the same court-martial, Captain Hutton was found guilty of having sent Captain Cutts a challenge to a duel, but was sentenced merely to a presidential reprimand. Major Cutting was found not guilty of the charge of having carried the challenge from Hutton to Cutts.

Lincoln approved the proceedings in the cases of Cutting and Cutts, but in view of Cutts' "previous good character . . . and gallant conduct in battle" remitted the sentence after reprimand. (*General Orders No. 330*). The proceedings in the case of Captain Hutton, Lincoln disapproved, because "The penalty fixed by the 25th Article of War for the offence of which the accused is found guilty, viz., sending a challenge to another officer, is cashiering, and admits of no alternative. . . . The President directs that Captain Hutton be dismissed the service of the United States from the 28th day of September, 1863." (*Ibid.*). Hutton was reappointed, however, as of October 30, 1863, and served throughout the war.

To Ladies in Charge of Northwestern Fair[1]

Executive Mansion, Washington,
Oct. 26. 1863.

Ladies having in charge of the North-Western Fair
For the Sanitary Commission   Chicago, Illinois

According to the request made in your behalf, the original draft of the Emancipation proclamation is herewith enclosed. The formal words at the top, and the conclusion, except the signature, you perceive, are not in my hand-writing. They were written at the State Department by whom I know not. The printed part was cut from a copy of the preliminary proclamation, and pasted on merely to save writing.

I had some desire to retain the paper; but if it shall contribute to the relief or comfort of the soldiers that will be better Your obt. Servt.   A. LINCOLN

[1] ADfS, DLC-RTL. On October 11, 1863, Mrs. D. P. Livermore of the Chicago Sanitary Commission wrote Lincoln:

"The patriotic women of the Northwestern States will hold a grand Fair in Chicago, on the last week of Oct., and the first of Nov., to raise funds for the Sanitary Commission of the Northwest, whose head-quarters are in Chicago. This Commission labors especially for the sick and wounded soldiers of the

South western States, of whose bravery, and persistent endurance, we are all justly proud. I enclose you circulars, which will explain to you our entire plan, and show you the magnitude of the enterprise, by which we confidently hope to realize from $25,000 to $50,000.

"The greatest enthusiasm prevails. . . . Artists . . . are painting pictures for it, manufacturers are making elegant specimens of their handiwork for the occasion, tradesmen are donating the choicest of their wares, while women are surpassing their ordinary ingenuity and taste in devising beautiful articles for sale, or decorations for the walls of the four spacious halls we are to occupy.

"The Executive Committee have been urgently requested to solicit from Mrs. Lincoln and yourself some donation to this great Fair—not so much for the value of the gift, as for the eclat which this circumstance would give to the Fair. It has been suggested to us from various quarters that the most acceptable donation you could possibly make, would be *the original manuscript of the Proclamation of emancipation.* . . . if it is at all consistent with what is proper, for you to donate it. There would be great competition among buyers to obtain possession of it, and to say nothing of the interest that would attach to such a gift, it would prove pecuniarily of great value. We should take pains to have such an arrangement made as would place the document permanently in either the State or the Chicago Historical Society.

"There would seem great appropriateness in this gift to Chicago, or Illinois, for the benefit of our Western soldiers, coming as it would from a Western President. We hope it may be possible for you to donate it to us.

"But if it be not possible, then allow us to ask for some other simple gift—from Mrs. Lincoln and yourself—sufficient to show that you are cognizant of our efforts. . . . Our Fair opens on Tuesday, Oct. 27th. . . ." (DLC-RTL).

On October 21, Isaac N. Arnold telegraphed, "I am desired by the ladies having charge of the North western fair to remind of it & beg you will send the original of proclamation of Freedom if possible. Answer to U.S. San Com Here." (*Ibid.*).

Concerning the fate of the manuscript, see note to Emancipation Proclamation, January 1, *supra.*

To Elihu B. Washburne[1]

Private & confidential

Hon. E. B. Washburne   Executive Mansion,
My dear Sir   Washington, Oct. 26. 1863.

Yours of the 12th. has been in my hands several days. Inclosed I send the leave of absence for your brother,[2] in as good form as I think I can safely put it. Without knowing whether he would accept it, I have tendered the Collectorship at Portland, Me, to your other brother, the Governor.[3]

Thanks to both you and our friend Campbell,[4] for your kind words and intentions. A second term would be a great honor and a great labor, which together, perhaps I would not decline, if tendered. Yours truly   A. LINCOLN

[1] ALS, owned by Hempstead Washburne, Chicago, Illinois. Representative Washburne wrote Lincoln on October 12:

"Notwithstanding the troubles that surround us, the time has come when we must confront the question of our next presidential candidate. I think you ought to let some of your confidential friends know your wishes . . . I have a recent letter from Hon. Thompson Campbell . . . one of the most effective and vigorous champions of our cause in California, before the late election, and is a member of the Legislature from San Francisco. Speaking of the Presidential candidate, he says: 'If he wishes the nomination, I am clearly for your friend, Mr. Lincoln.' He says he consented to go into the Legislature for the purpose of being better able to shape things in regard to the delegates to the National Convention next year. He says further, and it is well to heed it, that if he be not greatly mistaken, the whole patronage of the Government in California, will be wielded against you next summer. Campbell has done more to sustain your administration for the last six months, than all the office-holders in the State put together, and if he only knew your wishes and views I think he can be relied upon for an equally efficient service hereafter.

"Should you deem it best to make any suggestions to me in regard to these things, you know me well enough to be assured they will be openly and discreetly used.

"I enclose you a private letter from my brother Maj. Genl. Washburne [Cadwallader C. Washburn, September 20, 1863, DLC-RTL], and you will see what he says about a leave of absence. He went into the service at the sacrifice of immense business interests, and he has, served faithfully and acceptably in the most sickly climate for the last two years. His business imperatively requires his presence at home for a short time, and I think . . . his request is not unreasonable. A longer leave than twenty days must be granted by Genl. Halleck. Twenty days would not more than enable him to get home from where he now is. If you will ask that such leave be given and transmitted to me here, at Galena, Illinois, it will be a favor for which I will feel very grateful. . . ."

2 The leave of absence for Major General Cadwallader C. Washburn has not been found.

3 Israel Washburn, Jr., accepted the appointment as collector at Portland, Maine.

4 Lincoln's old friend and former U.S. representative from Galena, Illinois, Thompson Campbell, who was a member of the California legislature in 1863-1864.

Opinion on the Loss
of Robert H. Milroy's Division[1]

[October 27, 1863]

In June last a Division was substantially lost at, and near Winchester, Va. At the time it was under Gen. Milroy as immediate commander in the field Gen. Schenck as Department commander at Baltimore and Gen. Halleck as General-in-Chief at Washington. Gen. Milroy, as immediate commander, was put in arrest, and subsequently a Court of Inquiry examined, chiefly with reference to disobedience of orders, and reported the evidence. The foregoing is a synoptical statement of the evidence, together with the Judge Advocate General's conclusions. The disaster, when it came, was a surprize to all. It was very well known to Gen. Schenck and Gen. Milroy for some time before that Gen. Halleck thought the division was in general danger of a surprize at Winchester, that it was of no service there commensurate with the risk it incurred, and that it ought to be withdrawn; but although he more than once advised it's withdrawal he never positively ordered it. Gen. Schenck, on the contrary, believed the service of the force at Winchester, was worth the hazard, and so did not positively order it's withdrawal, until it was so late that the enemy cut the wire and prevented to [*sic*] order reaching Gen. Milroy. Gen. Milroy seems to have concurred with Gen. Schenck in the opinion that the force should be kept at Winchester at least till the approach of danger, but he disobeyed no order upon the subject. Some question can be made whether some of Gen. Halleck's despatches to Gen. Schenck, should not have been construed to be orders to withdraw the force, and obeyed accordingly; but no such question can be made against Gen. Milroy. In fact the last order he received, was to be prepared to withdraw, but not to actually withdraw till further order, which further order never reached him. Serious blame is not necessarily due to every serious disaster, and I can not say that in this case, any of their officers is deserving of serious blame. No Court-Martial is deemed necessary or proper in the case.

[1] ADf, DLC-RTL. In the *Official Records* (I, XXVII, II, 197), this opinion appears as an endorsement on the "Review of the Judge Advocate General of the Record of the Court of Inquiry Relative to the Evacuation of Winchester by the Command of Maj. Gen. R. H. Milroy."

To Edwin M. Stanton[1]

Hon. Sec. of War, please see these ladies a moment.
Oct. 27. 1863   A. LINCOLN

[1] ALS, CSmH. The ladies have not been identified.

To Thomas Swann[1]

Hon. Thomas Swann   Executive Mansion
Dear Sir: Washington DC. Oct. 27. 1863.

Your letter, a copy of which is on the other half of this sheet is received. I trust there is no just ground for the suspicion you mention; and I am somewhat mortified that there could be any doubt of my views upon the point of your inquiry. I wish all loyal qualified voters in Maryland & elsewhere, to have the undisturbed previlege of voting at elections; and neither my authority, nor my name can be properly used to the contrary. Your Obt. Servt.

A LINCOLN

Private. Publish both letters, if either   A L.

¹ ADfS, DLC-RTL. Thomas Swann of the Union State Central Committee, Baltimore, Maryland, wrote Lincoln on October 26, 1863:

"A suspicion having taken possession of the minds of many loyal Union voters of . . . Maryland, that the election . . . on the 3d. of November, will be attended with . . . interference on the part of persons claiming to represent the wishes of the Government, I am induced . . . to ask . . . that you would place me, as chairman of the Union State Central Committee, in possession of your views upon this object, in order that they may be communicated to loyal voters throughout the state.

"I will beg you to believe . . . that it is with no doubt or distrust on my part, as to what will be your response . . . but, simply to satisfy a large class of persons, who believe that an expression of opinion on your part, would not be without its benefit to the people of this State in promoting what we all desire, a fair expression of the public voice." (DLC-RTL).

See further, Lincoln to Bradford, November 2, *infra*.

To Andrew Johnson¹

"Cypher"

Hon. Andrew Johnson   Executive Mansion
Nashville, Tenn.   Washington D.C. Oct. 28. 1863.

If not too inconvenient, please come at once, and have a personal consultation with me.   A. LINCOLN

¹ ALS, RPB. Governor Johnson replied on November 2, 1863, "Since your dispatch of the twenty eighth (28) ulto I have been trying every way to start for Washington but it has been impossible. . . . I will be there the earliest moment practicable. . . ."

To John M. Schofield¹

Private & Confidential²   Executive Mansion Washington,
General John M. Schofield,   October 28th. 1863.

There have recently reached the War Department, and thence been laid before me, from Missouri, three communications, all similar in import, and identical in object. One of them, addressed to nobody, and without place or date, but having the signature of (apparently) the writer, is a letter of eight closely written foolscap pages. The other two are written by a different person,³ at St. Joseph, Mo., and of the dates, respectively, October 12th and 13th. 1863, and each inclosing a large number of affidavits. The general statements of the whole are, that the Federal and State authorities are arming the disloyal, and disarming the loyal, and that the latter will all be killed, or driven out of the State, unless there shall be a change. In particular, no loyal man, who has been disarmed, is named; but the affidavits show by name, forty two persons, as disloyal, who have been armed. They are as follows:

Jackson Christopher	Ratcliffe Baker	John Keyes
Henry Highsmith	Thomas J Nolan Capd	Enos Woodward
Richard Highsmith	Calvin James	William Marsh
David Alderman,	James Raneer	Barney Clark
& two sons	Milton R. Singleton	Caswell Goodman
William Jones	John Smedie	John Smith
Perry McVay	Anderson Cameron	Geo. Cunningham
John Goslin	John Utz	Fleming Tate
Newton Rogers	John Register	A. H. Leach
Alfred Rogers	Joseph Register	David Fitzpatrick
Jacob Cox. Capd	Lewis De Voss	Samuel Wyatt
Perry Hamilton	Joseph Corton	Aquilla I. Morrow
John Chestnut	P. Burge	William Morrow
William Ferrill	Dillard Woodward	Thomas Fly
Tip Russell		

A majority of these are shown to have been in the rebel service. I believe it could be shown that this government here have deliberately armed more than ten times as many, captured at Gettysburg, to say nothing of similar operations in East Tennessee. These papers contain, altogether, thirty one manuscript pages, and one newspaper in extenso; and yet I do not find it any where charged in them, that any loyal man has been harmed by reason of being disarmed, or that any disloyal one has harmed any body by reason of being armed by the Federal or State government. Of course I have not had time to carefully examine all; but I have had most of them examined and briefed by others, and the result is as stated. The remarkable fact, that the actual evil is yet only anticipated—inferred—induces me to suppose I understand the case. But I do not state my impression, because I might be mistaken; and because your duty and mine is plain in any event. The locality of nearly all this, seems to be St. Joseph, and Buchanan County. I wish you to give special attention to this region, particularly on election day. Prevent violence from whatever quarter; and see that the soldiers themselves, do no wrong. Yours truly   A. LINCOLN

[1] LS copy or DfS, DLC-RTL. General Schofield replied on November 9: "On my visit to Kansas, and North-West Missouri, during the troubles there in September last, I examined personally into the difficulties in Platte, Buchanan, and other Western counties, and learned fully their nature and origin. I at once ordered the organization of the militia which created so much commotion for a time, but which has restored that portion of the State of Missouri to a condition of profound peace. . . . The rule I established for the militia organization . . . was that the *Officers* should be of undoubted loyalty—*Original* Union men—and that both officers and privates, as far as possible, should be men of wealth and respectability whose *all* depended upon the preservation of the peace. . . . I have yet to hear the first report of a murder, robbery, or arson in that whole region, since this new organization was made. The late election was conducted in perfect peace and good order. . . . The prospects of future peace in the State are highly encouraging." (DLC-RTL).

2 In Lincoln's autograph.

3 Emended in Lincoln's autograph from "the above person" to "a different person." Benjamin F. Loan signed the letters dated October 12 and 13, enclosing affidavits (DLC-RTL). The third letter mentioned has not been located.

To Edwin M. Stanton[1]

October 28, 1863

I would like, if possible, to ascertain the facts.

1 Copy, DNA WR RG 107, Secretary of War, Letters Received, P 190, Register notation. The copy of Lincoln's endorsement preserved in the register notation indicates that it was written on a petition of Second Lieutenant Michael Towers, Company F, Seventh Iowa Cavalry, who had been mustered on June 3 and dismissed on August 26, 1863. No further reference has been found.

To Timothy J. Carter[1]

T. J. Carter   Executive Mansion
New-York.   Washington, D.C. Oct. 29. 1863

I made your appointment yesterday, and the Secretary of the Interior undertook to send it to you. I suppose it will reach you to-day.   A. LINCOLN.

1 ALS, RPB. See Lincoln to whom it may concern, October 5, *supra*. Carter telegraphed on October 29, "Has my appointment Director Pacific Rail Road been sent, when, where." (DLC-RTL). The appointment document has not been located.

To Clinton B. Fisk[1]

Gen. Clinton B. Fisk   Executive Mansion,
My dear Sir   Washington, Oct. 29. 1863.

I have just received and read your very kind and instructive letter of the 24th. for which please accept my thanks. It is so free from passion, and so full of charity and good will, that I regret not having time to do more than acknowledge the receipt of it. Yours very truly   A. LINCOLN

1 ADfS, DLC-RTL. See Lincoln to Fisk, October 13, *supra*. General Fisk wrote Lincoln on October 24, 1863:

"I have this day had the pleasure of perusing your communication to Hon. Chas. D. Drake and others of Missouri . . . I trust Your Excellency will pardon a Missouri soldier for briefly saying to you that you have hit the nail squarely on the head.

"I have been pained to see party disputes carried to such a length. . . .

"I am a Missourian. My home is in St. Louis where in April A.D. 1861 I shouldered a musket in defence of the old flag. I believed Slavery to be the cause and strength of the rebellion, and I desire that *Slavery should die.* I am counted orthodox among the radicals. I endorsed heartily your proclamation of freedom, save only that Missouri was excepted from its operation. . . .

"The war upon Gov. Gamble and Gen'l Schofield has been wicked, and prejudiced to the promotion of unity and peace. Gov Gamble although not my choice and some of whose acts I can not endorse—yet I *know* him to be as *loyal* as any *man* in Missouri. . . .

"It is probably not proper that I write either in praise or censure of my immediate Commanding Officer Genl. Schofield, but you will pardon me for saying that I wish every man in Missouri and the Country be he Citizen or Soldier were as loyal, patriotic and earnest for the Nation's welfare, as I believe Maj Genl John M. Schofield to be.

"Since my transfer from Genl. Grant's Department in July last, I have been in command of the District of South East Missouri, which district includes about thirty counties in the south east portion of the State. . . . Your orders to Genl Schofield in your communication of the 1st. inst., if cheerfully adopted, and vigorously carried out by his subordinate commanders and complied with by 'those not of the Military' are *just what will* restore kindly feeling—fraternal fellowship—unity and peace to the State. . . ." (DLC-RTL).

To James W. Grimes[1]

October 29, 1863

AN ACT to regulate the duties of the Clerk of the House of Representatives in preparing for the organization of the House.

Be it enacted by the Senate and House of Representatives of the United States of America in Congress assembled, That, before the first meeting of the next Congress, and of every subsequent Congress, the Clerk of the next preceding House of Representatives shall make a roll of the representatives elect, and place thereon the names of all persons, and of such persons only, whose credentials show that they were regularly elected in accordance with the laws of their States respectively, or the laws of the United States.

Approved March 3, 1863.

Hon. James W. Grimes   Executive Mansion
My dear Sir: Washington D.C. Oct. 29, 1863.

The above act of congress was passed, as I suppose, for the purpose of shutting out improper applicants for seats in the House of Representatives; and I fear there is some danger that it will be *used* to shut out proper ones. Iowa, having an entire Union delegation, will be one of the States the attempt will be made upon, if upon any. The Governor doubtless has made out the certificates, and they are already in the hands of the members. I suggest that they come on with them; but that, for greater caution, you, and perhaps Mr. Harlan with you, consult with the Governor, and have an additional set made out according to the form on the other half of this sheet; and still another set, if you can, by studying the law, think of a form that in your judgment, promises additional security, and qu[i]etly bring the whole on with you, to be used in case of necessity. Let what you do be kept still   Yours truly

A. LINCOLN

¹ ALS, IaHA. The act reproduced preceding the letter appears in the manuscript as a printed text below which Lincoln wrote his letter. On the verso appears the printed form for certification of elected members of congress by the governor of the state:

BY HIS EXCELLENCY

....

Governor of the State of...........................

I,........................., governor of the State of...............,
do hereby certify and make known that the following persons, namely:

Names.   Districts.

have been regularly elected members of the House of Representatives of the United States for the thirty-eighth Congress, and for the districts above mentioned, in accordance with the laws of the said State and of the United States, and that they only have been so elected.

IN TESTIMONY WHEREOF, I have hereunto set my hand and caused the .... seal of the said State to be affixed.

....
....

Secretary of State.

Senator Grimes replied on November 3, 1863: "Yours of the 29th ultimo, is recd. The Iowa delegation in congress will not fail to be present at the opening of the session & I will see to it that additional & specific credentials be furnished to each member of the House of Rep." (DLC-RTL).

To Hannibal Hamlin¹

Executive Mansion, Washington, D.C., October 29, 1863.

My dear Sir: The above act of Congress was passed, as I suppose, to exclude improper applicants from seats in the House of Representatives and there is danger now that it will be used to exclude proper ones. The attempt will be made, if at all, upon the members of those States whose delegations are entirely, or by a majority, Union men and of which your State is one.

I suppose your members already have the usual certificates— which let them bring on. I suggest that for greater caution, yourself, the two senators, Messrs. Fessenden and Morrill, and the Governor consider this matter, and that the Governor make out an additional certificate, or set of certificates, in the form on the other half of this sheet, and still another, if on studying the law you gentlemen shall be able to frame one which will give additional security; and bring the whole with you, to be used if found necessary. Let it all be done quietly. The members of Congress themselves need not know of it. Yours truly,   A. LINCOLN.

[1] NH, IX, 190-91. This letter like the preceding one to Grimes, *supra,* is written on a printed copy of the act, the verso of which contains the form for certification. On November 4 Hamlin acknowledged receipt of Lincoln's letter and promised to act on the suggestion made (DLC-Nicolay Papers).

To George G. Meade[1]

Major General Meade   Executive Mansion,
Army of Potomac   Washington, Oct. 29, 1863.

I see in a newspaper that you have recently approved sentences of death for desertion, of Thomas Sands, James Haley, H. H. Williams, Mathias Brown, alias Albert Brown, H. C. Beardsley, and George F. Perkins. Several of these are persons in behalf of whom appeals have been made to me. Please send me a short statement of each one of the cases, stating the age of each, so far as you can.?   A. LINCOLN

[1] ALS, IHi. See Lincoln to Meade, October 15, *supra.* Meade replied at 9:40 P.M., "Your telegram is received. The sentence to be shot to death in the cases of private James Haley 116 Penna & Private H. C. Beardsly 5th Michigan was ordered to be carried into execution on the sixteenth (16) inst & they were, accordingly shot on that day. The records of courts in these cases together with the order of promulgation was forwarded to the Judge Advocate General on the 23d. The record of the court in the case of private Thomas Sands 118th Penna was forwarded for your orders on the thirteenth (13) that in the cases of Sergeant H H Williams 11th. Penna & private Mathias Brown alias Albert Brown 90th Penna was forwarded for your orders on the twenty fifth (25). No communication was received from you in relation to Haley and Beardsley. Nothing is known here in relation to Geo. T. Perkins & no order has been issued from these Head Quarters to carry out the sentence of a court in his case." (DLC-RTL).

Of the men named, rosters show Thomas Sands wounded at Dabney's Mills, Virginia, on February 6, 1865, but "not accounted for" thereafter, and James Haley, executed on October 16, 1863; Henry H. Williams' and Albert (Mathias) Brown's sentences were commuted to imprisonment in Dry Tortugas by AGO, *Special Orders No. 166,* May 3, 1864. Henry C. Beardsley and George T. Perkins do not appear in the records, but William Pitt Fessenden wrote Lincoln on October 26, enclosing appeals in Perkins' behalf (DLC-RTL).

Reply to Matias Romero[1]

October 29, 1863

Mr. ROMERO: You have hitherto resided with us, and for a considerable period have been the chief diplomatic representative of your country at this Capital. You know how sincerely and how profoundly during that residence the United States desired that Mexico might always enjoy the blessings of domestic and foreign peace with perfect security, prosperity, independence and freedom. You know also that, during the previous residence to which I have referred, you enjoyed the respect and esteem of this Government and the good-will of the people of the United States. I have the pleasure of assuring you that in all things, as well affecting your country as yourself personally, these feelings remain unchanged. Thanking you for the liberal sentiments you have expressed for the United States, and congratulating you upon the renewed confidence which your Government has reposed in you, it is with unaffected pleasure that I bid you welcome to Washington.

1 New York *Times*, October 30, 1863. Lincoln replied to a brief speech made by Romero upon being presented by Secretary Seward as envoy extraordinary and minister plenipotentiary of Mexico.

To Zachariah Chandler[1]

Hon. Z. Chandler   Executive Mansion
My dear Sir   Washington D.C. Oct. 30. 1863.

There is danger that the above act of congress, intended to exclude improper applicants from seats in the House of Representatives, will be *used* to exclude proper ones. Your State is one upon which the attempt will probably be made if upon any. If the Governor has already made out the ordinary certificates, let the M.C's bring them along. In addition, I suggest that you, Senator Howard, and the Governor, have a consultation, and that another certificate or set of certificates be made out according to the form on the other half of this sheet, and still another, if you gentlemen can frame one that you shall think will give additional security, and bring them with you to be used, if needed. Let it be quietly done. Publicity might stir up the danger we wish to guard against. The M.C's themselves need not to know it   Yours truly   A. LINCOLN

1 ALS, DLC-Chandler Papers. This letter like the preceding ones to Grimes and Hamlin on October 29, *supra*, is written on a printed copy of the act, the verso of which contains the form for certification. Senator Chandler replied on November 13 that "the Governor has directed triplicate certificates to be made out for for [*sic*] each of our members of Congress, one to be sent immediately to the Clerk of the HR & the others to be retained by the Members *all* the certificates to be made in accordance with our own State Law. If any thing more is required please advise me. . . ." (DLC-RTL).

To Jacob Collamer[1]

                                                 Executive Mansion
Hon. Jacob Collamer.   Washington, D.C., Oct. 30, 1863.

My Dear Sir:—There is danger that the above Act of Congress, intended to exclude improper members, will be used to exclude proper ones. May I ask that you, Senator Foot and your Governor will study the Act, and have certificates made out in two or three different forms and bring them on with you to be used if needed? On the other half of the sheet is a form which I have thought might do for one. Let it be done quietly, as publicity might increase the danger. The members themselves need not to know of it. Yours truly,   A. LINCOLN.

[1] *Week by Week in Springfield, Illinois,* July 9, 1932, p. 8. Although the source does not reproduce the text of the act, presumably this letter, like that to Chandler, *supra,* and the ones to Grimes and Hamlin dated October 29, was written on a similar printed form. No reply from Collamer has been found.

To Frederick F. Low[1]

"Cypher"

Hon. F. F. Lowe   Executive Mansion
San Francisco, Cal.   Washington, D.C. Oct. 30. 1863

Below is an Act of Congress, passed last session, intended to exclude applicants not entitled to seats, but which, there is reason to fear, will be used to exclude some who are entitled. Please get with the governor and one or two other discreet friends, study the act carefully, and make certificates in two or three forms, according to your best judgment, and have them sent to me, so as to multiply the chances of the delegation getting their seats. Let it be done without publicity. Below is a form which may answer for one. If you could procure the same to be done for the Oregon member it might be well.   A. LINCOLN.

[1] ALS, RPB. The act and the form of certificate which appear in the manuscript telegram are clipped from a printed form such as the ones upon which Lincoln wrote his letter to Chandler, *supra,* and the preceding ones to Grimes and Hamlin on October 29. Low telegraphed on November 7, "Your dispatch received. Commissions in two forms were sent on the 6th. inst, one of each to each member and one to you. The certificates cover every point that I can think of If I knew the grounds of your apprehensions perhaps I could act more intelligently" (DLC-RTL).

To George G. Meade[1]

Major Genl. Meade   Executive Mansion
Army of Potomac   Washington D.C. Oct. 30. 1863

Much obliged for the information about deserters contained in your despatch of yesterday, while I have to beg your pardon for troubling you in regard to some of them, when, as it appears by yours, I had the means of answering my own questions.

        A. LINCOLN

[1] ALS, IHi. See Lincoln to Meade, October 29, *supra.*

To George Stoneman[1]

Gen. Stoneman, please see and hear patiently my friend, George I.
Bergen, who will hand you this.   A. LINCOLN.
Oct. 30, 1863.

[1] Stan. V. Henkels Catalog, April 8, 1908, No. 189. George I. Bergen was a
former resident of Springfield, Illinois. No further reference has been located.

To Edward Bates[1]

October 31, 1863
Inclining to believe that this boy has been sufficiently punished in
the four months imprisonment he has already endured, I have concluded to say "Let a pardon be made out in the case["]
Oct. 31. 1863   A. LINCOLN

[1] AES, DNA RG 204, U.S. Pardon Attorney, A 491. Lincoln's endorsement
is written on a petition from L. A. Whiteley, Washington, D.C., October 30,
1863, asking pardon of "Hamilton Anderson, a young colored man . . . sentenced to hard labor for one year in the Albany Penetentiary. . . ." on conviction for larceny.

To Edward Bates[1]

Will the Attorney General please have a pardon made out in this
case as soon as convenient & transmitted to me for signature.
October 31. 1863   A. LINCOLN

[1] ES, DNA RG 204, U.S. Pardon Attorney, A 491. Lincoln's endorsement is
written on a petition from Clarence Bate, Jefferson County, Kentucky, October
21, 1863, asking pardon from sentence imposed for opening a Confederate recruiting station.

Memorandum Concerning Troops in New York[1]

Executive Mansion Washington, Oct. 31. 1863
The Provost-Marshal-General has issued no proclamation at all.
He has, in no form, announced anything recently in regard to
troops in New-York, except in his letter to Governor Seymour of
October 21st. which has been published in the newspapers of that
State. It has not been announced nor decided, in any form, by the
Provost Marshal-General, or any one else in authority of the government, that every citizen who has paid his three hundred dollars
commutation, is liable to be immediately drafted again, or that
towns that have just raised the money to pay their quotas will have
again to be subject to similar taxation or suffer the operation of

the new conscription, nor is it probable that the like of these ever will be announced or decided.

¹ AD, DLC-RTL. This memorandum provided the substance of a telegram from John Hay to Abram Wakeman of this date in reply to a telegram from Simon Hanscom to Hay, received at 2:45 P.M. as follows: "Dean Richmond Chairman Democratic State Committee has distributed a circular over State announcing the Pro Mar Genl Fry claims in Proclamation that this State still owes forty seven thousand six hundred (47600) men under draft just completed & that every citizen who has paid his three hundred (300) dollars commutation is liable to be immediately drafted again & that towns that have just raised the money to pay their quotas will have again to be subject to similar taxation or suffer the operation of the new conscription. The effect of this is bad. I am requested by Post Master Wakeman to ascertain by Telegraph the proper answer to make to this which must be done immediately. Will you please ask Mr. L & give me the fact in a nutshell by Telegraph soon as possible." (DLC-RTL).

On this telegram James B. Fry endorsed: "I made in a letter to Gov. Seymour a full statement of his quota under the call for 300 thousand, and then told him what his quota was for the present (current) draft, and how many men had been held up to the date of my letter, and how their amount of men stood *up to that date.* The draft is still going on as is volunteering & the deficiency or credit for next draft if another is necessary cannot be foretold. Governor Seymour has published that letter. I know of nothing else on"

The New York *Tribune* for November 2, 1863, printed a despatch from Fry to Colonel Robert Nugent, acting provost marshal general at New York, November 1, denouncing the circular issued by Richmond and giving the substance of Lincoln's order of November 1, *infra.*

To St. Nicholas Hotel Office¹

St Nicholas Hotel Office   Washington, D.C.,
New York   Oct. 31 1863

Not knowing whether Col. Parsons could be spared from duty elsewhere to come to Washington, I referred Gov. Yates despatch to the Secretary of War, who I presume still holds it under advisement.   A LINCOLN

¹ ALS, RPB. The address is added in a different handwriting. A telegram from "St. Nicholas Hotel," received at 1:45 P.M. by the War Department, reads "Please get answer from President Lincoln. Message sent Thursday signed Richard Yates Gov. of Ills." (DLC-RTL). Governor Yates' message concerning Lewis B. Parsons, assistant quartermaster at St. Louis, has not been located.

To William Sprague¹

Hon. William Sprague   Executive Mansion
My dear Sir   Washington D.C. Oct. 31. 1863

There is danger that the above act of congress, intended to exclude improper applicants from seats, will be used to exclude proper ones. I propose that yourself, Senator Anthony and the

Governor[2] maturely consider the subject, and frame credentials for the members in two or three different forms, and bring them on with you to be used if needed. The form on the other half of this sheet will perhaps answer for one. Let it be done qu[i]etly, as publicity might increase the danger. The members themselves need not to know of it. Yours truly   A. LINCOLN

[1] ALS, RPB. See similar letters to Grimes and Hamlin, October 29, and to Chandler and Low, October 30, *supra*. No reply from Senator Sprague has been located.   [2] James Y. Smith.

To Edwin M. Stanton[1]

October 31, 1863

The bearer of this L. B. Goggin, resides in Kentucky and is well vouched as an unconditional Union man. He also is brother of W. L. Goggin of Va., whom I know, and whose honor I would take to any extent he would pledge it. Please see him and allow him to bring away from Va. a widowed daughter, whom he expects to meet at City Point.

[1] American Autograph Shop Catalog, June, 1941, No. 97. According to the catalog description, this partial text is from an autograph letter signed. No further reference has been found.

To Lyman B. Todd[1]

L. B. Todd   Washington, D.C.,
Lexington, Ky.   Oct. 31 1863

I sent the pass by Telegraph more than ten days ago. Did you not receive it?   A. LINCOLN

[1] ALS, RPB. See Lincoln to Todd, October 15, *supra*. On October 31, Todd telegraphed, "Your pass for Mrs. Robert Todd has not reached me." (DLC-RTL).

Order Concerning the Draft[1]

[November 1, 1863]

The State receives the same credit for a man who has paid commutation as if the drafted citizen had gone in person or furnished a substitute; and, in like manner, towns which have raised the money to pay for their quotas receive the same credit as if actual substitutes had been furnished. It is ordered that every citizen who has paid the $300 commutation shall receive the same credit therefor as if he had furnished a substitute, and is exonerated from military service for the time for which he was drafted, to wit, for three years.

1 OR, III, V, 629. In the source this order is given as part of Provost Marshal General James B. Fry's report on activities of his bureau, March 17, 1866. On November 1, 1863, the language of this order was incorporated in Fry's order to Colonel Robert Nugent, acting provost marshal general in New York, as printed by the New York *Tribune* on November 2. See Lincoln's memorandum, October 31, *supra*.

To William H. Seward[1]

Hon. W. H. Seward   Washington, D.C.,
Auburn, N.Y.   Nov. 1 1863

No important news. Details of Hooker's night fight do great credit to his commanand [*sic*], and particularly to the 11th. Corps, and Geary's part of the 12th. No discredit on any.   A. LINCOLN

1 ALS, RPB. On October 28-29, at Wauhatchie, Tennessee, "about 12. p.m. rebels fell upon Geary, seeking to crush and capture him before succor could be brought up. The moonlight was almost as bright as day . . . and Geary . . . got timely warning. Howard, marching to the relief of Geary, was heavily struck . . . but his corps behaved splendidly. . . . The enemy was successfully repulsed, and withdrew at 4 a.m. . . ." (Charles A. Dana to Stanton, October 29, OR, I, XXXI, I, 72-73). General John W. Geary commanded the Second Division of the Twelfth Corps, General Oliver O. Howard, the Eleventh Corps.

To Justus B. Sheppard[1]

J. B. Sheppard   Washington, D.C.,
Harper's Ferry, Md.   Nov. 1 1863

Yours of this morning received, and the Secretary of War is attending to your request.   A. LINCOLN

1 ALS, RPB. Regimental Adjutant Justus B. Sheppard telegraphed on October 31, "All the Maryland troops in this division have been ordered home to vote at the coming election and we the Second (2nd) E S Md Vols are exempt. We the officers and soldiers of the regt most earnestly and respectfully request that we may be granted the privilege to vote the unconditional Union ticket with our sister regiments. . . ." (DLC-RTL).

To Montgomery Blair[1]

Hon. Montgomery Blair: Executive Mansion,
My dear Sir.   Washington, Nov. 2. 1863.

Some days ago I understood you to say that your brother, Gen. Frank Blair, desires to be guided by my wishes as to whether he will occupy his seat in congress or remain in the field. My wish, then, is compounded of what I believe will be best for the country, and best for him. And it is, that he will come here, put his military commission in my hands, take his seat, go into caucus with our friends, abide the nominations, help elect the nominees, and thus aid to organize a House of Representatives which will really support the government in the war. If the result shall be the election of himself as Speaker, let him serve in that position; if not, let him re-take his commission, and return to the Army. For the country this will heal a dangerous schism; for him, it will relieve from a dangerous position. By a misunderstanding, as I think, he is in danger of being permanently separated from those with whom only he can ever have a real sympathy—the sincere opponents of slavery. It will be a mistake if he shall allow the provocations offered him by insincere time-servers, to drive him out of the house of his own building. He is young yet. He has abundant talent—quite enough to occupy all his time, without devoting any to temper. He is rising in military skill and usefulness. His recent appointment to the command of a corps, by one so competent to judge as Gen. Sherman, proves this. In that line he can serve both the country and himself more profitably than he could as a member of congress on the floor. The foregoing is what I would say, if Frank Blair were my brother instead of yours. Yours very truly

A. LINCOLN

[1] ALS, PHi; LS copy, DLC-RTL. Francis P. Blair, Jr., presented his credentials as congressman and served from March 4 to June 10, 1864, when his seat was successfully contested by Samuel Knox. On April 23, 1864, however, he resumed his commission and was assigned to command of the Seventeenth Army Corps.

To Augustus W. Bradford[1]

Gov. Bradford   Executive Mansion
Baltimore, Md.   Washington, Nov. 2 1863.

I revoke the first of the three propositions in Gen. Schenck's general order No. 53, not that it is wrong in principle, but because the Military, being of necessity, exclusive judges, as to who shall be arrested, the provision is too liable to abuse. For the revoked part, I substitute the following: That[2] all Provost-Marshals, and other military officers do prevent all disturbance and violence at or about the polls, whether offered by such person as above described or by any other person or persons whomsoever

The other two propositions of the order, I allow to stand. My letter at length will reach you to-night.   A. LINCOLN

¹ ALS, RPB. The text of this telegram was also incorporated in Lincoln's letter, *infra*. On October 27, General Robert C. Schenck issued his *General Orders No. 58*, instructing provost marshals (1) to arrest all persons "who have been engaged in rebellion . . . or have given aid and comfort or encouragement to others so engaged" if "found at, or hanging about, or approaching any poll. . . ."; (2) to require an oath of allegiance "of any one whose vote may be challenged on the ground that he is not loyal. . . ."; (3) to "report . . . any Judge of an election who, shall refuse his aid in carrying out this order . . . or who, . . . shall refuse to require the oath of allegiance. . . ."

On October 31, Governor Bradford wrote Lincoln:

"Rumors are today current . . . that detachments of soldiers are to be dispatched on Monday next to several of the counties of the State with the view of being present at their Polls on Wednesday next, the day of our State Election. These troops are not residents of the State and consequently are not sent for the purpose of voting, and as there is no reason in my opinion to apprehend any riotous or violent proceedings at the Election, the inference is unavoidable that these Military detachments if sent are expected to exert some control . . . in that Election. I am also informed that orders are to be issued from this Military Department on Monday presenting certain restrictions . . . in the right of suffrage. . . .

"From my knowledge of your sentiments on these subjects as expressed to Hon R Johnson in my presence on 22d Inst, as also disclosed in your letter of instructions to Genl. Schofield since published, in reference to the Missouri Election, I can not but think that the orders above referred to are without your personal knowledge. . . . I can not but feel that to suffer any Military interference in the matter of our Election, or to prescribe any test oath to voters, when all the Candidates . . . with the exception perhaps of two or three in one Congressional District, are all loyal men, would be justly obnoxious to the public sentiment of the State . . . would appear as an offensive discrimination against our State. Our citizens are aware that highly important Elections have recently taken place in other States, without . . . any such interference . . . with no limit upon the Elective franchise other than the State laws prescribe, and where one at least of the Candidates so supported was considered so hostile to the Government that for months past he has been banished from the County, certainly any such interference as between the loyal men now candidates in this State would under such compassions, be more justly objectionable and find nothing in the present condition of things here to justify it.

"I rely therefore upon your Excellency for such an order as will prevent it. . . ." (DLC-RTL).

² The remainder of this sentence is in John Hay's handwriting.

To Augustus W. Bradford¹

His Excellency A. W. Bradford
Governor of Maryland.

Executive Mansion,
Washington, Nov. 2. 1863.

Sir: Yours of the 31st. ult. was received yesterday about noon, and since then I have been giving most earnest attention to the subject matter of it. At my call Gen. Schenck has attended; and he assures me it is almost certain that violence will be used at some of the voting places on election day, unless prevented by his provost-guards. He says that at some of those places Union voters will not attend at all, or run a ticket unless they have some assurance of protection. This makes the Missouri case, of my action in regard to which, you express your approval. The remaining point of your letter is a protest against any person offering to vote being put to any test not found in the laws of Maryland. This brings us to a difference between Missouri and Maryland. With the same reason in both States, Missouri has, by law, provided a test for the voter, with reference to the present rebellion, while Maryland has not. For example, Gen. Tremble, captured fighting us at Gettysburg, is, without recanting his treason, a legal voter by the laws of Maryland. Even Gen. Schenck's order, admits him to vote, if he recants upon oath. I think that is cheap enough. My order in Missouri, which you approve, and Gen. Schenck's order here, reach precisely the same end. Each assures the right of voting to all loyal men; and whether a man *is* loyal, each allows that man to fix by his own oath. Your suggestion that nearly all the candidates are loyal, I do not think quite meets the case. In this struggle for the nation's life, I can not so confidently rely on those whose elections may have depended upon disloyal votes. Such men, when elected, may prove true; but such votes are given them in the expectation that they will prove false.

Nor do I think that to keep the peace at the polls, and to prevent the persistently disloyal from voting, constitutes just cause of offence to Maryland. I think she has her own example for it. If I mistake not, it is precisely what Gen. Dix did when your Excellency was elected Governor.

I revoke the first of the three propositions in Gen. Schenck's general order No. 53; not that it is wrong in principle, but because the military being, of necessity, exclusive judges as to who shall be arrested, the provision is too liable to abuse. For the revoked part I substitute the following:

"That all Provost Marshals, and other Military officers, do prevent all disturbance and violence at or about the polls, whether offered by such persons as above described, or by any other person, or persons whomsoever"

The other two propositions of the order I allow to stand.

Gen. Schenck is fully determined, and has my strict orders besides, that all loyal men may vote, and vote for whom they please. Your Obt. Servt   A. LINCOLN.

[1] ADfS, DLC-RTL; LS, MdAA. On November 3, Governor Bradford answered Lincoln:

"Your letter of 2nd inst. in reply to mine of 31st ulto. reached me to-day after I had already read it in the Baltimore papers of this morning.

"Your Excellency has in this respect the advantage of me, for although, following your example, I shall send a duplicate of this to the Press, the probabilities are, looking to recent events, that the military authorities will not allow its publication.

"When I wrote to you on Saturday last I had not been able to procure a Copy of the Military Order in reference to the Election and acted merely on the rumor of its character. When I saw it, as I did for the first time on Sunday I found it even more objectionable . . . and when I was shown on the same day a copy of your letter to Mr. Swann, in which you say you 'trust there is no just ground for the suspicion' he had expressed and declaring that you felt (mortified that there could be a doubt upon this point of your (his) enquiry' &c., which point was a suggestion by Mr. Swann, that 'the election about to take place will be attended with undue interference on the part of persons claiming to represent the wishes of the Government.' I rested satisfied that I should receive from you a prompt countermand of the Order in question. If the sending out one or more Regiments of troops distributed among several of the Counties to attend their places of Elections in defiance of the well known laws of the State prohibiting their presence; ordering Military Officers and Provost Marshals to arrest voters guilty, in the opinion of such officers, of certain offences; menacing Judges of Election with the power of the Military arm in case this Military order was not respected, is not an 'undue' interference with the freedom of elections, I confess myself, unable to imagine what is.

"The purport of your Excellency's remarks in your letter to me is confined chiefly to a justification of the exclusion of disloyal voters from the Polls by means of the administration of an oath of allegiance; without stopping to analyse the particular oath in question it may be sufficient to say that this clause of the Order is by far the least objectionable of the three. If any who were once citizens of the United States have been guilty of such conduct as justly disfranchises them, let them take the consequences . . . But I insist that the Judges whom the State has provided are the exclusive Judges of the question of such citizenship and that they shall be allowed to exercise their own judgment upon that question, and I shall never cease to protest against any attempt of the Military power in a loyal State to control that judgment and especially against the use of any threats tending to coerce. . . .

"The first and third Sections of the Order are the most remarkable items of the arbitrary authority it assumes. . . .

"I am aware that your Excellency has so far modified the first of said Sections, . . . but . . . whilst the modification may relieve that part of the order of some of the most immoderate of its powers it still leaves these Officers the exclusive judges of who are guilty of violence or disturbances . . . opportunity for . . . abuse of power,—the probabilities of which you may the more readily estimate when I inform you that several of them are themselves candidates for some of our most important offices. . . ." (DLC-RTL).

To James H. Hackett[1]

Private

James H. Hackett   Executive Mansion,
My dear Sir: Washington, Nov. 2. 1863.

Yours of Oct. 22nd. is received, as also was, in due course, that of Oct. 3rd. I look forward with pleasure to the fulfilment of the promise made in the former.

Give yourself no uneasiness on the subject mentioned in that of the 22nd.

My note to you I certainly did not expect to see in print; yet I have not been much shocked by the newspaper comments upon it. Those comments constitute a fair specimen of what has occurred to me through life. I have endured a great deal of ridicule without much malice; and have received a great deal of kindness, not quite free from ridicule. I am used to it. Yours truly   A. LINCOLN

[1] ALS, owned by Alfred W. Stern, Chicago, Illinois; LS copy, DLC-RTL. See Lincoln's letter to Hackett, August 17, *supra*. On October 3 Hackett wrote that he expected to present performances in Washington, December 21-23, and enclosed a copy of *The Man of the World* by C. Macklin: "I would propose to represent upon those evenings,—first, the *Falstaff* of KING HENRY V; next, *Sir Pertinax Mac Sycophant* in the comedy called—THE MAN OF THE WORLD; & immediately after it, *Monsieur Mallet, an exiled general of Napoleon* in my popular interlude of 'THE POSTOFFICE MISTAKE;' & upon my last night, the *Falstaff* of the comedy of THE MERRY WIVES OF WINDSOR; if it may happen to be convenient to Your Excellency to attend upon each or either one of those three evenings named." (DLC-RTL).

On October 22 Hackett wrote again:

"About a month since my son John K. Hackett of New York wrote to me how vexed he had been at the unwarrantable liberty taken by certain News-paper-Presses in publishing your kind, sensible & unpretending letter to me of '17 Augt.' last & more particularly at the Editorial remarks upon & perversion of its subject-matter to antagonistic political purposes, accompanied by satirical abuse in general.

"In order to calm my son's fears that it might give you cause to regret your having thus favored me, with such original materiel, I replied that I felt assured that, as a man of the world now and an experienced politician you were not likely to be so thin skinned, and that in my humble opinion such political squibs would probably affect your sensibility about as much as would a charge of mustard seed shot at forty yards distance, fired through a pop-gun barrel at the naturally armed Alligator, touch his nerves. Pray excuse the il-lustration! But, my son being a first rate shot with gun or pistol & thoroughly aware of their comparative effects, it was therefore an *argumentum ad hominem*.

"I have just recd. from my son the enclosed cut from the N.Y. Herald of 16th inst, transcribing an Editorial from '*The Liverpool* (Eng.) *Post of Oct 1st*'; and as I perceive your letter was not quite correctly quoted therein & has been very improperly in Sept. last by the *Boston Courier*, and also because you may not have retained a copy, allow me to send you one of some which I caused to be printed for my friends' perusal without subjecting the original to conse-quent mutilating.

"I wrote your Excellency hence dated '3d Oct.' inst with a small package by mail which I hope came duly to yr. hand; and I intend to depart hence within a week for New York, there to pass the Winter." (*Ibid.*).

Memorandum of Instructions for Test of Diller's Powder[1]

[c. November 2, 1863]

I select you to make the test of the new gun-powder, according to the foregoing documents. Having expended some five thousand dollars to be prepared for making the test, it is desired that it be most carefully and thoroughly made, and answers thereupon given to all the following questions, and any others which may occur to you as pertinent.

Does this powder contain saltpetre or sulphur?

Does it bear any relation to gun-cotten?

Can the ingredients for making it always be obtained in sufficient quantity in the United States?

Is it's manufacture simple, requiring no complicated apparatus, and is it attended with less danger than the manufacture of ordinary gun-powder?

Do atmospheric changes, whether of moisture or heat, injure the powder?

Will it explode with as little or less pressure than ordinary gun-powder?

Will it ignite under 300°. Celsius?

Will it ignite by a spark, or percussion-cap, like common gun-powder?

Are *seven* parts of it, in weight, as effective in smooth bored guns as *nine* parts of common gun-powder?

Is *one* part of it, in weight, as effective in rifled guns, as *two* parts of common powder?

Will it, or the ingredients of it, deteriorate in store?

Will it heat a gun less than common powder? and in what proportion?

Does it give a weaker report?

Does it make less smoke?

Does it foul a gun less?

Is it less liable to burst or damage a gun?

In proportion to effect produced, is it cheaper than common gun-powder?

Has it any fault or faults not stated, or suggested in and by the answers to the foregoing questions? and if so, what?

[1] ADf, DLC-RTL. See Lincoln to Isaac R. Diller, December 15, 1862, *supra*. As cataloged in the Lincoln Papers, this undated memorandum is assigned the date "[November?, 1862]" but a notation "Apr. 4 1863(?) (Evidently to Dr. [Charles M.] Wetherill)" appears on the first page, not in Lincoln's handwriting. Lincoln's reference to the amount of $5,000, however, definitely places this memorandum after his memorandum to Stanton and Welles of July 21, *supra*. A letter from Diller dated November 2, 1863, reads as follows:

"I have the honor to enclose, at your request, a true copy of the agreement entered into between your Excellency and myself, on the 15th. of December, 1862, respecting a new article of gun powder.

"I very respectfully beg leave to inform you, that I have delivered to Major T. T. S. Laidley, U.S.A. at the Frankford Arsenal, Penna. the *maximum* amount of powder as specified in the within agreement, and have the honor to request that a board of 'officers, or other skilled person or persons' may be selected by your Excellency to test the same, according to the terms of the agreement, before mentioned." (DLC-RTL).

Thus Lincoln's memorandum, which follows closely the specification given by Diller on December 10, 1862 (see note to Lincoln's letter to Diller, December 15, 1862), would seem to have been meant for the board of "officers, or other skilled person or persons" who were to test the powder.

See also Lincoln to Diller, November 7, *infra*.

On December 14, Diller wrote from Virden, Illinois, that he was awaiting orders, and that if the government did not intend to do anything about the manufacture of the powder, he would want to patent it. John Hay endorsed the letter, "Ansd. Dec. 26. The Prest. declines appn'g a new Board Mr D. has permission to patent his invention. The Prest. sends his best wishes for success." (DLC-RTL).

To Edwin M. Stanton[1]

November 2, 1863

I think this officer should be paid for services actually rendered, the sum, which is in equity due him.

[1] Copy, DNA WR RG 107, Secretary of War, Letters Received, P 198, Register notation. Although Lincoln's original note has not been located, the copy preserved in the register indicates that Lincoln referred to a statement of First Lieutenant Frank E. Yates, Company D, Ninth Excelsior. Other records show Frank E. Yates as an officer in the Seventy-third New York Volunteers, which was known as the Fourth Excelsior Regiment.

To George G. Meade[1]

Major General Meade   Executive Mansion,
Army of Potomac   Washington, Nov. 3, 1863.

Samuel Wellers, private in Co. B. 49th. Penn Vols. writes that he is to be shot for desertion on the 6th. Inst. His own story is rather a bad one, and yet he tells it so frankly, that I am some what interested in him. Has he been a good soldier, except the desertion? About how old is he?   A. LINCOLN

[1] ALS, owned by Edward C. Stone, Boston, Massachusetts. See Lincoln to Meade, November 5, *infra*. The sentence of Samuel Wellers was commuted to imprisonment in Dry Tortugas by AGO, *Special Orders No. 166*, May 3, 1864.

Recommendation for (Edward L.?) Baker[1]

I know the bearer—Mr. Baker—very well, and he can be safely trusted with a pass to see the Monitor.   A. LINCOLN
Nov. 3. 1863.

[1] ADS, U.S. Naval Academy Museum, Annapolis, Maryland. Edward L. Baker of Springfield, Illinois, was probably the man who received this recommendation.

To Abram Requa[1]

Abram Requa   Washington City,
New-York.   Nov. 3 1863

I know nothing whatever of Lt. Sebring, about whose case you telegraph.   A. LINCOLN

[1] ALS, RPB. Abram Requa telegraphed at 9 A.M., "Pray dont act in the case of Lt. Sebring convicted at St. Louis of acts contrary to rules of war before Henry Winter Davis & Moses F. Odell can be heard in his behalf. Please answer by Telegh" (DLC-RTL). Requa's letter to Lincoln, dated November 2, set forth that his nephew "Lt. Wm H Sebring a prisoner from the rebel Army has been tried by a court martial at St Louis Mo, and found guilty of the following charge, 'violation of the Laws and customs of War.' . . . . *such facts will be laid before you, as will I trust cause you to remit his sentence* upon his taking the oath of allegiance. . . ." (*Ibid.*). The record in Sebring's case contains Lincoln's undated endorsement, *infra,* but gives no further action by the president.

Endorsement Concerning William H. Sebring[1]

[c. November 3, 1863]

Sebring's relatives are all loyal Northern people, & a brother of his died in our service.

[1] AE, DNA WR RG 153, Judge Advocate General, MM 1055. See note to Lincoln's telegram to Requa, *supra.* This endorsement is written on an envelope filed with the record of Sebring's case.

To William H. Seward[1]

Hon. W. H. Seward   Washington City,
Auburn, N.Y.   Nov. 3. 1863

Nothing new. Despatches up to twelve last night, from Chattanooga show all quiet and doing well. How is your son?

A. LINCOLN

[1] ALS, RPB. Seward replied to Lincoln's telegram the same day: "Thanks. William is better. Our friends reckon on (25,000) majority in the state." (DLC-RTL).

DATE DUE

FEB 19 '66			
OCT 1 2 1971			
FEB 1 8 1972			
APR 1 2 1974			
MT. UNION			
MAY 2 3 1974			
GAYLORD			PRINTED IN U.S.A.